How to Use Objects

How to Use Objects

Code and Concepts

Holger Gast

✦ Addison-Wesley

Boston • Columbus • Indianapolis • New York • San Francisco • Amsterdam • Cape Town
Dubai • London • Madrid • Milan • Munich • Paris • Montreal • Toronto • Delhi • Mexico City
Sao Paulo • Sidney • Hong Kong • Seoul • Singapore • Taipei • Tokyo

Many of the designations used by manufacturers and sellers to distinguish their products are claimed as trademarks. Where those designations appear in this book, and the publisher was aware of a trademark claim, the designations have been printed with initial capital letters or in all capitals.

The author and publisher have taken care in the preparation of this book, but make no expressed or implied warranty of any kind and assume no responsibility for errors or omissions. No liability is assumed for incidental or consequential damages in connection with or arising out of the use of the information or programs contained herein.

For information about buying this title in bulk quantities, or for special sale opportunities (which may include electronic versions; custom cover designs; and content particular to your business, training goals, marketing focus, or branding interests), please contact our corporate sales department at corpsales@pearsoned.com or (800) 383-3419.

For government sales inquiries, please contact governmentsales@pearsoned.com.

For questions about sales outside the U.S., please contact international@pearsoned.com.

Visit us on the Web: informit.com/aw

Library of Congress Cataloging-in-Publication Data

Names: Gast, Holger, 1975- author.
Title: How to use objects : code and concepts / Holger Gast.
Description: New York : Addison-Wesley Professional, 2015. | Includes
    bibliographical references and index.
Identifiers: LCCN 2015038126 | ISBN 9780321995544 (hardcover : alk. paper)
Subjects: LCSH: Object-oriented programming (Computer science)
Classification: LCC QA76.64 .G39 2015 | DDC 005.1/17—dc23
LC record available at http://lccn.loc.gov/2015038126

ISBN-13: 978-0-321-99554-4
ISBN-10: 0-321-99554-6
Text printed in the United States on recycled paper at RR Donnelley in Crawfordsville, Indiana.
First printing, December 2015

To Dorothea, Jonathan, and Elisabeth
—HG

Contents

Preface

In roughly 15 years of teaching software engineering subjects at the University of Tübingen, from introductory programming courses through software engineering to software architecture, with a sideline on formal software verification, I have learned one thing: It is incredibly hard for those with basic—and even advanced—programming skills to become professional developers.

A professional developer is expected to deliver workable solutions in a predictable and dependable fashion, meeting deadlines and budgets, fulfilling customer expectations, and all the while writing code that is easy to maintain, even after the original project has long been declared finished.

To achieve all of this, the professional developer has to know both concepts and code. The concepts of software engineering, software design, and software architecture give high-level direction toward the goal and provide guidelines toward achieving it. Above all, they provide recurring solution patterns that are known to work and that other professionals will recognize. The concrete coding techniques must complement this knowledge to create good software. The guidelines come with many pitfalls and easy misconceptions, and the patterns must be put into a concrete shape that follows implicit conventions to be recognized. This is the second thing I have learned: It is incredibly hard to translate good concepts to good code.

I have written this book to present professional strategies and patterns side by side with professional code, in the hope of providing precisely the links and insights that it takes to become a professional developer. Rather than using classroom-sized toy examples and leaving the remainder to the reader's imagination, I select and analyze snippets from the code base of the Eclipse IDE. In many cases, it is the context of the nontrivial application that explains why one code structure is good, while a very similar structure fails.

Acknowledgments

In finishing the book, I am deeply grateful to many people. To my academic advisor, Professor Herbert Klaeren, who taught me how to teach, encouraged me to pick practically relevant topics for my lectures, and improved the original manuscript by reading through every chapter as it came into existence. To my editor, Christopher Guzikowski, for trusting me to write this book and for being generous with his advice and guidance in the writing process. To the reviewers, who have dedicated their time to help me polish the manuscript into a book. To my wife, Dorothea, who taught me how to write, encouraged me to write, and suffered the consequences gladly. And finally, to my students, who entrusted me with their feedback on and criticism of my lectures, and who were always eager to discuss their design proposals and solutions freely. The core idea of this book, to present code and concepts side by side, would not have been possible without these constant and supportive stimuli.

About the Author

Holger Gast graduated with a degree in computer science from the University of Tübingen, Germany, in 2000, and received a Ph.D. with a dissertation on type systems for programming languages in 2005 (Tübingen). As a post doctoral fellow, he worked on formal correctness proofs for software and finished his Habilitation for Computer Science in 2012 (Tübingen).

Since 2000, he has being teaching in the area of software engineering at different levels of the computer science curriculum, starting from introductory programming courses to lectures on software design and architecture. His other interests include scientific databases for the humanities and the model-driven construction of data-driven web applications.

Introduction

What makes a professional developer? The short answer is obvious: A professional developer produces good-quality code, and reliably so. It is considerably less obvious how the professional developer achieves this. It is not sufficient to know all the technical details about a language and its frameworks, because this does not help in strategic decisions and does nothing for the communication within a team. It is also not sufficient to know the buzz words of design and architecture, because they give no hints as to the concrete implementation. It is not sufficient to read through catalogs of design patterns, because they focus on particular challenges and are easily misunderstood and misused if seen out of context. Instead, the professional developer has to have a firm grasp of all of these areas, and many more. He or she must see the connections and must be able to switch between the different perspectives at a moment's notice. The code they produce, in the end, is just a reflection of a large amount of background considerations on many different details, all of which are interconnected in often subtle ways.

This book aims to cover some of the difficult terrain found along the path to professionalism that lies ahead of a developer who has just finished an introductory course on programming, a university curriculum on computer science, or a first job assignment. It presents the major topics that have proved relevant in around 30 years since the mainstream adoption of object-oriented development. Beyond that, it highlights their crucial points based on my 15 years of experience in teaching software development at all levels of a university curriculum and working through many and various software projects.

The Central Theme: Code and Concepts

The main theme of this book is that object-oriented development, and software development in general, always requires a combination of concepts and code. Without code, there will obviously be no software. Without concepts, the code will have an arbitrary, unpredictable structure. Concepts enable us to talk about the code and to keep it understandable and maintainable. They support us in making design and implementation decisions. In short, they explain why the code looks the way it does.

The field of object-oriented development offers a particularly fair amount of time-proven concepts. Here are just a few examples. At the smallest scale, the idea of replacing "method calls" with "messages" helps to keep objects independent. The approach of designing objects to take on "responsibilities" in a larger network of objects explains how even small objects can collaborate to create substantial applications. It then turns out that networks of objects often follow "patterns" such that standard problems can be solved consistently and reliably. The idea of describing method calls by "contracts" gives a consistent guide for obtaining correct code. "Frameworks" and "inversion of control" have become essential for building large applications effectively.

Concepts are useful and even necessary for writing good-quality object-oriented code, but it takes a fair amount of diligence, insight, and experience to translate them into code faithfully. Teaching experience tells us that the concepts are easily misunderstood and that subtle deviations can sometimes have disastrous consequences. In fact, the same lesson applies to many tutorials and introductory expositions. For instance, the famous MODEL-VIEW-CONTROLLER pattern is often given with a "minimal" example implementation. We have seen several cases where the model holds a reference to the concrete view class, and a single instance, too. These blunders break the entire pattern and destroy its benefits. The fact that the code works is just not good enough for professional developers.

Because code and concepts are both essential and must be linked in detail, this book always takes you all the way. For each topic, we introduce the central concepts and explain the general lay of the land with a few illustrations. But then we go on immediately to show how the concepts are rendered in concrete code. We do not stop at giving minimal examples but also explore the more intricate points. In the example of the MODEL-VIEW-CONTROLLER pattern, it is easy to get right for small examples. But as soon as models get more complex, the professional developer makes sure that only those parts that have changed are repainted. Similarly, attaching an event-listener to a button in the user interface is simple enough, but the professional must avoid freezing the display by executing long-running operations. This, in turn, requires concurrent execution.

Of course, there might still be the danger of oversights in "minimal" examples. Wherever feasible, we therefore present code taken from the Eclipse platform and highlight those elements that exhibit the concept at hand. This choice has a further advantage: It shows the concepts in action and in context. Very often, the true value of an approach, and sometimes even its justification, shows up only in really large applications. For instance, it is essential to keep software extensible. Convincing examples of extensibility can, however, be found only in modular systems such as Eclipse. Finally, if you want to dig a bit deeper into a particularly interesting point, you can jump right into the referenced sources.

In connection with the resulting code, there is one final story that is usually not told: the story of how the code actually gets written. Professional developers can become amazingly productive if they do not insist on typing their code, but know all the tricks that will make their IDE generate the code for them. For instance, knowing about the concept of "refactoring" is all right and useful. But professionals must also master the refactoring tools in Eclipse, up to the point where they recognize that three particular tools in sequence will bring about the desired code change. On the theme of code and concepts, we will therefore also highlight the Eclipse tools that apply to each concept.

The Structure of the Book

The book is organized in four parts. They approach the topic of object-oriented development by moving roughly from the "small" aspects of individual language elements to the "large" aspects of design and architecture. However, they also provide complementary answers to the same question: What does a professionally designed "object" really look like?

Part I: Language Usage Professional code always starts with professional language usage: A professional applies the language elements according to their intentions, rather than misusing them for seemingly nifty tweaks and hacks. The term "usage" is actually meant as in "usage dictionary" for natural languages; that is, if code obeys the idioms, the phrases, and the hidden connotations of the language constructs, it becomes more readable, understandable, and maintainable.

Part II: Contracts Professional code must above all be reliable. It must work in all situations that it is constructed for and it must be clear what these situations really are. The idea of design-by-contract gives a solid foundation for the necessary reasoning. It carries all the way from high-level descriptions of methods down to the details of formal software verification. As a complementary approach, the behavior of objects must be established by comprehensive testing.

Part III: Events Software of any size is usually event-driven: The application functionality is triggered by some framework that establishes the overall structure and fundamental mechanisms. At the core, the interpretation of methods changes, compared to Part II: A method does not implement a service that fulfills a specific request by the caller, but a reaction that seems most suitable to the callee. We follow this idea in the particular area of user interfaces and also emphasize the architectural considerations around the central model-view separation in that area. Because almost all applications need to do multiple things at once, we also include a brief introduction to multithreading.

Part IV: Responsibility-Driven Design One goal of object-oriented development is to keep the individual objects small and manageable. To achieve a task of any size, many objects must collaborate. The metaphor of assigning "responsibilities" to individual objects within such larger networks has proved particularly useful and is now pervasive in software engineering. After an introductory chapter on designing objects and their collaborations, we explore the ramifications of this approach in taking strategic and architectural decisions.

Together, the four parts of this book are designed to give a comprehensive view of object-oriented development: They explain the role of individual objects in the overall application structure, their reactions to incoming events, their faithful fulfillment of particular service requests, and their role in the larger context of the entire application.

How to Read the Book

The topic of object-oriented software development, as described previously, has many facets and details. What is more, the individual points are tightly interwoven to form a complex whole. Early presentations of object-oriented programming tended to point out that it takes an average developer more than a year in actual projects to obtain a sufficient overview of what this approach to programming truly entails. Clearly, this is rather unsatisfactory.

The book makes an effort to simplify reading as much as possible. The overall goal is to allow you to use the book as a reference manual. You can consult it to answer concrete questions without having to read it cover-to-cover. At the same time, the book is a proper conventional textbook: You can also follow longer and more detailed discussions through to the end. The central ingredients to this goal are the following reading aids.

Layered Presentation The presentation within each chapter, section, and subsection proceeds from the general points to the details, from crucial insights to additional remarks. As a result, you can stop reading once you feel you have a sufficient grasp on a topic and come back later for more.

Core Sections Each chapter starts with a self-contained section that explains the chapter's core concepts. The intention is that later chapters can be understood after reading the core sections of the earlier ones. By reading the core sections of all chapters, you get a "book within a book"—that is, a high-level survey of object-oriented software development. The core sections themselves are kept to a minimum and should be read through in one go.

Snappy Summaries Every point the text explains and elaborates on is headed by a one-sentence summary, set off visually in a gray box. These snappy summaries give a quick overview of a topic and provide landing points for jumping into an ongoing discussion.

Self-Contained Essays All top-level sections, and many subsections, are written to be self-contained treatments of particular topics. After reading the core section of a chapter, you can usually jump to the points that are currently most interesting.

Goal-Oriented Presentation The book's outline reflects particular goals in development: How to write good methods? How to use inheritance and interfaces? How to structure an application? How to use multithreading? How to work with graphical user interfaces? How to obtain flexible software? Everything else is subsumed under those goals. In particular, design patterns are presented in the context to which they contribute most. They are kept very brief, to convey the essential point quickly, but the margin always contains a reference to the original description for completeness.

Extensive Cross-Referencing Jumping into the midst of a discussion means you miss reading about some basics. However, chances are you have a pretty good idea about those anyway. To help out, all discussions link back to their prerequisites in the margin. So if you stumble upon an unknown concept, you know where to look it up. It is usually a good idea to read the core section of the referenced chapter as well. In the other direction, many of the introductory topics have forward pointers to more details that will give additional insights. In particular, the core sections point to further information about individual aspects.

The cross-referencing in the margin uses the following symbols:

    📖   Reference to literature with further information or seminal definitions, ordered by relevance

    ↰   Reference to previous explanations, usually prerequisites

    »   Reference to later material that gives further aspects and details

Furthermore, many paragraphs are set apart from the normal presentation by the following symbols:

⚠ Crucial details often overlooked by novices. When missed, they break the greater goals of the topic.

💡 An insight or connection with a concept found elsewhere. These insights establish the network of concepts that make up the area of object-oriented development.

💡 An insight about a previous topic that acquires a new and helpful meaning in light of the current discussion.

🔎 An additional remark about some detail that you may or may not stumble over. For instance, a particular detail of a code snippet may need further explanation if you look very closely.

⇄? A decision-making point. Software development often involves decisions. Where the normal presentation would gloss over viable alternatives, we make them explicit.

🪄 A nifty application of particular tools, usually to boost productivity or to take a shortcut (without cutting corners).

🌍 A (small) overview effect [259] can be created by looking at a language other than Java or by moving away from object-oriented programming altogether. Very often, the specifics of objects in Java are best appreciated in comparison.

Hints for Teaching with the Book

The book emerged from a series of lectures given by the author in the computer science curriculum at the University of Tübingen between 2005 and 2014. These lectures ranged from introductory courses on programming in Java through object-oriented programming and software engineering to software architecture. For this book, I have chosen those topics that are most likely to help students in their future careers as software developers. At the same time, I have made a point of treating the topics with the depth that is expected of university courses. Particularly intricate aspects are, however, postponed to the later sections of each chapter and can be omitted if desired.

If you are looking at the book as a textbook for a course, it may be interesting to know that the snappy summaries actually evolved from my transparencies and whiteboard notes. The style of the lectures followed the presentation in the book: After explaining the conceptual points, I reiterated them on concrete example code. The code shown in the book is either taken from the Eclipse platform or available in the online supplement.

The presentation of design patterns in this book, as explained earlier, is geared toward easy reading, a focus on the patterns' main points, and close links to the context to which the patterns apply. An alternative presentation is, of course, a traditional one as given in [100,59,263], with a formalized structure of name, intent, motivation, structure, down to consequences and related patterns. I have chosen the comparatively informal approach here because I have found that it helped my students in explaining the purpose and the applications of patterns in oral exams and design exercises. In larger courses with written exams, I have often chosen a more formalized presentation to allow students to better predict the exam and to prepare more effectively. For these cases, each pattern in the book points to its original publication in the margin.

The layered presentation enables you pick any set of topics you feel are most appropriate for your particular situation. It may also help to know which sections have been used together in which courses.

CompSci2 This introductory programming course is mostly concerned with the syntax and behavior of Java and the basics of object-oriented programming (Section 1.3, Section 1.4, Section 1.6, Section 1.5). I have included event-based programming of user interfaces (Section 7.1) because it tends to be very motivating. Throughout, I have used the view of objects as collaborating entities taking on specific responsibilities (Section 11.1). This overarching explanation enabled the students to write small visual games at the end of the course.

Software Engineering The lecture gives a broad overview of practical software engineering so as to prepare the students for an extended project in the subsequent semester. I have therefore focused on the principles of object-oriented design (Section 11.1, Section 11.2.1, Section 11.5.1). To give the students a head start, I have covered those technical aspects that would come up in the projects—in particular, graphical user interfaces (Section 7.1), including the principle of model-view separation (Section 9.1, Section 9.2.1), the challenges of frameworks (Section 7.3), and the usability issue of long-running jobs (Section 7.10). I have also covered the fundamental design principles leading to maintainable code (Section 11.5), focusing on the Single Responsibility Principle (Section 11.2.1) for individual objects and the Liskov Substitution Principle for hierarchies (Section 3.1.1). Throughout, I have discussed prominent patterns— in particular, OBSERVER (Section 2.1), COMPOSITE (Section 2.3.1), ADAPTER (Section 2.4.1), PROXY (Section 2.4.3), LAYERS (Section 12.2.2), and PIPES-AND-FILTERS (Section 12.3.4).

Object-Oriented Programming This bachelor-level course builds on CompSci2 and conveys advanced programming skills. We have treated object-oriented design (Section 11.1, Section 11.2.1, Section 11.3.2, Section 11.3.3) and implementation (Section 1.2.1, Sections 1.3–1.8) in some depth. Because of their practical relevance, we have covered user interfaces, including custom-painted widgets and the MODEL-VIEW-CONTROLLER pattern (Section 7.1, Section 7.2, Section 7.5, Section 7.8, Section 9.2). Finite State Machines served as a conceptual basis for event-based programming (Chapter 10). As a firm foundation, I have included a thorough treatment of contracts and invariants, including the practically relevant concept of model fields (Section 4.1). I have found that practical examples serve well to convey these rather abstract topics (Section 4.2) and that interested students are happy to follow me into the realm of formal verification (Section 4.7.2).

Software Architecture 1 This lecture treats fundamental structuring principles for software products. Because of the varying backgrounds of students, I started with a brief survey of object-oriented design and development (Section 11.1, Section 11.3.2, Section 10.1). This was followed by the basic architectural patterns, following [59] and [218]: LAYERS, PIPES-AND-FILTERS, MODEL-VIEW-CONTROLLER, and INTERCEPTOR (Section 12.2.2, Section 9.2, Section 12.3.4, Section 12.3.2). Because of their practical relevance, I included UNDO/REDO (Section 9.5) and the overall structure of applications with graphical interfaces (Section 9.4). The course ended with an outlook on design for flexible and in particular extensible and reusable software (Section 12.2, Section 12.3, Section 12.4).

Software Architecture 2 This lecture covers concurrent programming and distributed systems. For space reasons, only the first area is included in the book (Section 7.10, Chapter 8).

Part I

Language Usage

Chapter 1

Basic Usage of Objects

To learn a natural language properly, one goes abroad to live among native speakers for some time. One learns their idioms, their preferences in choosing words, and the general feeling for the flow of the language. But even so, when composing texts afterward, one turns to thesauri for alternative formulations and to usage dictionaries to acquire a desirable style.

This first part of the book will take you on a tour among Java natives, or at least their written culture in the form of the Eclipse IDE's code base. We will study common idioms and usages of the language constructs, so as to learn from the experts in the field. At the same time, the categorization of usages gives us a vocabulary for talking about our daily programming tasks, about the purposes of objects, classes, methods, and fields, and about the alternatives we have encountered and the decisions we have made. In short, it helps teams to code more efficiently and to communicate more efficiently.

Like any usage dictionary, the presentation here assumes that you are in general familiar with the language; thus we will discuss the meaning of language constructs only very briefly. Furthermore, the chapter focuses on the technical aspects of usage. Advanced design considerations must necessarily build on technical experience and are discussed in Chapters 11 and 12. However, we give forward pointers to related content throughout, and encourage you to jump ahead if you find a topic particularly interesting. Finally, we discuss the Eclipse IDE's tool support for the usages, because effective developers don't write code, they have the code generated by Eclipse. Here, we encourage you to try the tools out immediately, just to get the feel for what Eclipse can do for you.

1.1 The Core: Objects as Small and Active Entities

Because programming languages are designed to offer relatively few, but powerful elements that can be combined in a flexible way, it is not the language, but rather the programmer's attitude and mindset that determines the shape of the source code. As the well-known saying goes, "A real programmer can write FORTRAN programs in any language."

To get a head start in object-oriented programming, we will first formulate a few principles that set this approach apart from other programming

📖210

paradigms. From a development perspective, these principles can also be read as goals: If your objects fit the scheme, you have got the design right. Because the principles apply in many later situations, we keep the discussion brief here and give forward references instead.

It's the objects that matter, not the classes.

Learning a language, of course, requires mastering its grammar and meaning, so introductory textbooks on Java naturally focus on these subjects. Now it is, however, time to move on: The important point is to understand how objects behave at runtime, how they interact, and how they provide services to each other. Classes are not as flexible as objects; they are merely development-time blueprints and a technical necessity for creating objects. Learn to think in terms of objects!

»1.4.12 »1.3.8 »1.4.8.4

▢85

Indeed, not all object-oriented languages have classes. Only in *class-based* languages, such as Java, C++, C#, and Smalltalk, is each object an instance of a class fixed at creation time. In contrast, in *object-based* languages, such as JavaScript/ECMAScript, objects are lightweight containers for methods and fields. Methods can even be changed for individual objects.

We start our overview of the characteristics of objects by considering how entire applications can be built from them in the end:

An application is a network of collaborating objects.

»11
▢32,264,263

The idea of many small objects solving the application's task together is perhaps *the* central notion of object-oriented programming. While in procedural programming a few hundred modules are burdened with providing the functionality, in object-oriented applications a few hundred thousand objects can share and distribute the load. While classical systems feature hierarchical module dependencies, objects form networks, usually with cycles: No technical restrictions must impede their collaboration on the task at hand.

»11.1

Objects are lightweight, active, black-box entities.

»11.2

When many objects solve a task together, each object can focus on a small aspect and can therefore remain small and understandable: It contains just the code and information relating to that aspect. To achieve a clear code structure, it is helpful to assume that you can afford as many helper objects as you like. For instance, Eclipse's `SourceViewer`, which is the basis for almost all editors, holds around 20 objects that contribute different aspects to the overall component (and around 50 more are inherited). Indeed, without that additional structure, the `SourceViewer` would become quite unmanageable. Finally, objects are handled by reference—

»1.8.2 »2.2 »1.8.6

»1.4.13

that is, passing objects around means copying pointers, which are mere machine words.

Objects are also active. While modules and data structures in classical software engineering primarily have things done *to them* by other modules, objects are best perceived as *doing things*. For example, a `Button` does not simply paint a clickable area on the screen; it also shows visual feedback on mouse movements and notifies registered objects when the user clicks the button.

Finally, objects are "black-box" items. Although they usually contain some extensive machinery necessary for performing their task, there is a conceptual box around the object that other objects do not penetrate. Fig. 1.1 gives the graphical intuition of how black-box objects should collaborate. Object B employs several helper objects, of which C implements some functionality that A requires. Since B is a black box, A should not make assumptions about its internal structure and cannot call on C directly. Instead, A sends B a message m; that is, it calls its method m. Unknown to A, m now calls on C. Black-box objects do not publish their internal structure.

72,205

»7.8

»7.1 »2.1

»2.2.3 »11.5.1 »12.1.4

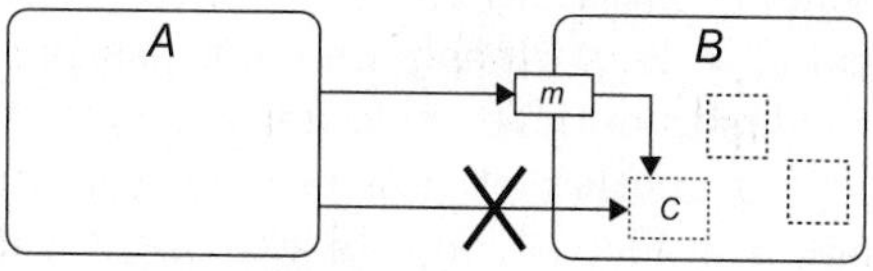

Figure 1.1 Collaboration Between Self-Contained Objects

⚬ Being "black-box" means more than just declaring data structures and helpers as `private` or `protected`. Preventing others from accessing an object's fields and internal methods at the language level is only the first step and really just a technical tool. This practice is called *encapsulation*, from the idea that the language enables you to establish an impenetrable capsule around the object. Beyond that, the concept of *information hiding* addresses creating "black-box" objects at the design level. What is hidden here is information *about* an object, which encompasses much more than just the definition of its technical internals. It may comprise its strategies for solving particular problems, its specific sequence of interactions with other objects, its choice in ordering the values in some list, and many more details. In general, information hiding is about hiding design decisions, with the intention of possibly revising these decisions in the future. In this book, Parts I–III deal mainly with encapsulation. Information hiding is discussed as a design concept in Part IV.

»1.4.5 »1.4.8.2

216(§7.4)
»11.5.1 205
216(§7.6)

Creating black-box objects demands a special mental attitude, and skill, from developers:

Think of objects from the outside.

Developers adore the nifty code and data structures that they use to solve a problem. In a team, however, it is essential to learn to speak about an object from the perspective of the other team members, who merely wish to use the object quickly and effectively. Consider a combo box, of class CCombo on the screen. It enables the user to select one item from a given list in a nice pop-up window. Providing this simple functionality requires 1200 lines of code, using 12 fields with rather complex interdependencies.

»4 »6
»10

For a smooth development process, professionals must learn to describe their objects' behavior—their reactions to method invocations—in general terms, yet precisely enough for other objects to rely on the behavior. Their implementation is treated as a private, hidden internal, and is encapsulated behind a public interface. You know that you have succeeded when you can describe your object in 1–2 brief sentences to your fellow team members.

»11.2

Objects are team players, not lone wolves.

»1.4.1 □□109

To emphasize the point of collaboration: Objects can focus on their own tasks only if they don't hesitate to delegate related tasks that other objects can perform better. Toward that goal, it also helps to imagine that objects communicate by sending *messages* to each other. A "method call" comes with many technical aspects, such as parameter passing and stack frames, that deflect the thoughts from the best design. It's better to see this process as one object notifying another object, usually that it wants something done. Note also how the idea of objects working together requires lean public interfaces: Delegating tasks works well only if the other object states succinctly and precisely what it can do—that is, which tasks it can perform well.

Objects have an identity.

»1.8.4 »1.4.13

Objects are commonly used to represent specific things. Domain objects stand for things that the customers mention in their requirements; other objects may manage printers, displays, or robot arms. An object is therefore more than a place in memory to store data—its unique identity carries a meaning by itself, since the object is implicitly associated with things outside the software world. Except in the case of value objects, one cannot simply exchange one object for another, even if they happen to store the same data in their fields.

Note that this arrangement stands in contrast to classical data structures. Like objects, they reside in the program's heap space. But, for instance, one hash map is interchangeable with another as long as both store the same key/value associations. The actual addresses of the hash map's parts are irrelevant.

Objects have state.

Objects store data in their fields and—apart from a few special cases—   »1.8.4
that data changes over time. As we have just seen, objects frequently relate
closely to the real world or our concepts about the world. The world is,
however, stateful itself: When you write on a piece of paper, the paper is
modified. When you type into an editor, you expect that the document
is modified correspondingly. Unlike the real world, its software counterpart
can support undo, by reversing modifications to the objects' state. Further-   »9.5
more, the computer hardware is stateful by design, and objects at some
point need to match that environment to work efficiently.

Objects have a defined life cycle.

Java makes it easy to work with objects: Just create them and keep a
reference to them as long as they are required; afterwards, the garbage   ▢133
collector reclaims them to reuse the memory.

   To understand objects, it is often useful to consider the things that
happen to an object during its existence more explicitly. The term *life cycle*
captures this idea: An object is allocated, then initialized by the constructor   »1.6.1
or by ordinary methods taking its role; then, its methods get called from the   »1.6.2
outside to trigger certain desired reactions; and finally, the object becomes   »1.4.1
obsolete and gets destroyed.

   From the object's point of view, these events are represented by calls
to specific methods: It is notified about its creation and initialization, then   »12.3.3.4
the various operations, and finally its own upcoming destruction. These
notifications serve to give the object the opportunity to react properly—for
instance, by freeing allocated resources before it gets destroyed.

Don't worry too much about efficiency.

Developers coming to Java often wonder whether it will be efficient enough.
Unlike in C or C++, it is simply very difficult to estimate the actual runtime cost of their code. Their preoccupation with efficiency then sometimes
leads them to trade object-oriented design for perceived improvements in
efficiency. As Donald Knuth puts it, "Premature optimization is the root of   ▢140 ▢44(Item 55)
all evil."

   Efficiency of code is, indeed, a dangerous goal: When it is stressed   ▢258
too much, developers are likely to spend much effort on complex special-
purpose data structures and algorithms. With the computing power now
available on most devices, the trade-off between expensive developer time
and cheap execution time is rapidly moving toward optimizing development
and maintenance.

 The trade-off might be obvious at the present time. But it is interesting that it
has been valid from the infancy of modern computing. One of the seminal papers

236(p.125)

on good software organization states, "The designer should realize the adverse effect on maintenance and debugging that may result from striving just for minimum execution time and/or memory. He should also remember that programmer cost is, or is rapidly becoming, the major cost of a programming system and that much of the maintenance will be in the future when the trend will be even more prominent."

115

Code optimization therefore requires a strong justification, ideally by demonstrating the bottlenecks using a profiler. Without such a tool, a good guide is Amdahl's law, which briefly says: "Make the common case fast." The overall system performance improves only when we optimize code that runs frequently and that takes up a high portion of the system runtime anyway. Usually, this is the case in inner loops that are processing large amounts of data or performing nontrivial computations in each iteration. Symmetrically, it is not worth optimizing methods that run infrequently and usually work on very little data. As a case in point, consider the choice of *linear* data structures in `ListenerList` and `AbstractListViewer` in the Eclipse code base.

🔍 A profiler may actually be instrumental in finding the bottleneck at all. Because object-oriented code works with lots of small methods rather than long and deeply nested loops, the time may be spent in unexpected places like auxiliary `hashCode()` or `equals()` methods. The author once found that his program analysis tool written in C++ spent around 30% of its runtime in the `string` copy constructor invoked for passing an argument to a central, small method. Using a `const&` parameter eliminated the problem.

50(§C.1) 174
»9.4.3
»7.10
»8 148

Furthermore, efficiency is not the same as program speed perceived by the user, and this speed can often be improved without using sophisticated data structures. For applications with user interfaces, it is usually sufficient to reduce the screen space to be redrawn and to move more complex tasks to background threads, or even to just switch to the "busy" mouse cursor. Multithreading can help to exploit the available CPU power. As these approaches suggest, optimization of perceived program speed is not so much about data structures and algorithms, but about good software organization. Moreover, this kind of optimization actually clarifies the structure, rather than making it more complex. The software will become more—not less—maintainable.

Finally, the concept of encapsulation ensures that you will not lose too much by starting with simple data structures and algorithms, as long as you keep their choice hidden inside objects. Once a profiler identifies a bottleneck, the necessary changes will usually be confined to single classes.

In summary, there is rarely a need for real optimization. You can design your code based on this assumption:

Objects are small and method calls are cheap.

You should not hesitate to introduce extra methods if they better document your overall approach and to introduce new objects (even temporary ones to be returned from methods) if they help to structure your solution.

» 1.4.6

📖 133,199

🔍 A particular concern of many C/C++ developers is the garbage collector. The HotSpot JVM's collector offers many state-of-the-art collectors, among them a generational garbage collector. It acts on the assumption that "many objects die young"—that is, the program uses them only temporarily. The garbage collector keeps a small heap in which objects are created initially, and that heap is cleaned up frequently. Since the heap is small, this approach is very cheap. Only objects that survive a few collections are moved to larger heap areas that are cleaned less frequently, and with more effort.

📖 133

1.2 Developing with Objects

Software development is more than just designing and typing code. It means working with and working on code that already exists or that is being written. Being a professional developer, then, is measured not only by the final outcome, but also by the process by which one arrives there.

1.2.1 Effective Code Editing in Eclipse

Programming is, or should be, a rather creative activity in the quest for solutions to given problems. Typing and formatting code, in contrast, is a mere chore, which easily distracts you from the solution. The goal is this:

Don't type your Java code—let Eclipse generate it for you.

While going through the language constructs in detail, we will point out the related Eclipse tool support. Here, we give a first, brief overview. To avoid lengthy and redundant enumerations along the menu structure, we give a motivational choice and encourage you to try the tools whenever you code.

1.2.1.1 Continuous Code Improvements

Two tools are so useful that developers usually invoke them intermittently, without special provocation: code formatting and organization of imports.

TOOL: Format Code

Press Ctrl-Shift-F (for *Source/Format*) in the Java editor to format the current source file according to the defined code conventions.

📖241

Code conventions define rules for formatting—in particular, for line breaks and indentation—that make it simpler for developers to share source code: If all source of a project is laid out consistently, developers get used to the style and are not distracted by irrelevant detail. With Eclipse, obeying code conventions is simple and there is no excuse for ill-formatted code. In the *Preferences/Java/Code Style/Formatter*, you can even fine-tune the conventions used to fit your requirements.

💡 You can also change these settings from a project's *Properties* dialog, which writes them to the `.settings` folder within the project. As a result, they will be checked into version control systems with the code and will be shared in the team. Alternatively, you can export and import the workspace-wide formatting settings.

🔍 Formatting does not work for source code with syntax errors. If `Ctrl-Shift-F` does not react, fix any remaining errors first.

Java requires `import` declarations to access classes or static methods from other packages. Of course, these are not meant to be written by hand:

TOOL: Organize Imports

Press `Ctrl-Shift-O` (*Source/Organize Imports*) to remove unused imports and add imports for unresolved names. If there are ambiguities, Eclipse will show a selection dialog to resolve them.

🔍 Since the compiler by default issues warnings about unused imports, Eclipse can even invoke the tool whenever a file is saved (see *Preferences/Java/Editor/Save Actions*).

1.2.1.2   Navigation

In real-world projects, it is necessary to keep an overview of large code bases. When learning APIs and new frameworks, you also need to see related code quickly. It is worthwhile to get used to the keyboard shortcuts.

The *Navigation* menu offers a huge selection of available tools. Here are some appetizers: `F3` jumps to the declaration of the name under the cursor; pressing `Shift` and hovering with the mouse over an identifier shows the definition in a pop-up (enable in *Preferences/Java/Editor/Hovers*); `F2` shows the JavaDoc. With `Ctrl-Shift-T` you can quickly select a class, interface, or enum to jump to; `Ctrl-Shift-R` jumps to general resources.

There are also many special-purpose views, which are placed beside the editor: `F4` shows the position of a class in the *type hierarchy*; that view's context menu then lets you move through the hierarchy by focusing on different classes. The *outline* reflects the structure of the current class, and a double-click jumps to the element; you can even rearrange elements by drag-and-drop. With `Ctrl-Alt-H`, you can navigate through the *call hierarchy* view to understand the collaboration between methods across classes. A second access path to such views is found in the *Show in ...* menu, which you reach in the Java editor by `Alt-Shift-W`. This menu will save you a lot of manual tree navigation in the *package explorer*.

To move within a class, invoke the *quick outline* with `Ctrl-O`, then type the beginning of the target method's or field's name. To also see declarations in the super-types, press `Ctrl-O` again.

1.2.1.3 Quick-Fix

Quick-Fix (`Ctrl-1`) was historically intended to fix simple errors. More recently, it has developed into a standard access path to powerful tools for code generation and modification. Very often, it is simpler to deliberately write wrong or incomplete code and then use Quick-Fix to create the intended version. We can give here only a few examples, and encourage you to invoke the tool frequently to build a mental model of what it can do for you.

First, Quick-Fix still fixes simple errors. It adds required imports, changes typos in names, and rearranges arguments of method calls to resolve type errors. When you call a nonexistent method, it creates the method for you. When you write an `abstract` method, it proposes to make the class `abstract` for you; when the method has a body, Quick-Fix can remove it. When your class implements an interface, but does not have the methods, Quick-Fix adds them. When you call a method that expects an interface, it offers to add an `implements` clause to the argument object or to add a cast. When you assign to a local variable of the wrong type, or call a method with a wrong parameter, it can change the target type, or the source type, to achieve a match.

The real power of these fixes comes from using combinations. For instance, if you want `this` to receive notifications about changes in a text field on the screen, just type `txt.addModifyListener(this)`. Quick-Fix first adds the required `implements` clause, then creates the required method declarations for you. »7.1

Quick-Fix is also good at generating and modifying code. Sometimes, while the code may compile, it may not be what you had in mind. When you have written an expression, Quick-Fix can place the result in a new variable declaration. It will even extract the subexpression under the cursor to a new variable. When you declare a variable and initialize it on the next line, Quick-Fix can *join the variable declaration* when the cursor is in the variable name on either line. In `if` and `while` statements, Quick-Fix can add and remove curly braces in single-statement `then`/`else` blocks and the loop body, respectively.

✿ *Linked positions* are shown as boxes in generated code when the generation involves
    choices or ambiguities. Using `tab`, you can navigate between the linked positions
and then choose the desired version from the appearing pop-up menus.

1.2.1.4   Auto-Completion

Auto-Complete (`Ctrl-Space`) in many editors means finding extensions to
the name under the cursor. In Eclipse, it means guessing what you were
probably about to write. As with Quick-Fix, it is useful to invoke the tool
very often to learn about its possibilities.

In its basic capacity, Auto-Complete will propose extensions to type,
method, and field names. It will also add `import` declarations as necessary. Using CamelCase notation often simplifies the input. To get, for instance, `IFileEditorInput`, just auto-complete `IFEI`; since there is only
one completion, it expands immediately. When looking for method names,
Auto-Complete uses the type of the invocation target. But it does even
more: If the current position is guarded by an `instanceof` test, it offers
the methods of the specialized type and adds the required cast.

𝒫 Under *Preferences/Java/Editor/Content Assist*, you can include or exclude names
   that are not actually available at the current point. In exploratory programming, at
the beginning of projects, or with new libraries, it is often useful to get all proposals,
even if they result in a compilation error; you can always quick-fix that error later on.

❱12.3.3 ❱A.1.2

𝒫 When working with plugins, it is often useful to auto-complete even types from
   plugins that are not not yet referenced by the current project. To enable this, open
the *Plug-ins* view, select all entries, and choose *Add to Java Search* from the context
menu. You can later use Quick-Fix to add the missing dependencies.

Auto-Complete also includes many code templates. Expanding the class
name, for example, yields a default constructor. At the class level, a method
name from the superclass creates an overriding method; completing `get`
or `set` offers getters and setters for fields; `static_final` completes to a
constant definition. Expanding `toarray` calls the `toArray()` method of a
collection in the context; you can choose which one through linked positions.

1.2.1.5   Surround With

Developing code is often an explorative process: You write down part of a
larger computation and only later realize that it should actually be guarded
by an `if`, or must run in a different thread altogether, so that it must be
packaged into a `Runnable` object. The tool *Surround With* (`Alt-Shift-Z`)

📖148

offers a choice of handy modifications that often need to be applied as an afterthought in daily work.

1.2.1.6 The Source Menu

An obvious place to look for code generation patterns is the *Source* menu. We have saved it for last because many of its tools are also available more easily through Auto-Complete or Quick-Fix. Yet, this menu often offers more comprehensive support. For instance, you can generate getters and setters for several fields, or override several methods at once. In practice, you will soon get a feel for whether the extra effort in going through the menu and a dialog offers any advantages over invoking the tool through other access paths. It is also worthwhile to get used to keyboard shortcuts to the menu items. For instance, Alt-S R is handy for generating getters and setters for fields; Alt-Shift-S shows a pop-up version of the menu over the editor.

1.2.2 Refactoring: Incremental Design Improvements

In the early days of computing, it was commonly thought that a software project should progress in a linear fashion: Gather the requirements from the users, lay down the system architecture, then the design, then specify the single classes and their methods, and finally implement and test them. This was called the waterfall model. Unfortunately, the waterfall has washed away many a software project.

Later software processes acknowledge that one learns during development by including cycles that allow going back to earlier project phases. Agile software development then established truly iterative development, and demanded a focus on the code, rather than on plans and documents. The challenge is, of course, that the design will change when the code already exists.

At a smaller scale, every developer knows that coding an object yields new insights on how the object should best be designed. After having written out the solution, one simply understands more of the solution's structure.

54

233
28

Expect to adapt objects to new design insights.

When you find that a new base class is a good place for shared functionality, introduce it. When you find that your colleague's tangled method can be perceived as a few high-level processing steps, introduce them. When you think of a better name for some variable, change it. A slogan in the community nowadays is "Leave the campground cleaner than you found it."

Of course, it won't do to anarchically change the design every few days. There must be some discipline to avoid breaking other classes and delaying the project's progress.

»3.1.3
»1.4.5 »1.4.6

»1.2.3
172

92

Refactoring means improving the design without changing functionality.

»5.4.8

Refactoring applies to existing, working, running, productive code. To avoid accidental breakage, the overall code base should be well tested. However, you can also write tests just to capture the current functionality of a specific object, and then go ahead and refactor it.

Refactoring is a transaction that takes a running application to a running application.

Writing tests for "obvious" modifications such as changing names seems, of course, so cumbersome that no one would do it. More generally, many frequent refactorings are syntactic in nature, and there is little danger of accidents. Eclipse provides a broad and stable tool support for refactorings, which we will introduce throughout this chapter, together with the constructs that they apply to.

Learn to use the Eclipse refactoring tools.

The Eclipse tools for reliable refactorings are accessible through a common menu, very often through the context menu:

TOOL: Eclipse Refactoring Tools

In most circumstances, select the element to be modified and press Alt-Shift-T to invoke the refactoring context menu.

One word of warning is in order: Cleaning up the structure often yields opportunities to add new functionality "while you're looking at the class anyway." Indeed, refactorings are often applied precisely because new functionality will not fit the existing structure. However, you should not yield to temptation. First, apply the planned sequence of refactorings and restore the old system behavior. Then, commit the changes to your versioning system. Only at that point should you change the functionality.

Don't introduce new functionality during refactoring.

This rule is often used to argue that refactoring is a wasted effort: The point is not to change the functionality, but then functionality is what the customer pays for. This argument is short-sighted, because it neglects the internal cost of implementing the requested functionality:

Refactoring makes developers more productive.

Refactoring is usually essential to achieve a project's goals with less effort and sometimes to achieve them at all. Refactoring changes the software structure so that new functionality will fit in more easily. It can separate special logic from general mechanisms and can enable reuse of the general parts. It makes the code more readable and more understandable. As a result, it reduces the time spent on debugging and on digging into the code written by other team members. During maintenance—and maintenance is the most cost-intensive part of the software life cycle—developers will find their way around the code more easily and will make the necessary adaptations with more confidence and in less time. In the end, refactoring is not a matter of taste in software design, but rather translates into direct gains in the cost of software production.

1.2.3 The Crucial Role of Naming

Whenever we code, we choose names: for variables, fields, methods, classes, packages, and so on. These names are for the human readers: for your fellow team members, for the later maintenance developers, and for yourself if you happen to come back to the code a few months later. Carefully chosen names can convey meaning and intention, while poorly chosen names may mislead and confuse readers and make them spend more time trying to decipher the code than necessary. The literature contains many guidelines and hints on naming. Here, we give a general overview to encourage you to consider naming a central activity in software development.

55 172(Ch.17,N)
263(p.67,p.69,p.88ff)

Think of names as documentation.

Most developers dislike documentation, because it takes away time from coding, gets outdated quickly, and is not read anyway. Not writing documentation means, however, that others will have to understand the code. Luckily, there is a simple way out: All language elements, from classes to local variables, have names that you can use to express your intention in writing the code. Knowing your intention will help future readers to grasp the working of the code. This gain in productivity motivates a simple guideline:

» 11.2.1

Invest time in finding the most appropriate names.

Suppose you are writing a data processing tool that deals with table-like structures, similar to relational database systems. You will have objects representing single data records. Without much thought, you could call these "data items"—but then, that's not very specific, since "item" has a rather fuzzy meaning. When focusing on the table structure, you might prefer "data row" or simply "row." In the context of databases, however, you might speak of a "record." Try out different variants, drawing on established names and your experience. You may also employ a thesaurus for inspiration about closely related words.

141

  As with any choice, you may find that the name that was best at one point later turns out to be unsuitable. For instance, when writing a loop that traverses a string, you may have introduced an index `pos` for the current position. As you proceed, you discover several further "positions": the first occurrence of some character, the end of some substring, and so on. To make the code more readable, you should change `pos` into `curPos` or even `searchPosition`, to describe the content more precisely. Fortunately:

There is no excuse for keeping bad names.

Changing names is so common that Eclipse provides extensive support for this operation. For novices, it may be daunting to go through the *Refactoring* menu, but that place was chosen merely to emphasize that renaming is a proper structural code modification that does not alter the meaning of the code.

↰1.2.2

TOOL: Renaming

Place the cursor over any name in the editor, or select an element in the *package explorer*. Then press `Alt-Shift-R` or use the *Refactoring/Rename* menu (`Alt-Shift-T`).

One important exception to changing bad names immediately is, of course, in the public interface of your software: If you offer functionality to others, your clients' code will be broken. As an extreme example, there is the case of the function `SHStripMneumonic` in the Windows API—once it was published, there was simply no way to correct the name to `SHStripMnemonic`.

📖61

A general guideline for choosing good names derives from the fact that humans tend to jump to conclusions:

Use similar names for similar things, and different names for different things.

When humans see a `ScreenManager` and a `Display` in the system, they will assume that someone was sloppy and the former actually manages the latter. If this is the case, rename `ScreenManager` to `DisplayManager`; otherwise, choose a completely different name, such as `WindowLayoutManager` (if that is its task). To make the point very clear, let's look at an example where the rule has been disobeyed. The developer guide of Eclipse's Graphical Editing Framework (GEF) states somewhat awkwardly:

📖214

> The "source" and "target" nodes should not be confused with "source" and "target" feedback. For feedback, "source" simply means show the feedback for the connection, while "target" means highlight the mouse target.

Since names serve communication purposes, they often crop up in discussions among the team. For this situation, it is important to obey a simple rule:

Make names pronounceable.

This strategy also implies that abbreviations should in general be avoided, unless they have an obvious expansion, which can then be pronounced. Note that auto-completion invalidates the excuse that abbreviations reduce the typing effort. In fact, use of CamelCase often makes it easier to enter the longer, pronounceable name.

↰1.2.1.4

The goal of communication also implies that names should conjure up associations in the reader's mind.

Use names to refer to well-known concepts.

For instance, if a name includes the term "cache," then the reader will immediately be aware that it contains temporary data that is kept for efficiency reasons, but is really derived from some other data.

If a concept is very general, you should qualify it further through composite names. For instance, the associations of a "hash map" are clear. The more specific class `IdentityHashMap` then turns out to associate values to objects based on object identity, instead of its `equals` and `hashCode` methods. However, the reference to well-known concepts is not unproblematic, since it depends on the intended group of readers. Therefore:

↠1.4.13

Choose names to fit the context.

Names are often linked to the project, team, and and part of the system. At a basic level, coding conventions may dictate, for example, that fields are prefixed by `f`. Look at, for instance, `JavaTextTools` and other classes from the Eclipse Java tooling for examples. Default implementations of interfaces are often suffixed with `Adapter`, such as in SWT's `MouseAdapter`. Further, patterns come with naming conventions. For example, observer interfaces in Java usually have the suffix `Listener`. Similarly, in the Eclipse platform the `update` method from the pattern is called `refresh`. Examples are seen in JFace's `Viewer` class and the `EditPart` from the Graphical Editing Framework. Finally, the layer of the object is important: Domain objects have domain names, such as `BankAccount`, while technical objects have technical names, such as `LabelProvider`.

↠3.1.4

↠2.1

↠9.3.1 ▯▯214

Sometimes, it can help to merge several views:

Choose compound names to indicate different aspects.

For instance, a `BankAccountLabelProvider` clearly is a technical object that implements a `LabelProvider` for domain-level `BankAccounts`.

One distinction to be obeyed painstakingly is that between the external and internal views of an object: The `public` methods' names must not refer to internal implementation decisions.

↠4.1 ↰1.1

Public names must be understandable without knowing the internals.

You can see whether you have got the naming right if you have achieved a simple overall goal:

Choose names such that the source code tells its own story.

📖141

»1.4.5

Code telling a story is easy to recognize. Suppose you read through a longish piece of code that calls some methods, accesses a few fields, and stores temporary results in local variables. At the same time, you have a good sense of what is going on, because the names establish conceptual links between the various steps and data items: This is code that tells a story. Make it a habit to look through code that you have just finished and to rearrange and rename until you are satisfied with the story.

Developers are a close-knit community, and one that is partly held together by common jokes, puns, and folklore. Nevertheless, we hope that you are by now convinced that names are too important to sacrifice them to short-lived merriment:

Don't joke with names.

Here is an example.[1] At some point, someone found it funny to use a Hebrew token name for the namespace separator :: in PHP. Unfortunately, this "internal" choice later turned up in error messages to the user, confusing everyone not in the know:

```
parse error, unexpected T_PAAMAYIM_NEKUDOTAYIM
```

Such occurrences are so common that there are collections of rules to avoid them.[2] Names referring to the author's favorite movie, pseudo-random words such as starship, and "temporary" names with my and foo in them are known to have made it into releases.

1.3 Fields

↰1.1 »4.1

An object's fields are usually at the core of operations: They store the information that the object works on, the knowledge from which it computes answers to method calls, and the basis on which it makes decisions. From the larger perspective of the overall system, however, this core of an object is a private, hidden detail. Consequently, other objects must not make any assumptions about which fields exist and what they contain.

---

1. http://php.net/manual/en/keyword.paamayim-nekudotayim.php
2. See, for example, http://thc.org/root/phun/unmaintain.html and http://c2.com/cgi/wiki?BadVariableNames

An object's fields are its private property.

The seminal object-oriented language Smalltalk takes this goal very seri-   📖109
ously: Only the object itself can access its fields (including those inherited
from its superclass); field access across objects is impossible. In Java, access   📖232
rights follow the philosophy of "participating in the implementation": An ob-   📖111
ject can access `private` fields of other instances of its own class, `protected`
fields can be accessed from all subclasses and classes in the same package,
and default visible fields (without modifiers) are shared within the package.
`public` fields are even open to the world in general.

   While all fields, technically speaking, store data, general usage differentiates between various intentions and interpretations associated with that
data. Anticipating these intentions often helps in understanding the fields
of a concrete object and their implied interdependencies. Before we start,
one general remark should be noted:

An object's fields last for its lifetime.

Fields are initialized when the object is created by the constructor. After-   ≫1.6.1
ward, they retain their meaning until the object is picked up by the garbage
collector. At each point in time, you should be able to say what each field   ≫4.1
contains and how it relates to the other fields. In consequence, you should
refrain from "reusing" fields for different kinds of data, even if the type fits.
It is far better to invest in a second field. Also, you should avoid having
fields that are valid only temporarily, and prefer to introduce helper objects.   ≫1.8.6

1.3.1   Data Structures

At the most basic level, objects use fields to maintain and structure their
data. For instance, the `GapTextStore` lies at the heart of text management
in the Eclipse source editors. It maintains a possibly large text efficiently
in a flat array and still provides (mostly) constant time manipulations for
frequent operations, such as typing a single character.

   Figure 1.2 depicts the meaning of the following fields:

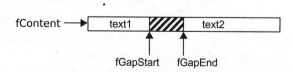

Figure 1.2 The GapTextStore Data Structure

---
org.eclipse.jface.text.GapTextStore

```
private char[] fContent;
private int fGapStart;
private int fGapEnd;
```

The fContent is the flat storage area. The *gap* between fGapStart and fGapEnd is unused; the remainder stores the actual text in two chunks. Text modifications are performed easily at fGapStart: New characters go into the gap and deletions move the gap start backward. To modify other positions, the object moves the gap within the buffer, by copying around the (usually few) characters between the gap and the new start. The array is resized only in the rare event that the gap becomes empty or too large.

📖72

This is a typical data structure, like the ones often found in textbooks. In such a structure, primitive data types are combined to represent some abstract value with operations, here a text with the usual modifications. It is also typical in that the object's interface is very simple and hides the intricate case distinctions about moving and resizing the gap—that is, clients merely invoke the following method to remove length characters at offset and insert the string text instead.

»4.1

---
org.eclipse.jface.text.GapTextStore

```
public void replace(int offset, int length, String text)
```

Data structures can also be built from objects, rather than primitive types. For instance, the JDK's HashMap uses singly linked lists of Entry objects to represent buckets for collision resolution. As in the case of primitive types, the HashMap contains all the logic for maintaining the data structure in the following fields. Entry objects have only basic getter-like methods and serve as passive containers of information, rather than as active objects.

📖72

---
java.util.HashMap

```
transient Entry[] table;
transient int size;
int threshold;
final float loadFactor;
```

🔎 The transient modifier states that the field is not serialized to disk in the default manner. Instead, Java's serialization mechanism invokes writeObject and readObject from HashMap.

The final modifier states that the field must not be altered after it has been initialized in the constructor. The compiler also tracks whether the field is, in fact, initialized.

Data structures are frequently constructed from larger and more powerful building blocks, in particular from the collections framework. For instance, the JFace AbstractListViewer displays lists of data items. It maintains

»9.3.2

these items in a general list, rather than an array, because that facilitates operations:

org.eclipse.jface.viewers.AbstractListViewer

```
private java.util.List listMap = new ArrayList();
```

The common theme of these examples is that the main object contains all the logic and code necessary to maintain the data structure fields. Even if those fields technically do contain objects, they are only passive information holders and do not contribute any functionality on their own—they perform menial housekeeping tasks, at best.

> Don't implement tasks partially in data structure objects.

Mentally classifying fields as "data structures" helps to clearly separate concerns, and you know that the contained objects are uninteresting when it comes to maintenance and debugging. At the same time, the work is clearly divided—or rather *not* divided in that the host object takes it on completely. If you do want helper objects to contribute, do so properly and give them self-contained tasks of their own.

»1.3.2 »1.8.2 »1.8.5

1.3.2   Collaborators

↞1.1

Objects are team players: When some other object already has the data and logic for performing some task, they are happy to delegate that task. One can also say that the objects *collaborate*. Very often, an object stores its collaborators in its fields, because it refers to them frequently throughout its lifetime. In contrast to data structures, an object entrusts collaborators with some part of its own specific responsibilities.

»11.1

The Eclipse platform's JobManager provides a good example. Its purpose is to schedule and track all background Jobs, such as compiling Java files. This task is rather complex, since it has to account for priorities and dependencies between jobs. The manager therefore delegates some decisions to JobQueue objects held in three fields, for different groups of jobs. The method JobQueue.enqeue(), with its helpers, then takes care of priorities and resource dependencies.

»7.10

org.eclipse.core.internal.jobs.JobManager

```
private final JobQueue sleeping;
private final JobQueue waiting;
final JobQueue waitingThreadJobs;
```

In contrast, the management of the currently running jobs is a core task of the JobManager itself, and the necessary logic belongs to that class. The bookkeeping is therefore performed in mere data structures, rather than self-contained objects. The JobManager is responsible for keeping up the

↞1.3.1

expected relationships between the two sets—we will later see that these relationships become part of its class invariant.

»4.1

org.eclipse.core.internal.jobs.JobManager

```
private final HashSet running;
private final HashSet yielding;
```

»2.2

All of these examples incorporate the notion of *ownership*: The JobManager holds the sole references to the collaborators, the manager creates them, and their life cycle ends with that of the manager.

↰1.1

↰1.1
»12.3.3.4

Collaboration is, however, not restricted to that setting; indeed, true networks of collaborating objects can be built only by sharing collaborators. As an extreme example, the Eclipse IDE's UI is composed from different *editors* and *views*, both of which are special *workbench parts*. Each such part holds a reference to the context, called a *site*, where it appears:

org.eclipse.ui.part.WorkbenchPart

```
private IWorkbenchPartSite partSite;
```

Through that site, views and editors can change the title on their tabs, and even access the overall workbench infrastructure, to observe changes, open and close parts, and perform other tasks.

1.3.3   Properties

↰1.1

In general, objects treat their fields as a private matter that is no one else's concern. In this manner, they are free to change the internal data format if it turns out that the current choice is inadequate. However, sometimes the task of some object is precisely to hold on to some information, and its clients can and must know about it. Such fields are called *properties*, and the object offers *getters* and *setters* for their properties—that is, methods named get⟨*property name*⟩ and set⟨*property name*⟩, respectively. For Boolean properties, the getter is named is⟨*property name*⟩. These methods are also collectively called *accessors*.

»1.8.3

»9.3.4

For instance, a JFace Action encapsulates a piece of functionality that can be put into menus, toolbars, and other UI components. It naturally has a text, icon, tool tip text, and other elements, so these fields are directly accessible by setters and getters. For more examples, just search for method declarations named set* inside Eclipse.

TOOL: Generating Getters and Setters

Since properties are so common, Eclipse offers extensive tool support for their specification. The obvious choice is *Source/Generate Getters and Setters* (Alt-S R or Alt-Shift-S R). You can also auto-complete get and set in the class body, possibly with a prefix of the property name. When the cursor is on the field name, you can choose *Encapsulate Field* from the refactoring menu (Alt-Shift-T), or just invoke Quick-

Fix (Ctrl-1). The latter two tools will also make the field private if it was public before.

⚠ Don't generate getters and setters lightly, simply because Eclipse supports it. Always remember that an object's data is conceptually private. Only fields that happen to fit the object's public description are properties and should have accessor methods.

⚠ Beware that the generated getters return objects stored in fields by reference, so that clients can *modify* these internal data structures by calling the objects' methods. This slip happens often with basic structures such as ArrayLists or HashMaps, and Eclipse does not recognize it. You must either return copies or wrap the objects by Collections.unmodifiableList() or similar methods. Similarly, when clients pass objects to setters, they may have retained a reference, with the same problematic results.

Sometimes, the stored information is so obvious and elementary that the fields themselves can be public. For instance, SWT decides that a Rectangle obviously has a position and a size, so making the fields x, y, width, and height public is hardly giving away any secrets. Besides, the simplicity of the class and the data makes it improbable that it will ever be changed.

»7.1

Even more rarely, efficiency requirements may dictate public fields. For instance, Positions represents points in a text document. Of course, these must be updated upon each and every text modification, even when only a single character is typed. To enable DefaultPositionUpdater to perform these frequent updates quickly, the position's fields are public (following Amdahl's law).

↰1.1

It is also worth noting that sometimes properties are not backed by physical fields within the object itself. For instance, the accessors of SWT widgets often delegate to a native implementation object that actually appears on the screen. In turn, a Label's foreground color, a Text field's content, and many more properties are stored only at the native C layer. Conceptually, this does not change their status as properties, and tools such as the WindowBuilder do rely on the established naming conventions.

»7.1

»7.2

Finally, the *JavaBeans* specification defines further support. When *bound properties* are changed, beans will send notifications to PropertyChange Listeners according to the OBSERVER pattern. For *constrained properties*, observers can even forbid invalid changes.

▭202

»2.1

1.3.4 Flags and Configuration

Properties usually contain the data that an object works with, or that characterize its state. Sometimes, they do more: The value of the property influences the object's behavior and in particular the decisions that the object makes. Knowing that the property has more influence than mere passive data is essential for understanding and using it correctly.

↰1.1

As a typical example, consider an `URLConnection` for accessing a web server, usually over HTTP. Before it is opened, the connection can be configured to enable sending data, by timeout intervals, and in many other ways. All of these choices are not passed on as data, but influence the connection's behavior.

java.net.URLConnection

```
protected boolean doOutput = false;
private int connectTimeout;
private int readTimeout;
```

Boolean configuration properties are called *flags*. Very often, they are stored in bit masks to save space. In the following snippet from SWT's text field, the `READ_ONLY` bit is first cleared, then perhaps reset if necessary. The `style` bit field here is shared through the built-in `Widget` hierarchy.

org.eclipse.swt.widgets.Text

```
public void setEditable(boolean editable) {
    style &= ~SWT.READ_ONLY;
    if (!editable)
        style |= SWT.READ_ONLY;
}
```

Beyond elementary types, configuration properties may also contain objects. An object is given a special collaborator, with the intention of defining or modifying its behavior by specifying the desired collaboration. For instance, all `Composite` widgets on the screen must somehow arrange the contained child elements. However, there are huge differences: While toolbars create visual rows of their children, forms often place them in a tabular arrangement. A composite's behavior can therefore be configured by a `Layout`, which computes the children's positions on behalf of the composite widget. The predefined choices such as `RowLayout`, `GridLayout`, and `StackLayout` cover the most common scenarios.

»7.5

Configuration by objects in this way is an application of the STRATEGY pattern:

»12.3 📖100

PATTERN: STRATEGY

Encapsulate algorithms (i.e., solutions to a given problem) with a common interface so that clients can use them interchangeably.

1. Identify the common aspects of the various solutions and define an interface (or abstract base class) *Strategy* capturing the access paths and expected behavior.

2. Define *ConcreteStrategy* objects that implement *Strategy*.

3. Optional: Rethink your definitions and refactor to enable clients to provide their own concrete strategies.

After you have performed these steps, objects can be parameterized by a strategy by simply storing that strategy in a property.

A second use of the STRATEGY pattern is to encapsulate algorithms as objects, without the goal of abstracting over families of algorithms. In this case, the complexities of the algorithm can be hidden behind a small, readable interface. If the family of algorithms is not to be extensible, the pattern might degenerate to a reified case distinction.

»1.8.6

»3.1.6

1.3.5 Abstract State

An object's state consists, in principle, of the current data stored in its fields. Very often, it is useful to abstract over the individual fields and their data structures, and to assign a small number of named states instead. For example, a button on the screen is "idle," "pressed," or "armed" (meaning releasing the button now will trigger its action); a combo box has a selection list that is either opened or closed. These summary descriptions of the object's state enable clients to understand the object's behavior in general terms. For instance, the documentation may state, "The button sends a *released* notification if it is in the *armed* state and the user releases the mouse button."

»10

Sometimes, the abstract state is reflected in the object's fields. While direct enumerations are rare, combinations of Boolean flags that determine the state are quite common. For instance, a ButtonModel in the Graphical Editing Framework has a bit field state for that purpose (shown slightly simplified here):

»10.3

214

←1.3.4

```
org.eclipse.draw2d.ButtonModel

protected static final int ARMED_FLAG = 1;
protected static final int PRESSED_FLAG = 2;
protected static final int ENABLED_FLAG = 16;
private int state = ENABLED_FLAG;
```

A second, very instructive example is found in Socket, whose state fields reflect the sophisticated state model of TCP network connections.

237

While it is not mandatory to make the abstract state explicit in the concrete state, it often leads to code that tells its own story. For instance, the setPressed() method of ButtonModel is called whenever the user presses or releases the mouse button. The previously given documentation is then directly expressed in the method's control flow, especially in lines 5–6 (value is the new pressed/non-pressed state).

←1.2.3

```
org.eclipse.draw2d.ButtonModel.setPressed

1 setFlag(PRESSED_FLAG, value);
2 if (value)
3     firePressed();
4 else {
5     if (isArmed())
6         fireReleased();
```

```
7   else
8       fireCanceled();
9 }
```

1.3.6   Caches

Designing networks of objects sometimes involves a dilemma between a natural structure that reflects the specification and problem domain directly, and the necessity to make frequently called methods really fast. This dilemma is best resolved by choosing the natural structure and method implementations to ensure correctness, and by making the methods store previously computed results in index data structures, such as `HashMaps`.

Caches hold derived data that could, in principle, be recomputed at any time.

A typical example is found in the Eclipse JDT's Java compiler. The compiler must track super-type relationships between defined classes and interfaces, and the natural structure is simple: Just store the types from the source code directly (a `ReferenceBinding` is an object representing a resolved type, either from the source or from a library):

org.eclipse.jdt.internal.compiler.lookup.SourceTypeBinding

```
public ReferenceBinding superclass;
public ReferenceBinding[] superInterfaces;
```

For any assignment c=d, the compiler will determine the types C and D of c and d, respectively. It must then decide whether a D object is valid for a C variable. This question clearly shows the dilemma mentioned previously: It is central for the correctness of the compiler, and should be implemented along the language specification by just searching through the `superclass` and `superInterfaces`. At the same time, it must be answered very often and very fast.

   Caching comes to the rescue: A `ReferenceBinding` implements the specification directly in a private method `isCompatibleWith0`. The method implements a linear search through the super-types and is potentially expensive. The public method `isCompatibleWith` therefore wraps calls by consulting a cache. The following code is slightly simplified. Line 1 looks up the previous result, which can be either `true`, `false`, or `null`. If the result is known (i.e., `result` is not `null`) then that result is returned (lines 2–3). Otherwise, the linear method is called. However, there is a snag: The search could end up in an infinite recursion if the type hierarchy contains a cycle. This is resolved by placing `false` into the cache and letting each recursion step go through the public method—a cycle ends in returning `false` immediately in line 3; at the same time, the recursion itself can take advantage of the cache. If despite this check the call in line 7 returns `true`, then no cycle can be present, so the result is updated to `true` (line 8). With this

setup, the answer to the subtyping query is computed only once for any
pair of types.

```
    org.eclipse.jdt.internal.compiler.lookup.ReferenceBinding.isCompatialbleWith
1 result = this.compatibleCache.get(otherType);
2 if (result != null) {
3     return result == Boolean.TRUE;
4 }
5     // break possible cycles
6 this.compatibleCache.put(otherType, Boolean.FALSE);
7 if (isCompatibleWith0(otherType, captureScope)) {
8     this.compatibleCache.put(otherType, Boolean.TRUE);
9     return true;
10 }
```

Caches are also a prime example of encapsulation, which is often motivated   ↰1.1 ↠4.1 ↠11.5.1
precisely by the fact that the object is free to exchange its internal data
structures for more efficient versions. Callers of isCompatibleWith are not
aware of the cache, apart from perhaps noting the superb performance. The
presence or absence of the cache does not change the object's observable
behavior.

⚠ One liability of caches is that they must be kept up-to-date. They contain information   ↠6.1.5
derived from possibly large object structures, and any change of these structures must
be immediately reflected in the cache. The OBSERVER pattern offers a general approach   ↠2.1
to this consistency problem. However, you should be aware of the trade-off between the
complexity of such a synchronization mechanism and the gain in efficiency obtained by
caching. The question of optimizations cannot be evaded by caches.   ↰1.1

⚠ Caches are effective only if the *same* answer is demanded several times. In other
contexts, this behavior is also called *locality of reference*. In the case of a cache
miss, the ordinary computation needs to be carried out anyway, while the overhead of
maintaining the cache is added on top. In the case of the compiler, it is probable that a
medium-sized code base, for instance during the recompilation of a project or package,
will perform the same type conversion several times.

🔎 For long-lived caches, you must start to worry about the cache outgrowing the original data structure, simply because more and more answers keep accumulating. The
central insight is that cache entries can be recomputed at any time, so you are free to
discard some if the cache gets too large. This strategy is implemented by the JDT's   📖99
JavaModelCache, which uses several ElementCaches to associate heavyweight information
objects with lightweight IJavaElement handles. Sometimes, a more elegant solution is   📖50
to leverage the garbage collector's support for *weak references*: A WeakHashMap keeps an   📖133
entry only as long as its key is referenced from somewhere else.

1.3.7   Data Shared Between Methods

»1.4.5

A central goal in coding methods is to keep the individual methods short and readable, by introducing separate methods for contained processing steps. Unfortunately, passing the required data can lead to long parameter lists, which likewise should be avoided. The obvious solution is to keep the data required by several methods in the object's fields.

←1.3.4 »1.8.6

This approach applies in particular when complex algorithms are represented by objects according to the STRATEGY pattern. Examples can be found in the `FastJavaPartitionScanner`, which maintains the basic structure of Java source code within editors, or in Zest's graph layout algorithms, such as `SpringLayoutAlgorithm`, but also in simple utilities such as the JDK's `StringTokenizer`.

When coding methods and their submethods, you often find out too late that you have forgotten to pass a local variable as a parameter. When you expect that the data will be needed in several methods anyway, Eclipse makes it simple to keep it in a field directly:

> **TOOL: Convert Local Variable to Field**
>
> Go to the local variable declaration in the Java editor. From the *Refactoring* menu (`Alt-Shift-T`), select *Convert local variable to field*. Alternatively, you can use Quick-Fix (`Ctrl-1`) on the variable declaration.

»7.1

This tool is particularly useful when the local variable contains an intermediate node in a larger data structure. For instance, when building a widget tree for display, you cannot always anticipate all the UI widgets that will need to be accessed in event listeners. Luckily, the problem is remedied by a quick keyboard shortcut.

⚠ Avoid introducing fields that contain valid data only temporarily; it can be rather tricky to ensure that all accesses will actually find valid data. If you find that you have several temporary fields, try to extract them to a separate class, together with the methods that use them. Very often, you will find that you are actually applying the STRATEGY pattern and are encapsulating an algorithm in an object.

1.3.8   Static Fields

The first rule about static fields is a simple one: Don't use them.

Reserve `static` fields for special situations.

←1.1

Static fields go against the grain of object-oriented programming: They are associated with classes, not objects, and classes should be an irrelevant, merely technical necessity. While you can reuse functionality in objects by creating just another instance, you cannot clone classes. That is, a class exists once per JVM.[3] When you find that you are using `static` fields very often, you should probably rather be writing in C (and even good C programmers shun global variables). However:

Do use constants.

Fields declared as `static final` are constants, meaning named values. They are not associated with classes at runtime, the compiler usually inlines them, and they disappear from the binaries altogether. Whenever you find in the code a stray literal value that has some meaning by itself, consider introducing a constant instead.

TOOL: Extract Constant

From the *Refactoring* menu (`Alt-Shift-T`), choose *Extract constant*.

It is sometimes inevitable to have global data for logical reasons. That is, when running Eclipse, there is only one `Platform` on which the application runs, one `ResourcesPlugin` that manages the disk state, and one `JobManager` that synchronizes background jobs. In such cases, you can apply the SINGLETON pattern. It ensures at least that clients keep working with objects and the implementation itself can also refer to a proper object.

»7.10

📖100

PATTERN: SINGLETON

If for logical reasons a particular class can have only one instance, then ensure that only one instance can ever be created and make it accessible globally.

To implement the pattern, maintain a static instance (line 2) with a global getter (line 4) and make the sole constructor private (line 3) to disable the creation of further instances. Lazy creation (line 6) can increase efficiency, since very often singletons are rather comprehensive classes.

```
1 public class Singleton {
2     private static Singleton instance;
3     private Singleton() {}
4     public static Singleton getInstance() {
5         if (instance == null)
6             instance = new Singleton();
7         return instance;
8     }
9 }
```

---

3. Technically, this is not quite true: A class is unique only within a class loader, and different class loaders may well load the same class several times, which leads to separate sets of its `static` fields coexisting at runtime. You should never try to exploit this feature, though.

⚠ Be very conscientious about the logical justification of single instances. Singletons may appear an easy way out if you have forgotten to pass around some required object and need just any instance quickly. Don't yield to that temptation: You lose the benefits of object-oriented programming, because your object's fields are essentially global variables.

⚠ As a special implication, singletons make testing harder, because it is not possible to change the type of created object. Tests have to work with exactly the same object as the production scenario. It is not possible to provide mock objects in creating a simplified fixture, so that its unit tests no longer run in the minimal possible context.

⚠ Be careful with SINGLETONS in multithreaded applications: When two threads invoke `getInstance()` simultaneously, it must be guaranteed that only a single instance is created. You can, for example, make the `getInstance` method `synchronized`, which uses the class's built-in lock. Beyond that, the singleton object itself must, of course, be thread-safe. If you feel you need a global object in a multithreaded environment, you can also consider using thread-local variables, which are supported in the Java library by class `ThreadLocal`.

1.4   Methods

If objects are to be active, collaborating entities, it is their methods that must make them active and that enable them to collaborate. In other words, simply invoking a method on an object is sufficient to induce the object to perform actions, compute results, or make decisions. Understanding methods is therefore key to understanding objects. We will also discuss many design patterns already in this section, because their intention is best motivated and explained from the behavior of the occurring methods.

1.4.1   An Object-Oriented View on Methods

In most presentations of object-oriented programming, methods are linked tightly with classes. You will know the approach: Classes define methods, the classes get instantiated, and one can invoke the defined methods on the instances.

```
public class BaseClass {
    public int op(int x) {
        return 2 * x;
    }
}
```

Margin references: 226, 163, »5.3.2.1, »5.3.2, »8.1, 148, 100

```
BaseClass obj = new BaseClass();
System.out.println(obj.op(18));
```

Object-oriented programming is then characterized by *polymorphism*: One can define derived classes (or subclasses), and override the methods introduced in the base class (or superclass).

```
public class DerivedClass extends BaseClass {
    public int op(int x) {
        return x + 24;
    }
}
```

The term polymorphism captures the fact that an object appears to have several "shapes." An object of the derived class can be used wherever the base class is expected. The object appears to have acquired a new shape. The transition from shape `DerivedClass` to shape `BaseClass` is explicit in the call to method `work()` shown next. Technically speaking, we must distinguish between the *static type* of a variable or field, as declared in the source code, and the *dynamic type*, which is the class instantiated at runtime to create the contained object. Under the typing rules of Java, the dynamic type is always a subtype of the static type (where subtyping is reflexive, meaning it includes the case of the types being the same).

```
public void workWithObjects() {
    DerivedClass obj = new DerivedClass();
    work(obj);
}
public void work(BaseClass obj) {
    System.out.println(obj.op(18));
}
```

We will not go into the details—you already know this material by heart.

To acquire a truly object-oriented coding style, it is, however, best to start out from a radically simple point of view:

Methods belong to the object, not to the class.

The language Smalltalk makes this view explicit: One does not "invoke" a method at all, but rather sends a *message* to the object and the object itself decides which *method* it will execute in response. The object-based language JavaScript takes an even more literal approach and says that "methods" are merely functions stored in an object's fields. In Java, the previously described simplification has the virtue of deliberately blurring the technical details of inheritance hierarchies: No matter *how* the method ended up in the object, the important thing is that it exists and can be invoked.

📖123,109

📖85

📖111

📖239

🔎 You will appreciate the simplicity of the formulation if you follow the details in the Java Language Specification. The core is in §15.12.4.4, which defines the *dynamic method lookup* procedure in method invocations, or more precisely *virtual* method invocations. Dynamic method lookup involves both the *runtime class* R of the target object and the *compile-time type* X of the object reference used to invoke the method m. It searches classes S, starting with R and traversing the hierarchy upward, until the central case applies: "If [...] the declaration in S overrides (§8.4.8.1) $X.m$, then the method declared in S is the method to be invoked [...]." Not only does this definition involve the interaction of several concepts, but it also gives only a procedural description of the lookup through a linear search in the inheritance hierarchy. If you think through these steps for every single method call, you will never get any coding done.

For practical purposes, the following understanding is sufficient:

When a class declares a method, then this method will be stored into all of its instances.
    Furthermore, a class inherits all methods declared in its superclass that it does not declare itself.

This formulation has the advantage that the runtime behavior remains simple: To find the invoked method, just look what has ended up in the object. The usual Java terminology is just a more detailed version:

📖111(§8.4.2)

- A method's *signature* consists of its name and parameter types.

- If a superclass happens to have declared a method with the same signature, then that method is said to be *overridden*.

- If a superclass or interface happens to have declared only an *abstract* method with the same signature, then that method is said to be *implemented*.

Method overriding replaces an inherited method with a new, completely independent version. Again, however, the important point is not the process, but the result:

➤➤3.1.1

Callers are not aware of the replacement of a method by overriding.

📖111(§15.12.4.4)
📖3,19,239

🔎 The technically minded reader may find it helpful to know that this is what actually happens internally: The JVM keeps a *method dispatch table* per class, which has a slot for every method declared in the hierarchy. Each slot contains a code pointer to the currently valid method; overriding replaces the code pointer. To invoke a method, the JVM merely looks up the table from the object, then the code from the table. C++ uses the term *virtual table* for the same concept.

TOOL: Override Method

To override one or more methods, choose *Source/Override or Implement Methods* (Alt-S V) and follow the steps in the dialog. For single methods, you can also type the name of an inherited method in a derived class, auto-complete it, and choose *Override Method*.

A second, more advanced tool takes care of slips in methods' signatures. It is often the case that you want to add new parameters—for instance, if a generalized implementation of a method requires more information, or if design changes require further collaborations and passing along further objects.

TOOL: Change Signature

To modify a method's signature consistently throughout the code base, place the cursor in the method's header, or its name at a call site, and use Alt-Shift-C (or Alt-Shift-T and the refactoring menu).

Finally, let us look at a special aspect of methods:

Use methods to enforce encapsulation.

Since the fields containing an object's state are its private concern, methods are the only way of accessing the object at all. At the same time, the methods' definition determines whether the fields really remain private. We have seen some pitfalls when passing and returning internal objects by reference, which enables clients to modify these internals. As a positive example, think back to the GapTextStore: Its public methods present a consistently simple view of a "stored text document" and never mention any aspects of its internal organization. You should always strive to write methods that do not allow the client even to *guess* at what goes on inside the object.

↰1.3 ↰1.1

↰1.3.3

↰1.3.1

1.4.2   Method Overloading

It remains to introduce briefly a second language feature concerning methods: *overloading*. Overloading is completely orthogonal, or complementary, to the question of overriding: The two can be used in isolation or can be combined arbitrarily.

Compared to overriding, overloading is very simple and happens completely at compile-time. If an object contains two methods with the same name, but different signatures, then the method is said to be *overloaded*. For a method call, the compiler *resolves* the overloading by choosing the "closest match" based on the types of the arguments. A method call in the created class file does not contain just the method's name, but its entire

📖111(§15.12.2)

signature. Consequently, there is no longer any ambiguity and no need for runtime choice. The usage of overloading is simple:

Overloading expresses a close logical relation between methods.

For instance, the Eclipse API for working with resources in the workspace offers two methods for obtaining a file from a surrounding folder:

org.eclipse.core.resources.IFolder

```
public IFile getFile(String name);
public IFile getFile(IPath path);
```

Indeed, the two methods are so closely related that the results of the following calls are the same (by `equals()`, since resource objects are handles):

```
IFile resultByString = folder.getFile("b/c");
IFile resultByPath =
folder.getFile(Path.fromPortableString("b/c"));
```

A special form of overloading is convenience methods, to be discussed
» 1.4.4   shortly. They represent simplified versions of very general methods.

↰ 1.1 ↰ 1.2.3 » 1.4.3   ⚠ You should take the logical connection implied by overloading seriously: The reader expects that basically the same thing will happen in all variants of the method. Think from the callers' perspective and aim at keeping their code readable. When in doubt, add some suffix to the name to disambiguate it.

🔎 Overloading and overriding interact at one special point: Overriding takes place only if two methods have the same signature. Up to Java 1.4, a common source of errors was that a method seemed to override an inherited one, but introduced a small variation in the parameters, so that the old method remained in place. The @Override annotation reduces that risk, since the compiler can at least check that *some* method has been overridden.

1.4.3   Service Provider

The first and most fundamental approach to using methods is to consider
↰ 1.1   them as services offered by the object to the outside world. Other objects can collaborate by invoking these methods, and can make use of the object's functionality instead of reimplementing it. Foremost, services are offered as `public` methods, because these are accessible to any other object in the system.

As a simple example, an `IFile` object in the Eclipse platform offers the following method to write data to disk. The data is given as an `Input Stream`, from which the bytes are read. Additional parameters specify whether changes not yet noticed by Eclipse should be ignored and whether a history entry for undo should be created. In the background, the object performs the disk updates, changes the internal resource data structures, and sends out change notifications—a complex service provided to the client object for free.

---

org.eclipse.core.resources.IFile.setContents

```
void setContents(InputStream source, boolean force,
        boolean keepHistory, IProgressMonitor monitor)
```

Further typical examples are found in the class GC from SWT, which enables drawing on the screen. They demonstrate the idea of "services" very well, because simple calls by the client require complex interactions with the operating system in the background. For example, just passing a position and a string to drawString() will take care of all font issues, such as rasterization and measuring.

    When writing service provider methods, the fundamental guide-line is:

»7.8

> Always think of methods from the clients' perspective.

A service method will be written once, but will potentially be used in many places throughout the code base. It is therefore essential to keep its use simple, even if this leads to a more complex implementation. Simplicity can often be gauged by a few basic questions: How many parameters must be provided? Is their meaning clear? Can the method's effect be described in 1–2 sentences? Are there complex side conditions on the use? It is also very helpful to write out a few use scenarios, possibly in the form of unit tests, to get a feeling for what the client code will look like, whether the code "tells its own story."

»4.1
»5.4.3
◄1.2.3

    Designing service methods always involves decisions. For example, consider again GapTextStore, which handles text documents for editors throughout Eclipse. Its core functionality is provided by a method replace(pos,len,txt), which performs the obvious text replacement. The Swing counterpart GapContent, in contrast, offers two separate methods insertString() and remove(). Both alternatives are certainly viable. While Swing's choice may be more natural from an application perspective, SWT's choice is more uniform from a technical point of view and also leads to further uniformity in other objects. For instance, undo/redo can be implemented in a single command class, instead of two. In any case, the crucial consideration is the expected use of the methods, not their implementation.

◄1.3.1
»9.5

    Certainly, not all public methods perform complex services. Sometimes, the services are extremely simple, such as accessing a property field. It is nevertheless necessary to consider such methods as full service providers. In particular, you should ask yourself—again—whether these methods should

◄1.3.3 ◄1.3.4

»2.1

actually be public. Furthermore, they may require new functionality along the way—for instance, they may notify observers about the change, or may maintain internal consistency conditions with other fields.

»3.1.2

»9.3.2

So far, we have looked at public methods, which are offered to the overall system. Objects usually also provide services for more restricted audiences. Services to subclasses are usually given by `protected` methods and require special care in calls, since the caller must understand more of the object's implementation. For instance, an `AbstractListViewer` maps linear data structures into lists or combo boxes on the screen. Internally, it keeps a mapping between data items and screen texts. The mapping is considered an implementation detail in general, but subclasses can still access it through methods like `indexForItem()`. Similarly, objects in a package sometimes collaborate closely, and their services to each other are presented as default visible methods.

»1.7

1.4.4   Convenience Method

Sometimes a service method is so general that calls become rather complex. When restricting the generality is not an option, it may be useful to provide convenience methods, which are sufficient for the most frequent applications and which internally delegate to the general method.

For instance, a tree widget on the screen can be told to expand the topmost levels of the displayed data structure through the following method `expandToLevel`. Really, this delegates to a more general method that expands below a given node:

org.eclipse.jface.viewers.AbstractTreeViewer

```java
public void expandToLevel(int level) {
    expandToLevel(getRoot(), level);
}
```

Similarly, a `Document` manages a text document with *positions*, which are markers that move according to modifications. The following convenience method allows simple clients to forget that there are actually several different categories of positions:

org.eclipse.jface.text.AbstractDocument

```java
public void addPosition(Position position)
        throws BadLocationException {
    addPosition(DEFAULT_CATEGORY, position);
}
```

»7

Whether to introduce convenience methods is, however, a decision not to be taken lightly. Having too many clutters up the API that users of the class have to learn. Worse, the semantics may become unclear. In `swt.Control`, for example, the general `setBounds(rect)` makes the widget cover a rectangular screen area; unexpectedly, `setLocation()` not only moves the widget, but also re-sizes it to width and height 0 (which is not stated in the documentation). It may also become unclear which method is the real implementation, so that it becomes hard to change the behavior by overriding. For instance, `Figures` in the Graphical Editing Framework have methods `setBounds()` and `setLocation()`; code inspection reveals that the latter is a convenience method for the former. However, from the documentation alone, the first might also call `setLocation()` and `setSize()`.

» 3.1.7
214

⚡ To clarify which one is the core method and to avoid confusion in overriding, you can make the convenience method `final` (in the example from `Figure`, `null` means "no layout constraint" and `-1` means "at the end"):

```java
public final void add(IFigure figure) {
    add(figure, null, -1);
}
```

Convenience methods should not be introduced for a particular client's convenience, but rather created only if they are useful as an additional interface. Their design is subject to the same considerations as that of general service methods.

1.4.5 Processing Step

The services of an object are rarely so simplistic that their implementation fits into the service provider method itself. Methods that span several screen pages are a maintenance nightmare, as they are write-only code. Realistically, once you get the test cases running, you will be only too happy to free your mind from the burden and move on to the next task. Then you have to keep hoping that the code will never be touched again.

Here is a typical example of how to get it right. Opening a new window on the screen seems simple enough: The client just calls `open()` on a `Window` object. The implementation shows the complexity: The window object negotiates with the operating system for resources, makes sure that the result fits on the screen, shows the window, and finally dispatches all events to the new window, if desired.

» 9.3.2

» 7.1
» 7.10.1

org.eclipse.jface.window.Window

```java
public int open() {
    create();
    constrainShellSize();
    shell.open();
    if (block) {
        runEventLoop(shell);
    }
    return returnCode;
}
```

This code shows good structuring; you can grasp the essence of the solution without knowing any of the details.

Use methods to break up the implementation into meaningful steps.

The steps are usually part of the object's implementation. That is, they are internal and therefore declared `private` or `protected`. Making them `private` clarifies their auxiliary status and there are no further difficulties. Making processing steps `protected`, in contrast, needs some reflection: Can subclasses reuse the steps for their own purposes? Then the methods become part of the subclass interface, which needs extensive consideration in itself. Or do you want subclasses to influence the behavior, by extension or according to the TEMPLATE METHOD pattern? All of those questions will be discussed in due course. For now, it is sufficient to summarize:

»1.4.8 »3.1.2

»1.4.11
»1.4.9

Take care not to expose internal processing steps inadvertently.

»1.4.8.3 »1.8.6 ☐27
Sometimes breaking up a method into smaller steps does not work out, because it requires complex parameter passing or temporary fields. In such cases, it is useful to factor out the method into a separate object according to the METHOD OBJECT pattern.

A more fundamental question is how to identify useful processing steps in the first place. The simplest approach is to allow yourself some wishful thinking: While coding some functionality that you know to be complex, just look out for bits that you know to be solvable, even if that resolution requires some further effort. Choose a descriptive name and just write down a call that you would think sensible, even though you know that the method does not yet exist.

TOOL: Create Method from Call

Place the cursor on the closing parenthesis and activate Quick-Fix (`Ctrl-1`). Eclipse will create a method below the current one that fits the call. Use `Tab` to jump to the linked positions at which Eclipse has made choices—for example, of parameter types and names—to amend those choices quickly.

The problem with wishful thinking is that it requires experience. In other words, you can think of useful steps only if you recognize a familiar pattern—that is, if you have coded something similar before. Making the right wishes can be surprisingly hard.

A complementary approach is to recognize processing steps after the fact, either in existing code or while you are coding. Eclipse's extensive tool support in this area testifies to the practical importance of this strategy.

> **TOOL: Extract Method**
>
> Select statements or a (sub)expression in the Java editor, then invoke the *Refactoring/Extract method* (by `Alt-Shift-M`, or through `Alt-Shift-T`). A pop-up dialog enables you to customize the result.

Eclipse is really amazingly intelligent: If it detects that some statement has a side effect on a local variable, it passes the current value as a parameter and returns the variable's new value from the method.

Tools, especially powerful tools, always need to be applied with care and consideration. Suppose that in the context of a spreadsheet application, you were to write a method that gets the cell content of a particular cell, ensuring that the cell exists. The row and column are given in 1-based, user-oriented notation. You may come up with the following code (`cells` is a `HashMap`):

»9.4

```
                    methods.refactoring.ExtractExampleCells00
1  public String getCellContent(int userRow, int userCol) {
2      Cell c = cells.get(new CellRef(userRow - 1, userCol - 1));
3      if (c != null) {
4          c = new Cell();
5          cells.put(new CellRef(userRow - 1, userCol - 1), c);
6      }
7      return c.content;
8  }
```

When you extract lines 2–6, you get a method `getOrCreateCell` with a tangle of functionality: It shifts indices to internal notation, adds cells as required, and so on. Very often, you have to clean up the code before extracting methods, and in many cases, a second tool comes to the rescue.

> **TOOL: Extract Variable**
>
> Select an expression and bind its result to a local variable by `Alt-Shift-L` (or refactor with `Alt-Shift-T`; or Quick-Fix with `Ctrl-1`). Variable extraction can also replace multiple occurrences of an expression simultaneously.

To select an expression for extraction, it is sufficient to place the cursor onto a character that belongs to none of its subexpressions, such as the operator in a binary expression.

For instance, if you want to capture only the on-the-fly creation of new cells, you would extract the `CellRef` objects into a variable and would end up with this code:

---
methods.refactoring.ExtractExampleCells01

```
public String getCellContent(int userRow, int userCol) {
    CellRef key = new CellRef(userRow - 1, userCol - 1);
    Cell c = getOrCreateCell(key);
    return c.content;
}
```

If you like this better, you can immediate inline the parameter, and the variable c as well.

> **TOOL: Inline Variable**
>
> Select a variable declaration or a variable reference and press Alt-Shift-I (or Alt-Shift-T for the menu).

This leaves you with the following neat code:

---
methods.refactoring.ExtractExampleCells02

```
public String getCellContent(int userRow, int userCol) {
    return getOrCreateCell(
        new CellRef(userRow - 1, userCol - 1)).content;
}
```

Looking at this code, you might see another piece of useful functionality lurking inside, and obtain the following final version. Note also how introducing an additional method makes the code "tell its own story."

↶1.2.3

---
methods.refactoring.ExtractExampleCells03

```
public String getCellContent(int userRow, int userCol) {
    return getOrCreateCell(convertExternalCoordinates(userRow,
            userCol)).content;
}
```

This example demonstrates a general guideline:

Plan method refactorings carefully and judge the result by readability.

Nevertheless, you will note that modifying code with the Eclipse tools is fundamentally different from writing code. The code is no longer a stiff, unmodifiable, fixed mass of statements, but becomes malleable, so you can easily mold or massage it into new shapes at the expense of a few keyboard short-cuts. Also, an *undo* will revert all modifications simultaneously, which leaves you free to experiment until you are satisfied with the result.

Despite the ease of code editing and experimentation, the original goal for introducing methods as processing steps remains valid:

Identify processing steps from the meaning and context of the code.

Methods, even internal helper methods, are never merely technical. Always be aware that methods structure your solution and shape the way that you, and later your team, will think about the solved problem.

Going one step beyond, this thought touches on the old debate about whether code should be written bottom-up, from the smaller steps to the larger, or top-down, by wishful thinking, from the general strategy to the details. In practice, the question arises very rarely, because both require experience with similar problems solved. When solving new problems, your first concern is to find and understand any solution. In the words of Tim Budd:

📖55(§2.3)

> [...] design might be said to progress from the known to the unknown.

In the extreme, this might actually lead to bottom-up code development, if you are working in an area that you are very familiar with. If you know that a particular bit of functionality will come in useful, you should not hesitate to write it down as a building block for the later development.

Write down what you clearly understand is necessary.

In summary, Eclipse's powerful tool support enables you to start coding, perhaps along test cases to be solved, and later restructure the code to facilitate maintenance. We close the discussion on methods as processing steps with one final guideline, which holds regardless of the way by which you have arrived at your code:

📖92
»5.2

Don't forget to clean up your code once you have understood the solution.

1.4.6   Explanatory Methods

Method names are extremely powerful documentation. In the declaration, they head the method body and leave the reader with an anticipation, an expectation of what that code will probably achieve. At the same time, the method name appears at the call sites. There, it gives a summary of a particular computation that needs to be performed. Methods can therefore be used as named pieces of code.

↰1.2.3

Use method calls to express and document your overall solution strategy.

This advice is actually at the heart of agile software development. This approach encourages you to cut down on wasted work. For instance, rather than writing documentation that no one reads or updates, it is more sensible to put an extra effort into creating good code structure to make the code self-documenting. Having short methods with descriptive names is a first, fundamental step.

📖28 📖172

When tempted to write an inline comment, introduce a method instead.

↰1.3.1

To see what can be achieved, consider the following excerpt from the Gap TextStore. To prepare for an insertion, it can just move the gap, or else it must reallocate the backing array because of insufficient space. The core of the method exhibits that choice, and also the contained parallelism, beautifully:

org.eclipse.jface.text.GapTextStore.adjustGap

```
if (reuseArray)
    newGapEnd = moveGap(offset, remove, oldGapSize, newGapSize,
        newGapStart);
else
    newGapEnd = reallocate(offset, remove, oldGapSize, newGapSize,
        newGapStart);
```

»12

Introducing explanatory methods also does not require deep thought or weighing of alternatives. The goal is not reusability or extensibility, but merely a place to put an expressive name. Making the methods private ensures that no one learns about their existence and that you remain free to restructure your code if you happen to find a better solution later on. Don't hesitate to extract methods with the tools *Extract Method* and *Extract Variable* for the purpose: Having a good, explanatory name is better than having no name at all. And in case you ever follow a dead-end street, there is always a simple solution:

> **TOOL: Inline Method**
>
> Place the cursor on a method name and press Alt-Shift-I to inline the method's body (or use Alt-Shift-T for the *Refactoring* menu).

1.4.7   Events and Callbacks

Very often methods defined by an object are not services or functionality offered *to* others, but rather points where the object accepts notifications *from* others. Observers are interested in state changes of other objects; visitors are called back for each node encountered in a hierarchical data structure. In the context of frameworks, inversion of control dictates that the framework decides when to run which application code. Callback methods are usually defined in interfaces and are then implemented in different objects. Examples can be found in the corresponding sections.

»2.1
»2.3.2
»7.3

»3.2.6

Technically, there is nothing special about a callback: The method gets called and the object executes the code to update its state and carry out suitable operations. Conceptually, however, callback methods cannot be understood from the caller's perspective, but only from the object's perspective—that is, the object alone determines the suitable reaction to the method call. Furthermore:

»7.11
↰1.1 ↰1.4.3

Understanding callbacks requires understanding the framework's mechanisms.

You also need complementary knowledge about the framework's mechanisms to understand when and why the method will be called. The method achieves its purpose only because the environment makes guarantees about the circumstances under which it will call the method. For instance, the JFace *viewers* display application data on the screen. They use *content providers* to access that data. These must provide, among other things, the following method:

»1.4.9 »3.1.2

»9.3.2

---
org.eclipse.jface.viewers.IContentProvider

```
public void inputChanged(Viewer viewer, Object oldInput,
    Object newInput);
```

To properly understand and implement this method, you have to know that it will be called whenever `setInput()` is invoked on the viewer, that `oldInput` can be `null` (for the first call), and that there will be one last call with `newInput==null` when the display widget is removed from the screen. That last case is important to de-register any observers that the content provider may have registered. The method name alone does not always tell the whole story.

»2.1.2

1.4.8 Reused Functionality

Code reuse is a fundamental and continuous challenge in software development: We simply cannot afford to recode a solution whenever we re-encounter a known problem. At a technical level, methods form the basis of reuse; they contain the solution's code and make it available as a service to any client that requires it. This approach to reuse raises the deeper question of which object, or class, should contain the code—that is, where a solution to a recurring problem is best placed to be as widely available as possible. Of course, the answer goes beyond single methods, to objects or even subsystems, if the solution requires more infrastructure.

»12.4

»1.8.6 »1.7
📖243

For the moment, we will start with methods. Also, in practice, you will often be faced with this situation: You see a method that implements a functionality that you require—how can you reuse it without reverting to copy-and-paste? The different answers to that question structure the subsequent discussion.

1.4.8.1 Reuse Within a Class

At the most basic level, an object offers the reusable functionality only to itself. Technically, the methods are `private`, or `protected` if they are to be available within the inheritance hierarchy. As a tiny but typical example, the developers of `GapTextStore` have realized that the representation of the *gap* by indices `gapStart` and `gapEnd` may not be ideal, since in many

◄1.4.5

◄1.3.1

situations the representation by `gapStart` and `gapSize` would be more adequate. They have therefore introduced a reusable service that converts to that representation on the fly, rather than inlining the computation, which would be simple enough.

```
org.eclipse.jface.text.GapTextStore.gapSize
```
```
private int gapSize() {
    return fGapEnd - fGapStart;
}
```

1.4.8.2 Reuse Through Inheritance

The availability of `protected` methods throughout the inheritance hierarchy was considered a prime motivation for object-oriented programming in the early days. When developers required new functionality, they would simply extend a suitably close class in the library and then have to provide only the missing bits, building on the existing infrastructure.

»3.1.7

»9.3.2

As an example of such reuse, consider `StructuredViewer`, which is a base class for many of JFace's viewers, including lists, tables, and trees. Each such viewer maintains an association between application data items and widgets on the screen, such as rows in lists, tables, and trees. A fundamental service then is to map a data item to its widget. The corresponding `protected` method `findItem()` is called at roughly 20 places throughout the hierarchy.

Achieving reuse requires careful planning and broad experience.

↰1.4.5

132,130,131,71

If it was hard to identify suitable processing steps, it is harder still to identify reusable services, methods that will be useful beyond the context in which they were invented. This task requires experience as well as forethought; it requires an overview of common problems, their best solutions, and an anticipation of their usage. What is more, there is a high danger of spending a lot of effort on "reusable," "general" solutions that will turn out not be used in the end. The task is daunting, perhaps too daunting to be attempted.

92

Fortunately, agile software development has taught us not to aspire to the one, ultimate solution immediately. Rather, it advocates that we just "do the simplest thing that could possibly work." If later on that solution turns out to be no longer good enough for the newest challenge, you can always refactor it.

28
92

↰1.2.2

For instance, suppose you have a fairly complex `private` processing step in one of your classes, which works with several fields and invokes several sub-steps. The class was never intended for reuse, and it does not yet have subclasses or a superclass (apart from `Object`, of course). But the code is readable, stable, and general, and you want to reuse it. Inheritance can be put to use as shown in Fig. 1.3: You move the reusable code to a place where it can be accessed from outside its current context, by introducing a superclass. Eclipse makes it simple to implement this solution:

> **TOOL: Extract Superclass**
>
> In the Java editor, choose *Extract Superclass* from the *Refactoring* menu (Alt-Shift-T). Choose the members that embody the desired functionality. The preview within the dialog is useful for detecting broken dependencies and fixing them by extracting further members. If a class already has an explicit superclass, the tool pushes the new class in between the two.

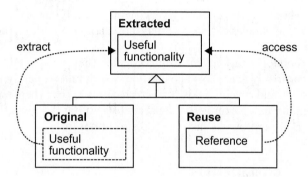

Figure 1.3 Extracting a Superclass for Reuse

If you already have a class hierarchy set up and later realize that some processing step is more generally useful, you can invoke a more specialized extraction on methods and fields only.

> **TOOL: Pull Up**
>
> In the Java editor, choose *Pull up* from the *Refactoring* menu (Alt-Shift-T). In the dialog, select the members to be moved up. The member in which the cursor was placed is preselected.

As an example, the classes `MouseController` and `KeyboardController` »9.2 in the online supplement were actually created in this way, starting from the first one. Looking at the code, and in particular their superclass `Controller`, you can still trace the process.

Note that, as in the case of processing steps, the ability to massage and mold code into place by powerful tools does not free us from careful planning: we were able to extract the `Controller` only because we had written a few dozen controllers previously and knew their commonalities. ▭71

Focus on conceptual commonalities, extract them to methods, and then to superclasses.

The Eclipse tools do not provide any intelligence; that part remains with the developers. They merely free developers from the technical chores and enable them to focus on conceptual decisions.

1.4.8.3   Reuse Through Separate Objects

»3.1.2 »3.1.11 ▢232

Although reuse through hierarchies may appear particularly "object-oriented," and hence nifty or desirable, it is by no means the only approach to reuse. Indeed, it is not even the best option, since it leads to rather severe complications: It fills the single available superclass slot and

»3.1.4 »3.1.2
»3.1.11

couples the classes in the hierarchy very tightly. Modifying a base class can easily break the subclasses, so you may not be able to adapt the class to new challenges.

Let us therefore start again: You recognize that some useful, complex functionality already exists in some method, which unfortunately uses other helper methods and several fields. An alternative strategy then is to extract the functionality into a completely separate object. Fig. 1.4 gives the desired result, and Eclipse provides just the tools to obtain it.

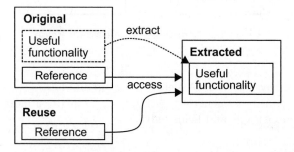

Figure 1.4 Extracting an Object for Reuse

TOOL: Extract Class

Invoke *Refactoring/Extract Class* (Alt-Shift-T) and select the fields on which the functionality will work. The tool will introduce a helper object in a new field and redirect all references to the extracted fields to that helper.

Compared to the *Extract Superclass* dialog, this one may be disappointing: You cannot even extract the methods you were interested in! Fortunately, Eclipse remedies this with a second tool:

TOOL: Move Method to Helper

Place the cursor into a method and invoke *Refactoring/Move* (Alt-Shift-V) to move it to the extracted helper object. Again, the tool will update the references within the method and to the method accordingly. You can also keep the original method, if other clients wish to refer to it and you do not want to publish the helper object (even though you will publish the helper class).

In Eclipse 4.3, you *cannot* move fields to the helper object in the same way. You have to extract them in the initial step.

When you follow these steps, you obtain a completely independent object that acts as a container for the desired functionality. This solution is actually closer to the guidelines on objects than the one based on inheritance: The extracted object is small and self-contained; its fields and methods are not lumped into the objects that require its services. Also, the object can be used more flexibly; you can even create temporary instances on the fly, within arbitrary methods.

»1.8.5 »1.8.6

←1.1

Another way of looking at the newly created object is to say that it encapsulates a method or algorithm. This leads to the more general idea of capturing a complex piece of code as a separate object with the aim of making it more self-contained and understandable.

»1.8.6

1.4.8.4   Reuse Through Static Methods

In rather rare cases, the functionality to be reused is an algorithm or a mathematical calculation that does not relate to any hidden state in some object. Examples are `Collections.sort()`, `Array.binarySearch()`, and `Math.sin()`. Furthermore, utility methods often take this form, such as `SwingUtilities` or `Geometry` in SWT.

In principle, however, static methods are not properly object-oriented: They do not belong to objects, but rather to classes. If some later extension of the functionality happens to require fields after all, you have to rearrange your software quite severely, by passing along suitable object references. The general guideline, as with static fields, therefore is:

»1.3.8

Reserve static methods for special occasions.

When considering whether to introduce a static method, always recall the *bon mot* and ask yourself: Am I perhaps being a FORTRAN programmer writing my FORTRAN program in Java?

210

109(Ch.16)

A fundamental conceptual reason for avoiding `static` is that classes in Java are second-class citizens: The objects accessible through `.class` or `getClass()` do not exhibit dynamic dispatching, they cannot implement interfaces, and so on. In contrast, Smalltalk starts from the premise that "everything is an object"—even the classes. The question follows: What is the class of a class? It is a *meta-class*, which defines the (static) methods of the class, and inheritance on classes induces inheritance on their meta-classes—in consequence, one can override static methods. The flexibility ends, however, one step further: The class of all meta-classes is `MetaClass`, a fixed entity, just like `Class` in Java.

1.4.9   Template Method

1.4.5

We have examined the idea of wishful thinking for inventing processing steps: While writing some larger method, you postpone implementing the details by introducing methods as placeholders. You can do this because you know that there is a suitable implementation, but writing it down would sidetrack you at this point. One step beyond, you may be aware that there are several useful implementations of a step, each of which would give rise to a useful variant of the overall algorithm. This is a typical scenario for introducing a TEMPLATE METHOD: You write a method that is merely a template, a blueprint where some steps are intentionally left out.

70
100

PATTERN: TEMPLATE METHOD

Template methods provide the main structure of a computation, while keeping some steps flexible to cater to different application scenarios.

1. Implement the blueprint of a service in a base class.

2. Make steps that allow different implementations into `protected abstract` methods.

3. Introduce different derived classes to fill in the variants of the steps.

You may also choose to provide default implementations for some steps. This reduces the effort that clients have to spend in simple cases.

Introducing a method as `abstract` is a generally useful trick to force subclasses to decide on an implementation. Also, Eclipse will guide the developer a long way: It will display an error and will also offer to Quick-Fix it by declaring the missing methods. The `abstract` tag here serves as a technical reminder of missing functionality.

9.3.2

As an example, consider JFace's `AbstractListViewer`. It provides the infrastructure for displaying application data in simple widgets such as lists and combo boxes. A central task is this: Whenever the application data changes, the corresponding display must be updated. Toward that end, one must determine the row in the list, compute the new text to be shown, and finally display that text. All but the last step in lines 7–8 are generic; that is, they work for any kind of list:

```
1  protected void doUpdateItem(Widget data, Object element,
2    boolean fullMap) {
3      if (element != null) {
4          int ix = getElementIndex(element);
5          ILabelProvider labelProvider =
6              (ILabelProvider) getLabelProvider();
7          listSetItem(ix, getLabelProviderText(labelProvider,
8              element));
9      }
10 }
```

The only place where the kind of display widget does matter is the actual update of the displayed text. That is left to be implemented in subclasses:

```
protected abstract void listSetItem(int index, String string);
```

The example also shows that experience and analysis are necessary in applying the pattern: Passing the text to be displayed might be an easy deduction, but how can you be sure that an index alone will be sufficient information for actually placing it at the correct position? That knowledge can be gained only by looking at the API of concrete SWT widgets—that is, `List`, `Combo`, and `CCombo`. All of them offer a `setItem(pos, text)` service method, so that the different variants can, in fact, be implemented directly.

» 7.1

⚠ The example indicates not to use TEMPLATE METHOD lightly. To emphasize the point, if you take the pattern to the extreme, you would write methods that consider each substep as a possible point of variation. You would end up with classes that can be adapted flexibly to different situations, just by introducing subclasses. You would, in fact, be creating a white-box framework. At the same time, the danger of introducing and paying for "Speculative Generality" would be extremely high.

» 7.3.3
📖 92

Since template methods are extremely common, Eclipse provides support for creating them. In a first scenario, you might find that method reuse through a common superclass does not quite work out, because some parts of the method must differ between the original and the new calls.

↰ 1.4.8.2

TOOL: Pull Up for Templates

The tool *Pull Up* (`Alt-Shift-T`) allows you to pull up methods as abstract declarations only, through the action *Declare abstract in destination*. To introduce a TEMPLATE METHOD, pull it up as usual, but pull up some of its steps as declarations only. The same applies to the tool *Extract Superclass*.

»3.1.5
»1.4.5
A second scenario occurs when you have a general method in a base class that has so far worked uniformly for all subclasses in your system. At some point, however, a new subclass (i.e., a new special case) requires a slightly different behavior. You can first use *Extract Method* to factor out the changed behavior into a separate processing step. Then, you can override the method in the new subclass. In effect, you have created a TEMPLATE METHOD with a default implementation.

One step further, you might also notice that, in fact, many subclasses require different implementations of the step. To force their developers to make a decision, you wish to make the step `abstract` in the base class, and to push down the default implementation into the existing subclasses. Eclipse enables you to do just that:

TOOL: Push Down

To enable different implementations of a method in the hierarchy, place the cursor in the method and choose *Refactoring/Push down* (`Alt-Shift-T`). When you choose *Leave abstract declaration* as the action, you effectively turn all callers of the method into template methods.

1.4.10   Delegated to Subclass

📖48 »3.1.5
A classical usage of inheritance involves modeling of abstraction hierarchies: The base classes capture some abstract concept that exhibits some general behavior and promises general services to its clients, while the derived classes represent special cases that will implement that behavior according to their own specific natures.

»9.3.2
In this context, it is natural that some of the services cannot be implemented at all at the general level. For instance, JFace introduces the abstraction of a *viewer*, which maps application data into display widgets on the screen. Any type of viewer takes some data structure as its *input* and, among other things, enables the user to *select* items from the data structure. The following two methods capture this promise to the client, yet they are abstract because text viewers and structured viewers, such as lists or tables, require completely different implementations.

---
org.eclipse.jface.viewers.Viewer

```
public abstract void setInput(Object input);
public abstract ISelection getSelection();
```

»2.3
A further field for such delegated services is the COMPOSITE pattern, where recursive operations are declared in the root class of the hierarchy and are implemented in each concrete subclass. This structure enables clients to work uniformly with any objects in the composite structure.

1.4.11   Extending Inherited Behavior

In general, method overriding is used to adapt an object's behavior to fit its special purpose. The adaptation is usually arbitrary. There is one special case, though, that is often found in abstraction hierarchies: The overriding method must only add to, not replace, the behavior of the overridden method. In other words, the superclass relies on its own method being called by the subclass.

»3.1.7 »6.4.1

A typical example is found in the hierarchy of JFace *viewers*. They take a widget on the screen and augment it to display application-specific data. Toward that end, they must initially *hook* themselves to the widget. The class `ContentViewer` therefore introduces a method `hookControl()`, which performs the necessary work. Subclasses add further hooks according to their needs. A `StructuredViewer`, for example, must react to double-clicks and similar actions that indicate the user wants to "open" the current selection. Note how the first action of the subclass is to invoke the superclass method to preserve its behavior.

»9.3.2

»7.1

```
org.eclipse.jface.viewers.StructuredViewer
protected void hookControl(Control control) {
    super.hookControl(control);
    OpenStrategy handler = new OpenStrategy(control);
    ...
}
```

When extending methods to *destruct* objects, such as to unregister hooks or free resources at the end of an object's life cycle, it is important to call the superclass's method *at the end*. Otherwise, the added code would work on a partially invalid object. Examples can be found in the `dispose()` methods of the Eclipse editor hierarchy—for instance, below class `TextEditor`. It is useful here to think in terms of parentheses: When *adding* structure, you invoke `super` first; when *removing* structure, you invoke `super` last—the `super` calls bracket your own code. Typical examples are given in the `EditParts` from the Graphical Editing Framework, in methods `activate()` and `deactivate()`.

◄1.1

»12.2.1.2

▢214

1.4.12   Factory Methods

We claimed in Chapter 1 that classes are second-class citizens that are conceptually less important than objects. One reason is their lack of flexibility. While you can pass objects around at runtime, once you write `new Label()`, that's it—you get a plain, simple text label for your UI. There is no chance of creating a more sophisticated display with style markups under different circumstances. Fortunately, this universal problem also has a universally applicable solution:

»7.1

PATTERN: FACTORY METHOD

Delegate the choice of a concrete class to be instantiated to subclasses, by introducing a method that subclasses can override.

1. Think about a common interface that all *products* must implement and make it the return type.

2. Think about the information that possible *concrete products* may require and pass it as parameters. Note that the object's fields are also accessible.

3. If a default implementation is not sensible, make the method `abstract`.

↰1.4.1
↰1.4.9

Because factory methods effectively postpone the choice of the class to runtime, analogously to virtual method dispatch, they are also called *virtual constructors*. Usually, FACTORY METHODS are called from TEMPLATE METHODS: they are part of a larger algorithm where at one point an object must be created to proceed.

📖214

Examples can be found throughout any larger framework. However, they usually mix object creation with initialization. A typical case is found in the Graphical Editing Framework, where *tools*, such as for creating new drawing elements or connections between them, send a *request* to the element currently under the mouse. The type of request naturally depends on the kind of tool, which is solved by a FACTORY METHOD:

org.eclipse.gef.tools.TargetingTool

```
protected Request createTargetRequest()
```

↰1.3.4

Note that factory methods are a rather heavyweight tool: Whenever clients want to adapt the behavior, they must derive a new class and override the method. That's a lot of work and boilerplate code. If only a single instance will be created anyway, it is more flexible to let clients pass in that instance as a configuration parameter. Especially when you are about to introduce several factory methods, stop to think twice: Clients must create a new subclass for each useful *combination* of products.

Prefer parameterization by objects to factory methods when possible.

Of course, factory methods can create several instances over the object's lifetime and can access the entire context of the host object's fields. So in the end you must make a design decision:

Prefer factory methods if the product is tightly integrated with its context.

Between these two opposite poles, there is a third solution that sometimes balances the forces: Instead of integrating the factory method tightly, you can pass an object containing the factory method. This construction then resembles STRATEGY, if you say that creating an object is just a particular kind of "algorithm." ↰1.3.4

A typical example is the JFace `SourceViewer`, which lies at the core of most of Eclipse's text editors. On the one hand, that class is fairly complex, so it is not advisable to force developers to subclass it for configuration, because they would be exposed to that complexity. On the other hand, the class needs to be highly configurable by tightly interacting objects. The solution is to have many configuration fields, but to fill them through an ABSTRACT FACTORY, an object that creates objects on demand. The relevant method (greatly abbreviated) then asks the configuration object to create all the features that you also recognize as a user (from the Auto-Complete, Quick-Fix, and Format tools):

org.eclipse.jface.text.source.SourceViewer

```
public void configure(SourceViewerConfiguration configuration) {
    fContentAssistant = configuration.getContentAssistant(this);
    fQuickAssistAssistant =
        configuration.getQuickAssistAssistant(this);
    fContentFormatter = configuration.getContentFormatter(this);
    ...
}
```

Note that each of the creation methods gets `this` as a parameter. For instance, the content assistant can be linked to the viewer at creation time:

org.eclipse.jface.text.source.SourceViewerConfiguration

```
public IContentAssistant
    getContentAssistant(ISourceViewer sourceViewer)
```

The pattern behind this code is summarized here: ▱100

PATTERN: ABSTRACT FACTORY

You want to enable families of logically related objects to be chosen or exchanged at runtime. Then hide the details of how the objects are created behind an interface.

1. Decide which interfaces the *products* need to implement to fit into the intended context of use.

2. Decide which information from the context should be available to the products—that is, how they can interact with their context.

3. Define an interface containing one method for each kind of product you require. Steps 1 and 2 give the return and parameter types.

> As with FACTORY METHOD, it simplifies the life of clients if the interface is given as an abstract class and some products have useful defaults.

»12.3

📖214

Abstract factories have the drawback of fixing the kinds of products, since each product needs a separate method—abstract factories are not extensible. *Extensible* abstract factories are obtained by introducing more comprehensive categories of products. For instance, the Graphical Editing Framework uses *edit parts* to access application data and display it on the screen. For each data item, GEF creates a new edit part. It is very liberal about which edit parts are allowed and does not make too many assumptions about them. Therefore, the abstract factory has a single method. It is extensible, because concrete factories can introduce new kinds of edit parts, one for each kind of `appData`.

---
org.eclipse.gef.EditPartFactory
```
EditPart createEditPart(EditPart context, Object appData);
```

Abstract factories also have the effect of hiding the classes of the concrete products completely: Clients of the factory can access the products only through the interfaces given in the creation methods. For instance, the W3C has specified Java language bindings for the XML document object model (DOM) as a set of interfaces. The concrete implementation is hidden completely. At the entry point, the library searches for any implementation available in the system; from there, you create documents, their elements, and other things.

---
xmldom.ReadXML.readXMLDocument
```
DocumentBuilderFactory builderFactory = DocumentBuilderFactory
        .newInstance();
```

A classic example is the `Toolkit` of the *abstract window toolkit* (AWT) introduced in early Java versions. A `Toolkit` has abstract methods for creating concrete native widgets on the screen, one for each kind of widget supported. To port the AWT to a different operating system, it is sufficient to implement a new `Toolkit`.

↩1.3.8 📖235

Specializing one step further, abstract factories that intend to hide the implementation are often SINGLETONs. For instance, the Eclipse Modeling Framework (by default) hides the implementation classes behind a factory, and creates one instance in a static field `eINSTANCE`. The same goal can be attained with a different implementation, by making the factory methods themselves `static`. This choice is applied frequently in the Eclipse platform to hide the implementation of subsystems. For instance, `JavaUI` provides factory methods for common dialogs related to Java editing. `JavaCore` can create handles on Java source or class files, Java projects, and so on. Both classes hide the actual implementation classes behind interfaces. Since clients are shielded from subsystems, these factories can also be considered instances of FACADE.

»3.2.7
»1.7.2

The size of this section on factory methods and the breadth of their applications reflects their practical relevance. At the end, however, you may be left with the impression that you should be using more factory methods anyway, since they seem to offer so many advantages. However:

Decide to use factory methods only after careful consideration.

Coming back to the initial example, when you write `new Label()`, you know what you get: a plain, simple, easy-to-use text on the screen. If you delegate the creation, you may still get a "label-like thing," but you know less about its behavior, so you may be less able to depend on its behavior. Debugging then involves understanding which object has been created and why in the first place. Remember to start with "the simplest thing that could possibly work." You can always use *Extract Method* and then *Push Down* or *Extract class* to introduce factory methods later on.

▱28

1.4.13 Identity, Equality, and Hashing

Objects in Java, and other object-oriented languages, are handled *by reference*. In other words, variables, parameters, fields, and arrays always contain pointers or *references* to objects, never the objects themselves. Passing or storing an object means passing or storing a pointer, a really cheap operation. Testing `a == b` with objects `a` and `b` tests whether they are identical, the very same object (i.e., whether `a` and `b` are identical as pointers).

Since objects are always handled by reference, they have *reference semantics*. In the following code, `s` and `r` refer to the same object. The call `r.translate()` modifies that object and the modification is visible through `s`. The fact that `r` and `s` refer to the same object is also called *aliasing* of the references.

core.JavaObjectsTest.referenceSemantics
```
Rectangle r = new Rectangle(100, 200, 40, 50);
Rectangle s = r;
r.translate(20, 30);
assertTrue(s.x == 120 && s.y == 230);
```

The meaning of an object usually depends on its identity, since it often represents some entity outside of the software world. However, some objects are conceptually values: One `Integer` is as good as another `Integer` as long as they store the same `int` value; one `String` is as good as another `String` as long as both contain the same characters. Comparing such *value objects* by == does not make sense. In particular, there is a common mistake among Java novices:

↰1.1
↠1.8.4

Do not compare `Strings` by ==, with the sole exception of constants.

Value objects by convention declare a method `equals()` that determines whether two objects represent the same value. That method is introduced in `Object`, where by default it just checks identity by `==`. The method is used throughout the library. For instance, collections like `List` use it to find elements, such as in the methods `contains()` and `indexOf()`. The requirement on the method's behavior there is that it is indeed a proper "equality" check (mathematically speaking, an *equivalence relation*):

1. An object is always equal to itself: `a.equals(a)`. Mathematicians call this property *reflexivity*, and so does the JavaDoc.

2. An object is *never* equal to `null`: `a.equals(null)` yields `false`.

3. The argument order does not matter: `a.equals(b)` is always the same as `b.equals(a)` (provided neither a nor b is `null`, of course). Technically, this is called *symmetry*.

4. Groups of equal objects can be identified: if `a.equals(b)` and `b.equals(c)`, then `a.equals(c)`. This property is called *transitivity*.

Obtaining these properties may be, in fact, a bit intricate, as the following implementation for an object with a single `int` field `val` shows. Lines 2–3 take care of the special case 2. Lines 4–5 play a double role. First, they ensure that the downcast in line 6 will succeed. Second, they ensure property 3; simply using `other instanceof IntVal` in line 4 would break symmetry in case `other` is an instance of a subclass that itself overrides `equals()`. Property 4 then follows, because the checks in lines 4 and 7 are transitive if both are successful.

```
equality.IntVal.equals
 1 public boolean equals(Object obj) {
 2     if (obj == null)
 3         return false;
 4     if (getClass() != obj.getClass())
 5         return false;
 6     IntVal other = (IntVal) obj;
 7     if (val != other.val)
 8         return false;
 9     return true;
10 }
```

⌕ Just in case you care to double-check: `Integer.equals()` in the library does use `instanceof`, but that class is `final`, so that no subclasses can break symmetry.

Fortunately, Eclipse has a tool that takes care of these details for us. In fact, it has generated the preceding example code.

> **TOOL: Generating `equals` and `hashCode`**
>
> Use *Source/Generate hashCode and equals* to obtain a correct implementation that checks selected fields for equality.

The second method generated here, `hashCode()`, is also declared in `Object`. It is employed in `HashMap`, `HashSet`, and their variants, for hash-based indexing in large collections. Roughly speaking, they look at a few bits of an object's hash code first and then search linearly only through the (relatively few) objects that happen to have the same bits. For this scheme to work out, `hashCode()` should exhibit the following behavior:

📖72

1. The result is compatible with `equals()`; that is, `a.equals(b)` implies `a.hashCode()==b.hashCode()`, since otherwise the equal objects will not be found by the above search.

2. The method returns the same value, as long as the object's fields do not change.

3. The hash code should be pseudo-random, to minimize the chances that non-equal objects have the same hash code.

The default implementation `Object.hashCode()` must therefore match the default implementation of `equals`, which checks object identity `==`. The corresponding hash code is computed by `System.identityHashCode()`, which is usually based on the object's address.

🔍 Conscientious readers will note that there is a possible interaction with efficient moving garbage collectors: Moving an object to a new address must not change its hash code because of property 2. The solution is to tag the (relatively few) objects whose hash code has been computed and that have actually been moved, and to store the original hash code explicitly in this case.

↰1.1 📖133
📖19(§3.3)

You may ask at this point why it is necessary to know these requirements at all, if Eclipse will generate the methods anyway. The answer is simple: As a developer, you are still responsible for the code, you will work with the code, and you may at some point need to understand and maintain `equals` and `hashMap` implementations that have not been generated by Eclipse. And even if Eclipse has generated them, you are still responsible for regenerating them if your class acquires new fields.

1.4.14 Refused Bequest

In principle, subclasses must offer all services that their superclass and interfaces specify; after all, the client cannot know whether a method has been overridden. Every once in a while, however, a subclass simply cannot

↠3.1.1
↰1.4.1

provide the services efficiently—for instance, because it uses a representation optimized for space rather than speed. Then it inherits a method that it does not want, a *refused bequest*. In such cases, clients are responsible for working around that limitation. For instance, they might have opted for a space-efficient implementation precisely because they do not require the more complex services anyway.

Avoid refusing bequests; if you must, be loud and throw an exception.

One usually throws an `UnsupportedOperationException` to indicate a refused bequest. It signals that the client has used the full generality of the object, even though the client should have been aware of its limitations. If you search in Eclipse for this type with *Match Locations* set to *Instance creation*, you will be surprised at the number of hits (roughly 1500 in Eclipse 4.3).

For instance, a `ListLineTracker`, according to its documentation, is a *read-only* implementation of the `ILineTracker` interface. It determines the lines once, when the text is set. Correspondingly, notifications that the text has changed are refused:

org.eclipse.jface.text.ListLineTracker

```java
public final void replace(int position, int length, String text)
        throws BadLocationException {
    throw new UnsupportedOperationException();
}
```

▶5.3.2.1
There is one context in which refused bequests are common and acceptable: Mock objects for testing purposes must be lean and provide only as much functionality as required in the test scenarios. Otherwise, we might as well wait for the real implementation to be ready before commencing testing.

1.5   Exceptions

Exceptions are not an object-oriented feature themselves. We discuss them briefly nevertheless, because they heavily influence the style of collaboration between objects. Independently of whether we choose to declare them explicitly in methods' interfaces or use unchecked exceptions throughout, callers must be aware of possible exceptions and must be prepared to react correspondingly. At the same time, robustness and proper error handling are major requirements for professional code.

▶1.5.7

1.5.1   Basic Usage

Java's exception mechanism is really straightforward: `throw` stops normal execution; code in the block is skipped, methods are terminated, and so on until a `try`/`catch` block is found. This behavior is called *abrupt termination*. If a `catch` clause matches the thrown exception, the exception is *caught* and normal execution resumes in that *exception handler*. Any `finally` blocks encountered on the way are guaranteed to be executed as well.

□111

From a broad perspective, the conceptual contribution of exceptions is this:

> Exceptions indicate circumstances that prevent code from achieving its purpose.

The real benefit of exceptions is that `return` statements are also skipped, so that methods are freed from the obligation to compute the expected return value, or more generally to achieve the effect that the caller expected. At the same time, the caller is notified of this fact and can try to recover from the failure.

»6.3

For instance, a `ProjectDescriptionReader` reads the `.project` files from Eclipse projects. Clients simply call the method `read()` shown next. Of course, a number of things can go wrong on the way: The file may not exist, the user may lack access rights, the content may not be valid XML, and so on. When anything happens that keeps the method from fulfilling its purpose, it will just throw an `IOException`.

```
                    org.eclipse.core.internal.resources.ProjectDescriptionReader
public ProjectDescription read(IPath location) throws IOException {
    ...
    file = new BufferedInputStream(
            new FileInputStream(location.toFile()));
    return read(new InputSource(file));
    ...
}
```

From the client's perspective, the exception shows that the project description could not be read. What is it supposed to do? There are really several routes open:

- It can *recover from the error* by catching the exception and, for instance, looking elsewhere for the missing file.

- It can *pass the exception on* to its own caller by declaring `throws IOException` as well.

- It can *throw a different* exception to its own callers to indicate that it cannot achieve its own purpose.

The second and third options deserve special attention. The client will quite often have a purpose that does not agree with the exception that occurred.

□161

Choose exceptions to match the method's purpose.

For instance, the `ProjectDescriptionReader` is a helper to `Workspace`, which implements the functionality of the overall Eclipse workspace you are familiar with. Clients of `Workspace` expect higher-level error messages, about resources in the workspace. Therefore, the following method wraps the low-level message into a higher-level one. Note how the new exception includes the original one, so that the details do not get lost.

org.eclipse.core.internal.resources.Workspace

```
public IProjectDescription loadProjectDescription(IPath path)
    throws CoreException {
    try {
        return new ProjectDescriptionReader().read(path);
    } catch (IOException ex) {
        IStatus status = new Status(/* more information */ex);
        throw new ResourceException(status);
    }
}
```

This pattern is encountered so frequently that all exception types in the library offer a `cause` argument, by which you can attach arbitrary exceptions.

Use the `cause` argument to exceptions to preserve error details while achieving the right level of abstraction for the message.

44(Item 45) Similarly, you should strive to capture in the exception's message enough information for maintainers to figure out what went wrong when they see the stack dump in a log file.

  To summarize, you should use exceptions to indicate that a method was not able to deliver the promised result, and to explain precisely what went wrong and why. Inside methods, abrupt termination then indicates that pieces of code have failed to achieve their purpose. Exception handlers, in the form of `catch` clauses, then resume normal execution. However:

Catch an exception only if you can recover from the failure.

Exceptions indicate that something in the planned course of events went wrong. When you catch an exception, you must be able to achieve the expected result of your own code *regardless of that failure*—for instance, by trying a different strategy or by retrying the same strategy.

Never catch and ignore an exception out of laziness or for your convenience.

⚠ For a compiler error *Uncaught exception*, Quick-Fix offers *Surround with try/catch* or *Add throws declaration*. The "surround" option is tempting, because the "throws" might require changes elsewhere. Nevertheless, "throws" should be your default option, unless you can really handle the error. A third option is to catch the exception and wrap it with an unchecked exception.

»1.5.7

If you decide to ignore an exception, document the decision. For instance, the method `close()` in I/O streams formally throws `IOException`, but there is really nothing you can do about it: Either the resource is freed, or you can't retry anyway. The Eclipse code base even contains a utility method for this situation:

```
org.eclipse.core.internal.utils.FileUtil
public static void safeClose(Closeable stream) {
    try {
        if (stream != null)
            stream.close();
    } catch (IOException e) {
        // ignore
    }
}
```

Very often, an error message to the user is the only recovery strategy.

Most operations and computations are triggered directly or indirectly by the user, usually by pushing some button or selecting some menu entry in the UI. The user then expects the operation to be carried out successfully, unless notified differently. Depending on the operation, the user will not appreciate it if your application tries various strategies, since that gives the user a sense of losing control. When displaying an exception, keep in mind that the user, like each method, has a particular level of abstraction: He or she is not interested in the implementation, but rather in why the original command failed.

»7

Finally, there is `finally`.

Use `finally` to free resources and leave objects in consistent states.

Fields and variables tend to be in a somewhat "messy" state in the middle of operations: Some assignments have been performed, while others have been aborted by the occurrence of an exception. The `finally` clause of a `try` block gives you the opportunity to free resources—for example, to close files or network connections, that may still be in use, make sure that locks are released, and perform similar cleanup operations.

»1.5.6 »4.1

📖148

1.5.2 Exceptions and the System Boundary

A premier source of exceptions is the system boundary. There, the input received from the user or from other systems, the data read from the hard-disk, and several other things are frequently faulty. Similarly, the network

»1.8.7 »4.6

connection you are about to read from may turn out to be closed, and the directory you are writing to may not be accessible to the user. In short:

Be paranoid whenever you reach beyond your own software system.

Being paranoid here means two things. First, you should check any data you receive into your system and check that any operation you perform has actually succeeded (unless that operation already throws an exception). Second, you should abort an ongoing operation by an exception rather than keep going despite previous faults, on a shaky and insecure basis. Suppose, for instance, that you need a particular directory to create files in. The following method checks for the different failure conditions and returns normally only if the directory exists in the end. (mkdirs() does *not* throw an exception.)

exceptions.CreateDirectorySafely

```java
public void ensureDirectoryExists(String absolutePath)
    throws IOException {
    File dir = new File(absolutePath);
    if (!dir.exists() && !dir.mkdirs())
        throw new IOException("Failed to create "+absolutePath);
    if (!dir.isDirectory())
        throw new IOException("File already exists: "+absolutePath);
}
```

Further caution is in order when applying the guideline to recover by returning an error message. Users will start to distrust your system if they see long stack traces they do not understand. These traces are for the log files. Worse still, if the operation was triggered from an external system, it may actually be dangerous to return the stack trace, as it may potentially reveal internal structure that attackers can exploit—for instance, because they know of the weakness in one of the libraries your system employs.

1.5.3　Exceptions to Clarify the Program Logic

Code is readable when it reflects the solution strategy clearly, so that human readers can align the technical details with their general understanding. The solution strategy usually assumes that intermediate steps work out correctly. It captures the salient points of the plan and defers the details of error handling to a later point, even though they are essential for achieving robustness.

Use exceptions to separate the control flow of normal and failed executions.

Exceptions enable the developer to transfer this mode of presentation to the code: to state the salient points in a sequence of processing steps and

📖31
↰1.4.5

to keep error handling implicit, until the catch clause adds the required logic for the unexpected cases in a single place.

Distinguish "normal" and "failed" executions from the client's perspective.

When defining a method's interface, one has to think twice whether a par- ≫6.1.3
ticular result constitutes a failure. For instance, HashMap.get() returns
null if the given key is not found. For most clients, this is just right, since
they fully expect that some keys are not present. The SymbolTable of a ▥2
compiler, which stores the definitions of names in the current context, is
quite a different matter: When get() does not find a binding for a variable,
this is in fact a failure, because normal compilation will not be able to continue without that information. It is therefore better to throw an exception
within the method. Note that this choice also follows the previous guideline
about "normal" and "failed" executions.

1.5.4 Exceptions for Checking Expectations

When coding, you make all sorts of assumptions. For example, when calling
a method in obj.m(), you assume obj is not null; when accessing a[i],
you assume a is not null and i is between 0 and a.length (exclusive);
when calling Math.sqrt(x), you assume that x is not negative, because
that is what sqrt() demands in its documentation. You might consider
testing these assumptions to make sure there will be no problems. Here is
some sample code that initializes the first part of an array a up to index end
(exclusive):

```
                    exceptions.CheckingAssumptions.initUpto
if (a == null) throw new IllegalArgumentException("a is null");
for (int i=0; i!=end; i++) {
    if (i < 0 || i >= a.length)
        throw new IllegalArgumentException("index");
    a[i] = data;
}
```

Although in general this checking will be cumbersome, there are some
situations in which you'd better make sure your reasoning is correct.

Check before irrevocable operations with possibly dramatic consequences.

For examples, look into Eclipse's abstraction over the file system called
resources, such as in class File (in package org.eclipse.core.internal.
resources). The *workspace* is a complex data structure on which the entire
Eclipse platform depends. If anything goes wrong there, the user's work
may be lost. Similarly, you can double-check before performing external ≫1.8.7
operations, such as moving a robot arm.

◄1.5.2 ►►1.8.7

Check when in doubt about the caller.

A situation analogous to the system boundary occurs at the beginning of methods. You will document which parameter values you allow and perhaps under which circumstances the method can be called, but you cannot be sure that the caller has read, understood, and obeyed the documentation. When conditions get complex, this is a good reason to double-check.

►►7

To give an example for the last two guidelines, SWT builds on a native implementation of user interface elements. Since that is written in C, accessing it incorrectly may bring the entire JVM crashing down, and the running Eclipse application with it. Even such an apparently trivial thing as setting a label's text therefore checks that the assumptions, such as the label not being destroyed and the current thread being the distinguished UI thread, actually hold before proceeding to the native code.

►►7.10

org.eclipse.swt.widgets.Label

```java
public void setText(String string) {
    checkWidget();
    ...
    OS.gtk_label_set_text_with_mnemonic(labelHandle, buffer);
    ...
}
```

A typical idiom is to throw `IllegalArgumentException`, such as in Eclipse text editors shown next. Here, the justification for checking lies in the fact that it may depend on the concrete class of the editor whether the passed mode is allowed, so that there are complex interdependencies that the caller may not be aware of.

org.eclipse.ui.texteditor.AbstractTextEditor

```java
public void setInsertMode(InsertMode newMode) {
    List legalModes = getLegalInsertModes();
    if (!legalModes.contains(newMode))
        throw new IllegalArgumentException();
    ...
}
```

When in doubt about the program logic, use `assert` or `Assert.isTrue`.

Lengthy case distinctions and complex control flows possibly involving exceptions may leave you in doubt about your own reasoning: Under which conditions and after which operations can a specific statement actually be reached? Usually there are one or two crucial deductions that you make from those circumstances. The best option is to simplify the control flow, so that your doubts dissolve because the deductions are obviously correct. The second best option is to write an `Assert.isTrue` (or `assert`) and state the outcome of your reasoning process: During the entire testing phase, your

►►4.1

results will be reconfirmed on each run of the code.[4] What is more, the maintenance developer who comes after you will find your central insights well documented and won't spend time on reestablishing or refuting your reasoning.

Check the `else` branch after long or complex `if-then-else` chains.

This is a special form of the previous strategy: After a sequence of cases tested by `if`, the final `else` must handle the remaining situations. At this point, you know that all previous `if` tests have returned `false`. Unfortunately, humans are very error-prone in deducing from many things that do *not* hold the things that *do* hold. Who has never made mistakes in applying de Morgan's laws? Better introduce an assertion.

As a reminder, de Morgan's laws state $\neg(P \vee Q) = \neg P \wedge \neg Q$ and $\neg(P \wedge Q) = \neg P \vee \neg Q$. The first one, read backward, captures the situation of nested `if`s.

Check when you rely on some place *not* to be reached.

In several situations, you know that a specific place in the code can never be reached: You have handled all allowed cases through `if` or `switch` statements, or you have caught an exception that will never be thrown anyway. In this case, you would be justified in leaving the `else` branch, the `default` case, or the `catch` block, respectively, empty. It is better, however, to be careful: Your reasoning may be faulty or a new case may crop up in the future. Just throw some `RuntimeException` with a message like "This can't happen." It will save you or a fellow team member much debugging effort later on. As a special case:

142(Ch.27)

Don't leave out the `default` in `switch`. Throw an exception.

In all of these instances, professional developers would check whether their reasoning, or the reasoning of some caller, is correct. Novices, in contrast, tend to check too much and in too many places. This section therefore concludes with some converse advice:

In general, do not check expectations and assumptions.

The reason is simple: Any code that you write for checking, you also have to debug, maintain, document, and manage throughout its lifetime. In the introductory example in this subsection, more than half the code went into

»6.1 »4.5

---

4. When using `assert`, you must start the JVM with the *enable assertions* flag `-ea`. Look at the launch configuration of your tests or the default arguments of the JVM in the Eclipse preferences.

checking assumptions. Checking has completely cluttered the very simple logic itself. Besides, it also costs runtime. And the code does not deliver any benefit in return; it just confirms what you already knew anyway.

1.5.5   Exceptions to Signal Incompleteness

»5

Exceptions are also a wonderful tool for prototyping, exploratory programming, and test-driven development. With exceptions, you first handle only the cases that you need for now, while you are well aware that some other cases need to be handled, perhaps with more knowledge and further specifications, later on. The central rule for such a strategy is this:

> Never continue silently when you know something is not (yet) handled correctly.

Perhaps your `if` statement is thought through for the `then` branch, which you need for the current test. In that case, just throw an `Unsupported OperationException` or `IllegalArgumentException` in the `else` branch, as a reminder to yourself that this part of the code is not finished. As soon as you write the first test case that relies on the missing functionality, you will get the exception and can fill in the right code there: The test will drive you to code the functionality, as intended.

Exceptions thrown to signal incompleteness are always derived from `RuntimeException`, so that they do not have to be declared in method interfaces. After all, they won't be thrown in the production version.

1.5.6   Exception Safety

Unfortunately, exceptions can easily get out of hand when a longer block of code can throw them in different locations. *Exception safety* denotes the property that no severe damage is done regardless of where an exception occurs. Damage can have several meanings here, up to physical damage done by robot arms that fail to stop and rockets that are blown up in mid-air for safety reasons.[5]

»6.3

In most cases, consequences are not so dramatic, since they are confined to the software itself. Here, damage usually means broken object structures and leaked resources. Consider a simple list of sensor readings that are arranged in a linked list (Fig. 1.5). A new reading `rn` is to be inserted after a given node.

The code seems simple enough; it just implements the pointer diagram in left-to-right fashion:

---

5. This has actually happened, as is well known: On the maiden flight of the Ariane 5, a floating-point measurement of the vehicle's horizontal velocity was unexpectedly high, so it was out of range in a conversion to an integer. This triggered an exception that caused the navigation system to stop itself due to an unexpected failure. As a consequence, the on-board system could no longer control the flight and initiated the rocket's self-destruction [87, §2.1].

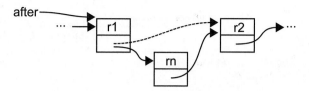

Figure 1.5 Example of a Destroyed Invariant

---

exceptions.SensorReadingsList.insertCurrentReadingWrong

```
1 Node newNode = new Node();
2 Node tmp = after.next;
3 after.next = newNode;
4 newNode.value = readSensorCurrentValue();
5 newNode.next = tmp;
```

Unfortunately, it is not exception-safe: When the reading of the sensor in line 4 throws an exception, the list structure is destroyed, because the partially initialized node `newNode` is found in its middle. The entire list is rendered unusable and the application will likely have to be shut down, even if the next reading succeeds.

To localize damage, one has to keep the list structure intact regardless of exceptions. The following code does just this: It allocates the new node, but reads the sensor before even touching the list. If line 2 throws an exception, there is no problem at all; the caller will be informed that this one reading failed, but it can decide to retry the operation at a later point.

---

exceptions.SensorReadingsList.insertCurrentReadingRight

```
1 Node newNode = new Node();
2 newNode.value = readSensorCurrentValue();
3 newNode.next = after.next;
4 after.next = newNode;
```

A further major kind of damage is that of leaked resources. Resources, such as open files, network connections, or system-level images and icons, are not cleaned up by the garbage collector, but must be released explicitly. Leaking resources means that the software allocates them and then loses control of them. Over time, this fills up memory and makes the application crash. The `finally` block is a good point to take care of that concern, since it is executed regardless of how the `try` block is left: by exception, with or without a `catch`, or even by `return`, `break`, or `continue`.

A typical example is found in `ImageIO`, from the JDK. Its method `read`, shown here, is supposed to read an image from the disk. It opens an input stream (line 2). If that throws an exception, nothing is lost, since the stream is not actually opened. In contrast, if `read` in line 6 throws an exception, then the stream would be leaked. The `finally` takes care of this concern. (Note that `istream!=null` at this point by line 2.)

```
                          javax.imageio.ImageIO
1  public static BufferedImage read(URL input) throws IOException {
2      InputStream istream = input.openStream();
3      ImageInputStream stream = createImageInputStream(istream);
4      BufferedImage bi;
5      try {
6          bi = read(stream);
7      } finally {
8          istream.close();
9      }
10     return bi;
11 }
```

The call to `createImageInputStream` in line 3 is *not* protected by the `finally` clause—it would seem that the developer was very sure that this method will never throw an exception. In fact, this assumption is not justified at all, as a quick look at the method's code reveals: It creates a cache file and that step may, of course, fail. The library code is not exception-safe at this point.

To be on the safe side, you can adopt the following coding idiom, which derives from a corresponding guideline for locks:

☐148

```
                exceptions.AllocReleaseResourceIdiom.demoOperation
resource = allocateResource();
try {
    // work with resource
} finally {
    resource.release();
}
```

☐111(§14.20.3)

Java 7 recognizes the importance of this idiom and provides language support in the try-with-resources construct: Objects initialized in parentheses after `try` are guaranteed to be automatically closed before leaving the `try` block. Initializations of several objects are separated by semicolons; all variables declared here must have subtypes of `AutoCloseable`.

```
                exceptions.AllocReleaseResourceIdiom.tryWithResources
File file = File.createTempFile("output", "tmp");
try (FileOutputStream out = new FileOutputStream(file)) {
    ...
}
```

1.5.7   Checked Versus Unchecked Exceptions

☐111(§11.1.1)

Java distinguishes three kinds of exceptions. First, there are *errors* that signal fundamental problems such as `OutOfMemoryError` or `ClassFormat Error`. They are neither thrown nor caught by applications, and are derived from the special class `Error`. You won't meet them in daily practice. Second, subclasses of `Exception` denote failures from which applications may try to recover. These are called *checked* exceptions, because the compiler tracks where they are thrown and requires a method to either catch them or declare them in a `throws` clause. Third, a special case of `Exceptions` includes subclasses of `RuntimeException`, which are called *unchecked* exceptions, because they are not tracked by the compiler.

In the Java community, a long and sometimes heated debate has arisen about whether checked or unchecked exceptions should be preferred. Some claim that the debate is over and that the "unchecked" party came out victorious. However, many professionals do use checked exceptions, and with very good reasons. As usual in software development, there is no simple answer to the question of which is best.

172(Ch.7)

We already know the arguments for checked exceptions: They clarify the behavior of a method, because they also make explicit its limitations and possible failures. Clients that are aware of these limitations can take precautions to guarantee exception safety. If the system uses unchecked exceptions throughout, code must be really paranoid, because exceptions may be lurking in *any* method call, or else developers must be really disciplined, and document all thrown exceptions. Furthermore, coding idioms can be introduced, but must then be obeyed meticulously. All of those tasks are greatly simplified when one knows which operations may actually fail.

»6.3 «1.5.1

«1.5.6

240
161

The argument for unchecked exceptions looks beyond single methods, to strategic planning of entire applications. Very often, their structure contains situations like that shown in Fig. 1.6. In this example, the application uses some library or framework, such as SWT or SAX parsers for XML. In each case, the library or framework calls back application code when it encounters specific situations. The problem with checked exceptions at this point is that the framework cannot be modified, so that the callbacks cannot throw checked exceptions at all. In effect, they must not fail, so that they cannot, for instance, reach beyond the system boundary. Similar arguments also apply to mechanisms inducing flexibility into systems themselves.

172(Ch.7)

»7
»7.3.2

«1.5.2
»12.2

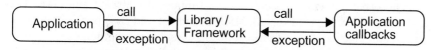

Figure 1.6 Motivation for Unchecked Exceptions

In software engineering, being dogmatic is usually the worst option. Before deciding for one or the other side, let us first analyze the usage in state-of-the-art code. This is useful to understand existing software, if nothing else. The general strategy found there can be summarized as follows:

44(Item 58)

Use checked exceptions for expected failures.

If exceptions indicate that a method could not fulfill its purpose, then expected failures are those that the software cannot be held responsible for—for instance, those occurring during I/O.

↰1.5.2

Use unchecked exceptions for failures that should not occur.

Failures that should not occur usually indicate an error in the program logic. The subclasses of `RuntimeException`, which are just the unchecked exceptions, bear witness to that usage: `NullPointerExceptions` are thrown when the developer thought they had a proper object reference; `ClassCast Exceptions`, when they thought they had a special subtype; `Illegal ArgumentExceptions` when the caller disobeyed the rules stated for a method; and so on. At crucial points, code will also actively check its expectations.

↰1.5.4

Since there are good reasons for both styles, let us be pragmatic—we can often convert one style into the other. The first direction is simple: You can always catch a checked exception and wrap it in an unchecked exception. The following snippet from SWT exchanges an `IOException` for an `SWTError`.

---
org.eclipse.swt.graphics.ImageLoader

```
try {
    stream = Compatibility.newFileInputStream(filename);
    return load(stream);
} catch (IOException e) {
    SWT.error(SWT.ERROR_IO, e);
}
```

This wrapping idiom is also useful if according to the program logic, the checked exception should not have been thrown in the first place.

If an exception should not occur logically, catch it and wrap it.

The other direction requires some support from the framework. For instance, a SAX parser scans an XML document and calls back methods in a `ContentHandler` for each tag it encounters. Those methods are allowed to throw a generic `SAXException`, which applications can use to wrap their own specific failures. The invoking part on the left of Fig. 1.6 then unwraps the original using `getCause()`.

---
org.xml.sax.ContentHandler

```
public void startElement(String uri, String localName, String qName,
        Attributes atts) throws SAXException;
public void endElement(String uri, String localName, String qName)
        throws SAXException;
```

1.6 Constructors

Before an object can be used, it must be initialized. In other words, data structures and helper objects must be created and connected, primitive indices have to be set up, and so on. The object must be in working order at the time the first public method gets called. Constructors are special methods that perform this initialization and are invoked within `new` expressions, right after the memory for the new instance has been allocated. Conceptually, they start on a raw memory area and leave a proper object. This view is also reflected in the byte code. For an example, run `javap -c` on class `CtorCall` from the online supplement.

> The constructor leaves a new object in ready-to-use condition.

In a different formulation, one can say that the object is *consistent* after the constructor finishes: Everything within the object is just as it should be. In yet another view, the constructor must establish the object's *invariants*.   **»**4.1

1.6.1 Initializing Objects

Allocation of an object presets all fields to their default values, such as `null` for references, `0` for `int`, and `false` for `boolean` variables. Basically, the object's memory area gets overwritten with 0 bytes to ensure that no stale pointers or data is left that would confuse the JVM's machinery. Beyond that, the programmer is responsible for proper initialization.

Let us first consider a typical case with data structures. The doubly linked list in `LinkedList` uses a *sentinel* node—that is, a node that does not contain data, but enables a uniform treatment without case distinctions for the empty list. The initialization code sets up precisely this data structure.   `□`72

```
                        java.util.LinkedList
1 private transient Entry<E> header = new Entry<E>(null, null, null);
2 private transient int size = 0;
3 public LinkedList() {
4     header.next = header.previous = header;
5 }
```

Lines 1–2 initialize the fields using variable initializers; the compiler prepends these to the constructor code. Then, the sentinel node is set up to be the only node in the list. For the details of this inlining, you can run `javap -c` on class `DemoInitializers` from the sample code.

The preceding constructor is called a *default constructor*, which does not have any arguments. You can create a default constructor by placing the cursor into the class body, outside any method, and invoking Auto-Complete.

» 1.3.3

Not all objects require data structures. Many information holders basically store properties, which can be initialized by values provided by their clients.

> **TOOL: Create Constructor for Fields**
>
> To initialize an object's properties with given values at creation time, use *Source/Generator Constructor Using Fields*.

◄ 1.3.3

⚠ Beware of breaking encapsulation by enabling the client to pass unsuitable values or objects for internal fields. As a rule of thumb, if a field is not accessible otherwise, its initial value should not be provided by the client.

◄ 1.4.5

Constructors can also be created by wishful thinking, similar to *Create Method from Call*: You just write down the constructor call passing all desired information, and create the constructor by Quick-Fix. Then, you go through the new constructor's parameters using the following tool:

> **TOOL: Create and Initialize Field**
>
> Place the cursor on a constructor's parameter. Open Quick-Fix (`Ctrl-1`) and choose *Assign parameter to new field*. The tool also works for parameters of other methods and also offers a variant *Assign parameter to field ...* that initializes an existing field.

Make constructors run quickly. Make long-running initializations lazy.

◄ 1.1

» 1.6.2

◄ 1.3.8

A fundamental assumption of object-oriented programming is that objects are small and cheap. Clients expect to create an object quickly, so the constructor should not open network connections, read files, or perform other tasks. Clients do, however, accept that methods can run longer. One alternative to full initialization in the constructor is to defer initialization to a life-cycle method called. We will discuss this approach shortly. Another option is lazy initialization, which we have already seen in the SINGLETON pattern. With this technique, the constructor sets up only rudimentary structures and marks those parts of the object that have not yet been initialized—for instance, by setting the fields to `null`. Typically, one then creates a getter that initializes the structure on the fly:

```
                          ctor.LazyInitializationDemo
private DataStructure getHugeData() {
    if (hugeData == null) {
        hugeData = new DataStructure();
        hugeData.fetchFromDisk();
    }
    return hugeData;
}
```

At a larger scale, platforms like Eclipse or Netbeans rely on lazy initialization to make the startup process bearable. Plugins, their classes, and data structures are initialized only when the user first accesses their functionality—that is, at a point where the user is prepared to wait for a bit. Also, plugins that never get used are not initialized at all.

174(§27.8) 50

1.6.2 Initialization by Life-Cycle Methods

While constructors and initializers work in most cases, it is sometimes necessary to make initialization an explicit step in the object's life cycle. A frequently encountered case is an object that is constructed by reflection. Extensibility mechanisms like Eclipse's plugins or Netbeans' modules take class names from XML documents and instantiate the classes basically as follows, where `newInstance` requires a public default constructor to succeed. The interface `CreateByReflection` in the example captures the minimal expectations, similar to the situation with factory methods.

» A 50

↰1.4.12

---
ctor.CreateByReflection.main
```
Class<?> namedClass = Class.forName(className);
CreateByReflection inst =
    (CreateByReflection) namedClass.newInstance();
```

Looking up a proper constructor for specific arguments would greatly complicate matters. However, once the static type is known after the cast, it is a simple matter to invoke methods for further initialization. For instance, *views* in Eclipse, such as the *Package Explorer* and *Outline*, are created by reflection and are wired to their context by the `init()` method afterward:

» 12.3.3.4
» 12.3.2

---
org.eclipse.ui.IViewPart
```
public void init(IViewSite site) throws PartInitException;
```

The idiom of a separate initialization method is used very widely, as the following example from the Servlet API shows. A servlet is a Java object that lives in a *servlet container* and is called back to answer incoming service requests, typically HTTP requests. When the container first instantiates the servlet, it invokes the following method:

---
javax.servlet.Servlet
```
public void init(ServletConfig config) throws ServletException;
```

A further benefit of using life-cycle methods is that they can be defined in an abstract base class once and for all. The passed information is then available "magically" to all subclasses.

» 3.1.4

1.6.3 Constructors and Inheritance

Unlike ordinary methods, constructors are not inherited. The reason is very simple: An inherited constructor would initialize only the inherited fields, but would leave the newly introduced fields with their raw default values. This is in general insufficient, and rarely desirable. Instead, initialization best proceeds in stages along the inheritance hierarchy:

> Each constructor initializes the fields declared in its own class.

»6.4.2

This general rule goes together with the insight, to be discussed later, that derived classes must not modify the consistency conditions, or invariants, of their superclass.

To enable this initialization strategy, Java allows one `super` call at the beginning of a constructor. This call delegates the responsibility for the inherited fields to the superclass constructor.

> **TOOL: Generate Constructor from Superclass**
>
> If you wish to "inherit" a constructor, invoke the tool *Source/Create Constructor from Superclass* (`Alt-S C` by menu mnemonics).

»1.8.8

🔎 A few restrictions apply in the `super` call. Since the object is not yet initialized, `this` cannot be accessed. In particular, the object's methods cannot yet be called to compute the arguments to the `super` call. Also, non-static nested classes cannot be instantiated, because they require a `this` reference internally.

🔎 Even though Eclipse usually generates it, a call `super()` to the superclass's default constructor is not necessary. It is inserted by the compiler if no superclass constructor is invoked. You can disable the generation of the call in the creation dialog.

There is one pitfall lurking in the interaction of method overriding and the nice strategy of initializing along the levels of the inheritance hierarchy: The super-constructor might invoke a method that is overridden in the subclass—and that can access a part of the object that is not yet initialized at all. In such a situation, of course, a multitude of things can go wrong.

Suppose you design the following (faulty) base class for windows on the screen. The `createContents` method is supposed to actually set up the displayed elements.

```
                              ctor.WindowBase
public WindowBase() {
    createContents();
}
protected void createContents() {
    ...
}
```

Derived classes overriding that method must be aware that their own constructors have *not yet run*. The following method actually sees 0 in the special field:

```
                          ctor.WindowDerived
private int specialField = 2;
protected void createContents() {
    super.createContents();
    System.out.println("Current content of specialField: "
        + specialField);
}
```

> Think carefully about the expected runtime behavior when invoking methods in constructors.

These complexities are the reason that some initializations are best deferred until later in the life cycle. For instance, the real class Window does not invoke createContents() within the constructor, but rather when the client uses open().

↰1.4.5

1.6.4   Copying Objects

Some constructors are used for copying objects, especially those of mere information holders and value objects. For instance, the collections framework generally provides constructors to initialize a collection from another collection.

≫1.8.3 ≫1.8.4

```
                          java.util.ArrayList
public ArrayList(Collection<? extends E> c)
```

This style of construction is very common in C++, under the designation of *copy constructor*. Copy constructors are particularly relevant there because not all objects are handled by reference. Those that are stack-allocated must be copied for initialization and parameter passing. For a class C, the compiler recognizes a constructor with parameter const C& (i.e., a reference to an immutable object) as a copy constructor and invokes it implicitly in these situations.

▢239 ▢144

   Similarly, the compiler will recognize *conversion constructors*, which have a parameter const D& as implicit conversions from D to C, and will apply them according to the overload resolution and conversion rules.

1.6.5   Static Constructor Methods

Constructors always have the same name as the class, so that you cannot use their names to express intentions. If there are several useful ways to initialize an instance, you can use only overloading, which does not capture

↰1.2.3 ↰1.4.5

↰1.4.2

the differences at all. Imagine different calls to the constructors of URL shown next; to understand what happens, you have to trace the types and resolve the overloading in your head.

java.net.URL

```
public URL(String spec) throws MalformedURLException
public URL(URL context, String spec) throws MalformedURLException
public URL(String protocol, String host, int port, String file)
        throws MalformedURLException
public URL(String protocol, String host, int port, String file)
        throws MalformedURLException
```

44(Item 1)

»1.7.2

In such circumstances, it can be sensible to make the constructor(s) private or protected and to provide public static constructor methods instead. The methods can also be located in a separate class, to gather entry points to the API in a single spot in the manner of a FACADE. You gain the same benefit as with well-named methods:

Static constructor methods can make the client code more readable.

148

A typical example is found in Java's concurrency library. Executors take on *tasks* and schedule them for background processing according to configurable heuristics and strategies. Clients can use executors in a simple fashion because static constructor methods capture the most common cases. For example, the client might decide on a fixed number of threads, with the constructor method configuring a generic thread pool accordingly:

java.util.concurrent.Executors

```
public static ExecutorService newFixedThreadPool(int nThreads) {
    return new ThreadPoolExecutor(nThreads, nThreads, 0L,
            TimeUnit.MILLISECONDS,
                new LinkedBlockingQueue<Runnable>());
}
```

This example also shows that constructor methods can be smart. Since the constructor itself is private, you can move some of its responsibilities for a "proper" initialization to the static method. This smartness can even include figuring out the correct (sub)class to be instantiated, similar to an ABSTRACT FACTORY. For example, MessageDigest.getInstance() takes the name of the desired algorithm and searches through the available implementations at runtime and instantiates a suitable subclass of MesssageDigest.

◄1.4.12

Two differences from earlier methods performing object construction must be pointed out. First, in contrast to factory methods, we are now talking about static methods. The intention of substituting the instantiated class at runtime is not present. Second, in contrast to the SINGLETON pattern, several instances can be created. Static constructor methods are really just that: wrappers around the private constructors.

◄1.4.12

◄1.3.8

1.7 Packages

Packages serve two technical purposes in Java. First, they introduce name spaces, so that the same class name can be reused in different libraries without clashes. Second, they introduce a visibility scope: If none of `public`, `private`, or `protected` is specified, then the class or member is visible within the defining package. Incidentally, `protected` elements are also visible throughout the package, because, like subclasses, the package members are supposed to contribute to the implementation of the protected elements.

111(§6.6.2)

The use of packages as namespaces keeps apart the code from different libraries, frameworks, or (sub)projects. It is good practice to choose hierarchical naming schemes, starting with the organization, then the (sub)project. The *Organize Imports* tool enables you to work effectively with such namespaces. This use is, however, a rather crude structure that does not tell anything further about the classes contained in the packages.

1.2.1

> ⚠ As a rule of thumb, don't reuse class names in different packages, because that makes the clients' code less readable. When naming classes, think at the application level.

263(p.92) 1.2.3

1.7.1 Packages as Components

The use of packages as a naming scope is much more fine-grained and reflects design decisions at the level of objects and classes. Usually, groups of objects work closely together to accomplish some task—they form a *neighborhood*. However, clients that employ this functionality are often not aware of the inner object structure behind its accomplishment—the objects form a *component* that can be reused as a whole, while the constituent objects are not useful outside the given context. In such a situation, only a few objects are offered to the client as `public` classes; the others are default-visible. The package creates a common, trusted space where the neighborhood can work without interference from the outside.

1.1

»11

A typical example is SWT's `Browser`. It enables you display web pages within your own Eclipse-based application. Because the functionality is rather complex, the package `org.eclipse.swt.browser` contains many default-visible helper classes that provide specific aspects of the overall behavior.

»7

> ⌿ The default visibility constraint does not offer any protection against malicious users. For instance, if different libraries (i.e., JAR files) contain the same package, these are actually merged at runtime. By just specifying the same name for a package, one can easily gain access to the default-visible members. The projects `chapter02pkg1` and `chapter02pkg2` in the sample code demonstrate the behavior.

» A.1

The OSGi (Open Services Gateway initiative) infrastructure strengthens the role of packages as components further. A *bundle*, OSGi's notion of a module, by default hides all contained classes, and the OSGi class loader actually enforces the restriction. Only the content of packages explicitly mentioned in the bundle's description, or *manifest*, will be accessible from the outside. Eclipse exploits this restriction by placing the public class of each component into a public package, and placing the helper classes into separate subpackages named `internal` by convention.

1.7.2   The Facade Pattern

When designing a component there is always a trade-off between powerful functionality and complexity of use: The more configurations and application scenarios that are supported, the steeper the learning curve before simple uses can be accomplished. For instance, if your Eclipse plugin for enhanced Java editing just wants to prompt the user to select some existing class or interface, you don't want to be bothered about finding available types, extracting their names to a list, filtering the list in a background job, and so on. All you want is a "type selection dialog." Fortunately, the Eclipse platform offers just the method(s): `JavaUI.createTypeDialog()`. You specify essentially the context in which the dialog is used, and the method then plugs together and configures the necessary objects from the subsystem.

» 7.10

⊓⊔ 100

> **PATTERN:** FACADE
>
> ---
>
> You want to facilitate the use of a subsystem by providing a uniform, clean interface that hides the collaboration between objects within the subsystem.
>
> ---
>
> Designate or create a number of `public` facade classes through which clients can access the subsystem's services in the most frequent cases.
>
> The facade can also hide the subsystem's internals, if you make other classes package-visible or, in the context of OSGi, move them to non-public subpackages.

Examples can be found throughout the Eclipse platform. For example, `JavaCore` provides access to the structured model of the Java source code in the system, and for manipulating aspects of Java projects. The `JavaPlugin` provides ready-made, reusable elements such as configurations for Java source editors. The `ASTParser` is really just a facade for Eclipse's internal Java compiler. The `JET2Platform` allows you to run *Java Emitter Templates*, which are then used, for instance, by the Eclipse Modeling Framework, without delving into the details of the code generation process.

⊓⊔ 235

1.8 Basics of Using Classes and Objects

We have finally reached the core of the matter: How to use objects? Much has already been said about the different elements that objects contain, and about their specific purpose and usage. Having gathered the pieces, we can now turn to the question of arranging them into objects. To avoid redundancy, the presentation here frequently refers to previously introduced material. It can therefore also be read as a restatement of previous principles in a larger context.

As we delve into the question of using objects, you might feel that we are really discussing object-oriented design. Indeed, it won't do any harm if you take a peek at Section 11.1 if you are getting curious. Design in general is, however, a complex activity that relies on further concepts and technical idioms that will be discussed up to Chapter 11. For now, we will draw the dividing line between analysis and creation: We will look at existing objects to find out how they work and how they achieve their purpose. Strategies for arriving at these objects will have to come later.

In this section and the next two chapters, you will acquire practical blueprints for your work. Together with the design patterns already introduced, they give you a repertoire for being creative with objects. Indeed, an essential prerequisite for becoming a successful designer is being an experienced developer. So don't hesitate to apply and test your new working knowledge immediately in your current projects.

1.8.1 General Facets of Objects

In the basic mindset of object-oriented programming, we have already seen   ↰1.1
essential characteristics of objects: They are small, lightweight, and black-box structures; they focus on specific tasks; and they collaborate to achieve larger goals. Also, they have identity and usually represent entities outside the software world, either from the real world or just concepts we invent while writing the software.

Now it is time to take one step closer and ask: What is it that objects actually *do*? Speaking very generally, objects will do three kinds of things: 📖263(Ch.4,p.110)

- They maintain *information*, by storing data in their fields.

- They perform *actions*, by executing code in their methods and thereby modifying the state of the software (and real) world. They may collaborate with other objects as part of their actions.

- They make *decisions* relating to other objects, by analyzing available information and then calling back on the other objects to make them perform the corresponding actions.

Usually, an object's overall behavior contains aspects from all three categories, where decisions about other objects are perhaps less frequent.

📖261
📖263(p.4, p.159ff)

↰1.3.3 ⏩1.3.3

⏩7.1 ⏩9.3

However, it is also useful to look out for objects in which one of the aspects predominates. Then, one arrives at *role stereotypes*:

- *Information holders* manage pieces of data important to the application, but do not implement the corresponding logic themselves. They may be entirely passive, such as an SWT `Rectangle` or a JFace `Document` for storing text. But they may also actively request the information they are supposed to know from others.

⏩1.3.4 ⏩1.8.6 ⏩7.1

- *Service providers* implement special algorithms or application logic, but rely on information obtained elsewhere. For instance, a `Layout` in SWT computes the position of widgets on the screen, based on constraints attached to these widgets.

⏩9.2

- *Controllers* mainly make decisions, but delegate the resulting actions to others rather than carrying them out themselves. In this way, they orchestrate or direct more complex operations. Prototypically, the controller in the well-known MODEL-VIEW-CONTROLLER pattern receives the user input and decides which application logic must be invoked in response.

Three further roles are specific to the software machinery that is necessary to get the application running:

⏩2.2
⏩7.6

- *Structurers* manage groups of objects and their relationships. Think of a dialog window, such as `Dialog` in JFace: It creates a main area and some buttons, and makes sure that the button clicks are received. Similarly, think of a pool of database connections: When a client requests a connection, the pool either creates a new one or reuses an existing one.

⏩1.8.7 ⏩2.4

- *Interfacers* link together parts of the system that are logically independent, and they connect the system to the outside world, to its users, and to other systems. For instance, they may perform I/O, parse and interpret requests coming in over the network, or transform data passed between different subsystems.

⏩7.7

- *Coordinators* mainly pass on requests between other objects. They enable, facilitate, or channel the communication of these objects, thereby centralizing the logic that is behind that communication.

Stereotypes offer a useful characterization of objects from a broad perspective. It is important to keep in mind, though, that they seldom occur in pure form. Instead, service providers typically keep some information themselves, structurers also make decisions on behalf of the managed objects, and interfacers may need to simulate some services, rather then merely delegating requests to a different part of the system.

1.8.2 Service Provider

In a broad sense, all objects provide services to the community: Their services are the justification for their existence. There is no place for "lazy classes" or "middle men." In a more narrow sense, objects collaborate on specific tasks: One object, the service provider, implements a piece of logic that another object, the client, requires. The client then usually invokes a method on the service provider to avoid reimplementing the logic. One of the core challenges in structuring object-oriented software entails distributing the logic in a way that avoids reimplementation—in other words, inventing suitable service providers.

📖92
↰1.1

Service providers can be typical library objects, such as a `FileInput Stream`. Whenever a client needs to read from a file, it creates such an object and invokes its `read()` method to access the data. When it is done, it disposes of the service provider. (We leave out precautions for exception safety here.)

↰1.5.6

```
                    serviceProvider.ReadingFiles.main
FileInputStream input = new FileInputStream(file);
while ((readCount = input.read(buf)) != -1) {
    // do something with data in buf[0..readCount]
}
input.close();
```

More often, the service provider is part of the application's object network and clients just contact the desired object whenever they need its services. For instance, a *workbench page* contains the main content of an Eclipse window (i.e., the window minus menu, toolbar, and status bar). It contains the open editors and their surrounding views, such as the *package explorer*. A workbench page offers, among many other things, the service of showing one more view (or bringing the given view to the front, if it is already shown):

↰1.1 ↠11.1

↠12.3.3.4

```
                    org.eclipse.ui.IWorkbenchPage
public IViewPart showView(String viewId) throws PartInitException;
```

If you invoke, in the Java editor, *Show in view* (via `Alt-Shift-W`), your command is finally dispatched to the following method (greatly abbreviated), which determines the page you are currently working with and asks it to open the target view.

---

org.eclipse.ui.internal.ShowInHandler

```
public Object execute(ExecutionEvent event)
    throws ExecutionException {
    ...
    IWorkbenchWindow activeWorkbenchWindow = HandlerUtil
        .getActiveWorkbenchWindowChecked(event);
    ...
    IWorkbenchPage page = activeWorkbenchWindow.getActivePage();
    IViewPart view = page.showView(targetId);
    ...
}
```

Services are often represented as methods: The client invokes a specific method to get at a specific service, and when the method returns, the service has been performed. One can, however, take a broader view. For instance,

the OBSERVER pattern can be understood as a notification service: The clients register for the notifications with one method call, but these are delivered only later on, when state changes actually occur. This kind of

service reflects the view on objects as active entities.

When placing services in objects, you should recall two general guidelines. First, think of objects from the outside. Services must be understandable and easily usable for clients who do not know about the object's internals. In particular, method names, parameters, and return values must

not give away the internal structure. Second, objects should remain *small*; that is, their services should be logically coherent, and they should not become bloated with different kinds of services. If you suspect your class is getting too heavy, extract parts of it into separate classes.

1.8.3   Information Holder

Objects in general are active: They offer services, they perform tasks, they react to method calls. A few selected objects nevertheless mainly store data and have that data manipulated by others. For instance, event objects have the purpose of packaging and transporting information, as can be seen in SWT's MouseEvent or KeyEvent. Similarly, SWT's Rectangle and Point capture areas and positions on the screen. In connection with

the PROXY pattern, the real subject might be a pure information holder that is managed by the proxy. An example from Eclipse's Java tooling is SourceMethodElementInfo, which contains data about a method in a Java file. The data is manipulated by a Method object.

A large domain for information holders is the application boundary,

where data is exchanged with other systems. For instance, the Java Persistence API is used to access relational databases. It deals in *entities*, which

are plain old Java objects that map to database rows. The application logic often resides outside the entities in a separate layer of the application.

Similarly, the *Java Architecture for XML Binding* (JAXB) uses objects to represent hierarchically nested XML elements. It is used as the basis for

SOAP web-service servers and clients, to shield them from dealing with DOM objects directly. 📖201(Ch.28)

From a system perspective, however, pure information holders are rare. They go against the grain of object-oriented programming, as they throw away the expressiveness of method overriding, and even avoid creating proper black-box objects. Whenever you design a data object, look out for functionality that goes well with the data, for active behavior that could—eventually—be sufficiently powerful to hide the data altogether, because no one accesses the data directly anymore.

📖92("Data Class")

»1.4.1
↰1.1

Place services together with the data that they work on.

For example, the designers of SWT have placed common operations on Rectangles as static methods in a separate class Geometry, while the designers of the Graphical Editing Framework's Draw2D layer have chosen to enhance their Rectangles with these operations. The neutral guideline can also be phrased somewhat more emphatically:

»7
↰1.4.8.4
📖214

📖92

When you have a lazy information holder, make it do some work.

1.8.4   Value Object

Information holders may or may not have identity: JPA entities represent specific database rows, while SWT Rectangles are exchangeable as long as their position and extent are the same. Prototypically, Strings are just containers for the characters they manage. Information holders without identity are *value objects*, meaning that they are nothing but a representation of the stored value. Value objects will usually override equals and hashCode to express the exact conditions under which objects are treated as "the same value" and are therefore interchangeable. For instance, the different Rectangle classes in the Eclipse platform override these methods. Value objects usually support copying or cloning, either through methods or constructors. For this reason:

↰1.1

↰1.4.13

↰1.6.4

Be sure to compare value objects using equals() instead of ==.

🔎 The only exceptions are string constants. The method String.intern() yields a unique object with the same character value as the argument, so that interning two equal strings yields the exact same object. Such an object is also called the *canonical representation* of the value. All string literals, including final static constants, are interned, so that you can compare them by ==. Interning symbols is a common technique in compiler construction, where declared names are made canonical to speed up the frequent search for names. If you are in a similar situation, you may want to use intern() yourself.

📖2

Furthermore, value objects are often immutable: Their fields are `final` and operations work by creating new instances representing the result values. For instance, `BigInteger` provides arbitrary precision integers, based on an immutable sign/magnitude representation. The operations then have the usual mathematical meaning, although for syntactic reasons they cannot be written infix:

📖143

java.math.BigInteger

```
public BigInteger add(BigInteger val) {
    ...
    return new BigInteger(resultMag, cmp == signum ? 1 : -1);
}
```

📖239

🌍 C++ includes comprehensive support for value objects. Infix operators such as +, -, and so on can be overloaded, so that mathematical operations can be written in familiar notation. Implicit copies, such as in variable initialization and parameter passing, can be coded as *copy constructors*, and the syntax *a=b* is considered as just a special *assignment operator*, which can likewise be overloaded. Finally, value objects can be stack-allocated, which circumvents, especially for small objects, the possible inefficiency of heap allocation and garbage collection. Beyond that, C++ objects that do not have `virtual` methods do not have any object header; they contain just the object's data fields. In consequence, an object wrapping an `int` stores just that single `int`.

📖245,42

When using value objects extensively, the programming style and software design change dramatically—when going all the way, one will effectively employ functional programming. The advantages of this paradigm are well known:

- Statements once true for an object remain true, since the object does not change. It will therefore be simpler to argue about correctness.

- Because the correctness arguments are simpler and there are no side effects, debugging becomes simpler as well.

- The computations building on immutable value objects can reflect mathematical rules and algorithms. In many cases, the specification of a method may be expressed directly in its implementation.

📖196

- Internal data structures may be shared between objects, which may outweigh the cost of creating new instances and *decrease* memory consumption.

📖148(§2.1)

- Immutable objects are inherently thread-safe, so that no synchronization is required.

📖44(Item 15)
📖194

Some argue that these consequences are worth working with immutable objects as far as possible. With special language constructs, such as case matching, working with value objects becomes even more attractive.

In the end, the decision of how many immutable objects you use depends on your style of problem solving and thinking. If you feel comfortable with purely functional solutions, try them out.

There is one possible caveat. Many object-oriented frameworks assume mutability, so purely functional solutions may stand alone, and you may end up re-creating, in your own functional framework, much of the logic that is already available in principle.

Conversely, many problem domains lend themselves to a purely functional treatment, and frameworks covering these domains will use immutable objects. For instance, symbolic manipulation of deeply nested trees benefits particularly from structure sharing and therefore from functional programming. For instance, Microsoft's open-source .NET tooling platform "Roslyn" is largely about syntax and code manipulations, in the context of compilation, code transformation, static analysis, and many other operations. Its API therefore uses immutable objects. As a result, syntax rewriting can be done in the style of mathematically precise term rewriting.

📖184

📖17

1.8.5   Reusable Functionality

A prime motivation for introducing a class is that it can be instantiated many times, so that its functionality is reused and need not be reimplemented in different places. We have already seen such classes in their role as service providers; there, one creates a new instance to access its operations. Of course, reuse also encompasses objects that become part of the application's network of objects more permanently, such as an Eclipse `TextEditor` or an SWT `MenuItem`. When browsing through the examples given earlier, you will notice that reusable objects are really composed from many parts and helpers. It is, indeed, usually necessary to look beyond single objects when trying for reuse:

↰1.4.8.3

↰1.8.2

↰1.1

↰1.7

Components are often a more suitable unit of reuse than individual objects.

Although reuse is highly desirable, there is a fundamental problem: Achieving it is exceedingly difficult.

Plan reusable classes carefully based on extensive experience.

The challenge in creating reusable classes is one of return on investment. When writing "the simplest thing that could possibly work" for your current application, it is clear that you will spend the minimal possible effort on a solution for today's problems. When writing a reusable class, you must make further investments, since you are creating a solution for tomorrow's problems as well. Instead of calling back a single object, for example, you may need an OBSERVER pattern; instead of closely collaborating with an object in the neighborhood, you might need to reimplement some functionality to make your class a stand-alone entity. The additional effort spent today will be justified only if you actually save effort tomorrow—avoid the smell of "speculative generality."

↠12.4.1

↠2.1.4
↰1.7

📖92

The expected return on investment will occur only if you have predicted the needs of tomorrow's application correctly. This, in turn, will be more likely if you are experienced in the area you are working in. While you are new to an area, your attempts at reuse will often be futile and frustrating.

Follow the "Rule of Three" when aiming at reuse.

A succinct guideline on the benefits of reusable components is given by the "Rule of Three": Do not attempt to define an abstraction before you have seen three concrete examples. The rule helps because it covers both the necessity of some previous experience and the expected return on investment in later applications.

After this rather discouraging outlook on reuse, we end on a more positive note:

Look out for potential reuse and discuss it with experienced colleagues.

Reuse will not happen at all unless you actively collect opportunities, and unless you recognize the three examples that make reuse worthwhile. This, in turn, will be possible only if there is a culture of reuse, a culture that values a clear code structure over short-time savings achieved by quick-and-dirty copy-and-paste solutions. You can start such a culture by discussing the opportunities you see, as long as you are prepared to take the advice of experienced colleagues if the opportunity is not so promising after all.

1.8.6   Algorithms and Temporary Data

↰1.1

When looking back at the mindset of object-oriented programming, you will notice that code does not figure very prominently. Objects are entities that often represent things outside the software world; they exhibit identity and behavior, and it is only incidentally that the behavior is captured by code.

📖214,269

In some objects, however, the code is really the main thing, since they embody an algorithm. For instance, Zest is a graph drawing library for Draw2D figures in the Graphical Editing Framework. All of its layout algorithms are captured as objects, whose classes derive from `AbstractLayout Algorithm`.

Enclose algorithms with their auxiliary data structures as objects.

↰1.4.5

Bundling an algorithm with its data structures achieves two things. First, the data is readily available throughout subroutines—that is, in `private` helper methods. Second, and more importantly, the data is encapsulated and hidden from clients. When tomorrow you find a better implementation,

you can always replace the old one. Its original presentation also ascribes
these goals to the STRATEGY pattern.

📖100
↰1.3.4

> Extract temporary fields with few referencing methods into separate
> objects.

Very often you recognize such algorithms only after you have coded them
as helpers within a larger object. Then, you may sometimes find that their
data structures are kept in fields that are valid only while the algorithm
is in progress. Rather than forcing the maintenance team to understand
at which points which fields are valid, you may extract the algorithm to a
separate object, using the tools *Extract Class* and *Move Method to Helper*.
In the best case, you even make your algorithm reusable.

↰1.4.8.3
↰1.8.5

Sometimes, the shared temporary fields do not become obvious until you
start dissecting a large and complex method into different processing steps.
This is the whole point of the METHOD OBJECT pattern:

↰1.4.5
📖27

PATTERN: METHOD OBJECT

When you find that breaking a complex method into smaller parts requires complex parameter passing, create an object to represent one invocation of the method. The class name reflects the method name, the
constructor takes the original method parameters, and the fields hold
temporary values.

At a lower level, it is sometimes necessary to wrap code in objects to pass
it around, most often as `Runnables`. If you already have the code, you can
ask Eclipse to create the object:

TOOL: Surround With

Select the code you wish to pass around in an object and use the menu
entry *Source/Surround With/Runnable* (`Alt-S W` or `Alt-Shift-Z`).

1.8.7   Boundary Objects

Objects within a software system work in a protected clean-room environment: They know their collaborators, their respective services, their demands and guarantees. As long as there are no bugs, the object machinery
runs smoothly and reliably. Interfacing with the outside world is quite a
different matter: You cannot rely on files to have the expected structure,
on users to enter only well-formatted data, or on other systems to send only
allowed requests over the network. Instead, you must expect the network
to break down unexpectedly, the disk to overflow, and the communication
partner to be a malicious intruder.

»4.1

↰1.5.2 »4.6

»4.6

Guarding against these uncertainties requires a lot of effort and fore-thought. The required logic is best kept in specialized *boundary objects* (Fig. 1.7), so that the core of the system can remain clean and simple.

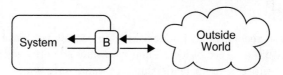

Figure 1.7 Boundary Objects

Boundary objects implement demarcation lines of trust.

The main goal of boundary objects is to insulate the internal software structure from the vagaries of the outside world. In other words, you trust the objects inside the system, but never the data or requests from outside the system. Boundary objects therefore check incoming data and requests meticulously before passing them on to the core that processes it.

Boundary objects transfer external to internal formats.

Very often, the process of validating incoming data is integrated with the process of translating it to some internal format that matches the process-ing demands. For instance, Eclipse stores information about a project's name, builders, and other details in a file .project in each project's root directory. The ProjectDescriptionReader translates that external XML format into an intern ProjectDescription. In this way, the logic for in-ternalizing the data is localized in one object. Thus, if ever the external format should change, you know which code needs to be adapted.

1.8.8   Nested Classes

↰1.1

The ideal picture of objects is that they are stand-alone entities that col-laborate rather loosely, just when others can perform specific tasks more effectively. Unfortunately, this ideal cannot always be reached, simply be-cause a corresponding distribution of tasks is not achieved easily.

»2.4.1

Suppose one of your classes called A is interested in changes to Eclipse's Java model, but really only in a special summary, not the details. As de-picted in Fig. 1.8(a), it would employ a helper B that analyzes the change reports relative to A's current state and passes on only a digest. B then requires a lot of information from A and even modifies its state directly. This requires A's interface to be larger than would be judged from its own

»11.2
↰1.7

purpose. Of course, the methods can be package-visible, but still they must be there; or else, uglier still, A's fields would have to be package-visible. *Nested classes* allow you to resolve this problem (Fig. 1.8(b)). Specifically, placing B inside A allows it to access A's fields directly, even if they are private—the outer class's fields are visible to its nested classes.

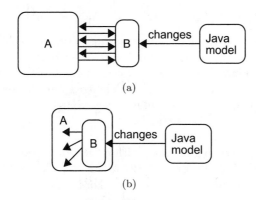

(a)

(b)

Figure 1.8 Motivation for Nested Classes

Nested classes enable proper structuring of closely collaborating objects.

The structure in Fig. 1.8(b) greatly enhances readability and maintainability: A's fields remain private, yet the nested class B can access them. The scoping rules of Java make it clear that no other class will access A's internals, so maintainers of A do not need to look further than B to understand the implementation.

Put the other way around, readers will also know that B is not a standalone class at all, but must be understood in connection with and in the context of A.

1.8.8.1   Inner Classes

Inner classes are nested classes that hold an implicit reference to an instance of the outer class, so that they can access that instance's fields at runtime. In most cases, this happens by referring to a field from the outer class. Explicit references use the syntax *OuterClassName*.this. Inner classes can occur at class level as *(non-static) member classes*, inside methods as *local classes*, and in expressions as *anonymous classes*. The last case warrants a separate discussion in Section 1.8.8.3.

Inner classes are proper classes. Apply the same care as for top-level ones.

The goal with usual objects is to keep them as independent from one another as possible, so that they can be understood, developed, and maintained independently. You should spend the same effort on your inner classes: Make them as stand-alone as possible, give them their own purpose, choose descriptive names. If an inner class is just a lump of code that accesses

↰1.1

↰1.2.3

the outer class's state all over the place, no further structure is gained and readability is not improved.

↰1.1
↠4.2.3

Delegate to the outer class to modifiy the data of that class.

Technically, inner classes can both read and write the fields of their surrounding instance. The guideline emphasizes the idea that you should strive to create explicit interfaces between your inner and outer classes wherever possible. If the outer class's fields are changed only by methods of that class, you get a self-contained outer object that can be understood and maintained on its own. In particular, the consistency of the outer object does not depend on the code of the inner class.

Let us study the two guidelines within `AbstractTextEditor`, which is the base of most editors in Eclipse. Because it has a lot of different aspects, it factors some of them into inner classes. For instance, the user can toggle insert/overwrite mode by some key sequence, which invokes the following action. While the `isChecked()` method reads the editor's current state, its `run()` method does not dare to modify that state, but delegates to the outer class instead.

---

org.eclipse.ui.texteditor.AbstractTextEditor

```
class ToggleInsertModeAction extends ResourceAction {
    public boolean isChecked() {
        return fInsertMode == SMART_INSERT;
    }
    public void run() {
        switchToNextInsertMode();
    }
}
```

🔍 This class happens to be package-visible in the original sources. It might as well be private, since it is referenced only from within `AbstractTextEditor`.

The conceptual boundary between inner and outer class becomes especially important in more involved cases that require more logic. You may want to look at the `TextListener` in Eclipse's text editor `AbstractText Editor` for example code; it contains a fair number of fields itself, yet it takes meticulous care to access the outer class only through method calls.

Hide inner classes to express that they are internal.

Inner classes usually depend on the outer class and are not usable outside that context. To emphasize this fact, the classes should not be public in most cases. The only exception would be an aspect or part that obviously contributes to the outer class's purpose and that you want to share with its clients. It this case, the nested class is often `static` (see the discussion in the next subsection).

> ⌕ The reference to the outer object is usually determined implicitly as the *immediately*   ▢111(§15.9.2)
> *enclosing instance* at the point where the instance of the inner class is created. Briefly
> speaking, this must take place in some method of the outer object. It is also possible
> to create instances of inner classes from the outside, at arbitrary points, by making the
> reference to the outer object explicit in *qualified class instance creation expressions*:   ▢111(§15.9)

```
Inner innerInstance = outerInstance.new Inner();
```

Such object creations are usually not desirable. If the inner class is really linked intricately
to the outer class, then it should be nobody else's business to create instances of the
inner class. In such cases, it is more readable to make the reference to the outer class
explicit and pass it to the inner class's constructor.

1.8.8.2   Static Member Classes

The goal of nested classes is to express clearly which code can access the
outer class's private aspects. Static member classes—that is, member classes
with modifier `static`—go one step beyond inner classes in that they do not
contain an implicit reference to an outer object. The maintenance developer
can deduce two things. First, the inner object is stand-alone, so it can be
understood without looking at the outer class. Second, the outer object's
state is not accessed implicitly in the inner class, so it can be understood
without looking at the inner class.

Static nested classes clarify the insulation between inner and outer objects.

Typical examples are found in helpers that parameterize reusable com-   ↰1.3.2
ponents. The concrete nested class is specific to its surrounding class, yet
conceptually it works inside a different object. For instance, `TableViewers`   ↠9.3.2
use a `ViewerComparator` to categorize and sort the displayed entries. The
clients of table viewers usually have very specific needs, so they subclass
`ViewerComparator` in `private` nested classes. Conversely, their specific
comparators usually do not depend on the clients' state, so they can be
`static`. For instance, the `JARFileSelectionDialog` from the Eclipse Java
tooling prompts the user for a JAR archive or a folder when specifying build
paths for projects. Inside the dialog, a nested class `FileViewerComparator`
keeps folders and files separate:

```
         org.eclipse.jdt.internal.ui.wizards.buildpaths.JARFileSelectionDialog
private static class FileViewerComparator extends ViewerComparator {
    public int category(Object element) {
        return element instanceof File &&
            ((File) element).isFile() ? 1 : 0;
    }
}
```

For more examples, open the *Type Hierarchy* (F4) on `ViewerComparator` and look out for private and/or static subclasses.

↰1.3.1

A different category of examples occurs in internal, nonreusable data structures. Since these are often passive, the outer object determines what happens and the inner objects do not access the outer one at all. Here is a typical example from the library's `HashTable`, whose entries form singly linked lists for collision resolution:

---
java.util.Hashtable.Entry

```
private static class Entry<K, V> implements Map.Entry<K, V> {
    int hash;
    final K key;
    V value;
    Entry<K, V> next;
}
```

1.8.8.3 Anonymous Classes

Sometimes objects are required just for technical reasons, but their logic and purpose are negligible. A typical case involves callbacks: You cannot pass a method as a callback, but instead have to construct a whole object. The object is really irrelevant; it is the code that matters. In such cases, Java allows you to define a new class and instantiate it in a single step:

↰1.4.7

```
new InterfaceOrClassName() { Field and Method Declarations }
```

Use anonymous classes as containers for code snippets.

»7.1

As an example, `SelectionListeners` are notified, among other things, when a button has been pressed. Here is a typical example from the wizard you get when you invoke *Team/Share project* on multiple projects. The second page has a list of projects and a button labeled "Share project." To react to button clicks, the wizard attaches the following listener object:

---
org.eclipse.team.internal.ui.wizards.ProjectSelectionPage

```
shareButton.addSelectionListener(new SelectionListener() {
    public void widgetSelected(SelectionEvent e) {
        shareSelectedProject();
    }
    public void widgetDefaultSelected(SelectionEvent e) {}
});
```

Another typical application area of anonymous classes comprises objects that are really functions. For instance, a `Comparator` is really an order predicate. The following code from a refactoring tool just sorts hits by their positions in the source file:

---
org.eclipse.jdt.internal.corext.refactoring.code.IntroduceFactoryRefactoring
---

```
SearchMatch[] hits = rg.getSearchResults();
Arrays.sort(hits, new Comparator<SearchMatch>() {
```

```
    public int compare(SearchMatch m1, SearchMatch m2) {
        return m2.getOffset() - m1.getOffset();
    }
});
```

Don't put extensive logic into anonymous classes.

Anonymous classes do not have names that could document or explain their purpose. As a consequence, they are rather hard to understand and maintain if they contain extensive code.

↶1.2.3

Use variable or method names to specify the anonymous class's purpose.

In contrast, the context of anonymous classes often implies their purpose. In the `SelectionListener` example, the button's variable name, together with the called method's name, clearly documents the point of the listener. Likewise, the `Comparator` is used to sort the array `hits`. There is one more technique along this line, which involves storing the created instance in a field or variable. For instance, the Eclipse platform's `JavaPlugin`, among other things, keeps track of Java-related font settings through the following listener:

org.eclipse.jdt.internal.ui.JavaPlugin

```
fFontPropertyChangeListener = new IPropertyChangeListener() {
    public void propertyChange(PropertyChangeEvent event) {
        ...
    }
};
```

🔍 Novices are sometimes surprised that they must declare local variables and parameters `final` in connection with inner classes, and in particular anonymous classes within methods. The reason is this: Conceptually, the inner class should be able to access the surrounding *scope*, meaning the language's nesting constructs such as classes, methods, and blocks. Using the compiler-generated reference, they can immediately access the outer object's fields. Local variables and parameters are a different: Although they are visible from classes inside the method, they reside in the method's stack frame. Since the compiler cannot store a reference to that stack frame in the inner object, it copies the variables' values *as seen at the point of object creation*. To make this very clear, the language prescribes that the variables must, in fact, be `final`.

1.8.9 The `null` Object

The object named `null` is very special. First, it is not a proper object at all, but rather a "non-object." Since one cannot invoke methods on `null`, it is actually very hard to work with it. Especially when used as a return value from methods, it burdens the client with a subsequent case distinction. Some authors therefore recommend that you avoid `null` altogether.

📖172(Ch.7,p.110f)

Many practitioners are not quite so severe. They use `null` to represent "no object," "no return value," "no options given," "default value," and other scenarios—just anywhere that the statement "there is no object" has a meaning in itself. As an example of a return value, `HashMap.get(key)` yields `null` when no value is associated with the *key*. The client will be aware that indeed this can happen from a logical perspective, so that the case distinction is useful and sensible anyway. Inside a class, `null` fields often denote, for instance, "not yet initialized."

↰1.3.8 ↰1.6.1

From a pragmatic point of view, one has to consider the alternatives. We focus on return values, but parameters and fields are similar. First, one could throw an exception if "no object" can be returned from a method. This would be justified if it is unexpected or unusual that no object can be returned. Since clients must then catch the exception, this solution introduces just a different form of case distinction. In some cases, one can return a "default" or "neutral" object, such as `Collections.emptyList()`. This has the disadvantage that the client cannot determine whether the result is empty because of a nonexistent object, or because the list is genuinely empty. It works well, however, for objects that merely get called back, as seen in `NullProgressMonitor`, which has empty method stubs and does not report progress at all.

↰1.5 ↠6.3

↠7.10

Taking the idea of default objects one step further, one can manufacture a proper object that behaves like a nonexistent object. For instance, Eclipse's resource layer always returns *handles* to resources: Whether a file on disk exists or not does not matter; `getFile()` always gives you a proper `IFile` object that you can work with. When accessing the file's content, an exception may be thrown, of course, but one expects this anyway with I/O. Also, the client can check `exists()`.

↠2.4.3

In a variant of this approach, a special `Null` object may be used to replace explicit case distinctions in the code by method dispatch. The following pattern has been introduced as a refactoring to remove repeated checks for `null` that clutter the code base:

↠3.1.6

📖92

PATTERN: Null Object

If many clients of a class C check for `null` and then execute some (common) default behavior, introduce a subclass `Null`C of C and override the methods to exhibit the same default behavior. You can then remove the checks for `null` in all clients. If checks for `null` remain necessary because some clients execute a deviating default behavior, introduce a method `isNull()` in C and have `Null`C return `true`, or use `instanceof` directly.

The Objective-C language includes a `nil` object. It accepts all messages (i.e., provides all methods), but these methods do nothing and return default values.

The NULL OBJECT pattern can also be understood as the object-oriented counter-part of introducing artificial *sentinel* elements into data structures with the aim of reducing case distinction in the operations. For instance, an empty doubly linked list usually contains a single sentinel node, which has its `next` and `previous` pointers point to itself. In a non-empty list, the sentinel remains as an extra element. The first node's `previous` pointer and the last node's `next` pointer both point to the sentinel, and the sentinel points back as expected. The code for insertion and deletion of nodes then does not have to check for these special cases, because the right thing happens automatically. Every node technically has a successor and a predecessor, even if it happens to be the sentinel.

📖72

The pragmatic advice therefore is: Don't use `null` lightly, since it in-duces case-distinctions in the code that may blur the code's meaning and make it more complex than necessary. Go through the alternatives, and decide to use `null` objects only when you feel that a "no object" can be justified logically.

There is one final technical aspect concerning `null` objects that professional devel-opers must be aware of, because it can lead to memory leaks: Whenever a field or array holds a reference to an object, but that object is no longer logically required, the reference should be set to `null`. In this way, the garbage collector can reclaim the object if it is no longer referenced elsewhere. For example, the `ArrayList` takes care to clean up after removing an element from the sequence, by setting the newly freed slot to `null` (the comment is from the original sources):

java.util.ArrayList

```java
public E remove(int index) {
    ...
    elementData[--size] = null; // clear to let GC do its work
    return oldValue;
}
```

Chapter 2

Fundamental Object Structures

In Chapter 1, we analyzed Java's perception of "objects" and their usage in professional software development. Chapter 3 will add the aspect of abstraction by inheritance and interfaces. After that, we will have discussed the most prominent language features, and by working and experimenting with the guidelines you will have become a sound and reliable developer.

Professional software development is, however, more than just the goal-oriented application of elementary language constructs in code. For one thing, it involves strategic planning and effective communication about goals and software structures. For these purposes, individual objects, with their various methods and fields, are too fine-grained. It would take forever to explain all the method interactions to colleagues one-by-one. One viable tool for thinking in more comprehensive terms is design patterns, many of which have already been presented as a conceptual background for using individual language constructs properly. Nevertheless, the discussion has remained mostly focused on single objects, sometimes with a hypothetical client or service provider to complete the picture.

📖100

This chapter presents frequent constructs involving several objects. First, the OBSERVER pattern explains how objects communicate about state changes. Given that state is a central ingredient to objects, it is necessary to handle changes effectively, predictably, and uniformly. Next, we discuss a few fundamental terms and guidelines concerning compound objects in general and move on to recursive or hierarchical structures, which we approach by the COMPOSITE and VISITOR patterns. Finally, it is often the case that an existing object must be wrapped: by an ADAPTER because its interface does not suit its clients, by a DECORATOR because the interface is incomplete, or by a PROXY because the real object is hard to work with.

↰1.1

2.1 Propagating State Changes: Observer

An object's fields, including the contained data structures, are summarily referred to as the object's state. In object-oriented programming, the usual case is that the state can change by side effects on these fields and data structures. This is in stark contrast to other paradigms, such as functional

↰1.8.4 📖245,42,196

📖63,164

📖72 ↰1.1

programming or logic programming, where data structures *never* change
once they have been initialized. An object's behavior is also in contrast to
imperative data structures, since objects are active: They do not passively
suffer modifications, but they react to these changes in a suitable manner.
Furthermore, because objects collaborate to perform common tasks, it is
very common that their own state reflects that of their collaborators in
some way.

📖100

The quintessential design pattern, from this perspective, is the OB-
SERVER pattern, as depicted in Fig. 2.1. In this pattern, a *subject* sends
out notifications about state changes to an arbitrary number and type of
observer objects.

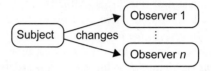

Figure 2.1 Basic Idea of Observer Pattern

PATTERN: OBSERVER

One object, the *subject*, holds some state on which several *observers* of
diverse kinds depend. The *subject* offers a service to register the observers
and to notify them whenever a state change occurs.

---

1. Think about the possible ways in which the subject's state may
   change. Define an `interface` whose methods represent messages
   about those possible changes. It is also customary to have a single
   method taking an *event object* that describes the change in detail.

2. Add to the subject a field `listeners` to hold the registered observers. Add also methods `addListener()` and `removeListener()`
   so that observers can register and de-register.

3. Add a `private` or `protected` method `fire ... ()` for each possible change that iterates through the observers and invokes the
   right method. Invoke the `fire` method whenever a change has
   taken place.

4. Let all observers implement the defined interface and register them
   with the subject, so that they receive the change notifications. Make
   sure to de-register observers that are no longer interested in the
   subject's state.

Since the OBSERVER pattern is central to the craft, this section explores its
implementation and consequences in some detail. Further details are also
added in connection with compound objects.

»2.2.4

2.1.1   Example: Observing Background Jobs

Let us start to explore the pattern by examining an extended example. We choose a nontrivial case here, because it also demonstrates the more intricate points and decisions. In addition, it shows to what extent the pattern can be adapted without losing its overall structure. If you would like to see a simpler example, we encourage you to trace the pattern for text changes in JFace class Document, the principal text storage in Eclipse.

We have already looked at Eclipse's JobManager, which orchestrates all background jobs in the Eclipse platform. It is clear that several objects will be interested in when a job starts or ends, and whether it has finished successfully. You will be familiar, for example, with the progress information displayed to the far right in the status line and the *progress* view.

◀1.3.2

We start with step 1 and consider the possible "state changes." First, the job manager itself is rather static; observers will be interested in the states of the managed Jobs. So what can happen to a Job? It can be scheduled, eventually started, can finish execution, and some more things. This enumeration is represented in the IJobChangeListener interface, by one method for each change. The IJobChangeEvent then contains the details of the change—for example, the job to which it applies.

```
             org.eclipse.core.runtime.jobs.IJobChangeListener
public interface IJobChangeListener {
    public void scheduled(IJobChangeEvent event);
    public void aboutToRun(IJobChangeEvent event);
    public void running(IJobChangeEvent event);
    public void done(IJobChangeEvent event);
    ...
}
```

Defining this interface was the main design challenge, because it fixes all further decisions. The remainder of the implementation is merely technical.

▶2.1.2

For step 2, the job manager keeps a listener list in a field. It employs a specialized class, because the notification process makes some special provisions (see below):

```
             org.eclipse.core.internal.jobs.JobManager
private final JobListeners jobListeners = new JobListeners();
```

It provides two methods that enable observers to register and de-register:

```
             org.eclipse.core.internal.jobs.JobManager
public void addJobChangeListener(IJobChangeListener listener) {
    jobListeners.add(listener);
}
public void removeJobChangeListener(IJobChangeListener listener) {
    jobListeners.remove(listener);
}
```

The methods according to step 3 are not contained in the `JobManager` itself, but in the helper object `JobListeners`. For each kind of change, it offers a corresponding method to send out events, as prescribed by the pattern. The following one, for instance, notifies the listeners that a job has just been started. It creates an event object and delivers it to the observers via an internal helper method, which implements the behavior that "global" listeners interested in jobs in general are notified before "local" listeners interested in a particular job.

---

org.eclipse.core.internal.jobs.JobListeners

```
public void running(Job job) {
    doNotify(running, newEvent(job));
}
```

» 9.3.2   A more usual pattern of a `fire` method is found in `Viewer`, which shows data on the screen and enables the user to select items. It notifies listeners when the selection changes:

---

org.eclipse.jface.viewers.Viewer

```
protected void fireSelectionChanged(final SelectionChangedEvent
    event) {
    Object[] listeners = selectionChangedListeners.getListeners();
    for (int i = 0; i < listeners.length; ++i) {
        ISelectionChangedListener l =
            (ISelectionChangedListener) listeners[i];
        l.selectionChanged(event);
    }
}
```

⚠ It is essential to copy the listener list before traversing it, because some listeners might decide to de-register when they receive the notification, or to register new observers. In a direct traversal of the listener list, this would cause havoc.

To finish step 3, the observers must be notified whenever the state has changed. In the example, starting a new job results in that job being run, which is reflected directly in the code (`job` is started by the omitted code):

---

org.eclipse.core.internal.jobs.JobManager

```
protected Job startJob(Worker worker) {
    ...
    jobListeners.running(job);
    return job;
}
```

Finally, we turn to the observers for step 4. For instance, the progress display implements and registers a job tracker `changeListener` as follows.[1] Any subsequent changes to the jobs' status will be delivered to that object and will cause the progress manager to update its internal data structures.

---
org.eclipse.ui.internal.progress.ProgressManager

```
Job.getJobManager().addJobChangeListener(this.changeListener);
```

We have now walked through the overall implementation. It is important to note that the sequence of steps is not arbitrary: You should think about step 1 in some depth, because it contains the crucial design decisions. Then, you can quickly and mechanically implement steps 2 and 3. At this point, the pattern is complete, and arbitrary observers can be added to the system in step 4. That last step is in principle open ended; at any time, new observers can turn up and can register for change notifications.

»2.1.2

2.1.2   Crucial Design and Implementation Constraints

The implementation guideline gives the salient points for solving the problem of change propagation. However, there are further invisible or implied constraints on the actual solution that professionals follow but learners must first become aware of. This section makes those constraints explicit, because neglecting them means ruining the entire effort of using OBSERVER.

The observer interface does not reflect information about concrete observers.

The implementation guideline states that the observer interface is to reflect the possible state changes of the *subject*. Implicitly, this means that the interface does *not* reflect any concrete observer objects that the developer may have in mind. The reason is very simple: OBSERVER adds to the subject a general infrastructure for change propagation. If tomorrow a new kind of observer should turn up in the system, it must fit with that infrastructure.

Unfortunately, honoring this constraint requires some mental effort. Often the pattern is applied when the first object depends on the subject's state. At this point, it is natural that you should tailor the observer interface to this concrete observer's needs, because doing so simplifies the implementation of that observer—after all, it gets just the information that it requires.

If you decide to use the pattern, use it properly. Sit back, purge the first observer from your mind, and focus on the subject alone: What are the relevant aspects of its state? In which ways can those aspects change?

---

1. In fact, the story is more involved, due to the strict model-view separation (Section 9.1). If you use *call hierarchy* on the add-listener methods, you find a cascade of listeners, so that job changes propagate as follows: `JobManager` → `ProgressManager` → `ProgessViewUpdater` → `ProgressContentProvider` (Section 9.3.2).

The answers to those questions will shape the observer interface in such a way that tomorrow's observer will benefit from the infrastructure. Always keep in mind that the final goal is that *any* kind of interested object can attach itself to the subject. If you feel that you cannot come up with a good general interface, maybe it is best to avoid the pattern and to stick with special notifications for now.

»2.1.4

Notifications must not reveal the subject's internals.

↰1.1

↰1.3.3

It is easy to leak internal information accidentally. Suppose your subject has a list of data items that may be modified. In sending the notification, you want to be helpful and pass along the current list. Unless you are careful, the observer may now be able to modify the list. When you have finished your observer interface, you should therefore lean back again and compare it to the normal interface of the subject. The notifications must not leak information that is otherwise inaccessible.

The subject must be consistent before it sends notifications.

↰1.3.1

»4.4 »4.2.3

Changes to an object's state are rarely as elementary as setting a single field. For example, replacing some text in a Document updates not only the text (line 6 in the following code), but also the ranges of the lines (line 7). In between the two, the object is inconsistent—you might also say "broken." If at that point some client were to get the text of a line, it would get the wrong text, because the line positions have not been updated. Unfortunately, sending change notifications transfers the control to other objects, and they may invoke methods on the broken subject. The preceding rule must therefore be followed very strictly.

---
org.eclipse.jface.text.AbstractDocument

```
1 public void replace(int pos, int length, String text,
2         long modificationStamp)
3         throws BadLocationException {
4     ...
5     DocumentEvent e = new DocumentEvent(this, pos, length, text);
6     getStore().replace(pos, length, text);
7     getTracker().replace(pos, length, text);
8     fireDocumentChanged(e);
9 }
```

All is well if you can summarize all changes that have occurred in one notification: You can simply send it at the end of the public method that performs the changes. In the document example, the changes to the line information are not observable—only the text is. Otherwise, you might introduce compound notifications that list the individual changes that occurred during the run of a method. These notifications are then, again, sent at the very end, when the subject is consistent. You can find a typical example in Swing's `DefaultStyledDocument`, where methods `beginEdits()` and `endEdits()` bracket and aggregate modifications.

Beware of overriding methods that send notifications.

The previous problem occurs in general when a method that sends a notification gets extended by overriding. Suddenly, the notification is sent in the middle of the new method, and very probably, the object is "broken" at that point—otherwise, the extension would not be necessary. If you foresee future extensions, you might want to employ TEMPLATE METHOD to inject the extensions *before* the notification.

» 1.4.11

↰ 1.4.9

Beware of observers that modify the subject.

The previous two points lay out a clear sequence of events: first perform a modification, then send out the notifications once the subject's state is stable again. This sequence can be broken not only within the subject, but also from without. Suppose a subject has three observers a, b, and c. When b receives a change notification, it calls an operation on the subject, causing yet another state change. As a result, the subsequent notification to c is stale, because the state it reports may no longer be valid. For a concrete example, think of a subject holding some list. When it reports the addition of an element at the end of the list, b decides to remove that element. When c tries to look at the supposedly new element, it gets an index-out-of-bounds exception.

Ensure de-registration of observers.

Observers that are once registered hang around in the subject's listener list until they are de-registered explicitly. Even if the observer is technically "dead"—for instance, because the window that it represents was closed by the user—it will continue to receive notifications. (Also, it cannot be garbage collected.) Usually, this will lead to unexpected exceptions, such as null pointer exceptions, because the internal structure of the observer has been destroyed and is no longer in working order when it tries to react to notifications.

↰ 1.8.9

The general rule, then, is this: Whenever you register an observer, you must also set up a mechanism by which it will be de-registered when it is no longer interested. For example, suppose you have a window that displays running jobs. When that window is opened, it starts tracking jobs, as shown previously. At the same time, it sets up a mechanism for de-registering the observer when it is no longer interested in the jobs.

↰ 2.1.1

```
                   observer.JobDisplayWindow.open
Job.getJobManager().addJobChangeListener(jobListener);
addDisposeListener(new DisposeListener() {
    public void widgetDisposed(DisposeEvent e) {
        Job.getJobManager().removeJobChangeListener(jobListener);
    }
});
```

50(§7.2.2.2)

🔎 There is one technical approach to working around the requirement of de-registration. Especially in larger applications, where some modules may not be trusted to be conscientious about de-registration, one can keep listeners in *weak* references: When the listener is not referenced anywhere else in the system, the garbage collector sets the weak reference to `null`, which the subject recognizes when sending notifications. This solution is, however, only partial, since a notification may still be sent to a broken observer before the garbage collector runs.

Always include a subject reference in notifications.

When thinking about the first observer of a subject, you will usually have the feeling that the observer knows which subject it is working with. Since general observers, however, very often register with several subjects, the notifications should always include a reference to their sender.

2.1.3   Implementation Details and Decisions

Implementations of OBSERVER exhibit a rather large degree of flexibility. We now discuss a few decision points to exhibit some of that flexibility.

Management of Registered Listeners   The usage pattern of listener lists differs subtly from that of ordinary data lists in several ways. For instance, additions and deletions are relatively rare, while traversals with copies are very frequent. Furthermore, listener lists are usually very small or even empty, so that space concerns dominate runtime concerns. You should therefore avoid the space-intensive amortized addition strategy of `ArrayList` and `Vector`, as well as the overhead of `LinkedList`.

↰1.3.1

Frameworks usually offer special data structures for listener lists. Eclipse uses `ListenerList` (in package `org.eclipse.core.runtime`), which keeps listeners in a plain array with no extra space and optimizes the case of the empty list by a constant empty array. The generic `PropertyChangeSupport` goes together well with objects that are primarily information holders, such as JavaBeans. In the context of UIs, there are many types of listeners, but for each widget, only a few types are actually used. Swing's implementation `EventListenerList` therefore keeps different types of listeners together in one array, by tagging each with the type of registered listener. Similarly, SWT's internal `EventTable` keeps the listener type for each slot. The `Widget` base class further optimizes the case of no attached listeners, by creating the event table only on demand.

↰1.3.3

↰1.6.1

Push Versus Pull   The design of the observer interface involves a classic   📖100
choice: Should the subject send a detailed description of the change, or
should it just point out that its state has changed, but not mention any details? The first variant is called the *push* model, the second the *pull* model.
The general rule followed by subjects throughout the Eclipse platform, and
elsewhere, is to provide as much detail as possible about the change. In consequence, the JobManager describes which job has changed to what state,   ↰2.1.1
the resource framework sends tree-structured IResourceDeltas, and so on.

The reason to prefer the push variant is that the updates performed by
the observers in response to the notification may be expensive. Just consider a text document that merely says "I changed" when the user types a
character. Any display for the document would have to repaint the entire
text, or else perform an expensive difference computation. Always remember that the infrastructure you create must be good enough for tomorrow's
observers.

Sending Notifications Safely   Sending notifications always incurs the risk
that the receiver is buggy and will throw an unexpected exception. Having
one such observer ruins the whole scheme, because later observers will not
receive the notification at all. It is therefore common practice to wrap the
actual sending in a try/catch block, especially when the observers are
likely to come from other modules or the subject is central to the entire
application. Eclipse provides the SafeRunner class for that purpose. The
class also takes care of properly logging any thrown exception, if desired.

Different Methods or Event Types   Subjects usually send different kinds
of changes. This can be expressed in the observer interface through different methods, such as in the case of IJobChangeListeners or SWT's   ↰2.1.1 ⇥7.8
MouseListeners. Alternatively, you can introduce an enum or int constants that capture the different kinds of changes. The latter option can be
seen, for instance, in IResourceDelta or the low-level SWT Event. Both
approaches are viable, and you must weigh their relative benefits: With
separate methods, the client is spared a switch on the type. At the same
time, making the type explicit and packaging it the event makes it easier
to forward the change notification, since only one method call is necessary.
In the end, it is the client's perspective and its needs that matter.   ↰1.1

Event Objects   It is a common practice to wrap the information about
a change into an event object, rather than having observer methods with
different parameters. There are several advantages to this approach. Event
objects are extensible if new kinds of changes or new data occur, so that
the overall implementation remains more flexible. Also, sending objects is
usually more efficient: One must create the object once, but can then pass
the reference, which consists of one machine word, to observers, which may
again pass it on to helper methods.

> **TOOL: Introduce Parameter Object**
>
> To convert an observer method with several parameters to one with an event object, use *Refactor/Introduce Parameter Object* (Alt-Shift-T). The tool also modifies all call sites. You should, however, go back to the `fire` methods, because the tool does not move the object creation outside the loop.

Implementing the Observer Interface   Objects that are interested in the changes of the subject must register an observer. However, it may not always be the best choice to register *themselves* as observers, since they would need to implement the observer interface and the `implements` clause is public information: Some client might think that it can actually use the object *as an observer*. It is usually better to keep the `implements` hidden from clients.

»3.2.1

◄2.1.1

For example, we have already mentioned that the `ProgressManager` observes the background jobs inside Eclipse. It does implement `IJobChange Listener`, although it has a hidden field containing an observer object. The field is initialized with an anonymous nested class, so that the observer can access the surrounding `ProgressManager` directly.

»1.8.8.3

org.eclipse.ui.internal.progress.ProgressManager

```
IJobChangeListener changeListener;
```

It is common that the nested class merely delegates notifications to the outer class. An example is found in `CCombo`, SWT's custom implementation of a combo box. The shown listener is attached to all parts of the widget, so as to get notification of all user interactions.

org.eclipse.swt.custom.CCombo.CCombo

```
listener = new Listener() {
    public void handleEvent(Event event) {
        if (popup == event.widget) {
            popupEvent(event);
            return;
        }
        ...
    }
};
```

»1.8.8.1
»4.1

The benefit of this delegation is that the outer class remains self-contained: Its code alone defines its entire behavior and is responsible for keeping the object consistent.

◄1.4.5

⚡ You can create the methods to delegate to by wishful thinking. Specifically, within a nested class, *Create Method* lets you choose between creating a `private` method in the nested class or a `protected` method in the outer class.

Sometimes, however, an object so obviously *is* an observer that it is acceptable to implement the interface directly. In particular, this is the case for controllers or mediators. Their purpose is precisely to receive notifications and to decide how to process or to delegate them. Their role in the system justifies the declaration that they *are* observers.

»3.1.1

»9.2 »7.7

Similarly, you may find that an anonymous observer attracts more and more code, and more and more of the actual logic. It is then better to introduce a named class, so as to capture its intention clearly.

↰1.2.3

TOOL: Convert Anonymous to Nested

To introduce a name for an anonymous class, place the cursor after the new, Quick-Fix (Ctrl-1) or *Refactor* (Alt-Shift-T), and choose *Convert anonymous to nested class*.

Going one step further, the observer's logic may become so extensive that its interaction with the surrounding class becomes unclear: After all, the observer may access and modify the outer class's fields *anywhere* within its own code. It is then better to move it to a separate, package-visible class, so that it can access the surrounding object only through a well-defined method interface.

»1.7

TOOL: Move Type to New File

To extract a nested class that has become dominating from its surrounding class, invoke *Refactor* (Alt-Shift-T) and choose *Move Type to New File*.

2.1.4 Judging the Need for Observers

No pattern is compulsory. One can design great object collaborations without using OBSERVER. Indeed, there are strong reasons *against* using it: When there is only one observer, in the beginning, the pattern introduces a lot of implementation overhead, meaning code that must be written and maintained. Furthermore, the sole observer will not get messages tailored to its needs, but only the changes of the subject, from which it must *deduce* its own correct reaction. Both of these have a strong smell of "speculative generality"—an infrastructure that you pay for, but that you never exploit.

»11

□□92

If you suspect that your first observer may remain single for quite some time, and if it bears a strong logical relationship to the alleged subject anyway, for instance because they work on the same task, then it might be better to add to the "subject" a simple reference to the "observer." Instead of sending general change reports, the subject can directly call some methods in the "observer" wherever that object is interested in the developments. In the end, special-purpose "hooks" are sprinkled throughout the "subject," but these hooks cost no implementation overhead. There's nothing wrong

↰1.1

📖109 ↰1.4.1

with such collaborations. Indeed, objects sending messages to each other is at the very core of object-oriented programming.

OBSERVER, however, can help you to create a flexible and extensible system. Since the subject makes only the barely necessary assumptions about its observers, it will collaborate with any part of your system that is interested in its state, including future extensions. Fig. 2.2 gives a graphical intuition: The subject sends its message to some abstract observer, which is specified by an interface. It neither knows nor cares what is beyond that interface. In effect, it does not depend on these details. Software engineers

»12.1

summarize this by saying that the subject and observer are *loosely coupled*.

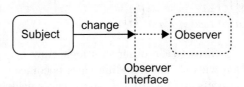

Figure 2.2 Decoupling in the Observer Pattern

A further benefit of the pattern is that observers can also be creative about what they do with the raw change information. Consider, again, the

↰2.1.1

management of jobs in the Eclipse platform. Job listeners are usually interested about when jobs finish, so that they can show their results to the user. They can, however, do arbitrary things. Suppose you want to implement a scheduler for regular tasks, such as cleanup or summary computations. You want to run such jobs when the platform is "idle"—when no background job has run for, say, half a minute. All your scheduler must do is observe the JobManager to gain that information; it can simply keep a time-stamp whenever a job is scheduled and finishes. The job manager was never written with that purpose in mind, nor would it have been easy to anticipate it. Yet, it fully supports this scenario.

In the end, providing OBSERVER is an investment: You believe that the infrastructure will come in useful in the future, so you pay a little more than would be strictly necessary right now. With some experience, you will become a shrewd judge of the expected return on investment. Furthermore,

»9.1
»2.2.4

some situations do demand OBSERVER. For instance, an object structure that will be displayed on the screen must support observers, although perhaps at some coarser level of granularity.

2.2 Compound Objects

↰1.1

Objects should not be large, monolithic entities that undertake substantial tasks by themselves—objects are small and share tasks among them.

In consequence, objects frequently hold references to, or are composed of, several other objects. This section explores this relationship and some of its implications.

Before we start, let us summarize briefly where compound objects have occurred previously: Data structures may be constructed from (dumb) objects (Section 1.3.1); some collaborators of an object may actually be private helpers (Section 1.3.2); reusable functionality may be extracted to separate objects (Section 1.4.8.3); lazy initialization keeps object creation cheap (Section 1.6.1). All in all, compound objects can structure the solution, can establish separation of concerns, and can help to avoid duplication and foster reuse.

2.2.1 Ownership

When working with objects that employ other objects to achieve their purpose, it is frequently useful to ask whether those other objects become in some sense a part of their employer. Fig. 2.3 shows the two extreme configurations: In (a), object A contains objects B and C, and they are logically parts of A. One also says that A *owns* B and C, and that A is the *host object* of B and C. In (b), in contrast, A merely employs B and C, and even shares C with another object D.

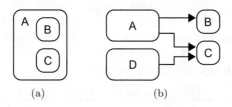

(a)   (b)

Figure 2.3 Ownership and Sharing

The UML differentiates further and introduces three levels of objects "belonging to" other objects (Fig. 2.4), by introducing relationships between their classes: 📖47 📖198(Table 7.3)

- The loosest form, *association*, merely means that instances of A somehow hold a reference to instances of B so that they can invoke the methods of that class. The fact that this relationship is directional can be made explicit by *navigability*, which is denoted by open arrow heads at the end of the association.

- *Aggregation* expresses whole–part relationships, which are associations that do not permit cycles. Another name for aggregation is "has-a" relationship. Unlike ownership, aggregation does not preclude structure sharing.

- *Composition* is full "ownership": It is an aggregation where the "whole" object controls the lifetime of the "part" and manages the part completely, and different "wholes" cannot share "parts."

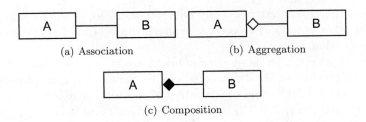

(a) Association   (b) Aggregation

(c) Composition

Figure 2.4 Class Relationships in the UML

We will now explore different aspects of aggregation and composition that developers usually connect with these concepts.

The "whole" manages the life cycle of its "parts."

First, and foremost, ownership implies linked life cycles. The host object, or "whole," manages the "part." Very often, it creates the "part." In the end, when the "whole" becomes invalid, it also destroys the "part." In many cases, this happens implicitly during garbage collection: Since the "whole" holds the only reference to the "part," the "part" is reclaimed with the "whole."

When one of the objects allocates resources, destruction must be arranged explicitly. A typical example can be found in SWT's CCombo implementation of a combo box. It combines, as usual, a text field and a selection list, which is available through an arrow button. The selection list must be displayed above other elements on the screen, in a separate pop-up window. This is arranged by two objects list and popup:

---
org.eclipse.swt.custom.CCombo

```
List list;
Shell popup;
```

The two elements are created, at the latest, when the list is to be shown. Note that in line 4, the first argument to list is the window popup; afterward, popup owns list. Fig. 2.5 shows the resulting nested ownership relations.

»7.1

---
org.eclipse.swt.custom.CCombo

```
1 void createPopup(String[] items, int selectionIndex) {
2     popup = new Shell (getShell (), SWT.NO_TRIM | SWT.ON_TOP);
3     ...
4     list = new List (popup, listStyle);
5     ...
6 }
```

When the life cycle of the combo box ends, for instance because the user closes the containing window, the combo box takes care to end the life cycle of its parts as well. This is accomplished by the following snippet. (Technically, it is executed as a part of a callback when the combo box is

»7.1

Figure 2.5 Ownership in the CCombo Example

destroyed.) Line 2 ensures that the object is not informed about the disposal of the list, which it initiates itself in line 3 by disposing its owner popup (Fig. 2.5).

org.eclipse.swt.custom.CCombo.comboEvent

```
1 if (popup != null && !popup.isDisposed ()) {
2     list.removeListener (SWT.Dispose, listener);
3     popup.dispose ();
4 }
```

Ownership can change dynamically.

The CCombo example also shows that the host object does not necessarily create the objects it owns, but can start to manage them when they are passed as arguments to constructors or methods: Starting at the point where it conceptually "owns" the parts, the host object also assumes responsibility for their life cycles. In the example, the popup will destroy the list whenever it is destroyed—regardless of how its destruction was actually triggered.

Ownership can be hierarchical.

If object A owns object B, and B in turn owns object C, then implicitly A owns C (i.e., ownership is a transitive relation). Thus, when A is destroyed, it will destroy B, which will cause C to be destroyed in turn (Fig. 2.5).

Parts often hold references to their owners.

Since a "part" can have only one single owner at a time, it is often useful to be able to navigate to this owner. Specifically, in hierarchical structures that do not imply encapsulation, clients will often want to navigate freely up and down the tree of objects.

»2.3.1

Provide a mechanism to enforce the consistency of parent references.

It is, of course, essential to keep the parent reference consistent with ownership: Whenever the ownership relation is established or changes, the parent reference must change immediately as well. In particular, you should not leave the update to clients, because some of those will not be aware of their duty and will break the link.

»7.1

There are two main techniques. First, as in the case of SWT, one can pass the parent to the child and add the child to the parent implicitly. Similarly, a `setParent` method can be made responsible for adding the part to its owner. Second, the parent can have methods for adding children. `Figures` in the Graphical Editing Framework use this technique. The `add` method then also re-parents the new child `figure`:

📖214

org.eclipse.draw2d.Figure.add

```
if (figure.getParent() != null)
    figure.getParent().remove(figure);
children.add(index, figure);
figure.setParent(this);
```

An alternative to re-parenting consists in requiring that the new child does not have a parent so far. This choice is exhibited in the abstract syntax trees used in the Eclipse Java tooling:

org.eclipse.jdt.core.dom.ASTNode

```
static void checkNewChild(ASTNode node, ASTNode newChild,
        boolean cycleCheck, Class nodeType) {
    ...
    if (newChild.getParent() != null)
        throw new IllegalArgumentException();
    ...
}
```

While parent links may simplify navigation in the data structure, they have the drawback of tying the part to the particular context. In other words, the type of the parent link determines where the part can be employed. Parent links therefore make the parts less reusable, a drawback that must be weighed against the benefit of navigation.

2.2.2 Structure Sharing

↰1.8.4

Ownership implies that objects are located in a particular place in a hierarchical structure. From the opposite perspective, they cannot occur in two places at once. In case of large and/or nested object structures, this is, however, very desirable: the same object can be shared between different parts of the overall structure to save memory. We have already seen that immutable objects in a functional programming style can benefit from structure sharing. UML's notion of aggregation captures just this case: hierarchical organization without ownership.

»2.3.1

Suppose, for instance, that we wish to capture mathematical expressions. In this case, each operator or function application is one object, and the arguments become the object's children. Then $\sin(e)$ is an object with a single child, which points to the representation of expression e. When we wish to compute the derivative, here $\cos(e)$, we can create a single new object for cos, which happens to share its argument with the original $\sin(e)$. No matter how deeply nested e is, derivation costs only a single new object. In general, structure sharing can be useful for symbolic computation.

📖17

Possible applications of sharing are, in fact, frequent. When representing Java code as abstract syntax trees, such as when generating code, it is useful to link some generated expression into different places, just wherever it happens to occur. In the hierarchical organization of file systems, hard or soft links can be represented by sharing `File` objects in different places.

238

In general, hierarchical object structures with sharing constitute directed acyclic graphs (DAGs). Whenever you recognize such special graphs, you can think about using aggregation with structure sharing. However, it must be clarified that not every DAG is aggregation. For instance, the JDT compiler represents classes and interfaces as `SourceTypeBindings`. In these, it maintains the `extends` and `implements` relationships in the following two fields:

72

org.eclipse.jdt.internal.compiler.lookup.SourceTypeBinding

```
public ReferenceBinding superclass;
public ReferenceBinding[] superInterfaces;
```

While they do establish a graph structure and a hierarchy with sharing, they do not constitute aggregation. The main entry point to accessing reference types is through the compiler's symbol tables, if there is any form of aggregation at all, it is the symbol table that "owns" the types.

In the other direction, full ownership does not preclude cross-referencing: If the object structure is public, any client can keep references to nested objects. These cross-references do not establish sharing in the sense of aggregation, nor do they destroy the property of unique parents. While each object still has a unique place, there can be more references to it elsewhere.

Similarly, structure sharing can be combined with parent links. In this case, however, each object can have multiple parents, which makes navigation quite awkward and often unusable.

2.2.3 Compound Objects and Encapsulation

When an object creates and manages several helpers, a natural question is whether other parts of the system will be aware of these auxiliary structures. A broad view will be taken in the discussion of design for decoupling. For now, let us stay with analyzing code.

12.2.1 12.1.4

Ownership can, but need not, imply encapsulation.

Ownership is a dynamic relationship about linked life cycles. As in the `CCombo` example of Section 2.2.1, it often implies as well that the parts are hidden from the clients—that their use is private. Fig. 2.3 and Fig. 2.5 indicate this by placing the parts inside their owners. This encapsulation is, however, not mandatory. For instance, the ownership between `popup` and `list` in the same example is public under the concept of a *widget tree*: Elements on the screen are nested hierarchically, so using `getChildren()` on `popoup` will yield `list`.

7.1

Ownership is often tied to consistency conditions.

»4.1 ▯23,21

An object creates and manages its parts to solve specific subtasks of its own overall task. Usually, the subtasks are not stand-alone entities, but rather are linked to one another, because only together can they contribute to the overall goal. This implies that there will usually be consistency conditions between parts, and the host object is responsible for maintaining these conditions.

In the CCombo example of Section 2.2.1, popup and list show the selection list when prompted by the user. Several consistency conditions apply—for instance, either both are null or both are non-null; if they are non-null, list is owned by popup and the list fills the entire popup window; the list contains all entries that the CCombo itself contains, and has the same font as CCombo. All of those conditions are enforced by CCombo.

Hide internal object structures, especially those with complex consistency conditions.

↰1.3.1

↰2.1

Revealing auxiliary object structures has the disadvantage that clients will start to rely on these structures, so that they cannot be modified later on. What is more, clients may invoke methods on the parts that destroy the overall consistency of the owner object. Especially in the case of objects used as data structures, this can be disastrous. In other cases, it might just mean more effort: The owner might have to observe its parts to maintain consistency despite changes triggered by clients.

Publish structure that constitutes a valid client interface.

↰1.1

»3.2.2

↰1.6.1

You must have compelling reasons for publishing helper objects. They are usually related to defining an interface that suits clients. As with methods, there is always the fundamental dilemma of hiding knowledge to change details later and publishing knowledge to enable effective work with the object. In some cases, the wisest path is to publish selected aspects as objects. For instance, all editors in Eclipse offer a getAdapter() method to access selected internals through well-defined interfaces. For instance, they offer a helper for performing find/replace operations (and create this helper lazily):

```
                    org.eclipse.ui.texteditor.AbstractTextEditor.getAdapter
if (IFindReplaceTarget.class.equals(required)) {
    if (fFindReplaceTarget == null) {
        IFindReplaceTarget target =
            fSourceViewer.getFindReplaceTarget();
        fFindReplaceTarget = new FindReplaceTarget(this, target);
    }
    return fFindReplaceTarget;
}
```

2.2.4   Compound Objects and Observers

The parts of a compound object cling together quite closely: They are
created and destroyed together, and may obey complex relationships during
their lifetime. It is therefore sensible to assume that:

↰2.2.1
↰2.2.3

> The owner's state comprises its parts' state.

In the context of state updates, the OBSERVER pattern technically addresses
updates to a single object's state. With the preceding insight, one would
therefore channel change notifications on parts to observers of their owner,
as shown in Fig. 2.6. In this situation, the parts themselves may not even
implement OBSERVER, but rather call hook methods, or even the `fire`
method, on their owner directly.

↰2.1

↰1.4.7

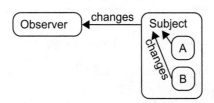

Figure 2.6 Compound Objects in the Observer Pattern

> Implement OBSERVER on the owner and forward changes from parts.

The benefits are clear: Observers have to register only once, instead of
for all parts separately. Especially when parts are created and destroyed
dynamically, this saves a lot of machinery. Similarly, the parts do not have
to store essentially the same lists of observers several times. The parts do
not even have to implement the observer pattern, but can rely on their
owner's infrastructure.

   A typical example is found in the deeply nested XML DOM trees. The
specification says that events generated at some node "bubble" upward and
are delivered to any event listener registered on the nodes encountered on
the way. Different types of events are available to meet the application's
demands. To receive notifications about any change at all at the granularity
of the nodes of the DOM, one registers for `DOMSubtreeModified` events at
the root. Registration is tied to a special interface `EventTarget`, which is
implemented by different kinds of nodes.

▭256(§1.6.4)

↠3.2.4

```
                     observer.XmlDomObserver.main
((EventTarget) doc).addEventListener("DOMSubtreeModified", listener,
                            false);
Element subsection1 =
    (Element) doc.getElementsByTagName("subsection").item(0);
subsection1.setAttribute("title", "New Title");
```

The change notifications then include information about which specific node has been modified:

observer.XmlDomObserver.main

```
public void handleEvent(Event evt) {
    MutationEvent mut = (MutationEvent) evt;
    Node changedNode = (Node) mut.getTarget();
    ...
}
```

↰2.1.1

A second example has already been seen in observers for background jobs. There, one can register with the system's (singleton) `JobManager` to receive status updates on any running job:

org.eclipse.ui.internal.progress.ProgressManager

```
Job.getJobManager().addJobChangeListener(this.changeListener);
```

In large structures, send out accumulated changes.

Eclipse has several object structures that are both large and widely used. Among them, the *resources* represent the workspace structure and the *Java model* keeps track of the current structure of the sources and libraries. Both offer the OBSERVER pattern, where clients register with the container. Because the data structures have a central position, many observers do get registered, so that sending every single change in isolation would involve some overhead. Instead, both accumulate changes through operations and send them in `IResourceChangeEvent` and `ElementChange Event`, respectively.

2.3 Hierarchical Structures

Computer scientists adore trees—at least in the form of file systems, XML data, language syntax, classification hierarchies, a book's table of contents, and many more. It is therefore a crucial question of how to organize hierarchical data in object-oriented systems. While the data representation using objects as tree nodes is straightforward, the proper treatment of operations, in particular recursive ones, requires some thought and decisions.

2.3.1 The Composite Pattern

Hierarchical data is easily stored as objects: Each object in the tree just owns its immediate child objects. Fig. 2.7 gives the idea. In part (a) of this figure, to represent an arithmetic expression $2 * x + 3 * y$, we build a tree according to the expression's structure (i.e., the nesting of a version with full parentheses added). In part (b), each node in the tree is an instance of `Expr`, of which there are several kinds: The numbers are `Literals`, the variables are `Vars`, and the operators are `Plus` and `Muls`, respectively. The latter two share the feature of having left and right operands, so these are extracted into a common superclass `Binary`.

»3.1.4

A crucial question is how operations on the nested compound object can be represented so that the clients do not have to perform case-distinction operations by using `instanceof`. The COMPOSITE pattern includes this aspect. In it, one declares the desired operations in the base class:

»3.1.9 ⌸100

expr.Expr
`public abstract double eval(Valuation v) throws EvalError;`

One then implements them in the concrete subclasses, according to the respective case. For variables, for instance, one can just look up their value:

expr.Var.eval

`public double eval(Valuation v) throws EvalError {`
 `    return v.get(varName);`
 `}`

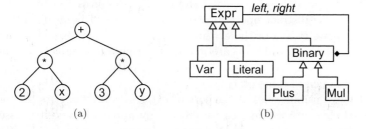

Figure 2.7 Representing Arithmetic Expressions

PATTERN: COMPOSITE

Represent hierarchical data structures and let clients work uniformly with different types of nodes.

1. Define a base class *Component* for all types of nodes in the tree.

2. Decide which operations clients should be able to use without knowing the concrete node type. Add them to the base class.

3. Derive one concrete class for each type of node.

4. If desired, introduce intermediate classes with supporting infrastructure. For instance, each node type with children can derive from a class *Composite* that provides management of children.

5. Implement the operations from step 2 for each concrete node. Use recursive calls to the operations on children as necessary.

COMPOSITE occurs throughout the Eclipse code base. Here are a few examples:

Base class	Meaning
ASTNode	Syntax of Java sources
JavaElement	Source and binary structure for package explorer
Resource	Files and folders in the workspace
Control	SWT user interface element
Figure	Lightweight drawing element in the GEF

None of these has the straightforward—not to say simplistic—structure of arithmetic expressions. Instead, they enable us to study more advanced questions. But let us start with a few implications and guidelines for the pattern.

Composite creates extensibility by new node types.

↰1.4.10

Clients of composed objects will work with references to the base class only, and the abstract operations declared there will be delegated to the concrete node types. In the arithmetic example, clients would invoke the eval method and will not care about the concrete node type at the expression's root. In consequence, it is always possible to add new types of operators, such as function calls.

This extensibility lies at the core of Figures and Controls: New kinds of visual elements will appear in almost any application, so it is essential that they can be added without changing the existing code. It is worthwhile to examine the hierarchy below Figure from this perspective: It comprises more than 100 cases, which range from simple textual labels, through buttons for GEF's palette, to layers of drawings and even special cases in anonymous classes.

↰1.8.8.3

Strive to include all necessary operations in the base class.

The above extensibility holds only as long as clients never have to downcast to access type-specific operations. Otherwise, their case distinctions will easily become incomplete if new node types are added. The pattern therefore works at its best if the operations required by clients are foreseen already in the definition of the base class. For example, all Figures can be moved and re-sized and they can have different kinds of observers.

Of course, this guideline does not address operations that are typically performed right after the creation of an object, because clients do know the concrete type at this point. For instance, Clickable figures comprise different kinds of buttons. They do offer specialized action listeners, which are notified when the user clicks the button, because such listeners are usually attached right after creation.

Furthermore, intermediate classifications offer advanced functionality. »3.1.5 The client does not downcast to single types, but to a super-type that captures some abstract concept useful in itself. For instance, generic nodes of type JavaElements from the Java model offer almost no functionality to clients. A Member, in contrast, allows clients to copy, move, and delete the element, regardless of whether the member is a field, method, or class.

> Exploit superclasses to extract common infrastructure.

Extensions by new node types must be as simple as possible to create a practical benefit. The rationale is simple: If every concrete type has to implement all offered operations from scratch, nobody will bother to do it. Even in very simple examples, it is therefore worthwhile to look out for common functionality, which can easily be shared in intermediate base »3.1.3 »3.1.4 classes. Very often, the abstract operations from the base class can then take the form of TEMPLATE METHODS, so that new node types have to «1.4.9 fill in only the really crucial points. For binary expressions, for instance, evaluation usually computes the results of subexpressions recursively and then applies an operator:

expr.Binary.eval

```
public final double eval(Valuation v) throws EvalError {
    return evalOp(left.eval(v), right.eval(v));
}
protected abstract double evalOp(double v1, double v2)
    throws EvalError;
```

New binary operations then need just fill in the operator itself:

expr.Plus.evalOp

```
protected double evalOp(double v1, double v2) {
    return v1 + v2;
}
```

Other functionality may have a default implementation. For instance, Figures are rendered by their paint method. As a TEMPLATE METHOD, it paints the figure itself, the children, and the border. By default, the first step fills its occupied area:

org.eclipse.draw2d.Figure

```
protected void paintFigure(Graphics graphics) {
    if (isOpaque())
        graphics.fillRectangle(getBounds());
    ...
}
```

↰1.4.11 Subclasses can then extend that behavior as they see fit:

org.eclipse.draw2d.ImageFigure

```
protected void paintFigure(Graphics graphics) {
    super.paintFigure(graphics);
    ...
    graphics.drawImage(getImage(), x, y);
}
```

Of course, the base class can also gather functionality ready for use: Generic `Figures` manage children (but optimize by lazy creation of the child list). `Resource` implements fundamental operations such as `copy` and `delete` using the workspace infrastructure.

Build the class hierarchy by commonalities, not case distinctions.

↱3.1 Even experienced programmers are sometimes led astray by the possibility of expressing detailed conceptual case distinctions in the hierarchy of node types. However, you should be aware that each class must justify its existence by making a contribution to the system's purpose: Each class creates costs in development, maintenance, and documentation, so it must have corresponding benefits. The best justification here is common behavior and infrastructure that does not have to be reimplemented in different concrete node types. Another one could be that some clients actually work at an intermediate level of abstraction, so that introducing an intermediate class can make these clients uniform over a set of node types. For instance, Eclipse introduces `Container` as an abstraction over resources that have recursive structure, such as folders or projects. Clients that merely wish to follow some path, for example, can do so independently of the concrete case.

Decide whether child management is in the base class.

The hierarchical object structure requires some management of children. In many cases, such as for `ASTNodes` or `JavaElements`, only the concrete type determines how many and which children exactly make sense. In other cases, such as for `Figures` and `Controls`, arbitrary numbers of children can be attached. Then, one must decide whether their management goes into the base class or a specialized subclass. Both are valid choices: `Figure` includes children, while `Control` defers their implementation to the subclass `Composite`. Here is a typical choice of methods:

org.eclipse.draw2d.Figure

```
public void add(IFigure figure, int index)
public void remove(IFigure figure)
public List getChildren()
```

The decision is between a greater uniformity in the first case, where clients can always work with `Figures`, and a restriction in using objects when many objects cannot have children for logical reasons.

`Composite` makes it hard to add new operations.

The downside of extensibility by node types is the loss of extensibility by new generic operations: Those would have to be added to the base class, so that any existing concrete node type would have to be adapted. Imagine the outcry if `Figure` were suddenly to acquire a new abstract operation that does not have a default implementation. In such a scenario, all applications depending on Draw2D would suddenly fail to compile! When defining the base class interface, you should therefore seek to be complete, and you should also write some actual client code to understand the requirements.

Offer a parent pointer if structure sharing is not intended.

Since clients are aware of the tree structure of the composite objects, they frequently wish to navigate upward in the tree to find surrounding elements. All of the listed examples have parent pointers. The only good reason against having them is the intention of structure sharing.

↰2.2.1

If the class hierarchy is closed, offer a type field.

In many cases, the class hierarchy of the pattern is not meant to be extended by applications, or is not likely to change at all. For instance, the various `ASTNodes` representing Java syntax trees will need to be extended only when the language changes; certainly, applications will never do it. The hierarchy is therefore, in effect, a closed case distinction. Clients can determine the concrete node type using the following method and can then `switch` over the result to avoid a linear search by `instanceof`. The base class `ASTNode` defines a constant for each node type. By throwing an exception in the `default` case, clients can guard against later language changes.

↠3.1.6

↰1.5.5

---
org.eclipse.jdt.core.dom.ASTNode

`public final int getNodeType()`

Wrap COMPOSITEs in top-level containers to simplify their use.

Trees are rather fine-grained objects that must be constructed, can be traversed, can change in nested locations, and so on. When the overall tree has a more comprehensive meaning, it can be a good idea to wrap it with a separate top-level object. For instance, clients of the Java model will

↰2.2.4

traverse and analyze `JavaElements` (through the interface `IJavaElement` and its subtypes), but the tree is really managed by the `JavaModel`, which in turn is contained in the (singleton) `JavaModelManager`. Such wrappers can then take care of observers, and can also organize the creation, update, and disposal of the entire tree.

2.3.2   The Visitor Pattern

↰2.3.1

The COMPOSITE pattern, as seen earlier, explains how to represent hierarchical object structures and how to implement (possibly recursive) operations on these structures. This pattern is great because it allows new node types to be added later on, without modifying existing code. Unfortunately, it is rather hard to implement new operations, because this may potentially break existing classes, which are perhaps developed by other teams or even other companies.

↰2.3.1

In many cases, however, the ability to add new operations is essential. For instance, there are too many application-specific operations on file systems to include all of them in the Eclipse's `Resource` class. Similarly, one can run so many analyses on Java sources that `ASTNode` will never provide all of them.

📖100

> **PATTERN: VISITOR**
>
> Make the set of operations on an object structure extensible by representing each operation by a *Visitor* object and letting the object structure pass each node in turn to the visitor.
>
> 1. Introduce an interface *Visitor*. Include a `visit` method for each type of node in the structure, and give it an argument of that node type.
>
> 2. Add a method `accept(v)` to each node type that takes a visitor `v` and passes `this` to the corresponding `visit` method of `v` and that invokes `accept` recursively on other nodes to pass the visitor on through the object structure.
>
> 3. Provide a base class of *Visitor* with empty stub implementations of all methods. Clients can then focus on the nodes they are interested in.

↰2.3.1

For a prototypical implementation, let's look again at arithmetic expressions. The interface for step 1 is clear; for simplicity, we integrate it with step 3 into an abstract base class:

```
                              expr.ExprVisitor
public abstract class ExprVisitor {
    public void visitLiteral(Literal node) {}
    public void visitVar(Var var) {}
```

```
    public void visitPlus(Plus node) {}
}
```

Step 2 is also straightforward and almost mechanical: The COMPOSITE's base has a new `accept` method, the leaf nodes pass themselves, and the inner nodes additionally recurse into subtrees.

expr.Expr

```
public abstract void accept(ExprVisitor v);
```

expr.Var.accept

```
public void accept(ExprVisitor v) {
    v.visitVar(this);
}
```

expr.Plus.accept

```
public void accept(ExprVisitor v) {
    left.accept(v);
    right.accept(v);
    v.visitPlus(this);
}
```

When working with predefined composite objects, look out for VISITOR.

VISITOR makes most sense for large, predefined data structures that have   ❱3.1.4
many clients and are general in nature. An example is found in the Eclipse
JDT's syntax trees for Java sources, which are represented by ASTNodes.
Any ASTNode can pass around a visitor:

org.eclipse.jdt.core.dom.ASTNode

```
public final void accept(ASTVisitor visitor) {
    ...
    accept0(visitor);
    ...
}
abstract void accept0(ASTVisitor visitor);
```

Suppose you wish to find all methods in a given Java source file. You would first parse the source into a syntax tree:

```
ASTParser parser = ASTParser.newParser(AST.JLS4);
parser.setKind(ASTParser.K_COMPILATION_UNIT);
  ... provide source as string
CompilationUnit cu = (CompilationUnit) parser.createAST(null);
```

Then, you can define a visitor that simply keeps all methods it encounters. (The return value `false` denotes that we do not wish to descend into the method.)

```
                    visitor.MethodAccumulator
public class MethodAccumulator extends ASTVisitor {
    private List<MethodDeclaration> methods;
      ...
    public boolean visit(MethodDeclaration method) {
        methods.add(method);
        return false;
    }
      ...
}
```

Finally, you ask the root node `CompilationUnit` to pass around your visitor and you extract the result:

```
MethodAccumulator accu = new MethodAccumulator();
cu.accept(accu);
List<MethodDeclaration> methods = accu.getMethods();
```

←1.8.8.3
In many cases, the tasks to be performed are so small that the visitor is best implemented as an anonymous class. This choice carries the additional implication for the human reader that the operation is used locally and does not have to be understood outside of the local context.

```
final List<MethodDeclaration> methods =
    new ArrayList<MethodDeclaration>();
cu.accept(new ASTVisitor() {
    public boolean visit(MethodDeclaration meth) {
        methods.add(meth);
        return false;
    }
});
```

Similarly, you can easily search for files with a specific extension below an `IResource`, or all classes defined in a JAR on the class path. Even change notifications for resources, which are very detailed and tree-structured, support visitors:

```
               org.eclipse.core.resources.IResourceDelta
public void accept(IResourceDeltaVisitor visitor)
    throws CoreException;
```

In all cases, the underlying object structure knows best how to reach all entries, so you just have to pass a visitor that is being "shown around."

»3.1.9
🔎 Visitors for resources and resource deltas do not adhere to the pattern precisely, as they receive generic `IResources` in a single method, rather than concrete files, folders, and other items in different methods. The case distinction on the type of resource must be implemented by `instanceof` and subsequent downcasts.

VISITOR is an instance of double dispatch.

When you come to think of it, VISITOR achieves something astoundingly general: You can execute an arbitrary operation on many different types of nodes. In other words, what it does is provide a generic binary operation execute(*operation*, *object*), where the concrete behavior of execute depends on the dynamic types of both the *operation* and the *object*. Unfortunately, the dynamic dispatch built into object-oriented languages works only for the this object on which a method is invoked, not for the arguments.

↰1.4.1

Binary operations depending on the dynamic types of both arguments are usually implemented by *double dispatch* (Fig. 2.8). That is, you use dynamic dispatch once on the first argument, passing along the second argument. Then, you use dynamic dispatch again on the second argument, this time passing along the first argument. The trick is that in the first dispatch, you gain the information about the dynamic type of this, which you can use to invoke a type-specific method in the second step. Since the dynamic type of this of b becomes available in the second step, the final methods can depend on both arguments, as required.

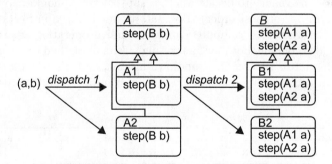

Figure 2.8 Double Dispatch

VISITOR can then be understood as an instance of double dispatch. Let us look through the case of ASTVisitors. The first dynamic dispatch is triggered by the accept() method in an ASTNode, which invokes accept0() on itself.

org.eclipse.jdt.core.dom.ASTNode

```
public final void accept(ASTVisitor visitor) {
    ...
    accept0(visitor);
    ...
}
abstract void accept0(ASTVisitor visitor);
```

Each type of node overrides `accept0()` and thereby gains the information about its own dynamic type in the `this` pointer. The second dispatch then occurs by invoking the corresponding method from the visitor. For instance, in the following implementation from `MethodDeclaration`, the call to `visit()` chooses the overloading for `MethodDeclaration`. The visitor can act correspondingly, as seen in the preceding example. The recursive traversal of the children follows the introductory expression example.

---
org.eclipse.jdt.core.dom.MethodDeclaration

```
void accept0(ASTVisitor visitor) {
    boolean visitChildren = visitor.visit(this);
    if (visitChildren) {
        ...
    }
    ...
}
```

Decide on top-down or bottom-up traversal, or combine both.

📖72

In a tree structure, you have several alternatives for the order in which nodes are visited. Top-down (or pre-order) traversal, as we have just seen, gives the visitor the chance to decide whether substructures should be visited at all. Bottom-up (or post-order) traversal, as we shall see in Section 2.3.4, enables the visitor to compute (some) recursive operations more easily. You can also combine both by "bracketing" visits in method calls: one when descending into a subtree in a top-down fashion, and one when leaving the subtree in a bottom-up manner. Here is an example from `ASTNode`, which does this throughout:

---
org.eclipse.jdt.core.dom.ASTVisitor

```
public boolean visit(MethodDeclaration node)
public void endVisit(MethodDeclaration node)
```

✗ XML documents can nowadays be regarded, perhaps, as the recursive data structure per se. A very efficient way of accessing external XML documents without reading them into memory consists of SAX parsers. In the current context, it is interesting to note that SAX parsers implement, in fact, VISITOR: They traverse the tree structure of the XML document and call back a `ContentHandler` for each node in that tree, once at the beginning and once at the end of the subtree traversal.

---
org.xml.sax.ContentHandler

```
public void startElement(String uri, String localName, String qName,
        Attributes atts) throws SAXException;
public void endElement(String uri, String localName, String qName)
        throws SAXException;
```

Beware that VISITOR fixes the set of node types.

Implementation step 1 of the pattern fixes the types of nodes that can occur in the object structure. Adding a new node type breaks all existing visitors, since they would be missing the corresponding method. Simply adding a default empty implementation is rather more dangerous, since it may break the visitors' logic without making the clients aware of it. You should add the VISITOR pattern only to structures that are unlikely to change.

It is also instructive to contrast the question of extensibility with that of COMPOSITE: There, it is possible to add new node types, but adding operations can break clients; here, it is possible to add new operations, but adding node types breaks clients. So when you need a new operation on a COMPOSITE, you have to decide whether adding it to the composite or introducing VISITOR is better in the long run. As usual, there is no silver bullet; rather, you will have to think carefully about the clients' needs before deciding on either strategy.

↰1.1

Visitors must build results by causing side effects.

VISITOR promises extensibility by all kinds of application-specific operations. In fact, this is only half the truth: While operations in COMPOSITE are usually recursive (i.e., they call themselves on children of a node), visitors cannot obtain any "result" computed on child nodes. We will take a closer look at the resulting stack structures using the concept of stack machines. For now, we observe that a visitor will have to build internal data structures with partial results while it traverses the object structure. In the introductory example presented earlier, this structure merely kept a list of relevant files. For an extended case study, look at the Eclipse Modeling Framework's persistence mechanism. It reads XML-based formats using `XMLHandler` (and subclasses), which is used as a visitor on external XML documents. It constructs the target in-memory objects on the fly. The class introduces around 60 fields that keep track of objects already constructed, their types, links that need to be resolved later on, and many other details.

📖100

»2.3.4

📖235

🕭 Even the entirely different paradigm of functional programming has devised a coding scheme similar to VISITOR, which emphasizes the importance of that pattern. Functional programmers have recognized early on that they tended to repeat themselves. That is, whenever they introduced a tree-structured data type, functions on the type roughly proceeded in three steps: (1) Switch on the type of node; (2) apply the same function recursively to all arguments of the node; and (3) combine the recursively computed results according to the type of node. They recognized that the redundancy could be avoided by introducing for each data type a *catamorphism* (with Greek prefix "cata-" for "downward" and "morphism" as a structure-related function, such as in "homomorphism"). Very briefly, a catamorphism is a function that implements steps 1 and 2. For step 3, it takes as arguments one function per node type, and invokes that function with the recursively computed values whenever it encounters that type of node.

📖245(Ch.7,9)
📖42(§4.5,§4.6)

📖178

2.3.3   Objects as Languages: Interpreter

Developers depend on languages to express the solutions they create for given problems. Mostly, this means programming in some general-purpose language such as Java, C++, C#, or Python. Surprisingly often, however, developers find that their solutions take similar shapes because the problems they solve stem from a common domain. Then, it may be worthwhile to create a special-purpose *domain-specific language* (DSL) that enables developers to express solutions for that domain straightforwardly and reliably. For instance, JSF facelets describe web pages, the Unified Expression Language (EL) captures data access in that context, SVG describes vector graphics, and Ant files describe a build process.

In fact, domain-specific languages are not always separate "languages." Often, they are simply libraries with a specific structure given by the INTERPRETER pattern discussed next. In this form, you will almost certainly create a domain-specific language before long.

> INTERPRETER guides the way to DSLs.

The core of many computer languages consists of a hierarchical, tree-like structure of operations. This is called the *abstract syntax* of the language, because it suppresses external detail such as whitespace, line breaks, and comments, as well as keywords such as if, else, and while, because they merely serve to mark and separate the language constructs in the source text. The abstract syntax would provide nodes ifthenelse and while, with children for the Boolean tests and the then, else, and body statements. As another example, the Expr nodes introduced earlier represent the abstract syntax of arithmetic expressions.

While COMPOSITE is sufficient for creating the tree structure, it says nothing about how to execute the language formed by the objects. INTERPRETER adds precisely this new aspect, in step 2 below. Very often, it is sufficient to interpret the language recursively along its tree structure. In other words, the interpretation or execution can be implemented according to the COMPOSITE pattern.

PATTERN: INTERPRETER

Represent the abstract syntax of a language together with its interpreter.

1. Define the language's abstract syntax and represent it by COMPOSITE.

2. Add an operation *interpret* to the COMPOSITE to execute the language.

35,249,179

100

2

↩2.3.1

↩2.3.1

100

3. Decide about the concrete syntax.

4. Write a parser that transforms source code to abstract syntax trees.

The original presentation does not include the parsing aspect in steps 3 and 4, but it clarifies the relation to the notion of a "language." We will explore these steps later.

But first, let us examine a real-world example for the first two steps—namely, the Unified Expression Language (EL) used in JSP and JSF to access data. We use the implementation from the Jasper JSP engine of Apache Tomcat (`jasper-el.jar`). Let us first consider step 1, the abstract syntax. It is given by a COMPOSITE with root type `SimpleNode`. The individual nodes in the abstract syntax reflect the language specification. So there are, for instance, nodes `AstIdentifier` for identifiers; nodes `AstInteger`, `AstTrue`, and `AstFalse` for literals; and nodes `AstPlus` and `AstMul` for arithmetic operators. Their common superclass `SimpleNode` already provides the child management. The field `image` holds the text of the operator, identifier, number, and other data that this node represents.

org.apache.el.parser.SimpleNode

```
public abstract class SimpleNode extends ELSupport implements Node {
    protected Node parent;
    protected Node[] children;
    protected String image;
    ...
}
```

🔍 Just in case you are fluent with the EL API and have never seen these classes: The API is given by the facade `ValueExpression` (package `javax.el` in `el-api.jar` of Tomcat). The Jasper implementation `ValueExpressionImpl` basically wraps a parser-level `Node`, whose implementation is given by `SimpleNode` and its subclasses.

But now for the core step 2. There are two basic modes of evaluating an EL expression: read the accessed data and write it. Correspondingly, `SimpleNode` provides two methods. Subsequently, we will focus on `getValue()` for simplicity:

org.apache.el.parser.SimpleNode

```
public Object getValue(EvaluationContext ctx) throws ELException
public void setValue(EvaluationContext ctx, Object value)
    throws ELException
```

Interpretation usually needs a context object.

The execution of nearly all programming languages uses some kind of context: to look up variables, to store data, to access external devices, and so on. But even the evaluation of simple arithmetic expressions, as we have seen, requires a mapping from variable names to values. In the EL example, the `EvaluationContext` similarly contains entities accessible from expressions:

↰2.3.1

---
org.apache.el.lang.EvaluationContext

```
public final class EvaluationContext extends ELContext {
    private final ELContext elContext;
    private final FunctionMapper fnMapper;
    private final VariableMapper varMapper;
    ...

}
```

It is good to think beforehand about the necessary information and to put it in a context object that can be passed around easily.

↰1.8.3

≫12.2

🔍 The first field `elContext` may look odd, given that `EvaluationContext` also implements `ELContext`. In fact, many methods of `EvaluationContext` just delegate to `elContext`. Evaluation of EL expressions uses many indirections to enable plugins to change the behavior. From the aspect of designing for flexibility, it is instructive to analyze Jasper's implementation, starting from `ELContextImpl`, as well as the substitution of objects from the EL evaluation process in the web application's deployment descriptor `web.xml`.

The interpretation method assigns a meaning to each operator object.

≫11.5.3

Designing any kind of programming language requires some experience. A good rule of thumb is compositionality: you define a number of elementary constructs that can be combined in arbitrary manners. The meaning of each construct must furthermore be defined on a stand-alone basis, without reference to the surrounding constructs (except implicitly through the context object). In the end, you will find that you implement in the interpretation method just the meaning of the construct that the operator class represents. You have applied the pattern well and designed the language well if that code is readable and understandable—if you can express clearly in a few lines of code what the construct really means.

Here are some concrete cases from the EL example. The binary "+" performs addition, as would be expected (loading off coercions and other tasks to a helper):

---
org.apache.el.parser.AstPlus

```
class AstPlus {
    ...
    public Object getValue(EvaluationContext ctx)
        throws ELException {
        Object obj0 = this.children[0].getValue(ctx);
        Object obj1 = this.children[1].getValue(ctx);
```

```
        return ELArithmetic.add(obj0, obj1);
    }
}
```

A literal integer is returned "as is" (parsing the `image` field in a helper method `getInteger()`).

org.apache.el.parser.AstInteger

```
public final class AstInteger extends SimpleNode {
    ...
    public Object getValue(EvaluationContext ctx)
        throws ELException {
        return this.getInteger();
    }
}
```

🔍 A central operation in the EL is, of course, the access of object fields, array elements, and map entries through dots "." and brackets "[]", both termed "suffixes." Because the exact types of the target and the suffix are not known until runtime, all cases are represented by a common node type `AstValue`. This makes the class too complex to study here, but we still encourage you to do so.

⚠️ Interpreters written with this pattern are not very efficient, because for each operation they must perform a dynamic dispatch and follow several references to different objects. For full languages, it is better to define a virtual machine to minimize the overhead of operations. Nevertheless, you should "do the simplest thing that could possibly work" and try INTERPRETER first—you can always move the code to the stack machine later on.

📖 100

▶ 2.3.4

🔍 A second example, which is more readily available than Tomcat's Jasper engine, is found in the JDK's implementation of regular expressions in `Pattern`. Internally, it represents regular operators as `Nodes` with an operation to recognize strings:

📖 122

```
boolean match(Matcher matcher, int i, CharSequence seq)
```

Note again the context object `Matcher`, which receives the start and end of matches and the text matched by groups in the regular expression. It is worthwhile studying the implementations of `match()` in the different subclasses of `Node`. Start with the simple case of `CharProperty` and work your way to `Branch` (operator "|") and `Loop` (operator "∗"). Concatenation is available with any node through its `next` field.

Parsers transform concrete syntax to abstract syntax.

So steps 1 and 2 of INTERPRETER describe how a language works at its core. After completing these steps, you can already stick together an "expression" in your language by creating and connecting objects. We now show that it

»9.1

←2.3.1

▭2,206,190

is not so hard to create a real language. The remaining steps are similar to building applications: After defining their functional core, we create a suitable user interface that accesses this core. We will walk through the steps using the abstract syntax of simple arithmetic expressions `Expr` introduced earlier.

The main task is to parse the source text, which is just a sequence of characters, into the structured form of the abstract syntax. There are a number of tools available to assist with this task, since writing parsers by hand is time-consuming and error-prone. For very simple languages, such as arithmetic expressions, you can consider shift-reduce parsers. For example, the online supplement includes such a parser, which we employ like this (the parser is generic over the concrete node type to make it reusable in different contexts):

»9.4.2 »12.4

---
interpreter.DSLOverall.evalExpression

```
Parser<Expr> parser = new Parser<Expr>(new SimpleNodeFactory());
```

Parsing the concrete syntax of an arithmetic expression then yields its abstract syntax tree as an `Expr`:

---
interpreter.DSLOverall.evalExpression

```
Expr ast = parser.parse(expr);
```

←2.3.1

Finally, we can evaluate the arithmetic expression, using a `Valuation` as a context object:

---
interpreter.DSLOverall.evalExpression

```
double res = ast.eval(v);
```

←2.3.2

»2.3.4

⚡ You get the parser, as well as the VISITOR pattern, for free when you base your language on XML and employ a SAX parser. As seen before, the `ContentHandler` can be understood as a visitor. Whenever an XML element ends, its children have been processed and the results are available. The implementation then leads to a stack machine, as will be seen in the next section.

2.3.4 Excursion: Composites and Stack Machines

←2.3.2

←2.3.3

Our treatment of hierarchical structures has revealed two shortcomings: VISITORs must build their results by creating side effects on some internal data structures and the INTERPRETER pattern can become too inefficient for implementing programming languages, because the overhead on executing a single operation is too high. In this section, we will highlight the connection of both issues to the concept of stack machines. This connection is, indeed, reflected in many of the more complex visitors occurring in practice. For instance, EMF's `XMLHandler` uses three stacks as its central data structure and treats XML elements as "instructions" for building

in-memory objects' structures. Understanding the connection is essential
for understanding and developing such complex visitors.

A *stack machine* is a (virtual) machine that stores temporary values on
a stack, rather than in named registers or in memory. The idea of stack
machines is ubiquitous in language implementations; the Java Virtual Machine
itself is only one example. The appeal of this type of machine is its
simplicity: The code can be stored efficiently in an array, one operation
after the other, instead of in objects as in INTERPRETER. The operations
are stored as numeric op-codes, usually bytes. In each cycle, the machine
loads one op-code from the code array, performs a `switch`, pops the corresponding
number of operands from the stack, performs the operation, and
places the result (if any) back on the stack.

231,135

159

To illustrate the connection to the previous material, let us start with an
example from Fig. 2.7(a) (page 117), which shows a tree for the expression
$2 * x + 3 * y$.

> Stack machine code is obtained by a post-order traversal of the syntax
> tree.

The stack machine code places the operations in the order in which they
will be executed. Since syntax trees are executed bottom-up, each node's
operator is placed after the code of all of its children. In other words, a post-order
traversal of the syntax tree yields the code. In the example, numbers
and variables mean "place that value on the stack," and operators mean
"take two values from the stack and push the result back on."

72

```
2 x * 3 y * +
```

The execution of this code yields the sequence of stacks shown in Fig. 2.9.

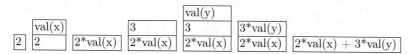

Figure 2.9 Example Expression on a Stack Machine

Implementing a stack machine `ArithVM` is straightforward: The class
defines numeric constants for the operators and offers an auxiliary class
`Code` as a linear container for an instruction sequence. The example can
then be coded up as a test case (`code` is a `Code` object; `val` is a valuation
for "x" and "y").

»5

interpreter.MachineTest.exampleExpr

```
Code code = new ArithVM.Code();
code.literal(2);
code.var("x");
code.op(ArithVM.MUL);
code.literal(3);
code.var("y");
```

```
code.op(ArithVM.MUL);
code.op(ArithVM.PLUS);
ArithVM vm = new ArithVM();
double res = vm.run(code, val);
```

Below you find the core of the machine, the execution loop. It demonstrates both the efficient storage and the low operation overhead enabled by numeric op-codes. We also introduce a special-purpose stack, whose push and pop operations are hard-coded. Its size is fixed, since the limit could in principle be derived from the code to be run. The two operations shown in the example illustrate the principle. The VAR operation is followed by an index into a pool of variable names, similar to the treatment of strings and identifiers in the JVM. The code then pushes the variable's current value onto the stack. The PLUS case is optimized even further: After popping the result of the right subexpression, the top pointer stays the same to overwrite the left operand with the result.

📖159

---
interpreter.ArithVM.run

```
int ip = 0;
VarName var[] = code.varNames;
int instr[] = code.instructions;
double tmp[] = new double[STACK_SIZE];
int top = -1;
while (ip != instr.length) {
    switch (instr[ip++]) {
    case VAR:
        tmp[++top] = val.get(var[instr[ip++]]);
        break;
    case PLUS:
        r = tmp[top--];
        l = tmp[top];
        tmp[top] = l + r;
        break;
     ...
    }
}
```

Let us now examine the connection to the VISITOR pattern somewhat further. If the visitor traverses the object structure bottom-up (i.e., post-order), it is simple to generate stack machine code in a visitor: At each node, just write out the operator corresponding to the node's type.

---
interpreter.CodeGenerator

```
public class CodeGenerator extends ExprVisitor {
    private Code code;
     ...
    public void visitLiteral(Literal node) {
        code.literal(node.getValue());
    }
     ...
    public void visitPlus(Plus node) {
```

```
        code.op(ArithVM.PLUS);
    }
    ...
}
```

📖100

For efficient execution of languages, introduce a virtual machine.

We can now make explicit an idea given in the original presentation of
the pattern: When INTERPRETER becomes too inefficient, use a recursive
operation in the COMPOSITE to compile the syntax to some machine code
and execute that code. Especially if the code contains loops, this will save
a lot of overhead. Building on the concepts discussed so far, we can code
the idea for the running arithmetic example: Line 1 parses the expression,
line 2 generates stack machine code, and lines 3–4 execute this code.

↰2.3.3

interpreter.MachineTest.codeGeneration

```
1 Expr expr = parser.parse("2*x+3*y");
2 expr.accept(new CodeGenerator(code)); // recursive code generation
3 ArithVM vm = new ArithVM();
4 double res = vm.run(code, val);
```

Complex visitors often contain conceptual stack machines.

So far, we have seen that visitors and stack machines build on common
ground: A post-order traversal of the syntax tree by the visitor creates
post-fix code that stack machines can execute directly. This scenario solves
the inefficiency of INTERPRETER. Let's now cut out the middle man, the
state machine, to arrive at a very common scheme for implementing visitors
for complex operations, such as reading XMI files in EMF and compiling
JSF pages.

The strategy is clear: The visitor contains a stack, and instead of emit-
ting an operation to be executed later by the stack machine, we execute
the operation within the visitor. Let us apply the strategy to the running
example. The stack is simple enough:

visitor.StackEvalVisitor

```
private Stack<Double> tmp;
```

Variables are again evaluated by fetching their value:

visitor.StackEvalVisitor.visitVar

```
public void visitVar(Var var) {
    tmp.push(vals.get(var.getVarName()));
}
```

For binary operators, just pop the results of the subexpressions and push
back the operation's result:

visitor.StackEvalVisitor.visitPlus

```
public void visitPlus(Plus node) {
    double r = tmp.pop();
    double l = tmp.pop();
    tmp.push(l + r);
}
```

The content of the stack during the run will be as shown in Fig. 2.9; after all, the very same sequence of computations is carried out. In the end, the result of the overall traversal will be left as the only value on the visitor's stack (we check this expectation because of the complex logic):

↰1.5.4

visitor.StackEvalVisitor

```
public double value() {
    assert(tmp.size() == 1);
    return tmp.peek();
}
```

Stack-based processing is a natural strategy for visitors.

To summarize, the hierarchical structure of COMPOSITEs in combination with the linear traversal of VISITOR require internal data structures to maintain intermediate results. Due to the connection of post-order traversal, post-fix code, and stack machines, the natural choice for data structure in post-order visitors are stacks: At each node, the visitor pops the results of the subtrees and combines them to a new result, which it moves on to the stack.

2.4   Wrappers: Adapters, Proxies, and Decorators

It is surprisingly commonplace to discover that the functionality that you are looking for is actually there in some subsystem or library, and is even packaged up as a nice, reusable service provider object, yet for some reason you still cannot employ it directly. Perhaps the interface is not quite what you need, it is lacking some functionality, or the object uses resources heavily and you can't afford to have it around all the time.

↰1.8.2

Fig. 2.10(a) gives the generic solution: You create a wrapper around your real collaboration target, and that wrapper provides just the missing bit of behavior. Specifically, the wrapper might translate the interface, add a bit of functionality, or transparently allocate and deallocate the object. These three purposes of wrappers, and some more, are captured by three patterns: ADAPTER, DECORATOR, and PROXY. Fig. 2.10(b) adds the detail that communication is often two-way: The client invokes services s, but expects notifications n through OBSERVER; both directions must be translated.

📖100

↰2.1

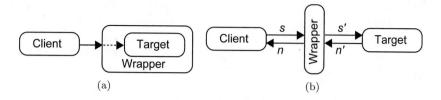

Figure 2.10 Wrapper Objects

2.4.1 The Adapter Pattern

Development folklore has it that some parts of the system will just need some *glue code* to stick together seamlessly. That is, it is imagined that some other team has invented an interface that you are supposed to use, but that does not precisely meet your demands—so you just put in some flexible glue, some adapters, to make it work. However, most adapters do not indicate bad design at all. Rather, it might simply be the case that the expected interface and the actual interface as they are make perfect sense in their respective subsystems. Then it is a valid—and even recommendable— decision to keep the subsystems in good shape separately, and to incur the slight overhead of writing adapters.

» 1.8.7
» 12.1

▢ 100

PATTERN: ADAPTER

Some client needs to work with a given object, but the interface does not meet the client's expectations. Write an adapter object that translates all communication between the client and the target object.

---

1. Define the interface *Target* that the *Client* expects, or would ideally wish to be present. Program the client against that interface.

2. Create an *Adapter* that implements the *Target* interface.

3. Translate method calls to the *Adapter* to the target object, which is also called the *Adaptee* in this context, as it is the object that has been adapted.

4. Translate any notifications that the *Adaptee* sends, for instance by the OBSERVER pattern, into notifications for the *Client*.

Very often, it is not necessary to create a separate `interface` in step 1. Instead, the interface of the adapter from step 2 is used directly.

A typical example of subsystems with different notions of "good inter- faces" occurs in UI programming: User interfaces are all about text and images to be shown on the screen. In contrast, the application's logic is

» 9.1

usually complex enough without bothering about those "fancy details." Suppose then that the UI is to show some data in a tree, so that the user can select some items. For step 1, an ideal interface lets it traverse the data in tree fashion, starting from the root elements, then navigating between nodes and their children. The interface uses generic `Object`s since it must apply to different data structures.

▶9.3.2

---
org.eclipse.jface.viewers.ITreeContentProvider

```
public interface ITreeContentProvider
                        extends IStructuredContentProvider {
    public Object[] getElements(Object inputElement);
    public Object[] getChildren(Object parentElement);
    public Object getParent(Object element);
    public boolean hasChildren(Object element);
}
```

For each node in the tree, the UI then retrieves the suitable text and icon.

---
org.eclipse.jface.viewers.ILabelProvider

```
public interface ILabelProvider extends IBaseLabelProvider {
    public Image getImage(Object element);
    public String getText(Object element);
}
```

One example of such a tree is the *Package Explorer* you are familiar with; it lets you look at and select parts of the Java code you are editing. Maintaining that information is heavy work, which is performed by the *Java Model* component. It keeps essentially a tree structure of `IJavaElements`, but does not bother with providing the UI-related methods. Instead, an adapter simulates that tree structure on the fly for steps 2 and 3. For projects, it retrieves the source folders and libraries; for those, it retrieves the packages, and for packages it finds the types and subpackages. A similar adapter exists for the texts and images.

▶2.3.1

---
org.eclipse.jdt.ui.StandardJavaElementContentProvider

```
public Object[] getChildren(Object element) {
    if (element instanceof IJavaProject)
        return getPackageFragmentRoots((IJavaProject) element);
    if (element instanceof IPackageFragmentRoot)
        return getPackageFragmentRootContent(
                        (IPackageFragmentRoot) element);
    if (element instanceof IPackageFragment)
        return getPackageContent((IPackageFragment) element);
    ...
}
```

Finally, the adapter within the package explorer must take care of step 4: Whenever the tree changes, because you edit your code, you expect to see

the modification immediately. Toward that end, the adapter registers for   ↶2.1
change notifications from the Java model.[2]

org.eclipse.jdt.ui.JavaElementContentProvider

```
public void inputChanged(Viewer viewer, Object oldInput,
                Object newInput) {
    ...
    JavaCore.addElementChangedListener(this);
    ...
    fInput = newInput;
}
```

Whenever the adapter receives such a notification, it determines what precisely has changed and sends suitable change notifications to the viewer. The following method runs, for instance, when a particular element in the Java model changes:

org.eclipse.jdt.ui.JavaElementContentProvider

```
private void postRefresh(final Object elem) {
    ...
    fViewer.refresh(elem);
}
```

In summary, ADAPTER implements Fig. 2.10(b): It translates the communications between the client and the adaptee in both directions.

A further application of adapters is to provide special views on an object   ↠3.2.2
to special clients. The EXTENSION OBJECTS pattern uses this device to avoid bloated interfaces and to enable unexpected changes to an object's interface without breaking existing clients.

2.4.2 The Decorator Pattern

The classic way of extending an object is to extend its class by inheritance and instantiate that class instead. Sometimes, this may not be practical. For   ↶1.4.12
example, you may be given the object at runtime and do not get the chance to create a different one. Or perhaps there are several possible extensions, so that it is infeasible to provide subclasses for all combinations. Finally, the original class may have complex invariants, which makes subclassing a   ↠4.1
tough job, or it may even be final. The solution is to wrap the original   📖100
object:

PATTERN: DECORATOR

To extend the capabilities of an object without using inheritance, wrap it with a *Decorator* object that has the same or an extended interface and that adds the desired behavior.

---

2. For historical reasons, this code is in a (now deprecated) subclass of StandardJavaElementContentProvider.

Typical examples are found in the Java I/O library. To read from a file, you create a `FileInputStream`. Then you add the capabilities that you need through decorators: `BufferedInputStream` will make the access more efficient by reading chunks of bytes from disk, `InputStreamReader` takes care of decoding bytes into characters, `ZipInputStream` decodes the ZIP file format, and so on.

That design is often sneered at for being cumbersome to use. For example, to read a plain text file line-wise, you write a monstrosity of code (there is also the shortcut `FileReader`):

```
new BufferedReader(new InputStreamReader(new FileInputStream(file)))
```

Sure, that's true, but you do nothing more than pay a bit extra in simple cases for the a huge flexibility you gain in the practically relevant complex cases. It is important to understand that the code is not a magic incantation, but rather a well-structured buying of additional functionality. It is like walking through a supermarket: You may be able to make pancakes from a ready-made mixture, but if you plan to bake a real cake, you'd better buy the ingredients separately.

»3.1.8
↰1.4.8.2
↰1.4.8.3

The DECORATOR pattern touches upon the fundamental question of delegation versus inheritance: Is it better to place a reusable piece of functionality into a base class or to offer it in the form of a separate object? The pattern suggests a new perspective: If the reusable functionality can be seen as a transparent addition to another object's behavior, then the option of a separate object is very flexible.

239
45 194
265

The problem of combining behavior in a flexible manner has always fascinated and inspired language designers. Multiple inheritance in C++, multiple inheritance and *standard method combinations* in the Common Lisp Object System (CLOS), *traits* in Scala, or *aspects* in AspectJ—they all serve to mix pieces of reusable behavior in a single object. Beyond decorators, this enables those pieces to interact and to collaborate. This is similar to the collaboration seen between subclass and superclass through method overriding. The gain in expressiveness is bought at the expense of more complex language definitions and even fragile corner cases. For example, in CLOS, the exact details of the *linearization algorithm*, which resolves names, matter for the runtime behavior.

2.4.3 The Proxy Pattern

Some objects are not readily accessible for collaboration. For instance, they may consume large amounts of memory so that keeping them around is impossible, or they may reside on a different machine in the network. Accessing such an object requires a fair bit of logic in itself, by loading it on demand or by serializing parameters and de-serializing return values in method invocations. It is a good idea to localize that logic in a small, local *proxy* object. Then, whenever a client wishes to collaborate with the *real subject*, it invokes a simple method on the proxy, and the proxy hides all

100

the details and the complications.

PATTERN: PROXY

Introduce a placeholder object, the *proxy*, that forwards collaboration requests to a different object, the *real subject*.

Make the proxy implement the same interface as the real subject, so that clients do not notice the extra level of indirection.

The kind of access logic encapsulated in the proxy leads to a classic categorization of proxies. *Remote proxies* hide the communication over process or network boundaries. Prototypical examples are found in the Java *remote method invocation* (RMI) mechanism, web services based on JAX-WS, and distributable *Enterprise JavaBeans* (EJB). *Virtual proxies* load heavyweight objects only on demand. In the Eclipse Java tooling, `JavaElements` do not contain the information about fields and methods all the time. Internally, they retrieve the information on demand from a cache that is managed with a least recently used (LRU) strategy. *Protection proxies* check and filter collaboration requests depending on the client's privileges. *Smart references* perform memory management by reference counting, in languages without garbage collectors or for special resources.

Proxies thus shield the client from some aspect of a potentially difficult collaboration. They keep the client-side interface clean and simple, thereby contributing greatly to the readability and maintainability of the system.

📖100
📖201
📖99
📖133

🔎 Proxies often override `equals()` and `hashCode()` in such a way that proxies for the same real subject are equal. The reason is that proxies are usually not unique for each real subject. Clients may even create their own proxies on the fly.

↩1.4.13

2.4.4 Encapsulation Wrappers

Proxies by definition have, at least conceptually, the same interface as the object that they wrap. The goal is to have clients work transparently with either the real object or the proxy. Sometimes, they deviate from this guideline a bit—for instance, by wrapping some native implementation or some basic functionality with the purpose of providing a clean, object-oriented interface. Let us call such objects *encapsulation wrappers*.

Typical examples are found in the SWT widget library. Each widget holds a reference to an operating system (or library) resource that is a native widget of the platform. It merely maintains a *handle*, an identifier of the resource that can be passed back to the operating system for later accesses (the exact type is, of course, system-dependent). For instance, a simple label holds the following handle:

»7
📖238

---
org.eclipse.swt.widgets.Label

```
int labelHandle;
```

To actually set the label's displayed text, the widget delegates to the native implementation. However, it also translates the request, similarly to an ADAPTER, to achieve a clean interface.

↰2.4.1

org.eclipse.swt.widgets.Label

```java
public void setText(String string) {
    ...
    char[] chars = fixMnemonic(string);
    byte[] buffer = Converter.wcsToMbcs(null, chars, true);
    OS.gtk_label_set_text_with_mnemonic(labelHandle, buffer);
    OS.gtk_widget_hide(imageHandle);
    OS.gtk_widget_show(labelHandle);
}
```

Encapsulation wrappers can thus serve as proxy-like gateways to functionality that would otherwise be hard to use. Again, the logic is centralized in one place and clients get more readable and maintainable.

Chapter 3

Abstraction and Hierarchy

The presentation so far has focused on objects and networks of objects. We ↰1.1 have discussed how objects manage their internals and how they collaborate on larger tasks. We have also seen fundamental recurring structures and patterns one finds in practical applications. To achieve this focus on the runtime behavior, we have deliberately neglected classes and interfaces as the static, compile-time foundations of objects. When questions of inheritance did crop up in the context of method overriding, we have restricted the presentation to technical arguments. In the end, we were interested only in the result: No matter how objects were constructed, how they obtained ↰1.4.1 their methods and fields, we have asked only how they perform their tasks in the very end.

This chapter fills the remaining gap in the presentation of Java usage: How do professionals use classes, interfaces, inheritance, and subtyping to build the objects that do the work at runtime? This question adds a new dimension to objects: While previously we have looked at the final resulting objects, we now ask how the objects' features are stacked one upon the other in their different superclasses of a hierarchy, and how the behavior of objects is classified by interfaces.

3.1 Inheritance

Many people consider inheritance the distinguishing feature of an object-oriented language, and the one on which a large part of the flexibility and reusability of objects rests. We have already seen a great deal of its me- ↰1.4 chanics in connection with method overriding. Now it is time to discuss the conceptual basis of inheritance itself. The challenge here lies in the very power of the mechanism, and in the creativity it inspires: Method overriding allows you to reuse code in intricate and sophisticated manners, but when applied without discipline, it becomes a maintenance nightmare, since later developers will have to untangle the web of calls between subclasses and superclasses. The goal must therefore be to find guidelines for a safe and predictable usage of inheritance.

Before we start, there's one word on wording: We will be using "superclass" whenever we start an argument from the subclass's (or derived class's) perspective. We will prefer "base class" whenever the discussion starts from that class and talks about possible derived classes or class hierarchies. These are, however, only stylistic considerations; the technical meaning of both terms is the same.

3.1.1   The Liskov Substitution Principle

It is common folklore that inheritance is all about "is-a relationships." This is also reflected in Java's typing rules: The compiler will allow assignments from a class to any of its superclasses. However, there are several different notions of what precisely constitutes an "is-a relationship." The possible confusion is exhibited in the classical circle/ellipse dilemma: On the one hand, a circle is-an ellipse, just one that happens to have two identical radii; on the other hand, an ellipse is-a circle, just one that happens to have an additional field "minor radius." More confusing still, a circle is not an ellipse at all, because unlike an ellipse, it cannot be stretched in two directions independently. So which one is it to be?

↰1.1
📖160,162

After long and wide-ranging debate, it has turned out that it is best to start from the behavior of objects, according to the premise that objects are active entities in a larger network. The focal point of this reasoning has been termed the *Liskov Substitution Principle*:

> An object of a derived class must be usable wherever an object of a superclass is expected.

In other words, clients that can work with an instance of a superclass must work as well with instances of a subclass, because the behavior that they expect is still present. These expectations can be made precise in the form of contracts. For now, an intuition is sufficient.

»6.4

Suppose, for example, that a client wants to copy the content of an InputStream to disk. The client merely fetches bytes into a buffer through the method read declared in the following snippet. It does not matter where these bytes really come from—whether from the local disk, over the network, or even from a pipeline of encryption and encoding steps. The behavior is determined solely by the idea of a "stream of bytes" from which the client takes an initial chunk.

↰2.4.2

```
                          java.io.InputStream
public int read(byte b[], int off, int len) throws IOException {
    ...
    for (; i < len; i++) {
        c = read();
        b[off + i] = (byte) c;
    }
    ...
}
```

The default implementation shown in this snippet reads single bytes one by one. This is actually inefficient in many situations. For local files, for instance, the operating system can fetch chunks of bytes directly (which is

📖238

done in the `native` method `readBytes` in the next example). The `File`
`InputStream` therefore overrides the method `read`. However, the client is   ↰1.4.1
not aware of this special implementation, since the object still exhibits the
behavior described in the superclass.

java.io.FileInputStream

```
public int read(byte b[], int off, int len) throws IOException {
    ...
    bytesRead = readBytes(b, off, len);
    ...

}
```

From a language perspective, the fact that a `FileInputStream` can be used where an
`InputStream` is declared is called *subtyping*. For s a subtype of t, one writes $s \leq t$.
Then, the language decrees that if *obj* has type s and $s \leq t$, then *obj* also has type t.
We now look briefly at different notions of subtyping in object-oriented languages.

The central question is how the types of different objects are related. In Java this
happens through `extends` and `implements` clauses: The subtyping between classes is
simply declared. The compiler checks that all technical side-conditions, such as on the
implementation of abstract methods, are fulfilled.

There is also a leaner and somewhat cleaner approach without explicit declarations.
Structural subtyping starts with a language that builds objects from three elementary   📖69,1,60,209
constructs: records, functions (as values), and fixed points. The question of how to do
that is in itself interesting, but beyond the current discussion. The point relevant for now
is that the subtyping rules on these elements are applied along the structure of objects.
In the end, they combine to yield a notion of subtyping for objects that basically ensures
that programs "can't go wrong" at runtime—that is, that all invoked methods are found   📖186
and all data items are used according to their types. In fact, these are the technical
side-conditions that the Java compiler must check as well.

In contrast, *behavioral subtyping* takes the view that structural subtyping must be   📖232,160,5,162
complemented by assertions about the object's reaction to method calls: The mere existence of a method does not guarantee that clients get the expected result from a call. The
declaration of super-types in the `extends` and `implements` clauses of Java can therefore
be seen as an explicit assertion by the programmer that the behavior of the resulting
object will be adequate—that is, that the subclass's instances will obey the rules set by
the super-type.

3.1.2   Interface Between the Base Class and Subclasses

The Liskov Substitution Principle explains how inheritance interacts with
the object's interface available to clients. If we consider classes just as a
tool for implementing objects, that's all there is to say. Inheritance, however, introduces a further visibility level `protected` between `private` and
`public`. It enables subclasses to be more intimate with their superclass,
to share some of its secrets hidden from the world at large. Unconstrained
access to the internals of the superclass will, unfortunately, quickly yield
complex and unmaintainable code. Furthermore, relying on these internals
too much means that the superclass can never change without destroying
the existing subclasses, a phenomenon termed the *fragile base class problem*.   📖185

📖232,160

It has been noticed early on that a firm conceptual basis for using inheritance in a safe way can be obtained by considering that each class really has *two* interfaces (Fig. 3.1): one toward its clients and one toward its subclasses.

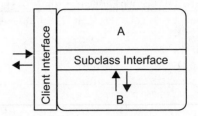

Figure 3.1 The Two Interfaces of a Class

Use `protected` to define and enforce an interface toward subclasses.

Developers of subclasses can be expected to be more familiar with the superclass's mechanics than is the general client. They can therefore be allowed greater license, more access points, and more services offered to them. We have already seen examples of this: In the one direction, reusable functionality in `protected` methods is accessible throughout the hierarchy. In the other direction, the superclass can explicitly invite the collaboration in specific operations through `protected abstract` methods in the TEMPLATE METHOD pattern.

↰1.4.8.2

↰1.4.9

📖111(§6.6.2)

🔎 In fact, the intention of the `protected` modifier is to allow access to any other classes that may be involved in implementing a specific functionality. In particular, classes in the same package and all derived classes are considered to belong to this group.

Design the interface toward subclasses with as much care as the interface toward other objects.

In the end, subclasses are still just consumers of the superclass's abilities. They are really clients of a different sort. In this capacity, they have a right to their own interface, a right to be told explicitly how the superclass can be used. There are two motivations for defining a narrow interface. First, it facilitates subclassing, and therefore reuse of your work, since it limits the amount of detail other developers have to understand. Second, it broadens your possibilities of later adaptations, since anything you keep hidden from subclasses can still be changed. If you think back, both points are really the same for `public` methods for general clients.

📖232

»12.1

Make fields `private` and define `protected` access methods.

A good strategy in general is to make each class responsible for its own
fields throughout the object's lifetime, first during initialization, then in
maintaining consistency. A class does not in general modify the fields it has
inherited, because this might destroy assumptions implicit in the superclass's code. A typical example is found in AbstractListViewer, whose
field listMap is private, but can be accessed by dedicated protected
service methods.

↰1.6.3
↠6.4.2

In fact, fields should be private even if they are final and therefore
cannot be modified by subclasses. Only if the fields are hidden completely
can the superclass change its implementation decisions whenever it sees fit.
Even read-only fields can break subclasses, when their content or interpretation changes unexpectedly—read-only fields, too, can lead to the fragile
base class problem.

↠3.1.11

3.1.3 Factoring Out Common Behavior

If the essence of objects lies in their behavior, then the essence of base
classes lies in the common behavior exhibited by all possible subclasses.
The first and best reason for introducing a base class is therefore to capture
that common behavior. There are really two kinds of behavior that could be
relevant here, analogously to the two interfaces of classes: one toward clients
and one toward subclasses. We will treat the first now, and the second in
the next section.

↰3.1.2

As an example, Eclipse's user interface contains many different kinds of
structured data displays, such as lists, trees, and tables. From a software
design perspective, they have many commonalities: The user can select displayed items, the data may be filtered and sorted, and so on. Furthermore,
one can observe changes in the selection and a viewer-specific "open" gesture, usually a double-click. It is therefore useful to introduce a common
base class StructuredViewer that offers corresponding methods:

📖70,71

↰2.1

---
org.eclipse.jface.viewers.StructuredViewer

```
public ISelection getSelection()
public void setFilters(ViewerFilter[] filters)
public void setComparator(ViewerComparator comparator)
public void
    addSelectionChangedListener(ISelectionChangedListener
        listener)
public void addOpenListener(IOpenListener listener)
```

Now other elements of the user interface that rely only on the common behavior of structured viewers can work independently of the concrete
viewer type. For instance, the OpenAndLinkWithEditorHelper opens the
current selection of a structured viewer in an editor. In the Java tools, it
is attached to the tree in the JavaOutlinePage as well as the table in
the QuickFixPage. The helper works because it relies on only the common

characteristics of structured viewers. First, it observes the selection and the "open" gesture:

org.eclipse.ui.OpenAndLinkWithEditorHelper.InternalListener

```
viewer.addPostSelectionChangedListener(listener);
viewer.addOpenListener(listener);
```

Then, when the selection actually changes, the helper can react correspondingly:

org.eclipse.ui.OpenAndLinkWithEditorHelper

```
public void selectionChanged(SelectionChangedEvent event) {
    final ISelection selection = event.getSelection();
    ...
    linkToEditor(selection);
    ...
}
```

It must be said, however, that factoring out common behavior for the benefit of clients is nowadays not usually done through inheritance, but through interfaces. A more precise delineation will be given at the very end, after both language features have been discussed by themselves. We have nevertheless put this point up front because it underlines the importance of the Liskov Substitution Principle: Inheritance is always about behavioral subtyping.

» 3.2.1
» 3.2.10

← 3.1.1

3.1.4 Base Classes for Reusable Infrastructure

← 3.1.1

Inheritance combines two aspects into one mechanism: that of subtyping, which enables clients to work uniformly over different subclasses, and that of a partial implementation, which enables subclasses get part of their own behavior for free. In the latter case, rather than working hard in the manner of self-made men, the subclasses just lay back and rely on their inheritance. Unlike real people, they can even choose a suitable parent.

Base classes are, however, more than just pieces of behavior that one takes as given. Good, powerful base classes provide an infrastructure that interacts with subclasses in several ways.

← 3.1.3
- They offer basic functionality to clients that the subclasses then do not have to rebuild themselves.

← 3.1.2 ← 1.4.8
- They offer an extended `protected` interface to the expected subclasses that lets the subclasses manipulate the internals.

← 1.4.9 ▭132
- They offer generic mechanisms that can be adapted at specific points through the TEMPLATE METHOD pattern.

Think of a base class as an infrastructure upon which concrete classes build.

You will note that we have studied all of these elements previously in isolation. We will now see that combining them in one class yields powerful abstractions. A second aspect of the guideline is that an infrastructure usually requires completion and cannot be used on its own. This is reflected in the fact that many base classes are abstract, or have Abstract as a prefix to their names. Others, such as LabelProvider, do implement all methods, but only with empty bodies and returning sensible default values.

Let's go back to the StructuredViewer and check for these three points. We have already seen the contribution to the client interface in the previous section: The structure viewer manages the selection, listeners, filters, and sorter, and similar publicly visible aspects. In terms of the second point, it maintains internal helpers, such as a caching hash map from ↰1.3.6 data items to display items that can speed up operations on large data sets.

```
org.eclipse.jface.viewers.StructuredViewer
```
```
private CustomHashtable elementMap;
```

On these data structures, the structure viewer offers protected operations for use in the subclasses. In the case of the cache, for instance, it provides the following method (the omitted code deals with cases where one data item is associated with several display items):

```
org.eclipse.jface.viewers.StructuredViewer
```
```
protected void mapElement(Object element, Widget item) {
    if (elementMap != null) {
        Object widgetOrWidgets = elementMap.get(element);
        if (widgetOrWidgets == null) {
            elementMap.put(element, item);
        } else
            ...
    }
}
```

All of these elements are usually reused as they are; that is, with the client or subclasss simply calling them to make use of the functionality.

The third point of the infrastructure is somewhat more intricate. Using ↰1.4.9 the TEMPLATE METHOD, the base class specifies the general outline of some operation, but leaves those parts that are specific to the subclasses to be implemented later. A simple example of this was given in the presentation of the pattern. For a more extended example, you might want to trace the workings of the following method, which must be called whenever some ↠9.3.2 properties of an element have changed locally, so that the display can be updated:

```
org.eclipse.jface.viewers.StructuredViewer
```
```
public void update(Object element, String[] properties)
```

The method takes care of multiple display items for `element`, each of which is treated by `internalUpdate`. That method first checks for a possible interaction with the current filters, then delegates, through intermediate steps, to the concrete subclass by calling:

org.eclipse.jface.viewers.StructuredViewer

```
protected abstract void doUpdateItem(Widget item, Object element,
        boolean fullMap);
```

Note that the infrastructure has taken care of the tedious details, caching, filtering, and so on, and has finally arrived at the conclusion that a specific display item needs to be refilled with the current data of a specific object. As a result, subclasses can concentrate on the essentials, on the task that they are really written for. Isn't that a great kind of infrastructure?

📖214

If you are longing for a yet more intricate example, you might want to take a look at the Graphical Editing Framework. Its `AbstractGraphical EditParts` add the further indirection of delegating part of their behavior not only to subclasses, but also to helpers called `EditPolicys`.

Finally, we point out that Eclipse actively supports the completion of an infrastructure base class by tools:

> **TOOL: Create Completed Subclass**
>
> In the *New/Class* wizard, choose the desired base class and then check *Inherited Abstract Methods* in the selection of method stubs to be generated.

⚠️ This tool does not excuse you from studying the documentation of the base class in detail to understand the provided mechanisms. Not all methods that you have to override are really `abstract`. Very often, you will have to use *Override Method* manually for specific further methods.

3.1.5   Base Classes for Abstraction

📖48(Ch.4)

A classic use of inheritance is to capture abstraction. Abstraction here means to construct a hierarchical case distinction, where superclasses are more general and comprise more concrete cases than their subclasses. Conversely, subclasses capture special cases of their superclasses. We can therefore also speak of a specialization hierarchy. Very often, the classes represent domain concepts, so that users see their own mental classification reflected in the software. The hierarchy then is an iterated refinement of concepts. The "is-a" relation has an intuitive meaning, both to users and to software engineers.

📖112,39

To give an example, Eclipse's Java Model classifies the different language concepts in a hierarchy below `JavaElement`. The hierarchy consists of 46 classes and has depth 7 (including the root). In comparison to usual hierarchies, it is rather detailed. For a detailed overview, use *Type Hierarchy*. Let us now look at some of the classes to understand how abstraction by inheritance works.

Some of the cases refer directly to language constructs, such as Source Field, SourceMethod, or ImportDeclaration. Furthermore, there are parts of the super-structure such as CompilationUnit (i.e., one source file), ClassFile (i.e., a compiled binary class file), or PackageFragment (where "fragment" indicates that the Java Virtual Machine merges different packages with the same name).

The hierarchy above these obvious types then captures their commonalities in a multistep case distinction. At the top, there are two kinds of Java Elements. First, SourceRefElements are elements that correspond directly to source code, either explicitly in source files or implicitly through the source information attached to binary class files. In contrast, Openable is a technical superclass of (largish) things that must be loaded into memory, or "opened," before their parts can be analyzed. For instance, a JarPackage FragmentRoot holds the file system path to a JAR file. When that element is opened, the infrastructure of Openable handles the general process and finally calls back the method computeChildren in JarPackageFragment Root, which reads the JAR file from disk and creates the corresponding entries in the Java model. ◄3.1.4

Within the source files, which are below SourceRefElement, the classification follows the Java abstract syntax. For instance, a SourceField is-a NamedMember, which is a Member, which is-a SourceRefElement. ▢111

Further examples of classification can found in the hierarchy below JFace's Viewer and that below SWT's Widget. »9.3.2 »7.1

Classify by dynamic behavior, not by static data or format.

It is important to note that the Liskov Substitution Principle is not invalidated only because the intention is to create an abstraction hierarchy. As we have seen, Openable provides an infrastructure for its subclasses. Also, it is used (through the interface IOpenable) in many places in the JDT to access the underlying source code. ◄3.1.1

Beware of deep or intricate abstraction hierarchies.

Novices in object-oriented programming are often overenthusiastic about creating classification hierarchies. You should always keep in mind that every class you introduce costs—for development, testing, documentation, and maintenance. It must therefore justify its existence by making a significant contribution to the system's functionality. Usually this means providing some facet of reusable infrastructure or a useful view on the object for some concrete clients. However, a mere case of implementation inheritance does not justify the existence of a base class. All in all, these demands are ▢92

◄3.1.4 ◄3.1.3 »3.2.2
»3.1.10

📖112

rather high and empirical studies suggest that hierarchies usually remain rather shallow and narrow.

3.1.6   Reifying Case Distinctions

📖208(No.32)

A developer's life is full of cases—so much so that Alan Perlis concluded, "Programmers are not to be measured by their ingenuity and their logic but by the completeness of their case analysis." Whenever the behavior of an object varies, whether because of external circumstances, parameters, or its internal state, the code must express corresponding case distinctions. Very often, the cases can even be made explicit by naming them.

A straightforward, if limited, approach is to use explicit `enums` to name the cases and then `switch` to perform the case distinctions. The limitation consists of two resulting problems. First, the code that treats each case is scattered throughout the sources, which makes it hard to grasp how the case is really handled. Second, adding new cases requires retouching all those case distinctions, so it usually cannot be done easily by arbitrary developers—they at least need access to the sources. If you neglected to throw an exception in the `default` case, you may also be in for lengthy debugging sessions.

↰1.5.5

> Inheritance can capture cases as objects.

Inheritance enables an object-oriented solution to keep the code of the individual cases together. First, you introduce a base class that essentially has one (abstract) method for each piece of code that depends on the case. Then you pass around the correct case as an object and invoke the required code as necessary. From a different perspective, you are replacing the `switch` statement by dynamic dispatch. A further angle is obtained by seeing the different code fragments as short algorithms; with this perspective, we arrive at an instance of the STRATEGY pattern.

📖100

↰1.3.4
📖82
📖201

Let us start by looking at an example. EclipseLink provides an object relational mapping (ORM)—that is, it implements persistent database storage for Java objects. Database systems do, however, differ in their exact SQL syntax and allowed language constructs. The class `DatabasePlatform` is the base of a corresponding case distinction. It has roughly 250 (!) methods representing the variabilities between database systems. For instance, every database system has the ability to generate unique primary keys, for instance by assigning increasing numbers to new rows. EclipseLink must later be able to determine the number assigned, a task for which it calls the method `buildSelectQueryForIdentity`. MySQL and PostgreSQL, for instance, use the following implementations:

org.eclipse.persistence.platform.database.MySQLPlatform

```java
public ValueReadQuery buildSelectQueryForIdentity() {
    ValueReadQuery selectQuery = new ValueReadQuery();
```

```
        selectQuery.setSQLString("SELECT LAST_INSERT_ID()");
        return selectQuery;
}
```

---
org.eclipse.persistence.platform.database.PostgreSQLPlatform

```
public ValueReadQuery buildSelectQueryForIdentity() {
    ValueReadQuery selectQuery = new ValueReadQuery();
    selectQuery.setSQLString("select lastval()");
    return selectQuery;
}
```

This example clearly shows the benefits of introducing cases as classes, compared to the solution by switch: The code for one database system remains together in one place, and it is possible to introduce new cases without touching existing code. Default implementations—in this case, along the SQL standard—can be placed into the base class and are then used across cases.

Of course, there are also some disadvantages: In smaller ad-hoc examples, the code infrastructure of base and derived classes, object creation and storage, and other supports can easily outweigh the actual case-specific code. Further, it becomes harder to grasp and exploit similarities between cases, because their code is scattered over different classes. The only remedy ↰1.4.8.2 ↰3.1.4 is to introduce infrastructure base classes, which requires additional effort and planning. Finally, the code that calls the case methods is in danger of becoming less readable, because the human reader may have to follow the dynamic dispatch mentally.

In the end you have to make a decision: Is the potential extensibility worth the overhead and code scattering? There is certainly no injunction to express case distinctions by inheritance, although you should consider the approach whenever the code of individual cases gets bulky, such that it is unreadable when cases are put side by side in a switch. If you do, you should follow a few guidelines.

Aim at behavioral abstraction.

If you perceive case classes only as places to dump the corresponding code, you are likely to pay out more than you receive back. Nevertheless, you can see the case distinction as a prompt to define some abstract behavior ↰3.1.3 that captures some common perspective on the different cases. Then, you have gained an additional insight. As a result, clients will be able to work at a more abstract level and their code becomes more readable through the ↰1.4.5 method calls, instead of becoming potentially less readable.

Aim at extensible case distinctions.

Ideally, the case distinction you introduce is open-ended: If other developers can identify and implement new cases even after your own code is complete, your software already caters to tomorrow's needs.

You may well ask: If I have to obey these rules anyway, what is the difference from previous uses of inheritance? Although the final result may, in fact, look very similar, there are two crucial differences. First, you started from the low-key observation of requiring a case distinction, rather than from the ambitious goal of creating a useful abstraction. Such a gradual development is often more to the point in practice. Second, you may always stop along the way. In the EclipseLink example, some methods look like behavior, while others are only code snippets that needed to differ according to the database. The preceding example may be read as behavior, in the sense that the database can retrieve the last assigned primary key. In contrast, the method `writeAddColumnClause`, which creates the syntax to add a column to an existing table, is necessary only because one supported database system happens to require parentheses around the column specification.

3.1.7 Adapting Behavior

When object-oriented programming first became popular, one of its attractions was the ability to adapt existing functionality by subclassing and method overriding. The general approach of *programming by difference* was to choose a class from an existing application and adapt those methods that do not fit the context of reuse. At the same time, it was recognized that reuse does not happen by chance or with hindsight. Rather, it happens due to the foresight of the original developer and judicious application of what has since been termed refactoring. Accordingly, adapting behavior usually occurs within a context of explicitly identified common behavior.

In some rare cases, the original idea of programming by difference can still be useful for internal classes that just need "a bit of extra functionality" beyond what is already there. For instance, the code assist system of Eclipse mainly deals in `JavaElements` extracted from the source. However, the original mechanism for unique identification of members seems to have been too slow so that caching needs to be added. Accordingly, `AssistSourceField`, `AssistSourceMethod`, and similar elements share a hash map that is consulted before recomputing identifiers. The fields mentioned in the following snippet are introduced for the purpose.

📖132

↰3.1.4 ↰3.1.5

»12.3.3.5
↰3.1.5

---

org.eclipse.jdt.internal.codeassist.impl.AssistSourceField

```
public String getKey() {
    if (this.uniqueKey == null) {
        Binding binding = this.bindingCache.get(this);
        if (binding != null) {
            this.isResolved = true;
            this.uniqueKey = new String(binding.computeUniqueKey());
        } else {
            ...

        }
    }
```

```
    return this.uniqueKey;
}
```

⚠ Whenever you feel like using inheritance in this way, you should be aware that you are really creating a hack: You are using a class—by subclassing—in a way that it was not specifically designed for. The chances that the class breaks with a change in the base class are therefore rather high. In fact, this use of inheritance is very near to implementation inheritance, to be discussed later.

➤3.1.11

➤3.1.10

3.1.8   Inheritance Versus Delegation

Whenever you wish to reuse functionality given in a class A, you must make a choice: Either you instantiate A and delegate the relevant subtasks to that object, or you inherit from A and incorporate A's functionality into your own object. Both approaches have specific advantages and disadvantages that you must be aware of to make an informed decision. As a general rule of thumb:

↰3.1.4

↰1.8.5

> Prefer delegation over inheritance, unless you need the extra expressive power.

The preference of delegation over inheritance can be widely seen in the Eclipse platform. For instance, the JFace `SourceViewer` incorporates over 70 aspects of its functionality through delegation. There are several rather obvious reasons for preferring delegation.

- There is only one inheritance slot anyway, so you have to choose carefully which class you inherit from.

- The inheritance relation is public knowledge, so you have to be wary of clients that seek to exploit the common base behavior.

📖232

- You always inherit the entire interface and cannot restrict the available methods.

↰1.4.14

- You cannot change the published choice of the base class later on, since it might break clients. At this point, encapsulation of implementation details is not achieved.

For all of those reasons, you can use inheritance only if you can argue that the Liskov Substitution Principle is obeyed—implementation inheritance is undesirable.

↰3.1.1 ➤3.1.10

Beyond these obvious reasons, inheritance makes reasoning about the code more complex, and poses corresponding challenges for understanding and maintenance. First, we have already seen that unlimited access to the

↰3.1.2 ➤6.4.2

superclass's fields is undesirable because it jeopardizes the object's consistency. Instead, you should define an explicit interface towards subclasses. Second, undisciplined use of method overriding can easily lead to the situation in Fig. 3.2(a), where arrows with solid heads represent explicit calls, while those with empty heads represent self-calls to an overridden method that are dynamically dispatched to the subclass. The only chance of taming this behavior is to designate explicit callbacks that subclasses can or must override.

📖232

↰3.1.4 ↰1.4.9

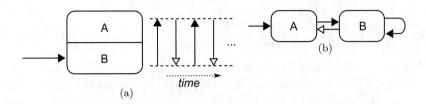

Figure 3.2 Coupling by Inheritance and Delegation

In contrast, delegation in Fig. 3.2(b) never incurs such inadvertent redirections of calls: The arrow with an empty head here represents explicit callbacks, such as notifications through an OBSERVER pattern. Furthermore, the DECORATOR pattern demonstrates that an incremental improvement akin to that achieved through inheritance can also be achieved through delegation.

↰2.1
↰2.4.2

Inheritance introduces tight coupling of the subclass to the superclass.

»12.1

All of these arguments are sometimes summarized by saying that the subclass is *coupled tightly* to its superclass. In other words, the subclass necessarily makes many assumptions about the superclass's mechanisms, its internal sequences of method calls, and the meaning of its fields. The more assumptions the subclass makes, the more likely it is to break when the superclass changes. Its implementation is tied to—is coupled to—that of the superclass.

3.1.9   Downcasts and `instanceof`

Type hierarchies are introduced, whether through inheritance or interfaces, to group objects in a meaningful way and to enable clients to work with different kinds of objects interchangeably. The compiler will always cast an object to any of its super-types, so the methods of these super-types are available to clients. Downcasts and `instanceof` expressions therefore go against the grain of classification: Clients single out special cases and are thus less widely applicable themselves. Nevertheless, both downcasts and `instanceof` are often used and required.

Try to argue that a special subtype will always be present.

The best situation is one where you actually know that an object must have a more specific type. Very often, this is the case because of basic consistency conditions (i.e., invariants). When you only ever put objects of a specific type into some list, as in this snippet:

»4.1

---
org.eclipse.jface.viewers.Viewer

```
public void addSelectionChangedListener(ISelectionChangedListener
    listener) {
    selectionChangedListeners.add(listener);
}
```

then you will always get those types of objects out afterward:

---
org.eclipse.jface.viewers.Viewer.fireSelectionChanged

```
Object[] listeners = selectionChangedListeners.getListeners();
for (int i = 0; i < listeners.length; ++i) {
    ISelectionChangedListener l = (ISelectionChangedListener)
    listeners[i];
    ...
}
```

You might feel that you are relying on some insubstantial reasoning here. In fact, no `instanceof` checks are necessary because the program's logic already dictates their outcome: This use of downcasts is completely safe. Bugs aside, the cast will always succeed.

Do not check with `instanceof` where the outcome is clear.

The reason why we advocate omitting the check is one of readability: If you write the check, the reader will start wondering what else can happen, and whether the other cases are handled correctly. Without the check, your code clearly states that no other cases can legally arise.

»4.5

In fact, this is how generics work under the hood: Java's type system keeps track of the list elements' type—in other words, the invariant over the list content.

📖53,52

---
downcasts.GenericsAndInvariants

```
1 private ArrayList<Integer> data = new ArrayList<Integer>();
2 public void useData() {
3     Integer d = data.get(0);
4 }
```

When one extracts an element (line 3), the compiler inserts a corresponding cast into the byte-code (at offset 8 in the following `javap -c` listing):

```
0: aload_0
1: getfield       #17 // Field data:Ljava/util/ArrayList;
4: iconst_0
5: invokevirtual #24 // Method java/util/ArrayList.get;
8: checkcast      #28 // class java/lang/Integer
```

»9.3.2
Another reliable source of information about specialized types comprises framework mechanisms. For instance, JFace viewers display application data on the screen. The viewer invokes `setInput` on the viewer to target it to the desired data structure. To access the data, the viewer employs a *content provider*. For instance, the *classpath* tab folder in a Java run configuration (go to *Run/Run configurations* to see it) displays a data structure called `ClasspathModel`. The viewer, in this case a tree viewer, is set up accordingly:

> org.eclipse.jdt.debug.ui.launchConfigurations.JavaClasspathTab.refresh

```
fClasspathViewer.setContentProvider(
    new ClasspathContentProvider(this));
fClasspathViewer.setInput(fModel);
```

Viewers promise to call back the content provider's `inputChanged` method first thing, with themselves as the `viewer` and the data structure supplied by the application. The casts in the following snippet are therefore completely safe, and no `instanceof` check should be done.

> org.eclipse.jdt.internal.debug.ui.classpath.ClasspathContentProvider

```
public void inputChanged(Viewer viewer, Object oldInput,
    Object newInput) {
    treeViewer = (TreeViewer) viewer;
    if (newInput != null) {
        model = (ClasspathModel) newInput;
    }
    ...
}
```

> Use `instanceof` whenever different subtypes may potentially be accessed.

◄1.5.2 »4.6

◄2.1.3
Finally, we reach the realm of uncertainty, where the concrete type may or may not be a subtype of some expected class or interface. One important source of uncertainty is the system boundary: One simply can *never* be sure that the user invokes some menu entry only at the appropriate point. Consider, for instance, the refactoring *Introduce Parameter Object*. It can be invoked only on methods, and the corresponding `Action` object should really be enabled only if a method is currently selected. Nevertheless, the `run` code checks that the restriction is indeed obeyed (line 3), before downcasting the selected object and proceeding (line 5).

> org.eclipse.jdt.internal.ui.actions.IntroduceParameterObjectAction

```
1 public void run(JavaTextSelection selection) {
2     IJavaElement[] elements = selection.resolveElementAtOffset();
3     if (elements.length != 1 || !(elements[0] instanceof IMethod))
4         return;
```

```
5   run((IMethod) elements[0]);
6 }
```

TOOL: Create `instanceof` Case

To create code for the idiom "`if instanceof` then downcast," type `instanceof`, auto-complete the code (Ctrl-Space), and choose *Dynamic type test and cast*. Use the linked positions, cycling them by `tab`, to fill in the details.

Finally, `instanceof` and downcasts may be necessitated by architectural considerations. Fig. 3.3 depicts a common situation. Some client in one module works with a hierarchy in a different module.

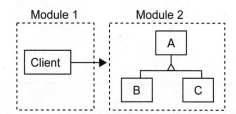

Figure 3.3 Downcasts for Architectural Reasons

Naturally, the client may wish to carry out operations that depend on the concrete class of an object. There are several different approaches.

1. Put an abstract operation into the base class and let dynamic dispatch handle the case distinction.

2. Include combinations of `instanceof` and downcast into the client.

3. If available, a VISITOR might be sufficient to implement the operation.

The last possibility really applies only to special case of recursive structures that happen to implement the VISITOR pattern. Since that pattern precludes extensibility of the hierarchy, it is rather uncommon. The first possibility applies only if your team controls the sources of the hierarchy. Furthermore, it incurs the grave danger of bloated classes: If *A*, *B*, and *C* are part of a central structure, then abstract operations will flow in from all parts of the system. Over time, these classes are heaped with more and more responsibilities. A very compelling reason for downcasts arises if the new responsibilities are fundamentally inconsistent with the purposes of the classes.

As an example, the Eclipse data structure of `IJavaElements` keeps track of the structure of the sources you are editing—that is, packages, classes, methods, and fields are all represented as objects within Eclipse so that you can easily access them. Even so, the visual appearance is a rather special need that is confined to special UI modules. The following code in Eclipse's

»12.1

↰3.1.6

»2.3.2

»9

UI layer therefore looks at the data structure, switches based on the node type, and then performs a downcast according to the case at hand. In the omitted code, the icons that you see, such as in the package explorer and outline view, get chosen.

org.eclipse.jdt.internal.ui.viewsupport.JavaElementImageProvider

```
public ImageDescriptor getBaseImageDescriptor(IJavaElement element,
        int renderFlags) {
    switch (element.getElementType()) {
    case IJavaElement.METHOD: {
        IMethod method = (IMethod) element;
         ...
    }
    case IJavaElement.FIELD: {
        IMember member = (IMember) element;
         ...
    }
     ...
    }
}
```

Try to avoid `instanceof` and downcasts.

We started this subsection by undertaking an analysis of situations requiring and at least suggesting case analysis and downcasts. It must be clear, however, that in general it is better to solve case distinctions in operations
↰1.4.1 ↰3.1.6 ↰2.3.1
by polymorphism and dynamic dispatch, since these mechanisms enable you to extend hierarchies later on; that is, when a new case surfaces, you can always create yet another class in the hierarchy. In contrast, explicit case distinctions limit the opportunities of evolving the software gracefully, since each and every case distinction needs to be touched on changes, something
📖92
that in refactoring is very aptly called "shotgun surgery."

Ad-hoc case distinctions do occur in practice. One common situation is that of special functionality associated with special cases. For instance, the
📖214
Graphical Editing Framework (GEF) introduces the concept of *connections*, which are lines attached automatically to other elements of a drawing. It is then useful to allow special elements to determine the exact attachment point, while in general the lines just continue to the bounding box of the element. The special case is captured in an interface `NodeEditPart`, which provides just the required support. The following snippet then determines the attachment of the line's start point:

org.eclipse.gef.editparts.AbstractConnectionEditPart

```
protected ConnectionAnchor getSourceConnectionAnchor() {
    if (getSource() instanceof NodeEditPart) {
        NodeEditPart editPart = (NodeEditPart) getSource();
        return editPart.getSourceConnectionAnchor(this);
    }
    IFigure f = ((GraphicalEditPart) getSource()).getFigure();
```

```
    return new ChopboxAnchor(f);
}
```

A similar situation occurs in connection with the extension interfaces.   »3.2.5

Encapsulating downcasts in methods leaves the client type-safe.

It is a common idiom to encapsulate the type test and downcast into a method that returns `null` if the test fails. In this way, the caller remains type-correct: It checks for `null`, but otherwise can assume it is working with an object of an expected type. The offending type checks are confined to a dedicated method.

For instance, many objects in the Eclipse platform offer a `getAdapter()` method that returns an adapter with a given interface, or `null` if such an adapter does not exist. Sometimes the result is the target `this` itself, if it happens to be a subtype of the given interface.

```
                    org.eclipse.core.runtime.IAdaptable
public interface IAdaptable {
    public Object getAdapter(Class adapter);
}
```

Conceptually, the method has the signature of the following dummy implementation, which follows that of `JavaEditor`. The interface `IAdaptable` does not use generics only for the historical reason that it was defined prior to Java 1.5.

```
                    downcasts.AdapterIdiom
public <T> T getAdapter(Class<T> adapter) {
    if (IContentOutlinePage.class == adapter) {
        // create the outline page if necessary
        return (T) fOutlinePage;
    }
    ...
    return null;
}
```

Consider client-specific interfaces when downcasts become necessary.

The deeper reason for having the method `getAdapter()` is that the client   »3.2.2
requires some functionality that was not envisaged in the object's original interface. Perhaps it is really specific for the client, or perhaps it was a simple oversight in the original design. In any case, understanding the new need as a stand-alone piece of functionality often helps to structure the design more clearly.

3.1.10 Implementation Inheritance

»6.4.1

The term *implementation inheritance* captures situations where a subclass is interested in the fields and methods of an existing class, but does not plan to honor the inherited behavior of that class.

Let us start with a typical example. A junior programmer wishes to implement the mathematical notion of a "valuation," referring to a mapping from variables to values. The programmer is supposed to provide `get()` and `put()` methods, so he decides he can finish the job quickly by just inheriting from `HashMap`:

implinh.Valuation
`public class Valuation extends HashMap<VarName, Double> {`   `}`

◄3.1.1

However, this class violates the Liskov Substitution Principle: A valuation is not meant to *be* a hash map, but merely *uses* the hash map's data structure. As a negation of the Liskov Substitution Principle, we get:

Avoid implementation inheritance.

The drawbacks of implementation inheritance have long been known.

□232
◄1.1

- Implementation inheritance exposes too much information. The inheritance hierarchy is public knowledge, while encapsulation requires that, the implementation of an object must be hidden. Implementation inheritance therefore exposes too much of the class's internals. In particular, clients of the class may upcast a reference to the subclass and use that reference with algorithms working directly on the implementation.

◄1.4.14

- The inherited interface is usually too large. In the example, iteration through the values is not part of a mathematical valuation. The subclass conceptually has a large number of refused bequests—that is, methods that it does not want but exposes for technical reasons.

»12.1

- The larger interface can increase coupling. In the example, the inherited method `putAll(Collection c)` ties the implementation to the Java collections framework, which might cause problems with porting later on.

»3.1.11

◄3.1.7

- Relying on the superclass's internals makes the fragile base class problem more likely. When choosing a class for its implementation, one usually takes a look also at the internals to determine whether all required mechanisms are actually there. Also, one adapts those methods that are not entirely as needed. This close link between subclass and base class makes it more likely that the subclass will break when the base class changes.

Hide the implementation object by delegation.

A better solution in the example is to move the implementation object to a field inside the `Valuation` class. Now only the specified methods are exposed; the implementation could be replaced later on. Furthermore, the behavior of the methods can be modified. For instance, they may throw an `UndefinedVariableException` if `get` is called with a nonexistent variable.

implinh.Valuation2

```
public class Valuation2 {
    private HashMap<VarName, Double> rep =
                new HashMap<VarName, Double>();
    public Double get(Object key) {
        return rep.get(key);
    }
    public Double put(VarName key, Double value) {
        return rep.put(key, value);
    }
}
```

TOOL: Generate Delegate Methods

To expose selected methods of a collaborator stored in a field, invoke *Source/Generate Delegate Methods* and choose the desired methods in the dialog.

C++ tackles the problem of implementation inheritance at its root: If clients of the subclass cannot "see" the superclass, then all of the previously given objections are resolved. The language therefore extends the usual concept of access privileges to inheritance. If the superclass is declared `private`, then its fields and methods are inherited as usual, but only the class itself (and its `friends`) can make use of the fact; they alone can access the inherited members and can upcast a pointer. If inheritance is `protected`, then only the class itself and its subclasses see the relation.   ☐239

In C++, one can express an "is-implemented-as" relation between subclass and superclass. The advantage over delegation is, of course, that the two involved objects are merged into one, such that the overhead of managing a separate object is avoided. Experts in C++ usage nevertheless advise that this feature be used only in special situations.   ☐183(Item 39)

(It also has to be said that the overhead of delegation is minimal. Since objects in C++ have value semantics by default, adding a field `rep` as in this solution would actually embed the hash map into the outer valuation object. Also, objects without virtual methods do not have a header, so the overhead consists of only the additional method call during delegation.)

3.1.11   The Fragile Base Class Problem

The discussion of inheritance so far has pointed out common usage that works well in practice. However, we must not ignore the reality that in using inheritance extensively, one always walks a narrow path, where Bad Things can happen if one takes a wrong step into uncharted territory. We have already seen some examples, when we discussed the need to introduce explicit interfaces of `protected` methods for subclasses and the guideline to prefer delegation over inheritance.

↰3.1.2
↰3.1.8

Development folklore has come to use the term *fragile base class problem* to summarize the undesirable phenomena related to inheritance: Developers find that a base class with many subclasses becomes "fragile," in the sense that changing the base class in seemingly minor ways that appear to concern only the class's internals nevertheless breaks many of the subclasses. This is, of course, an issue with extensible systems and (white-box) frameworks—that is, with software that is specifically intended to be reused in many applications. The same findings are also summarized by saying that inheritance results in tight coupling between subclass and base class: The subclass usually makes so many, often implicit, assumptions about the base class's behavior that even innocent changes to the base class will invalidate these assumptions. The problem can be recast in yet another way by saying that specifying the outside behavior of the base class is insufficient, because defining the allowed collaborations between the base class and its subclass clients requires talking about the internal mechanisms of the base class.

↦7.3.3

↦12.1

📖136

The plethora of reasons why a class can be "fragile" makes it hard to define the term "fragile base class problem" precisely and comprehensively. Mikhajlov and Sekerinski have given an extensive and formalized analysis of the problems involved. They derive and justify a number of rules that exclude the problematic cases and achieve a desirable goal, which they call the *flexibility property*. Expressed in the terms introduced here, this property yields the following strategic goal:[1]

📖185
📖185(§3.6,§5.2)

> Allow only changes to the base class that do not break the Liskov Substitution Principle for subclasses.

This goal can be justified from the previous discussions: A subclass is introduced to modify or concretize the behavior of its base class, with the aim of implementing the application's functionality. Such a modification is restricted by the Liskov Substitution Principle, which guarantees that the subclass will work smoothly within the existing context. If a modification of the base class were to break the substitution principle for the subclass, that

↰3.1.1

---

1. The original formulation is "If C is refined by C' and C is refined by $(M \bmod C)$, then C is refined by $(M \bmod C')$." In this definition, "refines" is used in the sense of [18] and means "fulfills all expectations," similar to the substitution principle. $M \bmod C$ expresses subclassing by viewing the subclass's definition as a modifier that is applied to the superclass's definition.

smooth integration would be destroyed and the overall application would be broken.

The question is how such a general goal can be achieved. The insight is that it is sufficient to follow a few rules in the code; given that this is the case, one can prove that the flexibility property is satisfied.

185(§3.6)

"No direct access to the base class state."

This first rule has already been explored extensively in Section 3.1.2 and does not need further discussion. If subclasses freely access the base class's state, then the base class internals can never be changed in any way without endangering the subclasses.

"No cycles requirement."

The fundamental challenge to the stability of base classes stems from the fact that (almost) all methods can be overridden, which can lead to undesirable interactions between the base class and the subclass. Each of the two classes can in principle make arbitrary self-calls, and these can get dispatched dynamically to either one of them.

One particular case is that overriding actually introduces an infinite recursion and nontermination of the program: If method f in the base class calls method g, and now the subclass overrides g to call f, the cycle is there. The immediate idea is, of course:

185

Be cautious about additional self-calls in overridden methods.

The deeper insight is that such cycles can be avoided only if there is a fixed linear order on methods so that methods always call "smaller" ones. (In the rare cases where mutual recursion is necessary for algorithmic reasons, the methods can be private or one can specify that they must be overridden together.) If "fixed linear order" seems rather abstract, then think of the call graph of the methods and perform a depth-first traversal: If you don't hit any cycles, you can number the methods as needed when finishing the visit. (In other words, you perform a topological sort of the call graph to obtain the numbers. The point is that a suitable numbering exists if and only if there are no cycles.)

185(§5.1)

136

72

Document the dependencies and call relationships between methods.

In practice, one does not number methods. However, the documentation of reusable classes usually excludes cycles by mentioning the intended call chains. For instance, the method paint() in Swing's JComponent makes a very explicit statement of this kind:

> This method actually delegates the work of painting to three
> protected methods: paintComponent, paintBorder, paint

`Children`. They're called in the order listed to ensure that children appear on top of the component itself.

Since clients will certainly refrain from calling `paint()` from within the three mentioned methods, cycles are avoided.

Specify the replaceable methods and the infrastructure mechanisms.

□136
□232

Another way of approaching the goal is to specify explicitly which methods should be replaceable. It was recognized early on that undisciplined overriding will lead to chaos, so the logical consequence is to allow overriding only at specific points. The implicit goal is, of course, to make sure that the mechanisms calling the overridable methods are cycle-free, and that the replacements will not call back into the generic mechanisms. The TEMPLATE METHOD pattern makes this very explicit; further conceptual foundations will be discussed in the context of frameworks.

↰1.4.9

↠12.3.2

Note also that this approach clearly prevents certain forms of implementation inheritance: If the designer decides and states which methods should be overridden, then the client cannot override methods just because they happen to implement something akin to their own requirements.

↰3.1.7

"No revision self-calling assumptions."

"No base class down-calling assumptions."

↠6.4.1

The last two rules touch the realm of contracts, in that the actual behavior of overridden methods must be discussed. However, they can also be understood from a technical perspective.

Fig. 3.4 illustrates the problematic cases underlying the two rules (following the code in [185, §3]). The levels B for the base class and S for the subclass are clear. We inject the revision B' of the base class in between, because it is able to intercept and redirect some of the method calls by dynamic dispatch. Also, B' is supposed to "behave essentially the same as B"—although technically there is no inheritance relationship, behavioral subtyping should hold.

↰3.1.1

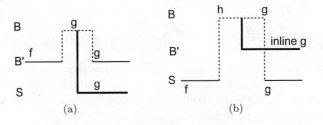

Figure 3.4 Self-Calls in Fragile Base Classes

Let us start with the situation in Fig. 3.4(a). The revision B' has a method f that at some point, either directly or indirectly through other methods, invokes g. Now the revision can make the mistake of expecting that dynamic dispatch will actually result in executing its own method g, whose behavior it knows exactly. But of course, the subclass S is not aware of that g and may override that method for its own purposes, probably with quite a different behavior. The revision B' breaks the application, because method f does not work as expected with the different g.

An analogous situation is shown in Fig. 3.4(b). The subclass has a method f that calls a method h, which probably implements some generic mechanism or infrastructure. From looking at the code of B, the subclass knows that h will eventually delegate to g and expects that dynamic dispatch selects it own method g, whose behavior it knows exactly. The method f therefore relies on the exact behavior of the final g, an assumption that gets broken when the revision B' overrides h and modifies the self-calling structure, for instance by inlining the code of g.

↰3.1.4

> Even in self-calls, methods must expect only the behavior of the base class.

In both cases, the problem arises from the additional and unjustified assumption that a particular method will be executed by dynamic dispatch. In both cases, special knowledge about the expected target method is exploited. The base class is fragile because revisions that invalidate this assumption break the overall application, even though the revision itself may be well within its rights: It overrides existing methods without changing their specified behavior.

But how can the inheritance hierarchy be made stable under such possible revisions? The core idea in both cases is simply this: Because it is uncertain which method will actually be executed in the end, all code must be written to work with the documentation stated in the base class, because then it will work with *any* possible overriding. In the case of Fig. 3.4(a), the method f in B' works with the overridden g in S if it assumes the behavior documented for g in B. In Fig. 3.4(b), f in S will not be derailed just because B' happens to change the call structure by inlining.

This reasoning will later be linked easily to the idea of contract inheritance, which states that methods must obey the contract of the method that they override, while all callers, including self-calls, always work with the contract specified for the overridden method.

↱6.4.1

3.2 Interfaces

While inheritance is an attractive mechanism for both code reuse and classification of objects, it creates an unfortunate link between implementation and classification. The accepted goal of behavioral subtyping sometimes

▭232,69,160
↰3.1.3

↰2.4.2   suggests several different views on the same object, which cannot be achieved
using a single available inheritance slot. Multiple inheritance, by comparison, introduces further complexities into the language.

Java's way out is its interfaces mechanism. Interfaces merely specify
which methods will be present in an object, but do not provide an
implementation.[2]

> Interfaces completely decouple the existence of methods from their
> implementation.

The compiler merely checks that the concrete class has all the required
methods. This point is actually central, because it establishes the freedom
associated with interfaces: The interfaces can be seen as behavioral "tags"
attached to objects for the benefit of their clients.

To illustrate the degree of independence, consider a base class with a
method `work`:

interfaces.Bases

```java
public class Base {
    public void work() {
        ...
    }
}
```

Suppose later on it is decided that "working" is a common behavior and
should be captured in an interface:

interfaces.Behavior

```java
public interface Behavior {
    void work();
}
```

Then, it is possible to tag the `Base` implementation in retrospect. In the
following class, the compiler just checks that the required method is present:

interfaces.Derived

```java
public class Derived extends Base implements Behavior {}
```

Similarly, an abstract class can promise to implement an interface and defer
the actual method implementations to its subclasses.

> **TOOL: Create Completed Implementation Class**
>
> Implementing interfaces in a class is so common that there are several
> ways to generate stubs for the necessary methods. In the *New/Class*
> wizard, you can select the interfaces and check *Create stubs for* ...

---

2. Java 8 features default implementations for interface methods that can be given directly in the interface. Their purpose is to enable extensions to interfaces, in particular
in the Collections API, without breaking existing code (see also Section 3.2.5).

Inherited Abstract Methods. Next, you can simply list the interface in the `implements` clause and Quick-Fix (`Ctrl-1`). Then, you can override the methods through *Source/Override or implement methods* or by writing the method name and auto-completing the code (`Ctrl-Space`).

  Those readers who are familiar with the internals of the efficient virtual method dispatch in C++ and the problems in extending it to multiple inheritance may wonder whether interfaces are sufficiently efficient for large-scale use. It turns out that with suitable engineering precautions, method invocations through interfaces require roughly one memory indirection more than method dispatch in single inheritance hierarchies. With the size of caches available today, this will hardly matter. The implementation effort saved through the clarified structure is always worth the very small runtime penalty.

📖239
📖3,4

Don't over-engineer your interfaces.

Before we embark on an investigation of interface usage, we point out that interfaces involve the danger of over-engineering a design. Because interfaces can be defined independently of an eventual implementation, there is the temptation to capture any facet of behavior that might seem important as an interface. Although this gives you the good feeling of writing down some actual code, it usually does not lead to the "simplest thing that could work." As a rule of thumb, any interface must be justified by some client object that uses the interface and that could not work with the concrete class directly. If you can eliminate an interface from your design, you will help your team members and the maintenance programmers, because they will have to understand one thing less and because they can work with calls to concrete methods whose code they can inspect without debugging.

3.2.1 Behavioral Abstraction

The central point of interfaces is that they can capture pieces of behavior that are exhibited by different objects throughout the system. It is not important how the individual objects are constructed; it only matters that in the end they show some expected behavior. In the context of design, we will speak of *roles* that are taken on by different objects.

»11.3.3.7

Interfaces capture common behavior exhibited by kinds of different objects.

A typical example is the concept of a "selection" in editing. Whether in text editors, in the outline view, in the package explorer, or in the problems view, the user can always pick some part of the data and manipulate it. The corresponding objects all give access to a "selection" of some sort (lines 2–3 in the next example). Of course, clients will usually be interested in changes to the selection as well. For instance, they may want to enable or disable menu entries or buttons depending on the current selection. The common behavior

↰2.1
therefore includes the OBSERVER pattern (lines 4–7), so that clients can register and de-register for change notifications. The converse also holds: The clients themselves are classified as `ISelectionChangedListeners`—that is, as objects capable of receiving the generated notifications.

org.eclipse.jface.viewers.ISelectionProvider

```
1 public interface ISelectionProvider {
2     public ISelection getSelection();
3     public void setSelection(ISelection selection);
4     public void addSelectionChangedListener(
5         ISelectionChangedListener listener);
6     public void removeSelectionChangedListener(
7         ISelectionChangedListener listener);
8 }
```

Here is a second example. There are many different kinds of editors and views in the Eclipse workbench. Some of them enable editing of files or other resources, so that they can become "dirty" and need to be "saved." Furthermore, Eclipse takes care of saving the changes to avoid data loss. Together, these common aspects of behavior are captured by the following interface:

org.eclipse.ui.ISaveablePart

```
public interface ISaveablePart {
    public boolean isDirty();
    public void doSave(IProgressMonitor monitor);
    public boolean isSaveOnCloseNeeded();
        ...
}
```

Design interfaces to match a concept, not the first implementing class.

In the preceding examples, the interfaces could be explained and understood from an abstract description of a conceptual behavior. It was not necessary to even look at concrete implementing classes to understand what the interfaces demand. This observation constitutes a good general guideline: The more you keep the definition of an interface independent of its eventual implementations, the higher the chances of reuse. Clients that work with the interface will work with any object implementing the interface, and the more objects that are able to implement the interface, the more objects that the client will work with.

»3.2.7
⚠ Eclipse offers a tool *Extract Interface*, which we will discuss later. Merely introducing an interface for an existing class does *not* enhance reusability. Instead, it clutters the source code with a useless abstraction that is, and in all probability will be, implemented only by a single class. Maintenance developers will see the interface and must take into

account the *potential* of several implementors, rather than working with their knowledge of a single concrete class.

Interfaces, like classes, must justify their existence by an added value.

3.2.2 Client-Specific Classification and Abstraction

The previous section advocated defining interfaces from some abstract concept that characterizes the behavior of several different objects. To find such concepts, it is sometimes useful to start from one particular client and its expectations on the objects it will work with. The Eclipse workbench contains several such examples.

- The *Properties* view shows the detailed settings on the current selection. Toward that end, it requests an `IPropertySheetPage` from the current editor.

- A *marker* is an annotation, such as a warning or an error, attached to some file. The interface `IGotoMarker` is then a behavior of an editor that allows outside clients to scroll the editor to a given marker without knowing anything about the editor's content. The interface is (essentially) used only in the following `IDE` facade method: ↰1.7.2

```
                          org.eclipse.ui.ide.IDE
public static void gotoMarker(IEditorPart editor,
    IMarker marker) {
    IGotoMarker gotoMarker = null;
    gotoMarker =
        (IGotoMarker) editor.getAdapter(IGotoMarker.class);
    if (gotoMarker != null) {
        gotoMarker.gotoMarker(marker);
    }
}
```

- The auto-completion pop-up in the Java editor is a generic component that internally delegates the choice of possible completions to any object implementing the following interface, which allows implementors to compute a list of proposals on demand.

```
            org.eclipse.jdt.ui.text.java.IJavaCompletionProposalComputer
public interface IJavaCompletionProposalComputer {
    List<ICompletionProposal> computeCompletionProposals(
                        ContentAssistInvocationContext context,
                        IProgressMonitor monitor);
    ...
}
```

This example is prototypical of a client-specific interface: There is a single call site for this method, and that caller is, again, called from only one point, and this continues four levels up the call hierarchy.

↰1.1
The first observation to be made from these examples is a special case of an earlier guideline:

Define interfaces from the clients' perspective.

Since the goal of interfaces is to enable clients to work with different kinds of objects, it is a good idea to start from the clients' expectations and to consider how the interface must be defined to make the clients' code look elegant and natural.

Client-specific interfaces enable generic, reusable clients.

We have previously stated that defining an interface from its first implementation can be harmful. In contrast, defining an interface from its first and perhaps only client's perspective usually enhances flexibility, since the client will work with different objects that may not even exist in the system as yet.

One possible pitfall is the inadvertent creation of an interface that can be implemented usefully in only one class. Thus, whenever you define an interface, make sure that there can be different useful implementations in the system.

Client-specific interfaces help tame change.

A complementary result of client-specific interfaces is that each client will depend on only those aspects of a concrete object that are accessible through its special interface. Any other methods and services not available here can then be changed without affecting the client. Especially for larger objects
📖170,169
»11.5.6
with many different sorts of clients, this is a distinct advantage. Martin terms this insight the *Interface Segregation Principle* (ISP): "Many client-specific interfaces are better than one general-purpose interface."

Use EXTENSION OBJECTS to provide extended views on an object.

In practice, it happens very often that a new client finds that its target ob-
»3.2.5
ject does not yet expose the functionality that the client requires. Extending an existing interface or superclass by new methods is problematic, because it breaks existing subclasses, since they do not yet provide these methods. Also, interfaces expressing key abstractions of the application will quickly become bloated.

The solution is to see such extensions as specific views on the target
📖98
object and to materialize them as extension objects, as the following pattern explains:

> **PATTERN:** EXTENSION OBJECTS
>
> To anticipate the need to extend an object's interface in the future, define a method `getExtension(type)` that returns an adapter implementing a newly introduced interface, or `null` if the interface is not supported. The `type` parameter identifies the view requested by the client.

🔍 This pattern is also known as EXTENSION INTERFACE, because you receive interfaces for extensions. This choice of name conflicts with the pattern of introducing extensions to interfaces described later on. The two patterns are entirely distinct and serve completely different purposes.

»3.2.5

As a result, objects can expose new functionality without breaking existing subclasses.

Because it avoids extending existing interfaces by using separate interfaces for the extensions instead, this pattern is also known as EXTENSION INTERFACE. Furthermore, client-specific views can be defined by client-specific interfaces, which avoids bloating the object's main interface with specialized functionality. Likewise, the implementation hierarchy remains independent of the abstraction hierarchies, which helps to build flexible systems. Finally, the different clients remain independent, since a change to one interface does not affect clients accessing the object through other interfaces.

»3.2.5
📖99,218

The Eclipse platform uses this approach in many places. It dubs the pattern's `getExtension()` method `getAdapter()`, which emphasizes the point that the returned object is in many cases really an adapter for the target object. For the pattern's `type`, Eclipse uses the class of the expected interface. The method must return an object implementing the requested interface, or `null` if the requested view is not available.

↰2.4.1

---
org.eclipse.core.runtime.IAdaptable

```java
public interface IAdaptable {
    public Object getAdapter(Class adapter);
}
```

For instance, editors offer their document's structure to the *Outline* view you are familiar with through an `IContentOutlinePage`. Each editor provides its own implementation of the interface to represent the structure of the edited content. Here is the example of the `JavaEditor`.

---
org.eclipse.jdt.internal.ui.javaeditor.JavaEditor

```java
public Object getAdapter(Class required) {
    if (IContentOutlinePage.class.equals(required)) {
        if (fOutlinePage == null)
            fOutlinePage = createOutlinePage();
        return fOutlinePage;
    }
```

```
        ...
    return super.getAdapter(required);
}
protected JavaOutlinePage createOutlinePage() {
    JavaOutlinePage page=
        new JavaOutlinePage(fOutlinerContextMenuId, this);
    setOutlinePageInput(page, getEditorInput());
    return page;
}
```

☐50(Ch.5)

The Netbeans Rich Client Platform employs the similar concept of Lookups. Lookups are conceptually bags of adapters, which are accessed through the method lookup(). Analogously to getAdapter(), clients can discover an object's capabilities, or can, at a global level, retrieve dependencies and service implementations from the *default lookup*.

3.2.3   Abstraction Hierarchies

Interfaces, like inheritance, can be used to create fine-grained abstraction or specialization hierarchies. In contrast to inheritance, one can define behavioral distinctions freely, without worrying about the implementation for the moment. Interfaces can capture specializations from the clients' perspective, without restricting at the same time the choices of the later implementors. For this reason, interfaces are nowadays preferred over inheritance for that purpose.

As an example, different kinds of "selections" naturally occur when editing in Eclipse: The user may select parts of text, or single or multiple elements in a table or tree. Correspondingly, the base interface ISelection has a single method isEmpty that determines whether anything has been selected. Buttons and menu items can use this, for instance, to determine whether they are enabled. Next, an IStructuredSelection deals with lists of data items that can be selected. It is used by tables and trees in the user interface and enables clients to access one or all selected elements.

org.eclipse.jface.viewers.IStructuredSelection

```
public interface IStructuredSelection extends ISelection {
    public Object getFirstElement();
    public Iterator iterator();
    public int size();
    public Object[] toArray();
    public List toList();
}
```

Tree-like displays explicitly allow the same data item to be shown at different tree nodes—for instance, when the data structure itself involves structure sharing. Selections in trees therefore can be described more precisely by capturing the entire path to the selected elements.

---

org.eclipse.jface.viewers.ITreeSelection

```
public interface ITreeSelection extends IStructuredSelection {
    public TreePath[] getPaths();
    public TreePath[] getPathsFor(Object element);
}
```

Text-based selections in `ITextSelection`, in contrast, are characterized by their offset and length, and the text itself.

A second example is seen in an interface hierarchy paralleling that below `JavaElement`, the representation of Java language constructs inside the Eclipse IDE. This parallel construction is suggested by the BRIDGE pattern. The interfaces derive from `IJavaElement`. For instance, an `IMethod` is-an `IMember`, which is-an `IJavaElement`; similarly, an `IField` is-an `IMember`. It is interesting to note here that the interface hierarchy is much cleaner than the class hierarchy, because it is not cluttered with considerations about data storage and resource accesses. For instance, the interface `IMethod` is implemented by `BinaryMethod` and `SourceMethod`, depending on whether the method is found in a JAR archive or in a source file. These classes are located below `BinaryMember` and `SourceMember`, respectively, because they require different access paths to the details such as the annotations and parameters. From a client's perspective, however, all that matters is that these details can be obtained. We conclude:

Abstraction by interfaces can concentrate on the clients' perspective.

3.2.4 Multiple Classification

One of the drawbacks of inheritance hierarchies is that one must decide on a single way of classifying objects that must, furthermore, be aligned with the objects' implementation. The latter point has already been discussed in the previous section. Now we will exhibit the utility of implementing multiple interfaces in one class.

Multiple classification can represent facets of behavior for different clients.

We have pointed out previously that it is useful to design interfaces based on particular clients' expectations. With respect to classification and abstraction, this guideline induces the idea of taking apart an object's behavior according to multiple possible views, and choosing corresponding abstraction hierarchies.

Consider again an `IMember` in Eclipse's Java model, which is the supertype of methods and fields. That interface extends four super-interfaces to capture different aspects of working with methods and fields: (1) As an `IJavaElement`, it is part of the tree structure extracted from the sources and compiled classes. (2) As an `IParent`, it is actually an inner node of that

↰3.1.5
↠12.2.1.5 ▢100

↰3.2.1

↠2.3.1

tree structure that exposes its children as generic `IJavaElements`. This can be used for displaying and browsing the structure in the user interface.

---
org.eclipse.jdt.core.IParent

```
public interface IParent {
    IJavaElement[] getChildren() throws JavaModelException;
    boolean hasChildren() throws JavaModelException;
}
```
---

(3) As an `ISourceReference`, it can be asked about its original location. For compiled classes in JAR archives, the information is taken from the class file and can be used to link to a separate source tree that you attach in the JAR's properties.

---
org.eclipse.jdt.core.ISourceReference

```
public interface ISourceReference {
    boolean exists();
    String getSource() throws JavaModelException;
    ISourceRange getSourceRange() throws JavaModelException;
    ISourceRange getNameRange() throws JavaModelException;
}
```
---

(4) As an `ISourceManipulation`, the member can be copied, deleted, moved, and renamed. Those methods are geared toward the corresponding refactoring operations.

3.2.5   Extension Interface

One strategic problem with interfaces is that they cannot be changed easily: Once they are published, you must assume that some classes out there implement them, so any change to the interface breaks all of those implementors, since they suddenly no longer match the interface. At the very least, it forces all implementing classes to be adapted accordingly. The first conclusion to be drawn is this:

> Design interfaces carefully when you introduce and publish them.

From a practical perspective, the challenge is often one of API versioning. Clients prefer backward compatibility in APIs, but sometimes this just cannot be achieved because the initial API design is known to be unstable. For instance, some of the expected uses of the API may not have been implemented, so that their requirements have not yet been integrated fully. In such cases, it is customary to make the status of the API explicit:

> Publish provisional APIs until you are sure of the design decisions.

One important change is the extension of interfaces. Even if you think broadly about the possible clients using the interface, you can never be sure that the next client will not need further support for its operations.

Sometimes, you may also learn about better ways of collaboration, simply by writing more client code that accesses the interface.

PATTERN: EXTENSION INTERFACE

To extend an interface, introduce a derived interface and use downcasts.

Naming convention: For the new interface choose the original name and append a number to document the various extensions, starting with 2.

As an example, we have seen the behavioral abstraction `ISaveablePart`, ↰3.2.1
which should be sufficient for editor-like implementors. When the editor is
closed in some way and its content has been modified, the workbench will
ask the user whether it should save the changes and then invokes `doSave()`
on the editor. Only later was it realized that some parts might profit from
an extended collaboration, where the saveable part itself prompts the user
in a specialized manner. This new collaboration is enabled by the following
extension interface (the interface defines constants for the return value):

org.eclipse.ui.ISaveablePart2

```java
public interface ISaveablePart2 extends ISaveablePart {
    ...
    public int promptToSaveOnClose();
}
```

For instance, the *Variables* view, which you are familiar with from debugging in Eclipse, just decides that it will always have its current state
saved to disk.

org.eclipse.debug.internal.ui.views.variables.VariablesView

```java
public int promptToSaveOnClose() {
    return ISaveablePart2.YES;
}
```

When it comes to working with the saveable parts, the extension interface must be taken into account by dynamic type checking and downcasts.
First, the logic in `SaveableHelper` checks whether the `saveable` happens
to implement the extension interface, and if so, gives it the chance of an extended collaboration. If the interface is not implemented, or the `saveable`
answers that the old-style prompt is sufficient, the logic falls back to that
prompt.

org.eclipse.ui.internal.SaveableHelper.savePart

```java
int choice = USER_RESPONSE;
if (saveable instanceof ISaveablePart2) {
    choice = ((ISaveablePart2) saveable).promptToSaveOnClose();
}
if (choice == USER_RESPONSE || choice == ISaveablePart2.DEFAULT) {
    // Standard Eclipse prompt
    ...
}
```

This example shows that extension interfaces come at the cost of making clients more complex. Furthermore, the implementors of the interface must make sure that they continue to work with old-style clients that are not aware of the extension.

> Consider EXTENSION OBJECTS as an alternative.

↰3.2.2

The EXTENSION OBJECTS pattern offers a partial remedy to the problems outlined previously: If the extension to an interface is done on behalf of specific clients, then it might be better to introduce a completely separate interface and have the object hand out an adapter implementing the interface.

3.2.6   Specifying Callbacks

The examples of behavioral abstraction seen so far have involved quite specific assumptions on the appropriate reaction of the implementing object. In short, the client expected the object to perform some specified service.

»7.11

»10 »7.3.2

In many cases, however, the situation is reversed. When the client calls a method through an interface, this is really a service *to* the object: The client notifies the object that something interesting has happened, but leaves the decision about an appropriate reaction entirely to the target object. The interface merely captures the technical necessity that some method exists.

↰2.1

»7.1

This situation occurs in particular with the OBSERVER pattern, where the caller notifies the target object about a state change. It also occurs prototypically in connection with user interfaces, where the application is notified about user interactions. For instance, to receive information about mouse clicks, the application implements the following interface:

```
                    org.eclipse.swt.events.MouseListener

public interface MouseListener extends SWTEventListener {
    public void mouseDown(MouseEvent e);
    public void mouseUp(MouseEvent e);
    public void mouseDoubleClick(MouseEvent e);
}
```

3.2.7   Decoupling Subsystems

Interfaces have the most wonderful property of purging concrete classes from client code: Clients can work with the interface alone; the concrete class is irrelevant. This property can be used to make subsystems less dependent on one another, a phenomenon known as *decoupling*. Fig. 3.5 gives the main idea. In this figure, Module B implements some functionality in a class Target. However, the developers are not sure about some of its aspects—whether it is the name, the inheritance hierarchy, or part of the class's API. They decide to publish only just enough information for the Client to start operating—that's API design on a need-to-know basis.

»12.1

Accordingly, the developers define an interface I that captures just those parts that they are sure about. If necessary, they also define an interface N that captures notifications issued by the Target. The final result is as desired: The developers remain free to change all the aspects of Target that are not yet published in either I or N. They can even make such far-reaching modifications as changing the inheritance hierarchy above Target. The interfaces on the module's boundary effectively form a shell around its internals.

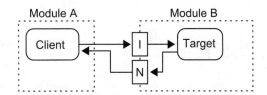

Figure 3.5 Decoupling Subsystems Through Interfaces

We have already seen an example of such decoupling, in the Eclipse Java model. That central module represents the structure of the projects and source code you are editing. It also updates the structure as you edit; the outline view and package explorer are adapted a few hundred milliseconds after you stop typing. Furthermore, memory consumption is kept acceptable by only caching the computed information on a most re- cently used basis and throwing it away when your focus of editing ac- tivities moves elsewhere. Surely, this behavior requires some rather nifty and probably complex internal logic, which is implemented in the pack- age org.eclipse.jdt.internal.core. Of these classes, we have already looked at the inheritance hierarchy below JavaElement.

↰3.1.5 ↰3.2.3 ↰3.2.4

▭99(Ch.33)

↰3.1.5

Decoupling through interfaces protects clients from a module's intricacies.

Clients, however, are not interested in these internals. Their expec- tation is quite simply the same as yours as a user: The data structure should roughly resemble the graphical display in the package explorer, where you start from projects, then dig down through packages, to individ- ual classes, and further down to the class's methods and fields. The Java model presents this nice outside view through interfaces in the package org.eclipse.jdt.core. At the top of the abstraction hierarchy, IJava Element is just one node in the nested structure. More specifically, an IJavaProject is clearly a project, an ICompilationUnit is a source file, an IType is a class or an interface, and so on. When you browse this hi- erarchy in Eclipse and look at the interfaces' methods, you will find that they correspond closely to the information displayed in the explorer views.

»2.3.1

TOOL: Extract Interface

If you have the concrete implementation ready and have decided which aspects of the class's API should be public, you can use *Refactor/Extract Interface* (Alt-Shift-T E) to create a corresponding interface.

Applying this tool results in a major inconvenience in the daily work with Eclipse: You can no longer jump from a method call to the method's definition with *Open Declaration* (F3), because that simply takes you to the interface. The Eclipse developers have seen this problem and have provided the solution in a separate tool:

TOOL: Open Implementation

To find the concrete method implementation hidden behind an interface, use the menu item *Navigate/Open Implementation*. This is also accessible in a pop-up menu by pressing Ctrl while hovering over a method call.

Provide abstract factories or facades to create objects.

One technical detail of decoupling by interfaces is that clients cannot create objects from the published interfaces alone. The module must offer other objects to perform those creations. We have already seen the relevant techniques: An ABSTRACT FACTORY is an object that creates objects conforming to some abstract type, in this case an interface. In the current context, this pattern can be combined with a FACADE to define a simple entry point and hide the internals of the module completely.

↰1.4.12

↰1.7.2

The Java model offers a facade JavaCore, whose static methods can create the desired objects. For instance, you can get the structure of a Java source file through the method:

org.eclipse.jdt.core.JavaCore

```
public static ICompilationUnit createCompilationUnitFrom(IFile file)
```

Make the insulation complete.

Hiding a few classes behind interfaces is certainly worthwhile if these are focal points of expected changes. However, the decoupling technique can be used to shield the client completely from the concrete types of a module. For instance, once you have a IJavaProject, you can manipulate its class path used for compilation:

org.eclipse.jdt.core.IJavaProject

```
void setRawClasspath(IClasspathEntry[] entries,
    IProgressMonitor monitor)
        throws JavaModelException;
```

The necessary class path entries are obtained from `JavaCore`—for instance, by using the following methods:

org.eclipse.jdt.core.JavaCore

```
public static IClasspathEntry newSourceEntry(IPath path)
public static IClasspathEntry newLibraryEntry(IPath path,
        IPath sourceAttachmentPath, IPath sourceAttachmentRootPath)
```

In the end, the interfaces that define the module's boundary form a complete capsule or shell around the concrete implementation classes. As a result, the entire implementation could be changed for the next release. Furthermore, clients can be sure that they do not need to understand the internals at all.

Use OSGi to enforce your restrictions.

The standard JVM class loader treats all JARs, packages, and classes on the class path the same: They all belong to a large, global pool of available types. OSGi (Open Services Gateway initiative) is a platform for build-   »A.1
ing modular Java software. The OSGi class loader, in contrast, honors the declaration of *exported packages* from each module's self-description in its `MANIFEST.MF` file. The Java model, for instance, exports the package `org.eclipse.jdt.core`, but not `org.eclipse.jdt.core.internal`. By putting all concrete types into hidden packages, clients cannot even work around the intended barrier by downcasting, because they cannot access the concrete types at all.

Interfaces for decoupling introduce an overhead that needs justification.

The preceding examples have shown not only the power, but also the draw-backs of introducing interfaces for decoupling:

- Clients cannot simply create objects, but must go through factory methods. Besides the notational overhead, clients can never argue about concrete types, but only about abstract behavior.

- Clients cannot subclass to adapt behavior according to their needs.   ↰1.4.11 ↰3.1.7
  This invalidates a major advantage of object-oriented programming.

- In consequence, the developers of the decoupled module must spend   ↰3.1.4 »7.3.3
  more effort to make explicit all possible points of adaptation, usually through notification interfaces (Fig. 3.5). That is, whenever an   »12.3.2
  adaptation point is reached, the client gets a callback to execute
  application-specific code.

This overhead needs to be justified and balanced by corresponding benefits to the concrete architecture: Do clients get simpler because they are shielded from the module's intricacies? Are the expected future changes actually likely to happen, and to the envisaged extent?

》12.3.3

In the case of the Java model, the decision is clear. The Eclipse platform is meant to be extended by many clients through the plugin mechanism. Making the details of one of its core modules public would mean that almost any change to that module would break at least some existing clients. At the same time, the Java model is so complex that subclassing by clients is not likely to be beneficial or even possible anyway.

3.2.8   Tagging Interfaces

The interfaces that an object implements can be determined at runtime using the `instanceof` operator, or the reflection mechanism starting with `getClass()`. It is therefore possible to use them as simple static "tags" attached to objects. For instance, neither `Cloneable` nor `Serializable` declares any methods. Their sole purpose is to act as flags that the generic field-wise object copy and object serialization by `ObjectOutputStream`, respectively, are applicable.

Similarly, empty interfaces can be used as bounds to type variables to introduce compile-time checks. For instance, an `EventListener` (in `java.util`) is an empty interface that ensures that one does not abuse Swing's `EventListenerList` for storing arbitrary objects. The `add` method of that class specifies that only objects tagged as `EventListeners` can be entered:

---
javax.swing.event.EventListenerList

```
public synchronized <T extends EventListener>
            void add(Class<T> t, T l)
```

Similar guards are added at other places in the library.

3.2.9   Management of Constants

↰1.3.8

Interfaces can define not only methods, but also constants. These constants become available in all classes implementing the interface. Mostly, this feature is used in connection with methods, such as to define cases for return or parameter values for these methods. Sometimes, however, the interface is used for the sole purpose of gathering constants. For instance,

▱214

`ColorConstants` from the Graphical Editing Framework provides standard colors; the `IContextMenuConstants` from the Java tooling declares constants that enable other plugins to place menu contributions at specific points; and so on.

3.2.10   Inheritance Versus Interfaces

We have seen established usage of both inheritance and interfaces, and in particular their ability to introduce classifications and abstractions. When you have to decide between the two mechanisms, it is necessary to gain a vantage point from which the differences can be judged and weighed in the particular situation.

Prefer interfaces for capturing and classifying behavior.

Both mechanisms are equally capable of capturing some abstract behavior. While traditionally class hierarchies were intended for this purpose, interfaces have nowadays taken over: They separate strictly behavioral subtyping from implementation issues, thereby avoiding the well-known problems with linking the two. The ability of multiple classification, up to the point of client-specific interfaces, gives you the expressiveness and freedom to differentiate views on an object in detail, without being restricted to a single classification scheme. Finally, the advances in efficient implementation of method dispatch for interfaces, together with the generally available computing power, have invalidated the need to optimize runtime or memory consumption by using single inheritance.

↰3.1.3 ↰3.2.1

▯▯232,162,160
↰3.2.4
↰3.2.2

▯▯3

Prefer class hierarchies if common infrastructure can be created.

The ability to define common functionality, and to enable clients to contribute through template methods, sets inheritance apart from interfaces. When creating such an infrastructure, be sure to obey the Liskov Substitution Principle and to give a well-defined interface toward subclasses. Also, be aware that subclassing is a rather heavyweight task, which often involves understanding the superclass's mechanisms, if not its implementation, in some detail. Sometimes, it is better to move reusable functionality outside the class hierarchy altogether, or even force clients to reimplement some small pieces of code.

↰3.1.4 ↰3.1.3
↰1.4.9
↰3.1.1
↰3.1.2

↰1.4.8 ↰1.8.5

Use inheritance for fixed or limited case distinctions.

The introduction of an interface gives a signal to the human reader: At this point, clients can define their own, often arbitrary behavior and can add it to the system. For case distinctions, this is often not the intention at all. There, new cases cannot be defined freely, but should be tied closely to the existing cases and the common abstraction. This can be expressed by inheritance: Since there is a single inheritance slot, clients cannot "link in" arbitrary implementations, but must fit their contribution into the existing hierarchy.

↰3.1.6

These few and rough guidelines on a very broad topic are certainly insufficient to decide whether to prefer inheritance or interfaces in specific cases. Even so, we hope that they have given you the general directions of the possible alternatives. At the same time, we would like to encourage you to find your own style and strategies: by reconsidering the different aspects in concrete situations you encounter in your daily work, and by studying existing code that you admire or find to be engineered soundly.

Part II

Contracts

Chapter 4

Contracts for Objects

One of the most vital questions in every programmer's life is: Does this code work? If it turns out that the code does not work properly, you're in for lengthy debugging sessions, the team will get irritated with their stalled progress, the boss will complain about ever-increasing backlogs, and customers will become frustrated with the reliability of the product. So how can you convince yourself, your team, your boss, and finally your customers that the code you write does work? And more importantly, how can you be confident that it does not just pass your test cases today, but will keep working tomorrow?

The fundamental problem in this area is that it is not obvious what good arguments for "this code works" really look like. Showing that the code is broken can be done by a single test case with an unexpected result, but how can you argue that your code will pass *any* test case or use case that your team, your boss, or your customers will come up with? In fact, the problem is so non-obvious that computer science has been struggling with it ever since its infancy: starting with the seminal papers by Floyd and Hoare in the late 1960s, through a surge of foundational computer-checked formal proofs in the 1990s, basic studies of heap-manipulating programs in the early 2000s, scalable implementations and the solving of some intricate subproblems in the late 2000s, and industrial applications around and after 2010. Judging from these latest breakthroughs on verifying core components of operating systems, we seem to be in the happy situation that the problem of arguing about the correctness of programs has been understood in all relevant facets.

90,119
110,121,254,253
213,49,176,246,102,103
22,12,79,168,36
188,167,134,230
66,67,153,138

What does all of this mean to practitioners? Depending on their general levels of politeness and honesty, they may call the above work "impressive," "intimidating," "irrelevant," or "formal rubbish." By comparison, Meyer's notion of *design-by-contract* has inspired software engineers and has found its way into everyday jargon: Mailing lists and bug trackers discuss "contracts" and "broken invariants" as a matter of course, and even books on object design naturally cover contracts of methods. In the form of the Java Modeling Language (JML), design-by-contract even progresses beyond practical tool support to formal reasoning.

182,181

263
149,151,150,56

The purpose of this and the following chapters is to provide a practical, self-contained, and understandable view on the question of correctness, always starting from the goal of "making the code work." From the huge amount of work sketched out previously, we will pick those concepts and arguments that do crop up in practical coding, in team meetings, and on mailing lists. Then, we will explain and connect them to create a solid conceptual framework for arguing about whether and why code works.

The material presented has one immediate benefit: Many of the lengthy and more intricate discussions from Part I can now be compressed in a few sentences: The central point of encapsulation is made precise by contracts and model fields. The question of when subjects fire change notifications in the OBSERVER pattern is clear from the idea of class invariants. The Liskov Substitution Principle and behavioral subtyping are contained in the idea of contract inheritance. The new view will therefore make your team's communication more effective, if nothing else. Given that communication has long been recognized as a major bottleneck of software development, the knowledge and understanding of contracts will boost productivity.

As a further point of motivation, you may be surprised to learn that practitioners actually follow the guidelines presented subsequently, especially when things get complicated. Indeed, when preparing the running example for Section 4.1, we found the following comment at the head of Gap TextStore.arrayCopy():

> A length < 0 cannot happen $\rightarrow$ don't hide coding errors by checking for negative lengths.

The statement "length ≥ 0" is an "assertion," as introduced later in this chapter, and obviously the developers assumed it would always hold, so that they can simplify their code. In fact, the goal not to "hide coding errors" refers forward to the "non-redundancy principle" in Section 4.5: The method just goes ahead and accepts that maybe an exception is thrown to alert the caller to a mistake.

In the presentation, we will omit all formal details and definitions, but we will never lie or cheat. If after following and applying the material of this chapter you have become keen to know more about the formal questions behind it, you can read up and fit in those parts that we have left out. You will not have to rearrange or even unlearn ideas. The presentation merely takes a few "skips" beyond details that are formally relevant, but "obvious" to the practitioner. The final section of this chapter, Section 4.7, gives you a taste of these additional details, just as an appetizer.

4.1   The Core: Assertions Plus Encapsulation

This core section, according to its purpose in the book, faces the daunting task of giving a guided tour of 50 years of computer science research in a few pages, while translating formal arguments into everyday insights. We solve this by introducing only the core concepts and their connections, while deferring discussions to the subsequent sections. Also, to avoid a formalistic style and to maintain the idea of a guided tour, we present the material in the form of a continuous narrative, in which we relive the discoveries of others in a running example.

Development practice knows many ways of arguing about whether some piece of code works: write a test case, start the debugger, execute the code mentally, compare it to code seen elsewhere, say that it combines a few well-tested steps in an obvious manner, and many more. However, none of these methods works all the time or is even practical for every piece of code: You cannot possibly understand a program of 50,000 lines by tracing it with the debugger, nor can you imitate or combine existing solutions in all situations.

To arrive at a solid framework for reasoning about code, let us assume that we have to convince a colleague—perhaps you even know such a person—who does not believe a single thing you say, except when confronted with really undeniable facts. We will start our quest by anticipating that nasty colleague's questions and will devise unimpeachable answers.

As a running example, we look again at Eclipse's `GapTextStore`, which ◄1.3.1 we considered earlier in the section on an object's data structures. To recap, a `GapTextStore` supports the modifications of text required by editors efficiently. For space-efficiency, the data is kept in a flat array of characters. For efficient modifications, that array contains a "gap," which does not contain actual data but is left open to receive additions and removals (see the following diagram, which replicates Fig. 1.2). For a modification, the gap is moved to the editing location, then the gap start is adapted to insert or delete characters. The main trick is that editing is a local activity, and moving the gap touches only the characters between the old location and the new location.

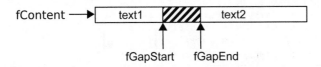

> Become wary about what you think you know about your code.

The purpose of our "conversational" approach to correctness is that it suggests a certain attitude toward code: To write correct code, it is necessary to start questioning the assumptions you are making and to argue that they do hold true. You will certainly have found yourself thinking about questions like the following: Why is this particular variable non-null? Why is that number always greater than 0? Why is this collection always non-empty? You will also have discovered, in debugging sessions, some such questions that you had not thought about. A main contribution of the conceptual framework established by computer science is that it leads up to finding *all* relevant questions systematically.

Suppose, then, that *you* have written the class `GapTextStore` and your disbelieving colleague has to use it. He comes up with a JUnit test case ▶5.4.9

and is annoyed to find that the object *does* meet his expectations (`set` initializes the gap store, `replace` combines a deletion with an insertion):

gapstore.GapTextStoreTest.inserting

```
1 store = new GapTextStore();
2 store.set("Hello, world");
3 store.replace(7, 0, "wonderful ");
4 String res = store.get(0, store.getLength());
5 assertEquals("Hello, wonderful world", res);
```

However, he wants to know whether he can rely on this behavior. You explain patiently what your class does. You may first say, in the manner of mental execution:

> The gap store really just maintains a string. So when you place "Hello, world" into the store in line 2, that string becomes the store's entire content. Unlike usual strings, you can modify the store: In line 3, you splice in "wonderful" at character position 7 (deleting 0 characters)—let's see—just before the "w." Naturally, you get "Hello, wonderful world." What is it you do not understand?

But, of course, your colleague really wanted to know whether this works *in general*, as shown in the following test. Also, he wanted to know how the thing *works*, not just the result.

gapstore.GapTextStoreTest.insertGeneral

```
1 store = new GapTextStore();
2 store.set(initial);
3 store.replace(pos, 0, insert);
4 String res = store.get(0, store.getLength());
5 String expectedResult = initial.substring(0, pos) + insert
6      + initial.substring(pos);
7 assertEquals(expectedResult, res);
```

Now the argument becomes a bit more involved, since you have to talk about arbitrary texts and positions, and you also have to connect the explanation to your data structures. So, drawing Fig. 4.1 on the whiteboard, you continue:[1]

> The nifty idea of the gap store is that it keeps the text in an array, but always leaves a "gap" into which new text can be inserted efficiently. Initially, after line 1, the gap fills the entire array. When storing the `initial` string in line 2, its characters are written to the beginning of the gap. So you see that the current content, as seen from the outside, is the array except

---

1. If you are of a disbelieving disposition yourself, which is good for a dependable developer, you may start looking at the original code now. You will find that several points in the subsequent presentation are slightly simplified. Even so, the omitted details do not invalidate our arguments.

for the shaded gap area. Line 3 now shows the heart of the gap store: Whenever a modification takes place, the gap is moved to the desired position, in this case `pos`. In this way, the new characters of `insert` can be placed into the gap, as I said before.

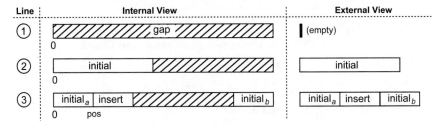

Figure 4.1 Tracing an Argument About `GapTextStore`

Your colleague now seems satisfied that you know what you are doing. He resolves to look at the code some more, but soon gets giddy with all the indices he finds there. So he comes back asking:

> Do I really *have* to know about those details you explained?

Having read Chapter 1, your answer is, of course:

> No, all of those are encapsulated. You need to understand only the external view.

At this point, let us leave the fictional conversation for the moment and consider which arguments have been used.

Contracts establish a consistent external view on an object's behavior.

The key point that we will pursue is that contracts save time and effort in software construction, because they enable developers to work with objects that they have not created themselves and do not understand in detail. For this to work out, the objects must be written to allow for consistent arguments using the external view only.

↰1.1

≫11.5.1

Let us then continue the explanation of `GapTextStore`. We must find an external view for the internal steps in Fig. 4.1, such that the external view remains in lockstep with the internal one. To explain the connection, we might say to the colleague, "So you see that the current content, as seen from the outside, is the array except for the shaded gap area." To be able to continue in a precise manner, let us add the actual field names to the internal view, as shown in Fig. 4.2. Since the external view is "really just a string," we describe that string by giving some of its properties in Fig. 4.3 [using notation $a[i..j]$ to denote the array slice from i (inclusive) to j (exclusive)]: The content consists of the non-gap parts of the array `fContent`, the length is just the number of characters in those parts, and a single character can be picked by case distinction. You should convince yourself that the overview is correct by comparing these descriptions with Figs. 4.2 and 4.1.

fContent | text1 | | text2 |
0   fGapStart   fGapEnd   fContent.length

Figure 4.2 Data Structure of a `GapTextStore` Object

External View	Internal View
content	`fContent[0..fGapStart]` `    + fContent[fGapEnd..fContent.length]`
length	`fContent.length - (fGapEnd-fGapStart)`
charAt(*p*)	`p < fGapStart ? fContent[p]` `    : fContent[fGapEnd + (p - fGapStart)]`

Figure 4.3 External and Internal Views of the `GapTextStore`

The external and internal views given in this way really offer different perspectives on the object's state. The internal one is phrased in terms of the object's actual fields, while the external one cannot be cast in these terms, because we wish to hide these internals.

Model fields present an external view onto an object's state.

📖155,154,62,188 ▶4.2.1 *Model fields* are a description of the object's state that does not give away the internals and conforms to the clients' understanding of the object's purpose. To find suitable model fields, just observe the terms you use to describe the object to someone else: You want the person to understand the object, so you invent summary "data" that explains the object's state closely enough.

Model fields are therefore essential for achieving encapsulation: They enable us to argue about an object's state without disclosing its actual fields and data structures. Without them, it would not be useful to hide an object's internals through language-level mechanisms, because a client would have to know them anyway. Model fields enable us to ban an object's

↰1.1 technical details from our discussions entirely and to create truly black-box objects.

↰1.3.3 The object's properties (i.e., those fields with getters and setters) are special: They are publicly visible through the accessors, so they are model fields; at the same time, they correspond one-to-one to implementation fields. In the gap store example, we could, for instance, formulate the post-condition of `getLength()` as follows (`\return` is the return value, as would be expected; the backslash serves as an escape symbol to identify JML keywords):

$$\verb|\return| = \mathrm{length} \tag{4.1}$$

Assertions describe snapshots of the program's state during execution.

Now that we can talk safely about an object's state, what do we say? Looking back at the argument, and in particular Fig. 4.3, it would seem that a good strategy is to point at specific lines in the code and to describe what the object, or the program's state in general, looks like at that point. This is, indeed, the fundamental idea behind software verification, as introduced by Hoare in 1969: An *assertion* is a statement about the program's state that holds at a particular point in the code whenever that point is reached during execution. For our purposes, the assertion can be formulated in precise English or pseudo-code Boolean expressions, but the approach can be refined to allow formulas as assertions and mathematical proofs to verify that they always hold (see Section 4.7 for a glimpse at this).

□119

Let us clarify this at the example. The previous lengthy explanation mentioning the different line numbers can be transformed into an assertion-style explanation by putting the assertions into comments. In line 2, we know that the gap store is empty; lines 4 and 6 trace the intermediate steps as before; line 9 captures the final outcome that we have derived by reasoning. Lines 10–12 then test our expectation: We recompute the expected result on strings, without using the gap store, and then compare it to the actual result using `assertEquals` from JUnit. That test will throw an exception if the expectation is violated.

»5.1

↰1.5.4 »4.5

---

gapstore.GapTextStoreTest.insertGeneral

```
1 store = new GapTextStore();
2 // store.content = ""
3 store.set(initial);
4 // store.content = initial
5 store.replace(pos, 0, insert);
6 // store.content = initial.substring(0,pos) + insert
7 //      + initial.substring(pos)
8 String res = store.get(0, store.getLength());
9 // res = store.content
10 String expectedResult = initial.substring(0, pos) + insert
11      + initial.substring(pos);
12 assertEquals(expectedResult, res);
```

⌕ One question that often arises on the first encounter with assertions is whether they include types. A purist would say that the type of some data item or object must, of course, be talked about when considering software correctness, because the type influences the behavior. The practitioner will, however, not bother with stating the obvious. In the following declarations, both `length` and `history` have declared types that match the types of their runtime content exactly. It would be redundant to point this out in an assertion. For `purchases`, one knows more about the actual object than is given by the type, and one might state an assertion `purchases` **instanceof** `ArrayList`.

```
private int length;
private ArrayList<Integer> history = new ArrayList<Integer>();
private List<ProductOrder> purchases =
                            new ArrayList<ProductOrder>();
```

↰3.1.9
⟫4.7.3

In particular, assertions about types are necessary to argue that a downcast will not fail. A typical situation is shown by the following `if` statement, where the test yields just the additional knowledge that guarantees the success of the downcast:

```
if (obj instanceof Integer) {
    Integer value = (Integer)obj;
    ... work with value
}
```

We would therefore propose to include type information into assertions only if the static and dynamic types differ and if that difference ever becomes important for the correctness arguments.

Assertions are conceptual breakpoints.

From a practical perspective, assertions can be understood as breakpoints that you set mentally inside the code. Each imaginary "stop" at an assertion would check whether the statement you have made is actually true.

Although we can now write down what we *think* we know about our program, we cannot yet argue that it actually *does* hold. In particular, we will have to describe what each method call in the test does to the gap store's state.

Contracts capture the behavior of objects.

The description of an object's state through model fields must be complemented by descriptions of its methods to answer this question: How do method calls modify the object's state? The crucial point of *design-by-contract* is that this goal is best accomplished by associating with each method a pair of special assertions:

📖182

- The *pre-condition* must hold at the beginning of the method, after the parameters have been set and just before the body starts executing.

- The *post-condition* must hold at the end of the method, after the return value (if any) has been computed and just before execution returns to the caller.

📖151

The post-condition may refer to the current state as usual and additionally to the pre-state, where the pre-condition holds, via `\old` (again using the backslash as an escape symbol). Also, it can access the return value as `\return`.

If assertions are like breakpoints, then pre- and post-conditions are like function breakpoints (Fig. 4.4): They are hit whenever execution enters or leaves a method, and at those points you can examine and describe the state.

The pre- and post-conditions together are also called the method's *contract*. The contracts of all methods together are the *class's contract*.

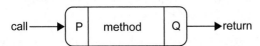

Figure 4.4 Illustration of a Method's Contract

Let us try this idea immediately on the example. The main method is `replace(pos,del,ins)`. The API documentation says that it "replaces the specified character range with the given text." The pre-condition states what must hold when the method starts executing. Here, the "character range" must be within the existing content; otherwise, the deletion operation does not make sense. In the form of a Boolean expression:

$$0 \leq \text{pos} \leq \text{content.length} \; \&\& \; \text{del} \geq 0 \; \&\& \; \text{pos} + \text{del} \leq \text{content.length} \quad (4.2)$$

The post-condition states what the method achieves, or what it leaves behind for the caller to work with. In the example, the replacement acts on the `content` of the gap store. The post-condition of `replace` then specifies the new content:

$$\text{content} = \backslash\text{old}(\text{content.substring}(0, \text{pos})) +$$
$$\backslash\text{old}(\text{ins}) + \backslash\text{old}(\text{content.substring}(\text{pos} + \text{del}))$$

🔎 We have to use pre-state $\backslash\text{old}(\text{ins})$, because in principle the method may have modified the parameter during execution. A post-condition that is stated in terms of the initial values of the parameters then gives a direct functional dependency from the outcome on the input—just as one would expect for a function-like construct such as a method.

With this new knowledge, we can actually *deduce* that the assertion in line 12 of the example holds, assuming that the assertion in line 4 holds and `pos` is within `initial`. This, in turn, can be derived from the post-condition of `set(text)`. That method, according to the API, "replace[s] the content of the text store with the given text." Its pre-condition is `true` (i.e., it can always be called with any `text` as a parameter), and its post-condition is

$$\text{content} = \backslash\text{old}(\text{text})$$

Great! So the assertion in line 4 also holds by deduction, and this time without checking anything else.

The theme of pre- and post-conditions has actually been explored in the literature in many different contexts and from many different perspectives. Let us briefly look at these definitions, because each new perspective offers a fresh angle for comprehension. Also, it connects your understanding to that of colleagues you might be talking to.

If the pre-condition holds when the method is called, the post-condition must hold when it finishes.

This view makes explicit a central logical dependency: Since we assume that the pre-condition holds at each method call, the method's body can work under the assumption that it holds *regardless of the actual call site*—it is possible to deduce the method's post-condition once and for all.

Garbage in, garbage out.

This is a popular negation of the previous view: If the pre-condition does *not* hold, we will not know anything about the post-condition—it might or might not hold, and the result can even be arbitrary "garbage."

The slogan's sloppy formulation also clarifies in an intuitive way that a method's developer cannot be blamed if the method is used outside its contract. For instance, if the skeptical colleague demands that "Appending should work in my test case!" you can simply reply by saying, "Garbage in, garbage out."

gapstore.GapTextStoreTest.insertTooFarRight

```
store.set("Hello, world");
store.replace(13, 0, "!");
```

The caller is responsible for ensuring the method's pre-condition, and the method is responsible for ensuring its post-condition under the assumption that the pre-condition holds.

Clearly, if the pre-condition is to hold before the method starts, then only the caller can provide the necessary argument. Conversely, only the method can argue that the post-condition holds based on the knowledge of its internal algorithm.

📖182
↰1.4.3
This view is, in fact, Meyer's original proposal, which has made contracts popular with a wider community: It points out the link of methods as service providers to real-world service providers. For instance, to buy a pizza from a delivery service, you have to choose a pizza that is on the menu, state your address clearly and correctly, and pay the bill to the driver. This is the pre-condition for using the service. Once it is established, the driver hands over the pizza in a moderately hot state; the post-condition is "you have got the pizza you ordered." In software engineering, the formulation

divides the responsibility for the proper working of the code fairly between the developer of a method and the developer invoking the method.

Despite its widespread use in the literature, this original formulation still does not quite link to everyday arguments used by developers. We would offer the following alternative:

> The pre-condition states when the method may be legally called; the post-condition states what it achieves.

This very high-level view explains contracts in terms of the method's purpose and also relates to the immediate questions of the caller: Can I call the method? And if so, what do I gain by calling it? The first is, of course, the same as asking for the caller's responsibility; the second rephrases the method's responsibility from an after-the-fact perspective: What has the method done for me when it finishes?

In summary, we have seen how the working of methods can be described and specified based on assertions, which capture the program state at specific points. In particular, we have seen that pre- and post-conditions act as contracts between caller and callee, and that they enable the caller to reason about an object's behavior without knowing its internal details.

> Contracts alone are insufficient for detailed reasoning.

We have not, however, discussed sufficiently how the method's developer can argue that he can guarantee the post-condition after execution. The central open question is this: When the method starts executing, how can the developer know that the object's internal fields are in proper working order? The model fields cover only the externally visible aspects—not the internal data structures.

For instance, the following method extracts a range of text into a string. How do we know that the case distinctions in lines 2 and 5 make sense? Can we be sure that fContent is not null, so that lines 3, 6, and 8–9 run through without a NullPointerException?

org.eclipse.jface.text.GapTextStore

```
1  public String get(int offset, int length) {
2      if (fGapStart <= offset)
3          return new String(fContent, offset + gapSize(), length);
4      int end = offset + length;
5      if (end <= fGapStart)
6          return new String(fContent, offset, length);
7      StringBuffer buf = new StringBuffer(length);
8      buf.append(fContent, offset, fGapStart - offset);
9      buf.append(fContent, fGapEnd, end - fGapStart);
10     return buf.toString();
11 }
```

To keep track of such internals, we have to complement the pre-condition by a statement about the object's fields. This assertion is called the *class invariant*.

Class invariants capture the consistency of objects.

So what does the method `get` have to know about the `this` object? Certainly that `fContent` is not `null` and that `fGapStart` and `fGapEnd` lie within that array, since otherwise lines 3, 6, and 8–9 will yield invalid character ranges—that is, character ranges that are not allowed by the pre-conditions of the `String` constructor and `append`, respectively. An object is "consistent" if it meets these basic criteria, if the statement you rely on holds "at all times" (well, almost, as we shall see). Incidentally, the term "invariant" relates precisely to this idea of not changing, of being invariably true. But where does this reasoning take us?

The invariant captures the intuitive understanding of a "proper object."

The reasoning takes us precisely to Fig. 4.2, which really just depicts a "normal" gap store's internal state. Let us repeat the figure here for convenience:

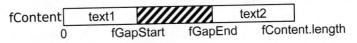

Of course, a picture is rather imprecise and open to interpretation. Fortunately, we can also write the invariant down as an assertion based on the picture—it should not be a great surprise that it is really what we have written up in English before:

$$\text{fContent} \neq \texttt{null} \ \&\& \ 0 \leq \text{fGapStart} \leq \text{fGapEnd} \leq \text{fContent.length}$$

The code of `get` makes sense if you relate it to these insights: Lines 2–6 treat the special cases in which the requested range is entirely to the left or to the right of the gap, and lines 7–9 treat ranges overlapping the gap.

You are already working with invariants all the time.

Invariants are not mysterious or incomprehensible. All experienced developers have a very good idea of the internal structure of their objects—otherwise, they would never get their code to run. The following, more everyday views on "invariants" might help you link the terminology to your own style of argumentation—whenever you find yourself thinking along these lines, start to formulate an invariant that is as precise as possible, in whatever form you find suitable and are comfortable with.

- My object internally *looks like this.*

- The object is *OK* now.

- The object is *usable.*

- Of course, *I always know* that ...

- This field *cannot contain / always contains* ...

- *This should not be the case!*

- This field is *always greater than* that field.

Fig. 4.5 depicts another useful intuition that might link to your development experience. While you "work with an object," you somehow "open up" the object, or you penetrate its encapsulation boundary, to get to the object's internals. When you are done, you "close" the object, at which point it becomes "whole" again. This intuition has the further attraction that it can be grounded in a solid formalization.

↰1.1

↠4.4

▥21

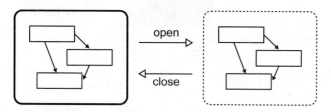

Figure 4.5 Intuition of Class Invariants

Writing down or drawing the invariant is, of course, an effort, but one that is certainly worthwhile: You can leave a note, to yourself or to others, of how an object's fields are interrelated and what their individual purposes are.

There is one question about invariants that has led to some controversy: When does that assertion actually hold? The term "invariant" itself suggests that it is true all the time, but this is, of course, nonsensical: The gap store's code will at some point allocate the array fContent, but will set fGapStart and fGapEnd only a few statements later; or it proceeds the other way around. For the duration of those few statements, then, the invariant does *not* hold—the diagram is "broken." So when does the invariant hold?

Over the years, many methodologies have been proposed to delineate precisely those times at which the class invariant must be shown to hold. Rather than follow these historical detours, let us start with a single general statement that comprises them all:

↠4.4

The class invariant holds for every instance whenever no code of the class runs.

This statement is so general that it might be hard to comprehend at first. Let us start from a practical perspective. As a developer, you will know that feeling of unease when working for a short time "against" the diagram of a "proper object" you have in your mind. Subconsciously, you start tracking what needs to be done to "repair" the object. When you have the diagram on paper, you will be retargeting references, moving index pointers, and so on. The point is always this: When your current code finishes working and your class yields control to something else, then the object must again be "in good shape." In other words, the invariant may be broken only as long as your own class is in control, as long as its code keeps running and can repair any damages before someone notices.

Another way of looking at the situation is by analogy. You will have seen the following label attached to critical doors in public buildings. Of course, "at all times" implicitly includes the qualification "except when someone is operating the door to pass through."

It is worth looking at other definitions, because they characterize special and common situations, even if they do not tell the whole story. Perhaps the most popular characterization of when the class invariant must hold is this one:

181

> Every public method can assume the invariant at the start and must establish it in the end.

The relation to our own formulation is clear: Whenever execution enters a `public` method, it potentially has come from the outside, so the invariant does hold. Whenever a `public` method returns, it potentially leaves the class's code, so the method should better leave the object intact. This guideline is very useful, as it establishes a warning bell inside the developers' minds: Before leaving the public method, the object must be put "in order."

Another benefit of this formulation is the clear link to an object's life cycle (Fig. 4.6). Throughout the life cycle, methods get called and return. At each entry, they assume that the invariant holds and they keep it intact when they finish execution. In this way, the next method call can always assume the invariant does, indeed, hold.

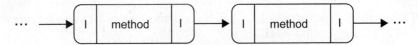

Figure 4.6 Invariants and Public Methods

Class invariants do not belong to the class's contract.

Finally, we wish to make explicit that although invariants belong to the conceptual framework of design-by-contract, they do *not* belong to a class's contract (which is the collection of all method contracts) since they deal solely with the internal view of the object. If anything, they are a contract of the class's developers with themselves (Fig. 4.6): They promise to themselves to keep the object in good shape, for the next time that a method should be invoked and the object's machinery kicks in.

📖182

Public invariants relate the model fields from a client's perspective.

There is, however, a second kind of invariant that does belong to the class's contract: *public invariants* (or *type invariants*), which describe consistency conditions on the client-visible, published state of an object. For instance, the model fields of a gap store in Fig. 4.3 obey the following constraint:

📖151(§3.3)

$$length = content.length$$

This published constraint then allows us to argue about the following method `appendGeneral()`, which is supposed to add the given string to the end of the gap store. The post-condition (4.1) of `getLength()` is phrased in terms of the model field `length`, while the pre-condition (4.2) of `replace` uses `content.length` instead, because this is more natural for a method modifying `content`. Without the public invariant, we could not deduce that the call to `replace` is legal.

```
public void appendGeneral(String txt) {
    store.replace(store.getLength(), 0, txt);
}
```

4.2 Elaborating the Concepts by Example

The previous section has introduced the core concepts of design-by-contract and of mainstream correctness arguments about code. The remainder of this chapter is dedicated to increasing the level of detail and to exploring some of the implications and ramifications of those concepts.

Despite its relative simplicity, the example of `GapTextStore` is too complex for this purpose. We therefore discuss a special iterator over an array instead. The task of the `ThresholdArrayIterator` is simple: Implement the `Iterator` interface for walking an array of `int`s, but return only elements that are no greater than a given threshold.

The code is brief and straightforward (Fig. 4.7). The general idea is that `a` is the input array, `threshold` is the given threshold, and `i` is somehow the current index. The constructor initializes everything, then `hasNext()`

and `next()` behave as specified in the `Iterator` interface. The main work happens in `findNext()`, which advances `i` and checks elements against the threshold on the way. But how do we know that the code works?

```java
public class ThresholdArrayIterator implements Iterator<Integer> {
    private int a[];
    private int i;
    private int threshold;
    public ThresholdArrayIterator(int [] a, int threshold) {
        // avoid side effects from outside
        this.a = Arrays.copyOf(a, a.length);          this.i = 0;
        this.threshold = threshold;
        findNext();
    }
    public boolean hasNext() {
        return i != a.length;
    }
    public Integer next() {
        Integer tmp = a[i];
        i++;
        findNext();
        return tmp;
    }
    private void findNext() {
        while (i != a.length) {
            if (a[i] <= threshold)
                break;
            else
                i++;
        }
    }
    public void remove() {
        throw new UnsupportedOperationException();
    }
}
```

Figure 4.7 An Iterator over Arrays

This section analyzes the necessary reasoning in detail. Before we proceed, here is a sketch of the overall contract we are aiming for. Since the iterator works on a sequence of elements, we capture an external view on its state by two model fields `seq` and `pos`. The field `seq` contains the elements returned by the `next()` method. It is an array, so that `seq.length` gives its length. The second model field `pos` is the iterator's current position within `seq`. Using these model fields, the contract of `hasNext()` is straightforward: It can be called at any time and checks whether the iterator has reached the end of the sequence.

$$Pre: \quad \texttt{true}$$
$$Post: \quad \texttt{\textbackslash return} = (pos \neq \texttt{seq.length})$$

The contract of next() also captures the intuitive behavior: It can be called as long as more elements remain, returns the current element, and advances the current position.

$Pre:$ pos $\neq$ seq.length
$Post:$ \return = seq[\old(pos)] && pos = \old(pos) + 1

This overview leaves many points to be considered: What exactly are the elements of seq in the case of a ThresholdArrayIterator? How are the model fields related to the object's concrete fields? What is the purpose of the constructor? And how are the public contracts related to the methods' actual code? These and many more questions will be explored now, including the question of how we have arrived at these contracts.

4.2.1 Invariants and Model Fields

We start by capturing the general setup of the class. The developer has, unfortunately, blundered a bit on the naming in the example class: i as a field name is too short and too generic to convey its meaning and purpose. It appears to be an index into the array a, but which one exactly? Furthermore, we need to state precisely which elements the iterator returns without looking into its internals. Both questions are relevant to understanding the class: The first question relates to the internal class invariant, the second to its external state description by model fields. As we shall see, the two are intertwined, because they are just two perspectives on the same thing: the object's state. Let us start with the class invariant: What does the developer know about an iterator object? Fig. 4.8 captures the essence (note that the class invariant is private and can therefore access the object's internals):

↰1.2.3

↰4.1

↰4.1

The index i references the next element to be returned by next().

This idea is supported by the code of next(), which just returns the element at index i. The traversal by findNext() will skip elements that are greater than the given threshold. This reasoning suggests that field i should be renamed to nextElement. As we will see later, it would be even better to call it currentElement, because it is the element that the iterator is currently positioned at.

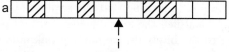

White elements are below the threshold; shaded elements are skipped.

Figure 4.8 Invariant of the ThresholdArrayIterator

The earlier statement about i is certainly understandable to developers, but it is not a proper assertion, and therefore not a proper class invariant.

Specifically, the meaning of "next" points to some *future* action, while assertions can talk about only the *current* state at the point when they are encountered.

Find formulations for assertions that talk about only the current state.

This restriction on assertions is perhaps the biggest challenge when first applying design-by-contract: Developers are so used to talking about the past and future execution of their program that they usually feel constrained when they can talk about only the present. The mental exercise to be practiced is this: Do execute the program in your head, but when you look at an assertion, detach yourself from the execution, interrupt the mental debugger, and talk about only what you know right now. Practicing this ability is really worthwhile. Indeed, once you get the knack of it, all those longish explanations about why and when you got to the current point in the execution can be cleared away. Your team's discussions will become much more focused and more precise.

◄1.4.1 ◄1.1 ►11.1

Another motivation for practicing this mindset is its connection to the fundamentally object-oriented perception of objects as entities that communicate by sending messages to each other: When an object receives a message, it reacts appropriately, but one disregards the sender or the sequence of messages. One thinks about the reception of a message and the subsequent reaction as an isolated occurrence, up to the point where messages are sent asynchronously, and the delivery occurs at some undetermined later point in time.

►8.4

To get back to the example, the point "now" for class invariants is really any point where no code of the class runs. How can we get rid of the term "next," with its implicit reference to a later call to next()? The essential insight here is that the "next element" really relates to the *outside* view, so that it cannot be captured by internal considerations alone. We first have to introduce suitable model fields.

Model fields provide a strong handle on the class's purpose.

From the clients' perspective, the iterator is always a specific position pos within the imaginary sequence seq formed by those elements from a that are no greater than threshold. As with usual arrays, the iterator can also be at position seq.length, indicating that the sequence has been exhausted. So we have already identified the model fields: seq and pos.

To relate them to the internals, we have to talk about "those elements in a up to some index j (exclusive) that are no greater than threshold." Since this phrase is rather unwieldy, let us introduce the notation $a_{\leq}[\ldots j]$ for the (imaginary) array containing these elements. Then, we can define the model fields precisely: seq encompasses all such elements—it spans the entire array; pos is the number of such elements that have already been traversed.

$$\mathtt{seq} := \mathtt{a}_{\leq}[\ldots \mathtt{a.length}] \tag{4.3}$$

$$\mathtt{pos} := \mathtt{a}_{\leq}[\ldots \mathtt{i}].\mathtt{length} \tag{4.4}$$

With these definitions, we have achieved the goal of eliminating the term "next" from the proposed invariant, by giving the meaning of i in the definition of pos: i is given as the *representation of* the element in the result sequence that the iterator is *currently* pointing to. Even the special case pos = seq.length is included in the representation as i = a.length.

Invariants usually include safety conditions.

For this scheme to work properly, however, we must make sure that i never stops at an element that is greater than the threshold; otherwise, the same position pos would be represented by different values of i. The term "never" indicates a consistency condition on the object, so we formulate the following class invariant. We also note in passing that, as a safety condition, i never leaves a (except at the one-past-the-end position).

$$0 \leq \mathtt{i} \leq \mathtt{a.length} \ \&\& \ (\mathtt{i} = \mathtt{a.length} \ || \ \mathtt{a[i]} \leq \mathtt{threshold}) \tag{4.5}$$

It is interesting to note that this invariant is really just what a developer would answer, after some thought, to the following questions by a disbelieving colleague: "What do you mean by 'i never leaves a'?" "Are you sure that next() will always return an element no greater than threshold?" "How do you know when you have hit the end?"

Model fields capture the abstraction implemented by the class.

Note that both model fields are wholly imaginary. In fact, defining the model fields well is a big step toward giving a useful outside view on the object, and therefore toward defining a useful API. In essence, we have postulated in the beginning that the clients' view should dominate an object's purpose and definition, and model fields are one essential ingredient to that view, since they capture the central aspects of the object's state.

↰1.1 ↰1.4.3 ↰1.8.2

4.2.2 Contracts in Terms of Model Fields

If the model fields capture a client's view on the object's state, then the method contracts capture the client's view of its behavior. The example has only two public methods that need to be described: next() and hasNext(). We will now discuss their contracts in some detail.

Phrase contracts in terms of public knowledge and model fields.

The purpose of contracts is to inform clients about what methods expect and what they guarantee in return. A necessary prerequisite is, of course, that clients can understand the contracts. Meyer calls this requirement the *pre-condition availability principle*: Contracts must not refer to the class's internals, but only to publicly available information such as model fields and public invariants.

  Let us start with the simpler method `hasNext()`, which does not modify the iterator's state. Here is the code again for convenience:

thresholditer.ThresholdArrayIterator

```
public boolean hasNext() {
    return i != a.length;
}
```

The pre-condition states under which circumstance the method may be called. According to the interface `Iterator`, clients may call the method at any time, so the pre-condition is `true`. The post-condition just describes the outcome of the test, but we cannot simply write

$$\texttt{\textbackslash return} = (\texttt{i} \neq \texttt{a.length})$$

because that would refer to the class's internals that the caller does not understand. Fortunately, `i` is closely related to the model field `pos` by (4.4), so that `i = a.length` is just the same as `pos = seq.length`, given that the invariant (4.5) forbids that `i` ever stops at an element not in the output sequence. All in all, we can simply state the post-condition of `hasNext()` as

$$\texttt{\textbackslash return} = (\texttt{pos} \neq \texttt{seq.length}) \tag{4.6}$$

  Again, let us relate this to the API documentation, which says: "Returns `true` if the iteration has more elements." Our check (4.6) expresses just this condition: The imaginary current result position still points to some element in the imaginary result sequence.

A contract must make sense from the method's purpose.

So far, we have used a syntactic meaning of "understanding": All fields mentioned in contracts must be public. However, "understanding" should also encompass the deeper meaning of "insight": When a method's pre-condition states a requirement that can be justified only by looking at its internals, nothing is gained—clients cannot know why the requirement is necessary and will be likely to overlook it. Also, they are likely to stop using the method altogether. Meyer therefore postulates the *reasonable pre-condition principle*: The contract of a method must be justifiable from the method's and class's purpose, without looking at their implementation.

The method `next()` is supposed to perform two things: (1) It returns the current element and (2) it advances the current position as a side effect. Fortunately, the contract can express this directly in terms of the introduced model fields: The post-condition (4.7) just states that the "next element" is returned, and that the field `pos` is incremented from its old value.   ↰4.1

$$\backslash\text{return} = \text{seq}[\backslash\text{old}(\text{pos})] \text{ \&\& pos} = \backslash\text{old}(\text{pos}) + 1 \qquad (4.7)$$

Just for illustration, let us translate this back to English (from left to right), by spelling out the meaning of the model fields: The return value is the next element in the output sequence (as it was found before the call), and the iterator is advanced to the next element (or to the end of the sequence, if no more elements remain).

Finding the pre-condition is at first not straightforward. The API documentation states "Returns the next element in the iteration," without mentioning any condition at all. However, it also states that the method throws a "NoSuchElementException if the iteration has no more elements." So   ↰1.5.4 ⇥4.5 ⇥6.3 the pre-condition really is that we have not yet reached the end:

$$\text{pos} \neq \text{seq.length} \qquad (4.8)$$

This pre-condition certainly is reasonable in the previously mentioned sense, because it can be understood from the idea that the iterator might have reached the end of the sequence so that no more elements can be extracted.

Another interesting thing about the contracts of the two methods is that they justify precisely the idiomatic loop for using an iterator:

```
1 ThresholdArrayIterator iter =
2     new ThresholdArrayIterator(data, threshold);
3 while (iter.hasNext()) {
4     Integer cur = iter.next();
5     // work with the element
6 }
```

The test in line 3 according to (4.6) allows the loop body to execute only if `pos` $\neq$ `seq.length`, but this is precisely the necessary pre-condition (4.8) for calling `next()` in line 4. Without knowing anything internal about our very special iterator, we can conclude that the code will work!

4.2.3 Contracts, Invariants, and Processing Steps

So far, we have written up contracts of methods by considering their purpose and expected behavior. This is, indeed, the way it should be done, since the clients' requirements are the best guide toward defining a useful API. Now   ↰1.1 it is time to consider the implementation of the iterator's methods. From the overall code in Fig. 4.7 it is clear that the logic is not very involved, yet a reusable processing step `findNext()` has been introduced to arrive at a   ↰1.4.5 ↰1.4.8 truly concise implementation.

This method is especially interesting in the present context, because we have actually found it when pondering how to maintain the invariant (4.5): At the core of the implementation, the index i must always point to a valid output element, or one past the end of the entire sequence. Whenever i accidentally points to an element of a that is too large, i must be advanced until "everything is again in order"—but "being in order" simply means that the invariant holds. So, let us look at the method in some more detail.

↰4.1

Non-public methods do not implicitly assume or guarantee the invariant.

Because public methods are the entry and exit points to the class's code, they implicitly assume that the invariant holds at their beginning and must guarantee that it holds in the end. In contrast, private and protected methods, as well as package-visible ones, are considered to be part of the implementation and to "look inside" the objects they are working on. Very often, they perform only a small step in a larger operation, so they may break the invariant and leave it to others to fix the invariant later on.

↰4.1

↰1.4.5 ↰1.4.8 ↰1.7

---

thresholditer. ThresholdArrayIterator

```
1 private void findNext() {
2     while (i != a.length) {
3         if (a[i] <= threshold)
4             break;
5         else
6             i++;
7     }
8 }
```

The purpose of findNext(), for example, is to skip elements not part of the result sequence seq, so as to reach the invariant (4.5). But what is the pre-condition of findNext()? Under which circumstance can it fulfill its task? From looking at the code, we must have (4.9): The first part ensures that lines 2 and 3 do not throw throw a NullPointerException, while the other part avoids an ArrayIndexOutOfBoundsException in line 3.

$$a \neq \text{null} \;\&\&\; 0 \leq i \;\&\&\; i \leq a.\text{length} \tag{4.9}$$

Of course, the latter two conditions derive from the invariant (4.5), as long as that part of the invariant does not get broken before the call—we will look into that presently. However, the first part is problematic, since it is not part of the invariant stated in Section 4.2.1. How can we deduce it?

It is normal to find invariants only with hindsight—document them!

The answer is that we cannot, because that condition is simply missing from the invariant. We deliberately omitted it earlier, because we felt that this textbook should guide you through the normal course of development, not through an artificial setup where the author has divined every detail by clairvoyance. It is usual to find during debugging that you have failed to identify an invariant and that you have consequently broken it at some point. Since this case is so common, you should make it a habit to document precisely those elusive, nonobvious details, because it will save the maintenance programmer from falling into the same trap. So, let us amend the invariant by adding the further condition:

$$a \neq \texttt{null} \qquad\qquad (4.10)$$

Provide meaningful contracts to internal methods.

Contracts capture the purpose of methods, so it will help the mainte-nance team immensely if internal methods are also well documented by a pre-condition stating when the method can be legally called and a post-condition stating what the method achieves. For `findNext()`, we have an-swered the first question already. The second question about its effect is also clear: It (re-)establishes the invariant, so its post-condition is the same as (4.5):

↰4.1

$$0 \leq \texttt{i} \leq \texttt{a.length \&\&} \left(\texttt{i} = \texttt{a.length} \mid\mid \texttt{a[i]} \leq \texttt{threshold}\right)$$

But is this really true? Does the method guarantee this post-condition? Let us briefly look at the code. The first part about the range of `i` is maintained by the loop, since the assertion holds initially and `i` is incremented in the body, where it is less than `a.length` by the loop's test. For the second part, we ask: When can the loop ever stop? Well, either when the loop test fails (i.e., `i` = `a.length`) or because of the inner `break`, where we have checked `a[i]` ≤ `threshold` just before.

»4.7

  In summary, we have been able to capture the behavior of `findNext()` very precisely by its contract, and because of this precision we have also been able to argue that the actual code meets the stated contract. We can now fit this contract to the context of the central method `next()`.

  We will actually give the explanation of the method `next()` twice: once in a high-level, trusting sort of way, and once for the disbelieving colleague. We hope to encourage you by the first to wade through the second, and to help you establish the links between the versions. The second version also fulfills our promise from the beginning of this chapter: that contracts enable you to argue very precisely in the presence of fierce opposition.

  The contract of `next()` has been given in Section 4.2.2: It may be called only when pos ≠ seq.length, which internally means `i` ≠ `a.length` (and so `i` is actually inside the array in Fig. 4.8). So line 2 in the following snippet will be OK, and line 3 makes `i` at most equal to `a.length`. Although `i` now potentially points to an element greater than `threshold`, that gets fixed by `findNext()` in line 4. As a result, we can safely return in line 5, delivering the promised element as the return value.

```
1 public Integer next() {
2     Integer tmp = a[i];
3     i++;
4     findNext();
5     return tmp;
6 }
```

Now for the second version. It is really the same as the previous one, except that it contains explicit references to earlier assertions and formulates all insights, again, as proper assertions. In this way, even the most distrustful team member will have to accept it. Let us first establish that the code runs through without exceptions. In line 2, the array access is OK: a is non-null by invariant (4.10); by invariant (4.5), the index i is in principle within the range of a, but may be one past the end. The latter case is excluded by the method's pre-condition (4.8). From both together, we can deduce $i < a.length$ at line 2. So after line 3, we have $i \leq a.length$ and can call findNext() in line 4 according to its pre-condition (4.9). But does next() achieve its purpose—that is, does it establish its post-condition (4.7) and the invariant? First, it obviously returns seq[\old(pos)], because that element is kept in tmp at line 2 and returned in line 5. Second, it establishes the invariant at the end, because findNext() establishes that in line 4 according to its post-condition. Done!

In summary, contracts for processing steps link the different parts of a class closely and ensure that they work together seamlessly. To exploit this behavior, it is not necessary to go all the way to a semi-formal argument. Rather it is sufficient to trace the assumptions and guarantees up to the level of detail that seems suitable for the desired level of dependability. If you do want to introduce more detail to the argument, read on in Section 4.7.

4.2.4   The Role of Constructors

↰4.1

↰1.6

📖111

The class invariant captures when objects are "OK" or "usable": Their internal structure is set up so that methods can perform their work properly when called from the outside. When an object is newly created, its memory area gets overwritten with 0 bytes, effectively filling the fields with the default values specified by the Java language. Any further setup beyond this safety precaution has to be done by the constructors (including the field initializers, which conceptually and technically become part of every constructor).

Constructors establish the invariant by initialization.

↰4.1

From the perspective of contracts, public methods can be called right after the constructor finishes execution. Since public methods expect the invariant to hold at the beginning, the invariant must be established by the constructors.

Let us check whether the example is correct in this respect. The constructor takes an array and a threshold and then searches for an element no greater than the threshold. The invariant (4.5) about i will hold: Setting i to 0 makes sure it remains inside the array a, and the call to findNext() according to that method's post-condition then establishes the second part of (4.5).

---

thresholditer.ThresholdArrayIterator

```
1 public ThresholdArrayIterator(int [] a, int threshold) {
2 // avoid side effects from outside
3     this.a = Arrays.copyOf(a, a.length);
4     this.i = 0;
5     this.threshold = threshold;
6     findNext();
7 }
```

The constructor's pre-condition enables it to establish the invariant.

The invariant (4.10) stating that a must not be null, which is also part of the pre-condition (4.9) of findNext() in line 6, cannot be guaranteed by the constructor without the caller's collaboration. The constructor therefore has the following pre-condition:

$$a \neq \texttt{null} \tag{4.11}$$

Constructors can have further post-conditions besides the invariant.

Every constructor must guarantee that the invariant holds after it finishes execution, but it can, of course, guarantee more. Very often, such constructors preset the object's state with some given value. For example, StringBuilders are set to a passed string and Sockets are connected to some remote port.

In the running example, the developer will expect the iterator to walk through the passed array. The constructor's post-condition therefore is that the seq comprises precisely the elements less than the threshold and that iteration starts at the first element of that sequence (we use a pseudo-function here, since the earlier notation $a_{\leq}[\ldots j]$ refers to the object's internals):

$$seq = elementsLessEq(\texttt{a}, \texttt{threshold}) \;\&\&\; pos = 0 \tag{4.12}$$

4.2.5 Pure Methods for Specification

Model fields give a completely external view on an object's state. They make explicit that the object does have a state, while at the same time hiding its representation. Very often, however, they merely make public some information that is accessible through methods anyway. As an alternative to using model fields in specifications, one can also allow calls to

150,124,151
152,23,74,73

such methods within contracts. To keep the contracts meaningful, one has to require, however, that these methods do not have any side effects on the object's state—the technical term used to describe this behavior is *pure method*.

In the iterator example, the method hasNext() is certainly pure: It just looks at the current content of fields a and i to decide whether another result element is available. We could then reformulate the pre-condition (4.8) of next() into

$$\text{hasNext}() \qquad\qquad (4.13)$$

↩4.2.2

This new pre-condition is clearly equivalent to the old one. It may, however, be more understandable for developers, because it reflects the idiomatic loop of iterators directly: Before calling next(), you have to call hasNext() to see whether a next element exists.

4.2.6   Frame Conditions: Taming Side Effects

↩4.1

Assertions capture the program's state at a particular point in the source code: Whenever that point is reached, the assertion must hold. If we take this view seriously, even for a single object each post-condition would have to describe every one of its model fields, since in principle *every* method call might change *every* model field—simply by modifying the underlying internal data. Clearly, this would be very unwieldy and cumbersome. Invariants contribute one aspect to a solution, since at least they capture the internals without repeating them at each public method's contract. This section discusses a complementary mechanism for stating which model fields are *not* influenced by a method's side effects.

In the iterator example, nonchanges to model fields would have to be made explicit as follows: The post-condition of hasNext() would have to include pos = \old(pos) and seq = \old(seq), while the post-condition of next() would include only seq = \old(seq), as it already states pos = \old(pos) + 1. Both assertions are really necessary from a logical perspective, because otherwise the caller could not argue that seq and/or pos are the same after the respective calls; the object may, for instance, modify the content of the internal array a.

»4.3

Of course, from the purpose of the class it is clear that seq does not change during the iteration, so the contracts we have given so far do make sense to any developer. They are also useful for arguing about the code's correctness, which is the main goal of this chapter. From a practical perspective, we would therefore like to keep the contracts as they are, merely adding that "nothing else changes."

Frame conditions capture your implicit knowledge of side effects.

The problem of stating such "nonchanges" has been investigated widely in the 2000s, because it is both a prerequisite and a fundamental problem when making contracts precise enough for formal verification. The term *frame condition* is used for such statements. In its simplest form, a frame condition consists of a `modifies` clause for a method's contract. The clause lists those model fields whose content may be influenced by the execution of the method. For instance, the `next()` method would have the additional specification

152,134,20,167,230
213,195,37,125

```
modifies pos
```

The developer must then argue not only that the post-condition is met, but also that the model fields not mentioned in the `modifies` clause remain unchanged. Unfortunately, making this argument precise involves a substantial logical machinery, which is certainly not suitable for the everyday practical correctness arguments we are aiming at here.

Make side effects explicit in the API.

When you read other developers' APIs and trust that they are conscientious about documentation, you assume that they will tell you when the object's state changes. The usual terminology of a "side effect" is revealing at this point: The change may not even be the method's main purpose; it may be effected only "on the way" toward achieving that purpose. Indeed, those hidden connections are a major motivation for the design guideline of keeping methods that merely read an object's state separate from those that modify that state.

Assume that model fields not mentioned in the contract remain unchanged.

When all developers obey the rule of making side effects explicit in their contracts, you can, in consequence, assume that any model field not mentioned does not change during a method call. In fact, this is just the usual development practice: API documentation focuses on what a method achieves and leaves implicit those things it does *not* do. While theorem provers in formal verification may have problems with such an attitude, humans tend to find it obvious and natural.

Pay close attention to assumptions about nonchanges.

The fact that frame conditions cannot be explained easily to theorem provers means that they have a high complexity. To deal with that complexity, professional developers are highly sensitive to situations where changes *might* occur: They have simply seen too many bugs caused by unexpected side effects that invalidated what they thought they knew about their objects. Whenever they sense possible effects, they will briefly stop to think, and they will try to convince themselves explicitly that a particular aspect of an object has, in fact, not changed.

4.3   Motivating Contracts with Hindsight

We have now discussed design-by-contract by examining two examples and considering varying levels of detail. In subsequent sections, we elaborate a few more points, but the framework is all in place: contracts to specify the behavior of methods, model fields to describe an object's state from an external perspective, and invariants to capture the consistency conditions on the private parts of an object as well as on its model fields. Now it is time to check what the framework achieves toward helping us write correct programs.

Contracts give you a checklist with the relevant questions.

We said at the beginning of this chapter that the whole purpose of contracts is to get your code working, and that their main contribution is to point you to all the relevant questions, so that you do not accidentally overlook the one crucial detail that breaks your code.

Contracts, then, are like a form that asks you for specific things to achieve a given goal: Have you thought about what the method assumes? Can you state precisely what it achieves and what the caller can expect? Can you describe the objects' state to clients? Can you sketch what your objects look like internally?

Another point of view is that contracts give you a mental checklist for describing code: Which self-respecting professional pilot would ever dare to take off without having gone through a detailed checklist? Professional software engineers also carry within them such detailed checklists, built from their experience, and design-by-contract is a standard checklist for ensuring the software's correctness.

Contracts facilitate communication.

If every developer asks the same questions about the code, or fills in the same mental form with the appropriate answers, communication becomes more efficient. If developers even use the same words for these questions, things get really quick. For instance, suppose you get back an unexpected `null` value from a method. You can then simply simply say to your teammate, "What's the precise post-condition of that method?" rather than saying, "You know, I have that test case where I call your method and get back `null`, as I saw in the debugger. Is that your bug or mine?"

Contracts help you write clearer documentation.

APIs are really just plain-language statements of contracts. They, too, must state when a method may be called, what it returns, and what its side effects are. Beginners often forget some of these points, which creates ambiguity and increases the likelihood of bugs. Thinking in terms of contracts reminds you of the points that must be mentioned and explained.

Contracts make you think twice about your code.

The examples have shown that the framework literally makes you think twice about the code: once about the meaning of an object at each point in time when defining the model fields and stating the invariant, and once in the contracts when stating what clients know just before and just after a method executes. The interconnection between those statements then serves to double-check your reasoning.

For instance, we introduced the model field `pos` into the threshold iterator because we wished to be precise about the post-condition of `next()`. At the same time, we found that `pos` could be employed to describe precisely the check performed by `hasNext()`.

Design-by-contract makes you think a third time.

Once the model fields, contracts, and invariants are written up and have been cross-checked, you actually have to think once again, to argue with quite some precision that the methods do obey their contracts. As we have seen with the example $a \neq$ `null`, invariants very often remain elusive until you go the extra mile of trying to exclude exceptions and to establish post-conditions by logical deduction, rather than by just testing and debugging.

The strong interdependencies between model fields, contracts, invariants, and arguments enable you to cross-check the individual reasoning steps in each of the areas. Overall, the confidence in the correctness arguments increases dramatically.

»4.7

4.4   Invariants and Callbacks

In the context of the OBSERVER pattern, we have pointed out using a concrete example that the subject must be consistent before it sends out notifications to its observers. The argument there involves a mental execution that eventually leads to an undesirable result. Now, we can be more precise and more general at the same time:

↤2.1.2

The invariant must hold before invoking other objects' methods.

This guideline now is really just an immediate consequence of the injunction that the class invariant must hold whenever no code of the class is running. Note that even if the other objects happen to be instances of the same class,

↤4.1

it is usually not a good idea to call their methods, because they nevertheless may get back to the caller.

Since the problem occurs so often in practice and is easily gotten wrong, let us make the point explicit. In Fig. 4.9, public method 1 in A at some point breaks the invariant, as indicated by the shaded area. It then decides to call method 2 in object B. That method, in turn, decides to call public method 3 inside A. At this point, the program will probably crash: Since method 3 is public, it assumes that the invariant holds, but during the actual execution, this is not the case at all. For instance, if method 1 had left some reference temporarily as `null`, method 3 will throw a `NullPointerException` when working with that reference.

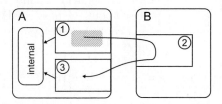

Figure 4.9 Invariants and Calls to the Outside

The proof obligations for class invariants are nonobvious.

↰4.1
📖243
📖181,151,187,188,21,124

The original proposal to connect invariants with public methods turned out to be insufficient only after some time, which indicates that the earlier guideline for calling outside code is not obvious at all. Indeed, researchers have not yet agreed on the best formal rendering of the proof obligations connected with invariants. To gain new perspectives, let us therefore trace a very influential approach.

📖21

The approach is to decouple invariants from designated syntactic code points like public methods altogether. Instead, the developer can state explicitly at which points the invariant does hold. "Unpacking" an object means starting to look into its internals, at which point the invariant is known to hold, while it can be broken subsequently. Conversely, "packing" an object requires the developer to argue that the invariant does hold. In this way, when the object is "unpacked" the next time, the invariant holds—because it cannot have been broken in between. The metaphor in the choice of terms is intended (Fig. 4.10(a); see also Fig. 4.1). An object is like a small package: To work with the content, you have to open it, but once you close the package, it remains safe until you reopen the package.

In this approach, the statement "the invariant holds" becomes just a mental "tag" to the object.[2] Fig. 4.10 illustrates this idea in the form of a state chart: An object is "valid" whenever the invariant holds and "invalid" otherwise. This choice of terms reflects the intuition that an object whose

↰4.1

---

2. Formally [22], such a "tag" is well understood as a special case of *ghost state*, which behaves like normal program state during verification but is not available at runtime.

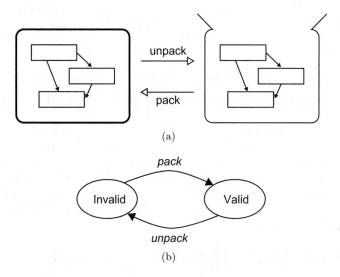

Figure 4.10 Packing and Unpacking Objects

invariant does not hold is somehow "broken." According to the state chart, "unpack" accepts only "valid" objects, so the situation in Fig. 4.9 is ruled out: Method 3 expects a "valid" object A, so method 2 expects a "valid" object A, which method 1 does not provide, since it has just "unpacked" this at the beginning of the gray area.

Think of "the invariant holds" as a mental tag to an object.

It is clear that this approach requires very precise bookkeeping of an object's invariant and is not suitable for informal, everyday reasoning. However, it shows that you are justified in treating "the invariant" as just an abbreviation when reasoning *within* methods' code. You can say, for instance, something like this: "Line 3 breaks the invariant, but line 6 reestablishes it after the new text has been inserted." This is particularly useful in the context of private and protected methods, whose pre- and post-conditions   ↰4.2.3
do not include the invariant implicitly.

Make public methods pay particular attention to the invariants.

The original guideline is nevertheless very useful, because it establishes a warning bell inside the developers' minds: Before leaving a public method, the object must be put "in order." Whether the leaving happens by returning   ↰4.1
or by calling outside code is irrelevant. When this rule is obeyed, then the next public method to be called can rely on the invariant.

Our own formulation steers a middle course: Since the class's code is allowed to break the invariant temporarily, one has to make those parts that *do* hold explicit in the assertions, or use the abbreviation "and the invariant holds."

4.5 Checking Assertions at Runtime

↰1.5.4

Getting programs correct can be a hard task, especially when the data structures and their invariants are complex. It is therefore common practice to check at crucial points whether the assumptions that the code relies on do actually hold and to throw an exception if they fail. Indeed, maintenance programmers prefer code to fail early with clear error messages rather than with obscure `NullPointerExceptions` that occur long after the causing code has been executed.

Make assertions executable and use them for debugging.

▭180
▭150,56

One influential approach, which was pioneered by Meyer's language Eiffel and later taken up by the Java Modeling Language (JML), is to write down the methods' pre- and post-conditions in a format that can be translated into executable code. During the debugging stage, that code checks the assumptions for the actual execution and signals a logical error when they do not hold. Similarly, Java's `assert` statement and Eclipse's `Assert.isTrue` evaluate a Boolean expression at runtime and throw an exception when it returns `false`.

The advantage of such sanity checks is clear: Invalid assumptions are detected early on and pinned down to particular points in the code. In the case of pre- and post-conditions, failures can also be compared directly to the specification and documentation to determine whether the assumption should, in fact, hold according to the code's goals. The blame can then be clearly attributed to the caller or the method, respectively. Also, developers understand the Boolean expressions immediately, since they remain inside the Java language.

»5.4.8 »12.2

A huge incentive for runtime assertion checking comes with the practical need to change code when its requirements change. Especially when a different team is involved in these changes, it is easy to miss and break some invariant or other or some implicit pre-condition that the original team had talked about in endless design discussions and that they never bothered to document, because everybody knew it anyway. Leaving the invariant or assumption in the form of an executable assertion, together with a number of test cases, makes it more likely that the maintainers will hit on their mistake early on.

↰4.2 »4.7

However, these checks are no more than that. In particular, they do not guarantee the absence of logical errors, as the next user interaction or the next test case can easily create a situation where the assertion fails. In contrast, logical deductions about assertions guarantee the absence of errors for all possible executions. Also, executable assertions can obviously cover only computable conditions, while even simple assertions involving "there is some ... " can easily become non-executable. A further disadvantage of runtime checks of assertions is that the checking code itself can be wrong, and must be debugged, maintained, refactored, and otherwise tended.

Methods should not check their pre-conditions.

It is this last disadvantage that motivates a contrasting point of view: Checking code does not contribute to the software's value and functionality, so it should be abandoned altogether. We have already hinted at this perspective in the discussion of runtime exceptions.

◂1.5.4
▢181

Meyer formulates this insight as the *non-redundancy principle*: Checking a method's pre-condition is redundant, because logical arguments show that it holds, so the effort of writing the checking code is wasted from the start. Instead, methods should trust their callers to take care of the pre-condition and should get on with their work. Only this approach allows the method's code to be brief and to the point. Of course, translating a pre-condition stated formally, as is done in Eiffel, does not negate this principle, because no further effort is involved here.

We have, however, pointed out some exceptions to the rule: When a pre-condition is complex or has been violated several times in the past, then it is very likely that it will be violated again in the future. Checking here is likely to save effort. When you cannot trust the caller to obey the pre-condition, you should check. When the consequences of mistakes would be disastrous, you should check. In these situations, the effort of checking must be weighed against the negative consequences of failure, and writing a simple test will usually win out.

◂1.5.4

▸▸4.6

4.6   The System Boundary

The non-redundancy principle decrees that methods should never check their pre-conditions because that work is wasted: The check will always succeed, or else the broken pre-condition will manifest itself in due course— for instance, through an exception signaling an index out of bounds or an access through a null pointer.

▸▸4.5

The basis of the non-redundancy principle is trust: The method trusts the caller to obey the pre-condition in each call and proceeds with its computation, taking the pre-condition for granted in making further deductions. Indirectly, this approach assumes an environment in which callers can be trusted, and in particular are neither malicious nor erroneous. Since both assumptions are not always met, the non-redundancy principle must sometimes be dropped to obtain a reliable system.

↶1.8.7

Every practically relevant system must at some point communicate with the outside world (Fig. 4.11). As part of such an interaction, the system will receive data to be processed and will invoke operations, usually by sending commands to other systems. We now examine these two directions separately to rephrase the earlier discussion from Section 4.5 in terms of contracts.

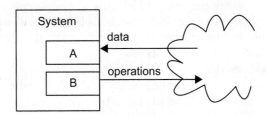

Figure 4.11 Methods on the System Boundary

Never trust incoming data.

The data flowing into the system should always be considered misconstructed and potentially harmful. To illustrate, consider the well-known exploit known as SQL injection. Suppose that the user can enter a new email address, which gets written to the database in the following method:

```
                         boundary.FormDataProcessor
public void updateEmail(int userID, String email) {
    String sql = "update systemUsers set email='" + email
          + "' where userID='" + userID + "';";
      ...
}
```

The new `email` in the SQL command is surrounded by quotes, as expected. However, a malicious user can simply close that quote to send along arbitrary SQL commands. For instance, here they get themselves root privileges by entering the following "email address," which starts and ends with a quote. (They have used the same trick before to query the database schema. The following is a string literal from the code.)

```
                       boundary.FormDataProcessor.inject
"got@you.com' where userID='1';
    update systemUsers set accountType='admin"
```

The resulting query sent to the database is:

```
update systemUsers set email='got@you.com'
    where userID='1';
```

```
update systemUsers set accountType='admin'
     where userID='42';
```

Don't trust the outside world to obey the system's pre-conditions.

In terms of contracts, the problem is that the preceding code has the pre-condition: "The `email` does not contain unescaped special characters." As long as the caller obeys this, everything works fine.

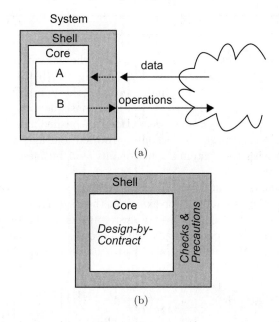

(a)

(b)

Figure 4.12 Protecting the System Boundary

A common approach taken to mitigate such threats is shown in Fig. 4.12(a): The system's functionality is contained in a core component, which never communicates directly with the outside world. That communication is performed by some outer layer, which protects the core like a shell. In the example, the shell would contain the following method, which preprocesses the input to establish the pre-condition of `updateEmail` by escaping any characters that have a special meaning in SQL.

```
                    boundary.FormDataProcessor
public void acceptFormInput(String email) {
    int userID = getSessionUser();
    updateEmail(userID, addslashes(email));
}
```

In the Java environment, the JDT driver accessing the database takes care of quoting and escaping during parameter substitution, as shown below. The protective shell here is found at the level of the database instead of the application. This setup is obviously more robust and also portable between database systems. Furthermore, the application can keep the original string, without escapes, for further processing.

boundary.FormDataProcessor.jdtSolution

```
String sql = "update systemUsers set email= ? where userID= ?";
PreparedStatement s = c.prepareStatement(sql);
s.setInt(2, userID);
s.setString(1, email);
s.execute();
```

From the perspective of design-by-contract, the separation between core and shell establishes a dividing line of trust (Fig 4.12(b)): Inside the core, the rules of design-by-contract, and especially the non-redundancy principle, apply and lead to all of their desirable consequences. For this to be possible, all necessary checks and precautions are pushed into the outer shell code. While the shell probably becomes crowded and ugly in the process, the core code with the system's functionality and business value remains clean and simple.

While malicious attacks certainly do happen, simple mistakes and errors are much more frequent—for example, the user does not enter a positive number as expected, the foreign system sends an ill-formatted XML document, or the data on the hard drive becomes corrupted. The link to design-by-contract remains the same: A method processing these data finds that its pre-condition has been violated.

Fail gracefully.

↶4.5

↶1.5.4

Checking the pre-condition here is different from checking it for debugging purposes: You want to give the outer world a meaningful answer, and one that does not give away internals, such as a stack trace. It is therefore necessary to spend some effort on the question of sensible error messages, as well as on logging the unexpected events.

Be paranoid when invoking potentially harmful operations.

📖157

The case of the system invoking operations in the outside can be problematic if damage can be done. Suppose the method B in Fig. 4.12(a) sends out some commands to perform a real-world operation that may harm or damage people or things in that world. One example would be software that controls some medical radiation device. It will contain one part that handles patient data, treatment plans, the user interface, and other administrative elements. Another part will be responsible for actually controlling the hardware to apply preselected radiation dosages, which are derived from the treatment plans.

Check pre-conditions if the consequences of disobedience are severe.

The methods of the hardware driver do have, of course, well-specified pre-conditions and the developers have probably taken special care in documenting them because they are aware of the potentially disastrous conse- 　157
quences. However, this is not enough: To exclude any possibility of an overdose, the hardware driver should check that its pre-conditions are obeyed. This code is therefore placed in the shell in Fig. 4.12(a).

　　The checking of pre-conditions may, in fact, not be trivial. For instance, in the railway control domain, the scheduling of trains to tracks is often 　43
separated from the actual execution of the schedule, which takes place only after checking that the schedule will not lead to collisions.

4.7   Arguing About the Correctness of Programs

A major motivation for applying design-by-contract is that it channels the 　↰4.3
arguments about whether code will work: After specifying the pre- and post-condition of a method, you have to show that, assuming the pre-condition holds initially, the post-condition holds at the end of the execution. Having done that for every method in the program, you know that the code will definitely work.

　　In most cases, it is sufficient to execute the code mentally to convince 　↰4.1 ↰4.2.3
oneself that it works. However, one can go one step further and argue very precisely, and even mathematically, about code. The seminal insights were laid out by Hoare in the late 1960s and have done much for computer science 　119
as a practical discipline ever since: Who would like to drive a modern car or fly a modern plane, where many vital systems are controlled by software, without a reliable assurance that these systems will work?

　　This section closes the remaining gap in the correctness arguments. Many practitioners will say that its content is of only theoretical interest, since all but the most safety-critical software projects lack the time and the resources to actually prove correctness. We have therefore structured the book so that you can skip this section.

　　We include this material because we hope to create a self-contained presentation that provides the essential insights and formal "tricks" in a form that is accessible to practitioners. Also, we wish to encourage you to think about two points that are highly relevant for any practical software development:

(a) Learn to formulate loop invariants.
(b) Learn to describe the content of your variables at every point.

In regard to point (a), it is almost impossible to write an extended piece of 　↠4.7.2
software without sophisticated loops, and it is very hard to get these loops

correct without understanding loop invariants. We have always found, both in teaching and in developing, that understanding loop invariants leads to both shorter and more lucid code and saves much trouble in debugging. Point (b) very often makes the difference between the professional developer and the amateur: The professional knows the meaning of every variable, field, and array in the program and can describe their content at every point in the program in a few succinct words. The amateur, in contrast, has to explain his or her code by describing the eventual execution. The idea of proof outlines makes this idea precise.

»4.7.1

4.7.1   Assignment

At the core of reasoning about contracts, we have to deal with side effects. The question to be answered is, after all, whether the state resulting from setting local variables, object fields, array elements, or something else will fulfill the specified post-condition. Essentially, the task is to capture the behavior of assignment precisely: Once we can handle one assignment, we can handle sequences of them and, as we will see shortly, assignments occurring in `if` and `while` statements. We cut the problem to size by considering first local variables and deferring an outlook on heap-allocated data to a later section.

»4.7.4.3

> Find a general way of reasoning formally about assignments.

»4.7.2

As an introduction to this topic, let us take a problem that lies at the heart of the later example of summing up the integers in an array. Here, we content ourselves with computing `i * j` by repeated addition of `j`. We keep the partial result in `s` (for "sum") and we use a counter `k`. In step number `k`, we have summed up $s = k * j$. The step is then shown below: We add one more `j` and increment `k` correspondingly. So if `s` is "correct" before that step, then it should be correct afterward. The assertions express just that.

reason.Assignment.assign1

```
1 // s = k * j
2 s = s + j;
3 k = k + 1;
4 // s = k * j
```

But how do we argue that the assertion in line 4 holds? Let us call the initial values of the modified variables S and K, respectively. We can then take a mental execution step: The initial value of `s` is $K * j$, so after the assignment in line 2, we have

$$s = S + j = (K * j) + j$$

For the next step, mental execution confirms that `k` has been incremented in line 3:

$$s = S + j = (K * j) + j \wedge k = K + 1$$

From this, we have to prove the assertion in line 4. We can do this by unfolding the current values of both variables, which leaves us with proving the simple equality

$$(K * \mathsf{j}) + \mathsf{j} = (K + 1) * \mathsf{j}$$

However, the juggling of new names for intermediate values can quickly become unwieldy. Also, we have introduced them on an ad-hoc basis, whenever we felt we needed to refer to "old values."

Make the reasoning steps mechanical.

Hoare has found an elegant solution to this problem, which is expressed in (4.14). There, you see a *Hoare triple*, which consists of a statement in the center together with a pre-condition to the left and a post-condition to the right. (We mark them as comments; traditionally, they are surrounded by curly braces.) The triple shown here is really a schematic program: The symbols must be replaced by concrete elements from an actual program. Later on, we will see such *Hoare rules* for the different language constructs. In the literature, the specific rule (4.14) is called the *assignment axiom*, because it expresses a true statement about an assignment.[3]

The meanings of x, e, and Q are then clear in (4.14): Expression e is assigned to variable x, and Q is the post-condition. The notation $Q[x \leftarrow e]$ means to perform syntactic substitution, in which you take the assertion Q and textually replace all occurrences of x by e (adding, of course, parentheses around e where necessary).

$$\text{/*}\, Q[x \leftarrow e]\, \text{*/}\ x = e\ \text{/*}\, Q\, \text{*/} \tag{4.14}$$

Herein, the expression e must not contain side effects.

»4.7.4.1

Compute proof obligations backward.

The point about Hoare rules is that they can be applied mechanically. However, the form of (4.14) forces us to proceed backward, starting from the post-condition and working toward the pre-condition. This may seem slightly bizarre at first, but before judging further, let us try whether it works.

In the example, we wish to have $\mathsf{s} = \mathsf{k} * \mathsf{j}$ in the end, so we apply (4.14) to the assignment in line 3 by setting the following equivalencies (we use

---

3. If you like mathematics, you might find it interesting that nowadays Hoare rules are not stated as axioms but as derived rules. An axiom is a proposition that is the basis for proving propositions but cannot be proven itself. Introducing an axiom always incurs the danger of inconsistency, referring to the possibility of proving `false`—in other words, to create a contradiction within the very basis of reasoning. The most famous example is perhaps Frege's axiomatization of set theory [96], which was later found to contain the well-known Barber paradox. Nowadays, the Hoare rules are proven from the definition of the language's semantics and the definition of correctness itself (e.g., [192,110,191,217]).

a different symbol $\equiv$ for equality *between* assertions, because $=$ is already used *within* assertions):

$$Q \equiv (\mathtt{s} = \mathtt{k} * \mathtt{j})$$
$$x \equiv \mathtt{k}$$
$$e \equiv \mathtt{k} + 1$$

The distinction between the two equality symbols reflects a distinction that is useful in computer science in many places: that between an *object level*, where the objects of our interest are described, and a *meta level*, at which we formulate statements *about* these objects. Another instance of this idea is the use of italics for the schematic variables x, e, and Q in (4.14), which are meta-level tools for talking about the object-level program variables $\mathtt{s}$, $\mathtt{i}$, and $\mathtt{k}$ set in typewriter font.

You also know the distinction from the escaping rules of string literals: The double quotes are reserved as meta-level symbols to talk about strings, to specify a string value. Consequently, at the object level of concrete string values, the double quotes are escaped, as in `"\""`. Another instance is compiler construction: Grammars are a meta-level tool for specifying the structure of object-level concrete programs.

Computer science simply loves creating languages and tools to talk about other languages, so it is useful to keep the distinction between meta and object levels in mind. For instance, XML is used to encode XSLT style sheets, which are used for transforming XML documents. When you write `<td><xsl:value-of select="..."/></td>`, the `td` tags are object-level output, and the `xsl:value-of` is a meta-level XSLT specification talking *about* a value to be inserted at the point; that value is computed by the meta-level XPath expression in the `select` attribute.

📖2

📖255

Let us proceed with the example. We have the replacements for Q, x, and e, so we can compute the pre-condition of line 3 by rule (4.14): $Q[x{\leftarrow}e]$ means replacing $\mathtt{k}$ by $\mathtt{k} + 1$ in the concrete Q, which yields

$$\mathtt{s} = (\mathtt{k} + 1) * \mathtt{j}$$

Surely, this is more concise than the previous combination of two equalities. Also, we do not have to invent extra names for previous values. Let us proceed with the assignment on line 2:

$$Q \equiv (\mathtt{s} = (\mathtt{k} + 1) * \mathtt{j})$$
$$x \equiv \mathtt{s}$$
$$e \equiv \mathtt{s} + \mathtt{j}$$

So, as the formal pre-condition of line 2, we get by mechanical substitution

$$(\mathtt{s} + \mathtt{j}) = (\mathtt{k} + 1) * \mathtt{j}$$

Finally, we can compute (and so could a theorem prover)

$$(\mathtt{s} + \mathtt{j}) = (\mathtt{k} + 1) * \mathtt{j} \;\equiv\; \mathtt{s} + \mathtt{j} = \mathtt{k} * \mathtt{j} + \mathtt{j} \;\equiv\; \mathtt{s} = \mathtt{k} * \mathtt{j}$$

But this is just the given pre-condition! Everything is mechanical computation, except for the very last step, which involves a slight arithmetic deduction that is easily carried out by a theorem prover: If the same thing is added on both sides of an equation, throw the additions away. Since we have reached the pre-condition merely by applying Hoare's rule, we know that the post-condition does indeed follow from the pre-condition; in other words, the code is correct.

Read Hoare rules backward, starting from the result to be guaranteed.

However, we have promised to justify the single reasoning steps, so it does not do to simply take (4.14) for granted. Formally, it can be deduced from the language semantics and the definition of what "correct" means. Intuitively, one can simply read the rule backward: Since e does not contain side effects, it is really just a value, and that value gets stored in x. The point to be seen is that Q will pick up that new value from x. If Q must be guaranteed to hold when reading e from x, it must already hold before the assignment, if we put in the value e immediately, without waiting to read it from x later on. This is just what substitution does in (4.14).

📖 192,110,191,217

⌕ Incidentally, the initial reasoning by mental execution can also be captured in a Hoare rule, known as the *forward-style assignment axiom*. Although you will not usully find it in the literature, it is equally valid and provable from the semantics of the language and the definition of correctness. It performs the choice of new names by existential quantification:

📖 102

$$/\!* P *\!/ \; x = e \; /\!* \exists x'.P[x'/x] \wedge x = e[x'/x] *\!/$$

This rule can be read as follows: If P holds before the assignment, then P continues to hold for the old value of x, which we call x'. Furthermore, the new value of x is e, where possible references to x will read the value x'. The disadvantage of cluttering the formulas with new names, of course, remains. We will therefore continue in the more widely used tradition of using the original assignment axiom (4.14).

Put the whole reasoning inline into the code.

Since the rule applications are purely mechanical, they do not have to be explained again and again for every program. Instead, we can simply put the assertions that we described inline into the program. The reader who knows (4.14) can then easily follow us from line 5 to line 3 and from there to the conclusion of line 1, which follows from the given pre-condition.[4] (We use $\Longrightarrow$ to denote meta-level implications between assertions, and $\longrightarrow$ to denote object-level implications within assertions.)

```
reason.Assignment.assign2
1 // s = k * j ⟹ s + j = (k + 1) * j
2 s = s + j;
3 // s = (k +1) * j
4 k = k + 1;
5 // s = k * j
```

---

4. This step is formally justified by a *consequence rule* [119], but we think it is fairly clear without the formalism.

This form of presentation is commonly called a *proof outline*, because the given assertions guide the correctness proof of the program. The lengthy argument from the previous pages now fits into 5 lines of commented code.

Correctness proofs start with verification condition generation.

Another point to be noted is that the only place where actual reasoning is necessary is the proof of the implication in line 1. The assertion on line 3 is derived mechanically by (4.14), and no intelligence or reasoning is involved here. The same holds for the right-hand side of the implication in line 1. This suggests a two-phase approach to arguing about correctness:

□77 ▶6.1.2

1. Apply Hoare rules mechanically, in a backward fashion, until you hit the stated pre-condition. This process yields a computed pre-condition. It is also called the *weakest pre-condition*, because it gives the minimal requirements under which the code will achieve the given post-condition.

2. Prove that the stated pre-condition implies the computed pre-condition.

□22,191,217,88

The first step is called *verification condition generation*. It reduces the task of proving the correctness of a program to merely showing a set of implications. The latter can then very often be *discharged* (i.e., proven) automatically by modern theorem provers.

4.7.2   Loops: Summing over an Array

Now that we have mastered the basics, let us get a bit more ambitious. Following you see the code for summing up the elements of an int-array nums. Initially, the array must not be null; in the end, we want sum to hold the sum of all elements. The code is certainly straightforward enough: It just runs an index loop through the array.

```
                          reason.ArraySum.sum
// nums ≠ null
int sum = 0;
int i = 0;
while (i != nums.length) {
    sum = sum + nums[i];
    i = i + 1;
}
//  ⟹  sum = $\sum_{j=0}^{nums.length-1}$ nums[j]
```

Reasoning about loops requires further, nonmechanical insights.

The new element in this example is, of course, the loop. At first, we may be tempted to just apply the assignment axiom (4.14) again and again, twice for each iteration. However, this does not work out, since we cannot know the length of the array nums beforehand.

So let us try to argue practically. Why is the loop "correct"? How does it achieve its purpose? The central insight is certainly that we sum up the array elements "left to right," as shown in Fig. 4.13. In the figure, the elements up to i (exclusive) have been added to sum, while those with higher indices remain to be processed.

To reason formally, we need to recast this statement in terms of asser-   ↰4.1
tions; we have to describe "snapshots of the program state." We could, for instance, capture the image by saying that "sum always contains the sum of all elements up to i (exclusive)."

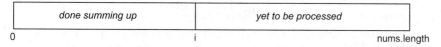

done summing up	yet to be processed

0   i   nums.length

Figure 4.13 Snapshot of Summation

This can be written a bit more precisely as (4.15). (Since summation in mathematics includes the upper limit, we subtract 1 from i.)

$$\text{sum} = \sum_{j=0}^{i-1} \text{nums}[j] \qquad (4.15)$$

If you think back, we had connected an assertion that "always holds" with   ↰4.1
the idea of an invariant: Except in specific code regions, the invariant holds. Therefore, the statement (4.15) is called the *loop invariant*.

Loop invariants are practically valuable.

Before we embark on a detailed discussion, let us start with a motivation. Experienced practitioners know the value of loop invariants. For instance, Koenig and Moo in their introductory textbook on C++ programming summarize their value [144, §2.3.2]:

> Every useful while statement that we can imagine has an invariant associated with it. Stating the invariant in a comment can make a while much easier to understand.
> [...]
> Although the invariant is not part of the program text, it is a valuable intellectual tool for designing programs.

The reason for such a strong statement is simple: All loops have to work independently of how many times they iterate, so we have to keep a precise understanding of the content of local variables and object structures through all iterations. The loop invariant is just that: a summary of that content and those structures. Without such a summary overview, there is always a danger that our loops will go astray and will fail to work at some point. Developers who cannot say precisely and succinctly what their variables contain will always be insecure about the working of their code.

Our own experience is that we write simple loops out of habit and complex ones out of a deeper understanding of their invariant. When you have written a few hundred iterations through an array, you do not make explicit the invariant of the next. However, when you encounter a new problem never solved, it is worth formulating an invariant.

A loop invariant holds just before the loop test is executed.

↰4.1

↰4.4

We had associated the class invariant with specific points in the code, whether we chose to use the entry and exit points to the class's code, the `public` methods, or explicit pack/unpack pseudo-statements. At the beginning of these code sections, the invariant was assumed to hold, and we had to argue that it held again when the code sections are left.

A similar reasoning applies to loops: At the beginning of the loop body, the invariant holds. Then, the body modifies the variables and objects involved and thereby breaks the invariant temporarily. However, at the end of the loop body, the invariant must have been reestablished.

↰4.2.3

Let us look at the example. If (4.15) holds at the beginning of the loop body, and the test ensures that `i` has not yet reached the end of the array, the invariant holds again after `nums[i]` has been added to `sum` and `i` has been incremented. When we look more closely, we have to ensure that the array access is valid. We next add a further invariant (4.16): Its first part excludes null-pointer exceptions; its second part, together with the loop test, excludes array-index-out-of-bounds exceptions. (Note that the case $i = \texttt{nums.length}$ is reached in the very last iteration, so $i < \texttt{nums.length}$ would not be an invariant.)

$$\texttt{nums} \neq \texttt{null} \land 0 \leq \texttt{i} \leq \texttt{nums.length} \tag{4.16}$$

Prove that the invariant holds when the loop starts.

If we wish to know that the invariant holds for the first iteration, we have to prove it. Only the code that sets up the local variables and objects can know something about that state, so it must also be responsible for establishing the invariant. Of course, it will usually have to rely on the method's pre-condition and the class invariant in the process. In the example, (4.15) holds by the initialization of `sum` and `i`; (4.16) derives the pre-condition and the initialization of `i`.

The invariant holds when the loop exits by the test returning `false`.

The real benefit of invariants is that we gain knowledge about the program's state at the end of the loop. By the preceding construction of the invariant, it always holds at the beginning of the loop body, just before the test: For the first run, we have to argue explicitly; afterward, the invariant is maintained from one execution of the body to the next, independently of how many times that body gets executed. So, the invariant will also hold at the very end, when the test returns `false` and the loop stops executing. (The treatment of `break` and `continue` is somewhat more involved.) In the example, the result deriving from (4.15) and `i = nums.length` is just the desired post-condition given in the beginning of this section—the loop will actually work!

»4.7.4.2

Loop invariants fit in well with verification condition generation.

Our general plan for correctness arguments is a two-stage process. First, we reduce the program to a set of implications by applying Hoare rules in a backward fashion. Second, we prove the remaining implications. To succeed, we have to give a rule similar to the one for assignment (4.14), but now for loops.

The required rule is actually very simple—it combines the guidelines about loop invariants stated earlier. The formulation (4.17) may look daunting at first, but there is nothing to it. First, the horizontal bar just means "derives" or "implies": When all the things above have been proven, the thing below has been proven. The thing below in this case is just "the loop is correct with pre-condition P and post-condition Q," written as a Hoare triple. The things above are just the previous insights: We have to prove that the invariant holds initially, that executing the body maintains the invariant under the assumption that the test yields `true`, and finally that the desired post-condition derives from the invariant when the loop ends (i.e., when the test returns `false`). That's it. (t must not have side-effects.)

»4.7.4.1

$$\frac{P \implies I \qquad \text{/*}\,I \wedge t\,\text{*/}\ b\ \text{/*}\,I\,\text{*/} \qquad I \wedge \neg t \implies Q}{\text{/*}\,P\,\text{*/}\ \textbf{while}(t)\{\ b\ \}\ \text{/*}\,Q\,\text{*/}} \qquad (4.17)$$

Applying the loop rule is mechanical.

Let us try out the rule on the example, using the notation of a proof outline as shown next, where we note the invariant down in front of the loop. The first proof $P \implies I$ at line 4 follows from the initialization of `sum` and `i`, since the empty summation from 0 to -1 yields 0. Then, let us check that the loop body maintains the invariant. We do so by noting the invariant at the body's end, then applying the assignment rule (4.14) backward; the result is noted in line 6, and we have to show that

$$\text{sum} = \sum_{j=0}^{i-1} \text{nums}[j] \implies \text{sum} + \text{nums}[i] = \sum_{j=0}^{(i+1)-1} \text{nums}[j]$$

which is clear by a short computation. For the last proof obligation in (4.17), we have to show that the result of the loop in line 12 implies the overall post-condition in line 13. But that, again, is just a simple computation.

```
                          reason.ArraySum.sum
```

```
1  // nums ≠ null
2  int sum = 0;
3  int i = 0;
```
4 // **Inv** : $\text{sum} = \sum_{j=0}^{i-1} \text{nums}[j]$
5 **while** (i != nums.length) {
6   // $\text{sum} + \text{nums}[i] = \sum_{j=0}^{(i+1)-1} \text{nums}[j]$
7   sum = sum + nums[i];
8   // $\text{sum} = \sum_{j=0}^{(i+1)-1} \text{nums}[j]$
9   i = i +1;
10   // $\text{sum} = \sum_{j=0}^{i-1} \text{nums}[j]$
11 }
12 // $\text{sum} = \sum_{j=0}^{i-1} \text{nums}[j] \wedge i = \text{nums.length}$
13 // $\implies \text{sum} = \sum_{j=0}^{\text{nums.length}-1} \text{nums}[j]$

> The loop invariant captures the partial result achieved so far.

A final question remains: How do you find the loop invariant? As we hope to have clarified, the central point is the practitioner's insight: The invariant is just a summary of why the loop works. The loop invariant then provides focus. It guides you toward thinking of about loops by asking the question "What do you know at the start of each iteration?" As with class invariants, it is a good strategy to picture the situation and then to describe the picture in words or formulas.

↰4.2.3

📖107,104–106

In our experience, a more specific question that very often yields new insights is this: What partial result has the loop achieved so far? In the example, Fig. 4.13 suggested that sum may contain the sum of "the left part of the array num," which was made more precise in (4.15). The beauty of this approach is that in the end, the loop test aborts the loop, at which point the overall result must have been achieved: The invariant's partial result together with the negated loop test must give the overall desired result.

4.7.3   Conditionals and Loops: Binary Search

The summation example has illustrated the main challenge in verifying code: to find the right loop invariant. At the same time, we have seen that the invariant can often be found by merely describing the partial result accomplished by the loop in the previous iterations. To strengthen this insight, we apply it to a second example, binary search.

📖72

The code that follows is simple enough, when read in the context of its illustration in Fig. 4.14. The code works on a sorted array vals and tries to locate value x. The lower bound l (inclusive) and upper bound u (exclusive) delineate the current search space. Each iteration looks at the value at the middle index m of the search space, decides whether x will be found to the left or to the right of m, and adjusts the search space accordingly.

---

reason.BinarySearch.find

```
1  int l = 0;
2  int u = vals.length;
3  while (l < u) {
4      int m = (l + u) / 2;
5      if (x == vals[m]){
6          return m;
7      } else if (vals[m] > x) {
8          u = m;
9      } else {
10         l = m +1;
11     }
12 }
13 return −1;
```

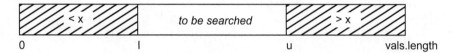

Figure 4.14 Loop Invariant of Binary Search

The result of binary search is either an index at which x has been found in vals or -1 if no such index exists. We can write this formally as the post-condition (4.18) (using ∈ also for containment in arrays):

$$(\backslash\text{return} \geq 0 \wedge \text{vals}[\backslash\text{return}] = x) \vee$$
$$(\backslash\text{return} = -1 \wedge x \notin \text{vals}) \tag{4.18}$$

The loop invariant captures the partial result achieved in previous iterations.

So why does this code work? Why does it always find x if it exists in vals? The main insight has already been sketched in Fig. 4.14: By the comparisons performed in the loop and the assumption that vals is sorted, the elements to the left of l are too small and the elements starting at u are too large to contain x—the value x can be found only in the region l to u, if at all. The partial result in this case consists in having eliminated parts of the array as possible locations of x.

To make the reasoning precise, we express this insight more formally. In fact, there are several possible ways of doing so. We might say, for instance, "If x is contained in vals, then it is also found between l and u." This idea would lead to invariant (4.19) [where we use vals[l..u] for the array slice from l to u (exclusive)]:

$$x \in \text{vals} \longrightarrow x \in \text{vals}[l..u] \tag{4.19}$$

This invariant would work out in the end. For instance, going backward through the assignment u=m; in line 8 would yield the proof obligation:

$$x \in \texttt{vals} \longrightarrow x \in \texttt{vals}[l..m]$$

Since we know in line 8 that $\texttt{vals}[m] > x$, this proof obligation is clearly solved, since x cannot be found in $\texttt{vals}[m..\texttt{\textbackslash old}(u)]$. However, this argument involves some hand waving, because it uses properties of the slice notation that we have not actually proven.

Aim at using elementary formalizations.

So, let us try again. We can, for instance, rephrase (4.19) by making explicit the index at which x occurs. Then we arrive at (4.20), which reads: "If x occurs (at all) at some index i, then that index is found between 1 and u." Now we have used only elementary notation, and the substitution for the assignment u=m; replaces u by m only at the end of (4.20). No hand waving is involved, as we shall see later.

$$\forall 0 \leq i < \texttt{vals.length.} \; \texttt{vals}[i] = \texttt{x} \longrightarrow 1 \leq i < \texttt{u} \qquad (4.20)$$

76,75

A further advantage of such a formulation is that modern theorems provers have highly optimized algorithms for dealing with elementary notation, so there is a good chance they will discharge the proof obligations automatically.

Conditionals yield the test as additional information.

Before we can proceed, we must integrate the if construct to the framework for generating proof obligations—we have to give a Hoare rule for if. Here it is:

$$\frac{/\!\!*\, P_1 \,*\!/ \; a \; /\!\!*\, Q \,*\!/ \qquad /\!\!*\, P_2 \,*\!/ \; b \; /\!\!*\, Q \,*\!/}{/\!\!*\,(t \longrightarrow P_1) \wedge (\neg t \longrightarrow P_2)\,*\!/ \; \textbf{if}\,(t)\, a \; \textbf{else}\; b \; /\!\!*\, Q \,*\!/} \qquad (4.21)$$

4.7.1

The formal rule (4.21) looks somewhat complex, but it can be understood easily by reading it backward: To guarantee a post-condition Q, that post-condition must be guaranteed by both branches a and b. We therefore compute the formal pre-conditions P_1 and P_2 for these (at the top), and then assemble the overall pre-condition by adding the information gained by the test. While proving P_1, we can assume additionally that the test returned true; for P_2, we can assume it returned false. As in the case

4.7.4.1 4.7.1

of while, the test cannot have side effects. (We use $\longrightarrow$ as the object-level implication within assertions, and $\Longrightarrow$ as the meta-level implication between assertions.)

Applying the if rule is purely mechanical.

With the above Hoare rules (4.14), (4.17), and (4.21), we are now ready to compute the proof obligations for binary search. The proof outline is shown below. As usual, it must be read backward. We start by injecting the post-condition (4.18) at each return statement. For the return at line 11, the post-condition is immediate from the if rule (4.21). Line 24 is the post-condition for return value −1; line 23 derives from the while rule (4.17), and since $u \leq 1$ contradicts $1 \leq i < u$, we have

▶4.7.4.2

$$(\forall 0 \leq i < \texttt{vals.length. vals}[i] = x \longrightarrow \texttt{false})$$

which implies

$$\neg(\exists 0 \leq i < \texttt{vals.length. vals}[i] = x)$$

which is just a more elaborate way of saying $x \notin \texttt{vals}$.

---

reason.BinarySearch.find

```
1  // sorted(vals)
2  int l = 0;
3  int u = vals.length;
4  // Inv:∀0 ≤ i < vals.length. vals[i] = x ⟶ 1 ≤ i < u
5  while (l < u) {
6      // ∀0 ≤ i < vals.length. vals[i] = x ⟶ 1 ≤ i < u
7      int m = (l + u) / 2;
       // (vals[m] > x ⟶ (∀0 ≤ i < vals.length.
       //                     vals[i] = x ⟶ 1 ≤ i < m))∧
8      // (vals[m] < x ⟶ (∀0 ≤ i < vals.length.
       //                     vals[i] = x ⟶ m + 1 ≤ i < u))
9      if (x == vals[m]) {
10         // x = vals[m] ⟶ Post
11         return m;
12     } else if (vals[m] > x) {
13         // vals[m] > x ⟶ (∀0 ≤ i < vals.length.
           //                     vals[i] = x ⟶ 1 ≤ i < m)
14         u = m;
15         // ∀0 ≤ i < vals.length. vals[i] = x ⟶ 1 ≤ i < u
16     } else {
17         // vals[m] < x ⟶ (∀0 ≤ i < vals.length.
           //                     vals[i] = x ⟶ m +1 ≤ i < u)
18         l = m + 1;
19         // ∀0 ≤ i < vals.length. vals[i] = x ⟶ 1 ≤ i < u
20     }
21     // ∀0 ≤ i < vals.length. vals[i] = x ⟶ 1 ≤ i < u
22  }
23  // u ≤ l∧ (∀0 ≤ i < vals.length. vals[i] = x ⟶ 1 ≤ i < u)
24  // ⟹ x ∉ vals
25  return −1;
```

We now examine the invariant according to the while rule (4.17). The invariant holds initially in line 4, simply by the fact that l and u span the entire array. To show that the body maintains the invariant, we proceed backward as usual: We start in line 21, then go backward through the different branches according to the if rule (4.21). The first branch returns, so nothing needs to be done. The second and third branches gain new information by the `if` tests, as shown in lines 13 and 17.

Line 8 now exhibits very clearly the idea of generating proof obligations: In combining the branches according to (4.21), it keeps only an implication for each branch, but we do not have to think about the original `if` statement anymore—we can argue just about the formula. The central point to be proven is this: Does line 8 follow from the invariant in line 6? (The exact value of `m` is irrelevant, so we do not substitute the assignment in line 7 to keep things brief.) A close look at the formula shows that this is the case: The array is sorted and the additional assumption in each case justifies the restriction of the search range. This was the last of the proof obligations— binary search is correct!

> Contracts support you all the way to formal reasoning.

We hope that you are convinced that the binary search works with the given invariant. It is, however, interesting to see that we can go even further: If the disbelieving colleague is not satisfied with taking "a close look at the formula," you can deliver an even more refined and more formal proof by making the implication between line 6 and line 8 precise. So here goes.

Since line 8 is a conjunction, we have to prove the two branches separately; we do only the one first here, as the second is similar. We have to show that

$$(\forall 0 \leq i < \mathtt{vals.length.}\ \mathtt{vals}[i] = \mathtt{x} \longrightarrow 1 \leq i < \mathtt{u})$$
$$\Longrightarrow (\mathtt{vals}[\mathtt{m}] > \mathtt{x} \longrightarrow (\forall 0 \leq i < \mathtt{vals.length.}$$
$$\mathtt{vals}[i] = \mathtt{x} \longrightarrow 1 \leq i < \mathtt{m}))$$

First, let us rename the first quantified variable from i to k to avoid confusion:

$$(\forall 0 \leq k < \mathtt{vals.length.}\ \mathtt{vals}[k] = \mathtt{x} \longrightarrow 1 \leq k < \mathtt{u})$$
$$\Longrightarrow (\mathtt{vals}[\mathtt{m}] > \mathtt{x} \longrightarrow (\forall 0 \leq i < \mathtt{vals.length.}$$
$$\mathtt{vals}[i] = \mathtt{x} \longrightarrow 1 \leq i < \mathtt{m}))$$

Then, we have to show the "for all" quantification on i. Let any i with $0 \leq i < \mathtt{vals.length}$ be given. We can then replace the repeated implication about by conjunction. The implication to be proven is

$$(\forall 0 \leq k < \mathtt{vals.length.}\ \mathtt{vals}[k] = \mathtt{x} \longrightarrow 1 \leq k < \mathtt{u}) \wedge$$
$$\mathtt{vals}[\mathtt{m}] > \mathtt{x} \wedge \mathtt{vals}[i] = \mathtt{x} \tag{4.22}$$
$$\Longrightarrow 1 \leq i < \mathtt{m}$$

We show this by contradiction. Suppose that $\neg(1 \leq i < \mathtt{m})$, which is the same as $i < 1 \vee i \geq \mathtt{m}$. So there are two cases: If $i < 1$, then the first line of (4.22) yields the contradiction $1 \leq i$ for $k = i$. If $i \geq \mathtt{m}$, then we have a contradiction in the second line of (4.22): vals[m] > x and vals is sorted, so that vals[i] > x, contradicting vals[i] = x. In summary, we have proven (4.22), so that the loop body maintains the invariant.

The invariant also captures unchanged facts from before the loop.

In the argument, we have frequently referred to the sortedness of the array. Also, the array accesses in the code work correctly only if l and u never go beyond the array. All in all, we have assumed the additional invariant (4.23), which is, however, maintained by the loop: The variable vals and the array vals do not change at all, and the computation of m in line 7 ensures the inequalities on l and u. (For l ≤ u, observe that m < u by the definition of m and the loop test l < u, so line 18 can never yield l > u.)

$$\text{vals} \neq \text{null} \wedge \text{sorted}(\text{vals}) \wedge 0 \leq \text{l} \leq \text{u} \leq \text{vals.length} \qquad (4.23)$$

4.7.4 Outlook

The material presented in this section has shown that contracts and assertions can serve as a solid foundation for different levels of reasoning, from informal pictorial arguments down to formal mathematical proofs. For brevity, we have omitted some practically relevant constructs. While these have been tackled successfully in recent research projects, full examples are beyond the scope of this book. To avoid leaving you with the unsatisfactory feeling that contracts are, in the end, only a theoretical toy, we conclude this chapter with a brief outlook on the main areas omitted so far. Other language constructs are discussed in Chapter 6.

153,138

4.7.4.1 Side Effects in Expressions

The Hoare rules (4.21) and (4.17) for if and while assume that the test t does not contain side effects. The practitioner, of course, immediately thinks of idioms such as the following one for reading from an input stream—do contracts fail even on such everyday code?

```
while ((n = in.read(buf)) != -1) {
    ...
}
```

The answer is simple: Theoreticians consider something like this as "obviously solvable" and usually do not bother to spell out the solution. The idea is, of course, that any expression with nested side effects can be unrolled into a sequence of simple expressions, similar to what a compiler does when generating linear machine code. The preceding idiom could, for instance be translated into the following equivalent version, for which proof obligations can be generated by the given rules (using also Section 4.7.4.2).

217(§4.2)

2

```
while (true) {
    int tmp01 = in.read(buf);
    n = tmp01;
    if (!(tmp01 != -1)) break;
    ...
}
```

4.7.4.2 Break, Continue, and Return

A second thing that practitioners do is to preempt the execution of loop bodies by break and continue: At some point, it is clear that some goal has been reached, so there is no use in continuing with the loop or at least with the current iteration.

217(§2.4.4,§4.5) The approach to formalizing this behavior is to introduce multiple post-conditions, which you can think of as different "channels" for assertions. The central insight is that any statement can do one of three things when it finishes: It can go on to the next statement as usual, it can break the current loop, or it can continue immediately to the end of the loop body. Each of these possible destinations is represented by a different post-condition that must hold at the respective jump target. In a backward application of the following rules, the right thing happens: Normal statements like assignment behave as before, and break and continue inject the correct post-condition.

$$/\!\!* \, Q[x \leftarrow e] \, *\!\!/ \; x = e; \; /\!\!* \, Q \mid B \mid C \, *\!\!/$$
$$/\!\!* \, B \, *\!\!/ \; \mathbf{break}; \; /\!\!* \, Q \mid B \mid C \, *\!\!/$$
$$/\!\!* \, C \, *\!\!/ \; \mathbf{continue}; \; /\!\!* \, Q \mid B \mid C \, *\!\!/$$

The post-conditions of the "side channels" B and C are initialized at the surrounding loop, in the proof obligation for the loop body [compare to (4.17)]: A break must establish the loop's post-condition Q immediately, and a continue must reestablish the loop invariant to admit the next iteration. The break and continue conditions B' and C' are irrelevant within the loop, because they relate to a possible outer loop.

$$\frac{P \implies I \quad /\!\!* \, I \wedge t \, *\!\!/ \; b \; /\!\!* \, I \mid Q \mid I \, *\!\!/ \quad I \wedge \neg t \implies Q}{/\!\!* \, P \, *\!\!/ \; \mathbf{while} \, (t) \, \{b\} \; /\!\!* \, Q \mid B' \mid C' \, *\!\!/}$$

Reasoning about return works exactly in the same way: We introduce yet another channel R in the post-condition, and the rule for the return statement selects that channel as its pre-condition. This rule makes precise the notion of "injecting the method's post-condition" used informally in Section 4.7.3.

4.7.4.3 Aliasing and the Heap

46,152 A major challenge of formal verification is the precise treatment of the heap and the possibility of aliasing between object references. Over time,

many approaches have been developed, and they all come with a substantial
formal and technical machinery. Here, we can only outline the problem and
show that the practitioner, unlike the mechanical theorem prover, solves
the challenge rather straightforwardly—by drawing pointer diagrams.

58,195,213,38
246,20,67,102,103

Let us start with a simple example of two `Point` objects, each of which
contains integer fields x and y. You will agree that the following test will
succeed: a and b are separate objects, and modifying a field in one will
leave the other object unchanged.

```
Point a = new Point();
Point b = new Point();
int bx = b.x;
a.x = 42;
assertEquals(bx, b.x);
```

Contrast this with a method that does the very same thing. The only difference is that we do not know that a and b are distinct objects. All we
could do is to capture this requirement in a pre-condition a ≠ b.

```
protected void modifyA(Point a, Point b) {
    int bx = b.x;
    a.x = 42;
    assertEquals(bx, b.x);
}
```

However, the approach of making non-aliasing explicit does not scale: For
n distinct objects, we would have to state roughly n^2 inequalities. Furthermore, frame conditions would have to refer to "all other objects." At their
core, recent approaches therefore seek to reason explicitly about the heap
layout and to deduce the necessary inequalities from the layout.

↰4.2.6
213,38,67,102,103,20

Formally, the challenge is to give a suitable assignment rule for heap-
allocated objects: Writes to the heap can hit, in principle, any object on
the heap (as C programmers can testify). The simple syntactic substitution
in the classical assignment rule (4.14), where the "hit" variable is identified
by its name, is no longer sufficient.

A classical and timeless approach is Burstall's memory model. Burstall
observes that different fields, whether in the same class or in different
classes, never overlap in any of the instances. For example, the following
test works correctly regardless of the concrete objects a and b involved,
because the fields x and y never overlap.

58,49,177,88,20,22

```
public void burstall(Point a, Point b) {
    int by = b.y;
    a.x = 42;
    assertEquals(by, b.y);
}
```

Burstall concludes that for verification purposes, one can treat the different fields as named global arrays that are indexed by object pointers. For the source code $p.f = e$, we generate verification conditions for the array access $f[p] = e$. As in the classical assignment rule (4.14), the different names of the fields then imply that the fields do not overlap in memory. As a result, a large number of inequalities do not have to be stated explicitly in assertions.

195,213

Separation logic gives a particularly elegant solution to the challenge. The operator $\star$, called *spatial conjunction* or simply *star*, is the logical "and" of two assertions about *disjoint* parts of the heap. The assignment rule (4.24) can therefore identify the "hit" heap location, again syntactically: If p points to any value e' before the assignment, then afterward it points to e, and the remainder of the heap, described by Q, is not influenced.

38

(In separation logic, Hoare rules are usually applied forward instead of backward.) The fact that Q remains unchanged is derived here from the meaning of $\star$: The memory modified by the assignment is found at p, and that area is disjoint from the area to which Q refers.

$$/\!*\, p \mapsto e' \star Q \,*\!/ \quad *p = e; \quad /\!*\, p \mapsto e \star Q \,*\!/ \tag{4.24}$$

From a practitioner's point of view, separation logic is particularly elegant because it usually makes precise the reasoning steps that developers carry out by drawing pointer diagrams on a daily basis. For instance, the running example could be drawn as Fig. 4.15. On a whiteboard, we would cross out the old value x_a and literally overwrite it with the value 42. This also makes it clear that the value x_b is not touched, because it is elsewhere on the whiteboard—it is this intuition of "elsewhere" that the spatial conjunction $\star$ captures.

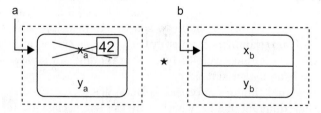

Figure 4.15 A Practical View of Separating Conjunction

Draw pointer diagrams for complex object structures.

The practical lesson to be gleaned from this outlook is that reasoning about the heap can become complex and tricky. It has taken computer science roughly 35 years, from 1969 to 2005, to progress from the first formalization of program verification itself to a general and scalable formalization of reasoning about the heap. The nice point about this eventual formalization is that it captures essentially the practice of drawing pointer diagrams,

119   38,213,195

which developers have been following in the meantime. Whenever you find yourself thinking about possible aliasing, you are now aware of two things: (1) that it is worth paying attention to details here and (2) that your diagrammatic reasoning rests on a solid foundation.

Chapter 5

Testing

Testing is an activity not much loved in the development community: You have to write code that does not contribute a shred of new functionality to your application, and the writing is frustrating, too, because most of the time the tests do not run through, so that you have to spend even more time on figuring out whether the test or the application code is wrong. Some people think that the reason for hiring special test engineers is to shield the real developers from the chores of testing and let them get on with their work.

Fortunately, the agile development movement has taught us otherwise: Testing is not the bane of productivity, but rather the backbone of productivity in software engineering. Testing makes sure we build the software we seek to build. Testing makes us think through the border cases and understand our own expectations of the software. Testing enables us to change the software and adapt it to new requirements. Testing lets us explore design and implementation alternatives quickly. Testing flattens the learning curve for new libraries. And finally, testing tells us when we are done with our task, and can go home and relax, so that we can return sprightly the next morning—if nothing else.

The purpose of this chapter is to show you that testing can actually be a very rewarding activity, and one that boosts both productivity and job satisfaction. The main point we will be pursuing is this:

Testing is all about checking our own expectations.

Whenever we write software, we are dealing with expectations of its future runtime behavior. In the previous chapter, we introduced assertions and contracts as a framework for reasoning about code to make sure it works once and for all. Many practitioners feel, however, that they need to see the code run to be convinced. Donald Knuth's formulation of this feeling has stuck through the decades: "Beware of bugs in the above code; I have only proved it correct, not tried it."

This chapter therefore complements the previous one by pointing out motivations and techniques for testing runtime behavior. Do not make the mistake of thinking that contracts become obsolete because you engage in testing: No serious software developer can develop serious software without forming a mental picture of assertions, contracts, and invariants that explain why the code works. Tests are only one (particularly effective) way of

28,29,172,171,92

4.1

139

capturing and trying out these assertions. Without having the assertions, you will not be able to write tests.

5.1   The Core: Unit Testing

Testing usually targets not whole applications, but rather single components and objects—most of the time, we perform *unit testing*. The underlying reasoning is, of course, that components conforming rigorously to their specifications will create a running overall application; to make sure that this is the case, we can always come back later and write tests targeting groups of components or even the entire application as their "units." These tests are then usually called *functional tests*, *integration tests*, or *acceptance tests*, if they concern use cases specified in the legal contract about the software. Because of its widespread use, good integration with Eclipse, and status as a pioneering implementation, we will use JUnit in this book.

📖34,30

Before looking any further, let us get in the right mindset about testing:

Testing is incredibly fast and cheap.

Since testing has become a central day-to-day activity in professional software development, the available Eclipse tooling supports the developer through all steps. Here is a very simple example that "tests" the built-in arithmetic:

testing.intro.Introduction

```
public class Introduction {
    @Test
    public void obvious() {
        assertEquals(42, 6 + 36);
    }
}
```

↰1.2.1

We have created this snippet in a few seconds by letting Eclipse generate the code: Typing @Test makes *Quick-Fix* (Ctrl-1) propose to add JUnit to the project's class path. Writing assertEquals proposes to add a static import for Assert.*, a common idiom for unit testing. Running tests is equally simple:

TOOL: Starting Unit Tests in Eclipse

Select *Debug As/JUnit Test Case* from the test class's context menu, either in the *Package Explorer* or in the editor. You can also press Alt-Shift-D T. When applying these steps to packages or projects, Eclipse will execute all contained test classes.

🔎 We typically use *Debug As* and `Alt-Shift-D`, rather than *Run As* and `Alt-Shift-X`, because the debugger will frequently come in handy. Thus it is a good idea, and one that comes with only a small overhead, to start the test in debug mode.

A little side view appears that announces by a bright, encouraging, green icon that the test has succeeded. The view also offers to rerun tests—the whole test suite, only the failed tests, or, through the context menu, selected test cases.

Tests boost productivity.

Compare this with the effort of manually trying out an application's behavior—for instance, because a user has reported a bug somewhere. Starting the UI, and then clicking through the various menus and dialogs until you can actually exercise the code deep down that you suspect of being faulty, can take several minutes, and does so every time you have to recheck the behavior after a change to the code.

Automatic JUnit tests, in contrast, let you run the suspected code directly, by creating a few objects and calling the method that seems to be the culprit. It is true that writing the first test for an object takes more time than clicking through the UI once. However, the effort is amortized quickly if for every attempt to fix the bug, you simply have to click a button to re-execute the test. Even the runtime of the test itself is much shorter than that of the application, because less infrastructure has to come up. In particular, if your application separates the core functionality from the user interface code, tests of the functionality will run an order of magnitude faster than the overall application.

»5.3.2.1
»9.1

Run tests frequently.

Tests are most beneficial if you run them after every change to the software: If you broke something in the software machinery, you will know immediately and you can fix it while the knowledge of the machinery is fresh in your mind. Since Eclipse makes running tests so simple, there is no reason not to make sure about the software every few minutes.

Make tests fully automatic.

Frequent testing is possible only if running the tests involves no more effort than pressing a button. For this to work out, all tests have to check the expected results automatically. It is not acceptable for tests to produce output for the user to inspect, because no one will bother checking the output manually, and the bugs introduced in a change will go unnoticed.

↰4.1

It is this automatic testing that creates the connection between testing and reasoning about software by assertions and contracts: Only if you have fixed your expectations in contracts will you be able to tell exactly which outcome to expect from a test. The test merely checks whether your expectation actually holds true. Conversely, writing automatic tests will advance your mastership of contracts. In the end, both techniques are complementary and mutually depending tools for achieving the goal of correctness.

Tests create fixtures for examining objects.

The challenge in making tests pay is to minimize the effort required to extract single functional units, whether they are objects or components, from the application and place them inside a test environment, which is also called a *fixture* in this context. Fig. 5.1 illustrates the point, in analogy to an electrical testing board (also sometimes called a fixture). You have to "wire up" the unit in an environment that enables it to perform its work. Some objects will "trigger" the unit by injecting data or calling methods; other objects will "observe" the behavior of the unit. Very often, these observers are just the assertEquals statements within the test case, which extract the result of computations from the unit and compare it with an expected value; sometimes they will be actual observers in the sense of the pattern. Finally, the target unit will need some collaborators, shown at the bottom of Fig. 5.1, which provide specific services.

↰2.1
≫5.3.2.1 ↰1.1

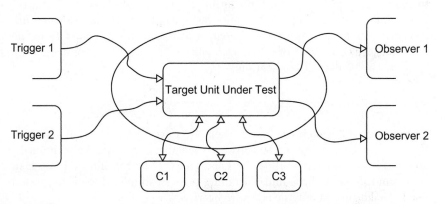

Figure 5.1 Creating a Fixture

Since fixtures are a common necessity, JUnit provides extensive support for them. It pays particular attention to the case where a number of test cases (i.e., a number of different trigger scenarios in Fig. 5.1) work in the context of the same fixture. The next sample code shows the procedure. For each method annotated @Test, the framework creates a new instance of the class, so that the test starts with a clean slate. It then runs the method tagged `@Before`, which can create the fixture by setting up the context of the unit under test. Next, it runs the actual `@Test` to trigger a specific behavior. Finally, it gives the method tagged `@After` the chance to clean up after the test, for instance by removing files created on disk. (The names `setUp` and `tearDown` reflect the JUnit3 naming conventions, which have stuck with many developers.)

```
                        testing.intro.Fixture
public class Fixture {
    private UnitUnderTest target;
    @Before
    public void setUp() {
        ... wire up target
    }
    @After
    public void tearDown() {
        ... free resources used in test
    }
    @Test
    public void test() {
        ... trigger behavior of target
    }
}
```

Sometimes it is useful to create a common environment for all test cases, such as by setting up a generic directory structure into which the different test files can be placed. This is accomplished by methods tagged `@BeforeClass` and `@AfterClass`.

Technically, each test case gets a fresh instance of the class, so the setup could also be done in the constructor or in field initializers. However, this is considered bad practice. First, exceptions thrown during setup get reported rather badly as "instance creation failed." Second, JUnit creates the instances of all test cases in the beginning, so that setups that acquire resources, open database connections, or build expensive structures can hit resource limits.

JUnit goes even further in creating fixtures by allowing you to parameterize the working environment of the target unit. Suppose you have written some code accessing databases. Since your clients will be using different database systems, you have to test your code on all of them. To accomplish this, you instruct JUnit to use a special executor (or runner) for the test suite, the pre-defined runner `Parameterized` (line 1 in the next snippet). That runner will query the test class for a list of values by invoking a static method tagged `@Parameters` (lines 8–15). The values are passed as arguments to the constructor (lines 5–7) and can then be retrieved later by the test cases (lines 18–19).

```
      testing.intro.ParameterizedTests
1 @RunWith(Parameterized.class)
2 public class ParameterizedTests {
3     private DBType databaseType;
4     private String host;
5     public ParameterizedTests(DBType databaseType, String host) {
6         ... store away the parameters
7     }
8     @Parameters
9     public static List<Object[]> getDatabaseTypes() {
10        Object parameters[][] = {
11                { new DBType("MySQL"), "localhost" },
12                ...
13        };
14        return Arrays.asList(parameters);
15    }
16    @Test
17    public void test() {
18        System.out.println("Accessing " + databaseType + " at "
19            + host);
20    }
21 }
```

Once such a fixture is in place, it is easy and lightweight to create yet another test, to cover yet another usage scenario for the target unit. Of course, the class can also contain further private helper methods that make it yet simpler to perform the elementary steps of triggering and observing the target unit.

↰1.4.5

See each test fail once.

Tests are only software themselves, and it is easy to make mistakes in tests. Very often, you might write a test with a particular special case of your software's behavior in mind, but not test the corresponding code segment at all.

Suppose you are unsure about whether the code for a special case in some method is correct. You trigger the method and observe the result. Because the result is as expected, you conclude that the code in question is correct. What may have happened, however, is that the actual execution has bypassed the existing bug. This problem can be avoided only if you see the bug manifest itself in the test once. Maybe you even check that the questionable code is executed using the debugger. If later the same test case succeeds, you can then be sure that you have tested the right thing and that thing is correct.

Write a regression test for every bug you find and fix.

There are many motivations and guidelines for testing. Since testing is all about the reliability of software, bugs are at its very core: Bugs, and the possibility of bugs, are the main reason for using tests. We therefore include one fundamental guideline here: Whenever you find a bug, write a test to expose the bug, then fix the bug, and finally see the test succeed. In this way, you document the successful solution and you ensure the bug will not resurface later on in case you just removed the symptom of the bug, rather than its source.

»5.4
»5.4.1

Let your testing inspire a modular design.

Before we go on to more detail, let us finish with one motivation for and outlook on testing that has always driven us to think carefully about the tests we write: Tests can help you create better designs.

»11.1 »12.1

The reason is a technical one: Whether it will be easier or harder to place a unit in a fixture clearly depends on how many connections the unit has with the objects in its environment, and how many assumptions it makes about these objects—the triggers and observers will have to replicate the machinery to fulfill these assumptions before testing can even begin. The underlying observation is that loose coupling provides for testability: An object that makes few assumptions, that is loosely coupled to its environment, will be easier to test.

»5.3.2.1

»12.1.2

The desire to write tests quickly can therefore guide you to structure your code in a more modular fashion, since a failure to achieve modularity shows up immediately in the increased effort of writing tests. Conversely, the effort put into creating a modular structure is partly compensated by the decreased effort required for writing tests.

163

»6.1.1

It is also interesting to see the situation in Fig. 5.1 as a form of reuse. That is, if a unit that was intended for an entirely different environment is placed into the testing fixture and still continues to work, then the likelihood that it can be reused in yet another, nontesting environment is increased.

»12.4

⇄? In fact, this argument describes the best possible outcome of extensive testing. The opposite outcome is also possible: If developers are forced to write tests and are measured only by how many acceptance tests are passed, they may be inspired to write quick and dirty code that gets them past the next release date. Be careful to take the right design cues from writing tests and to assign tests a constructive role in your software processes.

◄5.1

By now, you should be convinced that testing is beneficial beyond the nitty-gritty of tracing bugs and ensuring correct behavior. You should be itching to check your expectations on whether and how the software you are currently writing will actually work properly. JUnit, and other tools, are waiting to assist you in this quest.

5.2   The Test First Principle

Traditional software processes consider testing a post-hoc activity: You specify what your software is supposed to do, then you write the software, and finally you validate your implementation by writing tests. Unfortunately, this is often too late—by the time a bug is discovered, no one remembers clearly how the software was supposed to work in the first place; worse yet, very often a bug is only a manifestation of a misunderstanding in the specification, and substantial changes to the software will be required at the last minute. A conclusion that has been gaining more and more support in the community since the 1990s is the *test-first principle*:

92,29,171,172

> Start software development by writing tests.

At first, this is startling: How can you test something that is not even there? The explanation derives from the idea that the whole purpose of tests is to check your expectations. And the expectation of what the software under development will eventually do is clearly there right from the beginning—there is no reason not to write it down immediately.

Suppose that for your own source code editor, you want to build a text buffer that supports efficient modifications. Before you begin to write it, you capture some minimal expectations that you happen to think of:

1.3.1 4.1

```
                              testing.intro.TestFirst
public class TestFirst {
    private TextBuffer buf;
    @Before
    public void setUp() {
        buf = new TextBuffer();
    }
    @Test
    public void createEmpty() {
        assertEquals("", buf.getContent());
    }
    @Test
    public void insertToEmpty() {
        buf.insert(0, "hello, world");
        assertEquals("hello, world", buf.getContent());
    }
}
```

Unfortunately, the code does not even compile—you have not yet created the class `TextBuffer` or its methods `getContent` and `insert`. In fact, this is the intention of *test-driven development*: The test cases to be fulfilled drive which parts of the software need to be created and which behavior they should exhibit. Robert Martin proposes three laws that capture the essence:

5.4.3 5.4.5

171

1. You may not write production code unless you have first written a failing unit test.

2. You may not write more of a unit test than is sufficient to fail.

3. You may not write more production code than is sufficient to make the failing unit test pass.

These laws together suggest a particular way of developing software: Write a small unit test that fails, write just the functionality that is needed, ◀5.1
then proceed to the next test, and so on, until the tests cover the desired functionality. The interesting point is that the software developed in this way is correct—because it already passes all relevant tests.

In the previous example, we obeyed (1) but slightly bent (2), because we actually checked two expected behaviors. But the interesting point is (3): We have to make the tests succeed by adding just enough production code. Using *Quick-Fix* (`Ctrl-1`), we let Eclipse generate the missing class and the two missing methods. Then, at least, the code compiles, but the tests still fail, since the `getContent` always returns `null`:

---
testing.intro.TextBuffer

```java
public Object getContent() {
    // TODO Auto-generated method stub
    return null;
}
```

Even if the test fails so far, we have still gained something: We can run the test, it fails, and so by the second half of rule (1), we can start on the production code.

Tests keep you focused on what you want to achieve.

The interesting point in supplying the production code is that we are up against a concrete challenge: We do not want to find the ultimate version of `TextBuffer`; we just want the next test to succeed. In other words, we are looking for the "simplest thing that could possibly work." In this case, ▢28
we might first think about a `StringBuilder`. We get through the first test `createEmpty` by just defining:

---
testing.intro.TextBuffer

```java
private StringBuilder rep = new StringBuilder();
public Object getContent() {
    return rep.toString();
}
```

We can also solve the second task by adding:

testing.intro.TextBuffer

```
public void insert(int pos, String str) {
    rep.insert(pos, str);
}
```

Now both tests run through, and we can start the next round of testing-and-solving. For instance, we write a test for deleting a number of characters at a given position:

testing.intro.TestFirst

```
@Test
public void delete() {
    buf.insert(0, "hello, wonderful world");
    buf.delete(7, 10);
    assertEquals("hello, world", buf.getContent());
}
```

We can implement the new method immediately:

testing.intro.TextBuffer

```
public void delete(int pos, int len) {
    rep.delete(pos, pos + len);
}
```

The nice thing is that after every change, you rerun all tests to make sure immediately that the new functionality works and that the old functionality continues to work. You make steady progress on the goals at hand.

↰5.1

Test-first keeps you focused on the clients' perspective.

↰1.1

↰4.1 ↰4.2.2

»5.4.3

The initial depiction of objects already includes the injunction that in designing objects, we should always start from the clients' (i.e., the outside) point of view. This insight has resurfaced in the discussion of "good" contracts for methods. Test-driven development is a simple means of achieving this goal: If you start out by writing the client code before even thinking about the object's internals, these internals will not cloud your judgement about a good interface.

In the example of deletion, for instance, we translated the idea "a number of characters at a given position" into parameters (*pos*, *len*), and we discovered only afterward that the current representation uses parameters (*start*, *end*) instead. Since the representation is intended to be changeable, this is the way to go: The desirable client interface stays intact and sensible, and the details of the behavior are handled internally.

»11.5.1

Test-first ensures testability.

Another advantage of writing tests immediately is that the new unit does
not have to be extracted from its natural environment with a great effort—it   ↰5.1
first lives as a stand-alone entity and is then integrated into the application
context.

We remarked earlier that testing inspires modular design. Test-first in-   ↰5.1
creases this effect, because the units are created independently from one
another before they start collaborating. Since one writes only the minimal
test code that fails on the unit, the necessary fixture is kept to a minimum.
As a consequence, the unit will even be loosely coupled: As it makes few   ↠12.1
demands on the fixture, and since it works in that context, it will make few
demands on any context into which it will be deployed.

Test-first creates effective documentation.

Developers deplore writing documentation, because it does not contribute
to the functionality and becomes outdated quickly anyway. Conversely, developers love reading and writing code. Test code, when it is well structured   ↰1.2.3 ↰1.4.6
and readable, is a very effective documentation: Other team members can
read it as tutorial code that shows how the unit under test is supposed
to be used. With test-first, that explanation is even supplied by the original developer, who, of course, understands best the intention of the tested
unit. For the original developer, the test code serves as a reminder when
the developer comes back to the unit for maintenance.

5.3   Writing and Running Unit Tests

The basic usage of JUnit has already been explained: Just press `Alt-`   ↰5.1
`Shift-D T` to run the current class as a JUnit test suite. In most situations,
one needs to know a bit more about the concepts and the mechanics of testing. We treat these considerations here to keep this chapter self-contained,
even if they reference forward into later chapters.

5.3.1   Basic Testing Guidelines

Test development can be a substantial task, if it is taken seriously. Following a few guidelines will make this work much more effective, so that the
investment in tests pays off sooner.

Keep the tests clean.

Although tests may start out as ad-hoc artifacts created to explore and fix   ↠5.4.1
specific bugs, they must really be seen as a long-term investment. Much of   ↠5.4.8
their benefit shows up during maintenance, possibly long after the software

↰5.1

📖172(Ch.9)

↰1.4.5 ↰1.4.8
↰1.8.5 ↰3.1.4
↰1.2.3

has been developed and deployed. This means, however, that the tests them-selves must be maintained in parallel with the software and that they must be ready to be run at any given time. Running the tests frequently and making them automatic is one precaution, but it must also be easy to ex-tend the test suite to cover extensions of the software, and to adapt the tests to changes in the requirements and the behavior of the software.

Since tests in this way become an integral part of the software, they should be kept as clean and as maintainable as the production code. For in-stance, one can factor out common setup and test fixtures, either in separate methods, classes, or superclasses, and one should certainly spend time on good naming to make the code self-documenting. The immediate reward for these activities is the feedback that all tests are up and running. The long-term reward is a dependable software product.

Keep the tests up-to-date.

↰5.1

Tests must be maintained carefully to enable them to fulfill their role, in particular in the long range: If every month one test case gets broken and the developer does not bother to check out the problem, after a few years there will be so many rotten tests that no one dares to run them frequently, and newly broken tests will not be recognized. Such a test suite is a lost investment, one that consumes development time without ever producing any benefits.

Document known problems using succeeding tests.

↰5.1

A corner case arises with known problems and limitations of the software: On the one hand, they are bugs and should be documented by tests. On the other hand, you do not intend to fix them right away because they are low-priority items. Adding a test nevertheless will make JUnit report an overall "red bar," with the consequences just discussed. The solution is to write the test, say clearly that it constitutes a failure, but make it show as "green" nevertheless—for instance, by catching the (expected) exception. Later on, when there is some time, you can simply turn the test "red" and fix the known problem.

Test against the interface, not the implementation.

📖233

Software engineers usually distinguish between black-box and white-box tests. Black-box tests capture the behavior as stated in the specification. White-box tests look at the actual source code to ensure, for instance, that every branch in the code is covered by at least one test. The danger of looking at the implementation too closely is that the tests are blind to the border cases not covered there. Also, if the implementation changes later,

↰1.1

the original tests will no longer achieve their objective.

To integrate both perspectives, it is sensible to align tests with the specification, but to look into the implementation to discover those special cases that the specification does not mention. Such a case can be interpreted in two ways: Either the specification is incomplete, or the code does something that is not covered by its specification. If the case does not follow immediately from the specification, it should be mentioned explicitly, at least in some internal comment, so that the maintenance team can understand its necessity. In this way, the tests will finally target the software's interface and will provide a very effective documentation.

Make each test check one aspect.

Tests are useful for capturing contracts and checking for behavior in detail. This works best if each test covers one specific behavior or reaction of the software: The test's name links to that detail, the triggers are limited to the bare necessities, and the test's asserts check the one expected outcome. With this setup, a failing test points immediately to a specific mechanism that has been broken. In test-driven development, each test case corresponds to a use case, and each should be documented and described independently.

»5.4.2

↰5.1

↰5.2 »5.4.6

Writing a separate test for each aspect requires slightly more overhead than testing a multistep behavior in a single go, because one needs to apply similar triggers and check similar assertions in the end. This overhead can be minimized by keeping tests clean and by factoring out the common code.

We note, however, that sometimes bugs manifest themselves only in specific sequences of interactions; these should, of course, be written up as a single test case. This point does not contradict the general rule, because only the granularity of what constitutes an "aspect" has changed: The aspect here is the interaction between the different invoked features.

Keep tests independent.

The order in which tests are run is not defined, even if you might observe that your specific version of JUnit executes tests in alphabetical order. Tests that rely on such an order are not very useful: The larger context complicates bug tracking, while the main point of testing is to create a small, well-defined context for the purpose. Also, such tests cannot be rerun on their own for debugging if they fail.

Tests runs should be reproducible.

Tracking failures in tests is greatly simplified if the code is executed in exactly the same way each time the test is started. After the error is shown, you can use the debugger to step through the code, possibly restarting if you missed the crucial point at the first try. This implies that the fixture must be set up in the same way for each run.

Even so, it can still be useful to create randomized input data. First, of course, such tests might catch border cases that you had not identified previously. Second, creating bulk data by hand is hardly effective. There is certainly no harm in using randomized tests as a complementary set of usage scenarios besides the hand-coded fixtures. You might also consider saving the created input to disk explicitly to make the tests themselves deterministic.

Don't modify the API for the tests.

One crucial problem of tests is that their assertions can often be written up best by peeking at the internal state of the target unit. At some point in the test code you might think, "I'm not sure about whether this object is actually already broken." In such a circumstance, you would like to check its invariant, but that invariant is about the internal fields that are not accessible.

◄4.1

It is a bad idea to make fields public or to create getters just for testing purposes: Clients may think that these members belong to the official API and start using them in regular code, even if the documentation indicates that the member is visible only for testing purposes. Also, the test relies on the target's internals, so that an enhancement of these internals may break the test even though the final outcome remains correct. Testing the internals goes against the grain of encapsulation and destroys its benefits.

▶11.5.1

If you feel that you really must look at the internals of an object, you can make private and protected fields visible at runtime using reflection. Line 5 gets a handle on a private field in the target unit. Line 6 overrides the access protection enforced by the JVM, so that line 7 can actually get the value.

```
                     testing.basics.AccessPrivateTest
1 @Test
2 public void accessPrivateState() throws Exception {
3     TargetUnit target = new TargetUnit();
4     target.compute();
5     Field state = target.getClass().getDeclaredField("state");
6     state.setAccessible(true);
7     assertEquals(42, state.get(target));
8 }
```

Test the hard parts, not the obvious ones.

Writing and maintaining tests is always an effort, and it must be justified by corresponding benefits. Since the core benefit of tests is to check for the absence of bugs in specific usage scenarios, a test is futile if it checks obvious things. For instance, testing a setter by calling the corresponding getter afterward will not be very useful. Conversely, if the setter has further side

effects on the object's state and is expected to send out change notifications, ↰2.1
then it might be a good idea to include a test of these reactions. In general,
it is useful to test behavior

- That has a complex specification ↠5.4.2

- Whose implementation you have understood poorly

- Whose implementation involves complex, possibly cross-object invari- ↠6.2.3
  ants

- That is mission-critical to the project

- That is safety-critical ↠5.4.7

Focusing on such aspects of the product also increases the immediate reward of the tests and motivates the team to keep the tests up-to-date and ↠5.4.10
clean.

Write tests that leave the "happy path."

The happy path of a software is its defined functionality: Given the right
inputs, it should deliver the expected results. It is obvious that tests should
cover this expected behavior to verify that the software achieves its purpose.
Focusing tests on the happy path is also encouraged by the non-redundancy ↰4.5
principle from design-by-contract: The code remains simpler if a method ↰4.1
does not check its pre-conditions, so it is free to return any result or even
crash entirely if the caller violates the contract. Testing the happy path
respects such a behavior.

However, many components of a software must be resilient to unexpected inputs or must at least fail gracefully if something does not go according to plan. Foremost, the boundary objects must be paranoid about ↰4.6 ↰1.8.7
their input: Users or other systems will routinely submit erroneous inputs
and the system must cope without crashing. However, the safety-critical
internal components must also not do anything dangerous just because of
a bug in some other component.

In such cases, it is important to write tests that leave the software's
happy path. These tests deliberately submit ill-formatted input or input
outside the specified range and check that nothing bad happens: Negative
numbers in ordering items must not trigger a payment to the customer, ill-
formatted strings must not bring the server crashing down, and the robot
arm must not damage the surrounding equipment because of a wrong movement parameter.

Because professional software is, above all, reliable software, professional
developers routinely write several times as many tests for "wrong" scenarios
as for the happy path. If nothing else, writing many such tests spares you
the embarrassment of seeing your customer break the software in the first
demo session.

5.3.2   Creating Fixtures

↰5.1

One of the most time-consuming tasks in testing is the setup of the fixture, which is then shared between different related test cases. We therefore include a brief discussion of common techniques used here.

5.3.2.1   Mock Objects

↰1.1 ↱11.2

Since objects are small and focus on a single purpose, they usually require collaborators that perform parts of a larger task on their behalf. As Fig. 5.1 on page 246 indicates, these collaborators must be included in any testing fixture. However, this might be problematic: The collaborators might be developed independently and might not even exist at the time, especially in test-first scenarios. They might be large and complex, which would destroy the test's focus. They might be complex to set up, which bloats the fixture and increases the test's runtime. Put briefly, such collaborators need to be replaced.

Mock objects simulate part of the behavior of production objects.

📖163,29

Mock objects are replacements for collaborators that exhibit just the behavior required in the concrete testing scenario. They do not reimplement the full functionality; in fact, they might even fake the answers to specific method calls known to arise in the given test scenario.

↰2.1 ↱9.1

As a simple example, the Document in a word processor might be observed by a user interface component that renders the content on the screen. When testing the document, this rendering is irrelevant and blurs the test's focus. One therefore registers a mock observer that merely keeps all the events in a list (lines 2–3) and later checks that all expected events have arrived (line 6; the method merely loops through the given events and checks their data against that of the received events).

testing.mock.DocumentTest.testNotification

```
1 Document doc = new Document("0123456789");
2 MockObserver obs = new MockObserver();
3 doc.addDocumentListener(obs);
4 doc.replace(3, 2, "ABC");
5 assertEquals("012ABC56789", doc.get());
6 obs.checkEvents(new DocumentEvent(doc, 3, 2, "ABC"));
```

Mock objects can check early.

📖163

Tests are most useful if they fail early: If the final result of a test is wrong, then the bug must be hunted throughout the executed code. Mock objects make it simpler to create such early failures, because they naturally "listen in" on the conversation of the application object with its collaborators. In the preceding example, for instance, the `MockObserver` could also have been told the expected events up front, so that any irregularity would have been spotted early, and with a stack trace and debugger state leading to the point of the modification.

Mock objects can inject errors.

Robust software also handles error situations gracefully. To test this handling, it necessary to create these situations artificially, which might not be simple: You cannot simply unplug the network cable at a specific moment during the test to simulate network failure. However, you can create a mock network socket that behaves as if the network connection had been broken. The difference will not be visible to the target unit of the test—all it sees is an exception indicating the failure. (Note also the arbitrary result returned by `read()`; making the integer sequential might help debugging.)

---

testing.mock.MockBrokenNetwork

```java
public class MockBrokenNetwork extends InputStream {
    private int breakAt;
    private int length;
    private int currentCount;
    public MockBrokenNetwork(int breakAt, int length) {
        this.breakAt = breakAt;
        this.length = length;
    }
    public int read() throws IOException {
        if (currentCount == breakAt)
            throw new IOException("network unreachable");
        if (currentCount == length)
            return -1;
        return currentCount++;
    }
}
```

Separate components by interfaces to enable mock objects.

To work with the target unit of the test, the mock objects must be subtypes of the expected production classes. The easiest way to enable this is to anticipate the need for mock objects and to let the likely objects requiring testing interact only with interfaces. As a side effect, this leads to a desirable decoupling between the system's components. The goal of testing can then serve as an incentive to refactor the production code by introducing interfaces.

↰3.2.7 ↦12.1

Furthermore, the introduction of interfaces leads to a design where you think in terms of *roles* rather than concrete objects. Roles help to focus on the essential expected behavior of objects, rather than the concrete implementation. Also, they enable the designer to differentiate between client-specific interfaces, which structures the individual objects further.

↰3.2.1 ↦11.3.3.7

↰3.2.2

⚠ Do not introduce interfaces just because a mock object is required, since this will make the production code less readable. If the majority of types in the code are abstract interfaces, the human reader has to find, using the *Type Hierarchy*, that there is just a single implementation. Introduce interfaces for testing only if this also improves the production code.

Mock objects improve the design quality.

📖163

The original proposal of mock objects observes several beneficial effects of mock objects on the design and structure of the production code. Beyond the possible decoupling of interfaces mentioned previously, objects tend to become smaller and will make fewer assumptions on their environment, just because recreating this environment by mock objects for tests becomes so much harder. Furthermore, the use of the SINGLETON pattern is discouraged further, because it fixes the concrete type of the created object so that the object cannot be replaced. As a strategic effect, mock objects encourage the use of observer or visitor relationships, both of which tend to enable extensibility of the system by new operations and hence new functionality.

↰1.3.8

↰2.1 ↰2.3.2
↠12.3

5.3.3 Dependency Injection

📖201

Large frameworks, such as the JavaEE platform, offer applications a solid ground on which to build their specific functionality. Furthermore, they serve as containers that provide the application with predefined services such as database persistence or user authentication. To use a service, the application must get hold of the object(s) that constitute the entry point to the service's API. As more and more services are offered and consumed, the application gets tangled up with boilerplate code to access the required API objects.

📖251,137,252

Dependency injection is the way out. With this approach, the application declares, by simple annotations, which service objects it requires and relies on the container to provide them transparently. The boilerplate code is replaced by general framework mechanisms for providing dependencies before an object starts working. We will focus here on the core of dependency injection but note that injection frameworks usually offer much more, such as the management of the different components' life cycles and fine-tuned mechanisms for producing service objects.

Dependency injection helps in creating fixtures.

The central point in the current context is that dependency injection can be used to create fixtures: Once the general mechanisms are in place, they are not limited to a predefined set of container-provided services, but apply equally to different objects and components within the application. If the application uses this setup throughout, then it becomes straightforward to replace production objects with mock objects for testing.

Let us make a tiny example using the JavaEE Context Dependency Injection (CDI), mirroring the overview provided in Fig. 5.1 directly. Some target unit requires two collaborators: one basic `Service` and one `Collaborator`, which is specified through an interface to enable its replacement. We mark both as `@Inject` to request suitable instances from the injection framework. 📖251

```
                        testing.inject.TargetUnit
public class TargetUnit {
    @Inject private Service service;
    @Inject private Collaborator colleague;
    public int compute() {
        return service.compute(colleague.getData());
    }
}
```

The unit test must now set up the framework once (lines 1–4) and must access the target unit through the framework to enable injections (line 8). Otherwise, the test proceeds as usual (lines 9–10).

```
                       testing.inject.InjectionTest
1 @BeforeClass
2 public static void setup() {
3     weld = new Weld().initialize();
4 }
5 @Test
6 public void runWithInjection() {
7     TargetUnit target =
8         weld.instance().select(TargetUnit.class).get();
9     int result = target.compute();
10    assertEquals(42, result);
11 }
```

The framework will pick up any *beans*, which are Java classes with a default constructor that obey a few restrictions, from the class path and match them against the types, and possible other qualifiers, of an injection point. In this way, the local service can be provided as a standard class without further annotations. 📖137

```
                         testing.inject.Service
public class Service {
    public int compute(int data) {
        return data * 2;
    }
}
```

The mock implementation for the `Collaborator`, in contrast, is marked as an *alternative* implementation, so that it does not usually get picked up automatically.

---
testing.inject.MockCollaborator

```
@Alternative
public class MockCollaborator implements Collaborator {
    public int getData() {
        return 21;
    }
}
```

The container uses this special implementation only if the configuration file
`META-INF/beans.xml`, which can be specific to the testing environment,
contains a corresponding entry:

```
<alternatives>
  <class>testing.inject.MockCollaborator</class>
</alternatives>
```

Of course, the concept of alternative implementations also applies to concrete classes, so that we could replace the `Service` by a `MockService` in
the testing environment.

As an overall result, the testing context wires up all dependencies into
the target from the outside, so that the target unit contains the unmodified
production code. Dependency injection has helped to create an effective
fixture.

5.3.4   Testing OSGi Bundles

📖174
»A.1

The Eclipse platform provides a solid basis for your own application development. Its strength is a flexible and expressive module system, called
OSGi (short for Open Services Gateway initiative). OSGi enables components, called *bundles*, to coexist within a Java application. In Eclipse, the
term *bundle* is synonymous with *plugin* for historical reasons. The OSGi
framework provides many services, such as notifications at startup and shutdown of the application, and the dynamic loading and unloading of bundles,
which go beyond the capabilities of the standard Java runtime. Testing
OSGi bundles therefore requires this framework to be up to provide the
expected infrastructure.

> **TOOL: Quick-Start JUnit Plugin Test**
>
> As a shortcut to running tests on top of the OSGi platform, just use
> *Debug as/JUnit Plug-in Test* from the context menu of the current class
> or press `Alt-Shift-D P` (instead of `Alt-Shift-D T` for the usual unit
> tests).

»A.1.4
↰5.1

⚠ Unfortunately, this configuration is rarely useful: It selects all plugins in the current
workspace and from the Eclipse target platform, so that starting up the test is
unbearably slow and makes it impossible to run the test frequently.

TOOL: Launching JUnit Plugin Tests

Under *Debug/Debug Configurations*, the category *JUnit Plug-in Test* provides launchers for tests that require the OSGi platform. When you enter this dialog after selecting a test class, the *New Launch Configuration* toolbar item will create the same setup as the quick-start described earlier. However, you can configure it immediately. Once the test is configured, you can always reinvoke it with `Alt-Shift-D P`.

The first task in configuring is to select only the required plugins. Go to the new test, and then to the tab titled *Plug-ins*. You should first *Deselect all*. Then, you can reselect the plugin containing the test and click *Add required plug-ins*. At this point, the setup contains the minimal number of necessary bundles and startup time will be quick.

Try to use *Headless mode* whenever you are not actually testing the user interface. Starting tests with the Eclipse user interface up, even if it is never used, takes much time. In the tab titled *Main*, you should therefore set the selection *Run an application* to *Headless mode*.

As seen in the *Main* tab, the test is run in a special work area that gets erased when the tests are launched. However, for performance reasons, the work area is *not* deleted before the single tests, as the following code shows: The first test case creates a project that the second expects to be present. (We rely here on the alphabetic order behavior of our local JUnit implementation.)

testing.doc.ResourcesUsageTest

```
@Test
public void nonErasedBetweenTestsA() throws CoreException {
    ResourcesPlugin.getWorkspace().getRoot()
            .getProject("Retained")
            .create(null);
}
@Test
public void nonErasedBetweenTestsB() throws CoreException {
    assertTrue(ResourcesPlugin.getWorkspace().getRoot()
            .getProject("Retained").exists());
}
```

Plugin tests can exploit the powerful OSGi infrastructure. For instance, they can take advantage of libraries contained within bundles and can use a test workspace as a scratchpad for creating data. ≫A.2.1

In summary, testing on top of the OSGi platform is simple and cheap if you follow a few straightforward rules. Furthermore, it gives you the OSGi infrastructure for free.

5.3.5 Testing the User Interface

The user interface is, in some sense, the most important part of an application, because its quality will determine whether you earn the users' trust. Put simply, if the interface misbehaves too often, the users will deduce that the application is a bit flaky on the whole and will not apply it for critical tasks. It is therefore desirable to test the user interface. The Eclipse environment offers the SWTBot project for the purpose. Before we give a brief description, let us put the overall goal into perspective.

📖83

Minimize the need for user interface tests.

»7.1

»10.1

Unfortunately, user interface tests pose two new challenges, compared to tests of an application's business logic. First, user interfaces are event-driven, meaning they react to single user inputs, one at a time, and the sequence of these inputs will determine their reaction. Think of the *New Class* dialog in Eclipse. It should not matter whether you enter the class name or the package name first; the checks for legality should run in the same way. However, surprisingly often the concrete code does have a preference, because its developer thought of one particular input sequence. Thorough tests must encompass not just a simple collection of input/output scenarios; they also will need to drive at an expected result by several different interaction paths. A second, more fundamental problem is that user interfaces are volatile, since they have to be adapted to the users' changing requirements at short notice. However, even simple "style-only" changes, such as in the order or labels of buttons, can sometimes break the test cases and necessitate extensive and expensive rework.

»9.1

Invest in testing the core, rather than the user interface.

»9.1

Fortunately, well-engineered applications separate the user interface code from the core functionality. Ideally, the user interface is a simple, shallow layer that displays the application data and triggers operations in the core. The unit tests of the core functionality will then go a long way toward making the application well behaved. At the same time, these unit tests are rather straightforward. The testing of the actual user interface can then focus on the overall integration and on demonstrating that all use cases are covered.

»5.4.4 »5.4.6

The SWTBot simulates the events fired by the real widgets.

»7.1

User interfaces, very briefly, fill the screen with *widgets*, such as text fields, their labels, and buttons. Whenever the user interacts with these widgets, such as by typing into a text field or clicking a button with the mouse, the widgets send *events* to the application; in turn, the application takes corresponding actions. In a rough approximation, one could say that the

application observes the widgets, even if the notifications do not usually   ↰2.1
concern the widgets' state.

Consider the very simple application in Fig. 5.2. The user types two
numbers into the fields labeled A and B, and clicks the button. The application is to compute the sum of the two numbers.

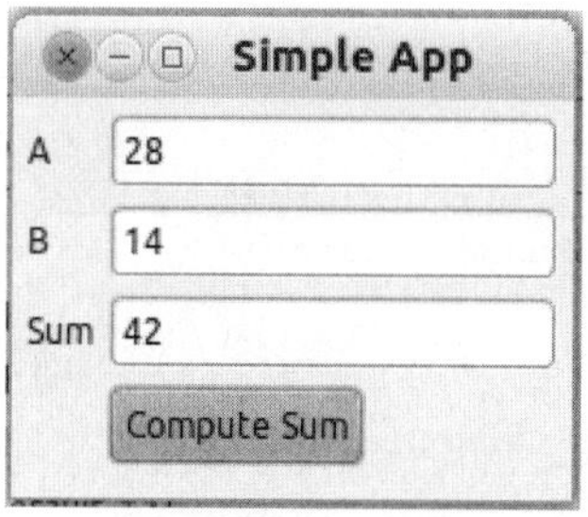

Figure 5.2 Simple Example Application for SWTBot

When the user interacts with the widgets, the application is notified
about these interactions. The SWTBot allows test cases to trigger the same
sequences of events automatically and repeatably. One challenge consists of
identifying the components on the screen. The SWTBot offers many search
methods, each of which returns a proxy for the real widget.   ↰2.4.3

Here is a simple example for this application. Line 3 looks up the first
test field (the tree of widgets) and uses the proxy to "type" some text. Line 4   ↠7.1
fills text field B accordingly, and line 5 searches for a button by its label
and "clicks" it through the proxy. Finally, line 6 checks the result text field.

---

testing.swt.SimpleAppTest

```
1 @Test
2 public void checkAddition() {
3     bot.text(0).setText("28");
4     bot.text(1).setText("14");
5     bot.button("Compute Sum").click();
6     assertEquals("42", bot.text(2).getText());
7 }
```

To apply the SWTBot, the JUnit test has to start the application under
test. If you are testing whole Eclipse applications, then the SWTBot run
configurations under *Run as/Configurations* will do the job. It is also possible to start applications programmatically. Because user interfaces involve
rather subtle threading issues, some care must be taken. The mechanics are   ↠7.10.1
already available in a JUnit runner class; you just have to fill in the actual
starting code:

---

testing.swt.SimpleAppTestRunner

```
public class SimpleAppTestRunner
    extends SWTBotApplicationLauncherClassRunner {
    public SimpleAppTestRunner(Class<?> klass) throws Exception {
```

```
        super(klass);
    }
    @Override
    public void startApplication() {
        SimpleApp.main(new String[0]);
    }
}
```

Then, you have to tell JUnit to run the test suite with that specialized runner:

---
testing.swt.SimpleAppTest

```
@RunWith(SimpleAppTestRunner.class)
public class SimpleAppTest {
    private static SWTBot bot;
    @BeforeClass
    public static void setupClass() {
        bot = new SWTBot();
    }
        ...
}
```

↰5.3.4

    🔍 The SWTBot works only for OSGi plugin tests. Since this is its main application area, it also starts up the Eclipse platform, which takes a few hundred milliseconds. Testing the user interface is therefore slightly less lightweight than unit testing, which is another argument for focusing tests on the core functionality.

In summary, it is feasible to test the user interface with JUnit, in much the same way that one tests any component. Because of the challenges mentioned in this section, however, it is a good idea not to test aspects of the functionality that could just as easily be tested independently of the user interface by targeting the core functionality directly.

5.4 Applications and Motivations for Testing

So far, we have explained the motivation for testing by exploring its benefits. For day-to-day work, this presentation might be too far removed from the actual decisions about what to test and when to test. Consequently, this section seeks to complement the previous material by identifying concrete challenges that can be addressed by tests. We hope that the list will serve as an inspiration for you to write more, and more varied, tests, and at the same time to be more conscious of the goals behind the single tests, as such an understanding will help you structure the test suites coherently.

5.4.1 Testing to Fix Bugs

A good point to start writing tests in earnest is when you encounter a really nasty bug, one that you have been tracking down for an hour or so.

One of the central and most fundamental strategies in the bug hunt is, of course, to dissect the software and to isolate the faulty behavior. Tests do just that: You have a suspicion of which component is the culprit, so you extract it from its natural surroundings to examine it in detail (Fig. 5.1 on page 246). If you already have a fixture for the component, the work is much simplified. If you don't, the potential gain in the concrete situation at hand might be a strong incentive to create one.

Write a test to expose the bug, then fix it.

Testing always starts with a failing test, after which one modifies the pro-   ↰5.1
duction code to make the test succeed. Afterward, the test can be run frequently, and can be used to make sure the desired behavior stays intact. This procedure matches the case of catching bugs perfectly.

Suppose you have written a component SortedIntArray, which keeps a set of ints in an array; it keeps the array sorted for quick lookups. The central point is an implementation of binary search to look up elements and to determine insertion points. As usual, a loop keeps bisecting a search   ↰4.7.3
range until a single possible occurrence has been isolated.

testing.bugs.SortedIntArray

```
 1 private int findPos(int n) {
 2     int i = 0;
 3     int j = cnt.length;
 4     while (i < j) {
 5         int mid = (i + j) / 2;
 6         if (n > cnt[mid])
 7             i = mid;
 8         else
 9             j = mid;
10     }
11     return i;
12 }
13
```

Unfortunately, colleagues complain that the code sometimes fails to terminate, but since they are not algorithmics experts, they do not want to touch the thing. Also, they cannot give you an exact case, because the code loops, so what can they do? (They could use the debugger and suspend execution.)

Your reasoning starts with the idea of the loop (or the loop invariant):   ↰4.7.3
The sought element occurs within $[i, j)$, if at all. If the loop does not terminate, it must fail to make progress in limiting that search range. But this can happen only if mid happens to be, again, i because of rounding down in integer division. This behavior should occur if you insert an element and then a greater element, which is just what the following test does.

testing.bugs.SortedArrayTest

```
@Test
public void bugNontermination() {
    SortedIntArray arr = new SortedIntArray();
    arr.insert(1);
    arr.insert(2);
    assertTrue(arr.contains(1));
    assertTrue(arr.contains(2));
}
```

After confirming that the code does, indeed, loop, you can fix the problem. The point is that line 7 does not take full advantage of the test in line 6 in limiting the search range, because we know that n cannot occur at mid. So the fix is as follows; after applying it, the test succeeds.

testing.bugs.SortedIntArray

```
i = mid + 1;
```

Tests make you more productive in this context because they allow you to check your conjecture about the source of the bug immediately and concretely, and in an isolated surrounding that excludes external influences.

A bug nailed down by a test will stay away.

The strategy of exposing bugs by tests also addresses the deeper reason for the existence of bugs that are not mere typos: Those bugs occur in complex parts of the functionality, at the interaction points between modules with complex APIs, or in the area of poorly understood requirements. If a bug occurs once in such a place, then it is likely to resurface after someone touches the code for maintenance. Running all bug-hunting tests immediately after each such change ensures that the bugs once found will keep away.

Each bug you find is a bug the customer won't find.

Another reason for excluding bugs by tests is that you document that it has been found and fixed. If your customers still find some kind of misbehavior, then at least you know you have to look elsewhere.

5.4.2   Testing to Capture the Contracts

While bug fixing may be a good motivation to start testing, more is gained by using tests right from the beginning, because they can document the API of components better than any JavaDoc. Whether you actually write the tests before the production code does not matter so much: You end up with test code that shows how to use the production components.

↰5.2

Tests document typical call sequences.

All components and objects in software are designed to be used in specific ways: Files must be opened before they can be read from, a database access layer needs to be set up with specific parameters before it works properly, and an application-specific data structure may impose usage restrictions, such as requiring clients to flush some cache after they have applied modifications.

Writing such details into the documentation is, of course, very helpful—but the reality is that developers do not like reading documentation. They prefer reading code, and they prefer running code even more. From this perspective, just writing up the expected usage in the form of test cases will be extremely helpful.

Suppose, for instance, that your team had written the Eclipse resource API. To explain how to create a file within the workspace, you could provide the following test case as an example usage; it sets up a new project within the testing workspace and creates a file in lines 10 and 11. These lines also ↰5.3.4 explain the fundamental principle that resources are first only *handles*, for which a concrete file may or may not yet exist on disk.

```
                    testing.doc.ResourcesUsageTest
1 @Test
2 public void createFile() throws CoreException {
3     prj = ResourcesPlugin.getWorkspace().getRoot()
4             .getProject("Testproject");
5     assertFalse(prj.exists());
6     prj.create(null);
7     prj.open(null);
8     ByteArrayInputStream bytes = new ByteArrayInputStream(
9             "Hello, world".getBytes());
10    IFile hello = prj.getFile("hello.txt");
11    hello.create(bytes, false, null);
12    assertTrue(hello.exists());
13 }
```

Tests can capture the border cases.

The preceding test also demonstrates the extreme detail that can be expressed in tests. Line 6 creates a project to contain the later file. One point that users of the API might stumble over is that even existing projects cannot be used immediately, but must be *opened* first. Line 7 clarifies the issue. A user confronted with an exception will look into test to see why it succeeds, and will spot the difference immediately.

Another point made implicitly in the test is that files must always be contained in projects. To make this explicit, you might explain the API further by the following test case:

```
                        testing.doc.ResourcesUsageTest
@Test(expected = IllegalArgumentException.class)
public void noTopFiles() throws CoreException {
    IFile top = ResourcesPlugin.getWorkspace().getRoot()
            .getFile(new Path("toplevel.txt"));
    top.create(new ByteArrayInputStream("top".getBytes()),
        false, null);
}
```

Tests remain in sync with the production code.

One of the principal complaints about documentation is that it is usually outdated, because there is usually too little time to keep the software itself up-to-date with requirements, let alone overhaul the documentation at the same time. Some developers take this observation as an excuse not to write any documentation at all.

Agile development, in contrast, takes the complaint as an incentive to write code that is self-documenting. However, this goal is best complemented by suitable testing: Since tests are run frequently, any inconsistency of the documentation provided through them is detected immediately.

5.4.3   Testing to Design the Interface

Choosing an appropriate interface for an object is not a simple task: The interface should be sufficiently general to make the object useful in different situations, yet it should be sufficiently specialized to enable clients to use the object easily in their specific situation. Furthermore, the interface must encapsulate the technical details of the object's implementation and must be understandable from the purpose of the class alone.

Achieving all of these goals requires a good feeling for what the client code will actually look like. One has to anticipate the use of names, the call sequences of methods, and the availability of information passed as parameters, and one has to make assumptions about the collaborators in the object's neighborhood.

Consider the test to be the first client.

Tests can offer guidelines, as they force you to write down the code that will later appear in the tested unit's clients. Especially with the test-first approach, you can judge the effectiveness of the interface before the implementation is in place.

Suppose you are to write an object for importing CSV data. A number of decisions need to be made: How will the object get its input? Is it passed to the constructor, as in the Java I/O library, or is there a method setInput(), as in the JFace library? Will the input data be given as a file or as a generic InputStream? Other questions also arise: What is a suitable output format? A sequence of String arrays can be implemented easily, but is this sufficient? If the client wants to store the result in a database, it might be better to wrap the data into JPA entities. But does this happen within the importer? The Single Responsibility Principle suggests rather not, and the PIPES AND FILTERS pattern proposes the alternative of creating entities in a postprocessing step. Still other details must be settled as well: How do we represent a sequence? Using the `Iterator` interface? Or like a SAX parser, which hands the read elements to a handler object one by one?

»5.4.9
»11.2
»12.3.4

All of these questions admit different answers, and most of these answers are valid options. In software engineering, there is seldom only one ultimate solution. The best way to proceed is to pick a likely path and use test cases to determine whether it can carry the load. Seeing that the importer will have to be configurable, we decide to pass the input via a setter (line 6), using a generic `InputStream` (line 3) as the basis. Next, `Iterators` can be hard to implement, because implementing `hasNext()` essentially has to pre-fetch the next entry. We therefore decide on a method `next()` that returns an array of strings or `null`, similar to `BufferedReader.readLine()`. This admits the elegant loop in line 12. The test is completed by checking the result (lines 9–11, 13, 16).

```
                         testing.interfaces.FirstClientTest
1  @Test
2  public void testCSVImporter() throws IOException {
3      InputStream sampleInput = getClass().getResourceAsStream(
4              "customers.csv");
5      CSVImporter importer = new CSVImporter();
6      importer.setInput(sampleInput);
7      String[] row;
8      int count = 0;
9      String[][] expected = {
10              ... test data matching customers.csv
11      };
12      while ((row = importer.next()) != null) {
13          assertArrayEquals(expected[count], row);
14          count++;
15      }
16      assertEquals(4, count);
17  }
```

Tests make for lightweight exploration of design choices.

The solution given here may not be ideal, but you can certainly evaluate its achievements. If in the end you decide that the interface needs to change, then at least no production code depends on the discarded version as yet. Furthermore, you will have the functionality behind the interface up and running, so there is no uncertainty about whether the revised interface admits an efficient implementation: Just refactor the implementation to fit the new choice.

◄1.2.2

Tests can preview notification behavior.

↰5.3.2
↰5.3.2.1 ↰2.1
↠7.1

So far, we have discussed the design of only the trigger part of the test fixture. However, you can also create mock objects for the notifications and events. This enables you to see the new object from its active side and check how it will interact with its collaborators. In the process, you will get a feeling for whether the interactions are useful to the collaborators, whether enough and the right information is passed on, and so on.

Use tests to specify your ideal API.

📖172

A special case of interface design occurs in developments that are spread over different teams. In this context, tests can be used to capture an ideal interface for components that are yet to be written.

Suppose, for instance, that your application needs to access some new hardware device, for which another team is just writing the actual low-level driver. There is a high probability that the driver's interface will reflect the device's characteristics, rather than the demands of your application. As a result, you will probably have to wrap the driver to avoid dealing with low-level details throughout the application code.

↰2.4.1

↰5.3.2.1

A better alternative is to write a mock driver first and create test cases that invoke its functionality. Once you are satisfied with the usage of the interface, you can try to integrate the mock driver into the real application. If it passes that check as well, you can hand the test cases to the hardware team as a succinct description of what the driver should be like.

5.4.4   Testing to Find and Document the Requirements

Very often you will come up against specifications and requirements that are rather vague, or to be more polite, visionary. They conjure up a piece of desirable functionality that is obviously attainable, but in their enthusiasm about the scope of the result, they fail to state the expectations in detail.

📖86

📖201

Suppose that your team has developed a really nice entity-relationship modeling tool that spits out SQL DDL (data definition language) statements and JPA entities. One fine morning, your project leader (who is not a technical person himself) walks into the room and announces, "Guys, I've just thought of the most amazing business case: If we could turn the legacy databases of our customers into nice ER diagrams, we could make *really* big money. Surely, that should be easy, right?"

The problem with that kind of demand is that one tends to underestimate the problem. It seems that the thing can obviously be done, but are there any lurking problems? Can one translate, in the end, any statement in the SQL DDL into an equivalent ER model element? And what is the goal? A guarantee that would certainly convince the customers of the tool's quality is that by translating the ER model back into DDL, one would get exactly the original statements. Can this be achieved?

Write test cases to make the intended applications precise.

The test-first principle comes to the rescue: Rather than studying the entire (rather bulky) standard of the SQL DDL, you hunt in your company's previous projects for real database definitions. Then, you create a series of test cases. For example, rather than writing a SQL parser, you first execute the SQL in a database engine. The import component can then query the structure using the JDK's Java Database Connectivity (JDBC) meta-data facilities. This yields an ER model in your own tool, which you can immediately use to create a second database. The test then checks that the created structure and the original structure are identical, again using JDBC.

  Great! Instead of a vision, you now have concrete applications of the component to be built. Furthermore, since your company does real work, it is likely that the challenges encountered in the collected database schemas will cover pretty much all the practical elements that your customers will come up with later on.

Tests can document business value.

If used in this manner, the tests do more than just exercise technical functionality; they prove that particular and practically relevant cases of real input can be processed correctly, which customers will take as an indication that your software will be valuable to them. The tests are, in fact, *functional tests*: They check the behavior from a completely outside perspective, from the customers' point of view.

Mark omitted cases and functionality by exceptions.

Unlike under the three laws of test-driven development, here you will usually   ↞5.2
try to collect a substantial number of use cases to get a feel for the real scope and ambition of the project. Naturally, you cannot attack all tests at the same time, so you may omit for now some branches of case distinctions that will be required only in other tests. Stay focused, and try to solve one thing after the next. It is a good idea to create all branches of case distinctions that you become aware of, but to throw an exception in those   ↞1.5.5
that would merely distract you from the case at hand. In this way, the test cases that are not yet handled will fail at first with an exception, and will   ↞5.1
later succeed once you add the missing code.

Tests can explore the feasibility of a project at low cost.

In the end, the database import tool will, of course, have a nice user inter-   ↠9.1
face. However, it might be a waste of time and money to build this interface, only to find later on that the actual functionality behind it cannot be created, because ER diagrams cannot, after all, capture every possible aspect of the SQL DDL.

A cheap way of assessing feasibility is to build just the most doubtful, the most challenging, the most advanced components, and to exercise them in test cases first. Once they are sure to meet all requirements, you can go ahead and wrap them up for the user.

5.4.5   Testing to Drive the Design

↰1.1
↠11.3.3.7
↰1.2.2 ↠5.4.8

↰5.4.4
▭86

↠5.4.9

The previous two applications of testing have suggested looking at the outside of a component through the test code: The tests capture the later usage and behavior of the production code. However, tests can do more. For instance, as you start to gather more and more use cases of your system, you may find that the initial software structure is too weak to carry the load. This is, in fact, not a fault but a virtue: It is a symptom of doing "the simplest thing that could possibly work." Now it is time to develop the inner structure further, by introducing more helpers, more collaborators, more roles that objects can fill. At best, this may be accomplished by applying multiple refactorings, at which point the tests ensure that existing functionality does not get broken.

Sometimes, however, your design will need to undergo major changes. Suppose that in the scenario of your ER diagram editor, you had relied on surrogate keys—that is, artificial primary keys generated by the database by incrementing some internal counter for each new row in a table. Also, you called these id and gave them type long, and you used that simple convention throughout your code generator for the JPA classes. While trying to import an existing table structure, you find that some tables already have primary keys that are not called id. At this point, you have to introduce a "primary key attribute" for entity types, and you have to revise all pieces of code that rely on the previous conventions.

▭92(Ch.3)

↰1.8.2 ↰1.8.6

The new test case capturing the unexpected use has driven you to redesign your software—in this example, by replacing an implicit convention by an explicit specification of primary key attributes. Such changes are notorious as "shotgun surgery": There is no single place at which a judicious change will have the desired effect; you have to apply many little changes in many different places. The good thing in the current case is that the change improves the design: After doing shotgun surgery once, you have introduced the new concept of a "primary key attribute." If you have taken the chance to encapsulate all logic related to key attributes in a single helper class, all later adaptations to the concept can be applied locally.

5.4.6   Testing to Document Progress

▭147

The requirements for a software project usually comprise a collection of use cases, each of which describes possible interactions of *actors* with the system. More precisely, the actor causes the system to perform sequences of *actions*, which in the end yield an observable reaction that is useful and valuable to the actor.

Align test cases with functional requirements.

When tests are aligned with use cases, they document the increasing use-fulness of the system to its stakeholders (e.g., its users and financers). Such tests can contain sequences of triggers that cause the system to perform precisely the desirable actions of a specific use case. The final assertions in the test then document the expected result of value.

Agile development calls such tests *acceptance tests*, which the user has   📖28,33
to supply, or at least has to specify in detail. When the test succeeds, the corresponding use case is ticked off the list and the developers go on to fulfill the next requirements.

Writing up tests for the different use cases also, as a side effect, helps you grasp the details of the requirements more precisely and spot omissions   ↰5.4.4
and inconsistencies in the specification early on.

Furthermore, your team gets a clear visualization of progress for free. With this process, you start out with all functional tests failing. However, as you progress to implement more and more of the system, more and   ↰5.2 ↱5.4.5
more of those tests will go green, which will give you an immediate sense   ↱5.4.10
of achievement. With each hour you spend on production code, more and more tests will succeed.

View the system from the outside.

The "unit" under test here is the entire system, or at least substantial parts of the system. Consequently, the fixture must include outside views, such as a desktop user interface, an endpoint for web services, or a web server.   ↰5.3.5

5.4.7   Testing for Safety

In most systems, there are things that must not happen under any cir-cumstances: A railway control system must not assign the same track to different trains at the same time and a word processor must not produce files it cannot read back in. Recognizing such crucial pieces of functional-ity can be a good incentive to start testing. Indeed, if the trust of your users depends on a particular behavior, you should test that behavior extensively.

Isolate crucial functionality into dedicated, small components.

The desire to test a crucial functionality again influences the design of   ↰5.4.5
the software, since the functionality must be available as a stand-alone component to be placed in a fixture. Very often, the critical parts are on   ↰5.1
the system boundary and should therefore be in a separate component in   ↰1.8.7 ↰1.5.2 ↰4.6
any case; the tests merely underline this goal from a technical perspective.

A second benefit of testing is that the critical components will remain   ↰5.2
small and have a few well-defined collaborators. As a result, the code base

»11.2
in which bugs can be hidden is reduced. The Single Responsibility Principle makes similar demands, but the tests make them concrete.

Include border cases, illegal arguments, and possible failures.

↰4.5
Unit tests in general will follow the non-redundancy principle: The target unit expects legal inputs and will not check them before starting its computation. Accordingly, the tests provide the unit with legal input and check whether they receive the expected answers in return.

Safety tests can deviate from this pattern, for the same reason that safety-critical components may deviate from the non-redundancy principle: If a Bad Thing must not happen under *any* circumstances, then this also includes logical errors in other parts of the system. Accordingly, the tests should encompass cases that test in particular the argument-checking code of the target. These tests should submit illegal arguments and use `@expected` to check that an exception is thrown. They can also check that no undesirable side effects have occurred, such as input files having become corrupted in the middle of processing.

↰5.3.2.1
As a special case, one can also simulate failures in collaborators by providing suitable mock objects. Suppose you wish to test a `DownloadJob` for some web browser. You would certainly want to check its behavior in the common case where the server breaks the connection before the data has arrived. For that purpose, you would pass a mock `InputStream` that after a fixed number of bytes suddenly throws an `IOException`. The `DownloadJob` should then clean up any partial files from the disk to avoid losing disk space.

Use observers to test for temporal safety conditions.

In some cases, the thing to be excluded is a temporal property phrased as "At no point in time must ... ." For such situations, it is necessary to inspect the state of the critical component or its outputs upon every change.

↰2.1
If the component supports the OBSERVER pattern, it is sufficient to register a mock observer that checks the desirable condition upon any state change.

5.4.8   Testing to Enable Change

Software will be most useful and most valuable if it matches the requirements and demands of its users as found in the real world. When these

📖92 ↰1.2.2
requirements change, the software has to change as well. Refactoring is a particular, internal kind of change: The software's structure does not fit a new requirement, so it has to change before the requirement can be tackled.

📖233
📖28,33
📖172
However, changing software is expensive and error-prone, and it demands the courage to drop a working system in favor of a new version that may or may not work immediately. There are stories of teams who, because they lacked the courage to restructure their product, made progress more and

more sluggish: The necessary refactoring that would enable further change would not be worked on, because the team feared breaking the existing functionality.

Extensive tests make changes predictable.

Suppose you are in a situation where you need to change only a single object because its internal data structures are no longer efficient enough for the growing amount of data to be processed. In principle, changing the implementation will not affect the remainder of the system, because it depends only on the published contracts. In practice, contracts are not so precise that they capture every detail of the object's behavior. Consequently, changing the object's internals may still break the border cases of its behavior, which will lead to particularly intricate bugs in other parts of the system. You will certainly and understandably be afraid to make that necessary change.

↰1.1 ↰4.1

Envision the same situation, but now suppose you have 30 or 50 tests for the object. In this scenario, everyone contributed a test case when they came across a border case in the behavior that they rely on. You will be confident about making the change in this circumstance, because you know you will probably not break the system elsewhere, as long as all the tests continue to succeed. What is more, no one will notice intermediate breakage, because you can get the tests up and running before you commit your working copy to the general repository. And finally, even if something does get broken due to your changes, the team members will all shoulder part of the blame, because they should have provided suitable test cases expressing their expectations in the first place.

↰5.4.2

See tests as a long-term investment.

Writing tests will always be an effort, and some propose the rule of thumb that you should write roughly as much test code as production code. While it may be a good idea to write tests specific to a planned refactoring so as to protect precisely the functionality that may get broken, testing must be a continuous activity to be successful: You invest some of the precious development time right now with the clear expectation that maintenance will become necessary at some point and that the availability of tests will reduce the effort required then.

▭92

5.4.9 Testing to Understand an API

Documentation in practice is often incomplete and tends to leave technical terms undefined. The reason is simple: It is usually the original developers who write the API documentation, and since they know the details, they may find it hard to approach their software from the perspective of a novice. Tutorials on the web, though well meaning, often fall into the same trap of omitting the conceptually "obvious" and the technically subtle. Finally, any form of writing about software will try to tell a consistent overall story while suppressing the details. In the end, developers are often faced with the need to close the remaining gaps by experimentation. Tests, which in this context are called *learning tests*, can help in the process. To demonstrate the power of this application, we use a more complex example: learning the Java Persistence API (JPA).

Tests force you to explore the technical details of an API.

Unlike documentation, tests cannot omit any technical steps. So we start by downloading Hibernate, a widely adopted implementation. First the basics: We create a plain Java project, unpack the Hibernate `lib/required` and `lib/jpa` into a folder `lib` in that project, and add the JAR files to the project's build path. Next, we need a relational database. For a simple test setup, we decide on an in-memory database with the HSQLDB engine. We download that software as well and place it on the `lib` folder alongside Hibernate. Actually, the story will not be quite so smooth: Chapter 4, "Tutorial Using the Java Persistence API," in the Hibernate guide says nothing about this setup; only Chapter 1 hints at the existence of `lib/jpa`. We have already learned quite a lot!

Let us start by managing some named "products." We create a `Product` entity following the templates in the quick-start guide. An ID attribute is used as a primary key, where the database is supposed to generate the actual unique value, and we add a name to contain some string. The `length` attribute tells Hibernate how much space it should reserve in the database when setting up the table. The class compiles, at least, so we have learned that all the annotations seem in order so far.

testing.learn.Product

```
@Entity
@Table(name="product")
public class Product {
    @Id
    @GeneratedValue(strategy=GenerationType.IDENTITY)
    private long id;
    @Column(name = "name", length = 128)
    private String name;
    ... getters and setters for properties
}
```

Let us set a first goal of writing our favorite dish to the product database. We use a fixture to set up the entity manager, so the test remains small and to the point: Create the `Product` entity and `persist` it. The database will assign a unique value to the `id` property.

testing.learn.LearnJPATest

```
@Test
public void writeSimpleEntity() throws SQLException {
```

↰5.1

```
final Product p = new Product();
p.setName("Marshmallows");
em.getTransaction().begin();
em.persist(p);
em.getTransaction().commit();
assertTrue(p.getId() > 0);
}
```

To get this test to succeed, we must create a configuration `persistence`
`.xml` in `META-INF`, list the `Product` there, and connect the persistence unit
to the database. The file can be found in the online supplement. Here, we
remark only that we use Hibernate's `hbm2ddl` option to set up the database
structure from the given entities.

Creating the fixture then is straightforward. We show here the setup;
the complementary teardown is to close both `emf` and `em`. Since creating
an `EntityManagerFactory` involves some work, we do this only once for
the whole class.

---
testing.learn.LearnJPATest

```
@BeforeClass
public static void setUpClass() {
    emf = Persistence.createEntityManagerFactory("learnJPA");
}
@Before
public void setUp() throws ClassNotFoundException {
    em = emf.createEntityManager();
}
```

Full of hope, we start the test, but of course we see it fail. In fact, the
author found he had made a spelling mistake in the entity's package in the
`persistence.xml` and had also forgotten to add the HSQLDB to the class
path in the first run. Such things will, of course, happen. The flaws fixed,
the test succeeded. We have learned *all* the steps that are necessary for
using Hibernate.

> Tests help you to keep on learning.

But how do we know that the data has been written to the database? We
decide to access the database through plain JDBC, bypassing the JPA layer
altogether. A web search tells us that we can get a JDBC connection from
Hibernate by first accessing the native Hibernate `Session`, for which the
`EntityManager` is only a wrapper (line 1). Next, the session provides us   ↰2.4
with the underlying connection on request (lines 2–3). Finally, we learn
how to write parameterized SQL (lines 4–6) without fear of SQL injection;
that `persist` will leave a new ID in the written entity (line 7); and how to
iterate through the result of a JDBC query (lines 8–11).

---
testing.learn.LearnJPATest.writeSimpleEntity

```
1 Session session = em.unwrap(Session.class);
2 session.doWork(new Work() {
```

```
3    public void execute(Connection conn) throws SQLException {
4        PreparedStatement sm = conn
5            .prepareStatement(
6                "select name from Product where id=?");
7        sm.setLong(1, p.getId());
8        ResultSet res = sm.executeQuery();
9        assertTrue(res.next());
10       assertEquals("Marshmallows", res.getString(1));
11       assertFalse(res.next());
12   }
13 });
```

Tests document usage for other team members.

↰5.4.2

Tests can be structured to tell the reader how to use a given API. Using tests to learn an API helps save work in the team: One member does the work once; the others can just see it is done. This goal can be strengthened by introducing helper methods with explanatory names. For instance, lines 1,

↰1.4.6

2, and 13 in the previously given checking code might be wrapped in a method accessRawJDBC, which takes the Work as an argument.

Tests can explore the subtleties of an API.

Once we have set up the fixtures, learning more becomes even simpler over time. Whenever you ask yourself a question like "Actually, what will happen if I ... ," you can easily write the test and try it out.

For instance, at some point we will have to deal with concurrent accesses to the database. Plain JDBC transactions do not help, because we usually wish to keep open an EntityManager for one unit of work as perceived by the user—and this may span many minutes. JPA uses a special

▢148

brand of *optimistic concurrency*: Each time a changed entity is written to the database, its *version* field is incremented; before writing back data, Hibernate checks that no one else has written a new version in the meantime. Here is the setup, in which we merely tag a special field (and make it long to avoid overflow):

testing.learn.Versioned

```
@Entity
@Table(name="versioned")
public class Versioned {
    @Id
    @GeneratedValue(strategy = GenerationType.IDENTITY)
    private long id;
    @Column(name="data", length = 128)
    private String data;
    @Version
    private long version;
    ... getters and setters for properties
}
```

Then, we can simulate a scenario where two users compete in modifying a single entity (which is persisted before the following snippet, with the ID testID). The otherEm is the access path by the other user. In lines 1–2, both users load their working copies into memory. In lines 4–7, the other user decides to update the entity first, before the first user writes her data in lines 9–12.

```
testing.learn.LearnJPATest.versioned
1 Versioned mine = em.find(Versioned.class, testID);
2 Versioned other = otherEm.find(Versioned.class, testID);
3
4 other.setData("02");
5 otherEm.getTransaction().begin();
6 otherEm.flush();
7 otherEm.getTransaction().commit();
8
9 mine.setData("03");
10 em.getTransaction().begin();
11 em.flush();
12 em.getTransaction().commit();
```

The final commit in line 13 is supposed to fail now, because the first user tries to overwrite the modification done by the second user. JPA specifies that an exception is thrown at this point, which we document in the test case:

```
testing.learn.LearnJPATest
@Test(expected = OptimisticLockException.class)
```

Tests are a cheap way of getting "into" an API.

At this point, we have demonstrated that learning tests are an effective way of approaching an API. Compare the effort spent here to that of developing an application using the API in question: You do not need user interfaces, web applications, or any kind of front end. You can get straight to the heart of the questions and treat them in a minimal setting. In the end, you have even provided yourself with a working test environment that can serve as a blueprint for the production setup.

Tests let you find the inadequacies early.

A common problem in selecting between rival libraries and frameworks is   ≫7.3.4
that one discovers their omissions and deficiencies only late in the day: The documentation gives a promising overview, and you make headway quickly at first for the common usage scenarios. After spending a lot of precious development time, you find that the library does not support the really hard

special cases of your application after all. Tests enable you to dig down to these special requirements faster, and with a smaller investment.

To extend the JPA example, suppose you wish to consider an *order* as "updated" if it receives a new *order item*. Conceptually, this seems sensible, because the *order* owns its items. Technically, the question is whether changing a @OneToMany relationship increments the object's version. To explore this point, we add one-to-many relationship parts to our Versioned test entity. We can then write the following test, in which we take an object, add a new part (lines 3–6), and flush the changes (line 7, calling em.flush() within a transaction). We expect the version field to be incremented (line 8).

↰2.2.1

testing.learn.LearnJPATest.persistingParts

```
1 Versioned mine = em.find(Versioned.class, v.getId());
2 long oldVersion = mine.getVersion();
3 Part p2 = new Part("B");
4 mine.getParts().add(p2);
5 p2.setOwner(mine);
6 em.persist(p2);
7 flush();
8 assertTrue(mine.getVersion() > oldVersion);
```

At first, with a plain @OneToMany relationship, this fails. After some web searching, we find that Hibernate provides an extension to the JPA standard for just this case: the annotation @OptimisticLock. With the following declaration of the parts property, the test succeeds:

testing.learn.Versioned

```
@OptimisticLock(excluded = false)
@OneToMany(targetEntity = Part.class, mappedBy = "owner")
private List<Part> parts = new ArrayList<>();
```

Tests are useful in this context because they are concrete: You do not have to argue about possible ambiguities in the documentation; you simply try out the actual behavior. Furthermore, if you do find the solution, your investment is preserved in the form of tutorial code that other team members can look up if they encounter a similar border case.

↰5.4.2

5.4.10 Testing for a Better Work–Life Balance

Before we leave the subject of testing, we would like to point out that tests are not only good for the software quality, which may be a rather abstract concept, but also for the developers. We will be very brief, however, on this nontechnical, though fascinating topic.

Testing keeps you motivated, happy, and productive.

⬜258

Software developers are known to be a very dedicated group of humans: They will work as hard as necessary to see their product run, and they

want to contribute to something outstanding. This kind of motivation is   📖118
created by many factors, among which social recognition and the ability to
work on challenging yet achievable tasks rank very high. Motivated people,
in turn, tend to be more focused and more productive.

Tests, and in particular the test-first principle, introduce a closed feed-   ↰5.2
back loop for many motivating factors: By documenting your progress, you   ↰5.4.6
have a constant sense of achievement. Since tests are shared, the team will
give you social recognition, as you are seen to work toward the team's
common goal. Since tests are small and concrete manifestations of open   ↰5.4.2 ↰5.4.5
challenges, they keep you going from one task to the next, and let you
finish each with the sense of a mission accomplished.

Tests tell the developers when they are done.

The high motivation of developers may also have the negative effect of driv-   📖258
ing them into unnecessary extensions, generalizations, and optimizations.
In many instances, for some perceived "elegance" in the software structure,
they will readily sacrifice progress on the required functionality.

Tests, together with the principle of building the "simplest thing that
could possibly work," discourage such deviations, because they signal that
a task has been accomplished. Once the test succeeds, there is no need
to work further on the production code until a new use case requires its   ↰5.4.5
modification.

Tests lessen anxieties about decisions and changes.

Software development involves making many decisions, and of course it is
easy to get them wrong. Being afraid of decisions is the worst case, because
it stalls progress altogether. Tests facilitate the decision-making process in
several ways. First, each successful test will boost your confidence in your
general plan and in your own capabilities. Second, the test-first approach
ensures that you have to make decisions based on only concrete challenges,
rather than abstract and long-term considerations. Finally, tests enable   ↰5.4.8
change, so that even if some decision turns out to be non-optimal, it can
be remedied easily.

Tests lessen anxiety about the final integration phase.

Developers in classical software processes dread the point where the software is first assembled and put to use on real data. Inevitably, the many
small misunderstandings in the API show up and cause tremendous amounts
of overtime in a brief time span.

Testing early helps to find misunderstandings and ambiguities early, so   ↰5.4.4 ↰5.4.2
that the chances of a successful integration increase dramatically. Only the
discrepancies between mock objects and actual implementation might still   ↰5.3.2.1
cause problems. If the entire software is available, *continuous integration*   📖28
with automatic testing will resolve this remaining problem.

Chapter 6

Fine Print in Contracts

Contracts form a solid framework for arguing about the correctness of code: Class invariants capture the consistency of the objects' internal structures, while the pre- and post-conditions of methods describe the objects' behavior to clients without requiring knowledge of the objects' internals. Within methods, the workings of the code can be traced in detail, down to formalizing the effects of individual statements.

↰4

↰4.2.3
↰4.7

The presentation so far has established the terminology and common reasoning patterns. However, a number of practically relevant questions have not yet been answered: The discussion was restricted to single objects with no internal helpers, and the interaction with the language constructs of exceptions and inheritance has not been been treated. The purpose of this chapter is to cover further material that is necessary in nearly all practical situations.

Unlike the previous chapter on contracts, this one will not lead up to a formalized treatment, simply because the formulas involved would become too complex to be handled usefully on paper. Instead, we will give miniature examples to establish the concepts, and then revert to the mode of discussing real-world code from Part I.

6.1 Design-by-Contract

Contracts capture the behavior of objects and in this way make precise the API commonly found in documentation. Just as the API is subject to design decisions, so writing down contracts involves decisions and planning. The general guideline for APIs is to start from the clients' perspective, and correspondingly the pre-condition availability principle and the reasonable pre-condition principle ensure that clients can understand contracts from an outside point of view. As we shall see now, the precision of contracts also enables detailed considerations about what the "best" API for a given object might be. We will actually approach design-by-contract.

↰1.1
↰4.2.2

📖182

6.1.1 Contracts First

The central point we will follow up on in this section is this:

Design contracts before writing the methods.

The more detailed presentation of contracts in Sections 4.2 and 4.7 has motivated the need for contracts primarily from the methods' code that relies on the invariants and pre-conditions for doing its work. While this is a useful device for pedagogical purposes, it is rarely an advisable procedure for introducing contracts in practice: You can easily end up with contracts that reflect a particular implementation, rather than the purpose of a method, and the contract does not help you to understand the demands on the method.

↰5.2

Compare this situation with the advice of test-driven development. There, the main point is to gain a detailed understanding of what a method or class will need to achieve before attempting to actually implement it. Contracts can serve as conceptual test cases: A method's pre-condition implicitly encompasses all possible tests, since it describes all possible situations in which the method can be called legally. Likewise, the post-condition encompasses all possible `assert` tests that can be expected to be passed on the method's result—all tests must be implied by the post-condition.

> Use contracts to capture the purpose of methods.

↰4.1

↰4.2

The contracts we gave in Chapter 4 do, in fact, conform to the intuition of the methods' purpose. For instance, the `replace` method in `GapTextStore` requires that the replaced text range is contained entirely in the current content according to the pre-condition (4.2). Likewise, the `next` method in `ThresholdArrayIterator` requires that the sequence is not yet exhausted,

↰4.2.2
↰4.2.5

which we have specified alternatively by model fields in (4.8) and in the form of the pure method `hasNext` in (4.13).

6.1.2   Weaker and Stronger Assertions

When designing an API, one often has to strike a balance between the interests of the clients and those of the implementors: Clients want classes that are simple to use and that can be reused flexibly in many situations, while the implementors would rather want to concentrate on a few well-defined, simple tasks that work in restricted scenarios. As an example, suppose you need an analyzer for HTML documents. Clients would like to throw any document they download from the Internet at that analyzer, while the implementors' lives would be simplified considerably if only valid XML documents needed processing—writing a robust HTML parser is just so much harder than using the SAX parser from the library. In the other direction, a method that generates text for inclusion in an HTML document is easier to use for the client if it already escapes the special characters, while it is easier to implement if escaping is left to the client as a second processing step. Such trade-offs between the responsibilities of the method and those of its callers are the everyday questions confronted by every software designer.

At the core, such decisions boil down to the question of how much is expected at specific points: How much must a client guarantee to be able to call a method and how much must a method guarantee when it finishes? An assertion is called *weaker* if it requires less; it is called *stronger* if it requires more than another assertion. We continue by exploring some salient aspects of these terms to illustrate them further.

Clients prefer weaker pre-conditions and stronger post-conditions.

Clients like it if they have to do less work before calling a method and if the method does more for them. The requirement of passing a well-formed XML document is stronger than that of passing a "reasonably well-formed HTML document displayable in a browser." The requirement of generating text with escaped special characters is stronger than just leaving the original characters in place.

Implementors prefer stronger pre-conditions and weaker post-conditions.

Implementors, in contrast, prefer calls that occur in very specific situations, where they know more about the parameters and the object's state. Of course, they would also like to do as little work as possible before returning.

Weaker and stronger have precise logical meanings.

The short-hand terms "weaker" and "stronger" can also be defined precisely: An assertion P is *stronger than* assertion P' if in all possible program states P logically implies P'. The qualification "in all possible states" refers, of course, to the values of the variables and heap locations referenced within P and P'. Conversely, an assertion P is *weaker than* an assertion P' if in all possible program states P' implies P. Two assertions P and P' are *equivalent* if P is both stronger and weaker than P' (which is, of course, the same as saying that P' is both stronger and weaker than P).

Unfortunately, the standard terminology is somewhat odd at this point: "Stronger than" and "weaker than" seem to signify strict relations, while the preceding definition would read the (trivial) implication $P \implies P$ as "P is stronger than P." From a linguistic point of view, you would expect "at least as strong as" and "at least as weak as." We prefer here to stick to the introduced terminology.

To illustrate, let us consider a few examples. Obviously, $i > 0$ implies $i \neq 0$, so $i > 0$ is stronger than $i \neq 0$. The assertion "p is a PDF 1.3 document" is stronger than "p is a PDF 1.4 document," because the PDF format is backward compatible, so that a 1.3 document is also a legal 1.4 document. The assertion "t is a text *and* the HTML special characters are escaped" is stronger than just "t is a text."

Methods remain correct with a stronger pre-condition and weaker post-condition.

Suppose we have a method with pre-condition P and post-condition Q and that we have proven that the method is correct. Assuming that the pre-condition holds initially, the code guarantees that the post-condition will hold in the end. Intuitively, the method is entered through P and left through Q, as shown in Fig. 6.1.

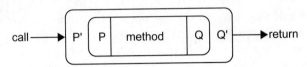

Figure 6.1 Weakening of Method Contracts

We now replace P with a stronger pre-condition P' and Q with a weaker post-condition Q'. Intuitively, we "wrap" the method in a new contract and inform callers only about that contract. Then the method is still correct: Initially, P' holds, from which we deduce that P holds; since the method was originally correct, we know that Q holds after its execution, from which we deduce that Q' also holds. This fundamental reasoning pattern of replacing assertions by variants will reappear when we study the connection between contracts and inheritances later on.

»6.4

6.1.3   Tolerant and Demanding Style

One of the central questions in designing contracts is this: What does the method expect from its callers? Which requirements does it specify in its pre-condition? As we shall see now, the remaining decisions about the contract largely hinge on this initial choice. We will now introduce the relevant concepts using the `ThresholdArrayIterator` and will give illustrative examples of the main conclusion in Section 6.1.4.

↰4.2

For motivation, let us go back to the `ThresholdArrayIterator`'s method `next` (see Fig. 4.7 on page 202 for the full code). The original pre-condition (4.8) states that the sequence must not be empty, which is expressed as

$$\text{pos} \neq \text{seq.length}$$

This condition can, however, be checked only by calling the method `has Next()`. Suppose clients find this checking too cumbersome. They would like to just call `next()` in any situation and can live with getting `null` when there are no more elements. Their version of an idiomatic loop for accessing all elements looks like this:

↰4.2.2

thresholditer_tolerant.ThresholdIteratorTest.dump

```
while ((data = iter.next()) != null) {
    // work with data
```

```
    . . .
}
```

Of course, such a variant of `next()` can be provided easily, by testing whether an element exists right at the start (lines 2–4 in the next code snippet). The original code in lines 5–8 then runs through because the `if` rule (4.21) guarantees its pre-condition i ≠ a.length in the `else` branch.

⬑4.7.3

---

thresholditer_tolerant.ThresholdArrayIterator.next

```java
1 public Integer next() {
2    if (i == a.length) {
3       return null;
4    } else {
5       Integer tmp = a[i];
6       i++;
7       findNext();
8       return tmp;
9    }
10 }
```

The new pre-condition of this method is `true`—that is, the method can be called in any situation.

Tolerant methods have weaker pre-conditions.

We said earlier that clients prefer methods that have weaker pre-conditions, because it is easier to call them. In the previous example, clients can still check `hasNext()` before calling `next()`, but they do not have to. The pre-condition `true` is certainly weaker than the original one.

⬑6.1.2

⬑6.1.2
📖181

Meyer proposes the term *tolerant* for such methods: They allow more inputs, they can cope with more situations, and they are more lenient toward the callers' possible shortcomings. Choosing the contracts of methods to be tolerant—in other words, aiming at weak pre-conditions—is then called the *tolerant style*.

Tolerance is a variant of robustness.

A method is robust if it fails gracefully in case its pre-condition is violated. This is especially important on the system boundary, where users, other systems, or hardware devices must be expected to misbehave. A tolerant method can be understood to be robust in a special sense: It deliberately requires less than it would do naturally, so as to allow clients some leeway to misbehave. The graceful failure for these cases is incorporated into the contract and comes with special guarantees about the result. In the example of a tolerant `next()`, the post-condition would be:

⬑4.6

⟫6.3

> Returns the next element in the sequence, or `null` if the sequence is exhausted.

In other words, if the client checks before the call in the usual way, it will receive an element. If it fails to check and the sequence is empty, the return value will be `null`.

Tolerance usually leads to weaker guarantees on the result.

There is a downside to choosing a tolerant contract: Because the method has to do something sensible even in border cases, it cannot guarantee to achieve its main purpose in all circumstances allowed by the pre-condition. In the preceding example, returning `null`, rather than a real result, is a workaround: Because there is no further element and yet something has to be returned, the method chooses `null` as the "non-object." The client gets fewer assurances about the result, so the post-condition is weaker. A further implication in this example is that `null` cannot occur as an element in the sequence, because clients would not be able to distinguish this case from the end of the sequence.

↰1.8.9

These examples show that tolerance induces uncertainty about a method's result. The client has to be aware of the different possible outcomes and must arrange a case distinction accordingly. The overall conclusion is this: A tolerant method is easier to call, but its result is harder to work with.

The tolerant style globally leads to more complex code.

The central insight by Meyer at this point is that, from a global perspective, tolerant methods are not desirable. The method code itself will contain more checks and special cases, and the caller's code will have to check the result for the various possible outcomes. In both places, the consequence of tolerance is more code that must be developed and maintained. The negative effect is multiplied by the fact that a method usually has several callers.

Not only the code itself, but also the reasoning about method calls becomes more complex. Suppose that, in the previous example, the client does check `hasNext()` before calling `next()`. Then it must deduce that the border case of an empty sequence does not apply and that therefore the result will not be `null` and can consequently be used as a proper object.

Prefer the demanding style.

📖181

Meyer introduces the term *demanding* as a contrast to *tolerant*. A method's contract is written in *demanding style* if the pre-condition requires everything that the method needs to be implemented straightforwardly and efficiently. The method is not a mere servant who tries to deal with every possible input that callers throw at it—the method, too, has clear preferences and a well defined scope for its contribution, and states these in its pre-condition.

The original specification of method `next()` is written in demanding ↰4.2.2
style. It is not sensible to require an iterator to produce a next element if
the sequence is finished, so the `next` method states the non-emptiness as a
requirement.

Demanding-style contracts achieve a fair distribution of work between
caller and method: The caller provides the method with the essentials it
needs, but no less. The method, in return, finishes its work quickly and
reliably.

Demanding-style contracts start from the method's purpose.

The question is, of course, how "demanding" a method can or should get:
If it requires too much, all callers, possibly in many different places, will
have to perform extra work. If it requires too little, the negative results of
tolerance start to emerge.

The solution has already been given in the earlier guideline of deriving ↰6.1.1
a method's contract from its purpose: If the method is to fulfill a particular
purpose, it can clearly ask its clients to provide everything that is necessary
toward achieving that goal. This strategy is also in line with the reasonable ↰4.2.2
pre-condition principle, since the clients will understand the justification for
the particular demands. It also aligns with the practical goal of designing
a method from the clients' perspective, since the method's purpose usually ↰1.1
answers a specific need of its clients. ↰1.4.3

Be demanding and do not check the demands.

A method is designed to be demanding because it requires a certain setup to
start working. Only when given that setup can the method get down to its
task. The `next` method's task, for instance, is to return the current element
and to advance the iterator. This is implemented in 4 lines of code (lines 5–8
on page 289). Since the method does state its demands, it should not waste
effort in checking that the demands are satisfied afterward; otherwise, it
could just as well not have stated them at all. This conclusion is, of course,
the same as the non-redundancy principle, which says that methods should ↰4.5
in general not check their pre-conditions.

6.1.4   Practical Examples of Demanding Style

Formulating demanding-style contracts is not always a simple matter, because it involves capturing the method's purpose in succinct assertions or ↰6.1.3
even formulas. As usual with such rather abstract recipes and strategies,
it is best to look at a few good examples.

In general, you will find that all methods that "look right" and are
"simple to use" conform to the rule. Reading their API with the particular
question in mind will clarify matters immediately.

- `StringBuilder.append(str,off,len)` requires that $off \geq 0 \wedge$ $len \geq 0 \wedge off + len > str.length$. This statement is explicit in the specification of the thrown `IndexOutOfBoundsException`.

- `ZipFile.getEntry(name)` requires that the ZIP file is open (i.e., that it has not yet been closed).

- `Matcher.getGroup(group)` can be applied only to groups that actually exist in the regular expression for which the matcher has been created.

- `URI(str)` constructs a URI from its given string representation, as specified in RFC 2396 (Uniform Resource Identifiers: Generic Syntax). The string must not be `null`.

- `ServerSocket(port)` requires that `port` is in the allowed range of a 2-byte unsigned value (0–65535).

In all of these examples, the stated restrictions are obviously sensible from what the method seeks to achieve on behalf of its caller.

You can deviate from the demanding style for good reasons.

Of course, software engineering is not an entirely rigorous discipline. As we have seen in many places in Part I, it is often necessary to take guidelines and rules with a grain of salt to improve the resulting code. In just the same way, there are good reasons for not taking the demanding style as a literal law in all situations.

The best reason for being a bit less demanding is the intended usage of a method. For instance, in `ZipFile` the method `getEntry(name)` "returns the ZIP file entry for the specified name, or `null` if not found." It is therefore a bit tolerant, because it does not require the client to check beforehand— using the collection obtainable by `entries()`, for example—whether the entry exists at all. The decision can be justified by saying that clients may often be looking for specific entries and would take their own measures if these are not found. It also points out the disadvantage of tolerant contracts: The client has to check that the result is non-null before using it.

↰1.5.3   The decision in `getEntry()` also links back to the earlier discussion of whether a particular situation is an error or a normal case of program execution. A demanding contract declares anything outside the method's purpose to be an error that results in an exception. A tolerant contract explicitly includes some of these border cases, thereby turning them into normal cases.

Similarly, established special cases can lead to tolerant contracts. Apart from its main purpose, the method covers several special inputs that lead to well defined results. For instance, the computation of the square root in `Math.sqrt(a)` intuitively can be applied only to non-negative `double` values. However, the relevant standard IEEE 754 for floating point computations defines special values `NaN` (not a number) and `infinity` that cover unavoidable rounding errors in numerical algorithms. Consequently, sqrt must be prepared to take these as arguments and to return something sensible—NaN or infinity, respectively. It also uses NaN as a designated return value for a negative input a.

Discerning the clients' expectations will usually require some interpretation and application of common sense. For instance, the URI constructor mentioned earlier in general accepts strings of the following format:

```
[scheme:][//authority][path][?query][#fragment]
```

The authority here comprises the host, with optional port and user information. However, the documentation of the method states the following explicit exception (among others):

> An empty authority component is permitted as long as it is followed by a non-empty path, a query component, or a fragment component. This allows the parsing of URIs such as "file:///foo/ bar", which seems to be the intent of RFC 2396 although the grammar does not permit it.

Even though these examples do show that a bit of tolerance can improve the usage of methods, let us end this section by emphasizing that disregarding the plea for a demanding style throughout the code base will lead to disastrous results: The global effects of tolerance are code bloat and complexity.   ↰6.1.3

6.1.5 Stronger and Weaker Class Invariants

If contracts can be tolerant or demanding, and pre- and post-conditions can be weaker or stronger, a natural question is this: Can class invariants also be weaker or stronger? Technically, this is certainly the case, since   ↰6.1.2
invariants are just assertions and can be implied by other assertions. The question is, however, also relevant in practice, because it links to decisions that software developers face on a daily basis.

The context of the question has been illustrated in Fig. 4.6, which we repeat here for convenience. In this figure, each public method leaves behind the invariant so that the next method call can start from a well-defined object state.

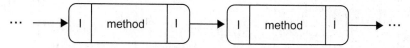

Considerations about the invariant's strength are always symmetric.

We pointed out earlier that the invariant can be seen as a contract of   ↰4.1
the class developers with themselves: The guarantees of one method are the assumptions of the next. Making that contract stronger or weaker will necessarily influence the complexity of the class.

The case of contracts between methods and their clients was asym- ↰6.1.? metric: The clients prefer weak pre-conditions and strong post-conditions, while the methods do the reverse. In the case of invariants, the view is symmetric: In the figure, the second method can, by relying on the invariant, save just the work that the first method has put into establishing the invariant.

Invariants can be used to "stash away" work performed internally.

As an example, suppose we write a class `IntSet` that just maintains a set's elements in an array. It uses linear search to check whether a value is an element in the set.

invariants.IntSet

```java
public class IntSet {
    private int elements[] = new int[0];
    public void add(int x) {
        if (!contains(x)) {
            elements = Arrays.copyOf(elements, elements.length + 1);
            elements[elements.length - 1] = x;
        }
    }
    public boolean contains(int x) {
        for (int i = 0; i != elements.length; i++) {
            if (elements[i] == x)
                return true;
        }
        return false;
    }
}
```

We could now strengthen the invariant by keeping the elements sorted. The method `add` would have to perform the extra work of finding the suitable insertion point in the first line below.

invariants.IntSetSorted.add

```java
1  int pos = Arrays.binarySearch(elements, x);
2  if (pos < 0) {
3      pos = -(pos + 1); // see API of binarySearch
4      int[] tmp = elements;
5      elements = new int[elements.length + 1];
6      System.arraycopy(tmp, 0, elements, 0, pos);
7      elements[pos] = x;
8      System.arraycopy(tmp, pos, elements, pos + 1,
9          tmp.length - pos);
10 }
```

That extra work is then "stashed away" in the invariant "the array `elements` is sorted." The second method `contains` can make use of that extra work by answering the question about membership in logarithmic time:

📖72

---
invariants.IntSetSorted.contains

```
return Arrays.binarySearch(elements, x) >= 0;
```

Stronger invariants can improve performance guarantees.

The effect of the strengthened invariant of the example can then be summarized as follows: While method `add` continues to take linear time, with a negligible logarithmic overhead, method `contains` becomes much faster. Assuming that `contains` is called very often, the optimization would make sense. If `add` is called very often, however, it would be advisable to get rid of the linear-time insertion and use an amortized-constant-time variant   ⬚72
as done in `ArrayList`. That change cannot be combined with sortedness, which in the worst case still requires linear time for moving elements.

In general, the invariant is a main source for deriving performance benefits. Due to encapsulation, objects can set up and continue to evolve their internal data structures to satisfy service requests more efficiently. Since   ↰1.1 ↰1.3.1 ↰1.4.3
clients do not know about these internals, the invariant is the only place where additional required information can be placed.

Once you start looking, such optimizations by strengthening invariants can be found in many core data structures. Even the simple `GapTextStore`   ↰4.1 ↰1.3.1
contains an instance. The concern here is that the flat array storing the text (Fig. 4.1, Fig. 4.2) is never cleaned up: When the user inserts a huge chunk of text and then later removes it, an unnecessarily large gap remains behind that might never be filled again—a huge piece of memory just sits there unused.

To mitigate this problem, `GapTextStore` strengthens the invariant: The current gap is never allowed to grow beyond twice its original size, referring to the size determined when the storage array was last reallocated. To implement this, the class introduces a threshold, the current maximum allowed gap size.

---
org.eclipse.jface.text.GapTextStore

```
private int fThreshold= 0;
```

The additional invariant comes, of course, with extra work for its maintenance. Whenever text gets replaced, the method `adjustGap` moves the gap to enable the modification to be performed at the start of the gap. The method computes the new gap size (elided) and then checks whether the gap has grown too large (lines 3–4). As a first step toward maintaining the invariant, it triggers a reallocation if this is the case (lines 9–10).

---
org.eclipse.jface.text.GapTextStore

```
1  private void adjustGap(int offset, int remove, int add) {
2      ...
3      boolean reuseArray = 0 <= newGapSize &&
4                      newGapSize <= fThreshold;
5      ...
```

```
6     if (reuseArray)
7         ...
8     else
9         newGapEnd = reallocate(offset,remove,oldGapSize,
10                                   newGapSize,newGapStart);
11    ...
12 }
```

The following reallocation routine first determines the new array size by an amortized strategy for insertions, similar to the one used by `ArrayList` (line 5), and computes the new gap size correspondingly (line 6). As the central point toward the new invariant, it then ensures by straightforward comparisons that the gap is never larger than `fMaxGapSize` (elided, line 8; the parameter defaults to 4kb). Finally, the new reallocation threshold is adjusted to the current gap size (line 9).

org.eclipse.jface.text.GapTextStore

```
1 private int reallocate(int offset, int remove,
2                         final int oldGapSize, int newGapSize,
3                         final int newGapStart) {
4     int newLength = fContent.length - newGapSize;
5     int newArraySize = (int) (newLength * fSizeMultiplier);
6     newGapSize = newArraySize - newLength;
7     // keep newGapSize between fMinGapSize and fMaxGapSize
8     ...
9     fThreshold = newGapSize * 2;
10    // perform allocation and copy
11    ...
12    return newGapEnd;
13 }
```

Caches make for stronger invariants.

One particular case of optimization by stronger invariants is the use of caches. We have pointed out in the language-level discussion that caches require constant maintenance. Now, we can make that point more precise: The cache contains, by definition, information derived from the remaining data accessible to the object. It therefore has an associated invariant that is basically an equation for that information:

$$cacheContent = deriveInformation(originalInformation)$$

Whenever the *originalInformation* changes, the cache must be updated accordingly to validate this equation. The equation itself becomes part of the class invariant, strengthening that invariant.

Strengthening the invariant has pervasive effects on the class's code.

The preceding example involving `GapTextStore` clearly shows a common phenomenon: Invariants are not maintained at single points, but by many

72

↰1.3.6

different pieces of code that may be scattered throughout the class and still work together toward the common goal of reestablishing the invariant. This observation tallies with the abstract guideline that every single (public) method must contribute its share of work toward maintaining the invariant; necessarily, the code of each such method is concerned with the invariant.

Deciding to maintain a stronger invariant can influence the concrete code rather dramatically, since any piece of code working with the associated data structures must be reviewed and revised. Especially when changing the class invariant after the initial development, you should consider very carefully whether the gain in efficiency is worth the increase in complexity and the risk of introducing bugs.

> Make the invariant just strong enough to implement all methods with ease.

We have seen many aspects and results of making a class invariant weaker or stronger. It is useful to sum up these individual points. Specifically, how strong should the class invariant be, and how much knowledge or previous work should it capture and guarantee?

A good guideline is found by starting from the case of contracts between client and caller, where the demanding style invariably leads to leaner code. Since invariants serve as implicit pre-conditions of public methods, a demanding style here would suggest that we should make the invariant so strong that all public methods can be implemented straightforwardly. Making it any stronger, however, would burden all methods with extra work that no one ever exploits. ↰6.1.3 ↰4.1 ↰4.4

The discussion in this subsection motivates this conclusion further using the resulting concrete code: Any invariant that is introduced must be maintained throughout the class, so it is advisable to choose carefully which constraints are really necessary and which ones are just "nice to have" or "intuitively useful."

At the same time, the conclusion underlines the earlier guideline to document the chosen invariants carefully: If only one method relies on the invariant, all other methods have to maintain it. It is therefore not possible to introduce an invariant on an ad-hoc basis, just because it would be convenient at the current point of coding. The other team members and later maintenance developers must be made aware of the invariant, since otherwise it will be broken sooner or later somewhere in the code. ↰4.2.3

6.2 Contracts and Compound Objects

Objects never work in isolation: They employ the services of other objects, or more generally collaborate with other objects, to achieve the common goal of delivering the application's functionality. Very often, an object "has" some parts that it uses for its own internal purposes, and the object's ↰1.1 ↰2.2.1

services are really an abstraction over the more basic services of the parts. For instance, `ArrayList` uses an internal array to store the data and a JFace `Document` uses a `GapTextStore` to maintain the raw text efficiently.

↰2.2.1

In this section, we will approach the question of how to reason about such compound objects. As there are many variants and degrees of the "part" relationship between objects, the analysis will have to be precise and careful, to clarify the context in which reasoning patterns apply. Also, there are no simple solutions. Fortunately, the literature on formal verification provides us with a solid foundation that can be translated into practical guidelines.

▢21

6.2.1   Basics

↰2.2 ↰1.3.1 ↰1.1

Before we investigate the more intricate relationships between a "whole" and its "parts," let us look back at the earlier practical discussions of these relationships. We will first translate them to the setting of design-by-contract.

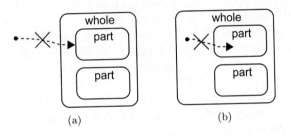

(a)   (b)

Figure 6.2 Basics of Contracts and Parts

The knowledge about existing parts is private.

↰4.2.2
↠12.1.4
↰1.3.1 ↰1.3.3

An object usually employs parts in the role of an internal data structure: The current implementation happens to be set up like this, but the implementation is, as usual, hidden from any clients of the object. Clients of the object must not be able to access the parts [Fig. 6.2(a)]. In particular, the whole object must be careful not to return internal parts from methods inadvertently.

↰4.2.2

In the context of contracts, these insights translate to the guideline that the parts do not appear in the contracts of the whole object's methods. In this way, clients cannot gain knowledge about the parts and cannot exploit that knowledge in their own reasoning. Of course, the whole object is still free to expose an abstract view on its parts through model fields.

↰4.1

Ownership does not confer additional powers.

The parts of an object are still self-contained objects in their own right. The whole object does not suddenly decide to dig into their internals [Fig. 6.2(b)], just because it happens to own the parts.

From the perspective of contracts, the whole object is a client of its parts, much like any other client in the system. It must work with the specified pre- and post-conditions of the parts' method and cannot assume additional details about their implementation.

Parts are responsible for their own invariants.

A particular aspect of the parts being self-contained is, of course, the treatment of their invariants: They are a private matter, so the parts are responsible for maintaining the invariants, just as they would be outside of the context of the whole object.

↰4.1
↰4.2.1 ↰4.2.3

Invariants of the whole usually concern its parts.

The whole object employs its parts as an internal data structure, but it does not merely re-export their functionality—otherwise, the clients could just as well work with the parts directly. The contribution of the whole object lies in the combination and coordination of its parts to faciliate the more comprehensive services that it offers to its own clients.

In terms of contracts, this means that the whole will usually establish additional invariants about these parts, just as it would about any internal data structures. As a simple example, an `ArrayList` has the invariant that its field `size` is an index into the underlying array store [Fig. 6.3(a)].

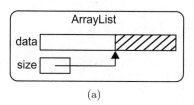
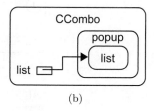

(a)   (b)

Figure 6.3 Invariants in Compound Objects

For a more complex example, we go back to the `CCombo` implementation of a combo box used in the previous discussion of ownership. The object maintains, among others, two objects `list` and `popup`. The list is the widget for displaying the choice of items, the pop-up window contains the list and enables `CCombo` to place it on top of the current window.

↰2.2.1

org.eclipse.swt.custom.CCombo

```
List list;
Shell popup;
```

The ownership structure is shown in Fig. 6.3(b). The invariant associated with the two owned objects is then "popup has a single child, which is `list`." [Note that the children of a widget are a public property, so the situation does not contradict Fig. 6.2(b).]

⇻7.1

It turns out that reasoning about these cross-object invariants is the hardest part of applying contracts to compound objects. We will discuss the conceptual basis in the following section.

The whole object is responsible for maintaining the cross-object invariants.

↰2.2.1

An object creates, maintains, and destroys its owned parts. During their lifetime, the object wires them up to create a data structure to fulfill service requests by its clients. This "wiring up" technically means, of course, to establish and maintain the invariant about the parts and their published model fields. For merely passive parts, this can be done by setting their ↱6.2.3.5 properties and fields accordingly; for more active parts, it might involve ↰2.1 registering observers on their state to adapt its own fields, as well as other parts, according to state changes in the parts.

6.2.2   Ownership and Invariants

The handling of invariants in connection with ownership and structure sharing requires careful attention. Fig. 6.4 outlines both cases to illustrate their difference. The `Whole` object owns object `O` but also holds a reference to an object `S` shared with object `Other`. The challenge is, of course, that both `Whole` and `Other` can modify `S` through their respective references.

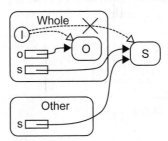

Figure 6.4 Invariants for Owned and Shared Objects

↰1.3.1

In this context, we have to let "references" include both fields containing data structures and temporary references stored in parameters and local variables. Anything that lets an object's code access another object constitutes a "reference" to that object.

In this section, we will discuss a solid foundation for delineating ownership from sharing and for reasoning about invariants including owned part objects. We will first establish its elements and then assemble the overall approach. In the end, we will reach an intuition that neatly extends the basic one from Fig. 4.1 to the new challenges and that comes, again, with practical guidelines.

Treat assertions as implicit references.

The main point of the illustration in Fig. 6.4 is the invariant I, which may mention the fields o and s and through them the properties and model fields of objects O and S. These conceptual, implicit references are shown as dashed arrows.

Invariants may reference only owned objects.

The central insight leading to a solution of the previously described chal-   📖21
lenge derives from the introduction of two rules:

- The invariant of an object may reference only owned parts.

- No other object may access the owned parts.

Together, these rules ensure that the invariant of a whole object never gets broken, since no other object can possibly modify its owned parts. We deliberately restrict the objects referenced in the invariant to only the owned objects to make the invariant "safe from destructive side effects." In Fig. 6.4, the reference from I to s is therefore forbidden and crossed out.

One possible precaution for preventing other objects from accessing the owned parts is, of course, to make sure that no one else has any references to these parts in the first place. In the earlier example of the   ↰4.2
ThresholdArrayIterator (Fig. 4.7), for instance, the constructor makes a copy of the passed array; otherwise, the situation of Fig 6.4 may have arisen, where the caller could have modified the passed array at some later point. This, however, would have invalidated the entire reasoning about the iterator's correctness in Section 4.2.

🌏 The idea of making assertions "safe from destructive side effects" by ownership even
supports the much more complex situation of multithreading. There, objects can be   »8.1
modified not only through all existing references, but also at unpredictable moments in
time. For example, an assertion that you knew to hold at some point can be broken even   ↰4.1
before the next statement starts executing, because the scheduler happens to interleave
the execution of a different thread in the meantime. The concept of *thread confinement*   📖148
extends ownership to this challenge: If only the current thread can possibly obtain a
reference to a given object, then assertions regarding that object will remain valid regardless of the scheduler's decisions and the side effects of other threads. In this context,
therefore, not only compound objects, but also threads, are said to own objects.

The proposed restriction can be explained and motivated by saying that the owned parts of an object effectively become part of the object's representation. Since they serve as an internal data structure, it is clear   📖21,193 ↰1.3.1
that the object should be able to state invariants about them.

The guideline introduces a restriction on programming techniques.

Before we progress further, however, it should be clarified that the proposal *is*, indeed, a restriction. For one thing, other objects cannot even perform

📖214

↰1.3.3

read accesses to the owned parts. Here is a practical example of such a situation. The standard Figure from the Graphical Editing Framework internally manages its current position and size in a rectangle bounds. The getter for this field actually returns the internal rectangle object, thereby violating the established principles for accessors.

---
org.eclipse.draw2d.Figure

```
public Rectangle getBounds() {
    return bounds;
}
```

The API documentation states this violation clearly:

> Implementors may return the Rectangle by reference. For this reason, callers of this method must not modify the returned Rectangle.

The reason for deviating from good practice here is efficiency: Most callers simply wish to peek quickly at some property of the bounds—for instance, the width or height. Creating (and later garbage collecting) a new object for each such access is unacceptable.

»4.1

↰2.1

»6.2.3.5

The second restriction is that the state of object Whole in Fig. 6.4 may actually depend on the state of the shared object S, which intuitively leads to an invariant involving S. Such a dependency, for imaginary fields width and children, might take the form of an invariant such as "the field width is always the number of elements in children of S." Such dependencies are encountered very frequently in practice. Indeed, they are the very motivation for the widely used OBSERVER pattern: They make it necessary to synchronize the states of otherwise unconnected collaborators. For the current example, Whole would observe S and adapt its width field whenever the children in S change. We will later examine such looser kinds of invariants on shared objects in more detail.

> The concept of ownership accepts some limitations to obtain simplified reasoning patterns and reduce the risk of bugs.

The question is, of course, Why should we deliberately restrict ourselves in writing code? That is, why should we give up efficient coding practices merely to fit our code into some conceptual framework? The answer is that the context created by the coding restrictions enables self-contained, reliable, and simple arguments about conforming code.

General code, in contrast, requires ad-hoc reasoning steps and easily leads to bugs. To continue the example of Figures, *anchors* attach connections to figures and keep them attached even when the figures move. Suppose some shape always attaches connections to the right-middle point of its bounding box. The following code seems to compute that point and even correctly reports the coordinates in the global system.[1] However, in view of the above documentation of getBounds(), it is wrong, because it implicitly modifies the bounds field of the figure to which the anchor is attached, with the effect that the figure paints itself in the wrong position.

---
ownership.RightAttachmentAnchor.getLocation

```
public Point getLocation(Point reference) {
    Rectangle b = getOwner().getBounds();
    getOwner().translateToAbsolute(b);
    return b.getRight();
}
```

The approach of restricting programming patterns with the aim of simplifying the reasoning about the resulting code becomes particularly relevant in the area of formal verification: Formalizing any possible ad-hoc arguments that inventive developers might employ leads to huge and complex formulas and is simply not viable. Also, the ad-hoc arguments used in different parts of the code usually do not combine well, so the overall program cannot be proven correct.

The term *methodology* refers to a coherent framework (or regime) of programming rules that dictate the usage of certain language features and gives a corresponding set of reasoning patterns that work on the resulting set of programs. The approach by Barnett et al. that we are following here is such a methodology. Other examples concern the meaning and use of "abstraction," the separation logic view that the heap should be seen as a set of non-overlapping areas, the use of Burstall's memory model, and a viable explicit encoding of disjointness assertions about heap objects. In all of these cases, certain kinds of programming patterns are supported by the reasoning infrastructure, while ad-hoc deviations can be treated, if at all, only with much more effort.

📖21

📖155 ↞4.7.4.3
📖38,247,126
📖58
📖67,102

Ownership is a dynamic property.

We have introduced ownership by saying that the owner determines the lifetime of an owned part object. However, this does not mean that the ownership relation persists throughout that lifetime. An owner can hand on the responsibility for managing one of its parts to a new owner. This happens, for example, with factory methods, where the object containing the factory method very briefly owns the created object, before returning it to the caller.

For instance, an ImageDescriptor in JFace is a lightweight reference to some image stored on an external medium. The specific implementation for files creates the actual image using the following method. Just after the FileImageDescriptor has created the new image, it assumes the duties of its owner; for instance, it must dispose of the image when it is no longer required. Immediately afterward, however, it passes these duties, along with the created object, on to its caller.

↞2.2.1

↞1.4.12

↠9.3

↞2.2.1

↠7.4.1

---

1. The naming of getOwner() here is an unfortunate coincidence: The "owner" of an anchor is the figure to which the anchor is attached. The anchor is not "owned" by the figure in the meaning of the current discussion.

---

org.eclipse.jface.resource.FileImageDescriptor

```
public Image createImage(boolean returnMissingImageOnError,
                         Device device) {
    String path = getFilePath();
    ...
    return new Image(device, path);
    ...
}
```

> Make ownership itself a proof obligation in establishing the owner's invariant.

The preceding discussion can be summarized in two points: Invariants can refer to only owned objects and ownership is dynamic. In conclusion, we somehow have to ensure that whenever the invariant on the owner has to be established, the ownership has to be established at the same time; that is, the owner must "be sure of its parts" before it can say anything about its invariant.

📖21 ↰4.4

This is, indeed, the main insight of the approach that we examined earlier: When "packing" the owner, and thereby establishing its invariant, we must fix the ownership of its parts. Fig. 6.5 illustrates this point from the perspective of the owned part. Since the invariant of that part must be reasoned about independently, the new state chart is an extension of Fig. 4.10, which depicts packing and unpacking of an individual object. Now, we add a new state "committed," where the local invariant of the part holds *and* the part is owned by a particular object. The state transition from "valid" (local invariant holds) to "committed" is not triggered by an action on the part, but on its owner.

↰6.2.1

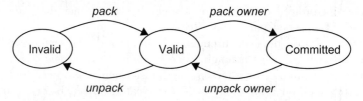

Figure 6.5 Objects States for Invariants with Ownership

Two observations are necessary to establish that the invariant of whole cannot be violated by side effects after whole has been "packed." First, the state chart in Fig. 6.5 ensures that each object can have only a single owner at any given time: The first potential owner that "packs" itself to establish its invariant will also "commit" the desired part. The next potential owner that tries to claim the part for itself cannot do so, because Fig. 6.5 does not allow it to "pack up" parts that are already "committed." Second, other objects are no longer able to invoke methods on the parts because those methods would require the parts to be in state "valid," instead of the state "committed." That state "committed" is not a somehow stronger form of "valid," but rather a completely distinct state.

Invariants with ownership extend the intuition for basic invariants.

In the introduction to contracts, we gave an intuitive illustration of invariants by depicting them as thick borders, as opposed to perforated borders when the object was currently working and was possibly violating the invariant (Fig. 4.5).

    The extension to the state of objects described in this section also translates to an extension to that intuition. Fig. 6.6 displays how first `whole`, then its part `p`, start working. On the left, all objects are "OK"—that is, their invariants hold. Additionally, `whole` has been able to "lock" its two parts `p` and `q` by setting their state to "committed," so that no other object can incorporate them into its own representation or work with them by calling methods. One step further, a method of `whole` is invoked and "unpacks" that object. At the same time, it releases the "locks" on the parts by changing their state from "committed" to "valid." Finally, on the right, a method of `p` starts working and "unpacks" that object. The reverse direction is executed when those methods finish executing: First `p` is again "packed"; then `whole` is "repacked," which also "locks" its parts.

The reasoning pattern enables dynamic transfer of ownership.

Although the introduced regime does not enable other objects to access, or even read from, owned objects, it does not forbid other objects to hold references to those parts—just as long as they do not try to work with the parts. In Fig. 6.6, for instance, the `whole` may hand out a reference to its parts, either before or after "unpacking." In the middle picture, it may then let go of its own reference to `p` or `q`, set the corresponding field to `null`, and repack itself. Now, another object can claim ownership of the released part.

The introduced reasoning patterns are reliable.

The interesting point about these reasoning patterns is that they are solid enough to satisfy even a theorem prover. By making the state of an object, as depicted in Fig. 6.5, into a *ghost state*, which exists only for proof purposes but not at runtime, the prover can keep track of the overall object population of the program and will guarantee that invariants, including cross-object invariants about owned parts, are never violated.

Mentally tag objects with their current owners.

In all of these proofs, the prover never has to be told explicitly *which* object really owns a part; it is sufficient that there is no owner in state "valid"

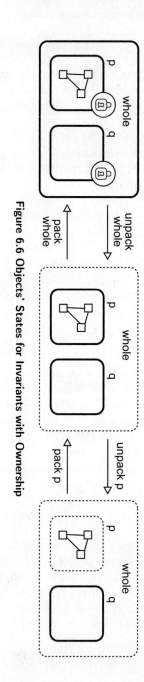

Figure 6.6 Objects' States for Invariants with Ownership

and "some owner" in state "committed." Humans, in contrast, usually have problems with such rather vague statements.

As a practical deduction, we therefore propose to mentally tag each object with its current owner. The owner becomes a pseudo-field (formally, a ghost field) of the object that points to its current owner. An object is in state "committed" exactly if that field is non-null.

Note the switch of perspective induced by this discussion: The important thing is no longer that some objects happen to own some objects that they reference. Rather, the important point is that any object at all can in principle be owned at any given point in time, and must then be immune to modification. If we always track whether this is the case, this approach enables us to ask, for any object at any place in the program,

"Who does currently own that object?"

It turns out that this perspective is, in fact, much more useful than the old one proposed in Section 2.2.1, because it enables you to make decisions that become necessary in the code you are currently working on.

Here is a practical example. The JFace `ColorSelector` creates a button ▶9.3 showing the current color in a filled image; when the user clicks the button, a dialog opens that enables the user to pick a new color. The question in the current context is: Who owns the filled image—the button or the selector? Let us track this through the following constructor. In line 1, the selector creates the image and owns it. Line 3 has the potential for dynamic ownership transfer, since the button obtains a reference to the image. The API of `setImage()` does not mention ownership, and indeed (under Linux/GTK) the button makes a private copy of the image data in an implementation-level pixel buffer. So in line 4, the selector still owns the image. It therefore remains responsible for freeing the resources when the image is no longer required, and makes the appropriate provisions in lines 4–11: Whenever the button vanishes from the screen, the image can also be destroyed.

---

org.eclipse.jface.preference.ColorSelector

```
1 fImage = new Image(parent.getDisplay(), fExtent.x, fExtent.y);
2 ... fill image with current color
3 fButton.setImage(fImage);
4 fButton.addDisposeListener(new DisposeListener() {
5     public void widgetDisposed(DisposeEvent event) {
6         if (fImage != null) {
7             fImage.dispose();
8             fImage = null;
9         }
10     }
11 });
```

Whenever you establish the invariant of a compound object, mentally check the owner-fields of all parts referenced in the invariant.

↰4.2.4
↰4.2

This guideline directly translates the formal rule that "packing" the owner requires its parts to be in state "valid" (rather than "committed"; see Fig. 6.5). It is useful because it establishes a warning bell for programming. For instance, constructors have to establish the invariant at their end. The invariant (4.5) of the `ThresholdArrayIterator` clearly involves the array a, a separate object:

$$0 \leq i \leq a.length \ \&\& \ (i = a.length \ || \ a[i] \leq threshold)$$

To establish the invariant with this reference to a, we also have to establish that the iterator may own the array a—that is, that it may set its state from "valid" to "committed." The original code in Fig. 4.7 enables this step by simply making a local copy.

As we have already pointed out, the new reasoning framework is somewhat more liberal, in that it allows others to retain references to the parts, as long as they do not access these parts. Suppose we were to omit the copy and use the following, more efficient code:

```
                 ownership.ThresholdArrayIteratorRisky
public ThresholdArrayIteratorRisky(int [] a, int threshold) {
    this.a = a;
    this.i = 0;
    this.threshold = threshold;
    findNext();
}
```

This code is legal, if somewhat risky. We have to add the pre-conditon

    a is not "committed," i.e., has no owner.

and the post-condition

    a is "committed" with owner `this`.

Then, we have to rely on the caller to respect the new state of the passed array, meaning it must no longer access the array. In short, it has transferred ownership to the iterator.

6.2.3   Invariants on Shared Objects

In the previous section, we introduced a methodology for reasoning about invariants that involve owned parts. In essence, whenever the invariant had to be established, the ownership had to be established as well. Furthermore, all other objects had to respect that ownership and were no longer allowed to access the part objects.

↰1.3.2 ⟫11.1 ↰2.2.2

Unfortunately, many programming practices do not fit this schema. In fact, object-oriented programming could be said to be all about structure

sharing and aliasing: If objects are to form networks of collaborating indi-   ↰1.1 ↠11.1
viduals, then naturally these individuals are not always arranged in some
artificial ownership hierarchy. Furthermore, the fundamental principle that
objects have identity naturally implies that several objects will access the
single object representing a particular concept or application-level entity.

As a consequence of the arising nonhierarchical, symmetric, and cyclic
relationships, it is very often not even possible to attribute invariants to
individual objects, but only to groups of objects. Typical and intuitive
examples arise in user interfaces, where fields in dialogs must frequently
be linked by some consistency condition. Fig. 6.7 shows such a dialog that
converts between dollars and euros, given the current rate. It is available in
class `CurrencyConverter` of the sample code. Whenever one of the fields
changes, the others must be updated to reflect, as an invariant, the equation

$$eur = rate \times dollar$$

This invariant can be established by attaching suitable observers to all   ↠6.2.3.5 ↰2.1
fields.

⊗ ⊖ ▢ **Currency Converter**		
Dollar	Rate	EUR
6.44❙	1.37	8.8228

Figure 6.7 Currency Converter

The general situation of object groups linked by invariants is illustrated
in Fig. 6.8. Objects a, b, and e access one another cyclically, while b and c
share d. The first group synchronizes their states such that I_1 holds; the
second maintains I_2. Let us call such invariants *global*, because they refer
to several objects at once, rather than being attached to a particular object
and the objects accessible to it.

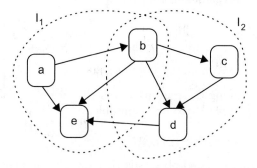

Figure 6.8 Global Invariants

> Avoid invariants spanning multiple objects.

Reasoning about such situations formally or even precisely involves substantial machinery. Practioners will not find this surprising: Object structures with much sharing and global invariants frequently cause bugs. The first advice is to avoid such invariants if possible. Since this is not always possible, we will discuss some practical approaches to taming the harmful consequences.

6.2.3.1 Immutability

↰1.8.4

We have already discussed the fundamental strategy of using immutable objects that essentially represent values. This approach is especially suitable for sharing potentially large internal representations. The class `BigInteger`, for instance, uses a sign/magnitude representation, storing the digits in an array. Since that array can be large, operations try to share it as far as possible. Prototypically, the negate operation uses the same array in the result value:

```
                      java.math.BigInteger
public BigInteger negate() {
    return new BigInteger(this.mag, -this.signum);
}
```

The constructor called here simply stores the passed array:

```
                      java.math.BigInteger
BigInteger(int[] magnitude, int signum) {
    this.signum = (magnitude.length == 0 ? 0 : signum);
    this.mag = magnitude;
}
```

In the current context, we can also discuss the invariants expressed in the class's documentation in some more detail. There, we find the following assertions about fields `signum` and `mag`, which serve to make the representation of a given integer value unique.

1. `sign` is -1, 0, or 1.

2. If the represented value is 0, then $\text{signum} = 0$ and $\text{mag.length} = 0$.

3. Otherwise, $\text{mag.length} \neq 0$ and $\text{mag}[0] \neq 0$.

Obviously, maintaining these invariants in the face of structure sharing is possible only if `mag` is treated as immutable.

6.2.3.2 Copy-on-Write

The core problem of shared objects is that the objects may change "while one is not looking" because someone else performs a modification: While one object describes the current state of the shared part in its invariant, another object modifies the part and breaks the invariant. Immutability of the shared parts is one, perhaps rather ruthless, method of preventing such destructive updates by disallowing updates altogether. Copy-on-write is a ↰1.8.4 somewhat softer form of protecting the invariants of different stakeholders in a shared part.

A typical example occurs with iterators over data structures. In principle, an Iterator must be a lightweight object and iteration must be fast, because it happens very often. The iterator must therefore share the underlying data structure with its container, as shown on the left-hand side of Fig. 6.9.

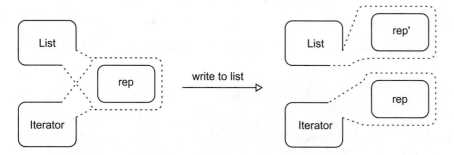

Figure 6.9 Sharing with Copy-on-Write

A typical example is found in the CopyOnWriteArrayList from the Java concurrency library. Here, the array list just passes on the internal array to the new iterator and the constructor of that iterator stores the reference directly. The next() operation can simply advance the cursor position (with pre-condition hasNext(), as usual) and remains lightweight.[2] ↰4.2

java.util.concurrent.CopyOnWriteArrayList

```java
public Iterator<E> iterator() {
    return new COWIterator<E>(array, 0);
}
```

java.util.concurrent.CopyOnWriteArrayList

```java
private static class COWIterator<E> implements ListIterator<E> {
    private final Object[] snapshot;
    private int cursor;
    private COWIterator(Object[] elements, int initialCursor) {
        cursor = initialCursor;
        snapshot = elements;
    }
    public E next() {
        return (E) snapshot[cursor++];
    }
}
```

2. Readers familiar with concurrency will sense that the access to the array field itself should be protected. Indeed, the field is declared volatile, so that writes and reads on that field occur in a well-defined, although unpredicatable, order under the Java memory model [111, §17.4.4].

```
   ... remaining iterator operations
}
```

The problematic case occurs, of course, when some client of the array list sets one of the elements. It then depends on the current position of the iterator, and in the case of concurrency also on the unpredictable decisions of the scheduler and the effects of the Java memory model, whether a next() call receives the old value or the new value. This undefinedness is clearly unacceptable.

The solution is shown on the right side of Fig. 6.9: Upon modification of the array, the list allocates a completely new array and leaves the previous, unmodified copy to the iterator to continue its work. The code of set() merely adds the detail of checking whether the write is necessary at all.

java.util.concurrent.CopyOnWriteArrayList

```java
public E set(int index, E element) {
    ... locking because of concurrency
    Object[] elements = getArray();
    E oldValue = (E)elements[index];
    if (oldValue != element) {
        int len = elements.length;
        Object[] newElements = Arrays.copyOf(elements, len);
        newElements[index] = element;
        array = newElements;
    }
    ... further measures because of concurrency
    return oldValue;
}
```

In copy-on-write, the modifier protects invariants of other stakeholders.

The central idea is that the "perpetrator," who could possibly break the invariants of other objects by its modification to shared parts, protects those invariants by performing modifications on a private copy only.

Copy-on-write behaves as an optimized variant of immediate copying.

The overall behavior is the same as if each iterator had made its private copy at the start of the iteration: Iterators, once they are created, continue to work on the same, unmodified array.

Copy-on-write works only for internal data structures.

For the strategy to be effective, all participants and possible owners of shared parts must be aware of the copy-on-write policy: Whenever they modify the part, they must first obtain their own copy.

Reference counting can improve performance.

Reference counting is a standard technique for managing memory objects. 📖133
Each memory object has an attached counter that keeps track of how many
pointers to itself currently exist. When the count reaches 0, the memory
can be freed and reused.

This technique can also be applied to the copy-on-write policy, as shown
in Fig. 6.10. Whenever A or B wishes to modify rep, it checks the current
reference count. If it is 1, as shown on the right, then "no one else is looking,"
so modifying the representation will not break their invariants and copying
can be avoided altogether.

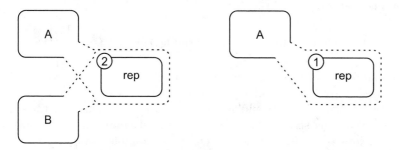

Figure 6.10 Copy-on-Write with Reference Counting

Of course, reference counting requires the active collaboration of the
referencing objects, A and B in Fig. 6.10: Whenever their references become obsolete, they must decrease the counter of rep. This is the case, in
particular, when their life cycle ends so that they no longer require rep.
Unfortunately, Java does not reliably notify objects before their destruction. However, in many cases, the life cycle of objects is well defined by   ◀1.6.2
the surrounding framework—for instance, because the management of ex-   ▶12.3.3.4 ▶7.4.1
ternal resources such as images and fonts for screen display demands an
explicit release. When copy-on-write is applied to large shared objects such
as styled text documents, these are often associated with similarly "large"
objects such as editors, and such parts usually do receive notifications by   ▶7.3.2
the framework about their own life cycle.

🌏 C++ requires all objects to be deallocated explicitly, because there is no garbage collector. For local, stack-allocated objects, this happens when the static block in which
they have been created is left; the compiler injects the necessary code automatically. For
heap-allocated objects, the application is required to use the delete operator. In each
case, the *destructor* of the destroyed object is called to give it a chance to free any other
memory objects and additional resources that it may have allocated. Also, any copy or
assigment can be intercepted by overloading the copy constructor and the assignment
operator, written in C++ as operator=. These facilities together then enable reference
counting: Copies and assignments increment the count, and the destructor decrements
the count and frees the referenced memory object if the count reaches 0. Concrete code
can be found in the classes string and, of course, shared_ptr in the library.

6.2.3.3   Versioning

The copy-on-write policy in the previous section avoids breaking invariants of sharing owners, but at the cost of permitting a somewhat sloppy behavior: The iterator may or may not access the current state of the collection, depending on other code that may not be under the control of the current developers. Also, the fundamental principle of object identity is weakened, because "the data structure" internally gets split into two—there are two different clones of what was previous one entity. In the context of concurrency, this is the best one can do, given that modifications can occur anytime anyway.

Detect problematic cases instead of avoiding them.

One can do better if instead of avoiding breakage, one can be content with detecting it. In the case of iterators, for instance, clients do not usually iterate through the data and modify it at the same time. In those rare cases where this step is necessary, they would simply have to make an explicit copy of the data structure. One such example has been seen in the OBSERVER pattern, where observers may wish to de-register themselves when they receive a change notification—that is, while the traversal of the observer list is in progress.

Inject runtime checks to detect harmful modifications.

In the vast majority of cases, however, that copy can be avoided, while still ensuring the invariants of the owner objects remain intact: The iterator simply has to recognize that a modification has taken place and throw an exception. This exception will alert the developer to a violation of the assumption that the collection remains unmodified throughout the traversal.

Let us look at the example of a HashMap, because it illustrates the point of complex structures better than a simple ArrayList, which applies the same scheme. Fig. 6.11 illustrates the hash map's internal structure: The array table is indexed by (a convolution of) the hash code computed for the key that needs to be found. Since usually several objects have the same hash code, all objects with the same code are kept in the same bucket, which is a linked list of Entrys. An Iterator for the set of entries must then follow that structure, as is indicated by the dotted line. Obviously, that iterator would easily go astray if the hash map was to change during the traversal.

Indeed, the iterator keeps two references into the hash map's internals: index points to the current bucket, and next is the next entry to be returned. Note that this description could be connected to model fields sequence and pos to formulate a precise invariant for HashIterator. It is this invariant that we seek to protect.

↰2.1.1

📖72

↰4.2

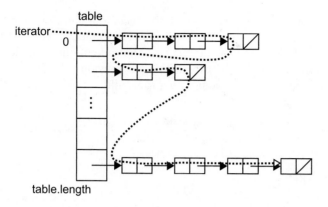

Figure 6.11 Internal Structure of a `HashMap`

---

java.util.HashMap

```
private abstract class HashIterator<E> implements Iterator<E> {
    int index;
    Entry<K, V> next;
    int expectedModCount;
    ...
}
```

The last field in the preceding code snippet, `expectedModCount`, is the key to the solution. The hash map keeps a similar field `modCount`, which it increments in `put()` whenever the structure changes in such a way that an existing iterator's invariant would be broken (line 7).

---

java.util.HashMap

```
transient int modCount;
```

---

java.util.HashMap

```
1 public V put(K key, V value) {
2         ... look up existing entry and update if it exists
3         e.value = value;
4         e.recordAccess(this);
5         return oldValue;
6         ...
7     modCount++;
8     addEntry(hash, key, value, i);
9     return null;
10 }
```

When the iterator is first created, it remembers the current count:

---

java.util.HashMap.HashIterator

```
HashIterator() {
    expectedModCount = modCount;
    ... advance to first entry
}
```

When next() starts running, it protects the iterator's invariant by checking whether the shared data structure is still intact. If it is, the iterator proceeds as usual to find the next entry. The code in lines 5–9 clearly relies on the internals being undisturbed from the previous visit, since otherwise both index and next may be pointing to invalid locations. Lines 2–3 signal a broken invariant to the developer.

```
                      java.util.HashMap.HashIterator
1  final Entry<K, V> nextEntry() {
2      if (modCount != expectedModCount)
3          throw new ConcurrentModificationException();
4      Entry<K, V> e = next;
5      if ((next = e.next) == null) {
6          Entry[] t = table;
7          while (index < t.length && (next = t[index++]) == null)
8              ;
9      }
10     return e;
11 }
```

6.2.3.4 Implicit Maintenance

In many situations, cross-object invariants are not as general as made out in the introduction to Section 6.2.3, and in particular Fig. 6.8. Instead, they concern only two objects that work together closely and that can easily negotiate the invariant between themselves.

↰2.2.1

📖214

For instance, the parent–child relationship in ownership usually comes with the invariant that the child's parent pointer refers to the uniquely determined object that currently owns the child. We have already seen the example of the Graphical Editing Framework's Figures, whose method for adding children maintains this invariant implicitly, as a side effect:

```
                     org.eclipse.draw2d.Figure.add
if (figure.getParent() != null)
    figure.getParent().remove(figure);
children.add(index, figure);
figure.setParent(this);
```

If you decide on implicit maintenance, do it properly.

However, the example is not perfect, since the invariant is not maintained in the reverse direction: Setting the child's parent does not add it to the parent's list of children:

```
                      org.eclipse.draw2d.Figure
public void setParent(IFigure p) {
    IFigure oldParent = parent;
    parent = p;
```

```
        firePropertyChange ("parent", oldParent, p);
}
```

Of course, such asymmetric behavior is very annoying and easily leads to bugs, since developers constantly have to keep track of which invariants are maintained under which circumstances. Another example will be seen in Section 6.2.3.7, where creating a new edge in a graph establishes some, but not all, necessary connections.

For a positive example, we turn to the concept of *opposite references* in the Eclipse Modeling Framework. We use a simple model of Nodes and Edges, which together form a graph structure. There is, of course, a local invariant that links the outgoing edges of a node to the start references of all of those edges (and similarly for the end references of incoming edges). EMF generates the following code for Edge.setStart(), which first removes the edge from the node it may have been attached to previously and then adds it to the node it is attached to now. (InvRel, for *inverse relationships*, is the name of the model; EMF generates several helpers for such a model.)

📖235

```
                              invrel.Edge
public void setStart(Node newStart) {
    if (newStart != start) {
        if (start != null)
            msgs = ((InternalEObject) start).eInverseRemove(this,
                    InvrelPackage.NODE__OUTGOING, Node.class, msgs);
        if (newStart != null)
            msgs = ((InternalEObject) newStart).eInverseAdd(this,
                    InvrelPackage.NODE__OUTGOING, Node.class, msgs);
        this.start = newStart;
    }
}
```

The reverse direction is supported symmetrically: The outgoing edges of a Node are not simply a list, but rather a list that actively maintains the opposite references.

```
                              invrel.Node
public EList<Edge> getOutgoing() {
    if (outgoing == null) {
        outgoing = new EObjectWithInverseResolvingEList<Edge>(
                        Edge.class, this,
                        InvrelPackage.NODE__OUTGOING,
                        InvrelPackage.EDGE__START);
    }
    return outgoing;
}
```

Regardless of whether the relationship between an Edge and a Node is established from the Edge's side or the Node's side, the local invariant between the two is always maintained.

6.2.3.5   Maintaining Invariants More Loosely

Let us go back to the initial example from Fig. 6.7 on page 309, a simple currency converter between dollars and euros that works in both directions. The conceptual invariant on the three text fields expresses that the computation has always been carried out faithfully so that

$$eur = rate \times dollar$$

←2.1

The standard approach to maintaining such interdependencies between dialog fields is to attach observers that propagate changes according to the desired result (Fig. 6.12): Observer (a) takes care of changing dollar entries, (b) takes care of changing rate entries, and finally (c) updates the dollars whenever the euros change. The dotted lines indicate which other value the observers will be using.

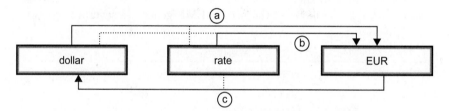

Figure 6.12 Updating in the Currency Converter

≫7.1

←3.1.4
←1.4.9

All three observers work alike: They wait for modifications of a text field and then change the other fields accordingly. User interface elements in general provide for such observers. To exploit the symmetries between the three, we introduce an abstract base class Updater that observes a text field, converts its value to a number, and uses the TEMPLATE METHOD to abstract over the concrete reaction.

```
                        globalinv.CurrencyConverter
abstract static class Updater implements ModifyListener {
    private static boolean updating;
    public void modifyText(ModifyEvent e) {
        ... break cyclic updates
                update(new BigDecimal(
                              ((Text) e.getSource()).getText()));
        ... take care of format exceptions
    }
    protected abstract void update(BigDecimal val);
}
```

As an example, the updater (a) in Fig. 6.12 reuses this infrastructure as follows (getRateValue() converts the entered text into a BigDecimal). Note how the computation in lines 3–4 express precisely the invariant between the fields. Similar observers are attached to the rate and euro fields.

```
                    globalinv.CurrencyConverter.createContents
1 txtDollar.addModifyListener(new Updater() {
2     protected void update(BigDecimal val) {
3         txtEur.setText(
4                 val.multiply(getRateValue()).toPlainString());
5     }
6 });
```

Observers maintain invariants by propagating necessary updates.

From the user's perspective, the dialog now works fine: Whenever the user types into one of the fields, the other dollar or euro field reflects these changes immediately and the display always shows the invariant.

Observers provide loosely coupled dependencies.

The attraction of using observers to establish invariants is their lightweight nature: With a few extra lines of code, you can wire up components that were not built to interact. In the example, the separate text fields do not even hold references to each other; it is only the observers that create their interaction. Components that know very little about each other are called *loosely coupled*.

» 12.1

Observers establish separation of concerns.

Another nice aspect of this solution is that the aspect of displaying and entering the information is completely separated from the aspect of maintaining the invariants. In the code, these aspects are managed by disjoint parts, which simplifies maintenance because the developers just have to understand the aspect that they are currently concerned with, or that exhibits an undesirable behavior.

Maintaining invariants by observers leaves consistency gaps.

A disadvantage of linking different objects through observers is that the apparent invariants do remain broken for some time, as Fig. 6.13 illustrates. When the user types a character, at some point the current text field will update its content and will notify its observers. The special Updater can then modify the linked fields correspondingly before all modified fields repaint themselves on the screen.

   In between the update of the edited field and the reaction of the Updater there is, of course, a brief time span in which the invariant is broken. Fortunately, the arrangements of the user interface framework make sure that the user cannot become aware of this: Each event-handling cycle processes user input completely before the screen is repainted, so that all fields are up-to-date at the time the results are actually shown to the user.

» 7.1

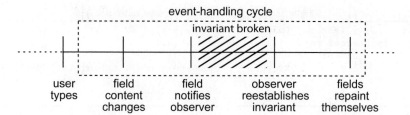

Figure 6.13 Maintaining Invariants with Observers

Other observers can see the broken invariant.

The question is: Does the broken invariant really matter if the user does not become aware of it anyway? The answer: Yes, it does matter, because the software itself can trip over the inconsistency and might make wrong decisions or incur runtime exceptions as a result.

↰1.5.4 ↰1.5.3

Technically, the sequence of notifications leaves only a very brief time span before the invariant gets repaired (Fig. 6.14). When the first field is set by the user's typing, it immediately notifies the updater, which in turn sets the dependent field. When the original call setText returns, everything is in order.

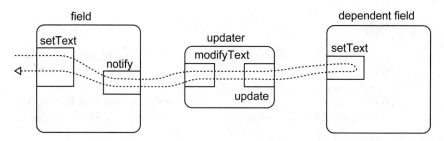

Figure 6.14 Method Calls in Observer-Based Invariants

The critical time span, which is shaded in Fig. 6.13, can therefore be defined more precisely: Since the inner execution sequence within the field cannot matter, the time span starts with the first outgoing call by notify and ends with the outgoing call to the updater.

To demonstrate that this is not a theoretical problem, let us write a small runtime checker for the invariant. It observes text changes in the fields, so as to be able to "listen in" on the ongoing update process.

---
globalinv.CurrencyConverter

```java
public class RuntimeChecker implements ModifyListener {
    ... keep a string tag 'which'
    public void modifyText(ModifyEvent e) {
        if (!getEurValue().equals(
                getDollarValue().multiply(getRateValue()))) {
```

```
        System.err.println("Invariant violation detected: "
            + which);
    }
}
```

It then remains to attach listeners "around" the actual updater. At runtime, these do, indeed, signal violated invariants.

---
globalinv.CurrencyConverter.createContents

```
RuntimeChecker checkA = new RuntimeChecker("A");
txtDollar.addModifyListener(checkA);
 ... register others
txtDollar.addModifyListener(new Updater() {
    ...
});
 ... the two other updaters
RuntimeChecker checkB = new RuntimeChecker("B");
txtDollar.addModifyListener(checkB);
 ... register others
```

The phenomenon encountered here can also be seen as a variant of the fundamental principle that objects must be consistent before sending out their notifications. The only difference in the current case is that the invariant is associated with a group of objects that conceptually, though not technically, are to behave like a single compound object.

↰2.1.2

Loosely coupled systems are likely to see the broken invariant.

The OBSERVER pattern is usually not applied in isolated spots, but pervasively throughout the system. One of the reasons is that it makes for a neat decoupling of different subsystems, because the fundamental principle of designing the observer interface according to the possible changes in the subject, and not the expected concrete observers, makes sure that subjects know next to nothing about their observers.

↠12.2.1.8 ↰2.1.2

In such systems, observers often function in cascades: When an observer receives a change notification, it notifies its own observers in turn, and so on. Because the order of observers cannot be influenced in a predictable fashion, this can easily lead to problematic situations, as illustrated in Fig. 6.15: Objects (a) and (b) are linked by an invariant that is maintained by an updater, in the manner seen earlier. Before the update takes place, however, (a) happens to notify (c), which notifies (d) and (e) in return. Now (e) is an object that happens to work with both (a) and (d).

The sketched problem occurs in systems where observers are used in many places, so that the potential for cycles, where some notified observer gets back to the original source of the cascading changes, becomes more likely.

Debugging with loosely coupled invariants can be cumbersome.

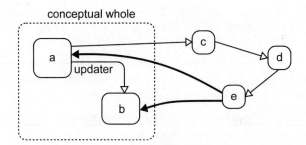

Figure 6.15 Cascading Notifications and Invariants

The crucial dilemma here is that each of the observer relationships is set up locally with the best intentions and according to the design goals. It is only in the resulting overall structure that the problem manifests itself. Furthermore, the order of registration can make all the difference: If the updater for (b) happens to run before the notification to (c), all is in order. Since there is no single place in the source code to which the misbehavior can be pinned, it becomes hard to track down and solve the problem.

Weigh the consequences of maintaining invariants by observers.

There are two conclusions to be drawn from the preceding discussion. First, it is very often possible to maintain invariants in a loosely coupled, minimally invasive way by simply attaching appropriate observers to pre-existing generic components. The observers can then propagate changes in such a way that the desired invariant holds once all observers have run to completion. Second, one should avoid such "ad-hoc invariants" between different objects, because they are not proper invariants in the strict sense of the word. Since they are broken on principle for short durations of time and since other objects in the system can easily become aware of that fact in practical situations, one would be well advised to avoid the construction altogether.

In the end, it is a question of whether the situation can be kept under control. Especially in the context of user interfaces, where the setup of the event-processing loop prevents, ultimately, the problematic output (Fig. 6.13), a looser maintenance of invariants can be acceptable. However, one might say the following:

»7.1

Protect crucial data structures by proper wrapping.

An alternative to the previously described dialog is obtained by taking the invariant between the three values seriously: If it is to be an invariant, we have to create a compound object that maintains it on its internal fields. Creating such a class in the current case is straightforward. The class has three properties (lines 2–4), provides change notifications (lines 5–6, 13) and reestablishes the invariant in every setter (line 12).

```
                        globalinv.CurrencyModel
1  public class CurrencyModel {
2      private double dollars;
3      private double rate;
4      private double eur;
5      private PropertyChangeSupport changes =
6                  new PropertyChangeSupport(this);
7      public double getDollar() {
8          return dollars;
9      }
10     public void setDollar(double dollars) {
11         this.dollars = dollars;
12         eur = rate * dollars;
13         fireChanged();
14     }
15     ... similarly for rate and eur
16 }
```

The dialog can then be attached to this core class using data binding, so   »9.3.3 that the overall effort is not much greater than for direct programming within the dialog.

A distinct advantage of separating out the data in this fashion is that such components can be tested indepedently of the actual user interface. It is, indeed, a common strategy to separate the data and functionality—in   »9.1 other words, to separate the core business value of the application from its mere display and editing capabilities, which might have to change anyway when porting to a different platform or when users wish for new ways of interaction.

6.2.3.6 Dynamic Checking

Invariants can also be read as constraints. An equation, for instance, constrains the referenced variables to contain values that fulfill the equation. Very often, the constraint is actually a restriction. For instance, all nodes in an XML DOM tree must belong to the top-level document—in other words, you cannot add a node that does not belong to that tree. The following code will therefore throw a DOMException:

```
                    globalinv.Constraints.domOwnership
Document docA = docBuilder.newDocument();
Document docB = docBuilder.newDocument();
docA.appendChild(docB.createElement("root"));
```

Of course, like any expectation, invariants can be checked at runtime,   ◄1.5.4 even if the non-redundancy principle decrees that this should not happen,   ◄4.5 because invariants, like all assertions, should be derived by logical reasoning rather than by brute-force error detection.

↰4.5 ↰1.5.4

Cross-object invariants can, however, justify a little more runtime checking, by arguments similar to those introduced earlier:

- Cross-object invariants are complex side-conditions that must be observed by different classes and objects. It is therefore likely that they will be broken sooner or later, which will require efforts in debugging. The additional effort of checking will be justified by avoiding the later problems.

↰6.2.3.5

- The clients of an object structure may be involved in obeying and maintaining the invariant. In the DOM example, the client is actively involved in composing the object structure, and even straightforward observer relationships might be problematic and therefore need to be restricted.

📖214

Such checks can also involve design decisions. Let us look at another tree structure, the Figure elements of a Draw2D image. On the one hand, they involve the global invariant that the tree never contains any cycles from a child to one of its parents. However, the generic method for adding children to a node can easily be used to create such cycles. Since nearly all processing steps of the Draw2D framework, such as painting, layout, and so on, depend on the absence of cycles for their termination, it is wise to report violations of the restriction as early as possible, rather than having to find out afterward at which point a specific cycle had been introduced. The method add() therefore checks the restriction in the very beginning:

```
org.eclipse.draw2d.Figure

public void add(IFigure figure, Object constraint, int index) {
    ...
    for (IFigure f = this; f != null; f = f.getParent())
        if (figure == f)
            throw new IllegalArgumentException(
                    "Figure being added introduces cycle");
    ... perform the addition and re-layout
}
```

↰2.2.1

On the other hand, trees also require that each node has a single parent. This invariant could also be enforced by simply checking. However, the figure elements, like the XML DOM nodes, choose to silently re-parent the new child if necessary.

```
org.eclipse.draw2d.Figure.add

if (figure.getParent() != null)
    figure.getParent().remove(figure);
children.add(index, figure);
figure.setParent(this);
```

However, this strategy is not the only possible one. The designers of the abstract syntax trees in Eclipse's Java tooling have decided that a new child is acceptable to an ASTNode only if it does not already have a parent.

---
org.eclipse.jdt.core.dom.ASTNode.checkNewChild

```
if (newChild.getParent() != null)
    throw new IllegalArgumentException();
```

Which of the two strategies is more useful depends on the expected needs of the clients: If they frequently move around subfigures, they may appreciate the silent re-parenting to maintain the invariants of the tree structure. At the same time, they must be aware of the fact that an existing figure that they insert at one place will suddenly disappear from its previous position in such a case. Since in the JDT case nodes are supposed to represent concrete spans of source code, such a side effect would certainly be rather surprising. Forcing clients to duplicate nodes explicitly, perhaps using ASTNode.copySubtree(), here is the more sensible choice.

↰1.1

6.2.3.7 Reconstruct Rather Than Synchronize

Cross-object invariants link the state of one object with the state of another object. If one of the objects changes, the other has to be adapted correspondingly, for instance using the OBSERVER pattern. In many cases, however, the dependency is asymmetric: One object depends on the other, but not the reverse. In such cases, it can be sensible to implement the invariant by recomputing the dependent object's state whenever its data is required.

↰6.2.3.5

As an example, suppose you want to lay out a directed graph displayed on the screen using the layout algorithms from the Graphical Editing Framework's Zest component. To accomplish that goal, you have to construct an instance of DirectedGraph that reflects your application-specific graph structure (Fig. 6.16). The nodes and edges in a DirectedGraph contain internal (package-visible) data that enables the layout alorithms to work efficiently. Technically speaking, it is necessary to create a graph structure that is isomorphic to the original one.

📖214,269

↰1.7.1

Certainly, the task can be solved by observers: Additions and removals of nodes and edges as well as possible reconnect operations on the application graph's edge can all be reflected faithfully in the DirectedGraph. However, doing so may not be the best choice, since it is easy to make mistakes. The DirectedGraph itself has, of course, internal invariants. For instance, an edge attached to any node must also be listed in the graph's edge list, as well as in the outgoing list of its source and the incoming list of its target node. Furthermore, some of these points are maintained implicitly, while others are not. For instance, the Edge constructor connects the new edge to its endpoints, but does not add it to the graph itself.

↰6.2.3.5

---
org.eclipse.draw2d.graph.Edge

```
public Edge(Object data, Node source, Node target) {
    this.data = data;
    this.source = source;
    this.target = target;
```

```
source.outgoing.add(this);
target.incoming.add(this);
}
```

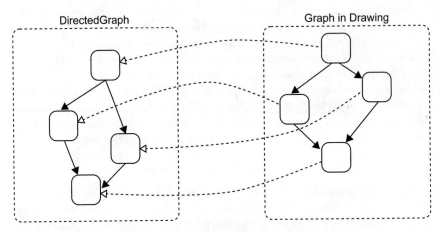

Figure 6.16 Synchronizing Graphs for Layout

Reconstruct if synchronization is complex and does not save runtime.

↰1.1

The alternative to mastering this mesh of side-conditions is to simply re-build the `DirectedGraph` for each layout operation, according to Amdahl's law: The layout algorithms decide on the placement of nodes and routing of edges essentially by solving constraint systems. Such optimizations take so much time that building the graph structure up front hardly matters at all. Just think of all the development time saved at the little expense of a few milliseconds at the beginning of what will be a lengthy computation anyway.

Prefer synchronization to enable incremental updates.

↰2.1.3

In contrast, the strategy of reconstructing the dependent state should be avoided if that state itself is observable. As we noted in the discussion of the push and pull variants of the OBSERVER pattern, updates usually cascade. As a consequence, it is necessary to send as detailed a change report as possible. The final operations that are triggered by the changes may be expensive, such as repainting parts of the screen, so that it is essential to keep changes focused throughout the chain of notifications.

↠9.4.3

Reconstruct and compute the difference as a compromise.

When you decide to rebuild a dependent data structure despite the exis-tence of OBSERVER objects, you can still aim at providing detailed change notifications, by comparing the original and the new structure after the new structure has been computed afresh. The usual way to do this is to merge the new structure into the old structure, and to gather changes on the way.

For instance, Eclipse's Java Model maintains a tree representation of the current Java sources, as well as the meta-structure of packages, archives, projects, and so on. Here, we have a typical cross-object invariant: The Java Model must be kept up-to-date when the sources change. However, incremental parsing is an art, or a complex craft, by itself. The actual update notifications in the form of `IJavaElementChanges` are therefore computed through differences. First, the Java Model tree is constructed from a new abstract syntax tree of the source (in `CompilationUnit.buildStructure()`). The new structure is passed on to a `JavaElementDeltaBuilder`, which recursively compares the new tree to the previous, cached version to detect the differences. Finally, these differences are sent out by the `DeltaProcessor`.

257,260,108

↰2.1.3

6.3   Exceptions and Contracts

Its contract places a method under an obligation: Given that the caller fulfills the pre-condition, the method must fulfill the post-condition—that is, it must provide the promised result. Sometimes, this obligation can be rather too severe. While technically the method can always be held responsible for failing to establish its post-condition, morally there are situations where it should be exculpated. Suppose, for instance, that we wish to submit mail to the local SMTP daemon for delivery by connecting to its local well-known port. The constructor of `Socket` certainly cannot be blamed if the administrator failed to start up the daemon and the connection is refused in consequence.

↰4.1

exceptions.SocketConnect.connectToLocalSMTP

```
Socket s = new Socket((String)null, 587);
```

Throw an exception to signal that the post-condition cannot be established.

Exceptions signal unexpected circumstances, such as the missing communication partner in the preceding example. This general usage coincides with the need for a method to intentionally break its contract because it simply cannot fulfill the post-condition.

↰1.5

Use checked exceptions to signal external reasons for broken post-conditions.

We argued earlier that checked exceptions should be used when the reason for aborting the processing is a problem that could be expected or forseen. This is the case, in particular, when a method needs to interact

↰1.5.7

↰1.5.2

with the outside world in the form of the network, the hard drive, or the user interface.

↰4.5

The perspective of contracts now adds another piece of support for that advice. The whole point of contracts, as made explicit in the non-redundancy principle, is trust: A method trusts its caller to establish the pre-condition, and the caller trusts the method in return to establish the post-condition. Now ask yourself: Which kind of business partner would you trust more—one who notifies you at the deadline that unfortunately he did not make it due to unforeseen circumstances, or one who notifies you well in advance of possible reasons for delay?

The checked exceptions become part of the contract.

Declaring a checked exception is like adding an exit clause to a contract. The exception stands for some specific circumstance under which the method can be relieved of fulfilling its promise to always honor the contract.

The API of the Java library contains many examples of such clauses. For instance, the `FileInputStream`'s constructor states when it will not be able to read the given file:

> Throws `FileNotFoundException` if the file does not exist, is
> a directory rather than a regular file, or for some other reason
> cannot be opened for reading.

Declared exceptions can be associated with alternative post-conditions.

Of course, a message that just says, "Sorry, I didn't make it," is not very informative. The textual information contained in an exception may be useful for maintenance purposes, but it does not help in handling the exception and recovering from the error.

↰1.5.1

📖23

It can therefore be useful to associate alternative post-conditions with the different exceptions a method declares in its header. The client might, in particular, be interested in guarantees about what has *not* changed, so that it can start again with the same object. Very often, however, such assertions are left implicit and are understood by a combination of exception safety

↰1.5.6
↰4.2.6

and the assumption that model fields not mentioned as being modified are assumed to stay the same.

A common case is to give further information about the conditions under which an exception is thrown in such a way that this information reveals new insights about the object's state. The additional post-condition is just this gained knowledge about the object's current state. For instance, the XML DOM API for method `appendChild()` in class `Node` says:

> `NO_MODIFICATION_ALLOWED_ERR`: Raised if this node is read-
> only or if the previous parent of the node being inserted is read-
> only.

When a client sees this specific exception, it knows not only that the insertion failed, but also that either the new parent or the old parent was read-only, so that the implicit re-parenting has failed. It can then take this information into account when devising recovery strategies.

↰6.2.3.4

Use unchecked exceptions for broken invariants and broken pre-conditions.

A second reason why a method might legally fail to establish its post-condition is, of course, that the caller has failed to provide the pre-condition. Although usually a method should not check for this, it might still be advisable in some situations where the consequences of silent failure would be unacceptable. We suggested earlier that unchecked exceptions should be used for this purpose.

↰4.5
↰1.5.2 ↰1.8.7

Again, this suggestion is backed up by the contracts point of view. When the caller breaks its part of the agreement by letting the method down on the pre-condition, the method can simply refuse to do any work at the earliest possible point. However, this kind of interaction is outside the world of contracts, so the corresponding exceptions should also not be mentioned in the contracts.

Similarly, when an object finds that it has broken its own invariant, this is not something that one would advertise to one's partners in the contracts. So unchecked exceptions are the right choice here, too.

Strive to maintain invariants despite throwing exceptions.

Once a class invariant gets broken, the corresponding object becomes useless, since the next call to a `public` method will probably fail and might even cause damage to the rest of the system. The contract view on the concept of exception safety is therefore that invariants should be maintained even if a method throws an exception: The only place where sufficient information for restoring the invariant is available is the place where the exception is thrown, so the object's internals should be repaired there and then.

↰4.1
↰1.5.6

6.4   Inheritance and Subtyping

Inheritance and interfaces are central abstraction mechanisms in object-oriented programming, and we have discussed their usage in some detail. At the heart, the usage guidelines derive from the Liskov Substitution Principle, which demands that an object of a subtype must be usable wherever an object of a super-type is expected. In this way, the object's clients can be adapted to new situations by simply substituting the object with collaborators that exhibit variants of a common abstract behavior. In some cases, the base class might even choose not to implement the behavior at

↰3
↰3.1.1
↰1.3.2 ↰1.4.8.3
↰1.4.11
↰1.4.10

↰1.4.9
all. Within a class, TEMPLATE METHODS define collaborations of an object with itself that can be adapted by subclassing.

↰4.1
The task in this section is to present a conceptual framework that covers these different uses of inheritance, integrates with the fundamental strategies for reasoning about correctness, and can in principle even be
↰4.7
extended to formal reasoning. Before we start, we point out a simplifying observation:

> Classes and interfaces behave the same way with respect to contracts.

↰1.4.1
Contracts specify the behavior of a method that a client can call. It does not matter how the client knows that the method exists, whether through an interface or through a concrete or abstract class. All that matters is that the client establishes the method's pre-condition and can expect the method's post-condition in return. In consequence, we can treat all kinds of subtyping, such as `extends` and `implements` for classes and `extends` for interfaces, simultaneously for the current purposes. To emphasize the commonality, we will speak generically of super-types and subtypes when we mean both interfaces and classes.

↰3.1.1

↰3.2.1

↰3.1.2
The subsequent presentation builds on the practical insights discussed previously and will derive the corresponding formulation from the perspective of contracts. We start with the Liskov Substitution Principle, which leads to the concept of contract inheritance. This covers the outside view of an object and addresses the use of interfaces as abstract specifications of some expected behavior. Then we look at the internal view, which relates back to defining the interface between a super-class and its subclasses. It involves two aspects: the maintenance of the invariants formulated at different levels of the hierarchy and the contracts of `protected` methods.

6.4.1   Contracts of Overridden Methods

↰4.1
↰1.4.1
A method's contract captures its behavior by specifying the legal calls in the pre-condition and the achieved result in the post-condition. Method overriding on its own can be understood best by considering methods to belong to objects, rather than to classes: Overriding replaces some method entirely with a new implementation, while the object's clients remain unaware of the substitution. The interaction between these two aspects is clear: The replacement must obey the original contract; otherwise, the new object is not substitutable because it behaves differently and may break the clients' expectations.

> An overriding method inherits the contract of the overridden method.

📖150,151,89,23
This point is really the foundation for treating inheritance in the context of contracts. The conventional term *contract inheritance* highlights the fact that a subclass inherits from its superclass not only the fields and methods, but also the methods' specifications. Viewed the other way
↰3.1.1
around, a behavioral subtype is one that honors the super-type's contracts.

Because of the crucial role of contract inheritance, let us examine this idea a bit more closely.

Suppose a superclass declares a method `meth()` with pre-conditon P_{super} and post-condition Q_{super} and publishes this contract to its clients.

inheritance.SuperClass

```
public class SuperClass {
    /**
     * PRE Psuper
     * POST Qsuper
     */
    public int meth(int param) {
        ...
    }
}
```

Now any client wishing to call that method has to obey the contract. In other words, it must make sure that P_{super} holds before the call and can only assume Q_{super} to hold after the call. Its reasoning therefore takes the following shape:

↰4.1

inheritance.DemoClient

```
public void operation(SuperClass obj) {
    ...
    // Psuper
    int res = obj.meth(arg);
    // Qsuper
    ...
}
```

Now a subclass `SubClass` might override the method `meth()`. Because of subtyping, an instance of that class could be passed for `obj` to the method `operation`. If the overriding method uses exactly the same contract as the method from the superclass, the client's reasoning remains valid, and the client code remains correct.

Let us illustrate the point with a tiny standard example. A `Cell` holds a single value in a field `content`. It publishes this state in model field content. The pre-condition of both methods `get()` and `set()` is `true`. The post-condition of `get()` is `\return = content`, while that of `set()` is `content = \old(c)`.

inheritance.Cell

```
public class Cell {
    protected int content;
    public int get() {
        return content;
    }
    public void set(int c) {
        this.content = c;
    }
}
```

The derived class `BackupCell` extends the behavior by providing a single-slot backup, with field and model field `backup`. Now the post-condition of `set()` is content $= \backslash$old$(c) \wedge$ backup $= \backslash$old$($content$)$.

---
inheritance.BackupCell

```
public class BackupCell extends Cell {
    private int backup;
    public void set(int c) {
        backup = content;
        super.set(c);
    }
    public void backup() {
        this.content = backup;
    }
}
```

The overridden method `set()` in particular guarantees the inherited post-condition and therefore honors the inherited contracts. Clients that know a particular object is an instance of the special case `BackupCell` can also take advantage of the additional knowledge about the `backup` state.

> Overriding methods can weaken the pre-condition and strengthen the post-condition.

The preceding example shows that inherited contracts do not have to be taken as they are. This raises the question of which modifications to the contract are permissible. Let us take a very general view. Suppose the `SubClass` specifies new pre- and post-conditions P_{sub} and Q_{sub}.

---
inheritance.SubClass

```
public class SubClass extends SuperClass {
    /**
     * PRE Psub
     * POST Qsub
     */
    public int meth(int param) {
        ...
    }
}
```

↰6.1.2   To validate the client's reasoning, we can go back to the idea of stronger and weaker assertions. If P_{sub} is weaker than P_{super}, such that the subclass requires less than the superclass, then P_{super} implies P_{sub} in all possible program states. Since the client establishes P_{super} before the call, it has also established P_{sub}.

Now assume the method in `SubClass` guarantees to achieve Q_{sub}. As long as Q_{sub} is stronger than Q_{super}, meaning the subclass guarantees more than the superclass, it also guarantees Q_{super}. In a logical formulation, this could be expressed as

$$P_{super} \implies P_{sub} \quad \wedge \quad Q_{sub} \implies Q_{super}$$

Although this generalization of contract inheritance is logically possible, it seems somewhat irrelevant from a practical perspective: Why should a subclass be content with less if it can get a stronger pre-condition, which means more information that it can work with? Why should it guarantee more than the superclass promises—why should it perform the extra work? The answer is simple: because the new contract captures the subclass's behavior more naturally.

Subtypes that are special cases do modify the contracts in practice.

A prototypical and small example of such special cases can be found in the JDK's collection framework. At the base, the interface Collection introduces a method for adding elements.   ↰3.1.5 ↰3.2.3

---
java.util.Collection

```
boolean add(E e);
```

Its documentation states:

> Ensures that this collection contains the specified element. Returns `true` if this collection changed as a result of the call. Returns `false` if this collection does not permit duplicates and already contains the specified element.

In the derived interface List, the same method is specified as follows:

> Appends the specified element to the end of this list.[...]
> Returns `true` (as specified by `Collection.add(E)`).

Both statements are clearly post-conditions, as they describe the methods' results. The post-condition of the derived method is actually stronger: It augments the assertion "contains" with the guarantee "at the end," and it does not involve a case distinction, but guarantees to choose the `true` case from the super-type's method.

Similarly, the interface Set states for the same method:

> Adds the specified element to this set if it is not already present. [...] If this set already contains the element, the call leaves the set unchanged and returns `false`.[...]
> Returns `true` if this set did not already contain the specified element.

The first sentence is logically the same as the formulation using "ensures" from the super-type. However, the second sentence makes the additional guarantee that the collection will not change if the element is already present. The two statements about the result are, again, equivalent to the original claims, since a Set, according to its documentation, will never contain duplicates.

»7.1

The documentation of abstract methods hints at the later specialization. For instance, a `Layout` in the SWT is responsible for positioning user interface elements. Its abstract method `layout` is specified as follows:

> Lays out the children of the specified composite according to this layout. This method positions and sizes the children of a composite using the layout algorithm encoded by this layout.

Checked exceptions are part of contract inheritance.

↩6.3

Checked exceptions are part of a method's contract: They announce in advance in which cases the method may not be able to fulfill its promise stated in the post-condition. It is therefore clear that an overriding method may not throw more or different exceptions than the method that it replaces, although it may, of course, throw fewer exceptions or subtypes of the original exceptions. This rule is also enforced by the compiler, in that the `throws` clause of the subtype must be contained in the `throws` clause of the super-type.

6.4.2   Invariants and Inheritance

↩3.1.2

In describing typical usage of Java, we have examined the relationship between a base class and its subclasses: Should a base class hide its fields or should it share them with its subclasses? Which of the two should initialize which fields? Is the base class a service provider to the subclass, or is it simply a foundation for building a derived implementation? The insights gained there can be rephrased easily in the language of contracts and invariants, where they become more precise and can even be formalized. From a practical perspective, we will gain a snug overview of the earlier discussions and discover new aspects to them. The central point to be observed is this:

📖243(§7.6.3)

📖21

Each class chooses and maintains its own invariant about its own fields.

From a technical perspective, inheritance accumulates the fields declared in different classes along the inheritance chain in a single object. Fig. 6.17 shows the case of class C deriving from B, which in turn derives from A. The suggestion of the guideline then is simply to treat the groups of fields, also called *class frames* in this context, individually. The overall invariant of the entire object is the Boolean conjunction of the three individual invariants: $I_A \wedge I_B \wedge I_C$.

↩6.1.5

The guideline can be justified in several ways. First, we observed earlier that it is complex and error-prone to either weaken or strengthen an existing invariant: A stronger invariant requires all `public` methods suddenly to do more work to maintain it, while a weaker invariant means that all `public` methods suddenly know less about the object's fields when they

↩4.1 ↩4.4

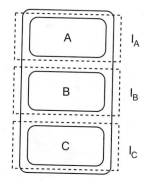

Figure 6.17 Invariants and Inheritance

start working. In both cases, the class's code will need to be revised thoroughly to keep working. It follows for the case of inheritance that a subclass cannot change the invariants of its superclasses, which means that those remain as they were stated in the superclasses. By a switch of perspective, the same argument also explains why a subclass should not be involved in maintaining its superclasses' invariants: Whenever those invariants change due to changes in a superclass, such as when its developers discover a more efficient data structure, the code of the subclass is broken.

≫3.1.11

A second explanation is obtained by starting from the view that a subclass is just a special client of its superclass and that the accesses to that class should be channeled through a well-defined interface of `protected` methods. The superclass's invariant, like every invariant, is private knowledge; it is a contract of the superclass developers with themselves that no client should be aware of.

↰3.1.2

↰4.1

<h2>Unpack classes along the inheritance chain.</h2>

We discovered earlier that it can be useful to make explicit those points where an object's invariant holds. The intuition was to imagine an object as a package [Fig. 4.10(a) on page 217]: When "packing" the object, the invariant is safely "contained" inside; when "unpacking" the object, we regain that information "stashed away" in the imaginary package.

↰4.4 ↰6.2.2

This idea links nicely with inheritance and the concept of protected interfaces for subclasses (Fig. 6.18). Each class along the inheritance chain only unpacks its own fields, which enables it to work on those fields. This unpacking happens in `public` methods, as before, or in `protected` methods in the context of inheritance. Each use of a superclass's `protected` interface unpacks precisely the layer of that class.

📖23

The unpacking and packing then happens in parallel with the call chain moving up the superclass hierarchy. In consequence, each class becomes responsible for maintaining its own invariants.

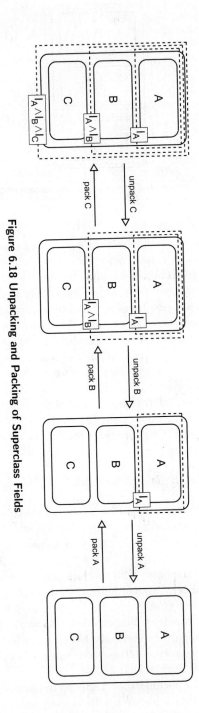

Figure 6.18 Unpacking and Packing of Superclass Fields

protected methods maintain the declaring class's invariant.

A practical consequence of this explanation is that protected methods should be treated like public methods with respect to invariants. In other words, they can assume the invariant at the beginning and must establish the invariant at the end. The only detail is that "the invariant" refers to an invariant about the current class frame, and implicitly to all those invariants from higher levels in the inheritance chain (Fig. 6.18).

↰3.1.2
↰4.4

The main challenge and the justification for this structure is that protected methods can be called from any point within the class hierarchy, not only from the subclasses. While many do act as service providers to subclasses, the TEMPLATE METHOD pattern, for instance, explicitly introduces protected methods to be called from the *superclass* code. A class's frame must therefore be "in good shape" whenever one of its protected methods is called.

↰3.1.4

Use private methods for processing steps.

The stronger obligations connected to protected methods also reemphasize the guideline of making mere processing steps, which are intended to be called from within a larger sequence, private. Such private methods can be liberal and flexible with the invariants; they can take their pick of which parts they assume in the pre-condition and guarantee in their post-condition.

↰1.4.5 ↰1.4.6
↰4.2.3

A subclass's invariants should not reference the inherited fields.

The goal of having each class along the inheritance chain maintain its own invariant can be reached only if those invariants never refer to a super-class's fields. In the context of invariants and ownership, we have seen that even such conceptual references, which never occur in the real code, can be problematic. We have also pointed out that they need to be restricted (Fig. 6.4). The same argument applies to invariants of subclasses: As soon as they reference the superclass's fields, the superclass is no longer free to maintain that invariant in the ways it sees fit and might inadvertently break the subclass's invariants.

↰6.2.2

Whenever a subclass invariant does reference a superclass's field, it is likely that any method modifying that field will need to be overridden in the subclass. To illustrate the point, consider a simple standard example of two versions of a linked list. The size() method in the basic version has to walk the list and therefore is linear in the length of the list.

📖185

inheritance.LinkedList

```
public class LinkedList {
    protected class Node {
        protected Object data;
        protected Node next;
```

```
    }
    protected Node head = null;
    public int size() {
        ... traverse the list starting at head
    }
    ...
}
```

The following subclass makes the `size()` function constant time, by adding a cache field `size` and stating the invariant:

`size` contains the length of the linked list in `head`.

↰1.4.11

To maintain that invariant, the subclass also has to extend the behavior of the inherited method `add()`:

inheritance.LinkedListWithSize.add

```
public void add(int pos, Object elem) {
    super.add(pos, elem);
    size++;
}
```

Treat references to superclass model fields as cross-object references.

Such problems are not, unfortunately, restricted to the superclass's implementation fields, which the subclass should certainly not reference. They also occur with conceptual references to model fields, because those fields always reflect the state of the superclass frame in Fig. 6.17. Any change to the inherited state can modify the model fields derived from that state, so the subclass invariant can be broken even if it relies only on the public model fields.

↰6.2.3.5

The remedy is, again, to override superclass methods to adjust the subclass's fields according to the change. This approach can, however, be understood as a special case of the observer-based maintenance of cross-object invariants: The subclass intercepts all calls to the superclass's method and thereby receives a "signal" that the method has been called. The code for the linked list with a cached size provides an obvious and small example.

↰6.2.3.5

There is, however, one detail that is simpler in the present case. The problem with "looser" invariants was that there were intermittent broken states that were visible to clients (Fig. 6.13) when these were registered as observers as well. When overriding superclass methods to update the subclass fields, in contrast, the control flow stays entirely within the class and clients cannot become aware of the intermediate illegal states. This is,

↰4.1

indeed, only analogous to the principal point that a class usually does break its invariant while it is working.

Part III

Events

Chapter 7

Introduction to the Standard Widget Toolkit

Object-oriented software at its technical core is constructed from objects that receive method calls, change their internal state, and compute some return value. Part II created a solid and detailed conceptual basis for reasoning about these method calls and about the correctness of software in general. Such a basis is indispensable for developing any substantial software product: If we are not able to capture the expected behavior of its different components precisely, we will never be able to divide the work among a team and still be confident that the parts will fit together seamlessly in the end.

The question of correctness naturally focuses on the caller's perspective: The caller always invokes a method to achieve a particular result. It obeys the method's pre-condition and expects the method to provide the result described in the post-condition. As a rather subtle consequence, that post-condition also determines the method's behavior to a large degree: The method will perform only such actions as are necessary to fulfill the post-condition, since any further effort is wasted and indeed unexpected from the caller's point of view.

↰1.1 ↰4.1
↰4.2.3

In many situations, the contracts cannot be as precise as would be necessary to specify the result completely. We have seen one instance in the case of the OBSERVER pattern: The subject sends out notifications about state changes to many different kinds of observers, by calling the methods of a common interface. Of course, the concrete behavior of the observers can then vary greatly, according to their respective purposes. The subject cannot prescribe a single contract for the method it calls. Similarly, at the system boundary, the network card may signal the arrival of a data packet and the operating system has to deal with it appropriately; when it hands the packet on to some application, it can, again, not prescribe the reaction of that application.

↰2.1

↠12.2.1.8

In all of these examples, the focus in reasoning about what is "correct" shifts from the caller to the callee. The observer, the operating system, and the networking application all exhibit some reaction that is appropriate from their own point of view, rather than serving to fulfill any expectation on the caller's part. Software structured in this way is called *event-driven*: Something relevant—the event—happens, the software is notified, and it reacts appropriately. Although internally such software will employ contracts

↠7.11

to specify the behavior of its objects, its overall structure is shaped by the view that events are delivered and must be acted upon.

Part III presents and examines the specifics of event-driven software. In this chapter, we look at an important and prototypical example, the construction of graphical user interfaces. It serves to approach the topic from a technical perspective, by just working out the concrete API of the Standard Widget Toolkit (SWT) used by Eclipse. Looking beyond, it analyzes the concept of frameworks and its central feature, inversion of control. Chapter 8 treats the additional complications arising when code is executed concurrently, in several threads. In particular, the communication between threads is best understood as being event-driven. Chapter 9 complements the discussion of user interfaces by examining a practically crucial aspect, that of model-view separation: Professional developers strive to keep as much of an application's functionality independent of the user interface as possible. Finally, Chapter 10 comes back to the original question: How can we talk about the correctness of event-driven software? It turns out that in many situations, the desired behavior of objects can be captured by finite state machines.

7.1   The Core: Widgets, Layouts, and Events

A graphical user interface is more than just a pixel-based image on the screen. The interface will reflect the user's mouse gestures, for instance by highlighting a button when the mouse moves in. A window will repaint itself when the user first minimizes and then reopens it. Different parts will interact when the user performs drag-and-drop gestures. In short, the user interface is a highly reactive piece of software.

»7.3

The technical structure of user interfaces is well understood and there are many frameworks that implement the fundamental mechanisms and graphical components. The Standard Widget Toolkit (SWT), which is used in Eclipse, is one prototypical example. Having mastered this specimen, you will easily find your way into the others as well.

📖84

The Eclipse web site offers a rich collection of SWT *snippets*, which show in a minimal environment how particular user interface elements are created and how the SWT API is supposed to be used. In short, they provide a helpful cookbook for creating your own user interfaces, covering basic patterns as well as special knowledge for experienced developers.

To examine the structure and usage of SWT, let us try to implement the simple web browser shown in Fig. 7.1. We need a field to type in the URL, a "Load" button, and a display area for the web page itself. Since SWT already contains a Browser component, as well as all the smaller elements shown in the figure, all we have to do is wire them up appropriately.

Figure 7.1 A Simple Browser

The user interface is represented in the software as a tree of widgets.

At the software level, the overall user interface is constructed as a tree of *widgets* (Fig. 7.2). Each widget covers a rectangular area of the screen, and it may have children according to the COMPOSITE pattern. In SWT, the top-level window is called a *shell* and is represented by an object of class `Shell`. Inside the shell, and below it in the widget tree, we have placed `top`, `browser`, and `statusBar`. The browser is simply a predefined object of class `Browser`. The other two are `Composites`, which is SWT's class that manages child widgets. The `top` composite contains the `url`, which is a `Text`, the `load` button of class `Button`, and a progress bar of class `ProgressBar`. The lower `statusBar` contains a single `Label` called `status` for displaying a text.

↰2.3.1

↰2.3.1

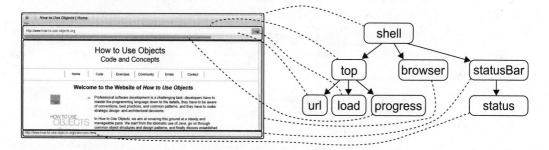

Figure 7.2 Widget Tree of the Browser

⌕ The class hierarchy of SWT may be somewhat misleading at this point. The visible widgets on the screen derive from `Control`. The root class `Widget`, from which `Control`

»7.4.1

also derives, covers all elements of the user interface that may be associated with resources and that may send notifications. Other subclasses of `Widget` represent, e.g., tool tips, rows in tables, and the system tray. In the following discussion, we will nevertheless continue to speak of "widgets" for anything that is painted on the screen.

↰2.3.1

Let us look at the code that creates the tree in Fig. 7.2. The COMPOSITE pattern suggests introducing methods `addChild` and `removeChild` for the purpose. SWT uses a different approach: Each widget is constructed below a specific parent and that parent must be passed to the widget's constructor. The construction of the tree from Fig. 7.2 then proceeds top-down, starting with the top-level window. The second parameter of each constructor is a generic bit set of *flags*, which can provide widget-specific customizations needed at creation time. Here, we do not use that feature and pass `SWT.NONE`.

---

swt.browser.SimpleBrowser.createContents

```
shell = new Shell();
top = new Composite(shell, SWT.NONE);
url = new Text(top, SWT.NONE);
load = new Button(top, SWT.NONE);
progress = new ProgressBar(top, SWT.NONE);
browser = new Browser(shell, SWT.NONE);
status = new Composite(shell, SWT.NONE);
statusText = new Label(status, SWT.NONE);
```

↰2.2.1
»7.4

The advantage of the top-down construction is that each widget is properly owned by its parent, except for the top-level shells, which transitively own all widgets in the tree below them. In this way, the operating system resources invariably associated with an SWT widget cannot be leaked easily.

SWT is very consistent in this approach. Even the single lines in tables and trees, which at the implementation level may allocate icon resources, are represented as `Widgets`. For instance, to create a table with random people (Fig. 7.3), we add each new line by the following code:

---

swt.intro.AddRemoveRowDemo.createContents

```
TableItem item = new TableItem(table, SWT.NONE);
item.setText(new String[] { randomName(), randomDate() });
```

To remove a row, or a widget from the tree in general, we dispose of that widget, rather than asking its parent to remove it as done in COMPOSITE. In the example, the following code removes the currently selected person:

---

swt.intro.AddRemoveRowDemo.createContents

```
int sel = table.getSelectionIndex();
if (sel != -1)
    table.getItem(sel).dispose();
```

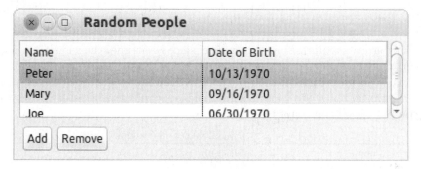

Figure 7.3 SWT Table

Layout managers position widgets within their parents.

Once the widget tree is created, the technical backbone of the user interface is in place. However, the visual position of the single widgets is unclear. For instance, how is SWT supposed to know that we expect `url`, `load`, and `progress` to appear in the configuration shown in Fig. 7.1?

The solution consists of making each `Composite` responsible for positioning its children—that is, for computing a *layout* for them. However, the positions must be computed in a very flexible, application-specific manner. Composites therefore employ the STRATEGY pattern: They are configured ↰1.3.4 by a `LayoutManager` and delegate any positioning requests to that object.

In the example, the `top` composite uses a `GridLayout` (lines 1–3 in the next code snippet; the parameters to `GridLayout()` in line 1 mean two columns, not using equal-width columns). That layout manager arranges the children in a table, but it is very flexible: Children may span multiple columns and rows (below the progress bar spans two columns), they are positioned within their table cell (e.g., left, center, fill), and some table cells may expand to fill the available space (`true`, `false`). These parameters are attached to the children as *layout constraints* of class `GridData` (lines 5–8).

```
                    swt.browser.SimpleBrowser.createContents
1 GridLayout gl_top = new GridLayout(2, false);
2 gl_top.marginWidth = 0;
3 gl_top.marginHeight = 0;
4 top.setLayout(gl_top);
5 url.setLayoutData(new GridData(SWT.FILL, SWT.CENTER, true,
6                               false, 1, 1));
7 progress.setLayoutData(new GridData(SWT.FILL, SWT.CENTER, false,
8                               false, 2, 1));
```

SWT offers a rich collection of layout managers that can be attached to arbitrary composite widgets. In practice, it is hardly ever necessary to write actual code to lay out children.

Do not specify pixel-based positions and sizes of widgets.

»7.2

Using layouts requires some experience, since sometimes the widgets do not come out as expected. The graphical WindowBuilder helps a lot, because you get an immediate preview of the later runtime behavior. However, you may still be tempted to just position widgets explicitly, because that gives you pixel-level control of the outcome:

---
swt.intro.XYLayoutDemo.createContents

```
text = new Text(shell, SWT.BORDER);
text.setBounds(53, 10, 387, 25);
```

»7.4

Do not yield to this temptation: If the font sizes or the behavior of the native widgets underlying SWT differ only very slightly on the user's platform, the display will be ruined. Also, users like resizing windows to fit their current needs, and this is possible only if the inner layout adapts automatically.

Laying out widgets is a recursive top-down process.

In most situations, it is sufficient to configure the local layout managers with the desired constraints for all children. Sometimes, however, the result is not exactly as expected, and then one needs to understand the overall process. Fortunately, that process is straightforward: Each composite widget assigns positions and sizes to its children and lays them out recursively.

The core of the process can be seen in the following snippet from `Composite`. The composite delegates the positioning of the children to its layout manager (line 2). This assigns all children a position and size via `setBounds()`. The process then continues recursively to the children (lines 4–7). The parameter `all` is an optimization for contexts where it is known that the children have not changed internally.

---
org.eclipse.swt.widgets.Composite

```
1 void updateLayout (boolean all) {
2     layout.layout (this, changed);
3     if (all) {
4         Control [] children = _getChildren ();
5         for (int i=0; i<children.length; i++) {
6             children [i].updateLayout (all);
7         }
8     }
9 }
```

At several places, layout managers may wish to take into account the preferred sizes of the children to ensure that the content fits the available screen space. This information is provided by the method `computeSize()` of each widget. Atomic controls just measure their texts and images and compute the size. `Composites` again delegate the decision to their layout managers (line 3) but ensure that only the available space, given by the hint parameters, is taken up (lines 4–5). It remains to add any local borders and margins (line 6).

---
org.eclipse.swt.widgets.Composite
```
1  public Point computeSize (int wHint, int hHint, boolean changed) {
2      Point size;
3      size = layout.computeSize (this, wHint, hHint, changed);
4      if (wHint != SWT.DEFAULT) size.x = wHint;
5      if (hHint != SWT.DEFAULT) size.y = hHint;
6      Rectangle trim = computeTrim (0, 0, size.x, size.y);
7      return new Point (trim.width, trim.height);
8  }
```

Since laying out widgets is a top-down process, it is usually triggered on the top-level window. The first choice is to set the size explicitly and then lay out the content again. Essentially the same thing happens when the user resizes the window.

---
swt.browser.SimpleBrowser
```
shell.setSize(550, 300);
shell.layout();
```

The second choice, which is often preferable for dialogs, is to *pack* the top-level shell.   ❱7.6

---
swt.browser.SimpleBrowser.open
```
shell.open();
shell.pack();
```

Packing is, in fact, available on any widget and means that the widget will be resized to its preferred size:

---
org.eclipse.swt.widgets.Control
```
public void pack (boolean changed) {
    setSize (computeSize (SWT.DEFAULT, SWT.DEFAULT, changed));
}
```

Events notify the application about the user's actions.

In user interfaces, many things can happen almost at any time: The user moves the mouse, clicks a mouse button, presses a key on the keyboard, moves a window, closes the application, and many more. The application can never keep track of all of those things all by itself. Fortunately, this is also not necessary: SWT will notify the application whenever something interesting happens. These "interesting things" are called *events* in this   ❱10.1
context. To be notified about events, the application has to register an *event-listener* with the widgets on which they can occur. Between events, the application can "lay back" and "relax"—there is no need to work unless   ❱7.3.2
the user makes a request by doing something to the application's windows.

In the browser example, the user will type in some URL, but there is no need to load the page until the user clicks the "Load" button. At this point, the entered URL has to be sent to the browser for display. In SWT, the event is called "selection" and is sent to a `SelectionListener`. The following event-listener contains the action to be taken directly in the method `widgetSelected`.

swt.browser.SimpleBrowser.createContents

```
load.addSelectionListener(new SelectionAdapter() {
    public void widgetSelected(SelectionEvent e) {
        if (!url.getText().isEmpty())
            browser.setUrl(url.getText());
    }
});
```

↰3.1.4

The generic selection event is used by many different widgets to signal that the user has "clicked" onto something, whether by selecting a table row or by pressing "enter" inside a text field. Simple selection calls method `widgetSelected`; double-clicks or pressing "enter" inside a text field are usually associated with some default action to be taken, so they are reported by calling `widgetDefaultSelected`. The base class `SelectionAdapter` provides empty implementations, so that the application simply has to override the interesting case.

↰2.1

Listening to events is very similar to the OBSERVER pattern. However, most of the time events do not refer to changes in the widgets' state, as in the pattern, but to some external action performed by the user. The message given to the listeners is not so much "something has changed" as "something has happened." While the change is persistent and can be queried by getter methods, the event is ephemeral and cannot be obtained otherwise. Nevertheless, the technical basis of event notification is the same as for the OBSERVER pattern, so the same design considerations apply.

↰2.1.2 ↰2.1.3

First-time developers of user interfaces sometimes find the event-based approach a little disconcerting: You add a tiny snippet of code and hope for the best, but can you really rely on being called by SWT? The abstract answer is that SWT is built to guarantee the delivery of the events, so that you can rely on the behavior. It may also help to take a look at the internal processing steps, shown in Fig. 7.4 (much simplified and generalized). When the user clicks, the mouse sends some signal to the computer's USB port, where it is picked up as a data packet and handed on to the computer's window system. That part of the operating system determines the top-level window over which the mouse is located and passes the relevant data about the click to that window, where SWT is ready to receive it. SWT determines the single widget at the mouse location, which in the figure is a button. The button first goes through the visual feedback. (Observe closely what happens between pressing and releasing the mouse button over

↠7.3.2

↠7.10.1

↠10.1

a button widget!) Finally, the button notifies the application code in the listener.

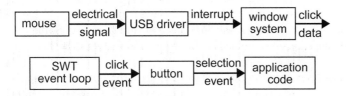

Figure 7.4 Overview: Events in a Button Click

Choose the correct event.

Every widget offers several events to which the application can react. The reason is very simple: Listening to events is all that an application can do to implement its functionality, so SWT has to be general and powerful enough to enable all desirable functionality to be implemented.

For instance, the `Browser` has to access the network and download possibly large amounts of data from possibly slow servers. It is absolutely necessary to provide the user with feedback about progress. The widget therefore offers progress reports as events. The following listener translates ❯❯7.10.2 these into a concrete display for the user, by setting the progress bar from Fig. 7.1 appropriately.

```
                    swt.browser.SimpleBrowser.createContents
browser.addProgressListener(new ProgressListener() {
    public void completed(ProgressEvent event) {
        progress.setSelection(0);
    }
    public void changed(ProgressEvent event) {
        progress.setSelection(event.current);
        progress.setMaximum(event.total);
    }
});
```

⚠ In choosing among the different events of a widget, it is sometimes easy to fall into traps. For instance, a `Button` offers to notify `MouseListeners` about mouse clicks. At first, this is what you want: When the user clicks, you receive an event. However, there are two problems. First, when the user presses a mouse button, moves the cursor outside the button, and then releases the button, then nothing should happen—the button is "armed" only as long as the cursor is inside. (Observe the visual feedback on your screen!) ❯❯10.1 Second, a button can be "clicked" by pressing "enter" on the keyboard as well, either by moving the focus to the button or by making the button the default one within the window. In summary, you always have to proceed based on the meaning of events—the precise conditions under which they will be signaled.

User interfaces offer different access paths to a given functionality.

⌑229

One of the core elements of usability is the goal of adapting the user interface to the user's work flows and expectations. Users will have different preferences on how to access some piece of functionality: Some prefer clicking with the mouse, some use keyboard shortcuts, yet others search through menus.

In the present example, novice users might actually click the "Load" button. More experienced users will expect that pressing "enter" in the URL field will start loading the page. So, let us set up this reaction (note that now we use `widgetDefaultSelected`):

---
swt.browser.SimpleBrowser.createContents

```
url.addSelectionListener(new SelectionAdapter() {
    public void widgetDefaultSelected(SelectionEvent e) {
        if (!url.getText().isEmpty())
            browser.setUrl(url.getText());
    }
});
```

Menus are similar to widgets in that they form a tree. The next code snippet shows the construction of a "Quit" entry in a "File" menu. The overall menu bar is attached to the shell (line 2). Menu items, like buttons, notify their selection-listeners when the user clicks on the item (lines 9–13).

---
swt.browser.SimpleBrowser.createContents

```
1 Menu menu = new Menu(shell, SWT.BAR);
2 shell.setMenuBar(menu);
3 MenuItem mitemFile = new MenuItem(menu, SWT.CASCADE);
4 mitemFile.setText("File");
5 Menu menuFile = new Menu(mitemFile);
6 mitemFile.setMenu(menuFile);
7 MenuItem mitemQuit = new MenuItem(menuFile, SWT.NONE);
8 mitemQuit.setText("Quit");
9 mitemQuit.addSelectionListener(new SelectionAdapter() {
10     public void widgetSelected(SelectionEvent e) {
11         shell.close();
12     }
13 });
```

To avoid re-implementing the same reaction in different event-listeners, you should usually factor this reaction out into a `protected` method of the surrounding class. From a broader perspective, the decisions involved here are really the same as in the case of implementing the observer interface, where we asked whether the event-listener or the surrounding class should contain the update logic of the observer.

↰2.1.3

»9.3.4

🔎 In most contexts, one does not create menus by hand. JFace wraps the bare functionality in a `MenuManager`, which keeps track of current "contributions" and reflects them in menus. It also enables navigation by paths for more declarative building of menu

structures. The Eclipse platform uses the latter feature to render additions by multiple   ▭174
plugins into one consistent menu structure.

The `Display` is the application's access to the window system.

A last element of SWT interfaces is the global `Display`. It represents the application's access to the underlying window system. In particular, it serves as an anchor point for resources such as `Images`, `Fonts`, and `Shells`. Furthermore, the `Display` offers global SWT functionality such as timer-based   ❱❱7.9
execution. Since the display is so important, it is passed to all created elements and can usually be retrieved by `getDisplay()`, for instance from the surrounding widget from within event-listeners. Globally, a special default display opens the connection to the window system when it is first requested:

```
                         swt.browser.SimpleBrowser.open
Display display = Display.getDefault();
```

Building user interfaces with SWT is technically straightforward.

This finishes the basic setup of any user interface: You create a widget tree, specify the layout of child widgets within their parent, and attach listeners to react to user interactions. The complexity of user interfaces results from keeping track of events and the proper reactions, and from matching the   ❱❱10
user's expectations.

Do not map data to widgets by hand.

User interfaces usually display some of the data managed by the application: A text field might contain the name of a customer; a table might show the orders placed by that customer, where each order is represented by the product's name and quantity, and the overall price. Such mappings are both tedious and commonplace. To deal with them, Eclipse's JFace layer, which resides on top of the SWT widget set, offers two abstractions: *Viewers* keep the displayed data synchronized with the underlying applica-   ❱❱9.3.1
tion's data structures through changes, and *data binding* links single input   ❱❱9.3.3
fields to properties of objects. Most user interface frameworks offer this kind   ◀1.3.3
of division, and it must be mastered before attempting any serious project.

7.2   The WindowBuilder: A Graphical Editor for UIs

The introduction in the previous section outlined the standard procedure for building user interfaces: create a widget tree, define the local layouts, and attach event-listeners to the relevant widgets. The process is, in fact, a little tedious and very time-consuming. Although the conceptual basis is fairly obvious, the technical code to be written quickly becomes lengthy and requires a detailed knowledge of the API, in particular for specifying the layout constraints.

Many widget toolkits come with a graphical editor for the user interface. With this tool, you can place widgets by drag-and-drop, specify layout parameters by simple clicks, and attach listeners through the context menu. We present here Eclipse's *WindowBuilder*.

From the start, we point out that such tools do not relieve you from knowing details of UI programming yourself. That is, the tools help you with standard tasks, but they will not support you through the detailed adaptations that customers invariably expect from professional user interfaces. In fact, most of the UI code of the Eclipse platform is written by hand, and standard code structuring techniques keep it readable and maintainable.

↩1.4.5 ↩1.4.8

7.2.1   Overview

Fig. 7.5 gives an overview of the WindowBuilder. The right-hand side pane contains a sketch of our simple browser application (Fig. 7.1), with the central `browser` widget highlighted. The controls at the top represent the layout constraints of the `GridLayout`, with the current choices depressed. Dragging handles on the selection changes the rows and columns spanned by the widget. To the left of this main area, the palette presents the available elements. The left-hand side gives the overall widget tree at the top and the detailed properties of the currently selected widget.

↩1.3.3

The lower-left corner shows a strength of the WindowBuilder: The tool does not keep a separate description of the user interface, for instance in XML. It extracts the graphical view from the source code instead, probably building an internal model for caching the analysis. As a result, you can switch freely between the two perspectives, according to the best fit for your current goals. Modifying the graphical representation generates the corresponding code in the background, while manual modifications of the code are integrated into the graphical view as well. This feature is also highlighted by the ability to reparse the code from scratch (at the top of Fig. 7.5), which is sometimes necessary if the graphical view has gotten out of sync.

»9.1

Events are handled via the context menu (Fig. 7.6). The WindowBuilder keeps track of the currently defined events for each widget and offers all available events as a simple choice. Selecting any menu item here jumps to the corresponding code section defining the event-listener. The Window-Builder is even a bit smarter: If the listener calls a single method, then it jumps to that method instead. This makes it easy to factor out common reactions.

↩7.1

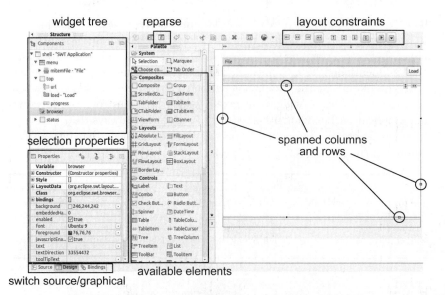

widget tree   reparse   layout constraints

selection properties

switch source/graphical   available elements

Figure 7.5 The WindowBuilder

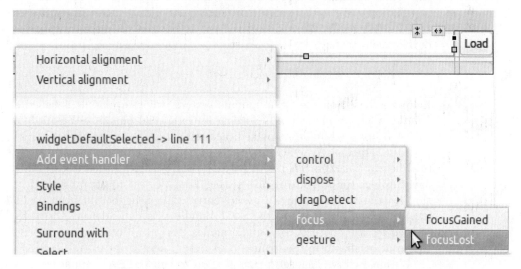

Figure 7.6 Events in the WindowBuilder

You still have to be able to write user interface code by hand.

The WindowBuilder certainly boosts the productivity of professionals, but it can easily lead the novice to make wrong decisions. For instance, the choice between attaching a selection-listener or a mouse-listener to a button, as mentioned before, must be made by the developer. Also, the abstraction offered by the tool is not perfect. For instance, it sometimes sets the preferred sizes of widgets in pixels, which later destroys the previews and application behavior. Finally, the tool does not always deal well with legacy code created by hand, so you will have to massage that into a more suitable form.

↰7.1

↰7.1

⟩⟩9.2
⟩⟩7.5

> ⚠ There is one possible trap when combining handwritten widgets with code generated by the WindowBuilder: Constructors must not take custom parameters, such as the application data that a widget is supposed to display. The WindowBuilder expects custom widgets to obey the SWT conventions, where the constructor accepts the parent widget and possibly some flags. For Swing, it expects a default, no-argument constructor.

7.2.2 Creating and Launching SWT Applications

SWT is not part of the regular Java library, but must be linked in from the Eclipse environment. The WindowBuilder offers a tempting shortcut: When you create a new SWT application window in a regular Java project through *New/Other/WindowBuilder/SWT Designer/Application Window*, the WindowBuilder will find the relevant JAR files from the local Eclipse installation and put them on the project's class path. Unfortunately, it uses the absolute local paths, so that the project cannot be shared within the development team.

Use SWT only in plugin projects.

⟩⟩A.1

Eclipse is based on the OSGi module system, where a module is called a *bundle*. A *plugin* in Eclipse is nothing but a special bundle. SWT itself is wrapped up as a bundle, to make it accessible to other parts of the Eclipse platform. Fortunately, OSGi is very lightweight and straightforward to use.

⟩⟩A.1.2

The way to access SWT is to create a *plugin project*, rather than a plain Java project (or to convert an existing Java project to a plugin project through the context menu's *Convert* entry). Then, in the plugin project's MANIFEST.MF, you can add the SWT bundle as a dependency. These dependencies are captured by bundle names instead of local paths and can therefore be shared in the team.

⟩⟩A.2.5

Within Eclipse, this setup enables you to run the SWT application as a simple Java application. The Eclipse launch configuration recognizes the OSGi dependencies and converts them to references to the corresponding JARs from the local Eclipse installation on the fly. What is more, the setup

also allows you to export the SWT application as stand-alone software,   »A.2.3
complete with a native launcher similar to the `eclipse` launcher of Eclipse
itself.

Let us summarize this explanation as a simple step-by-step recipe:

> **TOOL: Create and Run an SWT Application**
>
> - Create a plugin project through *New/Other/Plug-in Project*
> - Open the project's `MANIFEST.MF` and add a dependency on `org.eclipse.swt`
> - Create a package in the project as usual
> - Use *New/Other* in the context menu
> - In the dialog, type *Application* on top
> - Select the *SWT/Application Window*
> - Create the window's content with the WindowBuilder
> - Launch the window with *Run as/Java Application*

7.3   Developing with Frameworks

SWT offers a rich functionality for building user interfaces, but it is not
completely trivial to use and to learn. You have to understand concepts   ↰7.1
such as widget trees and layouts, and then you have to learn how to exploit
this infrastructure for your own applications. In practice, this often involves
looking for hours for the "right way" to do a particular thing. You will
encounter this phenomenon with many other reusable software products,
such as application servers, extensible editors such as GIMP, and IDEs such   📖201 📖117
as Eclipse: You browse tutorials at length to find out what to do and then
you do it within 15 minutes with a few lines of code. This experience can
be quite frustrating. It is then good to know the conceptual basis of these
complexities. This section explains that the approach taken by SWT and
other such tools is essentially the only possible way to go.

If you are currently more interested in learning SWT from a technical perspective, feel free to skip this section. But be sure to come back
later—knowing the concepts of frameworks is essential for any professional
developer, since they help in learning new frameworks more quickly.

7.3.1   The Goals of Frameworks

Many reusable software products come in the form of *frameworks* that   📖131,130,97,244
tackle complex tasks. Libraries such as the JDK's classes for I/O or collections offer small, stand-alone pieces of functionality in the form of individual

objects. You can take your pick and understand them one by one. Frameworks, in contrast, can solve their larger tasks only by providing entire networks of collaborating objects, which you have to buy complete or not at all. Some are finished but extensible applications, such as the Eclipse IDE. Some are semi-complete applications that just miss any specific functionality, such as the Eclipse Rich Client Platform. Some form only the backbone of applications, such as SWT or application servers. In any case, the framework you choose determines the overall structure of your application to a large degree.

Before we continue, we wish to point out that our subsequent description of "frameworks" follows the classical object-oriented definition from the cited literature. It is not uncommon, however, to find the term "framework" applied in a much broader sense. Often, it is used simply as an alternative for "complex library." MacOS uses it in the specific sense of a reusable software bundle installed on the system. Despite these different uses of the term, we find that the concepts attached to the classical definition are worth studying in any case, because they help developers to create and to understand professional software structures.

Frameworks provide ready-made structures for specific types of applications.

Frameworks offer complete or semi-complete networks of collaborating objects that support certain types of applications. When the framework starts working, everything falls into place, the large structures of the application are safely fixed, and the software is up and running.

It is useful to distinguish between two types of frameworks, because the type tells you what you can expect. *Application frameworks* offer infrastructure that is useful for building applications of certain shapes, independent of the particular domain that they address. For instance, the Eclipse Rich Client Platform, the SWT and JFace layers, and frameworks for developing web applications do not care about the content of the applications they support. You are free to develop just the application you need. At the same time, there is no support at all for the application's business logic.

Domain frameworks, in contrast, help in building applications for particular domains. For instance, bioinformatics is a discipline that is quickly maturing and that is developing standard processing steps for genome and other data. New scientific discoveries require building on existing techniques, and many frameworks seek to support this approach. Domain frameworks do include support for the application's business logic, but at the expense of also constraining the implementation of that logic to fit the framework's given structures.

7.3.2   Inversion of Control

The approach of building applications on top of existing networks of objects has dramatic consequences for the framework's API, which are summarized under the term "inversion of control." We will now examine this central switch of perspective, starting with a brief motivation.

Frameworks define generic mechanisms.

The tasks that frameworks take on are often complex and require an intricate software machinery. For instance, SWT handles layout, repainting, and event dispatching, among many other things. All of these tasks require collaborations among many objects, both along the structure of the widget tree and outside it.

↰7.1

Frameworks set up such mechanisms, such planned sequences of collaborations to relieve the application programmer from tedious standard tasks. The experience from building many applications has told the framework designers which mechanisms recur very often, and now the framework implements them once and for all. The application programmer can rely on the mechanisms, without understanding them in detail.

≫11.1

Frameworks rely on inversion of control.

Since the collaborations within the framework are complex, it is clear that the application cannot determine and prescribe every single step. With libraries, the application calls methods of service provider objects to get things going. With frameworks, things are already going on all the time. The application is notified only at specific points that the framework designers have judged useful based on their experience.

↰1.8.2

For instance, SWT offers buttons that the user can click. The button itself handles the visual feedback on mouse movements and the keyboard focus. The application is notified when the only really interesting thing happens—that is, when the user has clicked the button.

Since some applications require it, there are also low-level notifications about the mouse movements and the keyboard focus. These are not specific to buttons, but work for almost any widget. They are introduced higher up in the class hierarchy, at Control. Again, the framework designers had to anticipate the need for these events.

≫7.8

At the crucial points, the collaboration between framework and application is thus reversed, compared to the case of libraries: It is the framework that invokes application methods, while previously it was the application that invoked library methods. Since method calls are part of the software's control flow, one speaks of *inversion of control*. The framework determines the control flow in general; it passes control to the application only at designated points. A snappy formulation that has stuck is the *Hollywood Principle*: "Don't call us, we'll call you."

≫7.3.3 ▢▢242

If you already know SWT in some detail, you may feel at this point that SWT is not a framework at all. From a technical perspective, it is actually the application

≫7.10.1

that drives everything. The `main` method typically sets up the content of the application window and then keeps dispatching the incoming events by calling SWT methods:

swt.browser.SimpleBrowser.open

```
Display display = Display.getDefault();
... create shell and window contents
while (!shell.isDisposed()) {
    if (!display.readAndDispatch()) {
        display.sleep();
    }
}
```

From a conceptual point of view, however, the application does not really control anything: The whole logic of event handling is determined by SWT, after the application calls `readAndDispatch()`. The application code in event handlers is called back only when and if SWT sees fit.

For development purposes, it is better to understand SWT as a framework with inversion of control. In fact, the boilerplate code for the main method is a peculiarity of SWT: Other UI frameworks usually incorporate and encapsulate the dispatch loop completely.

» 7.6

Develop a laid back attitude toward frameworks.

We have found that novices often experience inversion of control first as a loss of control. That is, since they cannot see the code that makes things happen, they feel insecure about whether and when they will happen at all.

When working with frameworks, it is better to take the opposite perspective. You trust the framework to do its job properly. You can then conclude that you do not have to do anything until the framework explicitly asks you to do it. At this point, the framework will even hand to you all the information required for the task—you do not have to ask for it. Your software can "lay back" and "relax" in the meantime. As a developer, you can relax because you do not have to provide any code to make things happen, except for the special contributions at the callback points.

Know the framework's mechanisms.

The biggest hurdle in learning frameworks is to understand which mechanisms exist and which mechanism is supposed to be used for which purpose. Framework designers envision the applications that will be built on top of the framework, and they provide mechanisms for those use cases that are likely to arise. Your job as an application programmer is to take the reverse step: Based on your use case, you check out which mechanism the designer has provided.

The most common way of learning frameworks is by studying examples and tutorials. If they are created by the original designers, these tutorials usually show how to use particular mechanisms. It is important to see a tutorial not as a source for copy-and-paste programming, but as a prototypical case demonstrating a greater idea. Look for the point behind the code, and ask which larger purpose each statement in the example code fulfills.

Sometimes choosing a mechanism requires some thought. As a simple example, SWT provides two events that react to mouse clicks on `Buttons`: `mouseClicked()` and `widgetSelected()`. The second one is the correct one for ordinary "button clicks," because it also covers activations created by pressing the "enter" key and as the default button of a dialog.

↰7.1

Frameworks cannot be coaxed by force to exhibit some behavior you need. Until you have found the mechanism that supports your use case, there is nothing to do but keep looking. Many frameworks have forums on the web, and many discussions in these forums circle around the problem of finding the right mechanism for a particular purpose. The framework users with guru status are usually distinguished by having more mechanisms right at their fingertips.

Very often, finding a mechanism involves understanding it in some detail. For instance, it is simple enough to create application-specific SWT widgets that paint directly on the screen. For larger ones displaying complex data structures, however, you have to paint only the changed parts. Fig. 7.7 sketches the involved steps, and each step has a particular conceptual justification. (The "model" contains the application's data and business logic, the "view" displays the data, and the "graphics context" GC is used for painting on the screen.)

↠7.8

↠9.4.3

↠9.2.1

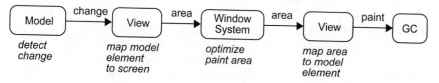

Figure 7.7 Preview: Process of Incremental Screen Updates

Do not look at the framework's internal implementation.

Even if mechanisms must be understood in some detail, their precise implementation is none of your business. It must be treated as encapsulated, even if it happens to involve `protected` or even `public` methods. The framework designers specify the possible points of interaction with the application, but apart from these, the framework code may change without further notice. Only novices use the debugger to examine sequences of method calls and to override arbitrary `protected` methods that they happen to find. Doing this causes the Fragile Base Class Problem and will almost certainly break the application within a few revisions of the framework.

↠7.3.3

↰3.1.11

To be entirely fair, it may be necessary to trace through the details of framework methods to understand the mechanisms. If the framework's documentation is sketchy and consists of just a few tutorials, looking at the execution is the only chance you get. However, having obtained the information you need to understand the tutorials, you should forget whatever internal details you have learned on the way.

7.3.3   Adaptation Points in Frameworks

↰1.4.1

Inversion of control demands that the framework code calls application code at specified points. In other words, application code is injected into the control flow established by the framework. In object-oriented frameworks, this is accomplished through polymorphism and dynamic method dispatch: The application code overrides or implements some method that the framework provides for the purpose. These designated methods are also called the *hot spots* of the framework. The remainder of the framework is supposed to be treated as a fixed, black-box setup called the *frozen spots*. The frozen spots constitute the infrastructure that the framework provides. Ignoring the frozen spots leads to the Fragile Base Class Problem: The framework's classes cannot change without breaking the application. With any framework you learn, it is therefore important to recognize the adaptation points and to understand their intended usage.

↰3.1.11

> White-box frameworks: Applications override methods in framework classes.

↰1.4.9

The most straightforward way of specifying adaptation points is the direct method overriding undertaken in the TEMPLATE METHOD pattern: The framework implements the general mechanisms and algorithms, but at specific points it passes control to designated `protected` methods. Applications can override these to add new behavior. The documentation of the framework class should then specify the method precisely: Which kind of behavior is expected to fit into it? Which kind of use case is it supposed to cover?

↰1.4.11
↰3.1.2

Frameworks that rely on this kind of collaboration are called *white-box frameworks*, because the application developer has to understand the framework's class hierarchy and some of the classes' internal mechanisms.

It is important to note that the application must not override just any `protected` method that it finds. Many of these methods are used for internal purposes, such as to factor out reusable functionality within the framework's own class hierarchy.

↰3.1.4

It can, however, be seen as an advantage of white-box frameworks that an application can in principle override any existing `protected` methods. It can therefore modify the framework's behavior even in cases that the framework developers had not foreseen. As a result, it is slightly simpler to develop white-box frameworks than black-box frameworks. Also, the risk that the framework might fall short of the application's expectations is reduced. Of course, this flexibility comes at the price of increasing the learning curve.

↠7.3.4

Black-box frameworks: Applications plug in objects with designated interfaces.

Black-box frameworks hide the implementation of their mechanisms completely from applications. They define special interfaces that applications can implement to receive notifications at relevant points in the mechanisms. The API then resembles that of the OBSERVER pattern: The framework defines notification interfaces; the application registers listeners for the notifications.   ↰2.1

In SWT (and JFace), all events are delivered through black-box mechanisms. Most widgets in SWT are entirely black-box, because they just wrap native widgets from the window system; the underlying, fixed C-implementation cannot easily call back `protected` methods on the Java side. Even the low-level callback for repainting a custom widget is invoked on a dedicated `PaintListener`, while Java's Swing, for instance, uses overriding of the `paint()` or `paintComponent()` methods from `JComponent`.   ↠7.4   ↠7.8

One advantage of black-box frameworks is that they are easier to learn. The application programmer can understand one adaptation point at a time and does not have to understand the framework's class hierarchy and its possibly intricate sequences of up-calls and down-calls. The application is not constrained in the choice of super-classes, which enables reuse of application-specific functionality through common super-classes. Also, the application is shielded from restructurings within the framework and the Fragile Base Class Problem is avoided. Many larger frameworks, such as the Eclipse platform, rely on black-box mechanisms because they are likely to change over time and have large user bases who depend on backward compatibility.   ↰3.1.4   ↰3.1.11

One disadvantage of black-box frameworks is that any use cases not envisaged by the framework designers cannot be implemented at all, not even by low-level tweaks found only through debugging. As a result, developing useful black-box frameworks is more difficult and takes much more experience.

Also, it may be harder to actually implement the objects to plug into the framework, because the framework itself offers no infrastructure for this step. Many black-box frameworks remedy this by providing abstract base classes for their interfaces. For instance, JFace asks the application to provide `ILabelProviders` to show data on the screen, but it offers a class `LabelProvider` that implements the obvious bookkeeping of listeners. Be sure to look for such classes: They can also help you understand what the object is supposed to do and which kinds of functionality are envisioned for an adaptation point.   ↠9.3.1

Most frameworks are hybrids between black-box and white-box.

Because white-box and black-box frameworks have complementary advantages and disadvantages, most frameworks are actually hybrids: They offer the most frequently used adaptations in black-box style, and the more advanced (or obscure) adaptations in white-box style. Be sure to understand which kind you are currently dealing with; also, try to find a black-box mechanism first, because it may be more stable through evolutions of the framework.

7.3.4   Liabilities of Frameworks

Frameworks are great tools if they work for your application, but they can bring your project to a grinding halt if they don't. Once you have decided on one framework, you are usually tied to it for the rest of the project. Be extremely conservative when choosing your frameworks.

Check early on whether the framework covers all of your use cases.

The biggest problem with frameworks is that their web pages look great and promise the world. But when it comes to actually coding the more advanced use cases of your application, you may find that the required adaptation points are missing. This is the most costly scenario for your company: You may have invested 90% of the project's budget, only to find that you will have to redo the whole thing, because your code is tied to the one framework and will usually not be portable to others.

Two immediate countermeasures suggest themselves. First, before fixing the decision for a framework, build a throwaway prototype of your application; be sure to include the most advanced and most intricate requirements you can think of. The code you produce will probably be horrible, because you are only just learning the framework. But at least you will know that everything *can* be done. The second idea is related: You should check whether your use cases fall into the broad, well-trodden paths covered in tutorials and examples. That functionality is well tested and stable. Furthermore, if you need something similar, you are likely to find it covered as well.

Check whether the developers are really domain experts.

A good strategy to estimate whether a framework is likely to cover your needs is to look at its design team. If they are experienced professionals who have long worked in the domain that the framework addresses, you can be pretty sure that they have thought of all of your needs even before you were aware of them. While exploring new corners of the Eclipse and Netbeans platforms, I'm constantly surprised by the amount of detailed thought that must have gone into the API design. Anticipating the use cases of a framework is foremost a question of experience in the domain.

174
50

$\mathcal{P}$ One reason why Eclipse has come out so well designed is certainly that IBM already had years of experience in building its Visual Age for Java development environment, and related products for other languages, starting with SmallTalk in 1993. The developers already knew the software structures that worked well, and more importantly those that did not work so well.

Opposite examples can be found in the myriad text editors written by hobbyists. Usually, the editors are the first ones that their developers have ever created. The projects start small, which means they do not have sufficient provisions for extensions. The authors have no strong background in software architecture, so they are likely to get the overall structures wrong and miss the important design constraints on APIs. If you build your application as a plugin to such an editor, your project is most certainly doomed to die within a few years (unless you get involved in developing the underlying platform, which will be a heavy investment).

Check whether there are detailed tutorials and examples.

Learning frameworks is best accomplished by studying their API definition and checking out the concrete use cases in their tutorials and examples. Finding the right way to do something in a tutorial saves you the effort of reading through the written documentation. To evaluate a framework, start by gathering the known requirements and checking whether they are covered in official tutorials.

    Beware of tutorials written in blog style. They may show a possible way of accomplishing something, but this may not be the way that the framework designers had planned for. As a result, the steps in the tutorial may be more complicated than necessary or may use fringe features broken with the next release. Tutorials are more reliable if the authors do not simply list the steps they have taken, but also explain their meaning and purpose in a larger context. If a tutorial does not do that, try to link its proposals to the official documentation.

Check whether the framework has reliable long-term backing.

Another problem with frameworks is that there is usually a flurry of activity when they first appear, but over time the developers have to move on to other projects. For your own company, the effects of this lack of support may be dramatic: You may be stuck with an old version of a software whose bugs will remain unfixed forever. Indications to look out for are rather obvious: the size of the user base, the organization supporting the framework development, and the history of the project.

7.4 SWT and the Native Interface

Java is designed to run anywhere, on top of the JVM installed locally. Accordingly, the Swing and JavaFX user interface frameworks provide a common look-and-feel across platforms. As a result, users familiar with Java applications will be able to work with it regardless of the operating system they are currently using.

> SWT lets you build professional applications that users will like.

SWT deviates from this Java point of view and accesses the native widget toolkit of the platform. As a result, an SWT application will look like a Windows, MacOS, or GTK application, depending on the environment. This is, in fact, what most users will prefer: A Swing application on Windows looks out of place to the ordinary Windows user, since everything looks a bit different, the keyboard shortcuts are different, and so on. The native toolkit also has the advantage of speed, since it is usually written in C and integrated tightly with the specific window system.

7.4.1   Influence on the API

Even if the native widgets themselves are encapsulated by the SWT widgets, the decision to target the native widget toolkit will influence the behavior of the SWT widgets at several places. It is therefore necessary to take a brief look at the relationship.

Fig. 7.8 gives an overview. The SWT widget tree is mirrored, although perhaps not one-to-one, in a native widget tree. Each SWT widget is a PROXY for its native counterpart: It holds a *handle* to the native widget and uses it to invoke native functionality. However, the SWT widget is also an ADAPTER, in that it translates an expected, cross-platform API to a platform-specific API.

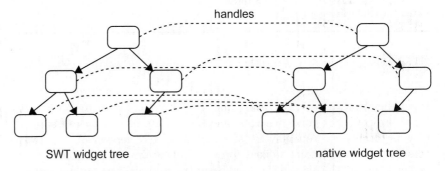

SWT widget tree   native widget tree

Figure 7.8 SWT and Native Widget Trees

> SWT widgets are not usable without their native counterparts.

Because of the close relationship, SWT widgets can work only if their native counterparts exist. Each constructor therefore creates the corresponding native widget immediately. Because the constructor receives the parent widget as a parameter, it can add the native widget to the tree and

↰2.4.3 ↰2.4.4

↰2.4.1

↰7.1

obtain any context information—for instance, about fonts and background colors—that may be necessary at this point.

Furthermore, any access to an SWT widget first checks this fundamental condition before possibly messing up the native C-level memory.

◀1.5.4

---
org.eclipse.swt.widgets.Widget

```
protected void checkWidget() {
    if (display == null)
        error(SWT.ERROR_WIDGET_DISPOSED);
    ...
    if ((state & DISPOSED) != 0)
        error(SWT.ERROR_WIDGET_DISPOSED);
}
```

The exception `Widget is disposed` occurs when you happen to access an SWT widget without a native counterpart.

Most widgets must not be subclassed.

Many user interface frameworks are white-box frameworks: You see a widget that suits your needs in general, but it would need to be modified in the details—for instance, by painting some fancy overlay when the mouse is moved over it. In such a case, you just subclass and override the method that paints the widget on the screen.

▶7.3.3

◀3.1.7

Since SWT widgets do not really live completely in the Java world, such ad-hoc adaptations by inheritance are not allowed. The interactions with the behavior of the native widgets could hardly be controlled. The method `checkSubclass()` in SWT widgets checks the restriction at run-time. Only a few widgets, such as `Composite` and `Canvas`, are meant to be subclassed.

▶7.5 ▶7.8

The application must dispose of any SWT widget or resource.

Java objects are managed by the JVM's garbage collector: When the program cannot access a given object, that object's memory is reclaimed and reused. This mechanism does not work for the C-level native widgets, because the garbage collector cannot work on the C stack and C data structures reliably.

📖133

When working with SWT, all widgets, as well as other resources such as images and fonts, must be freed explicitly by calling `dispose()` on the SWT widget. It is advisable to do so as soon as possible. For instance, if a dialog requires a particular image, then that image should be freed as soon as the dialog is closed.

⚠ Do not override `dispose` on widgets such as dialogs to free extra resources allocated. That method is used for the internal disposal of the native widgets. Attach a `Dispose Listener` instead.

The correct way to proceed is shown in the following snippet from a dialog that displays an image `sun.png`. Lines 1–2 load the image into memory. This data is an ordinary Java object that is handled by the garbage collector. Line 3 allocates a native image resource, which is not garbage-collected. Lines 4–8 therefore ensure that the image is disposed as soon as the dialog is closed.

swt.resources.DialogWithImage.createContents

```
1 ImageData imageData = new ImageData(
2         DialogWithImage.class.getResourceAsStream("sun.png"));
3 imageResource = new Image(shell.getDisplay(), imageData);
4 shell.addDisposeListener(new DisposeListener() {
5     public void widgetDisposed(DisposeEvent e) {
6         imageResource.dispose();
7     }
8 });
```

⚠ The WindowBuilder allows you to set the images of labels and buttons very conveniently through the widget's properties. However, it creates a class `SWTResource Manager`, which owns and caches all images loaded in this manner. This class remains in memory for the whole runtime of the application, and the loaded images will not be freed unless the `dispose()` method of the class is called. This strategy is acceptable for simple applications, but large images should always be freed as soon as possible. Simple icons and fonts are usually obtained from the platform or are cached in `ImageRegistrys` associated with plugins.

Test an SWT application on every window system that you support.

Even though SWT provides a pretty good abstraction layer over the native widgets, that abstraction is not perfect. The behavior of widgets and the framework may differ in subtle details that break your application in special situations. Before shipping a product, be sure to test it on each supported target platform.

7.4.2　Influence on Launching Applications

Since SWT widgets internally create and manage native widgets, the SWT implementation is platform-specific and the SWT OSGi bundle contains native libraries accessed through the Java Native Interface (JNI). When an application is launched from within Eclipse, the correct plugin is selected automatically from the Eclipse installation. Similarly, when using SWT within an Eclipse plugin, the SWT implementation from the host Eclipse platform is used.

» A.2

It is only when creating stand-alone applications that a little care must be taken to provide the right JAR file for the target platform. When that file is included in the class path, the application can be started as usual from the command line.

A more elegant approach is to use the Eclipse Rich Client Platform
directly. For this platform, the Eclipse developers provide a *delta pack* plugin, which contains the SWT plugins for all supported platforms. Also, the
Eclipse export wizards for building the product are aware of the different
target systems and will create different deliverables automatically.

⊞174
»A.3

7.5   Compound Widgets

Object-oriented programming makes it simple to aggregate combinations
of objects into higher-level components: Just create a new class to hold the
necessary helpers, then wire up the helpers internally to create the desired
functionality. The same can be done with widgets:

↰1.8.5 ↰2.2

Derive reusable compound widgets from `Composite`.

What is more, the WindowBuilder actively supports this strategy:

↰7.2

TOOL: Create Composite with WindowBuilder

From a package's context menu, select *New/Other* and then *SWT/Com-
posite* in the dialog. (Type "Composite" at the top.)

As a final touch, you can place any such widget easily into a larger
context.

TOOL: Reference Custom Widgets in WindowBuilder

In the WindowBuilder's palette, use the *System/Choose Component* button to select any widget from the class path and drop it into the preview pane. Alternatively, you can create new categories and items in
the palette from the palette's context menu. Finally, you can bundle
palette entries with the project using *New/Other/WindowBuilder/Pro-
ject Palette* (type "palette" into the filter).

⚠ Follow the SWT convention of passing only the parent widget and possibly a bit-set
of style flags to the constructor. Otherwise, the WindowBuilder might have problems
creating the preview.

As an example, we will build a calendar view that enables the user to
pick out a date in the expected way (Fig. 7.9, the upper component). That
is, first the user switches to the correct month (starting from the current
month), and then the user clicks on a day within the month. The widget
has a property `selectedDate` and implements the OBSERVER pattern, so
that the example can track the current selection in the text field.

↰2.1

Figure 7.9 The `DatePicker` Widget

We will also use this example as a walk-through of user interface development in general. After all, any window or dialog we construct is just a compound widget, one that serves as a root of the widget tree. Although it may not be as stand-alone and reusable as the `DatePicker`, the general programming guidelines outlined here still apply. The overall setup is this: We subclass `Composite` and fill in the desired behavior.

swt.compound.DatePicker

```
public class DatePicker extends Composite {
    ...
    public DatePicker(Composite parent) {
        super(parent, SWT.BORDER);
        ...
    }
    ...
}
```

↰7.4.1   ⚠ You might be tempted to derive your widget from something like `Text` or `Label`, because its behavior is similar to the one you need to create. However, most widgets in SWT must not be subclassed. `Composite` is an exception to the rule, as it explicitly allows for subclassing and disabling the corresponding safety check:

org.eclipse.swt.widgets.Composite

```
protected void checkSubclass() {
    /* Do nothing - Subclassing is allowed */
}
```

If your widget is essentially a variant of an existing one, set the existing one as the Composite's only child and let it fill the space with a FillLayout.

Make compound widgets into proper objects.

One thing to be aware of is that compound widgets are not just arbitrary collections of sub-widgets or nice visual gadgets. From a development perspective, they are first of all compound objects that function within the software machinery. In the best case, they adhere to the fundamental characteristics of objects: They provide a consistent API for a small, well-defined piece of functionality; they encapsulate the necessary machinery; and they communicate with their collaborators through well-defined channels. Furthermore, they take the ownership of their child widgets seriously, in creating and disposing of them. Also, they define and maintain invariants between their different parts and between their own fields and the parts. Because these aspects look slightly different in an event-driven, visual environment, let us look at them in some more detail for the date picker widget.

↶2.2
↶1.1

↶2.2.1 ↶2.2.3
↶6.2

Implement a small, well-defined piece of functionality.

The action of "picking a date" is certainly a small enough task, and it appears in many applications. Also, the conventions for picking dates from a calendar are quite obvious, so that we know how the widget is supposed to behave. The idea of objects taking on a single task is therefore obeyed.

↶1.1 ↠11.2

Give the widgets a proper API.

To work well as a software object, a compound widget must be a convenient collaborator for the software's other objects. It is therefore crucial to get the API right—just a nice visual appearance does not make for a great widget. As usual, it is a good idea to start from the clients' perspective. What is the result of picking a date, from a technical point of view? A date is commonly represented as a Date, so it is natural to provide a getter and setter for a property selectedDay:

↶1.1 ↶3.2.2 ↶5.4.3

```
swt.compound.DatePicker
public Date getSelectedDay()
public void setSelectedDay(Date date)
```

Fit compound widgets into the event-driven context.

User interfaces are all about the application reacting to user actions. If the new widget is to work well in such an environment, it must offer all

↶7.1

necessary events to its clients. For the example widget, it is sufficient to
↰2.1   implement the OBSERVER pattern for its single property. In doing so, we
have to follow one more guideline:

Adapt the design to the context.

It is a fundamental design strategy to solve similar problems by similar
means, since this keeps the overall software readable and understandable.
↰2.1.2   While the standard implementation of OBSERVER is clear, the context of
SWT widgets suggests a different solution: to use SWT's standard "selection" event and to reuse the notification infrastructure from the `Widget`
class. First, here are the methods for the clients:

swt.compound.DatePicker

```java
public void addSelectionListener(SelectionListener l) {
    TypedListener typedListener = new TypedListener(l);
    addListener(SWT.Selection, typedListener);
}
public void removeSelectionListener(SelectionListener l) {
    removeListener(SWT.Selection, l);
}
```

Sending the notifications is then straightforward, since the superclass
already provides the necessary method:

swt.compound.DatePicker.setSelectedDayInternal

```java
notifyListeners(SWT.Selection, new Event());
```

↰2.1.2   🔎 The default construction of `new Event()` might seem odd, since a subject should
at least provide a reference to itself. To simplify this common coding idiom, the
notification infrastructure in `Widget` fills in the basic fields of the event that have not yet
been initialized.

Encapsulate internal data structures.

Compound widgets will usually require internal data structures and maintain invariants on them. The `DatePicker` widget shows how these can be
used in the context of event-driven software.

↰7.1   🔎 Technically, the internal widget structure of compound widgets is accessible via
`getChildren()`, because compound widgets are part of the usual widget tree. However, clients are sure to know that such accesses are undesirable.

As a first point, the `DatePicker` (Fig. 7.9) must somehow maintain the
current month, chosen in the upper part of the widget, and display its days
in the lower part, aligned correctly with the days of the week. We can create

the upper part and place a `Composite` to maintain the month's days using the WindowBuilder:

```
                     swt.compound.DatePicker
private Label curMonth;
private Composite days;
```

But how do we represent the current month and the current selection? This question can be answered only by truly internal data structures. At the core of our application, we keep a `Calendar`, because this makes it simple to do arithmetic for the forward/backward buttons. We maintain the invariant that `cal` always contains the first day of the current month. We store the currently selected day separately.

↰4.1

```
                     swt.compound.DatePicker
private Calendar cal;
private Calendar selectedDay;
```

The choice of `selectedDay` is especially interesting, because it links the internal data structures and the external behavior. Since we already have the current month, we might have used a simple `int` to store the selected day within that month. However, this choice would entail that when switching to the next month, the selected day would also change, while the user probably perceives the upper part of the widget only as a browser for weeks. With the choice of `selectedDay`, we can simply highlight in the lower part just the day that is `equal` to the `selectedDay`.

↰1.4.13

The next question is how to perform the display of the days. The simplest choice is to set a `GridLayout` on `days` and place the different text snippets as labels, as shown in Fig. 7.10. The `GridLayout` has seven columns, so we can easily place the first row as a list of labels with bold font (`addDay` places a `Label` with fixed size into `days`).

```
              swt.compound.DatePicker.updateDisplay
for (String head : DAY_HEADS) {
    Label l = addDay(head);
    l.setFont(bold);
}
```

Next, we have to leave a few fields blank (Fig. 7.10; note that fields in `Calendar` are 1-based).

```
              swt.compound.DatePicker.updateDisplay
int startWeekDay = cal.get(Calendar.DAY_OF_WEEK);
for (int i = 1; i < startWeekDay; i++)
    new Label(days, SWT.TRANSPARENT);
```

Finally, we can fill in the actual days. In general, this is just a loop over the days of the month (line 4). To retrieve the label for a given day easily, we keep the index of the first such label (line 1); the others follow

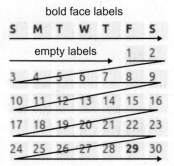

Figure 7.10 Days Area of the DatePicker Widget

sequentially. For each day, we create a label (line 6); if it is the currently selected day, we highlight it (lines 7–9). Finally, we make the label clickable by registering our own handler (line 10). That handler will have to find out the day that the label represents. We exploit the widget's generic data slot (line 11), which is meant to contain just such application-specific data associated with a visual element.

swt.compound.DatePicker.updateDisplay

```
1  firstDayChildIndex = days.getChildren().length;
2  int lastDay = cal.getActualMaximum(Calendar.DAY_OF_MONTH);
3  Calendar tmp = (Calendar) cal.clone();
4  for (int i = cal.getActualMinimum(Calendar.DAY_OF_MONTH);
5       i <= lastDay; i++) {
6     Label l = addDay(Integer.toString(i));
7     tmp.set(Calendar.DAY_OF_MONTH, i);
8     if (tmp.equals(selectedDay))
9        l.setFont(bold);
10    l.addMouseListener(selectionHandler);
11    l.setData(tmp.clone());
12 }
```

With this setup, it is straightforward to react to clicks: Just extract the data associated with the label and set it as the currently selected date. The helper method also unhighlights the previously selected label and highlights the new one.

swt.compound.DatePicker

```
private class SelectionHandler extends MouseAdapter {
    public void mouseUp(MouseEvent e) {
        Label clicked = (Label) e.getSource();
        setSelectedDayInternal((Calendar) clicked.getData());
    }
}
```

The example shows a particular characteristic of custom widgets, and
»7.11   event-driven programming in general: The event handlers require informa-

tion that must be set up beforehand, and about which invariants need to
be maintained.

Layouts are not automatic.

The process of computing layouts is comparatively expensive. It is therefore   ↰7.1
performed only at special points, such as when a window is first opened.
In the current context, we have to trigger the layout of the newly added
children of the compound `days` explicitly:

swt.compound.DatePicker.updateDisplay

```
days.layout();
```

Keep track of resources.

The `DatePicker` also contains an example of using resources: The `bold`
font set on labels must be allocated before it can be used. From a user's
perspective, a font is just given by its name, size, and flags such as "italic"
or "bold." Within the window system, each font is associated with actual
resources. Specifically, the relevant font definition (usually in the form of
splines) must be loaded from disk, and each character must be rendered
into a bitmap for quick rendering according to the font size, the screen
resolution, and the color depth.

SWT also differentiates between the two views: `FontData` objects contain the external description of a desired font, whereas a `Font` is the actual
window system resource associated with the loaded font data and bitmap
cache. The next code snippet first creates a `bold` variant of the currently
used default font by overriding the flag in the `FontData` (lines 1–3) and
allocating the corresponding resources (line 4). Lines 5–9 then make sure
that the resources are freed once the `DatePicker` is no longer used.   ↰7.1

swt.compound.DatePicker.DatePicker

```
1 FontData[] fds = getFont().getFontData();
2 for (FontData fd : fds)
3     fd.setStyle(SWT.BOLD);
4 bold = new Font(getDisplay(), fds);
5 addDisposeListener(new DisposeListener() {
6     public void widgetDisposed(DisposeEvent e) {
7         bold.dispose();
8     }
9 });
```

This kind of behavior is typical of compound objects. First, ownership   ↰2.2.1
dictates that the owner determines the life cycle of its parts; when the
`DatePicker` is disposed, so is its font. Second, there is a consistency con-   ↰2.2.3 ↰6.2.2
dition or invariant between the parts: The `bold` font will be allocated as
long as it may still be used in any `Label` created for the days.

> Keep widgets independent of their surroundings to enable reuse.

»12.1 »12.4

Developing user interfaces can be quite an effort. It is therefore highly desirable to develop elements such as the `DatePicker` that are reusable in different environments. To achieve this, it is necessary to decouple the elements from their context.

Let us briefly review the relevant decisions in the current example. One central element to achieve this is to use the Observer pattern rather than sending specific messages to specific collaborators. Since UIs are event-driven anyway, this choice also fits in well with the general style of programming. Furthermore, the `DatePicker`'s API offers a generic property `selectedDay`. In contrast, a widget `SelectFlightStartDate` with method `getSelectedFlightDate`, which might occur in a travel booking application, would certainly be not reusable immediately. Also, making the API of the Observer consistent with SWT's conventions will lower the effort required for reuse because other team members will understand exactly what to do.

> Refactor parts of existing widgets into compound widgets.

↰1.4.8.3

Reusable objects are often obtained by extracting reusable parts from larger objects. It is useful to consider compound widgets to be usual objects in this respect, too: Since the WindowBuilder parses the source code, you can actually use the *Extract Class* tool to create sub-widgets. When you find a UI element in one part of the application that might be reused in a different place, invest the bit of time needed to refactor the part into a stand-alone compound widget, if there is any chance that you can reuse it a third time.

↰1.4.12

The WindowBuilder itself similarly offers to introduce factory methods that create a chosen composite and can then be invoked from different points of the application as well, since they appear in the palette. Although it requires a bit more effort, creating a separate class gives you better control over encapsulation and makes you independent of the WindowBuilder.

7.6   Dialogs

Most applications have one window and the user interacts with the application mostly through that window. However, the same applications usually do employ additional or auxiliary windows. For instance, these windows may be used for the following purposes:

- To ask for more information or for a decision from within an event handler and wait for the answer before proceeding, such as in confirming the deletion of a file

- To display detailed information or enable editing of some element shown in the main window, such as in the "properties" dialog on files in the *package explorer*

- To show a small *direct editing* field for a specific aspect of the data displayed   ❱❱9.3.1 ▢▢214

- To display additional information or choices, such as in Eclipse's Java auto-completion

The common theme of these situations is that the application's main window is overlaid by a smaller window and that the new window receives all the input for the application, so that access to the main window is temporarily blocked. We will examine these elements of auxiliary `Shell` objects in more detail in this section.

If you wish to experience the different settings discussed, you can use the `DialogDemo` application from the online supplement (Fig. 7.11). The names of flags and choices in the figure correspond directly to the technical flags at the SWT level that we will discuss.

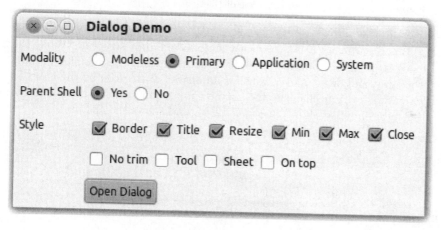

Figure 7.11 Dialog Demo

In the presentation, we encounter the slight problem that all windows are really "shells." To simplify the reading, we will speak of the "application window" and the "dialog," even if strictly speaking the "dialog" is yet another shell that does not differ from the "application window" at the technical level, and "dialogs" can even open "dialogs" themselves.

🔎 Both SWT and its abstraction layer JFace contain classes named `Dialog`. These are   ❱❱9.3
not shells themselves, but merely provide a framework for creating shells.

The modality of a shell determines whether it blocks other windows.

Dialogs are usually employed to focus users' attention on a particular point—for instance, to force them to make a decision or to enable them to edit the properties of a particular element of a data structure. From this perspective, it is sensible to block the remainder of the application as long as the dialog is being shown.

Dialogs that block the application window are called *modal*; those that do not are called *modeless*. The window system will silently ignore all input such as mouse clicks that the user may try to send to the application window.

SWT provides different levels of modality: The default, *primary modal*, means that only the window that opens the dialog will be blocked; *application modal* blocks all windows of the same application; and *system modal* blocks the remainder of the screen, if this capability is supported by the underlying window system. All of these modality levels should be read as hints given to the window system. For instance, if it does not support *primary modal* dialogs, it will silently fall back to *application modal*. It is therefore best for applications not to rely on these fine distinctions.

Blocking dialogs can also greatly simplify the code structure. While the dialog is open, the application's data structures cannot be modified in some other way, and one can even wait for an answer or decision by the user. To demonstrate the mechanism, the simple application in Fig. 7.12(a) asks the user for a name, as shown in Fig. 7.12(b), and shows the answer.

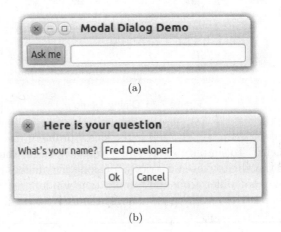

(a)

(b)

Figure 7.12 Modal Dialog Demo

The actual code can simply open the dialog. That call blocks until the dialog is closed again, at which point the result is available. (The parameter to the `AskMeDialog` constructor is the *parent shell* of the new window, to be discussed later.)

---
swt.dialogs.ModalDemo.ModalDemo
```
AskMeDialog dlg = new AskMeDialog(getShell());
String result = dlg.open();
if (result != null)
    txtResult.setText(result);
else
    txtResult.setText("- no answer -");
```

The `AskMeDialog` derives from SWT's `Dialog`. It demonstrates two important points in the event-listener attached to the "OK" button. When the user clicks that button, the dialog is closed in line 4. Before that, the user's answer is read from the input text field in line 3, and is stored in a field of the dialog class.

---
swt.dialogs.AskMeDialog.createContents
```
1 btnOk.addSelectionListener(new SelectionAdapter() {
2     public void widgetSelected(SelectionEvent e) {
3         result = txtName.getText();
4         shell.close();
5     }
6 });
```

⚠ Always retrieve values from widgets before closing the dialog. Otherwise, the contained widgets are disposed and are no longer accessible.   ↰7.4.1

A final question that needs to be addressed is how the result is actually returned to the caller after the dialog closes. In SWT, the answer can even be traced in the code: The `open()` method in the following snippet first makes the new shell appear on the screen and then keeps dispatching events until the dialog is closed (lines 6–10). At this point, the `result` has been set by the listener and can be returned to the caller.   ≫7.10.1

---
swt.dialogs.AskMeDialog.open
```
 1 public String open() {
 2     createContents();
 3     shell.open();
 4     shell.layout();
 5     Display display = getParent().getDisplay();
 6     while (!shell.isDisposed()) {
 7         if (!display.readAndDispatch()) {
 8             display.sleep();
 9         }
10     }
11     return result;
12 }
```

The parent element of a shell determines z-order and minimization.

The most important aspect of dialogs is that they appear "above the main window," where they are expected to catch the user's attention immediately. In practice, this simple demand has three facets: In a setup with multiple monitors or workspaces, dialogs appear on the same monitor and workspace as the main window. Within that workspace, they usually appear centered over the application window. And, finally, they appear *over* the application window, in the sense that the application window never partially conceals them. This visual layering of elements on the screen is usually referred to as their *z-order*. All of those aspects must be taken into account to achieve a satisfactory user experience.

The single most important setting toward that end is to pass the proper *parent shell* to the constructor of a new shell. That setting links the new window to its parent, so that the new window appears at the expected location on the screen and above its parent in the z-order. The dialog even remains on top if the user reactivates the main window by clicking into that window (which is possible only with modeless dialogs).

A shell without a parent, in contrast, will appear in the middle of the screen when opened. It may also be buried behind the main application window, or the user can place the application window on top of the dialog. However, that behavior is system-dependent and depends on further settings. For instance, a modal dialog may still appear on top of the window that was active before the dialog was opened, even if that window is not its explicit parent shell. Here, the window system has made an informed guess at what was probably the user's intention in opening the dialog. You should not rely on this behavior, but rather explicitly set a parent shell on each dialog.

Shells always involve interaction with the window manager.

Users appreciate and expect consistency: The windows on their desktop must look and behave the same, regardless of which application happens to open them. Window systems therefore include a *window manager* component that handles the drawing of and interaction with top-level windows. As a result, the visual appearance of a window is split into two parts (Fig. 7.13). The window's content is created by the application, possibly using a system-wide library of available widgets. The title bar and border, in contrast, are drawn by the window manager. The window manager also handles moving, resizing, minimizing, and maximizing of windows. SWT calls the elements collectively the *trimmings* of a window. (Other frameworks call these the window's *decorations*.)

The trimmings can be specified by many style-bits passed to the constructor of a Shell (see Fig. 7.11). However, many of these should be taken as only hints to the window manager, which is ultimately responsible for

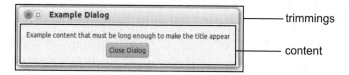

Figure 7.13 The Trimmings of a Shell

creating and handling the visual appearance consistently with the system's overall look-and-feel. Also, there may be interdependencies. For instance, some window managers will not provide minimize and maximize buttons if the shell is not resizable.

Place shells in global, absolute coordinates.

Several applications mentioned in the introduction require the dialog to appear at specific positions and even to be moved along programmatically. For instance, an auto-completion pop-up in a source code editor may follow the cursor to reflect the current insertion point. We demonstrate here only the basics: We open a list of selections below a button that triggers the appearance of the list (Fig. 7.14). The general style of the dialog is set by `SWT.NO_TRIM`, meaning that the window manager will not provide additional decorations.

Figure 7.14 Opening a Dialog at a Given Position

The code that follows demonstrates how the special layout requirements are fulfilled. Lines 1–2 first compute the desired size, by determining the preferred width of the list and enlarging the size by any borders that the window manager may wish to add despite the "no trim" flag. Lines 3–4 compute the lower-left corner of the widget below which the dialog is to appear. Line 3 works in coordinates local to the target widget, and line 4 translates the chosen point to the global coordinate system in which the top-level windows are placed. Lines 5–8 then lay out and display the dialog.

↰7.1

swt.dialogs.DialogDemo.openDialogBelow

```
1 Point listSize = select.computeSize(-1, -1, true);
2 Rectangle dialogSize = dialog.computeTrim(0, 0, listSize.x, 100);
3 Rectangle targetBounds = target.getBounds();
4 Point anchor = target.toDisplay(0, targetBounds.height);
5 dialog.setBounds(anchor.x, anchor.y, dialogSize.width,
6         dialogSize.height);
7 dialog.layout();
8 dialog.open();
```

Use standard dialogs where possible.

The discussion presented here has introduced the conceptual and technical points of using dialogs. Since dialogs are such a standard feature, it is not sensible to consider the details over and over again for each instance. Instead, many dialog-style interactions are already supported by standard dialogs. Choosing files, fonts, or printers, as well as requesting confirmation and displaying errors—all of these are hardly new challenges. Indeed, SWT, JFace, and the Eclipse platform layer already contain standard implementations for them—`FileDialog` (or `DirectoryDialog`), `FontDialog`, `PrintDialog`, and `MessageDialog`, respectively.

»9.3 »A

Using standard dialogs has the additional advantage that they are usually shared across applications, so that the user is familiar with them. Besides simplifying the implementation, they will increase the acceptance of your application.

7.7   Mediator Pattern

Event-driven software comes with one fundamental complexity: Each possible event can be fired at almost any time and events can be fired in almost any order, and by different sources of events. In the case of user interfaces, the user's mouse gestures and keyboard input, the state changes of widgets, as well as the scheduled timers all cause events that must be processed correctly and reliably. The MEDIATOR pattern helps in organizing the reaction to events.

📖100

PATTERN: MEDIATOR

In a situation where a group of objects sends messages, such as event notifications, to one another, a central *mediator* object can help to localize the necessary logic and to keep the other participating objects independent of one another.

↰7.1

For an example, let us go back to the introductory simple browser [Fig. 7.1; Fig. 7.15(a)]: The user can target the browser to a new URL either by pressing "enter" in the text field or by pushing a button. The browser then fires notifications about progress and address changes. The "load" button will be enabled only if some URL has been entered. The code implementing these reactions is scattered throughout the various listeners, so that it is hard to trace whether the desired behavior is achieved.

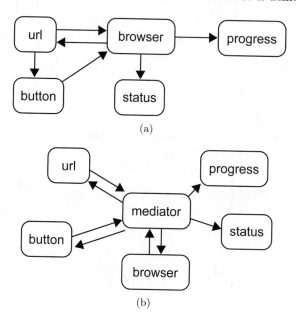

(a)

(b)

Figure 7.15 Motivation for Mediators

The situation changes dramatically if we introduce a central *mediator* object [Fig. 7.15(b)]. It receives all events, decides on the proper reaction, and calls the corresponding methods on the involved widgets.

```
swt.mediator.BrowserWithMediator.createContents
url.addSelectionListener(mediator);
url.addModifyListener(mediator);
load.addSelectionListener(mediator);
browser.addStatusTextListener(mediator);
browser.addProgressListener(mediator);
browser.addTitleListener(mediator);
```

We make the mediator a nested class within the application window so that it has access to all relevant objects. The mediator is then kept in a field of the browser object:

```
swt.mediator.BrowserWithMediator
private Mediator mediator = new Mediator();
```

The `Mediator` class is set up to receive all occurring events. As a result, it can also contain all the logic that is necessary for handling these events.

---
swt.mediator.BrowserWithMediator

```
private class Mediator implements SelectionListener, ModifyListener,
        ProgressListener, StatusTextListener, TitleListener {
    ...
}
```

↰7.1

The mediator's methods contain code that is similar to the original event handlers. This is not surprising, since they serve the same purpose and implement the same reactions. However, because in principle events can come in from several widgets, they check the source at the beginning (line 2 in the next code snippet). The example also shows an immediate benefit of the approach: Because the code is centralized within `Mediator`, it becomes simpler to extract reactions triggered by different access paths into helper methods such as `retargetBrowser`.

↰7.1
↰1.4.5

---
swt.mediator.BrowserWithMediator.widgetDefaultSelected

```
1 public void widgetDefaultSelected(SelectionEvent e) {
2     if (e.getSource() == url) {
3         retargetBrowser();
4     }
5 }
6 public void widgetSelected(SelectionEvent e) {
7     if (e.getSource() == load) {
8         retargetBrowser();
9     }
10 }
11 protected void retargetBrowser() {
12     if (!url.getText().isEmpty())
13         browser.setUrl(url.getText());
14 }
```

That's it for the basics. Let us now examine some consequences of using mediators.

Mediators can encapsulate complex logic.

In the example, the interdependencies between the objects were not really complex. However, in dialogs with many widgets that influence one another's state, the communication between those widgets can itself be substantial. Placing it in a separate mediator object helps keep the code readable.

This result is similar to that of introducing objects as containers for algorithms and the data structures that they work on. There, too, the complexity of a piece of logic suggests that it should be stored away in a separate object, rather than let it clutter its surroundings.

↰1.8.6

Delegating all events to the host object introduces an implicit mediator.

In the context of the OBSERVER pattern, we have discussed the approach   ↰2.1.3
of having observers call `protected` methods in a surrounding object. The
focus there was on handling the state changes induced by the events in one
class, rather than throughout the code.

Mediators serve a similar role, but they usually receive the events immediately, rather than providing specialized methods that are called from the
listeners attached to the different widgets. However, the resulting structure is similar, and the similarity creates a new perspective on the former approach: the surrounding object becomes an implicit mediator for its
parts.

> Mediators make the code more complex by an extra indirection.

Finally, it must be said that mediators are not the only possible solution to
handling events and that the original structure in Fig. 7.15(a) does, in fact,
have its merits: Each widget in the code immediately exhibits the reactions
associated with it. One can answer questions like "What happens if ... "
straightforwardly, because the event-listener is right there on the spot, close
to the creation of the widget. In the mediator, in contrast, one has to find
the called method and the right branch in the case distinction on the event
source.

Introducing MEDIATOR is therefore really a decision. You have to consider whether it is better to have localized reactions at the cost of scattering
the overall logic throughout the code, or a centralized logic at the cost of
introducing an indirection.

7.8   Custom Painting for Widgets

In some situations, the predefined widgets are not sufficient. For instance,
your application data may require special rendering, or you may want to   ⟫11.3.1
brand your application with special elements to make it stand out.

> Avoid creating custom widgets.

Custom widgets imply a lot of work. Besides the actual painting with pixel-
based computations of geometry, you have to place their elements manually,
compute the optimal size based on the local fonts, and deal with low-level
mouse and keyboard input. Also, it is best to check that the widget actually
behaves as expected on the different operating systems. Think twice before
setting out on that journey.

Very often what seems to be a special widget at first can still be created
as a compound widget with special listeners attached. In particular, static
graphics can often be simulated by setting icons on `Labels` without text;
the label will render only the given image.

Restrict the custom painting to the smallest possible element.

Since managing a custom widget entails so much work, it is good to keep the work minimal by restricting the new widget to just the things that really need special painting. For example, if you wanted to write a memory game, the largest solution would be a widget `MemoryBoard` that does everything: places the cards, handles the mouse clicks, implements the rules of the game, and so on. Of course, we need custom painting, because we want to have nice-looking cards with custom borders, and so on. However, the cards are laid out in a grid, so that part is already handled by the `GridLayout`.

So we decide to implement a custom widget `MemoryCard` instead. Fig. 7.16 shows two such cards placed side by side. One shows a checkered back-side, and the other shows the card's image.

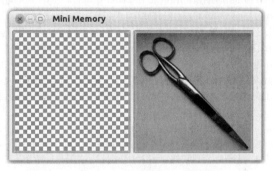

Figure 7.16 Memory Cards

Derive custom widgets from `Canvas`.

↰7.4.1

In SWT, one cannot simply subclass any likely-looking widget and adapt its behavior by method overriding. New widgets requiring custom painting are to be derived from `Canvas`, which is a raw rectangular space onto which arbitrary graphics can be painted.

---

swt.custom.MemoryCard

```
public class MemoryCard extends Canvas {
    ...
    public MemoryCard(Composite parent) {
        super(parent, SWT.NONE);
        ...
    }
    ...
}
```

⚠ `Canvas`, according to its documentation, does not handle children properly, so you can use it only for atomic special elements. Possibly, you will have to stitch together your desired component from a core `Canvas`, embedded into other elements as before.

Apply the object-oriented structuring guidelines.

As for compound widgets, the new widget should always be considered as   ◄7.5
a software artifact: How must its API and behavior be defined to make it a
useful collaborator that works well in different contexts? We have discussed
the relevant aspects for the compound widgets. For the current example,
they translate to the following decisions. We will be brief, because the
considerations closely resemble those from the `DatePicker`.

First, we see that the reaction to a mouse click is context-dependent.
While it would usually flip the card, it might also cause two revealed images
to be hidden at some other point in the game. We therefore decide to let the
`MemoryCard` provide a generic "selection" mechanism and give it a proper
`imageName` that serves as an identifier for the shown image. Also, the client
can explicitly choose whether the image is shown. In this way, different
decks of cards can be chosen. Together, these considerations lead to the
following API:

---

swt.custom.MemoryCard

```
public String getImageName()
public void setImageName(String name)
public boolean isImageShown()
public void setImageShown(boolean show)
public void addSelectionListener(SelectionListener l)
public void removeSelectionListener(SelectionListener l)
```

   ⌀ The `imageName` is a property rather than a parameter to the constructor because the
      WindowBuilder does not handle such constructors well.   ◄7.5

Painting on the screen is event-driven.

The central question is, of course, how to paint on the `Canvas`. In other
frameworks, such as Swing and the Graphical Editing Framework's Draw2D   ▢214
layer, the solution is to override one or several methods that are responsible
for drawing different parts of a figure in an application of the TEMPLATE   ◄1.4.9
METHOD pattern. SWT instead lets you register `PaintListeners` that
are called back whenever some part of the `Canvas` needs re-drawing. The
`MemoryCard`'s constructor sets this up, as shown in the next example. We
choose to delegate to the outer class here, because painting is one of the   ◄2.1.3
`MemoryCard`'s tasks and the `PaintListener` is only a technical necessity.

---

swt.custom.MemoryCard.MemoryCard

```
addPaintListener(new PaintListener() {
    public void paintControl(PaintEvent e) {
        paintWidget(e.gc);
    }
});
```

The actual painting code writes to the display through the given GC (for *graphics context*) object. Lines 2–5 paint either the image or back-side of the card; lines 6–13 draw a series of rounded rectangles with different shades of gray to create a 3D effect around the card (Fig. 7.16).

swt.custom.MemoryCard

```
1 protected void paintWidget(GC gc) {
2     if (imageShown)
3         gc.drawImage(image, BORDER_WIDTH, BORDER_WIDTH);
4     else
5         gc.drawImage(checkered, BORDER_WIDTH, BORDER_WIDTH);
6     Rectangle bounds = getBounds();
7     for (int i = 0; i != BORDER_WIDTH; i++) {
8         int val = 150 + 10 * i;
9         gc.setForeground(new Color(null, val, val, val));
10        gc.drawRoundRectangle(i, i, bounds.width - 2 * i,
11                              bounds.height - 2 * i, 5, 5);
12    }
13 }
```

⚡ The GC encapsulates the actual rendering. For instance, it is also possible to create a GC for an Image using new GC(image). Be sure to dispose of the GC after use.

swt.custom.PaintToImage

```
protected Image createImage() {
    Image img = new Image(getDisplay(), 100, 100);
    GC gc = new GC(img);
    try {
        gc.drawOval(30, 30, 60, 40);
    } finally {
        gc.dispose();
    }
    return img;
}
```

Restrict painting to the necessary area.

Drawing operations are comparatively expensive, because they must get back to the operating system and the actual hardware. In larger widgets, it is therefore mandatory to redraw only those parts that are actually no longer up-to-date. The PaintEvent passed to the paint-listener contains the rectangular bounding box of the region that needs redrawing. Use it to skip any drawing code that does not touch the area.

》9.4.3

Schedule repainting to cause the widgets to be updated.

Widgets encapsulate and manage internal state and data structures. At some point, they will discover that a state change influences their visual appearance, so that they have to repaint themselves. Since painting is event-driven, at this point they must trigger a suitable event—that is, they must tell SWT that their screen space needs to be updated. The method redraw() does this.

---
swt.custom.MemoryCard

```
public void setImageShown(boolean show)
{
    imageShown = show;
    redraw();
}
```

We pointed out earlier that a widget should repaint only those parts that are actually touched by the bounding box given in the paint event. That bounding box can be given in a variant of the redraw() request (the parameter all indicates whether children should also be repainted):

---
org.eclipse.swt.widgets.Control

```
public void redraw (int x, int y, int width, int height,
    boolean all)
```

⚠ Do not assume that the bounding box passed to the PaintListener is the same as the bounding box passed to redraw. For instance, the window system might discover that parts of the requested area are actually hidden below another window, in which case it clips the area further to make the painting even more efficient.

⚠ Do not force immediate repainting. The class GC also offers a constructor for painting onto arbitrary Drawables, and widgets on the screen are also Drawables. (Note that you have to dispose() of the GC obtained in this way.)

---
org.eclipse.swt.graphics.GC

```
public GC(Drawable drawable)
```

In principle, it is possible to repaint a widget directly at the point when the state change occurs. However, this short-circuits and disables all the fine-tuned optimizations implemented by the window system and SWT.

7.9   Timers

So far, we have created interfaces that react to user actions. Without user input, nothing happens. Many situations do, however, require a more dynamic behavior: Timeouts and delays can be used for implicit actions, such as to show auto-completions in an editor when the user stops typing for a while, or they can trigger expensive computations only after some period of inactivity. Animations can highlight certain aspects or conditions, such as an urgent error status, and they can make extensive changes in the displayed data, such as recomputing the layout of a graph, more comprehensible by providing intermediate states visually. User interface frameworks provide *timers* to implement such behaviors that proceed without explicit user interaction.

7.9.1   Timeouts and Delays

A prototypical delayed action is to show a pop-up on auto-completion text fields: As long as the user keeps typing, there is no need for the pop-up; after a period of inactivity, a list of selections is supposed to occur. To explore timers, we implement a small widget that auto-completes country names, as shown in Fig. 7.17: the user keeps typing, and after a delay of 500 ms, the list of possible countries matching the current entry is updated.

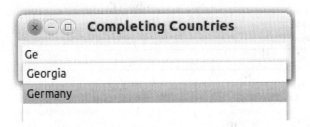

Figure 7.17 Auto-Completing Country Names

»9.3

↰7.3

JFace provides a mechanism for auto-completion in its `ContentProposalAdapter`, which can be attached to text fields. Do not implement auto-completion yourself, but learn to use the framework instead.

SWT provides timers in the form of callbacks scheduled to occur later on.

↰7.1

↰1.8.6

Timers in SWT are created through the `Display`, which provides a simple method: The given code, which is wrapped up in a `Runnable`, is executed after a given number of milliseconds. The "timer" in SWT is therefore not really an object, but rather an event, or a callback, that is scheduled to occur at some later point.

org.eclipse.swt.widgets.Display

```
public void timerExec(int milliseconds, Runnable runnable)
```

»7.10.1

The given timeout is not exact, as the callback may occur slightly later than the given delay. The reason is that it will always occur in the event-dispatch thread, and that thread may be busy processing other events at the time.

🌍 Other toolkits provide timers as proper objects with a proper API. For instance, the
Timer class of Swing provides methods to start and stop the timer, and to let it fire
events periodically. Watch out for timers in the library that are not related to the user
interface: They typically make use of background threads and require the corresponding
precautions.   》7.10

For the example, we implement a widget AutoCompleteCountries. It
contains a text widget input as a single child. The crucial point is that any
modification to the text field will result in a later pop-up with completion
proposals (line 5 in the next example). As a detail, line 4 serves to disable
this reaction for the case where the text replaced by a selected completion
proposal. Otherwise, selecting a proposal would immediately pop-up the
shell again.

swt.timer.AutoCompleteCountries.AutoCompleteCountries

```
1 input = new Text(this, SWT.NONE);
2 input.addModifyListener(new ModifyListener() {
3     public void modifyText(ModifyEvent e) {
4         if (!settingSelection)
5             getDisplay().timerExec(DELAY, showPopup);
6     }
7 });
```

Here showPopup is a Runnable that merely calls the following method   ↰2.1.3
showPopup() in the surrounding class. That method creates and places
the pop-up as a new Shell and then fills the list of proposals by searching through a fixed list of country names. Since all of this is not related
to timers, we will skip the details here. They can be found in the online
supplement.

swt.timer.AutoCompleteCountries

```
1 protected void showPopup() {
2     if (input.isDisposed())
3         return;
4     createPopup();
5     fillPopup();
6 }
```

Timers can be rescheduled and canceled.

Existing timers can be rescheduled and canceled by passing the same
runnable with a different delay. Line 5 in the modify-listener implicitly
makes use of this feature: While the user keeps typing, the pop-up is delayed again and again, until the user stops typing and the delay can elapse.

To cancel a timer, one uses a delay of -1. For instance, when the user
presses escape, the following listener unschedules any existing timers and
then hides the pop-up. (The listener is named because it is also attached

to the pop-up shell to catch the escape when the pop-up has the keyboard focus.)

swt.timer.AutoCompleteCountries.AutoCompleteCountries

```
closePopupOnEscape = new KeyAdapter() {
    public void keyReleased(KeyEvent e) {
        if (e.character == SWT.ESC) {
            getDisplay().timerExec(-1, showPopup);
            hidePopup();
        }
    }
};
input.addKeyListener(closePopupOnEscape);
```

> The example demonstrates several other techniques not related to timers: placing pop-up shells relative to a given widget, managing the focus between the text field and the pop-up, and moving along the pop-up when the user drags the window containing the text field.

↰1.8.8.3

> As a cross reference, we proposed in Part I to store instances of anonymous nested classes in named fields or variables to improve readability, or to clarify the intention by passing the instance to a method directly. Look again at these two styles in the code here to judge the relative merits.

Check for disposal of widgets in timed callbacks.

📖148

↰7.4.1

Working in an event-driven environment means that you have to expect things to happen while you are not looking. Suppose the user closes the dialog containing `AutoCompleteCountries` widget, but leaves the application running. When a timer is still scheduled, the method `showPopup()` above cannot work properly, because it accesses a disposed widget. Lines 2–3 in the code of that method catch this special case.

Encapsulate local state.

The `ModifyListener` method given earlier introduces a special flag `settingSelection` that works around an unintended behavior: When setting the text in `input` programmatically after a user selects a completion, the "modify" event is fired, which would make the pop-up reappear immediately. Fortunately, both the completion and the delayed trigger are contained within the class `AutoCompleteCountries`, so that we can introduce a workaround that remains hidden from clients. The following code attaches a listener to the selection list in the pop-up. When the user double-clicks or presses "enter," it sets the current selected text on the `input`. To suppress the undesired reappearance behavior, lines 6 and 8 set the local flag `settingSelection`.

```
                    swt.timer.AutoCompleteCountries.createPopup
1 list.addSelectionListener(new SelectionAdapter() {
2     public void widgetDefaultSelected(SelectionEvent e) {
3         int selected = list.getSelectionIndex();
4         if (selected != -1) {
5             String country = list.getItem(selected);
6             settingSelection = true;
7             input.setText(country);
8             settingSelection = false;
9             hidePopup();
10         }
11     }
12 });
```

7.9.2   Animations

Timers can also be used to implement animations. The only necessary addition to the techniques discussed previously is the repeated, periodic scheduling of tasks. Suppose we want to implement a `Ticker` widget that moves a message around in a `Text` widget (Fig. 7.18).

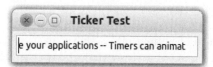

Figure 7.18 The Ticker Widget

Periodic behavior is achieved by rescheduling a timer.

The `Ticker` maintains an internal position `pos`, which designates the character where the overall text is split to achieve the effect. The central method is `tick()`, which sets the content of the `output` text field according to the current position and then advances that position cyclically through the given text. Finally, it schedules a timer `ticker`, which merely calls, again, the method `tick()` after the given delay (we use 80 ms).

```
                              swt.timer.Ticker
protected void tick() {
    if (text.isEmpty() || output.isDisposed())
        return;
    pos = (pos + 1) % text.length();
    String txt = text.substring(pos, text.length()) + " "
            + text.substring(0, pos);
    output.setText(txt);
    getDisplay().timerExec(DELAY, ticker);
}
```

↰7.9.1

↰4.1

🔍 Note again the check for the disposal of the `output` widget: The user might have closed the surrounding window in the brief time span after the timer has been last scheduled. To illustrate the danger of such intuitions, and to appreciate the necessity of precise reasoning here, consider the following argument: Processing `tick()` will take approximately 1 ms, so the chance of the user's closing the window between ticks is actually relatively high.

The first call to `tick()` is scheduled in `setText()`:

swt.timer.Ticker.setText

```
if (!text.isEmpty())
    getDisplay().timerExec(DELAY, ticker);
```

↰7.5

🔍 The choice of the name `text` for the property reflects an interesting decision. On the one hand, "message" would be a more appropriate name if one focuses on the API of the compound widget we implement. On the other hand, all widgets in SWT that display some form of text call their property "text." We have therefore opted to follow the conventions of the user interface context.

Animations keep a current state and advance it through timer events.

The general structure of animations is shown in Fig. 7.19. The animation takes place in short bursts of activity that update the display, and then the application schedules a timer and waits for it to elapse. To keep track of what the current and next display should be, the application maintains an internal state that captures the current progress of the animation abstractly. In each animation step, it updates the state and reflects it on the screen. In the example, the state is only `pos`, the point where the text was currently split, and moving the animation forward means incrementing `pos` cyclically through the given message.

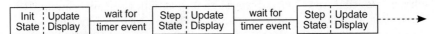

Figure 7.19 Structure of an Animation with Timers

↰4.1

⚠ Do not use `Thread.sleep()` to implement the waiting from Fig. 7.19, even if it is tempting. Maintaining the state in fields requires formulating and maintaining invariants. Here, we have "`pos` is the current point where the text gets split. It is always between 0 and `text.length` (exclusively)." Often the animation could be expressed more easily in a `while` loop that updates only local variables, like this:

swt.timer.NoThreadingExample.animate

```
int pos = 0;
while (!animationFinished){
    Thread.sleep(DELAY);
```

```
    pos = (pos + 1) % text.length();
    output.setText(splitText(pos));
}
```

However, because of the event loop, this code must run in a different thread, which causes all kinds of concerns. Also, in effect, the loop will have invariants that are very similar to those about the fields in the correct solution.

»7.10.1
◄4.7.2

7.10 Background Jobs

User interface toolkits in general make one important trade-off: They assume that event-listeners will run very quickly so as to gain the simplicity of handling the incoming events one after the other, without overlaps in the execution of the listeners. The downside is that listeners that do run longer block the user interface completely, up to the point where highlights under the mouse cursor will no longer show up, menu items do not respond, and it even becomes impossible to close the application window. To demonstrate the effect, you can just attach a "blocking" listener to a button:

```
                     swt.intro.BlockUIDemo.BlockUIDemo
btnBlockUI.addSelectionListener(new SelectionAdapter() {
    public void widgetSelected(SelectionEvent e) {
        Thread.currentThread().sleep(5000);
    }
});
```

The decision of the user interface toolkits works out well most of the time, but sometimes reactions to certain events will take more time. For example, downloading a page from the web or processing nontrivial amounts of data can easily take a several seconds, and even accessing a local file can be delayed if the file happens to be located on a network drive. Users, however, are not prepared to wait for long: They tolerate delays of roughly 200–300 ms before seeing a reaction; otherwise, they get uneasy and assume that the system has crashed. The least the system must do is display a "busy" cursor to indicate that it will take some more time. SWT provides a class BusyIndicator for this purpose.

□229 □50(§C.1)

Sometimes this is not good enough, in which case long-running tasks must be executed in separate *threads*. Threads are a runtime mechanism for executing different parts of the program conceptually in parallel, by quickly scheduling these parts on the CPU in a round-robin fashion or by executing them on different CPUs or different cores within one CPU. The result is that the user interface remains responsive and the user remains happy while background threads do the heavy processing.

»8 □148

This section explains the relation to user interfaces to multithreading. The topic of threads in general does, however, fill entire books. Chapter 8

□148

complements the current chapter by providing a succinct overview that should be sufficient for the purposes of user interface programming.

7.10.1   Threads and the User Interface

The goal of processing one event after the other is achieved by introducing one central *event dispatch loop*, which gathers events from different sources, decides on their relative order and their destination widgets, and dispatches them to the listeners registered on the widget (Fig. 7.20): The window system sends low-level user input, as well as high-level events such as the signal that the user has clicked the "close" button in a window's title bar. Timers may have elapsed, so that their associated handlers must be called. Also, as we shall see shortly, arbitrary `Runnables` can be injected into the event processing through a method `asyncExec()`. In concrete systems, further sources of events can be present.

◀7.9

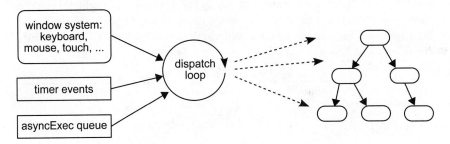

Figure 7.20 Event Dispatching in a Loop

Most user interface toolkits hide the event loop in one "run UI" method that must be called when the application starts up and that finishes only when the application terminates. In SWT, the event loop is actually visible as a very simple coding idiom (which the WindowBuilder generates for top-level windows): While the application window is visible, the loop keeps dispatching events, waiting for the next event if currently there is no work.

swt.browser.SimpleBrowser.open

```
while (!shell.isDisposed()) {
    if (!display.readAndDispatch()) {
        display.sleep();
    }
}
```

148

The call to `display.sleep()` might seem suspicious, since polling by checking for events every few milliseconds is bad coding practice and must be avoided. The method does the right thing, however: It checks for the internal sources of events and otherwise blocks on reading new events from the window system. When timers elapse, they also wake up `sleep()` to continue processing. An alternative, and possibly more suitable, name for the method would have been `waitForEvents`.

Widgets must be accessed only in the unique event dispatch thread.

One aspect associated with the event dispatch loop is that dispatching is always executed in a dedicated thread, the *event dispatch thread*. It is this thread that runs the event loop and calls the registered listeners. Indeed, no other thread must access any widgets, because quasi-parallel accesses to the widgets will easily break invariants, while synchronizing accesses is cumbersome and error-prone. The `checkWidget()` method, which is called at the start of any `public` method in SWT's widgets, excludes cross-thread accesses:

»8.2 ☐148 »7.10.2
↰7.4.1

---
org.eclipse.swt.widgets.Widget

```
protected void checkWidget() {
    ...
    if (display.thread != Thread.currentThread())
        error(SWT.ERROR_THREAD_INVALID_ACCESS);
    ...
}
```

Access the user interface from other threads via `asyncExec`.

Suppose you decide that you need to perform a long-running operation in a different thread. You will still have to access the user interface to display progress reports and the final result. The technical solution is a method in `Display` that takes a `Runnable` and executes that code within the dispatch thread:

»7.10.2

---
org.eclipse.swt.widgets.Display

```
public void asyncExec(Runnable runnable)
```

ഏ The abbreviation `async` expands, of course, to "asynchronous." "Asynchronous" in computer science is usually linked to the idea of "running independently" or "not being in lock-step." One important connotation in the current context is that the `Runnable` will be executed later on, whenever SWT finds the time for it, without further guarantees.

Of course, this procedure might feel a bit uncomfortable: You have some state change that you wish to report back to the user and now the report is delayed for some arbitrary (but short) time. From the user's perspective, the delay hardly matters, since it was not clear how long the job would take in the first place.

> **TOOL: Creating Runnables Quickly**
>
> In the current context, one needs to create many `Runnables`. Eclipse offers an easy support: Just type "runnable" and auto-complete (`Ctrl-Space`) it to a runnable with overridden method `run()`.

> Beware of the delay introduced by `asyncExec`.

» 8.2

From a technical perspective, the consequences of using `asyncExec` are rather more severe, because one has to consider the possible state changes that occur before the `runnable` gets executed. The overall situation is shown in Fig. 7.21, where each invocation of `asyncExec` incurs a brief delay before the user interface code runs. Within this delay, you should assume that anything can happen, both to the internal data structures and to the user interface—after all, the background thread keeps on working and the user interface keeps dispatching events.

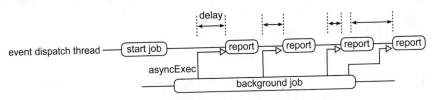

Figure 7.21 AsyncExec from Background Threads

To start from a concrete goal, suppose we simply wish to update a progress bar after a number of `steps` have been finished by the background job. We correspondingly schedule a runnable (line 2). However, it might be the case that the user has closed the window before the runnable executes, so we need to check that the target widget is still valid in line 4 before performing the update in line 5.

↰ 7.4.1

```
                    swt.threads.ProgressBarMonitor.worked
1 final int steps = work;
2 display.asyncExec(new Runnable() {
3     public void run() {
4         if (!progressBar.isDisposed()) {
5             progressBar.setSelection(
6                     progressBar.getSelection()  + steps);
7         }
8     }
9 });
```

⚠ Always check for disposed widgets before accessing them in code scheduled via `asyncExec()`. Otherwise, SWT will throw an exception.

⚠ Line 2 requires access to the current display. Note that it is not possible to use `getDisplay()` on the target widget, because that method fails if the widget has been disposed. It is therefore necessary to store the display in a field or local variable beforehand, when the background job is first created, because at that point the target does exist.

A second, slightly less dramatic point is seen in line 1. Suppose `work` is a field in the background job that is updated whenever the job finds it has made progress. By the time `Runnable` is executed, this field will have been altered, so that the report is actually wrong and the same work may be reported twice, leading to a wrong setting of the progress bar.

It is therefore useful to make a copy of any data structure or state of the background job that is needed in the display code. This is precisely what line 1 accomplishes. In this way, the report will always be accurate, independent of the time that it is actually delivered.

Think of `asyncExec` as producer–consumer.

A common pattern in coding with multiple threads, which furthermore keeps the involved complexity at a minimum, is called *producer–consumer* (Fig. 7.22): One thread keeps producing a sequence of data items that another thread then consumes and processes. Since the threads run in parallel and independently, a queue in the middle buffers data until it is consumed.   ▯▯148

»12.3.4

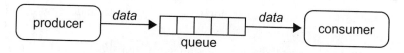

Figure 7.22 Producer–Consumer Pattern

In the case of `asyncExec`, one does not pass data, but `Runnables`, and the role of the queue is played by an internal data structure of `Display` that buffers the `Runnables`. The consumer is the event thread, which merely executes the `Runnables`.

To make this important coding idiom concrete, let us consider a tiny example where a thread computes several results that should be displayed one by one. Also, a progress bar should keep the impatient user informed about the remaining time. As shown in the example code, the overall loop runs in the background thread and the computation in line 2 presumably takes a longish time. Line 3 saves the current counter for the report, because the counter might change later on. Line 4 schedules the update of the user interface in lines 6–7. The call to `asyncExec` returns immediately, which enables the background thread to proceed without waiting for the sluggish user interface to finish the display.

↩1.8.8.3

```
                    swt.threads.ProduceConsume.ProduceConsume
 1  for (int i=1; i <= 100; i++) {
 2      ... compute next result
 3      final int cur = i;
 4      display.asyncExec(new Runnable() {
 5          public void run() {
 6              results.add(Integer.toString(result));
 7              progress.setSelection(cur);
 8          }
 9      });
10  }
```

The essential point of the producer–consumer pattern is that the data is never shared between the threads, so they never access the data simultaneously. The producer creates and initializes some objects, passes them into the queue, and then relinquishes the references. Of course, this also concerns references that are stored within the data: The object structure that arrives at the consumer must no longer be accessible, or at least not written to, from anywhere within the producer. The pattern, like the technical analysis given earlier, therefore suggests to make copies of any relevant data.

Keep track of which code runs in which thread.

When programming with background threads, it is essential to keep track of which code runs in which thread, because the different threads impose different restrictions:

- Background threads must not access UI widgets under any circumstances.

- Code in the event dispatch thread must run quickly and must not perform long-running operations.

While mistakes in the first point show up immediately in exceptions thrown by SWT, neglecting the latter may not become obvious until some user happens to process an unexpectedly large file or happens to access a file over the network rather than on the local hard disk.

It is useful to think of the event thread and the background threads as two separate worlds where different sets of rules apply. Getting confused between the two worlds is, unfortunately, rather simple. For one thing, Runnables may be nested inside each other, each one signaling a transition between the event dispatch thread and a background thread.

↶2.1 ↷9.1

A yet more complex case arises when observing objects with the purpose of keeping the user interface up-to-date: If the modification happens to be performed in a background thread, then the notification is also sent in that thread, even if the observer itself is statically contained in a widget.

Suppose we implement a complex task that involves summing up some data. The class Summation contains the current result and notifies any registered PropertyChangeListeners about new results.

---
swt.threads.ObserveBackground.ObserveBackground

```
final Summation sum = new Summation();
```

Then, the background thread creates such a summation and starts working.

---
swt.threads.ObserveBackground.ObserveBackground

```
for (int i = 1; i <= 100; i++) {
    ... compute next delta
    sum.add(delta);
}
```

Since the task takes some time, users would be happy to see the intermediate results on the screen, so that they get a feeling for the progress. This can be done easily enough by registering a change-listener with the Summation. The essential point is that the background thread calls sum.add(), so that the change notifications are also sent within that thread, and finally the listener in the next code snippet gets executed in the background thread. As a result, the listener cannot access the widget result immediately, but must do so through asyncExec (line 4).

---
swt.threads.ObserveBackground.registerObserver

```
1 final Display display = getDisplay();
2 sum.addPropertyChangeListener(new PropertyChangeListener() {
3     public void propertyChange(final PropertyChangeEvent evt) {
4         display.asyncExec(new Runnable() {
5             public void run() {
6                 if (result.isDisposed())
7                     return;
8                 result.setText(
9                         Integer.toString(
10                                (Integer)evt.getNewValue()));
11            }
12        });
13
14     }
15 });
```

🔍 Note that we need to keep the display in line 1, because a call to getDisplay() in line 4 would fail in case the widget has be disposed.

Treat the event dispatch thread as a scarce resource.

Once one gets used to the idea of scheduling code into the event thread, the asyncExec facility comes in very handy in many situations: Whenever something needs to be done, but cannot be done right now, one packages it up as a Runnable and hands it over to the event dispatch thread. Suppose, for instance, that your application tracks incoming network data. Whenever the receiving object has got hold of a message, it can simply pass a Runnable to the event thread and can immediately go on reading data.

The problem with such a setup is that it swamps the event thread with small pseudo-events. If thousands of them arrive in a second, as may easily be the case, then the processing of the actual user input becomes ever more delayed, with the result that the display appears to be "frozen." For instance, highlights under the mouse depend on the mouse events to be delivered to the respective widget in a timely fashion.

↰7.9

     ✎ If your application does receive bulk data in a background thread and has to somehow display a digest of the data on the screen, you have no choice but go through asyncExec. In such a case, you should accumulate data in the background thread and send updates to the screen only periodically—for instance, after a few hundred data items have been processed or after some timeout, such as 50 ms, has elapsed. This approach relieves the burden on the event thread; the user would not be able to track the faster changes anyway.

Use syncExec (only) if some feedback is required from the user.

In rare situations, the background thread may need to wait until the user interface code has actually run. The class Display provides a variant syncExec of asyncExec for this purpose.

                                    org.eclipse.swt.widgets.Display

public void syncExec(Runnable runnable)

↰7.6

In this way, the background job can, for instance, ask the user a question and proceed according to the answer.

                            swt.threads.AskFromBackground.startThread

```
1 final boolean decision[] = new boolean[1];
2 getDisplay().syncExec(new Runnable() {
3     public void run() {
4         decision[0] = MessageDialog.openConfirm(getShell(),
5             "Proceed?", "Do you want to delete the file?");
6     }
7 });
```

↰1.8.8.3

     ✎ Line 1 must declare decision itself final to make it accessible within the Runnable, but the array still provides a slot that can be filled with the result in line 4.

The first thread accessing a display becomes the event thread.

The question remains as to which thread is singled out as the unique event dispatch thread. SWT's answer is that a display is associated with the thread that creates the display. Usually, this happens just before the event dispatch loop in the main thread of the application.

While SWT reuses some existing thread in this way, many other frameworks create an internal, private thread and dispatch events from that thread. As a result, even the creation of the user interface must be performed explicitly in that thread. In Swing, for instance, the following code schedules the `Runnable` to be called in the event thread; lines 4–6 then create and display the window. Even though line 6 returns immediately, the application keeps running while the event thread keeps dispatching events.

swt.threads.StartSwingApp

```
1 public static void main(String[] args) {
2     SwingUtilities.invokeLater(new Runnable() {
3         public void run() {
4             JFrame window = new JFrame("Example");
5             ... create content
6             window.setVisible(true);
7         }
8     });
9 }
```

7.10.2   Long-Running Tasks

Whenever the user can trigger a task whose execution will potentially take longer than the bearable 200 ms, the task must be executed in a separate thread. Sometimes the actual processing consumes a lot of CPU time, but more often it is the waiting for input data that causes the overall delay. In a separate thread, one has basically all the time in the world.

Prefer timers to threads whenever possible.

Before we delve into the details, we would like to emphasize that the complexities involved in using threads suggest avoiding them if at all possible. In particular, most animations are *not* a case for a background thread: They wait most of the time, then perform some quick rendering, then return to waiting. Such behaviors are better solved by timers.

»8
↰7.9.2

As an example that does require background processing, we implement an application that merely connects to a web server and downloads a web page, displaying progress as it goes along (Fig. 7.23).

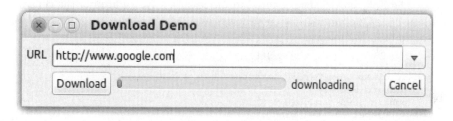

Figure 7.23 Download Job Demo

↰7.4.2

🔍 The Eclipse API discussed here is not part of SWT, but resides in the bundle `org.eclipse.core.runtime`. The parts of that bundle used here are, however, accessible outside of the Eclipse platform and work in standard Java applications. Since Eclipse provides a global display for progress, normal Java applications have to supply a substitute, which is done by calling the following method once at the beginning of the application.

swt.threads.DownloadDemo.DownloadDemo

```
Job.getJobManager().setProgressProvider(new ProgressProvider() {
    public IProgressMonitor createMonitor(Job job) {
        ... access suitable UI elements
    }
});
```

Use a task execution framework.

»8.1 ↰1.8.6

Starting raw threads is simple: Just wrap code in a `Runnable`, pass it to a new `Thread`, and start that thread. However, this has the disadvantage of always working at the lowest possible level. For background jobs, it is usually better to use some execution framework that distributes *tasks* to a given number of *worker threads*. These frameworks are also called *lightweight executable frameworks*, because the single tasks are lightweight, in contrast to threads, which consume actual system resources.

📖148

The Java library offers the `ThreadPoolExecutor` for the purpose. It is designed to be efficient and can be customized to handle large amounts of tasks efficiently. For instance, the Apache Tomcat servlet container uses it to handle incoming requests in parallel. The executor also offers callbacks `beforeExecute()` and `afterExecute()`, in the form of TEMPLATE METHOD, which allow applications to track single jobs.

↰1.4.9

Use the infrastructure provided by the user interface toolkit.

User interface toolkits usually offer a task execution framework with even more infrastructure. For instance, this infrastructure often includes observers for the tasks' state and progress—something that is usually required in this application area.

↰2.1

The Eclipse API for background processing revolves around the central class `Job`. One merely has to subclass and override the `run()` method to employ the framework.

swt.threads.DownloadJob

```
public class DownloadJob extends Job {
    private URL url;
    public DownloadJob(URL url) {
        super(url.toString());
        this.url = url;
    }
}
```

```
    protected IStatus run(IProgressMonitor monitor) {
        ... perform the download
    }
}
```

Starting a Job is similarly simple: Just create an instance and schedule it to be run at some convenient time. The framework will choose an available thread from an internal pool to execute the job.

---
swt.threads.DownloadDemo.DownloadDemo

```
curDownload = new DownloadJob(parsed);
...
curDownload.schedule(100);
```

The Job API is usable outside of the overall Eclipse workbench. However, the standard workbench offers more support—for instance, by displaying the progress in the status bar, in the lower-right corner of the window, and enabling the user to cancel running jobs.

When assessing the offered API, one has to be a bit careful. For instance, the ApplicationWindow abstraction offered by JFace also includes a facility to run jobs, ostensibly in the background by using an argument fork. The run() method provides a very convenient interface, as seen in the next example. (Its first argument is fork, the second is cancelable.) At second glance, however, these jobs are not properly run in the background, even if technically they execute in a separate thread: The call to run() blocks until the job finishes, so lines 5–6 must wait. The framework dispatches only just enough events to show progress and let the user cancel the job.

»9.3

---
swt.threads.ModalOperationsDemo.createContents

```
1 run(true, true, new IRunnableWithProgress() {
2     public void run(IProgressMonitor monitor) {
3         ... perform the actual work
4 });
5 MessageDialog.openInformation(getShell(), "Done",
6         "The job has finished now");
```

Keep track of the running jobs.

Jobs are usually not something that one fires and forgets. Users need to cancel jobs, and this may also happen implicitly. When a dialog starts a job, such as to validate some input file, and the user closes the dialog, then the job needs to be stopped as well. For such cases, one always keeps a reference to running jobs. When a job finishes, it must then be cleared from the list:

---
swt.threads.DownloadDemo.DownloadDemo

```
curDownload.addJobChangeListener(new JobChangeAdapter() {
    public void done(IJobChangeEvent event) {
```

```
        display.asyncExec(new Runnable() {
            public void run() {
                curDownload = null;
            }
        });
    }
});
```

↰7.10.1

🔍 Note that `curDownload` is a widget field, so it must be accessed only within the event thread to avoid confusion. For this reason, the actual reaction to the callback `done()` is scheduled via `asyncExec()`.

Reflect state and results in the user interface.

Users who trigger a job also wish to be informed about its status. In the Eclipse IDE, a global progress monitor is available in the status bar, and that monitor tracks all currently running jobs. In the current example, we also update a label `message` according to the status. Since the events are fired from a background thread, we have to switch to the event thread (omitted in the second method for brevity).

↰2.1.1

swt.threads.DownloadDemo.trackJob

```
curDownload.addJobChangeListener(new JobChangeAdapter() {
    public void running(IJobChangeEvent event) {
        display.asyncExec(new Runnable() {
            public void run() {
                message.setText("downloading");
            }
        });
    }
    public void done(final IJobChangeEvent event) {
        ...
                if (event.getResult().isOK()) {
                    message.setText("finished");
                } else if (event.getResult().getSeverity()
                    == IStatus.CANCEL) {
                    message.setText("canceled");
                } else
                    message.setText(event.getResult()
                        .getMessage());
        ...
    }
});
```

↰7.10.1

💡 This is a typical instance of the earlier injunction to know which code runs in which thread. In principle, the application merely translates a signal that the job has changed to a message to the user. In more detail, this message involves switching to the event thread.

Swing's `SwingWorker` anticipates the need to update the user interface. One derives new kinds of jobs from that class and implements the actual task in the method `do InBackground()`. When that method finishes, the framework calls `done()` in the event thread. During the processing, `doInBackground()` may invoke `publish()` with intermediate results, which get passed on to `process()`. That latter method is, again, run in the event thread. As a result, the code complexity of switching threads is avoided.

javax.swing.SwingWorker
protected abstract T doInBackground() **throws** Exception
protected void done()
protected final void publish(V... chunks)
protected void process(List<V> chunks)

Provide timely and accurate progress reports to the user.

Long-running jobs can make for a trying user experience, which can be much improved by the provision of accurate progress reports. The Eclipse API provides the mechanism of `IProgressMonitors` for the purpose: The job manager supplies each job with such a progress monitor and the job is supposed to invoke the methods of the monitor at suitable points. The IDE will display the information in a global progress view and in the status bar.

↰2.1.1

The general approach of reporting is as follows: At the start of a job, one determines the overall amount of work and calls `beginTask()`. When parts of the work have been performed, one reports `worked()`. Finally, one reports the end via `done()`.

swt.threads.DownloadJob.run

```
1 monitor.beginTask("download", length);
2 try {
3     ...
4     while ((n = in.read(buf)) != -1) {
5         ... read and write data
6         monitor.worked(n);
7     }
8 } finally {
9     monitor.done();
10 }
```

The API governing the use of progress monitors is rather strict: `beginTask()` must be invoked only once and `done()` must always be invoked. When starting delegating

▢197

↰1.3.2 ↰2.4

parts of jobs to collaborators, it is therefore customary to wrap the monitor into a `SubProgressMonitor`, which calls `subTask()` only on the original.

Estimating the work up front can, of course, be problematic. An accurate measure that also corresponds linearly to the expected time is the best option. Otherwise, one can also count subtasks to be completed and report each as `worked(1)`. In the worst case, one can pass `IProgressMonitor.UNKNOWN` and hope that the UI does something sensible, such as providing a flashing or cyclic progress bar.

Allow the user to cancel requests.

In the current example (Fig. 7.23), the user cancels the current task via a simple button.

```
swt.threads.DownloadDemo.DownloadDemo
```

```java
btnCancel = new Button(this, SWT.NONE);
btnCancel.addSelectionListener(new SelectionAdapter() {
    public void widgetSelected(SelectionEvent e) {
        if (curDownload != null)
            curDownload.cancel();
        curDownload = null;
    }
});
```

»10

In a real implementation, one should gray out the button if `curDownload` is `null` instead of checking this before proceeding.

▢148 »8.3

Canceling a job properly involves two steps: (1) send a signal to the respective job and (2) enable the job to terminate itself. The latter is achieved by providing suitable exit points, which usually occur before the job attempts a new piece of work. In the download example, the loop for reading data is a natural point. In the Eclipse API, the signal for canceling is sent through the `monitor` also used for creating progress reports.

```
swt.threads.DownloadJob.run
```

```java
while ((n = in.read(buf)) != -1) {
    if (monitor.isCanceled()) {
        return Status.CANCEL_STATUS;
    }
    ... work with data
}
```

Do not forget to clean up after the job. Background jobs usually involve resources such as network connections and file streams, and it is important to close these

whenever the job finishes. The standard idiom is using a `try-finally` block for the ↰1.5.6
purpose to ensure that the cleanup code runs regardless of why the job terminates.

7.10.3 Periodic Jobs

Background jobs can also tackle tasks that run infrequently but periodically. Typical examples would be querying an email inbox for new messages, cleaning up some temporary files, and checking the state of database connections available in a pool.

The Eclipse framework handles periodic jobs as jobs that just reschedule themselves (line 9 in the next example). To keep the runs spaced evenly, it makes sense to adapt the timeout according to the time spent on the actual job (lines 6–8).

```
                        swt.threads.PeriodicJob.run
1  protected IStatus run(IProgressMonitor monitor) {
2      long startTime = System.currentTimeMillis();
3      monitor.beginTask("clean up", WORK);
4      try {
5          ... do work
6          long timeTaken = System.currentTimeMillis() - startTime;
7          if (timeTaken > INTERVAL)
8              timeTaken = 0;
9          schedule(INTERVAL - timeTaken);
10     } finally {
11         monitor.done();
12     }
13     return Status.OK_STATUS;
14 }
```

7.11 Review: Events and Contracts

We started this chapter, and this part of the book, with the observation that events challenge the view that methods are basically service providers for their callers. In an event-driven setting, the proper behavior of an object is not determined by the expectations of the caller, but rather by the role that the object itself plays in the overall software machinery of the application. A listener attached to a button, for instance, will trigger operations that may loosely correspond to the label of the button, but unlike the client of a service provider, the button itself does not depend on this reaction for its future work.

But if methods are no longer essentially service providers, does the rather substantial and somewhat complex framework of contracts remain useful for talking about the correctness of event-driven software? We will now briefly investigate the salient points of the relationship between events and contracts to set the previous framework in a new perspective.

Contracts remain crucial for the machinery employed by event-listeners.

The first and most fundamental argument against dismissing contracts summarily is that an event-listener rarely works on its own. Very often, it will trigger computations and operations that are independent of the user interface and that are part of the application's core functionality. The situation is shown in Fig. 7.24: The call (a) from SWT to the registered listener is, indeed, not governed by conventional contracts, since SWT's widgets do not expect a particular behavior or "service." However, the event-listener often relies on some application-specific service provider objects in call (b) to implement the desired overall reaction. These objects, in turn, are usually based on some basic libraries such as for data structures, file I/O, or XML processing. Both calls (b) and (c) are then covered by the framework of contracts, because they clearly take place with a specific expectation on the side of the respective callers.

»9.1

←1.8.2

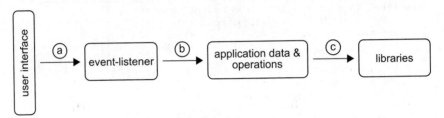

Figure 7.24 Event Handlers Based on Contracts

SWT's service methods do have contracts.

The second point where contracts remain important is the use of service methods in widgets and other SWT objects. For instance, when invoking `setText()` on a text entry field, you rightly expect that `getText()` will retrieve exactly the same string immediately afterward. The concepts of object state, model fields (here, the text value), and pre- and post-conditions therefore still apply to methods offered by SWT to the application.

In this context, there is only one minor deviation to be noted: The actual painting on the screen that follows the update of the widget's state will be delayed by a few milliseconds, because paint requests are queued and optimized before being carried out. In practice, this hardly matters, because the user is not aware of the delay and the software usually does not examine the screen's state at all.

←7.8

The concept of pre- and post-conditions does not fit event-listeners.

The initial observation of this part therefore mainly concerns the specification of event-listeners, for which no proper contract can be given. First, the caller usually supplies a detailed description of the event, which comes with the implicit pre-condition that this event has actually taken place. It should be noted that this pre-condition is not, in fact, a proper assertion, because it does not concern the current state of the program, but rather some past occurrence. Also, the pre-condition is generic for all interested event-listeners, while conventionally the pre-condition is specific to the single methods, as is made explicit in the advice of using a demanding style.

↰4.1

↰6.1.3

As for the post-condition, specifying one for a generic event-listener in the interface would mean that all possible implementations have to fulfill the expectation expressed in the post-condition. In summary, it is really the concepts of pre- and post-conditions that do not apply well to event-listeners.

↰6.4.1 ↰4.1

Class invariants become more important in event-driven software.

Class invariants, in contrast, become more important. When reasoning about the behavior of the code of a method, there are basically two sources of information about the current state at the start of the execution: the pre-condition and the class invariant, which captures the "proper state" of the object's encapsulated data structures. If the pre-condition is missing or generic, the class invariant must carry all the load.

↰4.7

↰4.1

Let us clarify this statement by examining a concrete example, the simple cash register application shown in Fig. 7.25. In this appication, the user enters 4-digit product codes and the application does all the bookkeeping: It looks up the code in the product database, adds the product's price to the current overall sum, displays the new sum and the new purchased product, and finally clears the entry field to receive the next product code.

```
                    swt.contracts.TillApp
1 private Map<String, Product> productDatabase =
2                          readProductDatabase();
3 private BigDecimal sum = new BigDecimal(0);
4
5 protected void addProduct(String code) {
6     Product p = productDatabase.get(code);
7     if (p != null) {
8         sum = sum.add(p.getPrice());
9         txtSum.setText(sum.toPlainString());
10        TableItem row = new TableItem(bill, SWT.NONE);
11        row.setText(0, p.getName());
12        row.setText(1, p.getPrice().toPlainString());
13        entry.setText("");
14    }
15 }
```

The heart of the matter is seen in lines 8–9: How do we know that the price we show to the user is the correct one? Why is sum actually the sum of the individual product prices? The answer is, of course, that this is just the class invariant: "The field sum contains the sum of the prices of products shown in the table bill." This invariant is maintained by the example code,

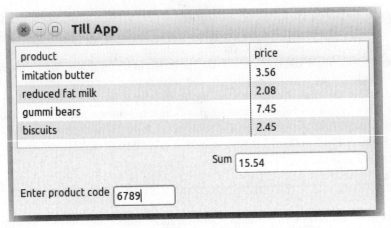

Figure 7.25 A Simple Cash Register Application

because just as it adds a new product to the bill in lines 10–12, it adds the product's price to the `sum` in line 8.

This situation is typical of user interface programming. That is, the incoming events do not carry any particular information about the application's purpose. That information is always kept in fields, and the class invariant explains how to interpret the fields.

Treat event-listeners as public methods with respect to contracts.

One central question in connection with class invariants is which code will be responsible for maintaining them. In the classical case of service providers, we have used the rule that `public` methods can assume the invariant at their beginning and must reestablish it at the end. The justification for the rule is that `public` methods serve as entry points to the class's code: Before they run, the invariant must hold, and after they finish, it must hold again.

From this perspective, we must now treat the event-listeners as entry points, because they get called from the outside, even if they do occur in private or anonymous classes and are therefore not accessible to the arbitrary clients. The rule to be obeyed is "Each event-listener can assume the class invariant initially and must guarantee it at the end." Here, "the invariant" refers to the invariant of the outer class surrounding the event-listener, since usually listeners do not have internal state themselves and often delegate the actual work to `protected` methods in the outer class.

Cross-object invariants can be broken temporarily.

↰4.1

↰2.1.3

Event-driven programming is very well suited to maintaining cross-object invariants, because events will signal any change that may violate an invariant so that the event handler can restore the invariant. For instance, different widgets in the same dialog or compound widget are often linked conceptually—for instance, because one displays the result of processing the input from the other. Fig. 7.26 shows a tiny example. The `Spinner` on top and the `Slider` at the bottom are linked by the invariant that "spinner and slider always hold the same value."

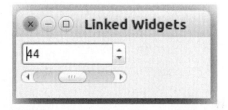

Figure 7.26 Linked Widgets Demo

As a result, when either of the widgets changes, the other must follow suit. This can be achieved directly by event handlers, because they are called precisely "whenever the value changes":

swt.contracts.LinkedWidgets.LinkedWidgets

```
spinner.addSelectionListener(new SelectionAdapter() {
    public void widgetSelected(SelectionEvent e) {
        slider.setSelection(spinner.getSelection());
    }
});
slider.addSelectionListener(new SelectionAdapter() {
    public void widgetSelected(SelectionEvent e) {
        spinner.setSelection(slider.getSelection());
    }
});
```

There is, however, a small caveat that has already been discussed in connection with invariants within compound objects. There, too, the connection between parts could be maintained by observers. However, the invariant was always broken for a brief time, and other observers were able to see this. The same reasoning applies to event handlers.   ↢6.2.3.5

The user interface belongs to the system boundary.

A final connection to contracts must be made in observing that the user interface belongs, of course, to the system boundary. There, the strict rule to be followed is that all input must be checked and no input can ever be trusted. In particular, the non-redundancy principle does not apply. In the case of the user interface, the software must never assume that the user obeys any rules about the order of entries or the values entered. Instead,   ↢4.6

↢4.5

229

every input must be checked and the user must be notified about any invalid inputs. Users will greatly appreciate and even expect this resilience of the software toward any errors on their part.

Chapter 8

A Brief Introduction to Threads

Programming with threads is in many ways very different from single-threaded code, and threads often exhibit surprising and unintuitive behavior. It would therefore be irresponsible to leave you with the impression that background threads in user interfaces are merely about how to start, stop, and track long-running tasks. This chapter highlights the new challenges and techniques that arise with using multiple threads, whether in the form of actual `Thread` objects or through task execution frameworks. We also hope to encourage you to follow up on this fascinating and practically highly relevant topic in the literature.

↰7.10

↰7.10.2

📖148

8.1 The Core: Parallel Code Execution

Modern users expect modern applications to do many things at once: to display animations, to perform extensive computations, to access the network, and many more. Managing these activities is much simplified if each task can be coded as if it were the only one, and then the Java platform takes care to execute the tasks at the same time, or at least virtually the same time. Threads enable precisely this programming model.

> Wrap code fragments in `Runnables` to start them in parallel.

Suppose, for instance, that one needs to download files and do heavy computation simultaneously. First, one wraps up the code as objects:

↰1.8.6

```
                    threads.MinimalThreads
class DownloadWorker implements Runnable {
    public void run() {
        ... perform work as if only task
    }
}
class ComputationWorker implements Runnable {
    public void run() {
        ... perform work as if only task
    }
}
```

Then, one can tell Java to execute the two fragments in the `run()` methods simultaneously, by constructing `Thread` objects and starting the threads.

threads.MinimalThreads.startActivities

```
new Thread(new DownloadWorker()).start();
new Thread(new ComputationWorker()).start();
```

⌨148

    This code shows the accepted way of creating threads. In principle, the API would allow overriding the `run()` method of `Thread` directly before starting the thread, but the solution presented here has the advantage of keeping the language infrastructure separate from the application objects.

The scheduler decides nondeterministically which threads get to run.

Fig. 8.1 shows the resulting runtime behavior. Code from the download task and the computation task is executed for brief periods of time, then is preempted and another thread gets to run. Since the switches happen so frequently, the user perceives the tasks as running simultaneously.

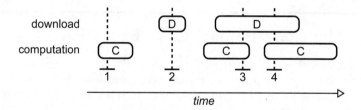

Figure 8.1 Interleaving of Code Execution by Threads

At this point, the connection between parallel and concurrent execution must be clarified. Because the scheduler makes tasks appear to be running simultaneously, one also says that the tasks execute *concurrently* and speaks of *concurrent execution*, *concurrent programming*, and so on. Since modern CPUs have multiple cores, threads very often will run truly in parallel: You cannot assume that other threads are stopped while your thread is working. The connection is captured succinctly by the popular characterization that "concurrency is potential parallelism."

Let us examine Fig. 8.1 in more detail. At points 1 and 2, the two threads run on their own, but the execution can actually overlap, as at points 3 and 4, if the system has multiple CPUs or a CPU with multiple cores. The question of which thread runs at which point in time is decided by a central *scheduler* component, which usually resides in the operating system. Its decisions are based on how many threads are waiting, their different priorities, whether a thread tries to read data that is not yet available, whether it is waiting for some lock, and many other details. From

»8.2

the application's perspective, its choices appear to be completely arbitrary and nondeterministic, so you should always assume that a thread might be running at any time, unless you actively prevent this—for instance, by using locks.

Threads create entirely new programming challenges.

The remainder of this chapter discusses solutions to the fundamental challenges arising from the use of threads (Fig. 8.2).

1. When two threads, with the unpredictable runtime behavior from Fig. 8.1, access the same data, the state of the data structure becomes unpredictable as well, because it is unclear which writes take effect before which reads. Because the central question is which one of several operations gets executed first, this problem is termed a *race condition*. The challenge is to restrain the nondeterministic behavior so that one can still create programs that are correct and perform reliably.

2. Sometimes, threads need to communicate, mostly about events. But each thread is running its own code, so they cannot simply call methods of one another. We need a mechanism for sending signals between threads and for waiting for signals within a thread.

3. The solution to the first problem consists of locking the data: Before a thread accesses the data, it must obtain the *lock* on the data. Since no two threads can ever obtain the lock at the same time, the order of writes and reads has become somewhat more predictable. However, a new problem arises: If threads access several pieces of data, it may happen that each of them acquires one lock and then waits indefinitely, because the other thread holds the other lock. Such *deadlocks* are dreaded because they are usually not reproducible, so that they are challenging to track down and fix.

Objects confined to threads do not require special attention.

Before we delve into the details, here is a shortcut that can be taken very often: If only a single thread holds a reference to an object, then it can work with that object as if there was no multithreading at all, since other threads cannot interfere with the object. This technique is called *confinement*. The object in question never "escapes from" a specific thread, and this is guaranteed by obeying a strict ownership discipline that avoids leaking object references to places where they might be accessible to other threads. Confinement is the deeper reason for introducing a dedicated event dispatch thread in user interfaces and using other threads only as "producers" of data that they hand to the event thread via `asyncExec()`. One effective strategy for coping with threads is to identify as many object structures as possible that can be managed within one thread. For the remaining cases, read on.

📖148(§2.3)

↰2.2.1

↰7.10.1

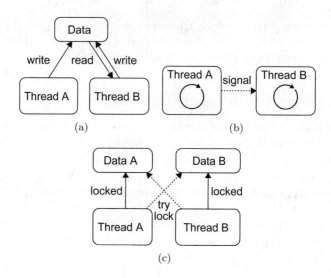

Figure 8.2 New Challenges with Threads

8.2   Correctness in the Presence of Threads

◄7.10

▶▶9.1
◄7.10.1

To keep the discussion focused, let us get back to the original motivation of background threads in user interfaces. Fig. 8.3 shows the pattern observed in many similar situations. The user interface spawns two threads A and B. Both collect data from somewhere and modify the application's data structures accordingly. The user interface mirrors that data on the screen. Since displaying the data already involves the event dispatch thread, the same problems will occur with a single background thread A alone. Here are some concrete examples of such situations:

- The application is a web browser and the threads perform different downloads simultaneously.

📖237

- The application is a server, and each thread is responsible for communicating with a single client.

📖235

- The application is Eclipse, and a builder thread transforms an EMF model into Java source code in a file that an editor is currently visiting.

Threads challenge the correctness arguments.

The primary challenge in the situation of Fig. 8.3 is that the access to *shared resources*, such as data structures or files, must be coordinated to avoid causing havoc in the resources' representations and endangering the

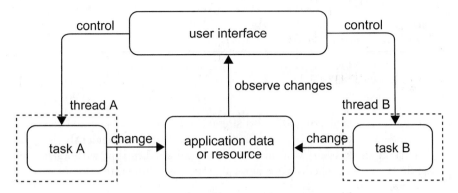

Figure 8.3 The Challenge of Multithreading

correctness of the software. After all, the entire correctness argument introduced with contracts at the core rests on the notion of assertions, which
capture knowledge about the program's behavior in statements of the form:
"Whenever execution reaches this point in the code, I know that … "

Threads introduce the problem of *interference*. That is, one thread
reaches an assertion and knows that it holds; in the next microsecond,
a second thread modifies the memory described by the assertion and the
assertion does not hold any longer. In other words, with threads you must
assume that unexpected modifications of memory can occur at any time—
unless you exclude them explicitly.

A particular danger lies in breaking the often intricate invariants of
objects. The invariant describes what a "proper object" looks like, and it
must hold whenever no code of the object's class runs. However, if the object
is currently "working," then it usually breaks the invariant temporarily. As
a result, a different thread accessing the same object can no longer assume
that the invariant holds.

To demonstrate the problem of interference, let us break a `GapText`
`Store`. Our previous analyses have convinced us that the code is correct.
Yet, the following code produces an exception: As soon as the access in line 7
happens to run simultaneously in the two threads created in lines 11 and 12,
some exception or other will be thrown; because of the intricate arithmetic
on indices, it is most probably an `ArrayIndexOutOfBoundsException`.

swt.threads.BreakRepresentation.main

```
1  final GapTextStore shared = new GapTextStore();
2  class Worker implements Runnable {
3      public void run() {
4          for (int i = 0; i != 10000; i++) {
5              String text = String.format("%03d ",
6                                          rand.nextInt(1000));
7              shared.replace(shared.getLength(), 0, text);
8          }
9      }
```

```
10 }
11 new Thread(new Worker()).start();
12 new Thread(new Worker()).start();
```

The minimal requirement is mutual exclusion.

Interference can occur at any time, unless one prevents it explicitly. *Mutual exclusion* means denying all but a single thread access to a shared resource for some period of time, so that the thread can work independently of other threads in the system. Mutual exclusion is minimal in that without it, the nondeterministic scheduling results in unpredictable states of the shared resource.

Mutual exclusion is usually accomplished by *locks*, as shown in the following code. First, we create a `Lock` object. Locks have two main methods `lock()` and `unlock()`. When a thread calls `lock()`, then it *acquires* the lock and *holds* it until it calls `unlock()`. The internal mechanisms guarantee that no two threads can ever hold the same lock simultaneously. If a thread calls `lock()` while another thread happens to hold the lock already, the first thread must simply wait until the lock becomes available again.

swt.threads.PreserveRepresentation.main

```
final Lock lock = new ReentrantLock();
```

🔍 The interface `Lock` specifies only the basic behavior, but there can be variations. A common one is a `ReentrantLock`, which allows a thread that already holds the lock to `lock()` it once more. The lock keeps a count of `lock()` and `unlock()` calls and frees the lock only when the counter reaches 0. This behavior is useful, for instance, when one `public` method calls another `public` method and both start by locking the entire object, as seen in the next example.

Using a lock, we can now protect the `GapTextStore` by replacing the problematic line 6 in the original with the following code block. In line 1, the thread executing the code obtains the lock, or waits until the lock is available. The crucial observation is that line 3 can be reached only by a single thread—namely, the thread that holds the `lock`. As a result, only a single thread at a time can perform the modification of the gap store, so that the correctness argument is not invalidated by interference, and no exception is ever thrown. The lock protects the code between `lock()` and `unlock()` from interference.

swt.threads.PreserveRepresentation.main

```
1 lock.lock();
2 try {
3     shared.replace(shared.getLength(), 0, text);
4 } finally {
```

```
5      lock.unlock();
6 }
```

Make sure to always release a lock you have acquired, since otherwise the shared resource can never be accessed again. The preceding code shows the idiom of using a `try-finally` combination for this purpose; regardless of how the protected region between `lock()` and `unlock()` is left, the lock is freed.

📖148
↰1.5.6

Very often, locks are conceptually associated with a specific object, or a group of objects. Code that wishes to work with the object has to acquire the lock beforehand and release it afterward. In such cases, one says that one holds the lock *on* the object, even if the connection is only conceptual, not technical.

Java offers a built-in locking mechanism through the `synchronized` keyword. Each object has an associated lock that `synchronized` acquires and releases, usually for the `this` object. Writing `synchronized` before all `public` methods of a class protects its internal invariants: Only one thread at a time can ever enter the class's code, so the normal correctness arguments apply. Such objects are also called *monitors*. (Unfortunately, that term is used by the Java Language Specification in a different sense.) Compared to `Lock` objects, this mechanism is much less flexible. We will discuss the inflexibility later at the appropriate points.

📖148

↰4.1

Multithreading on modern processors goes beyond nondeterministic execution of one thread or another. The threads may actually run in parallel, on different CPUs or different cores of the same CPU (Fig. 8.4). The memory hierarchy of the processor then introduces a new problem beyond mere interference: When one thread overwrites the memory accessed by a different thread, the other thread may not even become aware of the fact. Suppose one thread runs on CPU A and writes some data to a shared object. For efficiency, that data is not written through to main memory, but is kept in the CPU's local cache A until the cache is required elsewhere. The second thread, when it runs, reads only from its own local cache B and is not aware of the new data in cache A.

📖115

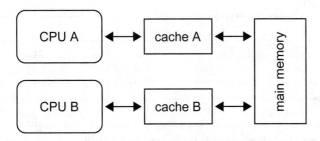

Figure 8.4 Threads and Caching

Java's mutual exclusion mechanisms also include a *memory barrier*, which synchronizes the different caches and the main memory at the hardware level, thereby ensuring that all threads do see the current data stored in an object. The keyword `volatile` also introduces a memory barrier, without providing locking at the same time. The details are specified in the *Java Memory Model*. The specification itself is rather daunting. Essentially, it guarantees that when using locking or `volatile`, the reads and writes to a memory location are always properly ordered in the sense that a read either sees or doesn't see a write, depending on the scheduler's decisions, but there is no state of undefinedness in between.

📖111,166

Make protection from interference part of the encapsulation.

The guard for the shared gap store in the example is rather unreliable, since all clients must obey the protocol of acquiring the lock before accessing the store. A better solution is to build objects in such a way that they protect their own data structures and invariants by its own locks. Such objects are called *thread-safe*.

↰2.4

In the example, we could just wrap the `GapTextStore` in a class that acquires a lock before accessing the wrapped store, as shown next. If each `public` method proceeds in the same way as `replace()`, then the invariants of the store are always safe and clients cannot circumvent the locking protocol.

swt.threads.ThreadSafeTextStore

```java
class ThreadSafeTextStore {
    private Lock lock = new ReentrantLock();
    private GapTextStore rep = new GapTextStore();
    public final void replace(int offset, int length, String text) {
        lock.lock();
        try {
            rep.replace(offset, length, text);
        } finally {
            lock.unlock();
        }
    }

    ... similarly for get() and getLength()
}
```

🔍 In such small examples, the coding overhead for lock acquisition and release does seem rather tremendous. In real-world code, the locks protect longer sequences of operations, so that the necessary `try-finally` block is not as intrusive.

🌍 The Java library offers wrappers for the classes of the collections framework. To make an `ArrayList` thread-safe, one wraps it by `Collections.synchronizedList()`. The concurrency library in `java.util.concurrent` also offers special data structures, such as `ConcurrentHashMap`, which are thread-safe but may also allow more concurrency—

for instance, for simultaneous traversals through iterators. For storing single values in a thread-safe manner, one use the classes `AtomicInteger`, `AtomicIntegerArray`, and so on from `java.util.concurrent.atomic`.

Since the new gap store objects are thread-safe, one can simply share an instance between threads.

swt.threads.ThreadSafeRepresentation.main

```
final ThreadSafeTextStore shared = new ThreadSafeTextStore();
```

The problematic access in the example no longer requires explicit protection.

swt.threads.ThreadSafeRepresentation.main

```
shared.replace(shared.getLength(), 0, text);
```

From a higher perspective, thread-safe objects encapsulate not only their data structures, but also the protection of those data structures. Their `Lock` objects become part of their internal representation, and one can formulate assertions about whether the lock is currently held at some given point. The main advantage is that clients no longer have to understand the necessity to lock, so this is one more encapsulated detail.

Beware of multistep operations and cross-object invariants.

Thread-safety is not the ultimate solution to threading problems, but addresses only a bare minimum requirement: When the invariants of objects are broken, there is no chance of ever obtaining correct software. However, it is important to remember that even a thread-safe object can potentially be modified *between* two calls to locking methods, so that the assertions *about* the object's state may get broken.

To demonstrate, consider the following very simple case: We append a string `text` to the thread-safe text store `shared` in lines 1–2 and read the text back immediately afterward in line 3. Lines 4–7 write an error message if the text has been changed unexpectedly.

swt.threads.MultiStepBroken.main

```
1 int insertAt = shared.getLength();
2 shared.replace(insertAt, 0, text);
3 String retrieved = shared.get(insertAt, text.length());
4 if (!retrieved.equals(text)) {
5     System.err.println("Unexpected text read back at position "
6             + insertAt + " and step " + i);
7 }
```

In a single-threaded setting, we can track the state of `shared` in detail by ↰4.7 assertions. After line 2, `shared` contains `text` at `insertAt`, so `retrieved` should be the same text. Surprisingly often, however, this is not the case.

In experiments with executing the preceding code 10,000 times in a loop in two threads, usually between 20 and 60 violations were detected.

Lock objects that are mentioned in assertions.

The previously mentioned experiments show that there is no such thing as "immediately afterward" with threads; thus, you should always assume that a different thread *will* happen to run at the most inappropriate moment. This attitude is very similar to the advice to be paranoid about the correctness of software.

↶4.1

↶4.1

In consequence, whenever one makes an assertion about an object in a multithreaded context, one must check at the same time that one holds a lock on the object. Assertions without locks will always be broken at some point by an unfortunate combination of thread interactions.

In the preceding example, the crucial lines 1–3 work with shared, and it is in this code region that we make assumptions about the state of shared. Lines 4–7, in contrast, work with local variables, which cannot be accessed from a different thread. The minimum required locking therefore protects the problematic steps, as shown here:

```
                    swt.threads.MultiStepCorrect.main
int insertAt;
String retrieved;
shared.lock();
try {
    insertAt = shared.getLength();
    shared.replace(insertAt, 0, text);
    retrieved = shared.get(insertAt, text.length());
} finally {
    shared.unlock();
}
```

Note that we must use the lock built into shared, because otherwise other clients of that object resource might still modify it at the same time. The ThreadSafeTextStore therefore exports its lock.

```
                    swt.threads.ThreadSafeTextStore
public void lock() {
    lock.lock();
}
public void unlock(){
    lock.unlock();
}
```

🔍 At this point, we see the first advantage of explicit locks over synchronized. That statement always releases the lock in the same method where it obtains the lock—it supports block-structured locking. Explicit `Lock` objects, in contrast, can be held for arbitrary periods of time, independently of the program's block structure.

Missing mutual exclusion makes for elusive bugs.

It is important to realize that a missing lock may not show up immediately, but may remain undetected for a very long time. Especially if the shared data structure is accessed only infrequently, chances are that the bug will lie dormant for months or even years. When it does show up, it will be hard to trace down and virtually impossible to reproduce. You should really be paranoid about holding all necessary locks.

8.3   Notifications Between Threads

We have seen the wide application and importance of notifications through the OBSERVER pattern. Event-driven software generalizes this idea to say   ↰2.1
that an object's behavior can be understood as reactions to events. It is therefore necessary to investigate the connection with threads: What happens if the execution of one thread discovers some state change or event that a different thread should be notified about or that it is even waiting for? Unlike with the usual pattern, one cannot simply call a method on a thread and pass some event object. Instead, the software must include mechanisms to synchronize the working of threads at specific points.

We use a simple example to understand the mechanics of interthread notifications [Fig. 8.5(a)]: The user enters a number that gets processed in a background thread. The result of the processing appears in the list below the entry field. Fig. 8.5(b) shows the sequence of necessary steps from a high-level perspective. The example involves two threads, the SWT event   ↰7.10.1
dispatch thread and a background worker thread. The new challenge is the synchronization in step 2 of Fig. 8.5(b), which passes the entered number across the thread boundary.

But let us treat the other steps first to get the overall picture. In step 1, when the user presses enter in the text field, an event-listener dispatches the number for processing:

```
                    swt.threads.ConditionsDemo.ConditionsDemo
number.addSelectionListener(new SelectionAdapter() {
    public void widgetDefaultSelected(SelectionEvent e) {
        int input = Integer.parseInt(number.getText());
        number.setText("");
        sendNumber(input);
    }
});
```

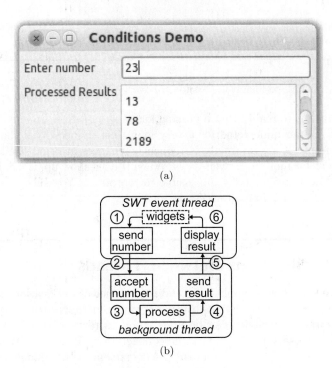

(a)

(b)

Figure 8.5 Mechanics of the Conditions Demo

↰8.1

🔍 In this code, we finish the UI-level work before sending off the number. Had we left `number.setText()` as the last statement, the answer might have arrived before the old number was cleared. Although in the specific example this does not matter, we prefer to keep the sequence clear: We complete fetching the number from the UI before starting the processing.

Step 3 in Fig. 8.5(b) is a simple method call to `processNumber()`, which is a no-op and passes the input on in step 4:

swt.threads.ConditionsDemo

```
public void processNumber(Integer number) {
    Integer result = number; // pseudo-"processing"
    sendResult(result);
}
```

↰7.10.1

In step 5, the worker thread accesses the user interface in the usual manner using `asyncExec()`. Step 6 is inlined in the following code:

swt.threads.ConditionsDemo.sendResult

```
display.asyncExec(new Runnable() {
    public void run() {
        if (!results.isDisposed()) {
```

```
            results.add(result.toString());
        }
    }
});
```

In case you are wondering about the asymmetry, recall that step 5 involves a second   ↰7.10.1
queue, with very similar coding idioms as the ones shown next. It is the SWT event
queue, but it remains hidden in the implementation of `asyncExec()`.

So the remaining task is to complete step 2 in Fig. 8.5(b). The general
approach is shown in Fig. 8.6. The two threads share a lock `dataLock`,
a *condition variable* `dataAvailable`, and a plain, unsynchronized queue
`postbox` for buffering data. Briefly speaking, condition variables enable
signals to be sent across thread boundaries. Here is what will happen: (1)
The worker thread keeps waiting for a signal that new data is available.
(2) When the user enters a new number, the SWT thread acquires the lock
for synchronization, (3) pushes the data into the queue, and (4) sends the
signal that the worker is waiting for. (5) The worker then acquires the lock
and fetches the newly arrived data from the queue.

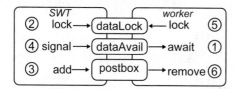

Figure 8.6 Using Condition Variables for Thread Synchronization

So much for the conceptual side. Because of interactions between the
lock and the condition variables, the technical details and coding idioms
are somewhat more involved.

Condition variables serve to signal state changes between threads.

Our example follows a standard approach to the producer–consumer pattern (Fig. 7.22, page 397): The producer drops data into a queue, where
the consumer can pick it up later. In the next code snippet, we create the
setup from Fig. 8.6: A `postbox` contains the actual data, and we choose a
plain linked list. Since different threads will work with the data, we need a
`dataLock` to protect the accesses.

---
swt.threads.ConditionsDemo

```
private Queue<Integer> postbox = new LinkedList<Integer>();
private Lock dataLock = new ReentrantLock();
private Condition dataAvailable = dataLock.newCondition();
```

The new element in the example is the *condition variable* data
Available. A condition variable enables one thread to suspend execution
until a particular condition on the program state may hold, which a different thread signals through the condition variable after it has changed the
program state. The qualification "may hold" is necessary, of course, because
the state may change again between the sending and the processing of the
notification. Also, the condition variable does not check whether the signal
is actually justified. Condition variables are always associated with locks,
because otherwise the notifications themselves may be prone to interference
and race conditions.

↰8.2

In the current example, the condition variable dataAvailable will be
used to signal the specific state that the postbox now contains data. When
the user presses "enter" in the number field, a listener for the widget
DefaultSelected event executes the following code. It locks the postbox
as usual to guarantee exclusive access. It then pushes the new number into
the queue (line 3). Finally, it uses the condition variable dataAvailable
to send a signal to any waiting thread that new data has arrived (line 4).

swt.threads.ConditionsDemo.sendNumber

```
1 dataLock.lock();
2 try {
3     postbox.add(number);
4     dataAvailable.signalAll();
5 } finally {
6     dataLock.unlock();
7 }
```

🔍 Like a lock, the condition variable is not technically associated with a specific data
structure or a state of that data structure. The chosen name reflects the conceptual
relationship to keep the code readable.

📖 148

🔍 The method signalAll() wakes up all threads waiting for the given condition. It is
customary to use signalAll() even if one expects only a single thread to be waiting,
because *lost signals* can easily occur if there happen to be several threads and the one
being woken up cannot handle the signal. The idioms for preventing lost signals would
complicate the code, while the gain in runtime would be marginal. It is better to be
conservative when programming with threads.

The background thread keeps on processing numbers from the postbox.
(The loop follows in the next code snippet.) Whenever it is ready for the
next input, it will look at the postbox. If no number has arrived as yet, it
must wait. Conditions enable the thread to implement just this behavior.
Since the thread needs to access the postbox, it acquires the corresponding lock (lines 1–2, 8–10). The counterpart of the signaling from the event

thread is found in lines 3–4: The background thread checks whether the postbox contains data and otherwise goes to sleep until the event thread announces that data is available. Once data becomes available, it is processed as usual in lines 5–7.

```
                        swt.threads.ConditionsDemo.run
1 dataLock.lock();
2 try {
3     while (postbox.isEmpty())
4         dataAvailable.await();
5     do {
6         processNumber(postbox.remove());
7     } while (!postbox.isEmpty());
8 } finally {
9     dataLock.unlock();
10 }
```

Three crucial details are worth mentioning. First, calling `await()` on a condition variable also releases the lock that it is associated with. In the preceding code, line 4 therefore releases the lock acquired in line 1. This is necessary to enable other threads to modify the data structure—here the postbox—at all, because they need the lock to do so. When a signal is received and `await()` is about to return, it reacquires the lock. (If several threads have called `await()`, the first one to acquire the lock proceeds; the others continue to wait for the lock to become available.)

As a related second detail, the entire region from line 1 to line 9 is protected by the lock from the thread's perspective. In particular, when the check in line 3 detects available data, then this assertion cannot be ↰8.2 invalidated by interference afterward, so that line 6 is justified in assuming that the call to `remove()` will not fail. (We have chosen a `do-while` loop to demonstrate this detail.)

Finally, the `while` loop in line 3 needs explaining: Would not an `if` be sufficient? After all, the intuition is to "wait *if* no data needs processing." The problem with this reasoning is that it assumes that the `await()` returns precisely if data is available. However, there are several reasons why this might not be the case. Not all are valid in the current context, but they explain the general idiom of using a `while` loop. First, several threads might wait simultaneously and the first one to reacquire the lock after `await()` would process all the data. The others would wake up to find that no data is available after all and would fail in line 6. Second, the condition might be signaled inadvertently, especially if the condition variable is used by many clients or is even `public`. Finally, the Java platform does not guarantee absolutely that `await()` returns only when a corresponding `signal()` has been called—*spurious wakeups* may make `await()` return without provocation. Since programming with threads should be very conservative, one *always* uses a loop to wait for the desired condition.

In summary, the example has introduced the fundamental idea of sending notifications between threads: One uses conditions to send the actual signal and employs data structures to contain the event objects or other data associated with the notifications. Conditions can be thought of as a predefined interthread observer pattern.

> Use predefined building blocks for synchronization wherever possible.

↰8.2

This idiom for sending and receiving notifications is extremely common. The Java library offers a set of *blocking queues* that encapsulate all the necessary locking and signaling. The term refers to the fact that these queues will block the execution of reading threads when no data is available and the execution of writing threads when the queue's capacity is exhausted. Blocking queues offer just the functionality for passing data items or events safely from one thread to the other.

As a result, blocking queues make programming with threads a breeze. In the previous example, we can replace the bare `postbox` with a synchronized queue.

---

swt.threads.BlockingQueueDemo

```java
private BlockingQueue<Integer> postbox =
            new LinkedBlockingQueue<Integer>();
```

Whenever the user enters data, the event dispatch thread puts it into the queue, relying on the queue's internal mechanisms to take care of all interthread communication issues.

---

swt.threads.BlockingQueueDemo.sendNumber

```java
postbox.put(Integer.parseInt(number.getText()));
number.setText("");
```

Likewise, the background thread can simply fetch the next item from the queue. The method `take()` blocks until data is actually available.

---

swt.threads.BlockingQueueDemo.run

```java
processData(postbox.take());
```

↰7.10.1 ▭148

🔍 Blocking queues are the basic ingredient to implementing producer–consumer relationships between threads: One thread keeps producing data and putting it into the queue; the other thread keeps taking data from the queue and processing it further. In such a situation, one more aspect of synchronization must be considered—namely, that of processing speed. If producing data is much quicker than processing it in the consumer, then memory will overflow with the items stored in the queue. For this reason, blocking queues in the library usually have a fixed *capacity*. When the producer calls `put()` and the queue is already full, then the call will block, making the behavior symmetric to that of `take()` on an empty queue. As a result, the producer will be slowed down to the speed of the consumer and a memory overflow is avoided.

In the preceding example, the `LinkedBlockingQueue` has unbounded capacity, which mirrors the previous behavior of the postbox and ensures that the call to `put()` will not block in the event thread, which would freeze the user interface. This situation is really special. In usual producer–consumer relationships, you should prefer queues with a limited capacity.

The library supports further common synchronization tasks. For instance, a `CountDownLatch` enables a thread to wait until one or more other threads have reached some specific point—for example, until all threads have started up or have finished processing different parts of a computation. A `CyclicBarrier` lets threads wait for one another repeatedly at specific points, such as when data needs to be exchanged. It is highly advisable to look through the library before attempting to implement a custom mechanism.

📖148

Stop threads using `interrupt()`.

The final notification between threads concerns their termination. Suppose the user interface has started a background thread, but the expected results have become redundant due to further user actions. How should one notify the thread about this event? Within the Eclipse framework, this is accomplished through the progress monitors. At the level of the threads themselves, *interrupts* serve the purpose.

↰7.10.2

In the running example of processing entered numbers, the background thread must be stopped when the dialog closes. We attach a `Dispose Listener` to the dialog and interrupt the background thread (line 5).

```
                    swt.threads.ConditionsDemo.ConditionsDemo
1 workerThread = new Thread(worker);
2 workerThread.start();
3 addDisposeListener(new DisposeListener() {
4     public void widgetDisposed(DisposeEvent e) {
5         workerThread.interrupt();
6     }
7 });
```

The thread being interrupted may receive the interrupt in two possible ways. When it is currently blocked in waiting for some signal or condition to occur, such as through `await()` on a `Condition` or `take()` on a `BlockingQueue`, the call will return with an `InterruptedException` (possibly after waiting to reacquire any released locks). Otherwise, the thread's built-in *interruption status flag* will be set to `true`.

The processing loop of the running example, shown next, exhibits a common idiom for handling interrupts. Before starting on any further work, the thread checks whether it has already been interrupted (line 2). Otherwise, it waits for more data and processes it. Furthermore, it expects an `InterruptedException` to be thrown while it waits for new data. Lines 5–8 exhibit the idiom of converting the exception to a set interruption status

📖148

flag to unify the two cases of receiving an interruption. In the example, the loop and the thread then terminate.

```
                         swt.threads.ConditionsDemo
1  public void run() {
2      while (!Thread.currentThread().isInterrupted()) {
3          try {
4              ...
5          } catch (InterruptedException exc) {
6              // convert to flag
7              Thread.currentThread().interrupt();
8          }
9      }
10 }
11
```

In summary, the thread terminates itself rather than being terminated from the outside. The interrupt sent by another thread is understood as a kind request. In particular, the receiver must be exception-safe for possible InterruptedExceptions, meaning it must close open resources and leave invariants of data structures intact.

↰1.5.6

⚠ Do not ignore InterruptedExceptions. When writing code, these exceptions often appear to be merely a nuisance to be dealt with later on, and one is tempted to add an empty catch clause to be rid of them. However, you should be aware that the proper termination of a thread is just as much a part of its life cycle and behavior as the actual processing that it performs. Properly handling InterruptedExceptions is part of the requirements.

⚠ Be aware of which blocking methods are interruptible. For instance, the method Lock.lock() blocks until the lock becomes available but it is *not* terminated with an InterruptedException when the thread receives an interrupt in the meantime. The reason is that usually one does not expect to wait long for locks, so that the behavior is a useful default. If your application does expect to wait longer, it might make sense to use lockInterruptibly() instead.

🔍 The ability to lock while accepting interrupts and the ability to lock with a given timeout are two more aspects that make Lock objects much more flexible than the built-in synchronized command.

⚠ Never use the stop() method on Threads. It aborts the computation immediately without giving the thread the chance to clean up. Even the finally clauses, which are used to protect against unexpected termination, will *not* be executed.

↰1.5.6

Ensure that all threads that get started are also interrupted.

Threads that are no longer required must be interrupted to free their resources. One further reason is that the JVM will not terminate until all started threads have terminated. In user interface examples, this means that even closing their shell and terminating their event dispatch thread will not be sufficient. It is necessary to add a dispose-listener as shown earlier. The requirement to stop threads is really no different from the general injunction of managing an object's life cycle, for instance, by unregistering the object from all subjects that it observes and freeing any resources it might hold.

↰2.1.2
↰7.4.1

⌕ The JVM offers *daemon threads* that get terminated automatically when the last non-daemon thread terminates. As a result, daemon threads never force the JVM to keep running. However, daemon threads are stopped abruptly, without any notification to the threads themselves, and the reasons against using `Thread.stop()` apply here as well.

8.4   Asynchronous Messages

Normal communication between objects consists of calling methods of each other. Since method calls are always associated with technical details of parameter passing and the call stack, it is simpler to use the abstraction that objects communicate by sending messages to each other, even if in the end "sending a message" really translates to calling a method. The objects in this abstraction become more independent of one another, with one sending a message and the other reacting appropriately.

↰1.4.1 ↰1.1

In the context of threads, this independence can be strengthened, since the receiving object does not have to react to a message immediately, but can defer processing until a convenient time. Such messages are called *asynchronous messages*. Fig. 8.7 gives an overview. Object A lives in a thread 1; its code is executed in that thread. Object B lives in a different thread 2. Usually, B will execute a loop to wait for messages and call the appropriate methods on itself. If A wants to send a message to B, it puts the message into a synchronized queue and proceeds with its own processing. At some later point, B will receive the message and react to it. Since the sender does not wait for a return value, any results are often transmitted again asynchronously through a second queue, shown as dashed lines in the figure.

↰8.3

For a concrete example, consider a user interface that downloads web pages in the background. Object A in Fig. 8.7 is part of the user interface

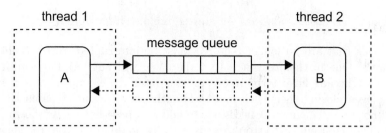

Figure 8.7 Asynchronous Messages

↰7.10.1 and lives in the event thread. It uses the following method `download()` whenever it requires a web page. Lines 2–4 create a request and display it in a table. Line 5 associates the table row with the request in a hash map. This is necessary because of asynchronous completion: When the answer to the request arrives, its result has to be shown in the correct table row.

swt.threads.AsyncMessages

```
1 public void download(String url) throws InterruptedException {
2     DownloadRequest req = new DownloadRequest(url);
3     TableItem item = new TableItem(table, SWT.NONE);
4     item.setText(0, url);
5     openRequests.put(req, item);
6     requests.put(req);
7 }
```

The results, through the dashed queue in Fig. 8.7, are received in a separate thread, which executes the following loop and displays the results ↰7.10.1 in the correct table row (switching to the event thread as usual).

swt.threads.AsyncMessages.run

```
while (true) {
    final DownloadResult res = results.take();
    final TableItem origin = openRequests.remove(res.request);
    display.asyncExec(new Runnable() {
        public void run() {
            origin.setText(1, res.message);
        }
    });
}
```

▯218 The ASYNCHRONOUS COMPLETION TOKEN pattern generalizes this approach to messages sent between processes and over the network. In this setting, the original request to which an answer belongs cannot be given by a simple object reference, as done in the preceding example, because the asynchronous message leaves the JVM's address space. Instead, each request contains a unique identifier, the completion token, which the receiver passes back unmodified with the answer. The sender keeps a table of open requests to assign the incoming answers correctly.

Functional languages—notably Erlang, ML, and Scala—have long since discovered that sending asynchronous messages through message queues is a viable model of concurrent execution itself. Rather than having to talk about bare-bones threads executing methods of objects, one can talk directly about objects, sometimes called *actors* in this context, which send and receive messages through *channels*. The fact that asynchronous messages can carry entire programming models highlights their practical utility.

📖16 📖212 📖113

Asynchronous messages introduce some extra complexity, since we cannot wait for the return value of a method call as usual. Sometimes it will be possible to hide this complexity. The ACTIVE OBJECT pattern gives the general idea.

📖218

PATTERN: ACTIVE OBJECT

The ACTIVE OBJECT pattern offers an abstraction over asynchronous message processing (Fig. 8.8) by encapsulating the details of queuing and multithreading. Internally, the active object contains a *servant*, which contains the real functionality. To the outside, the active object acts as a PROXY for that servant. It starts a *scheduler* thread, which repeatedly takes method calls from an *activation queue* and calls the corresponding method in the *servant*.

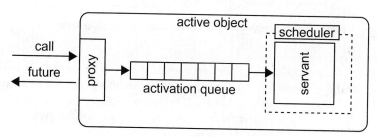

Figure 8.8 Active Object Pattern

Clients of active objects appear to simply call methods on the proxy, knowing that the calls will be processed asynchronously in the background. Active objects can maintain this abstraction of method calls for the return values by employing *futures*. Futures are simply containers for the value to be computed later on. The active object's methods return a future immediately, and the client can later obtain the result by calling `get()` on the future. If the processing has not yet been completed, the call blocks. The Java library contains a collection of future implementations, which are intended to be used with the executors framework.

📖148

8.5   Open Calls for Notification

↰2.1

User interfaces and event-driven software in general rely heavily on notifications, and in particular on the OBSERVER pattern. In connection with threads, a fundamental question is whether notifications should be sent while holding the lock or after releasing it. Notifications sent without holding on to the lock are termed *open calls*. We will now look at the consequences and the differences to the usual observer pattern that result from this relaxation of locking.

📖148

↰8.2

»9.1

Fig. 8.9 is a typical situation: The application data is stored in some thread-safe object, so that background threads can work with it by calling the available methods to perform operations. The user interface seeks to reflect the state of the data on the screen in a timely fashion. For that purpose, it registers an observer and updates the display according to the reported changes.

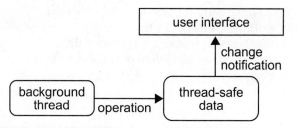

Figure 8.9 Reflecting Thread-Safe Data in the User Interface

As a concrete example, let us examine a class ThreadSafeData that maintains a single value data, as a representative for a larger data structure. The first and obvious way to implement the OBSERVER pattern here would be the following: We protect both the actual modification and the change notification by locking, so as to make the whole block behave just as in the single-threaded setting.

```
                    swt.threads.ThreadSafeData
1  public void setValueSync(int value) {
2      lock.lock();
3      try {
4          int oldData = this.value;
5          this.value = value;
6          changes.firePropertyChange("data", oldData, value);
7      } finally {
8          lock.unlock();
9      }
10 }
```

When we turn to the user interface, we see that this strict locking discipline may, in fact, not be necessary. The user interface registers a listener with the data structure, uses `asyncExec` to switch to the event thread, and updates the text field `value` with the new content of the data structure (lines 6–7).

---
swt.threads.ReflectThreadSafeData.setThreadSafeData

```
1  public void propertyChange(final PropertyChangeEvent evt) {
2      display.asyncExec(new Runnable() {
3          public void run() {
4              if (isDisposed())
5                  return;
6              int curValue = data.getValue();
7              value.setText(String.format("%03d", curValue));
8              int reportedValue = (Integer) evt.getNewValue();
9              state.setText(reportedValue == curValue ? "==" : "!=");
10         }
11     });
12 }
```

Lines 8–9 drive home the crucial point of the example: They check whether the current value of `data` is still the same as the value reported with the change event—that is, the value for which the event has been sent originally. When the background threads keep modifying the shared data structure, this will usually not be the case: Line 2 schedules the runnable to be executed on the event thread at some later point, so the code at line 4 does not start executing immediately and there is plenty of time for the thread to modify the data in between (see also Fig. 7.21 on page 396).

Notifications with locks provide strong guarantees.

Now suppose we attach a second listener to the shared data. It is independent of the user interface and simply checks whether the data is still intact when the listener receives the callback. In fact, this is always the case, because the lock in `setValueSync()` prevents a change between lines 5 and 6 of that method.

---
swt.threads.DifferencingObserver

```
public void propertyChange(PropertyChangeEvent evt) {
    int reportedValue = (Integer) evt.getNewValue();
    int actualValue = data.getValue();
    if (reportedValue != actualValue)
        System.out.format("detected difference %03d != %03d\n",
            reportedValue, actualValue);
}
```

From a more general perspective, sending notifications while still holding the lock ensures that the observers see exactly the state that is the result of a single modification. This behavior is just the same as in a single-threaded environment. This strong guarantee is bought at the expense that no other thread can work with the data structure until all observers have finished.

Open calls can decrease lock contention.

📖148

The example of the user interface also shows that in many situations the observers do not rely on finding exactly the state as it was after the change. That is, they will look at the data structure anyway to retrieve the most recent values, so it does not matter whether these have been changed in the meantime. We can therefore recode the setter in `ThreadSafeData`: Before sending out the notifications in line 10; we release the lock in line 8 to enable other threads to operate on the data.

---
                         swt.threads.ThreadSafeData

```
1 public void setDataOpen(int value) {
2     lock.lock();
3     int oldValue;
4     try {
5         oldValue = this.value;
6         this.value = value;
7     } finally {
8         lock.unlock();
9     }
10    changes.firePropertyChange("data", oldValue, value);
11 }
```

Open calls in general are notifications, whether to observers or calls to arbitrary collaborators, that are sent without holding on to locks after the actual operation has completed. When the data structure in question is central to the application and is heavily used by different threads, then switching to open calls for notifications can make the application more efficient, because fewer threads must wait for the lock—the potential for *lock contention* is reduced. Open calls can also help prevent deadlocks, as will be clarified by our later analysis of that phenomenon.

»8.6

Open calls can endanger correctness.

↰2.1.3

Suppose the data structure is a list and the observer pattern follows the usual *push* variant, in which the subject sends along detailed change information. One change might read "added item at position 5." However, when the observer finally receives the call, that item might already have been moved elsewhere, or the index 5 might be invalid because the list has been emptied in the meantime.

↰8.2 ↰4.1

In essence, this behavior once again reflects assertions invalidated by interference. At the end of the list operation, the index was valid because the assertion "the index is in the list" was protected by the lock. As soon as the lock is released, the assertion can be invalidated.

Use open calls only when no observer will rely on the stronger guarantees.

We have presented open calls here mainly to point out their challenges, and to discuss the decision necessary about holding onto or releasing a lock for notifications. Open calls can be useful in heavily used data structures, but they require all possible receivers of the calls to be aware of the fact that the message they receive may no longer be up-to-date.

Open calls are very similar to asynchronous messages in this respect: There, too, the reception of the message may be delayed to the point that the data that it concerns has changed in the meantime. The huge success of message-driven systems such as Erlang's actors shows that open calls do have a place in performance-critical applications.

↰8.4

📖16

8.6 Deadlocks

There is one more complication in connection with threads that needs to be discussed: *deadlocks*. In general, this term covers situations where one or more threads fail to make progress because a condition that they are waiting for can never occur. More particularly, deadlocks happen when threads cannot obtain the locks they require because other threads hold onto those locks and cannot make progress themselves.

Deadlocks arise easily in operations involving multiple objects.

We will illustrate the problem in the context of multistep operations. These must often obtain multiple locks on different objects from a collection that is shared with other threads, since they can exclude interference only by holding all the necessary locks for the entire duration of the operation.

↰8.2

Let us proceed with a simple example, where operations simply copy sections of text from one ThreadSafeTextStore to another. At the core, they perform the following actions (lines 4–6): They compute the section of text to be copied, obtain the characters from the source, and write them to the destination. Both src and dst are shared among different operations running simultaneously. Therefore, assertions established about the character range in line 4 hold true in lines 5–6 only if the whole sequence is protected by locks.

↰8.2

swt.threads.DeadlocksBroken.main

```
1 src.lock();
2 dst.lock();
3 try {
4     ... determine positions and length for
5     String text = src.get(srcOffset, srcLength);
6     dst.replace(dstOffset, 0, text);
```

```
7 } finally {
8     src.unlock();
9     dst.unlock();
10 }
```

So far, the code looks good, and no assertion can ever be broken by inter-ference. However, it can easily happen that operations prevent one another from obtaining the necessary locks in lines 1–2. Suppose, for instance, that two operations copy texts around between two buffers, as in the following setup: One copies from a to b, the other in the other direction. (`Worker` performs this action many times in its `run()` method.)

swt.threads.DeadlocksBroken.main

```
new Thread(new Worker(a, b)).start();
new Thread(new Worker(b, a)).start();
```

Now a new interaction between threads occurs. The action starts by locking both the source and the target, as would be expected:

swt.threads.DeadlocksBroken.main

```
1 src.lock();
2 dst.lock();
```

However, the two threads lock in a different order: The first thread locks a and then b, but the second thread locks b and then a. As a result, each thread may acquire in line 1 the very lock that the other thread is trying to acquire in line 2. Effectively, the threads prevent each other from proceed-ing beyond line 2, and the application, or at least some of its background threads, freezes completely.

As before, such a problem may or may not occur depending on the exact timing. If one thread happens to pass lines 1–2 while the other is doing something else, everything will be in order. Such bugs can be difficult to trace and to fix, because their manifestation depends on the exact timings of the run and the decisions taken by the scheduler.

↰8.1

Avoid deadlocks by resource ordering.

The core of the deadlock problem lies in the different order in which the threads acquire the locks. If both threads were to lock first a and then b, regardless of which is their respective source and destination, then nothing bad would happen: the thread which first locks a can also proceed to lock b, since the other thread is still waiting for its first lock on a. This seems simple enough, but does this idea also work with more than two objects? The answer is "yes", and the approach is called *resource ordering*.

To see the point, suppose there are many threads working on a collection of objects, as shown in Fig. 8.10(a). Each object is protected by a specific lock, which a thread must acquire before working with the object. The dotted lines indicate the order in which each thread would like to acquire

📖148

the necessary locks. In the example, all threads at some point require the object in the middle, but otherwise they access different sets of objects, sharing only some with other threads.

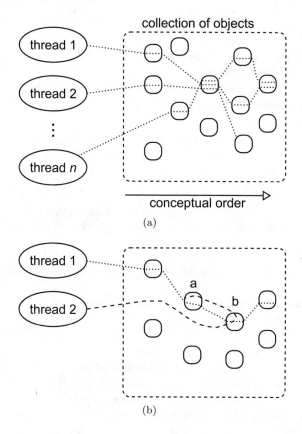

Figure 8.10 Intuition of Resource Ordering

The intuition of the picture suggests that deadlocks are avoided if threads always lock objects "left-to-right." A deadlock would require a situation like that in Fig. 8.10(b), where thread 1 locks a, thread 2 locks b, and then thread 2 goes "back left" to lock a. However, this cannot happen if locking proceeds from left to right.

The graphical notion of "locking left-to-right" can be made precise by imposing some conceptual order on the objects by expressing "a is left of b" by the symbol $a < b$. The figure suggests that it is not necessary to choose a *linear order*, such as for natural numbers, which arranges the objects strictly from left to right. It can be allowed that two objects occupy the same horizontal position, which leads to a *partial order*, where $a \leq b$ and $b \leq a$ imply $a = b$ (i.e., two different objects on the same horizontal position cannot be compared).

How can one establish such an order on objects? Since any partial order will do, we are actually quite free in the choice.

- One can use some intrinsic attribute of the locked objects. For instance, when moving money from one `BankAccount` to another, one could order bank accounts by their account numbers.

📖148(§2.4.5) ↰2.2.1

- *Hierarchical containment locking* proceeds along the ownership structure of objects, always locking owners before their parts. This strategy is particularly useful if the parts also protect their own invariants by locking, since then a call from the owner to a part's method locks in the correct order.

📖148(§2.2.6)

- One could use the technical value `System.identityHashCode`, which is usually based on the objects' addresses. Although it is not guaranteed to be unique, a failure is extremely unlikely.

↰4.7

Whatever the concrete order is in the end, it is guaranteed to prevent deadlocks in all possible situations, in the same way that proper reasoning about contracts ensures the correctness of the software in all possible circumstances.

Knowing all objects in advance can be challenging.

The intuition from Fig. 8.10(a) assumes implicitly that one has a well-defined collection of objects in the first place. In the most common case of hierarchical locking, for instance, one knows the owner and the parts. Furthermore, the compound operations of the owner are aware of which parts they will have to lock. In some situations, however, the objects to be locked in a multistep operation will become clear only at runtime.

↰2.1

One instance is a setting where arbitrary observers receive notifications about state changes and must act upon them. The subject sending out the notifications will not be aware of all observers, nor are the different observers aware of one another. If the subject holds any locks while sending out notifications, it is likely that deadlocks will occur, since observers usually go back to parts or collaborators of the subject and those may have been locked by other threads in the meantime. Imposing a resource order on these specific objects may help, if all observers can be relied upon to obey it. In other situations, evasive actions must be taken.

↰8.5

Open calls can prevent deadlocks, since here the subject notifies its observers only after releasing all of its own locks. The drawback that observers must again query the current state of the subject after obtaining their own locks in this context appears slight compared to the avoided deadlocks.

📖148

A different approach is to be pessimistic and to assume that deadlocks will occur anyway whenever callbacks to essentially arbitrary code, possibly residing in different modules in a large system, take place. Each of the participants in such a scenario can then prepare for the worst case by calling `lock()` always with a timeout and by assuming that a deadlock situation occurs when the timeout elapses. Then, the participant will release all of its locks and sleep for a random, brief time to give others a chance to complete their operations, before trying again to obtain all the locks.

Be conservative with locking.

Very often, there is a choice in locking: One can associate a lock with each individual object in a group, or a single lock with the entire group. The first option is preferable for performance reasons, since there is just the chance that several threads can work in parallel on different subsets of the objects. The latter option is clearly preferable since it excludes deadlocks altogether.

In the end, it is a question of optimization: Do you really want to spend the development overhead and incur the risk of deadlocks for the potential performance benefit? As with all optimizations, the "simplest thing that could work" should be chosen until a clear need for a more complex solution is demonstrated. For many years, the FreeBSD kernel's data structures were protected by a single global "giant lock"—and the system was known for its supreme performance nevertheless.

↰1.1

Chapter 9

Structuring Applications with Graphical Interfaces

Chapter 7 introduced the technical and conceptual basis for building user interfaces using the SWT framework that comes with Eclipse. At the core, development comprises two aspects: setting up a widget tree with layout information to create the visual appearance, and attaching event-listeners to the individual widgets to implement the application's reaction to user input. Although this seems simple enough, this basis alone is too weak for building larger applications: Since the application's functionality tends to be scattered throughout event-listeners, one will almost certainly end up with a code base that cannot be maintained, extended, and ported to different platforms—in other words, software that must be thrown away and redeveloped from scratch.

This chapter investigates the architectural building block that keeps applications with user interfaces maintainable and portable: In the code, one always separates the application's business logic strictly from its graphical interface. Section 9.1 introduces this approach, called model-view separation, and traces it through different examples within the Eclipse platform. Next, Section 9.2 discusses its conceptual and technical basis, the classical MODEL-VIEW-CONTROLLER pattern. Section 9.3 introduces the JFace framework, which complements the basic SWT widgets by connecting them to the application's data structures. Section 9.4 uses a running example *MiniXcel*, a minimal spreadsheet implementation, to give a self-contained overview and to explore several implementation details of model-view separation that must be mastered to create truly professional applications. Finally, Section 9.5 adds the aspect of making edits undoable, which is indispensable for achieving usability.

Throughout the presentation, we will pay particular attention to the fact that model-view separation is deceptively simple: While the concept itself is rather straightforward, its rendering in concrete code involves many pitfalls. We will discuss particularly those aspects that have often been treated incorrectly in the work of novices to the field.

Before we start to delve into these depths of software design and implementation, there is one general piece of advice to set them into perspective:

Always gear the application toward the end users' requirements.

📖258

The reason for placing this point so prominently is that it is neglected so often. As developers, we often get swept away by our enthusiasm for the technically possible and the elegance of our own solutions. However, software development is not a modern form of *l'art pour l'art*, but a means of solving other people's pressing problems. These people, called "users," do

📖229

not care about the software's internals; they care about their own workflows. So before you even start to think about the software's view and model and

📖28

the elegance of their separation, talk to the end users: What are their expectations of the software's concrete behavior? How do they wish to interact with the software? Which particular tasks must the software support? The conscientious professional software engineer starts application development by learning about the users' work—in other words, by learning about the software's application domain. Everything said subquently must be subject to this overall guideline.

9.1   The Core: Model-View Separation

Every application has a purpose for which it is built and which provides its unique value to its users. Correspondingly, the application contains code that implements the *business logic* to fulfill that purpose. Apart from that, most applications need a graphical user interface, simply because they have nontechnical users who do not appreciate command-line tools too much.

»9.2.2

Apart from all of the strategic considerations related to software quality and maintenance, to be discussed later, it is useful to keep the code implementing the business logic and the user interface separate simply because they have different characteristics (Fig. 9.1). Users buy, for instance, CAD software because its business logic can do CAD and nifty computations, but they accept it into their working routine because they like the way they can interact with it. The business logic of a CAD system must be extremely reliable to prevent bridges from collapsing, and it must be stable enough through different software releases, for instance, to read the same files correctly throughout projects running for several years. The interface, in contrast, must be visually appealing and must adapt to the changing working habits of its users so that they can, for instance, exploit new input methods such as 3D interaction devices. To achieve stability, the business logic must adhere to rigorous contracts and must be tested comprehensively,

↰7.11 ↰5.3.5

while the interface is event-based and cannot be tested easily, especially if it is liable to frequent changes. Finally, the business logic must deal with internal data structures and basic services such as file I/O, which are easily ported to different platforms. The API of graphical interfaces, in contrast, varies dramatically between platforms, and user interface code is usually not portable at all—for instance, from SWT to Swing. Keeping business logic and user interface separate is therefore first of all a matter of separation of concerns.

Business Logic	User Interface
Why users buy the application	Why users accept the application
The trusted, reliable, valuable core	Visually appealing front-end
Stable over a long time (e.g., file formats)	Volatile to adapt to changing user expectations [229]
Dominated by software-intrinsic concerns	Dominated by usability
Governed by contracts and service providers (Section 4.1)	Governed by events and reactions (Section 7.1, Section 7.11)
Demanding style and non-redundancy (Section 4.5)	Defensive programming (Section 4.6)
Comprehensive unit testing (Section 5.1)	Interface testing (Section 5.3.5)
Largely independent of operating system	Depends closely on window system (Section 7.1)

Figure 9.1 Characteristics of Business Logic and the User Interface

Keep the user interface and the business logic in different modules.

Accepting the goal of this separation, we have to investigate how it can be accomplished in the concrete software. Fig. 9.2 gives an overview, whose aspects we will explore in the remainder of this section. As a first step, one places the user interface and the business logic into separate modules, as indicated by the dashed horizontal dividing line in the figure. Referring to their roles in the MODEL-VIEW-CONTROLLER pattern, the business logic and the user interface are also called the *model* and the *view*, respectively, which explains the term *model-view separation* as a summary of the principle.

»9.2

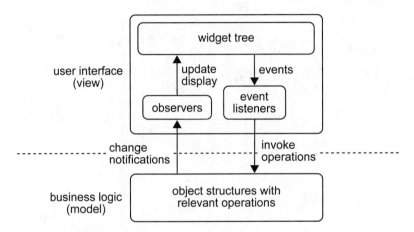

Figure 9.2 Overview of Model-View Separation

»A.1

In Eclipse, modules are implemented as plugins. Throughout the Eclipse code base, plugins with suffix `.ui` access the functionality provided by the corresponding plugins without that suffix. For instance, `org.eclipse.jdt.ui` accesses the Java Development Tools, whose logic comes in plugin `org.eclipse.jdt.core`, as well as `org.eclipse.jdt.launching`, `org.eclipse.debug.core`, and others.

»A.1.2

Introducing separate plugins will at first appear as a somewhat large overhead for small applications. However, the sophisticated support for plugin development in Eclipse removes any technical complexity and exhibits the benefits of the split: The functionality can be linked into different applications to enable reuse; unit tests run much faster on plugins that do not require the user interface to come up; the OSGi class loader ensures that the logic code cannot inadvertently access interface classes; the logic module remains small and focused on its task; and several more. And, finally, successful small applications have a tendency to grow quickly into successful large applications; the split into different plugins ensures that they will also grow gracefully.

»A.1

The model contains the application's core functionality.

From the users' perspective, an application is all about the user interface, since they are not and should not be aware of any other part. The interface creates simplifications and abstractions that keep all the technical complexity under the hood. When writing a letter with a word processor, for example, one certainly does not want to think about linear optimization problems for line and page breaking.

□□229

□□142

    The software engineer, in contrast, focuses on the business logic, or the model, in Fig. 9.2. That component contains the data structures and algorithms that solve the problems that the application is built for. Its objects constitute the machinery that the whole project relies on. Its answers to the technical, conceptual, and maybe scientific challenges make up the team's and the company's competitive advantage. The user interface from this perspective is merely a thin, albeit commercially all-important, wrapper that enables nontechnical users to take full advantage of the functionality.

»11.1

    We have chosen the term "core functionality" rather than just "functionality" in this summary because the user interface does provide its own nontrivial behavior. Visual highlights and effects, reactions to drag-and-drop gestures, and wizards to guide the user—they all require careful engineering in themselves. Yet, they do not belong to the "core," because they would need to be rebuilt from scratch on a new platform.

»9.4.4

Never mention user interface classes in the logic.

The goal of the proposed division is to keep the business logic independent of the user interface, because this will establish precisely the separation of concerns indicated in Fig. 9.2. This can, however, be accomplished only if the code implementing the business logic never mentions user interface classes, such as widgets, images, or other resources: A single reference to a specific user interface library destroys portability and testability. At the level of modules, this means that the user interface module will reference the logic module, but not the reverse.

Connect the user interface to the logic using OBSERVER.

The question is then how logic objects can ever communicate with interface objects at all. The key insight here is that the OBSERVER pattern enables precisely this communication: The subject in the pattern accesses its observers only through an interface that is defined from the perspective of the subject and is independent of the concrete observers.

↰2.1.2

    In the case of model-view separation, the observer interface is contained in the business logic module, and that module sends change messages to observers in the interface module (see Fig. 9.2). These observers will translate the generic change notifications into concrete updates of the widgets.

Let us look at the example of Eclipse's management of background jobs, which also exhibits several interesting facets beyond the bare fundamentals. We have already seen that the platform's `JobManager` allows observers to register for change notifications:

↰2.1.1

org.eclipse.core.internal.jobs.JobManager

```
public void addJobChangeListener(IJobChangeListener listener)
public void removeJobChangeListener(IJobChangeListener listener)
```

The interface `IJobChangeListener` is contained in the same package as the job manager itself, in `org.eclipse.core.runtime.jobs`. Neither that interface nor the `IJobChangeEvent` is connected in any way to possible user interfaces.

org.eclipse.core.runtime.jobs.IJobChangeListener

```
public interface IJobChangeListener {
    public void scheduled(IJobChangeEvent event);
    public void aboutToRun(IJobChangeEvent event);
    public void running(IJobChangeEvent event);
    public void done(IJobChangeEvent event);
    ...
}
```

↰2.1.2

The discussion of the OBSERVER pattern has pointed out that the definition of the observer interface must be independent of specific intended observers. It should focus instead on the possible changes occurring in the subject. This guideline becomes even more important in the case of model-view separation, because here the express intention is to keep the view exchangeable. Unfortunately, it is often tempting to reduce the complexity of the user interface code by sending along detailed notifications that meet the interface's needs precisely, especially to obtain efficient incremental screen updates. In the long run, the simplicity of the current implementation will have to be paid for during subsequent changes and extensions of the user interface.

↠9.4.3

The standard user interface for jobs is the *Progress* view, implemented in class `ProgressView` and several helpers. They reside in the user interface package `org.eclipse.ui.internal.progress`. The central class is the (singleton) `ProgressManager`, which registers to observe the (singleton) `JobManager`.

↰1.3.8

org.eclipse.ui.internal.progress.ProgressManager.JobMonitor

```
ProgressManager() {
    ...
    Job.getJobManager().addJobChangeListener(this.changeListener);
}
```

org.eclipse.ui.internal.progress.ProgressManager

```
private void shutdown() {
    ...
    Job.getJobManager().removeJobChangeListener(
```

```
            this.changeListener);
}
```

Construct view-related information at the view level.

The example of the *Progress* view also illustrates a typical aspect that accounts for a lot of the complexity involved in presenting the business logic adequately to the user: the need to create intermediate view-related data structures.

The model of jobs is essentially a flat list, where each job provides progress reports through progress monitors. Usability, however, is improved by arranging the display into a tree of running jobs, job groups, tasks, and subtasks that integrates all available information. The `ProgressManager` in the user interface therefore constructs a tree of `JobTreeElement` objects. Since the information is useful only for a specific intended user interface and might change when the users' preferences change, the maintenance of the tree is handled entirely in the view, not in the model.

↰7.10.2

⇄? This is actually a design decision. From a different perspective, the model itself might be structured. For instance, the JVM's bare `Threads` naturally form a tree.

The `ProgressManager`'s internal logic then integrates two sources of information into a single consistent tree: the running and finished jobs, obtained through the observer registered in the preceding example, and the progress reports sent by the running jobs, to be discussed next.

Let the model access the view only through interfaces.

The observer pattern is only one instance of a more general principle, if we perceive the view and the model as different *layers* of the overall application. In this context, a lower layer accesses a higher layer only through interfaces defined in the lower layer, so as to allow higher layers to be exchanged later on. Furthermore, the calls to higher layers usually take the form of event notifications (see Fig. 9.2). In a typical example, the operating system's networking component does not assume anything about applications waiting for data, but it will notify them about newly arrived data by passing that data into the buffers belonging to the application's sockets.

»12.2.2 ▢59

Both aspects—the access through interfaces and the notifications—can also be seen in the handling of progress reports. The model-level `Jobs` receive an object to be called back for the reports, but this object is given as an interface `IProgressMonitor`:

```
org.eclipse.core.runtime.jobs.Job
```
```
protected abstract IStatus run(IProgressMonitor monitor);
```

The user interface can then create a suitable object to receive the callbacks. In Eclipse, this is also done in the `ProgressManager` class, where `progressFor()` creates a view-level `JobMonitor`.

```
                         org.eclipse.ui.internal.progress.ProgressManager
public IProgressMonitor createMonitor(Job job,
                                      IProgressMonitor group,
                                      int ticks) {
    JobMonitor monitor = progressFor(job);
    ... handle grouping of jobs
    return monitor;
}
```

The guideline of accessing the user interface only through interfaces can also be seen as a positive rendering of the earlier strict rule that no class from the user interface must ever occur in the model code. If the model code must collaborate with a view object, it must do so through model-level interfaces implemented by view objects.

Event-listeners mainly invoke operations defined in the model.

>>12.1

We have now discussed in detail the notifications sent from the model layer to the view layer, depicted on the left-hand side of Fig. 9.2. This focus is justified by the fact that the decoupling between model and view originates from the proper use of interfaces at this point.

←7.1

The right-hand side of Fig. 9.2 shows the complementary collaboration between view and model. By technical necessity, the user input is always delivered to the application code in the form of events. The question then arises as to how the expected behavior of the overall application should be divided between the event-listeners in the view and the code in the model component.

←5.3.5
←5.4.8

The main insight is that the event-listeners are a particularly bad place for valuable code. The code cannot be tested easily, which makes it hard to get it stable in the first place, let alone keep it stable under necessary changes. Also, the code will probably be lost entirely when the users demand a different interface or the application is ported to a different platform (Fig. 9.1).

←4.1 ←5.1

It is therefore a good idea to place as little code and logic as possible into the event-listeners, and to move as much as possible into the model instead. There, it can be made reliable through contracts and testing; there, it can be reused on different operation systems; there, it can be maintained independently of the vagaries of user interface development.

>>9.4.4

In the end, the ideal event-listener invokes only a few methods on the model. The only logic that necessarily remains in the event-listeners relates to the interface-level functionality such as the handling of drag-and-drop of data and of visual feedback on the current editing gestures.

⚡ In practice, one often starts adding functionality to meet concrete user demands, and one usually starts at the interface. The user says, "I need a button right here to do this particular thing," and the developer starts developing right with the event-listener. Such event-listeners tend to become long and complex, and it is useful to refactor them in retrospect. First, try to factor code fragments that are independent of the user interface into separate methods within the listener, then move those methods into the model. There, they will also be available to other team members for reuse.

↰1.2.2
↰1.4.5

Design the model first.

It is tempting to start a new project with the user interface: You make rapid progress due to the WindowBuilder, you get early encouragement from prospective users, and you can show off to your team leader. All of this is important, since nifty data structures without a usable interface are not worth much—in the end, the users have to accept the application and use it confidently. For this reason, it can also be strategically sensible to start with the interface and even a mock-up of the interface, to check whether anybody will buy the finished product.

↰7.2

Because starting with the user interface is such an obvious choice, we wish to advocate the complementary approach: to start with the model. Here are a few reasons for postponing work on the user interface for a little while.

📖59

- You stand a better chance that the model will be portable and reusable. As with the test-first principle, the missing concrete collaborators in the user interface reduce the danger of defining the model, and in particular the observer interfaces (Fig. 9.2), specifically for those collaborators.

↰5.2

↰2.1.2

- Test-first is applicable to the model, and it will have its usual benefits.

↰5.2

- The model will naturally contain all required functionality, so that the danger of placing too much functionality into the listeners is avoided from the start.

- There is no danger that a mock-up user interface presumes an API for the model that cannot be supported efficiently.

- The mission-critical challenges, such as in algorithmics, will be encountered and can be explored before an expensive investment in the user interface has taken place. If it turns out that the application will take a longer time than expected or cannot be built at all, the company has lost less money. Also, there is still time to hire experts to overcome the problems before the release.

- The user interface can focus on usability. Once the functionality is available, the user interface team just has to provide the most effective access paths to that functionality; it does not have to delve into the business logic aspects.

»9.2.2

Together, these aspects maximize the benefits of model-view separation.

Envision the interface while creating the model.

Conversely, a strict focus on the model is likely to have drawbacks for the final product. From an engineering point of view, the API of the model may not suit the demands of the interface, so that workarounds have to be found:

- The event-listeners contain extensive logic to access the existing API. This means that this logic will be lost when the interface has to change.

↰2.4.1

- The model contains adapters to provide the expected API.

- The model has to be refactored.

From a usability perspective, the fixed model API may induce developers to take the easy way out of these overheads and to provide a user interface that merely mirrors the internals. A typical example comprises CRUD (CReate Update Delete) interfaces to databases, which are easy to obtain, but which are known to provide insufficient support for the user's workflows.

220,145,266
114

Model-view separation incurs an extra complexity that will pay off.

We have seen much motivation and many benefits of model-view separation, and we will discuss the details. At the end of this overview, however, let us consider not the benefits, but the costs of model-view separation.

»9.2.2

- Splitting the code into separate modules always involves the design of interfaces between the modules, and the communication about them can take a lot of time and presents the potential for mistakes that must be remedied later at high cost. When a data structure is kept right in the user interface, one can hack in a new requirement at the last minute. In contrast, if the data is encapsulated in a different module, one may have to negotiate with the developers who are responsible first.

- The collaboration from model to view always takes place by generic change notifications (Fig. 9.2), rather than specific method calls that update parts of the screen. In the model, one has to provide the general OBSERVER pattern for many objects, even if there is in the end only a single concrete observer in the user interface. Furthermore, the logic to translate the changes into screen updates itself can be substantial and complex, especially if it is necessary to repaint the smallest possible screen area to keep the application responsive.

↰2.1
↰2.1.4
»9.4.3

Model-view separation is therefore an effort that must be taken at the start of a project. The walk-through example of MiniXcel will give you a mental checklist of the single steps, which allows you to assess the overall

»9.4

effort up front. We hope that the checklist is then simple enough to convince you of using model-view separation in all but the most trivial throwaway applications. Even in projects of a few thousand lines, the investment in the extra structure will pay off quickly, since the software becomes more testable, maintainable, and changeable. And if the application happens to live longer than expected, as is usually the case for useful software, it is ready for that next step as well.

9.2 The Model-View-Controller Pattern

The MODEL-VIEW-CONTROLLER pattern (MVC) has proven a tremendous success in many different areas of user interfaces, starting from the original SmallTalk toolkit, through all major players such as Qt, GTK, SWT, Swing, and MFC, right to web application frameworks such as Ruby on Rails and ASP.MVC. Naturally, the different areas have produced different variants that suit their specific needs. Nevertheless, the fundamental concept remains the same. We will study here the classical version, which will also clarify the workings of the variants. We will use a minimal example to illustrate the conceptual details of the pattern clearly without swamping the discussion with unnecessary technical complications. A more extended example will be given in the MiniXcel application. Also, we start out with the classical separation of view and controller, even if most practical implementations unify these roles. Understanding the separate responsibilities of view and controller separately first will later help to create clearer structures.

📖146

📖59

➤➤9.4

➤➤9.2.8

9.2.1 The Basic Pattern

The structure of the MVC pattern is shown in Fig. 9.3. In essence, the pattern reflects the model-view separation: The business logic is kept separate from the user interface code, and the logic collaborates with the interface only through generic change notifications in the OBSERVER. The pattern adds a finer subdivision in the interface layer: The *view* is responsible for rendering the application data on the screen, while the *controller* contains the logic for reacting to user input.

The benefit of this additional split is mainly a stricter separation of concerns. We have seen in the discussion of the MEDIATOR that the event-listeners attached to widgets can quickly become complex in themselves. Moving this code into a self-contained object will keep the code of the view more focused on the visual presentation itself. Although many practical implementations reunite the two roles in the DOCUMENT-VIEW variant, is useful to consider them separately first, since this will lead to a clearer structure within the view component of this later development.

◄9.1

◄2.1

◄7.7

➤➤9.2.8

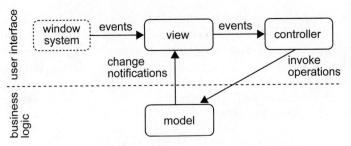

Figure 9.3 The Basic Model-View-Controller Pattern

In summary, the three roles of the pattern then perform these tasks:

↰9.1

- The model maintains the application's data structures and algorithms, which constitute its business logic. The model is the valuable and stable core of the product; it is built to last through revisions and ports to different window systems. It builds on precise contracts and is thoroughly unit-tested.

↰7.11

- The view renders the current state of the application data onto the screen. It accesses the model to retrieve the data, and registers as an observer to be notified about any changes and to keep the display up-to-date. By technical necessity, it also receives all user input as events and passes those events on to the controller.

↰7.1

- The controller interprets the user input events as triggers to perform operations and modifications on the model. It contains the logic for handling the events. In this role, it is a typical decision maker: It decides what needs to be done, but delegates the actual execution to others. In the basic pattern, this means calling the model's methods.

↰1.8.1

🔎 The pattern describes all three roles as if they were filled by single objects. However, this is hardly ever the case: The application logic is usually implemented in a complex component with many helper objects that collaborate intensively, and even the view may need helpers to fulfill its task.

To see the pattern in action, we implement a tiny widget that enables a single integer value to be incremented and decremented by clicking on different areas (Fig. 9.4). Rather than building a compound widget, we implement this from scratch to show all of the details.

↰7.5

The model maintains the application data and supports observers.

Following the earlier advice, we start with the model. Its "functionality" is to maintain a single integer value. To serve as a model in the pattern, the object also implements the OBSERVER pattern. The crucial point to be noted is that the model is in no way adapted to the intended presentation on

↰9.1

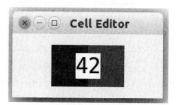

Figure 9.4 Minimal MVC Example

the screen. In particular, the observers are merely notified that the content has changed (line 21); there is no indication that this notification will trigger a screen update later on.

celledit.mvc.IntCell

```
 1  public class IntCell {
 2    private int content;
 3    private EventListenerList listeners = new EventListenerList();
 4    public void addCellListener(CellListener l) {
 5      ...
 6    }
 7    public void removeCellListener(CellListener l) {
 8      ...
 9    }
10    public int get() {
11      return content;
12    }
13    public void set(int cnt) {
14      int old = content;
15      this.content = cnt;
16      fireCellChanged(old);
17    }
18    protected void fireCellChanged(int old) {
19      for (CellListener l : listeners.getListeners(
20                                      CellListener.class))
21        l.cellChanged(this, old, content);
22    }
23  }
```

The view displays the data on the screen.

The view in the pattern must paint on the screen, so it derives from `Canvas`.   ↰7.8
It keeps references to the current model and controller, as well as the (larger)   ↰7.4.1
font used for painting and the computed preferred size.   ↰7.1

celledit.mvc.View

```
public class View extends Canvas {
    private IntCell model;
    private Controller controller;
    private Font fnt;
```

```
        private Point sizeCache;
           ...
    }
```

↰7.8

The main task of the view is to render the application data on the screen. The following excerpt from the painting method gives the crucial point: Line 3 gets the current value from the model and transforms it into a string to be drawn on the screen in line 7. The remaining code serves to center the string in the widget (bounds is the area available for painting).

celledit.mvc.View

```
1 private void paintControl(PaintEvent e) {
2     ... paint red and green fields
3     String text = Integer.toString(model.get());
4     Point sz = g.textExtent(text);
5     int x = bounds.width / 2 - sz.x / 2;
6     int y = bounds.height / 2 - sz.y / 2;
7     g.drawString(text, x, y);
8 }
9
```

The view keeps the display up-to-date by observing the model.

To keep the display up-to-date, the view must observe the model. Whenever the model changes, the view observes the new model.

celledit.mvc.View

```
public void setModel(IntCell c) {
    if (this.model != null)
        this.model.removeCellListener(modelListener);
    this.model = c;
    if (this.model != null)
        this.model.addCellListener(modelListener);
}
```

↰7.4.1

⚠ Do not forget to detach the view from the model when the view is disposed. This can be achieved reliably by setting the model to null in a DisposeListener.

↰7.8

↠9.4.3

The modelListener merely requests a complete repainting of the widget. In many scenarios, this is too inefficient for production use, so that incremental repainting must be implemented. To demonstrate the pattern, the simple choice is sufficient.

celledit.mvc.View

```
private CellListener modelListener = new CellListener() {
    public void cellChanged(IntCell cell, int oldVal, int newVal) {
        redraw();
    }
};
```

The view forwards user input to the controller.

Finally, the view must forward the events to the controller. This is usually achieved by registering the controller as an event-listener. For the current example, we delegate the actual registration to the controller itself to demonstrate an exchange of the controller later on.

»9.2.7

---

celledit.mvc.View.setController

```java
public void setController(Controller c) {
    if (controller != null)
        controller.detach(this);
    controller = c;
    if (controller != null)
        controller.attach(this);
}
```

Having finished with the model and the view, we have set up the main axis of Fig. 9.3: The display on the screen will always reflect the current data, independent of how that data will be manipulated. We will now add this last aspect by implementing the controller.

The controller receives all relevant user input.

The controller must receive all user input relevant to the expected reactions. Since the input is technically sent to the view, the controller registers itself as a listener on the view. In the current example, it becomes a mouse-listener to receive the clicks that will trigger the increment and decrement operations. (The super call merely remembers the view in a field view.)

---

celledit.mvc.MouseController.attach

```java
public void attach(View view) {
    super.attach(view);
    this.view.addMouseListener(this);
    this.view.addMouseTrackListener(this);
    this.view.addMouseMoveListener(this);
}
```

The controller interprets the events as operations on the model.

The summary of tasks given earlier states that the purpose of the controller is to translate raw input events into operations on the model. The implementation can be seen in the callback methods for mouse clicks. The controller accesses the model to be operated on (lines 2–3) and checks which area the click actually occurred in (lines 4 and 7). Based on this information, it decides whether the model value should be incremented or decremented (lines 6 and 8). As a detail, the controller decides not to decrement the value if it has already reached 0.

»9.2.3

```
                    celledit.mvc.MouseController.mouseUp
 1 public void mouseUp(MouseEvent e) {
 2     if (view.getModel() != null) {
 3         IntCell m = view.getModel();
 4         if (view.isInDecrementArea(new Point(e.x, e.y)) &&
 5             m.get() > 0)
 6             m.set(m.get() - 1);
 7         else if (view.isInIncrementArea(new Point(e.x, e.y)))
 8             m.set(m.get() + 1);
 9     }
10 }
```

The pattern processes input through view, controller, and model.

The overall goal of the MODEL-VIEW-CONTROLLER pattern can also be seen by tracing the user input through the different roles, until an actual screen update occurs.

1. The view receives the input and hands it to the controller.

2. The controller decides which action to take on the model.

3. The model performs the invoked operation and sends the resulting changes to the view, as one of possibly several observers.

»9.4.3

4. The view interprets the model changes and decides which parts of the screen need to be redrawn.

5. The view refetches the relevant data and paints it on the screen.

This sequence of steps highlights the contributions of the different objects. It also points out that each of them can influence the final outcome: The view will contribute the visual appearance; the controller implements the reaction, since the view simply forwards events; and the model implements the functionality, but does not see the input events.

The central point of model-view separation is seen in steps 2 and 3. First, the controller alone is responsible for interpreting the input events; the model is not aware of the real causes of the invoked operations. Second, the model is not aware of the precise view class, or that there is a user interface at all; it merely supports the OBSERVER pattern.

9.2.2   Benefits of the Model-View-Controller Pattern

The MODEL-VIEW-CONTROLLER pattern is, in fact, rather complex and requires some extra implementation effort, compared to the naive solution of implementing the application's functionality directly in event-listeners attached to the widgets. The investment into the extra structure and indirections introduced by the pattern must therefore be justified.

The user interface remains flexible.

The most important benefit of the pattern derives from its ability to keep the user interface flexible. Because the application's functionality stays safe and sound in the model component and does not depend on the user interface in any way, it will remain valid if the interface changes. This can and will happen surprisingly often over the software's lifetime.

The first reason for changing the user interface is the user. The central goal of a user interface is to support the users' workflows effectively. As these workflows change or the users develop new preferences, the interface should ideally be adapted to match them. Also, different user groups may have different requirements, and new views may need to be developed as these requirements emerge. The MVC pattern confines such changes to the actual interface, unless the new workflows also require new computations and operations.

229

The second reason for changes relates to the underlying window system. When APIs change or new widgets or interaction devices are developed, the user interface must exploit them for the users' benefit. Since these aspects are usually not related to the functionality in any way, the MVC keeps the application's core stable.

Finally, it may be desirable to port the application to an entirely different platform. Here, the problem lies mostly in the user interface. In the best case, an analogous set of widgets will be available: Whether you access Windows, MacOS, GTK, or Qt, their widgets offer basically very similar services and events. Nevertheless, the user interface must usually be redeveloped from scratch. The MVC pattern ensures that the valuable core of the application, its functionality, will continue to work in the new environment, since this core uses only standard services such as file or network access, for which cross-platform APIs are available or where the platform differences can be hidden behind simple adapters.

↰2.4.1

Multiple, synchronized views can better support the users' workflows.

Modern IDEs such as Eclipse give us a good grasp on our source code. For example, while we work on the source in a text editor, we see an outline of its structure on the side. When we rename a method in one of the two windows, the other window reflects the change immediately. The reason is simply that both windows are, possibly through an indirection of the Java Model, views for the same text document, which fulfills the role of the view component in the MVC pattern. Similarly, Eclipse's compiler reports an error only once by attaching an IMarker object to the file. The marker is reflected in the editor, the problems view, and as a small icon in the package explorer and project navigator.

The MODEL-VIEW-CONTROLLER pattern enables such synchronized views on the application's data structure because views observe the model and are informed about its current state regardless of why changes have occurred.

The display remains up-to-date with the internal state.

At a somewhat more basic level, users will trust an application only if they are never surprised by its behavior. One common source of surprises is inconsistency between the internal data structures and the displayed data. The MVC pattern eliminates this chance completely and ensures that the users always base their actions and decisions on the most up-to-date information about the internal structures.

The application's functionality remains testable.

↰5.4

The single most important technique for making a system reliable and keeping it stable under change is testing. By making the functional core, the model, independent of a user interface, its operations can also be exercised in a testing fixture (see Fig. 5.1 on page 246) and its resulting state can be examined by simple assertions in unit tests. Testing the user interface,

↰5.3.5

in contrast, is much more complex. Since the user interface itself tends to change very often, the effort of adapting the existing test cases and creating new ones will be considerable. The functional core, in contrast, is built to remain stable, so that the investment of testing will pay off easily.

Model-view separation enables protection of the system's core.

↰4.1

The stability of an application's functionality relies heavily on precise contracts. Within this reasoning framework, each method trusts its callers to fulfill the stated pre-condition—that is, to pass only legal arguments and

↰4.5

to call the method only in legal object states. The non-redundancy principle condenses the idea of trust into the development practice of never

↰4.6 ↰1.5.2

checking pre-conditions. At the system boundary, in contrast, the code can never trust the incoming data and requests. Methods must be written to be robust, and to check whether they really do apply.

Model-view separation offers the benefits of localizing these necessary checks in the user interface component and maintaining the functional core in the clean and lean style enabled by the non-redundancy principle.

9.2.3   Crucial Design and Implementation Constraints

↰2.1.2

As with the OBSERVER pattern, the concrete implementation of the MODEL-VIEW-CONTROLLER pattern must observe a few constraints to obtain the

↰9.2.2

expected benefits. We list here those aspects that we have found in teaching to make the difference between the code of novices and that of professionals.

Do not tailor the OBSERVER pattern to a specific view.

The first aspect is the definition of the *Observer* interface for the model. Especially when dealing with complex models and the necessity of incremental   »9.4.3
screen updates, there is always the temptation to "tweak" the change notifications a bit to simplify the logic that determines which parts of the screen
need to be updated. Certainly, one should use the "push" variant of the OB-
SERVER pattern; that is, the change notifications should be very detailed to   ↰2.1.3
enable any view to work efficiently regardless of its possible complexity.

When targeting the messages at specific views, however, one endangers
the ability to add a new view or to change the existing one, or to port the
application to an entirely different platform. Suppose, for instance, that
the model manages a list of objects with some properties. It should then
send a change message containing a description of the change. However, it
should not use a message `updateTableRow()` simply because the current
view is a `Table` widget. A better choice is a message `changedData()`, which
reflects the change instead of the expected reaction. If the view displays the
properties in a specific order, the model must not send messages `update`
`Table(int row, int col)`, but rather `changedData(DataObject obj,`
`String property)`. Even if this means that the view must map objects to
rows and the property names to column indices, it increases the likelihood
that the view can change independently of the model.

The controller never notifies the view about triggered operations.

A second shortcut that one may be tempted to take is to let the controller
notify the view directly about any changes it has performed on the model,
rather than going through the indirection via the model. First, this shortcut is marginally more efficient at runtime. What is particularly attractive,
however, is that it saves the implementation of the general OBSERVER pat-   ↰2.1.4
tern in the model and the perhaps complex logic for translating changes to
screen updates in the view.

However, the shortcut really destroys the core of the pattern, and nearly
all of its benefits. One can no longer have multiple synchronized views. Also,
the information on the screen may no longer be up-to-date if the controller
neglects internal side effects and dependencies of the model. Finally, the   »9.4.2
logic for the updates must be duplicated in ports and variations of the user
interface.

The controller delegates decisions about the visual appearance to the view.

A comparatively minor point concerns the relationship between the view
and the controller. If these roles are implemented as different objects at any   »9.2.8
point, then one should also strive for a strict separation of concerns—for
instance, to keep the controller exchangeable.   »9.2.7

One notable aspect is the possible assumptions about the visual appearance. The controller often receives events that relate back to that visual appearance. For instance, a mouse click happens at a particular point on the screen, and the visual element at this point must determine the correct reaction. If the controller makes any assumptions about this visual element, it is tied to the specific implementation of the view. If several controllers exist, then it becomes virtually impossible to change even simple things such as the font size and spacing, since several controllers would have to change as well.

»12.1.2

↰9.2.1

In the following tiny example, we have therefore made the controller ask the model whether the click event e occurred in one of the designated "active" areas. The controller now assumes the existence of these areas, but it does not know anything about their location and shape. That knowledge is encapsulated in the view and can be adapted at any time.

celledit.mvc.MouseController.mouseUp

```
if (view.isInDecrementArea(new Point(e.x, e.y)) && m.get() > 0)
    m.set(m.get() - 1);
else if (view.isInIncrementArea(new Point(e.x, e.y)))
    m.set(m.get() + 1);
```

»9.2.8

Even in the common DOCUMENT-VIEW variant of the MVC, where view and controller are implemented together in one object, it is still useful to obey the guideline by separating the concerns into different methods of the object.

The controller shields the model from the user input.

↰1.5.2 ↰4.6

The user interface is, of course, one of the system's boundaries. Accordingly, all user input must be treated with suspicion: Has the user really entered valid data? Has the user clicked a button only when it makes sense? Does the selected file have the expected format?

↰7.11
↰4.5

Many of these questions are best handled in the controller, because it is the controller that receives the user input and decides which model operations need to be called in response. Since the model is built according to the principles of design by contract, it does not check any stated preconditions. It is the controller's task to ensure that only valid method calls are made.

9.2.4   Common Misconceptions

The MODEL-VIEW-CONTROLLER pattern is rather complex, so it is not surprising that a few misunderstandings arise when first thinking it through. We have found in teaching that some misunderstandings tend to crop up repeatedly. They seem to arise mostly from the correct impression that the MVC is all about exchangeability and flexibility. However, one has to be careful about what really is exchangeable in the end and must not

»12.2

conclude that "all components can be exchanged and adapted to the users' requirements." We hope that highlighting the nonbenefits of the pattern in this section will enhance the understanding of the benefits that it does create.

Model-view separation is not a panacea.

The rather extensive mechanisms and logic necessary for establishing a proper model-view separation must always be seen as an investment. It is an investment that pays off quite quickly, even for medium-sized applications, but it is still an investment. The decision for or against using the MVC must therefore be based on a precise understanding of it benefits, so as to relate them to the application at hand. A small tool written for one project only will never need porting, for example, and if the developer is also its only user, there is little chance of having to change the user interface. A general understanding that the MVC offers "everything that can be wished for" is not enough.

The model is not exchangeable and the view is not reusable.

The view and the controller necessarily target a specific model: They ask the model for data and draw exactly that data; the view registers as an observer and expects certain kinds of change messages; and the controller translates user gestures into specific operations offered by the model. As a result, the model cannot usually be exchanged for a different one; by switch of perspective, this means that the view is usually not reusable.

Of course, it is still possible to implement generic widgets that access the model only through predefined interfaces. For instance, a table on the screen has rows, and the data in each row provides strings for each column. Both JFace and Swing provide excellent examples of generic and reusable tables. However, this is an exercise in library or framework design. To build a concrete user interface, one has to supply adapters that link the generic mechanisms to the specific application model, and one has to implement listeners for generic table events that target the specific available model operations. In this perspective, the generic table is only a building block, not the complete user interface in the sense of the MVC.

»9.3.1 📖80

↩2.4.1

The controller is usually neither exchangeable nor reusable.

The controller interprets user gestures, such as mouse moves, mouse clicks, and keyboard input. These gestures have a proper meaning, and hence a reliable translation to model operations, only with respect to the concrete visual appearance of the view. It is therefore usually not possible to reuse a controller on a different view. Exchanging the controller is possible, but only within the confines of the event sources offered by the view.

»9.2.7

9.2.5   Behavior at the User Interface Level

Effective user interfaces allow the user to invoke common operations by small gestures. For example, moving a rectangle in a drawing tool takes a mouse click to select the rectangle and a drag gesture to move it. Since many similarly small gestures have similarly small but quite different effects, the application must provide feedback so that the user can anticipate the reaction. For instance, when selecting a rectangle, it acquires drag handles— that is, a visual frame that indicates moving and resizing gestures will now influence this object.

Implement user feedback without participation of the model.

The important point to realize is that feedback is solely a user interface behavior: Different platforms offer different mechanisms, and different users will expect different behavior. The model does not get involved until the user has actually triggered an operation.

↰9.2.1   Suppose, for instance, that we wish to enhance the example widget with the feedback shown in Fig. 9.5. When the mouse cursor is *inside* the widget, a frame appears to indicate this fact (a versus b and c); furthermore, a slightly lighter hue indicates whether a click would increment or decrement the counter (b versus c), and which field is the current *target* of the click.

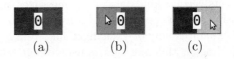

(a)   (b)   (c)

Figure 9.5 User-Interface Behavior: Mouse Feedback

Feedback is triggered by the controller.

The second aspect of feedback concerns the question of which role will actually decide which feedback needs to be shown. The answer here is clear: Because the controller will finally decide which operation is triggered on the model, it must also decide which feedback must be shown to apprise the user of this later behavior. It is similarly clear that the controller will decide on the feedback but will delegate the actual display to the view.

In the implementation of the example, the `Controller` tracks both the general mouse movements into and out of the widget, and the detailed movements inside the widget. The reaction to the `mouseEnter` and `mouseExit` events is straightforward: Just tell the view to draw the frame or to remove it. When the mouse leaves the widget, any target highlight must, of course, also be removed. The `mouseMove` proceeds in parallel to the `mouseUp` method in the basic implementation: It checks which operation it would perform and sets the corresponding highlight.

↰9.2.1

---
celledit.mvc.MouseController

```
public void mouseEnter(MouseEvent e) {
    view.setInside(true);
}
public void mouseExit(MouseEvent e) {
    view.setInside(false);
    view.setTargetField(View.TARGET_NONE);
}
public void mouseMove(MouseEvent e) {
    if (view.isInDecrementArea(new Point(e.x, e.y)))
        view.setTargetField(View.TARGET_DECREMENT);
    else if (view.isInIncrementArea(new Point(e.x, e.y)))
        view.setTargetField(View.TARGET_INCREMENT);
    else
        view.setTargetField(View.TARGET_NONE);
}
```

The naming of the `View` methods is worth mentioning. They publish the fact that some visual effect can be achieved, but the effect itself remains a private decision of the `View`. This parallels the earlier implementation of `mouseUp`, where the controller did not know the exact shape of the clickable areas within the view.

We said earlier that `mouseExit` must "of course" remove any target highlight. The question is whether this must be as explicit as in the code shown here: Would it not be better if the call `setInside(false)` would also remove the target highlight? In other words, shouldn't the connection between the feedback mechanisms already be established within the `View` class? It would certainly make the controller's methods simpler and more symmetric, and it would ensure a certain consistency within the view. We have chosen the variant in the example to emphasize that all decisions about feedback lie with the controller. In practical implementations, the other options can, however, be equally valid.

Feedback usually requires special state in the view.

In implementing the actual visual feedback within the `View`, we have to take into account one technical detail: Painting always occurs in a callback,   ↰7.8
at some arbitrary point that the window system deems suitable. The view must be ready to draw both the data and the feedback at that point. We therefore introduce special state components in the view:

---
celledit.mvc.View

```
private boolean inside = false;
public static final int TARGET_NONE = 0;
public static final int TARGET_DECREMENT = 1;
public static final int TARGET_INCREMENT = 2;
private int targetField = TARGET_NONE;
```

The `View` publishes the new state, but only to its related classes, such as the `Controller`. The setter for the state stores the new value and invokes `redraw()` to request a later painting operation. Since this is potentially expensive, one should always check whether the operation is necessary at all.

↰7.8

celledit.mvc.View

```
protected void setInside(boolean inside) {
    if (this.inside == inside)
        return;
    this.inside = inside;
    redraw();
}
```

The actual painting then merely checks the current feedback state at the right point and creates the visual appearance. Here is the example for highlighting the "decrement" field; the increment field and the "inside" indications are similar.

celledit.mvc.View

```
private void paintControl(PaintEvent e) {
    ...
    if (targetField == TARGET_DECREMENT)
        g.setBackground(getDisplay().getSystemColor(SWT.COLOR_RED));
    else
        g.setBackground(getDisplay().getSystemColor(
                                        SWT.COLOR_DARK_RED));
    g.fillRectangle(bounds.x, bounds.y, bounds.width / 2,
                    bounds.height);
    ...
}
```

Separate view-level state from the application functionality.

The example of the feedback given here has introduced the necessity of state that only lives at the view level but does not concern the application's core data structures. A plethora of similar examples comes to mind immediately: the selection in a text viewer or the selected row in a table; the folding and unfolding of nodes in a tree-structured display, such as SWT's `Tree`; the currently selected tool in an image editor; the position of scrollbars in a list and the first row shown in consequence; the availability of buttons depending on previous choices; and many more.

In the end, the view-level state and the model-level state must be merged in one consistent user interface with predictable behavior. Internally, however, the two worlds must be kept separate: The one part of the state is thrown away, and the other must be stable when the interface changes; the one part is best tested manually, and the other must be rigorously unit-tested. Consequently, one must decide for each aspect of the overall state to which of the worlds it will belong.

   The decision may seem rather obvious at first, but some cases might merit deeper discussions and sometimes one may have second thoughts about a decision. For instance, the GIMP image editor treats the selection as part of the model: You can undo and redo selection steps, and the selection even gets saved to the .xcf files. The reason is, obviously, that in the image manipulation domain, selection is often a key operation, and several detailed selection steps must be carried out in sequence to achieve a desired result. Being able to undo and redo selection helps users to remedy mistakes in the process.

»9.5

9.2.6   Controllers Observing the Model

In the basic MODEL-VIEW-CONTROLLER pattern, the view necessarily observes the model, because it must translate any changes in the data to updates of the display. In many scenarios, the controller will also observe the model.

◄9.2.1

> Controllers can observe the model to indicate availability of operations.

A typical example of this behavior is seen in menu items that get grayed out if an operation is not available. For instance, a text editor will gray out the "copy" and "cut" entries if there is currently no selection.

> The controller decides on the availability of operations.

It might be tempting to integrate the feedback on available actions directly into the view. After all, the view already observes the model and it can just as well handle one more aspect while it is at work anyway. However, since the controller decides which operations it will invoke for which user input, it is also the controller which decides whether these operations are currently available.

   Suppose, for instance, that we wish to gray out the decrement field if the current count is already 0. This requires an extension of both the View and the Controller classes: The view acquires a new bit-mask stating which of the fields need to be grayed out, and that information is used when choosing the background color in paintControl(). The controller observes the model and switches the "gray" flags of the fields according to the current model value.

℗ You might ask whether to bother graying out the "increment" field at all, since the widget's behavior does not assume an upper bound. We feel that keeping the implementation slightly more general and symmetric at very little cost at this point might help in future extensions. After all, similar widgets such as Slider and ScrollBar all do have upper limits.

Controllers must assume that others modify the model.

One possible pitfall that leads to nonprofessional code lies in the fact that the controller modifies the model itself and therefore seems to know precisely whether an operation causes some action to become unavailable. However, it should be noted that the MVC is built to support multiple synchronized views, and that other controllers may invoke model operations as well. Each controller that depends on the model's state must therefore observe the model.

9.2.7 Pluggable Controllers

»9.2.8

📖146

Even if, as we shall see shortly, the view and controller are often coupled so tightly that it is sensible to implement them in a single object, it is still instructive to consider briefly the concept of making the controller of a view pluggable to implement new interactions with an existing graphical presentation. This flexibility can be achieved only after understanding precisely the division of responsibilities between view and controller.

↰9.2.1

So, let us implement a controller that enables the user to access the number entry field from the introductory example (Fig. 9.4 on page 455) via the keyboard. The new `KeyboardController` waits for keyboard input and modifies the model accordingly. Since the view observes the model, the change will become visible to the user.

---

celledit.mvc.KeyboardController.keyReleased

```java
public void keyReleased(KeyEvent e) {
    IntCell m = view.getModel();
    switch (e.character) {
    case '+':
        m.set(m.get() + 1);
        break;
    case '-':
        if (m.get() > 0)
            m.set(m.get() - 1);
        break;
    }
        ...

}
```

↰7.6

Keyboard input is different from mouse input in that it is not the current location of some cursor, but the *keyboard focus* of the window system (and SWT) that determines which widget will receive the events. The keyboard focus is essentially a pointer to that target widget, but it has interactions with the window manager (because of modal dialogs) and the tab order of widgets in the window. It is therefore necessary to display feedback to the users so that they know which reaction to expect when they press a key. The new controller therefore registers as a `FocusListener` of the `View`.

---
celledit.mvc.KeyboardController.attach

```
public void attach(View view) {
    ...
    view.addFocusListener(this);
}
```

The controller then uses the existing "inside" indication on the view for the actual feedback:

---
celledit.mvc.KeyboardController

```
public void focusGained(FocusEvent e) {
    view.setInside(true);
}
public void focusLost(FocusEvent e) {
    view.setInside(false);
}
```

Another convention is that clicking on a widget with the mouse will give it the focus. This is, however, no more than a convention, and the widget itself has to request the focus when necessary. This reaction can be implemented directly. (Note that the actual indication that the focus has been obtained is shown indirectly, through the event-listener installed previously.)

---
celledit.mvc.KeyboardController.mouseUp

```
public void mouseUp(MouseEvent e) {
    view.setFocus();
}
```

Finally, it is also useful to give a visual indication, in the form of a short flash of the respective increment/decrement fields, when the user presses the "+" and the "−" keys. This, too, can be achieved with the existing feedback mechanisms. The keyReleased() event then resets the target field to "none." The flash will therefore mirror precisely the user's pressing of the respective key.

---
celledit.mvc.KeyboardController.keyPressed

```
public void keyPressed(KeyEvent e) {
    switch (e.character) {
    case '+':
        view.setTargetField(View.TARGET_INCREMENT);
        break;
    case '-':
        view.setTargetField(View.TARGET_DECREMENT);
        break;
    }
}
```

The new controller emphasizes the division of logic between the view and the controller: The display and highlights remain with the view, and the controller decides what needs to be done in reaction to incoming user input. It is this division that has enabled us to reuse the existing highlight mechanisms for new purposes.

»12.4

You might, of course, be suspicious of this reuse: Was it just coincidence that the existing mechanisms worked out for the new controller? Reuse always requires anticipating the shape of possible application scenarios and keeping the supported ones lean at the cost of excluding others. In the current case, we would argue that the feedback mechanisms that the view provides match the user's understanding of the widget: The user "activates" the widget by "zooming in," either by the mouse or by the keyboard focus, and then "triggers" one of the increment and decrement areas. All of these interactions are then mirrored by the highlights.

☐214

Nevertheless, it must be said that views and controllers usually depend heavily on each other, so that exchanging the controller is rarely possible. One example where it is enabled is found in the pluggable *edit policies* of the Graphical Editing Framework, which create a setup where reusable controller-like logic can be attached to various elements of the user interface in a flexible way.

9.2.8   The Document-View Variant

The view and controller in the MVC pattern are usually connected very tightly: The controller can request only those events that the view provides, and it can make use of only those feedback mechanisms that the view implements. Since it is therefore often not possible to use either the view or the controller without the other, one can go ahead and implement both roles in the same object. This leads to the DOCUMENT-VIEW pattern, where the document contains the application logic and the view contains the entire user interface code. In this way, the interface code can share knowledge about the widget's internals between the logic of the display and the event-listeners. This may facilitate coding and avoids having to design an API that enables the view and the controller classes to communicate.

↤9.1

↤9.2.1

↤7.8

↤2.1.3

Let us examine this idea through the simple example of incrementing and decrementing an integer value. We start from a technical perspective. Since we need to implement a widget with custom painting, the overall structure is that of a `Canvas` with attached listeners. The drawing part is actually the same as in the previous implementation. Only the code for the event-listeners is integrated. In the simplest case, we wait for mouse clicks. To avoid publishing this fact by making the `View` class implement `MouseListener`, we attach an anonymous listener that delegates to the outer class.

---
celledit.docview.View.View

```
addMouseListener(new MouseAdapter() {
    public void mouseUp(MouseEvent e) {
        handleMouseUp(e);
```

```
        }
});
```

Keep the code for display and reaction loosely coupled.

On the first try, one is liable to take the freedom of "sharing knowledge" between display and event-listeners very literally. For instance, we know that paintComponent() draws the dividing line between the decrement and increment fields right in the middle of the widget's screen space. The event-listener can therefore be written up like this:

celledit.docview.View

```
private void mouseUp1(MouseEvent e) {
    Rectangle area = getClientArea();
    if (cell.get() > 0 && area.width / 2 <= e.x &&
        e.x <= area.width &&
        0 <= e.y && e.y <= area.height)
        cell.set(cell.get() - 1);
    ...
};
```

However, this is highly undesirable: It is not possible to change the visual appearance without going through the entire class and checking which code might be influenced. It is much better to introduce a private helper method that decides whether a particular point is in the increment or decrement fields. Placing this helper near the paintComponent()—that is, splitting the class logically between display and reaction code—will greatly facilitate maintenance.

↰1.4.5

celledit.docview.View

```
private void handleMouseUp(MouseEvent e) {
    if (cell.get() > 0 && isInDecrementArea(new Point(e.x, e.y)))
        cell.set(cell.get() - 1);
    ...
};
private boolean isInDecrementArea(Point p) {
    ...
}
```

In the end, this implementation is very near the original division between view and controller. One crucial difference is that now the helper method is not an external API that may be accessed from the outside and must therefore be maintained, but rather a private, encapsulated detail that may be changed at any time without breaking other parts of the system.

With predefined widgets, access their API directly.

In many cases, the actual display consists of predefined widgets such as text fields or tables. These widgets already encapsulate all painting-related aspects so that it is not necessary to introduce helpers. The DOCUMENT-VIEW pattern then applies very directly, since listeners can get the content or the selection of widgets without further ado.

9.3   The JFace Layer

↰7.1

SWT is a typical user interface toolkit that provides the standard interaction elements, such as text fields, tables, and trees, out of the box. How-

↰7.4

ever, it is also designed to be minimal: Since it accesses the native widgets of the platform that the application executes on, the SWT classes must be ported to every supported platform. For that reason, SWT offers only bare-bones functionality. Any higher-level functionality is factored out into the JFace framework, which is pure Java and portable. JFace facilitates connecting the application data structures to the existing SWT widgets, and is therefore indispensable for effective development of user interfaces. It also provides standard elements such as message dialogs and application windows equipped with a menu, toolbar, and status bar.

From a conceptual point of view, JFace provides a complementary perspective on model-view separation. While usually the model is stable and the user interface remains flexible, JFace provides fixed but generic user interface components that connect flexibly to application-specific models. Studying its mechanisms will enhance the understanding of model-view separation itself.

↠9.3.3

🔍 The JFace layer is contained in the bundle `org.eclipse.jface`, with extensions in `org.eclipse.jface.databinding` and `org.eclipse.jface.text`. For historical rea-

↰7.4.2

sons, it also relies on some elements of `org.eclipse.core.runtime`, which can be used outside of the platform in just the way that we launched SWT applications as standard Java applications.

9.3.1   Viewers

↠12.2.2

The basic approach of JFace is shown in Fig. 9.6(a). JFace establishes a layer between the application's business logic and the bare-bones SWT widgets. JFace uses methods like `setText` and `setIcon` to actually display the data in widgets and registers for low-level events as necessary. It also offers events to the application itself, but these are special in that they translate from the widget level to the model level. For instance, when a user selects a row in a `Table` widget, SWT reports the index of the row. JFace translates that index into the model element it has previously rendered in the row, and reports that this model element has been selected. In effect, the application is shielded from the cumbersome details and can always work in terms of its own data structures. Of course, it still listens to events such as button

clicks directly on the SWT widgets, and translates those into operations on   ↰9.2.1
the model. JFace follows model-view separation in getting the data to be   ↰9.1
displayed from the model and listening to change notifications of the model
to keep the display up-to-date.

   We will now discuss the various roles and relationships depicted in
Fig. 9.6. This section focuses on the *viewers* and their collaborators. The
listeners, which implement the application's reactions to user input in the
sense of controllers, are discussed in Section 9.3.2.   ↰9.2.1

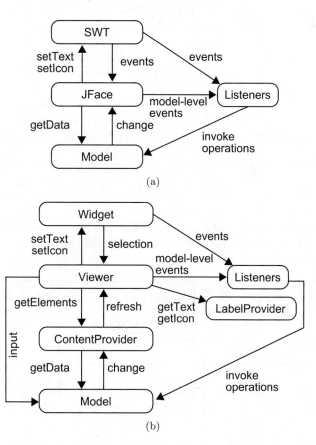

Figure 9.6 JFace Architecture

JFace viewers target specific widget types.

A core contribution of the JFace layer relates to its selection of generic *viewers*, each of which targets a specific type of widget: A `TableViewer` targets
`Table`s, a `ComboViewer` targets a `Combo` combo box, and so on [Fig. 9.6(b),
at the top]. Viewers use the widget-specific methods for displaying data and
listen for widget-specific events.

JFace viewers access the application data through adapters.

One question not addressed in Fig. 9.6(a) is how JFace will actually access the application-specific data: How is a generic viewer supposed to know the right `getData` method and the implementation of the OBSERVER pattern of the specific data structures? Fig. 9.6(b) supplies this detail. First, each viewer holds a reference to the model, in its property *input*. However, that input is a generic `Object`, so the viewer never accesses the model itself. Instead, the viewer is parameterized by two adapter objects that enable it to inspect the model just as required:

↰1.3.4 ↰2.4.1

- The *content provider* is responsible for traversing the overall data structure and for splitting it up into *elements* for display purposes. For a table or list, it provides a linear sequence of elements; for a tree-like display, it also accesses the child and parent links between the elements. Furthermore, the content provider must observe the model and notify the viewer about any changes that it receives.

↰2.4.1

- The *label provider* is called back for each element delivered by the content provider, usually to obtain concrete strings and icons to represent the element on the screen. A `ListViewer` will request one text/icon combination per element; a `TableViewer` or `TreeViewer` will request one combination for each column. The viewer will also observe the label provider to be notified about changes of the text and icons to be displayed.

⟋ The text-related viewers `TextViewer` and `SourceViewer` deviate from this schema in that they expect an implementation of `IDocument` as their model. The document itself then includes the text-specific access operations, without requiring a separate adapter.

⟋ The framework includes a deliberate redundancy regarding changes in the model: When values change within a data element, then those may be translated for the viewer either by the content provider, by calling the viewer's `update()` method, or by the label provider, by firing change events. Each mechanism has its merits. On the one hand, the content provider observes the model anyway, so the label provider can often remain passive. On the other hand, some generic label providers, such as those used in data binding, may wish to avoid relying on specific content providers.

≫9.3.3

Let us start with a simple example, in which an application accepts and monitors incoming TCP connections (Fig. 9.7). Whenever a new client connects, the corresponding information gets shown. When the client disconnects, its row is removed from the table.

Keep the model independent of JFace.

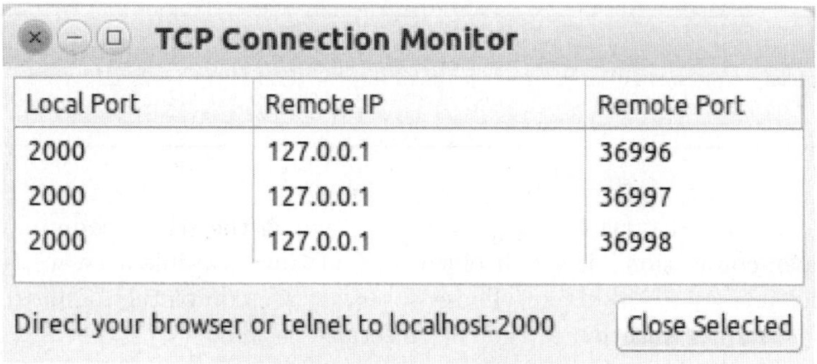

Figure 9.7 Connection Monitor

We start by developing the model of the application, with the intention of keeping it independent of the user interface, and more specifically the JFace API. The model here maintains a list of connections (which contain a `Socket` as the endpoint of a TCP connection). Furthermore, it implements the OBSERVER pattern, which explains the registration (and omitted de-registration) of listeners (lines 13–16), as well as the `fire` method for notifying the listeners (lines 18–20). The method `opened()` and corresponding method `closed()` will be called back from the actual server code. Since that code runs in a separate thread, all access to the internal data structures needs to be protected by locking. Finally, we decide that the notification of the observers can be performed in an open call (line 10), without holding on to the lock.

↰9.1

↰8.1

↰8.5

---

connections.ConnectionList

```
 1 public class ConnectionList {
 2     private ArrayList<Connection> openConnections =
 3                         new ArrayList<Connection>();
 4     private ListenerList listeners = new ListenerList();
 5
 6     void opened(Connection c) {
 7         synchronized (this) {
 8             openConnections.add(c);
 9         }
10         fireConnectionOpened(c);
11     }
12         ...
13     public synchronized void addConnectionListListener(
14                         ConnectionListListener l) {
15         listeners.add(l);
16     }
17         ...
18     protected void fireConnectionOpened(Connection c) {
19         ...
20     }
21         ...
22 }
```

🔎 We use `synchronized` for locking because the simplicity of the use case makes it
unlikely that we will ever need the flexibility of the library tools advocated in the
chapter on multithreading.

↰8

The important point about the model is that it is independent of the
user interface: It serves as a central list in which the server code manages
the open connections, it synchronizes the different possible accesses, and it
notifies interested observers. These observers are completely agnostic of a
possible implementation in the user interface as well:

---
connections.ConnectionListListener

```
public interface ConnectionListListener extends EventListener {
    void connectionOpened(ConnectionList p, Connection c);
    void connectionClosed(ConnectionList p, Connection c);
}
```

This finishes the model in Fig. 9.6(b). We will now fill in the remaining
bits.

Create the widget and its viewer together.

The viewer in Fig. 9.6(b) is linked tightly to its SWT widget: The type of
widget is fixed, and each viewer can fill only a single widget, since it keeps
track of which data it has displayed at which position within the widget.
One therefore creates the viewer and the widget together. If a viewer is
created without an explicit target widget, it will create the widget by itself.
↰7.1 The viewer constructor also takes the parent widget and flags, as usual for
SWT. The SWT widget is not encapsulated completely, since the display-
related services, such as computing layouts, are accessed directly.

---
connections.Main.createContents

```
connectionsViewer = new TableViewer(shell, SWT.BORDER);
connections = connectionsViewer.getTable();
connections.setLayoutData(new GridData(
                    SWT.FILL, SWT.FILL, true, true,
                    2, 1));
connections.setHeaderVisible(true);
```

Connect the viewer to the model through a special content provider.

Each model has, of course, a different structure and API, so that each model
will also require a new content provider class. The viewer then receives its
own instance of that class.

---
connections.Main.createContents

```
connectionsViewer.setContentProvider(
                    new ConnectionListContentProvider());
```

The reason for this one-to-one match between content provider object and viewer object is that the content provider usually has to be linked up very tightly between the viewer and its input [Fig. 9.6(b)]. The life cycle of the content provider clarifies this. Whenever the viewer receives a new input, it notifies its content provider through the `inputChanged()` method. The method must also make sure to de-register from the previous input (lines 8–9). When the viewer is disposed, with the SWT widget, it calls the method again with a new input of `null`. The logic for de-registering from the old model therefore also kicks in at the end of the life cycle. At this point, the viewer calls the content provider's `dispose()` method for any additional cleanup that may be necessary.

↰2.1.2

```
                    connections.ConnectionListContentProvider
 1 public class ConnectionListContentProvider implements
 2          IStructuredContentProvider, ConnectionListListener {
 3      private ConnectionList list;
 4      private TableViewer viewer;
 5      public void inputChanged(Viewer viewer, Object oldInput,
 6                      Object newInput) {
 7          this.viewer = (TableViewer) viewer;
 8          if (list != null)
 9              list.removeConnectionListListener(this);
10          this.list = (ConnectionList) newInput;
11          if (list != null)
12              list.addConnectionListListener(this);
13      }
14      public void dispose() {}
15      ...
16 }
```

Line 7 in this code assumes that the viewer is a `TableViewer`. This can be justified by stating in the class's contract that the content provider may be used only with that kind of viewer. The non-redundancy principle then decrees that line 7 must not check whether the contract is actually obeyed. Many content providers in the Eclipse code base are more defensive, or general, at this point and do something sensible for different kinds of viewers.

↰4.5

The content provider knows how to traverse the model's structure.

The content provider in Fig. 9.6(b) is an adapter that provides the interface expected by the JFace viewer on top of the application's model. Designing this interface is an interesting task: Which kind of common structure can one expect to find on all models? The approach in JFace is to start from the minimal requirements of the `TableViewer`, as the (main) client: A table is a linear list of rows, so the viewer has to be able to get the data elements behind these table rows. In the current example, each row is a `Connection` and the model already provides a method to obtain the current list. The

↰3.2.2

inputElement is the viewer's input model passed to inputChanged();
passing it again enables stateless and therefore shareable content providers.

---

connections.ConnectionListContentProvider.getElements

```
public Object[] getElements(Object inputElement) {
    return ((ConnectionList) inputElement).getOpenConnections();
}
```

To see more of the idea of generic interface components, let us consider
briefly a tree, rendered in a TreeViewer. A tree has more structure than a
flat table: The single elements may have children, and all but the top-level
elements have a parent. Tree-like widgets usually enable multiple top-level
elements, rather than a single root, so that the content provider has the
same method getElements() as the provider for flat tables.

---

org.eclipse.jface.viewers.ITreeContentProvider

```
public interface ITreeContentProvider
                      extends IStructuredContentProvider {
    public Object[] getElements(Object inputElement);
    public Object[] getChildren(Object parentElement);
    public Object getParent(Object element);
    public boolean hasChildren(Object element);
}
```

Now the JFace viewer can traverse the application model's data structure by querying each element in turn. As long as the model has a table-like
or tree-like structure, respectively, it will fit the expectations of the JFace
layer. In general, each viewer expects a specific kind of content provider
stated in its documentation, according to the visual structure of the tar-
geted widget.

□ 60

⌕ You may find it rather irritating that all viewers offer only the generic method shown
   next, which does not give an indication of the expected type. The deeper reason is
that it is in principle not possible to override a method and specialize its the parameter
types, because this *co-variant* overriding breaks polymorphism: A client that works with
only the base class might unsuspectingly pass a too-general object. Java therefore requires
overriding methods to have exactly the same parameter types.

---

org.eclipse.jface.viewers.StructuredViewer

```
public void setContentProvider(IContentProvider provider)
```

↰ 1.3.8

⌕ For simple display cases where the model does not change, one can also use the
   ArrayContentProvider, which accepts a List or an array and simply returns its
elements. Since it does not have any state, it implements the SINGLETON pattern.

The label provider decides on the concrete visual representation.

In the end, SWT shows most data on the screen as text, perhaps with
auxiliary icons to give the user visual hints for interpreting the text, such
as a green check mark to indicate success. The label provider attached to
JFace viewers implements just this transformation, from data to text and
icons. In the example, the table has three columns for the local port, the
remote IP, and the remote port. All of this data is available from the `Socket`
stored in the connection, so the label provider just needs to look into the
right places and format the data into strings.

connections.ConnectionListLabelProvider

```
public class ConnectionListLabelProvider
                    extends LabelProvider
                    implements ITableLabelProvider {
    ...
    public String getColumnText(Object element, int columnIndex) {
        Connection c = (Connection) element;
        switch (columnIndex) {
        case 0: return Integer.toString(c.getLocalPort());
        case 1: return c.getRemoteAddr().getHostAddress();
        case 2: return Integer.toString(c.getRemotePort());
        default:
            throw new IllegalArgumentException();
        }
    }
}
```

🔎 A corresponding `getIcon()` method remains empty here. If icons are allocated for   ↰7.4.1
the specific label provider, they must be freed in its `dispose()` method, which the
viewer calls whenever the widget disappears from the screen.

🔎 The base class `LabelProvider`, or actually its superclass `BaseLabelProvider`, implements an observer pattern that enables concrete label providers to notify viewers
about changes in the choice of text or icon. Model changes are usually handled through
the content provider, as seen next.

By separating the concerns of model traversal and the actual display,
JFace gains flexibility. For instance, different viewers might show different
aspects and properties of the same model, so that the same content provider
can be combined with different label providers.

The viewer manages untyped `Objects`.

We have found that at this point it is useful to get a quick overview of the viewer's mechanisms, so as to better appreciate the respective roles and the interactions of the viewer, the content provider, and the label provider. At the same time, these interactions illustrate the concept of generic mechanisms, which will become fundamental in the area of frameworks and for providing extensibility.

»11.1
»12.3

Fig. 9.8 shows what happens from the point where the application supplies the model until the data shows up on the screen. The input is forwarded to the content provider, which chops up the overall model into elements. The viewer passes each of these elements to the label provider and receives back a string. It then displays that string on the screen. For deeper structures, the viewer queries children of elements, and again hands each of these to the label provider, until the structure is exhausted.

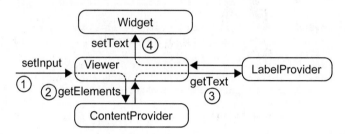

Figure 9.8 The Sequence for Displaying Data Through Viewers

In the end, the viewer's role is to manage untyped objects belonging to the application's model: It keeps references to the model and all elements as `Objects`. Whenever it needs to find out more about such an object, it passes the object to the content or label provider. In this way, the viewer can implement powerful generic display mechanisms without actually knowing anything about the application data.

Forward change notifications to the viewer.

We have now set up the display of the initial model. However, the model changes over the time, and it fires change notifications. Like any adapter [Fig. 2.10(b) on page 137], the content provider must also translate those notifications for the benefit of the viewer [Fig. 9.6(b)].

Toward that end, JFace viewers offer generic notification callbacks that reflect the possible changes in the abstract list or tree model that they envision in their content provider interface. A `TableViewer`, for instance, has callbacks for additions, insertions, deletions, and updates of single elements. The difference between `update()` and `refresh()` is that the first method locally recomputes the labels in a single table entry, while the latter indicates structural changes at the element, though it is relevant only for trees.

---

org.eclipse.jface.viewers.AbstractTableViewer

```
public void add(Object element)
public void insert(Object element, int position)
public void remove(Object element)
public void update(Object element, String[] properties)
public void refresh(Object element)
```

⚠ Even though these methods are `public` as a technical necessity, they are not for general use but are intended for the content provider only. In particular, they do *not* add or remove the given elements from the underlying model.

🔍 As a matter of optimization, viewers offer variants of these methods for bulk updates of several objects passed in an array. For large models, `TableViewer` and `TreeViewer` also support lazy population of the widget through the `SWT.VIRTUAL` flag passed to the constructor. In this case, the content provider can implement `ILazyContentProvider` or `ILazyTreeContentProvider`, respectively. The viewer will call the content provider only for rows that become visible—for instance, by scrolling or unfolding of tree nodes. The overhead of initially filling the entire widget is avoided.

In the running example, connections can be added to and removed from the list of current connections. The content provider listens to these changes and notifies the viewer accordingly. Since the server uses several threads for the processing of client connections, the content provider must also switch to the event thread to notify the viewer.

↰7.10.1

connections.ConnectionListContentProvider.connectionOpened

```
public void connectionOpened(ConnectionList p, final Connection c) {
    viewer.getControl().getDisplay().asyncExec(new Runnable() {
        public void run() {
            viewer.add(c);
        }
    });
}
```

🌍 Swing's `JTable` takes a different—and very interesting—approach to these notifications, which renders the idea of an "adapter" more clearly. Its method `setModel()` accepts any implementation of `TableModel`, and that model must provide the OBSERVER pattern for `TableModelListeners`. The generic `JTable` widget merely registers as one such listener. The JFace perspective, in contrast, is that the content provider is a close collaborator of a single viewer, which it notifies directly. This approach saves the effort of implementing the OBSERVER pattern.

↰2.4.1
↰2.1

↰2.1.4

Viewers provide higher-level services at the application level.

JFace viewers offer more services than just a mapping from application model to screen display. For instance, they enable the application code to work almost entirely at the level of the application model. Consequently, SWT widgets, for example, represent the concept of "selection" by publishing the indices of selected elements. JFace viewers, in contrast, publish `IStructuredSelection` objects, which are basically sets of model elements. Furthermore, viewers do not map elements directly, but perform preprocessing steps for filtering and sorting. As a final example, they implement mechanisms for inline editing: When the user clicks "into" a table cell, the table viewer creates a small overlay containing an application-specific `CellEditor` that fills the cell's screen space but is, in fact, a stand-alone widget.

↰7.6

↰9.1

💡 Sorting and filtering are interesting in themselves as an instance of model-view separation: The fact that a user prefers, in certain situations and for certain tasks, to see only a selection of elements in a particular order, must be dealt with independently of the core functionality—after all, the next view or the next user may have entirely different preferences. For instance, Eclipse's Java Model reflects the structure of the Java source code. The underlying abstract syntax tree keeps declarations in the order of their appearance within a class. At the interface level, the user may prefer seeing only `public` members or having the members be ordered alphabetically, as seen in the *Package Explorer*.

↰2.4.1

9.3.2   Finishing Model-View-Controller with JFace

↰9.2.1

JFace viewers already cover much of the MODEL-VIEWER-CONTROLLER pattern, in that the screen reliably mirrors the state of the application's functional core. The only missing aspect is that of controllers, which interpret the raw user input as requests for performing operations on the model. This will happen in the event-listeners shown in Fig. 9.6.

> JFace enables controllers to work on the application model.

Suppose that we wish to implement the button labeled "Close" in Fig. 9.7. Since the button itself is an SWT widget independent of any viewer, we attach a listener as usual:

↰7.1

```
                    connections.Main.createContents
Button btnClose = new Button(shell, SWT.NONE);
btnClose.addSelectionListener(new SelectionAdapter() {
    public void widgetSelected(SelectionEvent e) {
        handleCloseSelected();
    }
});
```

The method `handleCloseSelected()` then relies heavily on support from JFace. Line 3 retrieves the viewer's selection, which maps the indices of rows selected in the table widget to the model elements shown in those rows. As a result, line 5 can ask for the first (and only) selected element

and be sure to obtain a `Connection`, because the viewer's content provider ↰9.3.1
has delivered instances of only that class. The crucial point now is that
the actual logic for implementing the desired reaction in line 7 remains at
the application level: The model's `Connection` objects also offer a method
`close()` for terminating the TCP connection with the client.

connections.Main
```
1  protected void handleCloseSelected() {
2      IStructuredSelection s =
3          (IStructuredSelection) connectionsViewer.getSelection();
4      Connection selectedConnection =
5          (Connection) s.getFirstElement();
6      if (selectedConnection != null) {
7          selectedConnection.close();
8      }
9  }
```

🔍 The implementation of the `Connection`'s close method at first seems simple enough:
We simply have to close the underlying TCP connection.

connections.Connection
```
public void close() throws IOException {
    channel.close();
}
```

However, this method finally runs in the event thread, while the server is concurrently ↰7.10.1
processing client input in background threads. This use case is not supported by the basic ↰7.10
`Socket` API, but only by the *asynchronously closeable* TCP connections introduced with
the NIO API in Java 1.4. The details are explained in the documentation of the interface
`InterruptibleChannel`.

Screen updates follow the MVC pattern.

Let us finally reconsider the fundamental reaction cycle of the MODEL- ↰9.2.1
VIEW-CONTROLLER pattern: The window system delivers events to the
view, which forwards them to the controller, which interprets them as requests for operations on the model, which sends change notifications to the
view, which repaints parts of the data on the screen. So far, we have seen the
first half: SWT delivers the button click to the application's event-listener,
which serves as a controller and decides that the selected connection should
be closed.

And now something really interesting happens, because the model is
not a simple list, but involves side effects on the underlying TCP connections. Executing `close()` on the connection goes down to the operation
system, which will declare the connection terminated some time later. This,
in turn, causes the `read()` method accepting client input (line 4 in the next
code snippet) to return with result "end of stream," which terminates the
server loop (lines 4–6). As a result, this particular server thread terminates

(line 10), but not before notifying the `ConnectionList` about this fact (line 8).

connections.Server.run

```
1  public void run() {
2      list.opened(conn);
3      ...
4      while (channel.read(buf) != -1) {
5          ...  send input back to client as demo
6      }
7      ...
8      list.closed(conn);
9      ...
10 }
```

Upon receiving this latter signal, the MVC mechanisms kick in to effect the screen update: The `ConnectionListContentProvider` observes the model and translates the incoming `connectionClosed()` event into a `remove()` notification of the table viewer, which removes the corresponding row from the SWT display. That's it.

9.3.3 Data Binding

The mechanisms of JFace presented so far make it fairly simple to display data so that the screen is kept up-to-date when the data changes. However, the content and label providers have to be programmed by hand, and changing the data is not supported by the framework at all. The concept of *data binding* addresses both concerns. Broadly speaking, data binding maps the individual properties of beans to widgets such as text fields or lists. One also says that the properties are *bound to* the widgets, or more symmetrically that the property and the widget are *bound*.

↰1.3.3

↰7.2

The WindowBuilder includes a graphical tool for creating bindings, so that data binding makes it simple to bridge the model-view separation by quickly creating input masks for given model elements. The usage is mostly intuitive: Select two properties to be bound and click the "bind" button. We will therefore discuss only the few nonobvious cases.

▯201
▯234
▯222

Many frameworks cover the concept of data binding. For instance, *JavaServer Faces* (JSF) allows you to bind input components to model fields declaratively through special *Expression Language* (EL) annotations. *Ruby on Rails* is famed for its effective way of creating input masks through simple form helpers. Microsoft's *Windows Presentation Foundation* (WPF) offers an especially comprehensive treatment of data binding.

↰1.3.3

↰2.1

We will discuss the details of data binding in JFace using the example of editing an *address book*, which is essentially a list of *contacts* (Fig. 9.9). The `AddressBook` and its `Contact` objects are simple Java beans; that is, their state consists of public properties and they send change notifications. From top to bottom in Fig. 9.9, we see the following features of

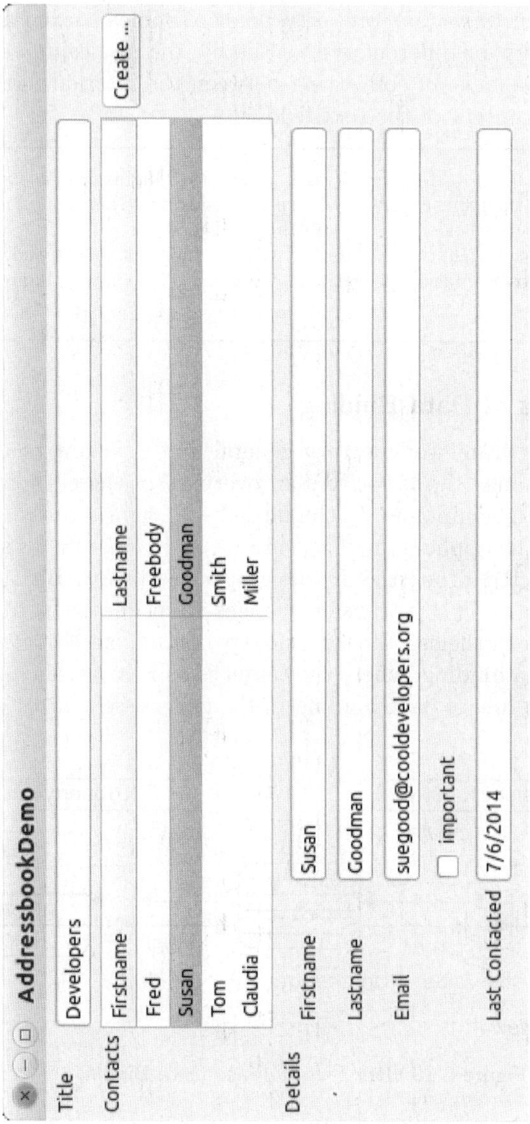

Figure 9.9 Address Book Editor

data binding, ordered by increasing complexity: The address book's *title* property is bound to a text field; its *contacts* property is a list of `Contact` beans shown in a JFace viewer. In a master/detail view, the details of the currently selected contact are shown in the lower part. Here, the *first name*, *last name*, and *email* properties of the contact are, again, bound directly to text fields. The *important* property holds a Boolean value and demonstrates the support for different types. Finally, the *last contacted* property introduces the challenge of converting between the internal `Date` property and the `String` content of the text field.

🔎 The JFace data binding framework lives in several plugins, which must be set as dependencies in the `MANIFEST.MF` of any plugin using the framework. In the spirit of model-view separation, those parts not dealing with the user interface reside in `org.eclipse.core.databinding`, `org.eclipse.core.databinding.beans`, and `org.eclipse.core.property`. Those connected to the display directly reside in the plugin `org.eclipse.jface.databinding`.

9.3.3.1   Basics of Data Binding

The data binding framework is very general and is meant to cover many possible applications. Fig. 9.10 gives an overview of the elements involved in one binding. The endpoints, to the far left and right, are the widget and bean created by the application. The purpose of a *binding* is to synchronize the value of selected properties in the respective beans. Bindings are, in principle, symmetric: They transfer changes from one bean to the other, and vice versa. Nevertheless, the terminology distinguishes between a *model* and the *target* of a binding, where the target is usually a widget. The figure also indicates the role of data binding in the general scheme of model-view separation.

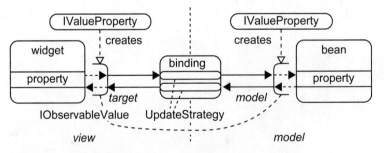

Figure 9.10 Overview of JFace Data Binding

To keep the data binding framework independent of the application objects, these are adapted to the `IObservableValue` interface in the next code snippet, as indicated by the half-open objects beside the properties in Fig. 9.10. The adapters enable getting and setting a value, as well as observing changes, as would be expected from the basic MVC pattern. The

↰9.3.1

↰7.2.2

↰9.1

↰9.1

↰2.4.1

↰9.2.1

value type is used for consistency checking within the framework, as well as for accessing the adaptees efficiently by reflection.

---

org.eclipse.core.databinding.observable.value.IObservableValue

```
public interface IObservableValue extends IObservable {
    public Object getValueType();
    public Object getValue();
    public void setValue(Object value);
    public void addValueChangeListener(
                    IValueChangeListener listener);
    public void removeValueChangeListener(
                    IValueChangeListener listener);
}
```

The `IObservableValue` in this code captures values of atomic types. There are analogous interfaces `IObservableList`, `IObservableSet`, and `IObservableMap` to bind properties holding compound values.

Creating these adapters often involves some analysis, such as looking up the getter and setter methods for a named property by reflection. The adapters are therefore usually created by `IValueProperty` objects, which serve as abstract factories. Again, analogous interfaces `IListProperty`, `ISetProperty`, and `IMapProperty` capture factories for compound value properties.

↰1.4.12

---

org.eclipse.core.databinding.property.value.IValueProperty

```
public interface IValueProperty extends IProperty {
    public Object getValueType();
    public IObservableValue observe(Object source);
    ...  observing parts of the value
}
```

We have now discussed enough of the framework to bind the *name* property of an `AddressBook` in the field `model` to a text field in the interface. Lines 1–2 in the next code snippet create an `IValueProperty` for the *text* property of an SWT widget and use it immediately to create the adapter for the `bookname` text field. The code specifies that the property is considered changed whenever the user leaves the field (event `SWT.FocusOut`); setting the event to `SWT.Modify` updates the model property after every keystroke. Lines 3–4 proceed analogously for the *name* property of the `AddressBook`. Finally, lines 5–6 create the actual binding.

---

databinding.AddressBookDemo.initDataBindings

```
1 IObservableValue observeTextBooknameObserveWidget =
2     WidgetProperties .text(SWT.FocusOut).observe(bookname);
3 IObservableValue nameModelObserveValue =
4     BeanProperties.value("name") .observe(model);
5 bindingContext.bindValue(observeTextBooknameObserveWidget,
6                     nameModelObserveValue, null, null);
```

🔍 A *binding context* manages a set of bindings. The two `null` values in line 6 indicate that no update strategies (Fig. 9.10) are required.

↰7.10.1
🔍 The framework anticipates the possibility of multithreading in the model, which requires switching to the event dispatch thread at appropriate moments. Each observable value is said to live in a specific *realm*. One realm, accessible by `SWTObservables.getRealm()`, is associated with the event thread. A *default realm* can be set with `Realm.runWithDefault()`, so that it is usually not necessary to specify a realm explicitly for individual values.

9.3.3.2   Master/Detail Views

Fig. 9.9 includes a typical editing scenario: The list *contacts* is a *master* list showing an overview; below this list, several fields give access to the *details* of the currently selected list element. The master list itself involves only binding a property, as seen in the following code snippet. On the viewer ↰9.3.1 side, special content and label providers then accomplish the data access and updates.

---
databinding.AddressBookDemo.initDataBindings

```
IObservableList contactsModelObserveList = BeanProperties
        .list("contacts").observe(model);
contactsViewer.setInput(contactsModelObserveList);
```

The actual master/detail view is established by a two-step binding of properties. Lines 3–4 in the next example create a possibly changing value that tracks the currently selected `Contact` element as a value: Whenever the selection changes, the value of the property changes. Building on this, lines 5–8 create a two-step access path to the *first name* property: The `observeDetail()` call tracks the current `Contact` and registers as an observer for that contact, so that it also sees its property changes; the `value()` call then delivers an atomic `String` value for the property. Through these double observers, this atomic value will change whenever either the selection or the *first name* property of the current selection changes.

---
databinding.AddressBookDemo.initDataBindings

```
1 IObservableValue observeTextTxtFirstObserveWidget =
2     WidgetProperties.text(SWT.Modify).observe(txtFirst);
3 IObservableValue observeSingleSelectionContactsViewer =
4     ViewerProperties.singleSelection().observe(contactsViewer);
5 IObservableValue contactsViewerFirstnameObserveDetailValue =
6     BeanProperties
7         .value(Contact.class, "firstname", String.class)
8         .observeDetail(observeSingleSelectionContactsViewer);
```

```
 9 bindingContext.bindValue(observeTextTxtFirstObserveWidget,
10          contactsViewerFirstnameObserveDetailValue, null, null);
```

> ⌕ At this point, the usage of the WindowBuilder is somewhat unintuitive, because the "model" side of the binding involves the JFace-level selection. The two panels shown here appear on the right-hand, model side of the WindowBuilder's *bindings* page. In the first, one has to select the *widgets* tree, instead of the *beans*, in the upper-right corner. From the table *contactsViewer* appearing in the second panel, one then chooses *part of selection*. The subsequent dialog requests a choice of the selection's content type and desired detail field.

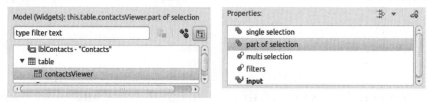

9.3.3.3   Data Conversion and Validation

We finish this section on data binding by discussing the crucial detail of *validation and conversion*. The need arises from the fact that the model's data is stored in formats optimized for internal processing, while the user interface offers only generic widgets, so that the data must often be displayed and edited in text fields. One example is the *last contacted* property of a `Contact`, which internally is a `Date`, but which is edited as a text with a special format (Fig. 9.9).

The basic property binding follows, of course, the master/detail approach. The new point is the use of *update strategies* (Fig. 9.10), as illustrated in the next code snippet. Each binding can be characterized by separate strategies for the two directions of synchronization. Lines 1–5 specify that the text entered in the interface should be converted to a `Date` to be stored in the model, and that this transfer should take place only if the text is in an acceptable format. The other direction in lines 6–8 is less problematic, as any `Date` can be converted to a string for display. Lines 9–11 then create the binding, with the specified update policies.

↰9.3.3.2

```
              databinding.AddressBookDemo.initDataBindings
 1 UpdateValueStrategy targetToModelStrategy =
 2                        new UpdateValueStrategy();
 3 targetToModelStrategy.setConverter(new StringToDateConverter());
 4 targetToModelStrategy.setAfterGetValidator(
 5                        new StringToDateValidator());
 6 UpdateValueStrategy modelToTargetStrategy =
 7                        new UpdateValueStrategy();
 8 modelToTargetStrategy.setConverter(new DateToStringConverter());
 9 bindingContext.bindValue(observeTextTxtLastcontactedObserveWidget,
```

```
10          contactsViewerLastContactedObserveDetailValue,
11          targetToModelStrategy, modelToTargetStrategy);
```

To demonstrate the mechanism, let us create a custom converter, as specified by the `IConverter` interface. The method `convert()` takes a string. It returns `null` for the empty string and otherwise parses the string into a specific format. It treats a parsing failure as an unexpected occurrence.

↰1.5.7

databinding.StringToDateConverter

```
public class StringToDateConverter implements IConverter {
    static SimpleDateFormat formatter =
                    new SimpleDateFormat("M/d/yyyy");
    ... source and destination types for consistency checking
    public Object convert(Object fromObject) {
        String txt = ((String) fromObject).trim();
        if (txt.length() == 0)
            return null;
        try {
            return formatter.parse(txt);
        } catch (ParseException e) {
            throw new IllegalArgumentException(txt, e);
        }
    }
}
```

The validator checks whether a particular string matches the application's expectations. In the present case, it is sufficient that the string can be converted without error, which is checked by attempting the conversion. In other cases, further restrictions can be suitable.

databinding.StringToDateValidator

```
public class StringToDateValidator implements IValidator {
    public IStatus validate(Object value) {
        try {
            StringToDateConverter.formatter.parse((String) value);
            return Status.OK_STATUS;
        } catch (ParseException e) {
            return ValidationStatus.error("Incorrect format");
        }
    }
}
```

Conversion and validation are specified separately since they often have to vary independently. Very often, the converted value has to fulfill further restrictions beyond being convertible, such as a date being within a specified range. Also, even data that is not constrained by the internal type, such as an email address stored as a `String`, must obey restrictions on its form.

🔎 Very often, it is simpler to validate the converted value rather than the raw format. Update strategies offer `setAfterConvertValidator` and `setBeforeSetValidator` for this purpose. Both work on the result of conversion. The only difference is that the latter may not be called in case the update strategy is configured not to update the model at all (see `ValueBinding.doUpdate()` for the details).

The class `MultiValidator` provides mechanisms for checking cross-field constraints, such as the end date of some activity being later than its start date.

Conversion and validation touch upon a central aspect of user interfaces—namely, the fact that the interface belongs to the system boundary. The boundary has the special obligation to check all incoming data to avoid corrupting the system's internal structures and to prevent malicious attacks. Furthermore, it must convert all data into the internal formats, to prepare it for efficient processing. Validators therefore do not simply check that the data is convertible, but also check that the data is acceptable to the system as a whole. Conversion and validation therefore create a uniform framework to handle these aspects, and this explains their presence in many of the major interface toolkits.

↶1.5.2 ↶4.6

Another observation concerns the relation between validation and conversion. Most converters cannot handle all inputs allowed by their expected input types. In other words, their `convert()` method has an implicit pre-condition. The role of the validator is to check that the pre-condition is fulfilled before the framework attempts the actual conversion. This relation also explains why the example validator refers back to the converter: It simply ensures a perfect match of the checked condition and the required condition.

↶4.1

9.3.4   Menus and Actions

We have seen that JFace viewers connect generic SWT widgets such as lists or tables to an application model [Fig. 9.6(b) on page 473]: The viewer queries the data structures and maps the data to text and icons within the widget. It also listens to model changes and updates the corresponding entries in the widget.

A similar mechanism is used for adding entries to menus and toolbars. SWT offers only basic `MenuItems`, which behave like special `Buttons` and notify attached listeners when they have been clicked. SWT menu items, just like other widgets, are passive: While they can show a text and icon, and can be enabled or disabled, they wait for the application to set these properties.

↶7.1

To keep this chapter self-contained, the presentation here refers to the example application MiniXcel, a minimal spreadsheet editor to be introduced in Section 9.4. For now, it is sufficient to understand that at the core, a `SpreadSheetView` displays a `SpreadSheet` model, as would be expected from the MODEL-VIEW-CONTROLLER pattern.

↶9.2.1

Actions represent application-specific operations.

↰1.8.6

↰9.1

JFace connects SWT menus to application-specific *actions*, which implement `IAction` (shown next). Actions wrap code that can act directly on the application's model (lines 6–7). But actions also describe themselves for display purposes (lines 3–4), and they identify themselves to avoid showing duplicates (line 2). Finally, it is anticipated that an action's properties will change, in much the same way that an application's model changes (lines 9–12).

org.eclipse.jface.action.IAction

```
1  public interface IAction {
2      public String getId();
3      public String getText();
4      public ImageDescriptor getImageDescriptor();
5
6      public void run();
7      public void runWithEvent(Event event);
8
9      public void addPropertyChangeListener(
10                     IPropertyChangeListener listener);
11     public void removePropertyChangeListener(
12                     IPropertyChangeListener listener);
13     ... setters for the properties and further properties
14 }
```

▢▢100 ⟫9.5.1

The concept of an "action" that acts as a self-contained representation of some operation is virtually universal. One variant of the COMMAND pattern captures the idea: Swing has a very similar interface `Action`, Qt has a `QAction` class, and so on.

Contribution items connect menu items to actions.

To connect SWT's passive menu items to the application's available actions, JFace introduces *menu managers* and *contribution items* (Fig. 9.11, upper part). Each menu is complemented by a menu manager that fills the menu and updates it dynamically when the contributions change. Each SWT menu item is complemented by a contribution item that manages its appearance. Initially, it fills the menu item's text, icon, and enabled state. Whenever a property of the action changes, the contribution item updates the menu item correspondingly. In the reverse direction, the contribution item listens for clicks on the menu item and then invokes the action's `run()` method (or more precisely, the `runWithEvent()` method).

Actions are usually shared between different contribution managers.

One detail not shown in Fig. 9.11 is that action objects are independent of the concrete menu or toolbar where they get displayed. They are not

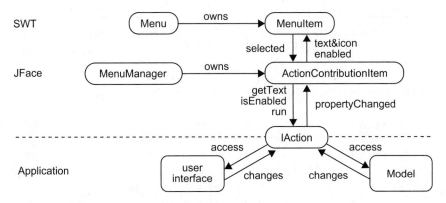

Figure 9.11 Menus and Actions in JFace

simply an elegant way of filling a menu, but rather represent an operation and thus have a meaning in themselves. Eclipse editors usually store their actions in a local table, from where they can be handed on to menus and toolbars. In the example, we use a simple hash map keyed on the action's ids.

───
                minixcel.ui.window.MainWindow
───
```
private Map<String, IAction> actions =
                    new HashMap<String, IAction>();
```

Create the menu manager, then update the SWT widgets.

Once the table holds all actions, a concrete menu can be assembled quickly: Just fill a menu manager and tell it to update the menu. For instance, the MiniXcel spreadsheet application has an edit menu with typical undo and redo actions, as well as a "clear current cell" action. Lines 1–8 create the structure of nested menu managers. Lines 9–11 flush that structure into the visible SWT menu.

»9.4

───
            minixcel.ui.window.MainWindow.createContents
───
```
1 MenuManager menu = new MenuManager();
2 ...  set up File menu
3 MenuManager editMenu = new MenuManager("Edit");
4 menu.add(editMenu);
5 editMenu.add(actions.get(UndoAction.ID));
6 editMenu.add(actions.get(RedoAction.ID));
7 editMenu.add(new Separator("cellActions"));
8 editMenu.add(actions.get(ClearCellAction.ID));
9 shlMinixcel.setMenuBar(menu.createMenuBar(
10                         (Decorations)shlMinixcel));
11 menu.updateAll(true);
```

🔎 The cast to `Decorations` in line 10 is necessary only because an overloaded method taking a `Shell` argument is now deprecated.

Actions are usually wired to some context.

The lower part of Fig. 9.11 highlights another aspect of action objects: They are self-contained representations of some operation that the user can invoke through the user interface. The `run()` method is the entry point; everything else is encapsulated in the concrete action. This means, however, that the action will be linked tightly to a special context. In the example, the action that clears the currently selected cell must certainly find and access that cell, so it needs a reference to the `SpreadSheetView`. (The command processor `cmdProc` is required for undoable operations, as seen later on.)

»9.5

```
                                minixcel.ui.window.MainWindow
private void createActions() {
    ...
    actions.put(ClearCellAction.ID,
            new ClearCellAction(spreadSheetView, cmdProc));
}
```

📖174

The same phenomenon of exporting a selection of possible operations is also seen in Eclipse's wiring of actions into the global menu bar. There, again, the actions are created inside an editor component but get connected to the global menu and toolbar. This larger perspective also addresses the question of how global menu items are properly linked up to the currently open editor.

9.4   The MVC Pattern at the Application Level

So far, we have looked at the basic MODEL-VIEW-CONTROLLER pattern and its implementation in the JFace framework. The examples have been rather small and perhaps a little contrived, to enable us to focus on the mechanisms and crucial design constraints. Now it is time to scale the gained insights to the application level. The question we will pursue is how model-view separation influences the architecture of the overall product. Furthermore, we will look at details that need to be considered for this scaling, such as incremental repainting of the screen.

The running example will be a minimal spreadsheet application *Mini-Xcel* (Fig. 9.12). In this application, the user can select a cell in a special widget displaying the spreadsheet, and can enter a formula into that cell, possibly referring to other cells. The application is responsible for updating all dependent cells automatically, as would be expected.

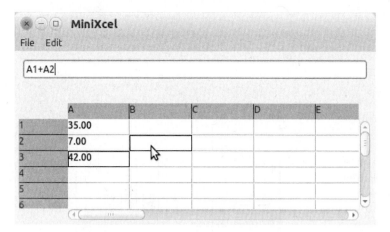

Figure 9.12 The MiniXcel Application

   The application offers enough complexity to explore the points mentioned previously. First, the model contains dependencies between cells in the form of formulas, and the parsing of and computation with formulas constitutes a nontrivial functionality in itself. At the interface level, we need a custom-painted widget for the spreadsheet, which must also offer view-level visual feedback and a selection mechanism to link the spreadsheet to the input line on top.

9.4.1   Setting up the Application

The overall structure of the application is shown in Fig. 9.13. The Spread Sheet encapsulates the functional core. It manages *cells*, which can be addressed from the outside by usual *coordinates* such as A2 or B3, as well as their interdependencies given by the stored formulas. A *formula* is a tree-structured COMPOSITE that performs the actual computations. A simple (shift-reduce) *parser* transforms the input strings given by the user into structured formulas. The core point of model-view separation is implemented by making all functionality that is not directly connected to the user interface completely independent of considerations about the display.

   The main window (Fig. 9.12) consists of two parts: the SpreadSheet View at the bottom and the CellEditor at the top. These two are coupled loosely: The SpreadSheetView does not assume that there is a single Cell Editor. Instead, it publishes a generic IStructuredSelection containing the currently selected Cell model element. When the user presses "enter," the cell editor can simply call setFormula on that Cell. This has two effects. First, the dependent cells within the spreadsheet are updated by reevaluating their formulas. Second, all updated cells will notify the view, through their surrounding SpreadSheet model.

↰9.1

↰2.3.1
⊞2
↰9.1

↠12.1

↰9.3.2

↰2.2.4

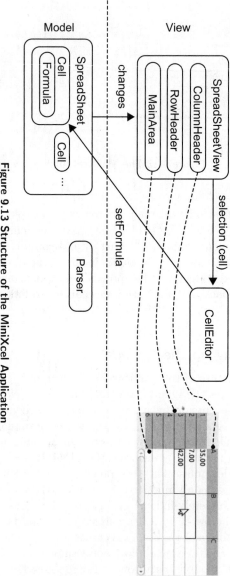

Figure 9.13 Structure of the MiniXcel Application

Despite the visual similarity between Fig. 9.13 and Fig. 9.3, the `CellEditor` is *not* the controller for the `SpreadSheetView`. The `CellEditor` is a stand-alone widget that, as we will see, contains a view and a controller, where the controller invokes the `set Formula` operation noted in Fig. 9.13.

9.4.2 Defining the Model

We can give here only a very brief overview of the model code and highlight those aspects that shape the collaboration between user interface and model. The central element of the model is the `SpreadSheet` class. It keeps a sparse mapping from coordinates to `Cells` (line 2) and creates cells on demand as they are requested from the outside (lines 5–12). The model implements the OBSERVER pattern as usual to enable the view to remain up-to-date (lines 4, 14–16, 18–20). The class `Coordinates` merely stores a row and column of a cell.

minixcel.model.spreadsheet.SpreadSheet

```java
public class SpreadSheet {
    private final HashMap<Coordinates, Cell> cells =
                     new HashMap<Coordinates, Cell>();
    private final ListenerList listeners = new ListenerList();
    public Cell getCell(Coordinates coord) {
        Cell res = cells.get(coord);
        if (res == null) {
            res = new Cell(this, coord);
            cells.put(coord, res);
        }
        return res;
    }

    public void addSpreadSheetListener(SpreadSheetListener l) {
        listeners.add(l);
    }
    ...
    void fireCellChanged(Cell cell) {
        ...
    }
    ...
}
```

A real-world implementation that scales to hundreds and thousands of rows full of data would probably create a matrix of cells, rather than a hash map. However, it must be noted that each cell in the spreadsheet will have to carry additional information, such as the dependencies due to formulas, so it might be useful to make cells into objects in any case. Only their organization into the overall spreadsheet would differ.

Application models usually have internal dependencies.

Each `Cell` in the spreadsheet must store the user's input (line 4 in the next code snippet) and must be prepared to evaluate that formula quickly (line 5). Since the view will query the current value rather frequently and other cells will require it for evaluating their own formulas, it is sensible to cache that value rather than repeatedly recomputing it (line 6). As further basic data, the cell keeps its owner and the position in that owner (lines 2–3).

↰2.2.1

⌕ We have decided to keep the original formula string, because the parsed formula loses information about parentheses and whitespace. Real-world spreadsheets keep an intermediate form of *tokens* (called "parse thing," or PTG in this context) resulting from lexing, rather than full parsing. If whitespace is kept, the original representation can be restored. If the tokens are stored post-order, formula evaluation is quick as well. A further advantage of this representation is that references can be updated when cell contents are moved.

⊞10
⊞2

↰2.3.4

The example of spreadsheets also shows that an application model is rarely as simple as, for instance, a list of Java beans. Usually, the objects within the model require complex interdependencies and collaborations to implement the desired functionality. In `Cells`, we store the (few) cross references introduced by the `formula` in two lists: `dependsOn` lists those cells whose values are required in the `formula`; `dependentOnThis` is the inverse relationship, which is required for propagating updates through the spreadsheet.

↰1.3.3

minixcel.model.spreadsheet.Cell

```
 1 public class Cell {
 2      final SpreadSheet spreadSheet;
 3      private final Coordinates coord;
 4      private String formulaString = "";
 5      private Formula formula = null;
 6      private Value cachedValue = new Value();
 7      private final List<Cell> dependsOn = new ArrayList<Cell>();
 8      private final List<Cell> dependentOnThis =
 9                          new ArrayList<Cell>();
10
11      ...
12 }
```

Clients cannot adequately anticipate the effects of an operation.

One result of the dependencies within the model is that clients, such as the controllers in the user interface, cannot foresee all the changes that are effected by an operation they call. As a result, the controller of the MVC could not reliably notify the view about necessary repainting even without interference from other controllers. This fact reinforces the crucial design decision of updating the view by observing the model.

↰9.2.3

In the current example, the prototypical modification is setting a new formula on a cell. The overall approach is straightforward: Clear the old dependency information, and then set and parse the new input. Afterward, we can update the new dependencies by asking the formula for its references and recomputing the current cached value.

---

minixcel.model.spreadsheet.Cell

```
1 public void setFormulaString(String formulaString) {
2     clearDependsOn();
3     this.formulaString = formulaString;
4     ... special cases such as an empty input string
5     formula = new Formula(spreadSheet.getFormulaFactory(),
6                           formulaString);
7     fillDependsOn();
8     ... check for cycles
9     recomputeValue();
10 }
```

The update process of a single cell now triggers updating the dependencies as well: The formula is evaluated and the result is stored.

---

minixcel.model.spreadsheet.Cell.recomputeValue

```
private void recomputeValue() {
    ...
    setCachedValue(new Value(formula.eval(
                          new SpreadSheetEnv(spreadSheet))));
    ... error handling on evaluation error
}
```

The cache value is therefore the "current" value of the cell. Whenever that changes, two stakeholders must be notified: the dependent cells within the spreadsheet and the observers outside of the spreadsheet. Both goals are accomplished in the method setCachedValue():

---

minixcel.model.spreadsheet.Cell

```
protected void setCachedValue(Value val) {
    if (val.equals(cachedValue))
        return;
    cachedValue = val;
    for (Cell c : dependentOnThis)
        c.recomputeValue();
    spreadSheet.fireCellChanged(this);
}
```

This brief exposition is sufficient to highlight the most important points with respect to model-view separation. Check out the online supplement for further details—for instance, on error handling for syntax errors in formulas and cyclic dependencies between cells.

9.4.3   Incremental Screen Updates

Many applications of model-view separation are essentially simple, with
small models being displayed in small views. Yet, one often comes across
the other extreme. Even a simple text viewer without any formatting must
be careful to repaint only the portion of text determined by the scrollbars,
and from that only the actually changing lines. Otherwise, the scrolling
and editing process will become unbearably slow. The MiniXcel example is
sufficiently complex to include a demonstration of the necessary processes.

↰7.8 Before we delve into the details, Fig. 9.14 gives an overview of the challenge. Put very briefly, it consists of the fact that even painting on the
screen is event-driven: When a change notification arrives from the model,
one never paints the corresponding screen section immediately. Instead, one
asks to be called back for the job later on. In some more detail, the model
on the left in Fig. 9.14 sends out some change notification to its observers.
The view must then determine where it has painted the modified data.
That area of the screen is then considered "damaged" and is reported to
the window system. The window system gathers such damaged areas, sub-
tracts any parts that are not visible anyway, coalesces adjacent areas, and
maybe performs some other optimizations. In the end, it comes back to
the view requesting a certain area to be repainted. At this point, the view
determines the model elements overlapping this area and displays them on
the screen.

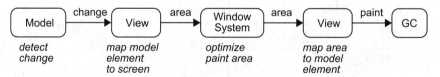

Figure 9.14 Process of Incremental Screen Updates

A further reason for this rather complex procedure, besides the possibility of optimizations, is that other events, such as the moving and resizing
of windows, can also require repainting, so that the right half of Fig. 9.14
would be necessary in any case. The extra effort of mapping model elements
to screen areas in the left half is repaid by liberating the applications of
optimizing the painting itself.

Let us track the process in Fig. 9.14 from left to right, using the concrete
example of the MiniXcel `SpreadSheetView`. At the beginning, the view
receives a change notification from the model. If the change concerns a
single cell, that cell has to be repainted.

```
           minixcel.ui.spreadsheet.SpreadSheetView.spreadSheetChanged
public void spreadSheetChanged(SpreadSheetChangeEvent evt) {
    switch (evt.type) {
    case CELL:
        redraw(evt.cell.getCoordinates());
        break;
```

```
        ...
    }
}
```

It will turn out later that cells need to be repainted on different occasions, such as to indicate selection or mouse hovering. We therefore implement the logic in a helper method, shown next. The method `redraw()`
called on the `mainArea` of the view is provided by SWT and reports the
area as damaged.

»9.4.4
↰1.4.8 ↰1.4.5

---
minixcel.ui.spreadsheet.SpreadSheetView

```java
public void redraw(Coordinates coords) {
    Rectangle r = getCellBounds(coords);
    mainArea.redraw(r.x, r.y, r.width, r.height, false);
}
```

In a real implementation, the method `getCellBounds()` would determine
the coordinates by the sizes of the preceding columns and rows. To keep
the example simple, all columns have the same width and all rows have the
same height in MiniXcel. This finishes the left half of Fig. 9.14. Now it is
the window system's turn to do some work.

---
minixcel.ui.spreadsheet.SpreadSheetView

```java
protected Rectangle getCellBounds(Coordinates coords) {
    int x = (coords.col - viewPortColumn) * COL_WIDTH;
    int y = (coords.row - viewPortRow) * ROW_HEIGHT;
    return new Rectangle(x, y, COL_WIDTH, ROW_HEIGHT);
}
```

In the right half of Fig. 9.14, the `MainArea` is handed a paint request
for a given rectangular area on the screen, in the form of a `PaintEvent`
passed to the method shown next. This method determines the range of
cells touched by the area (line 3). Then, it paints all cells in the area in the
nested loops in lines 7 and 11. As an optimization, it does not recompute
the area covered by each cell, as done for the first cell in line 5. Instead,
it moves that area incrementally, using cells that are adjacent in the view
(lines 9, 14, 16).

---
minixcel.ui.spreadsheet.MainArea.paintControl

```java
1 public void paintControl(PaintEvent e) {
2     ... prepare colors
3     Rectangle cells = view.computeCellsForArea(e.x, e.y, e.width,
4                                                 e.height);
5     Rectangle topLeft = view.computeAreaForCell(cells.x, cells.y);
6     Rectangle cellArea = Geometry.copy(topLeft);
7     for (int row = cells.y; row < cells.y + cells.height; row++) {
8         cellArea.height = SpreadSheetView.ROW_HEIGHT;
9         cellArea.x = topLeft.x;
10        cellArea.width = SpreadSheetView.COL_WIDTH;
11        for (int col = cells.x;
12                col < cells.x + cells.width; col++) {
13            paintCell(col, row, cellArea, gc);
14            cellArea.x += cellArea.width;
```

```
15          }
16          cellArea.y += cellArea.height;
17      }
18 }
```

≫11.1 ≫11.2

> 𝒫 Note that the `MainArea` delegates the actual computation of cell areas in lines 3–5 to
> its owner, the `SpreadSheetView`. Since that object was responsible for mapping cells
> to areas, it should also be responsible for the inverse computations, to ensure that any
> necessary adaptations will be performed consistently to both.

The actual painting code in `paintCell()` is then straightforward, if
somewhat tedious. It has to take into account not only the cell content,
but also the possible selection of the cell and a mouse cursor being inside,
both of which concern view-level logic treated in the next section. Leaving
all of that aside, the core of the method determines the current cell value,
formats it as a string, and paints that string onto the screen (avoiding the
creation of yet more empty cells):

minixcel.ui.spreadsheet.MainArea

```
private void paintCell(int col, int row,
                       Rectangle cellArea, GC gc) {
    if (view.model.hasCell(new Coordinates(col, row))) {
        cell = view.model.getCell(new Coordinates(col, row));
        Value val = cell.getValue();
        String displayText;
        displayText = String.format("%.2f", val.asDouble());
        gc.drawString(displayText, cellArea.x, cellArea.y, true);
    }
}
```

This final painting step finishes the update process shown in Fig. 9.14.
In summary, incremental repainting achieves efficiency in user interface pro-
↰2.1.3
gramming: The view receives detailed change notifications, via the "push"
variant of the OBSERVER pattern, which it translates to minimal damaged
areas on the screen, which get optimized by the window system, before the
view repaints just the model elements actually touched by those areas.

9.4.4   View-Level Logic

↰9.2.5
We have seen in the discussion of the MVC pattern that widgets usually
include behavior such as visual feedback that is independent of the model
itself. MiniXcel provides two examples: selection of cells and feedback about
the cell under the mouse. We include them in the discussion since this kind
of behavior must be treated with the same rigor as the model: Users consider
only applications that react consistently and immediately as trustworthy.

Treat selection as view-level state.

Most widgets encompass some form of selection. For instance, tables, lists,
↰9.3.2
and trees allow users to select rows, which JFace maps to the underlying

model element rendered in these rows. The interesting point about selection is that it introduces view-level state, which is orthogonal to the application's core model-level state.

We will make our `SpreadSheetView` a good citizen of the community by implementing `ISelectionProvider`. That interface specifies that clients can query the current selection, set the current selection (with appropriate elements), and listen for changes in the selection. The last capability will also enable us to connect the entry field for a cell's content to the spreadsheet (Fig. 9.13). For simplicity, we support only single selection and introduce a corresponding field into the `SpreadSheetView`.

minixcel.ui.spreadsheet.SpreadSheetView

```
Cell curSelection;
```

The result of querying the current selection is a generic `ISelection`. Viewers that map model elements to screen elements, such as tables and trees, usually return a more specific `IStructuredSelection` containing these elements. We do the same here with the single selected cell.

minixcel.ui.spreadsheet.SpreadSheetView.getSelection

```
public ISelection getSelection() {
    if (curSelection != null)
        return new StructuredSelection(curSelection);
    else
        return StructuredSelection.EMPTY;
}
```

Since the selection must be broadcast to observers and must be mirrored on the screen, we introduce a private setter for the field.

minixcel.ui.spreadsheet.SpreadSheetView

```
private void setSelectedCell(Cell cell) {
    if (curSelection != cell) {
        Cell oldSelection = curSelection;
        curSelection = cell;
        fireSelectionChanged();
        ... update screen from oldSelection to curSelection
    }
}
```

The remainder of the implementation of the OBSERVER pattern for selection is straightforward. However, its presence reemphasizes the role of selection as proper view-level state.   ↤2.1

Visual feedback introduces internal state.

The fact that painting is event-driven, so that a widget cannot paint visual feedback immediately, means that the widget must store the desired feedback as private state, determine the affected screen regions, and render the feedback in the callback (Fig. 9.14).   ↤7.8

For MiniXcel, we wish to highlight the cell under the mouse cursor, so that users know which cell they are targeting in case they click to select it. The required state is a simple reference. However, since the state is purely view-level, we are content with storing its coordinates; otherwise, moving over a yet unused cell would force the model to insert an empty `Cell` object.

↰9.4.2

minixcel.ui.spreadsheet.SpreadSheetView

```
Coordinates curCellUnderMouse;
```

Setting a new highlight is then similar to setting a new selected cell:

minixcel.ui.spreadsheet.SpreadSheetView

```
protected void setCellUnderMouse(Coordinates newCell) {
    if (!newCell.equals(curCellUnderMouse)) {
        Coordinates oldCellUnderMouse = curCellUnderMouse;
        curCellUnderMouse = newCell;
        ...  update screen from old to new
    }
}
```

The desired reactions to mouse movements and clicks are implemented by the following simple listener. The `computeCellAt()` method returns the cell's coordinates, also taking into account the current scrolling position. While selection then requires a real `Cell` object from the model, the targeting feedback remains at the view level.

minixcel.ui.spreadsheet.SpreadSheetView.mouseMove

```
public void mouseMove(MouseEvent e) {
    setCellUnderMouse(computeCellAt(e.x, e.y));
}
public void mouseDown(MouseEvent e) {
    setSelectedCell(model.getCell(computeCellAt(e.x, e.y)));
}
```

The painting event handler merges the visual and model states.

The technical core of visual feedback and view-level state, as shown previously, is not very different from the model-level state. When painting the widget, we have to merge the model- and view-level states into one consistent overall appearance. The following method achieves this by first painting the cell's content (lines 4–5) and overlaying this with a frame, which is either a selection indication (lines 9–12), the targeting highlight (lines 13–17), or the usual cell frame (lines 19–23).

minixcel.ui.spreadsheet.MainArea

```
1 private void paintCell(int col, int row,
2                        Rectangle cellArea, GC gc) {
3     ...
4     displayText = String.format("%.2f", val.asDouble());
5     gc.drawString(displayText, cellArea.x, cellArea.y, true);
```

```
6      Rectangle frame = Geometry.copy(cellArea);
7      frame.width-;
8      frame.height-;
9      if (view.curSelection != null && view.curSelection == cell) {
10         gc.setForeground(display.getSystemColor(
11                                 SWT.COLOR_DARK_BLUE));
12         gc.drawRectangle(frame);
13     } else if (view.curCellUnderMouse != null
14             && view.curCellUnderMouse.col == col
15             && view.curCellUnderMouse.row == row) {
16         gc.setForeground(display.getSystemColor(SWT.COLOR_BLACK));
17         gc.drawRectangle(frame);
18     } else {
19         gc.setForeground(display.getSystemColor(SWT.COLOR_GRAY));
20         int bot = frame.y + frame.height;
21         int right = frame.x + frame.width;
22         gc.drawLine(right, frame.y, right, bot);
23         gc.drawLine(frame.x, bot, right, bot);
24     }
25 }
```

According to this painting routine, the view-level state is always contained within the cells to which it refers. It is therefore sufficient to repaint these affected cells when the state changes. For the currently selected cell, the code is shown here. For the current cell under the mouse, it is analogous.

minixcel.ui.spreadsheet.SpreadSheetView

```
private void setSelectedCell(Cell cell) {
    if (curSelection != cell) {
        ...
        if (oldSelection != null)
            redraw(oldSelection.getCoordinates());
        if (curSelection != null)
            redraw(curSelection.getCoordinates());
    }
}
```

This code is made efficient through the incremental painting pipeline shown in Fig. 9.14 on page 500 and implemented in the code fragments shown earlier. Because the pipeline is geared toward painting the minimal necessary number of cells, it can also be used to paint single cells reliably and efficiently.

9.5   Undo/Redo

Users make mistakes all the time, especially with highly developed and optimized user interfaces, where small graphical gestures have powerful effects. Most of the time, they realize their mistakes immediately afterward, because the screen gets updated with the new application state and the result does not match their expectations. A fundamental requirement for any modern application is the ability to cancel operations immediately through an "undo" action and to "redo" them if it turns out that the effect

↰453

was desired after all. This section discusses the established technique for solving this challenge: The application maintains a list of incremental and undoable changes to the model. We first consider a minimal version to highlight the technique, then we briefly examine various implementations within the Eclipse platform to get an overview of practical issues involved.

9.5.1 The Command Pattern

↰1.1

The fundamental obstacle for undoing editing operations is, of course, the stateful nature of objects: Once existing data has been overwritten, it cannot be restored. For instance, the `CellEditor` in the spreadsheet application (at the top of Fig. 9.12 on page 495) enables the user to enter the new formula or value for the selected cell. When the user presses "enter," the new formula gets set on the model, as shown in the next code snippet. The model automatically updates the dependent cells. After executing this code, the previous formula is irretrievably lost and it is not possible to "undo" the operation.

↰9.4.2

---

minixcel.ui.celledit.CellEditor

```
protected void putFormula() {
    if (curCell != null) {
        curCell.setFormulaString(txtFormula.getText());
    }
}
```

To implement undo/redo, the overall goal is to create a conceptual *history* of operations, as shown in Fig. 9.15. At each point in time, the current model state is the result of executing a sequence of operations. These operations can be undone, with the effect that the model reverts to a previous state. Operations that have been undone become redoable, so that later model states can be reached again if necessary.

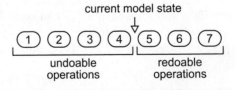

Figure 9.15 History for Undo/Redo

Controllers delegate the invocation of operations to *Command* objects.

To implement undo/redo, one modifies the MODEL-VIEW-CONTROLLER pattern from Fig. 9.3 (page 454) in one tiny detail into the version shown in Fig. 9.16: The *controller* no longer invokes model operations directly, but creates *Command* objects that invoke the operations.

This central insight is captured by the COMMAND pattern.

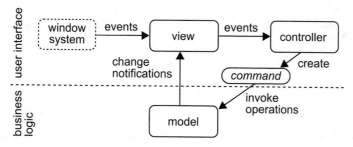

Figure 9.16 MVC with Undoable Operations

PATTERN: COMMAND

If you need undoable operations, or need to log or store operations, encapsulate them as objects with execute() and undo() methods.

1. Define an interface Command with methods execute(), undo(), and redo().

2. Provide an abstract base class defining redo() as a call to execute().

3. Define a command class, implementing the Command interface, for each operation on the model. Store all necessary parameters as fields in the *Command* object. This includes in particular references to the target objects that the operation works with.

4. Let each command's execute() method invoke methods on the model to perform the operation. Before that, let it store the state it destroys in fields inside the command.

5. Let each command's undo() method revert the change to the model using the stored previous state.

We will now explore the details of this concept and the implementation at the example of the spreadsheet editor. Steps 1 and 2, and their motivation, are deferred to Section 9.5.2.

Let the commands capture incremental state changes.

The central point of the pattern is that commands must capture enough of the previous model state to be able to restore it. In the example of setting the formula in a spreadsheet cell, we just have to keep the cell's previous formula. In the code snippet that follows, line 4 sets the new formula, but only after saving the old value in line 3. In this way, the operation can be undone in line 7.

---

minixcel.commands.SetCellFormulaCommand

```
1 public void execute() {
2     Cell c = model.getCell(coordinates);
3     oldFormulaString = c.getFormulaString();
4     c.setFormulaString(formulaString);
5 }
6 public void undo() {
7     model.getCell(coordinates).setFormulaString(oldFormulaString);
8 }
```

Making each operation into a separate command object then has the advantage of creating a space for that additional data. In the current example, it consists of a single field `oldFormulaString`, but more may be required for more complex operations.

It is important for efficiency to keep an incremental record of the changed data—that is, to store only those data items that are actually necessary for restoring the model to the previous state. For instance, when deleting a (small) part of a text document in a `DeleteTextCommand`, you should keep only the deleted text, not the entire document.

Do not fetch the old state already in the command's constructor. At first glance, the difference seems negligible, because one usually creates a command and executes it immediately afterward (by passing it to the command processor, as seen in Section 9.5.2). However, when composing commands, as seen later in this section, other commands may actually intervene between the construction and the execution of a command, so that the data stored for the later undo is actually wrong. The only reliable technique is to fetch the old state in the `execute()` method, just before actually changing the state.

↰4.1   Thinking in terms of assertions is the crucial trick at this point: If you want to establish, in the example, that "`oldFormulaString` holds the content seen before setting the new formula," the only reliable way of achieving this is to actually look up that string right before setting the new one.

Introduce a `CompoundCommand` to make the approach scalable.

Very often, one operation from the user's perspective requires a series of method invocations on the model. To achieve this effectively, it is useful to introduce a `CompoundCommand`, which maintains a list of commands and executes and undoes them as suggested by the concept of a history.

minixcel.commands.CompoundCommand

```
public class CompoundCommand implements Command {
    private List<Command> commands;
    ...
    public void execute() {
        for (int i = 0; i != commands.size(); i++) {
```

```
                    commands.get(i).execute();
            }
    }
    public void undo() {
        for (int i = commands.size() - 1; i >= 0; i--) {
            commands.get(i).undo();
        }
    }
    ...
}
```

The overall effort of implementing undo/redo then becomes manageable: One has to go through writing a command class for every elementary operation offered by the model once, but afterward the operations required by the user interface can be composed almost as effectively as writing a sequence of method calls.

The method `redo()` must leave exactly the same state as `execute()`.

Commands usually come with a separate method `redo()` that is invoked after `undo()` and must reexecute the command's target operation. More precisely, this method must leave the model in exactly the same state as the original `execute()` did, because the later operations in the history (Fig. 9.15) may depend on the details of that state.

In the current case of setting a spreadsheet cell, the `execute()` method is so simple that `redo()` can behave exactly the same way:

minixcel.commands.SetCellFormulaCommand.redo

```
public void redo() {
    execute();
}
```

In some situations, however, `redo()` may differ from `execute()` and will then require a separate implementation:

- If `execute()` creates new objects and stores them in the model, then `redo()` must store exactly the same objects, rather than creating new ones, because later operations may contain references to the new objects so as to access or modify them.

- If `execute()` accesses some external state, such as the clipboard, a file, or some data from another editor, which may not be governed by the same history of commands, then that state must be stored, because it might change between `execute()` and `redo()`.

- Similarly, if `execute()` makes decisions based on some external state, that state—or better still the decision—must be stored and used in the redo operation.

- If `execute()` asks the user, through dialogs, for more input or a decision, then that input or decision must be stored as well.

Again, the COMMAND offers just the space where such additional information is stored easily.

> Make a command a self-contained description of an operation.

To be effective, commands must store internally all data necessary for executing the intended operation. Obviously, this includes the parameters passed to the invoked method. It also includes any target objects that the operation works on. In the example, we have to store the spreadsheet itself, the cell to be modified, and the formula to be stored in the cell. For simplicity, we keep the coordinates of the cell, not the `Cell` object itself.

---
minixcel.commands.SetCellFormulaCommand

```java
public class SetCellFormulaCommand implements Command {
    private SpreadSheet model;
    private Coordinates coordinates;
    private String formulaString;
    private String oldFormulaString;
    public SetCellFormulaCommand(SpreadSheet model,
                                 Coordinates coordinates,
                                 String formulaString) {
        ...
    }
    ...
}
```

↰2.2.1

⇄? Alternatively, one could have said that the command is not about `SpreadSheets` at all, but about single `Cells`, which may happen to be contained in a `SpreadSheet`. Then, the first two fields would be replaced by a single field `Cell cell`, with a change to the constructor to match.

> Be sure to make `undo()` revert the model state exactly.

One challenge in defining the commands' methods is that they must match up exactly: Invoking `execute()` and then `undo()` must leave the model in exactly the same state as it was at the beginning. The reason is seen in Fig. 9.15 on page 506: Each operation in the sequence in principle depends on the model state that it has found when it was first executed. Calling `undo()` must then reconstruct that model state, because the later `redo()` will depend on the details. A `DeleteTextCommand`, for instance, may contain the offset and length of the deletion, and it would be disastrous if undoing and redoing a few operations were to invalidate that text range.

↰4.1

🔋 The necessary precision can be obtained by thinking in terms of assertions: The contracts of the invoked operations specify their effects precisely, so that the command can gauge which parts of the state need to be stored for the undo.

Do not neglect possible internal dependencies of the model.

Let us reconsider the example code from the perspective of a precise `undo()` method. The `execute()` method sets a given cell. Ostensibly, it just changes a single property in line 3 in the next code snippet. The `undo()` method reverts that property to `oldFormulaString`, so that everything should be fine.

```
                    minixcel.commands.SetCellFormulaCommand.execute
1 Cell c = model.getCell(coordinates);
2 oldFormulaString = c.getFormulaString();
3 c.setFormulaString(formulaString);
```

Two effects may cause the internal model state to deviate from the original.   ↰9.4.2
First, the call to `getCell()` in line 1 might actually create the cell object in the data structure. Second, and perhaps more importantly, the call in line 3 implicitly updates all dependent cells.

However, both points are irrelevant in regard to the overall goal of keeping the undo/redo history intact. Clients cannot distinguish whether a `Cell` they receive from `getCell()` has just been created or had already existed. The model treats the sparse representation of the spreadsheet content as a strictly internal issue. The dependencies between cells do not cause problems either, because the reevaluation of formulae is strictly deterministic, so that setting the old formula also resets all dependent cells to their previous values.

This explanation rests on the idea of the externally visible state, which is captured   ↰4.1 ↰4.2.2
in an object's model fields: The command stores all relevant public state before the modification and restores that state to undo the operations. Since clients cannot actually observe any internal difference between two states that are indistinguishable from an external perspective, their behavior cannot depend on the difference either.

One snag in the example concerns the external format of the spreadsheet written to disk: The model may choose to write out the cell created in line 1 of the previously given `execute()` method, even if that cell has been emptied out by `undo()` in the meantime. In the present case, one can argue that any programmatic access, after reloading the spreadsheet document, can still not observe the difference. In other cases, where the external format is the really important thing, such differences may not be acceptable. As an example, Eclipse's editor for OSGi bundles is really just a front-end   ↠12.3.3 ↠A.1.2
for the underlying configuration files such as `plugin.xml` and `MANIFEST.MF`. Adding some extension and then undoing that addition should leave the file structure untouched.

Java's Swing framework introduces an interesting alternative perspective on undo/redo, which already integrates the possible necessity of tracking changes to the model's internals. Rather than requiring commands to store the previous state, the model itself sends out `UndoableEdit` notifications upon any change. These notifications contain sufficient internal information to undo the change and offer public `undo()` and `redo()` methods. For a typical example, see Swing's `HTMLDocument`. Clients, such as editors, have to track only these notifications, using the provided `UndoManager`.

Use mementos to encapsulate internal state, but only if really necessary.

In some rare cases, the internal state is so complex that you would rather not rely on all effects being reliably undone when resetting the public state to the previous value. In particular, if the internal dependencies are non-deterministic, or may become nondeterministic in the future, some further measures have to be taken. We mention the idea only very briefly and refer you to the literature for the details.

100

PATTERN: MEMENTO

If clients must store snapshots of the internal state for later reference, package those snapshots into impenetrable *Memento* objects.

Define a `public` *Memento* class with only `private` fields and no `public` accessors as a nested class inside the model. The private fields hold copies of particular state elements from the model. Although clients can handle such objects—the pattern says they are *Caretakers*—they can never inspect the internal state wrapped up in the memento objects. For the *Caretakers*, introduce a method `createMemento()` that captures the current state and a method `setMemento()` to revert to that state.

Fig. 9.17 illustrates the idea: The application model has some complex internal state. It also offers public methods for copying out some of the state, but that state remains hidden inside the memento object, as indicated by the double lines. Further public methods enable the clients to restore old states by passing the memento back to the model. As suggested in the COMMAND pattern, it is usually sensible to keep only incremental updates inside the mementos.

100

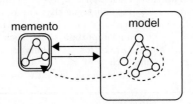

Figure 9.17 Idea of the Memento Pattern

⚠ Do not introduce MEMENTO without good reasons. The pattern is rather disruptive to the model's implementation, because any operation must track all changes it makes in a memento, which is both complex and possibly inefficient. For an example of such overhead, you might want to look at Swing's HTMLDocument class. Conceptually, one can also argue that the pattern partially violates model-view separation, because view-level requirements infiltrate the model's definition. As a benefit, the availability of the extra information might make undo/redo much more efficient.

9.5.2 The Command Processor Pattern

We have now finished examining the core of undo/redo: Any operation on the model is represented as a *Command* object, and that object is responsible for keeping enough of the previous model state for restoring that state later on. It remains, however, to manage the overall sequence of commands executed on the model. As Fig. 9.15 (on page 506) has clarified, each command in the overall history implicitly assumes that all previous commands have executed properly so that it can perform its own operation. The COMMAND PROCESSOR pattern handles exactly this new aspect.

↰9.5.1

▱59

PATTERN: COMMAND PROCESSOR

If you introduce COMMAND for undo/redo, also centralize the execution and reversal of the operations that they represent. The *Controllers*, or other parts wanting to interact with the model, create *Commands* and pass them to a *CommandProcessor*. The *CommandProcessor* alone decides about and keeps track of the proper order of calls to the *Commands*' methods.

---

1. Maintain the command history in fields (Fig. 9.15).

2. Offer public execute(Command), undo(), and redo() methods.

3. Implement the OBSERVER pattern for history changes.

As a preliminary prerequisite to introducing such a command processor, all commands must have a uniform structure. As already envisaged in the COMMAND pattern, we introduce an interface to capture the available methods. Since redo() in the majority of cases is the same as execute(), it is useful to have an abstract base class where redo() just calls execute().

↰9.5.1

↰3.1.4

---

minixcel.commands.Command

```
public interface Command {
    void execute();
    void undo();
    void redo();
}
```

The command processor can then implement the history from Fig. 9.15 in the form of two stacks of commands. We also lay the foundation for the OBSERVER pattern.

---

minixcel.commands.CommandProcessor

```
public class CommandProcessor {
    private Stack<Command> undoList;
    private Stack<Command> redoList;
    private ListenerList listeners = new ListenerList();
    ...
}
```

Associate each model with a unique command processor.

↰9.15

The nature of a command history implies that no modifications must ever circumvent the mechanism: If the current model state changes by a direct invocation of model methods, the undoable commands as well as the redoable commands may fail because they originally executed in different situations. For instance, when one deletes some text in a text document directly, then any command storing the start and length of a character range may suddenly find that it is using illegal positions.

≫9.5.4

It is therefore necessary to create a (or to choose an existing) unique command processor that manages all changes to a given model. One command processor may, of course, manage several models at once to enable operations that work across model boundaries.

Channel all operations on the model through its command processor.

Whenever the user, or some part of the system, wishes to work with the model, it will create a command object and pass it to the command processor. In the MiniXcel example, the CellEditor enables the user to input a new formula for the selected cell by creating a SetCellFormula Command.

minixcel.ui.celledit.CellEditor

```
protected void putFormula() {
    if (curCell != null) {
        cmdProc.execute(new SetCellFormulaCommand(getCurSheet(),
                curCell.getCoordinates(), txtFormula.getText()));
    }
}
```

↰2.1

The command processor's execute() method executes the given command (line 3 in the next code snippet). However, because it is responsible for managing all command executions, it does some more bookkeeping. Since the new command changes the model state, all previously redoable commands become invalid (line 2), and the new command becomes undoable (line 4). Finally, the command processor is observable and sends out commandHistoryChanged messages (line 5), for reasons shown in a minute.

minixcel.commands.CommandProcessor

```
1 public void execute(Command cmd) {
2     redoList.clear();
```

```
3       cmd.execute();
4       undoList.add(cmd);
5       fireCommandHistoryChanged();
6   }
```

Undo and redo are services offered by the command processor.

Of course, the overall undo/redo functionality is not itself implemented in the form of commands, but rather resides in the command processor. Its `undo()` method must be called only if there is, indeed, an undoable command. The method then moves that command to the redoable stack and calls its `undo()` method. Finally, it notifies the observers.

minixcel.commands.CommandProcessor

```
public void undo() {
    Assert.isTrue(!undoList.isEmpty());
    Command cmd = undoList.pop();
    cmd.undo();
    redoList.push(cmd);
    fireCommandHistoryChanged();
}
```

The user triggers undo usually through a toolbar button or menu item. These should be disabled if no command can currently be undone. The JFace method of achieving this is to create an `Action` that listens for state changes. In the current example, the base class `CommandProcessorAction` already implements this mechanism in a template method and calls `checkEnabled()` whenever the command history has changed. The action's `run()` method does the obvious thing.

↩9.3.4

↩1.4.9

minixcel.commands.UndoAction

```
public class UndoAction extends CommandProcessorAction {
    public static final String ID = "undo";
    public UndoAction(CommandProcessor cmdProc) {
        super("Undo", cmdProc);
        setId(ID);
    }
    public void run() {
        cmdProc.undo();
    }
    protected boolean checkEnabled() {
        return cmdProc.canUndo();
    }
}
```

The implementation of a corresponding `RedoAction` is analogous.

9.5.3   The Effort of Undo/Redo

After finishing the standard mechanisms for implementing undo/redo, it is useful to pause briefly and consider the overall effort involved. Although in the end there will be no alternative to going through with it to satisfy the users, it is best to maintain a good overview so as not to underestimate the effort, but also to look actively for supporting infrastructure.

All serious UI frameworks come with undo/redo infrastructure.

The first observation is that the overall mechanisms are fairly rigid and will reoccur whenever undo/redo is required: `Commands` capture and revert changes, and some `CommandProcessor` keeps track of all executed `Commands`. The interaction between the two is limited to generic `execute()`, `undo()`, and `redo()` methods, probably together with some similarly standard extensions.

»9.5.4

◀3.2.1
▢▢235

▢▢214

Many frameworks and libraries provide variants of this scheme, and one then simply has to create new types of commands for the application-specific models. For instance, the Eclipse Modeling Framework defines a `Command` interface and a `BasicCommandStack` command processor; the Graphical Editing Framework defines an abstract class `Command` and a `CommandStack` command processor; and Eclipse's core runtime defines an interface `IUndoableOperation` for commands and a class `Default` `OperationHistory` as a command processor.

Create commands for atomic operations, then build `CompoundCommands`.

◀9.5.1

When using command processors, any operation on the model must be wrapped in a command at some point. However, writing a new command class for every single task that the user performs in the user interface simply does not scale. It is better to create a set of basic commands for the single operations offered by the model and to combine these as necessary using a `CompoundCommand`, which will also be available in any framework.

Write `Commands` at the model level.

◀9.1

A second concern is to keep the command definitions as independent of the concrete user interface as possible. When modifying or porting the user interface, as enabled by model-view separation, the effort spent on more specific commands may be lost. At the same time, commands and the command processor are solely concerned with the model, and not with the user interface, so that they can be implemented at the model level.

⇄? In contrast, undo/redo is an interface-level concern, so one might argue that commands should be defined in the interface-level components. Both alternatives can be found in the Eclipse platform: EMF provides generic commands on the models and in the model-level package `org.eclipse.emf.common.command`, while the IDE places workspace operations in `org.eclipse.ui.ide.undo`.

»9.5.2

Many model-level frameworks provide atomic operations as commands.

Many libraries and frameworks are, of course, aware that professional applications require undo/redo. For instance, Eclipse's resources come equipped with commands to create, copy, move, and delete resources. The Eclipse Modeling Framework provides modifications of bean properties of general EObjects, such as those created from a specific EMF model.

📖235

9.5.4 Undo/Redo in the Real World

So far, everything has been rather straightforward and to the point: While executing a command, keep enough data to enable reverting the change; to undo a command, play back that data. In real-world applications, things become somewhat more complex because side-conditions and special cases must be observed. These intricacies also explain why one cannot give a single implementation that covers all applications. We will look at three examples from the Eclipse platform: GEF, EMF, and the core platform. In each case, it is sufficient to analyze the various definitions of the command, since the command processors follow.

The Graphical Editing Framework provides powerful abstractions and mechanisms for creating general drawing editors, in the form of editors that are not limited to standard widgets for displaying the model but create truly graphical representations. Its Command class defines the three basic methods execute(), undo(), and redo(). The first practical extension is the label property, which is used for indicating the nature of the change in undo and redo menu items. The remaining methods are discussed subsequently.

📖214

↰7.1

↰1.3.3

```
                    org.eclipse.gef.commands.Command
1 public abstract class Command {
2     public void execute()
3     public void undo()
4     public void redo()
5     public String getLabel()
6     public void setLabel(String label)
7     ...
8 }
```

> Test the applicability of commands before execute() and undo().

One detail about commands not yet discussed is that the execute(), undo(), and redo() methods do not declare any thrown exceptions. This is not a careless omission, but a conceptually necessary restriction following from the overall approach: Commands are executed and undone as atomic steps in a history and they must execute either completely or not at all—any model left in a state "in between" can never be repaired, in particular not by calling undo(). In short, commands are best understood as transactions on the model.

📖86

Practical frameworks therefore add methods canExecute() and canUndo() that are called before the respective methods are invoked. The

command must return `true` only if these methods can run through without
faults immediately afterwards.

---
org.eclipse.gef.commands.Command

```
public boolean canExecute()
public boolean canUndo()
```

🔍 You may rightly ask whether there should not be a `canRedo()` as well. However,
since `execute()` and `redo()` must essentially perform the same operation, the latter
is covered by `canExecute()` as well. An exception is seen and explained later.

GEF's implementation of the command processor will silently ignore
any commands that are not executable, to avoid corrupting the model.

---
org.eclipse.gef.commands.CommandStack

```
public void execute(Command command) {
    if (command == null || !command.canExecute())
        return;
    ...

}
```

↰4.1
↰6.4.1

💡 A deeper reason for having the checking methods is that the model operations invoked by `execute()` and `undo()` will in general have pre-conditions. However, these
special pre-conditions cannot be declared for `execute()` and `undo()`, because both inherit
their pre-conditions from the `Command` interface (or abstract base class). The only solution
is to make `canExecute()` the pre-condition of the interface's `execute()` method, so that
clients are responsible for calling `canExecute()` before calling `execute()`. This reasoning
also explains the implementation of `execute()` in the `CommandStack` shown here. For a
similar example, you can go back to the class `ThresholdArrayIterator`, where `next()`
has pre-condition `hasNext()`.

↰4.2

🔍 Be aware of the interaction between `canExecute()` and `CompoundCommands`. The
method `canExecute()` in a `CompoundCommand` usually asks each of the commands
in turn whether it can execute. This means, however, that each one checks this condition
on the initial model state. During the actual execution, the contained commands are
executed in order, so that they see a different state—the earlier commands in the sequence may invalidate the condition of being executable for the later commands. In most
situations, this is not problematic, as long as the developer is aware of the limitation. A
more faithful rendering would have to execute the commands in sequence and undo them
later on—an overhead that is usually not justified. In case this becomes relevant to your
application, look at `StrictCompoundCommand` from the Eclipse Modeling Framework.

Chaining enables the framework to accumulate commands easily.

In many situations, the overall operation on a group of objects can be constructed by performing the operation on each object in turn. For instance,

when the user selects several elements in a drawing and presses the "delete" key, then each element can be deleted by itself to achieve the effect. The `chain()` method of a command supports the framework in assembling this operation.

org.eclipse.gef.commands.Command
public Command chain(Command command)

Expect commands to have proper life cycles.

Commands may in general need to allocate resources, such as to store some image copied from the clipboard, or they may need to listen to the model. When the command is no longer held in the history, it must free those resources, or de-register as an observer. Like other objects, commands therefore need a well-defined life cycle. The command processor is responsible for calling their `dispose()` method when they are removed from the history and are no longer required.

↰7.4.1

↰1.1

org.eclipse.gef.commands.Command
public void dispose()

EMF adds the ability to define results and highlight target objects.

The `Command` interface defined by EMF offers the same methods as that of GEF shown earlier, and adds two more. First, the method `getResult()` allows commands to provide some abstract "result" of their execution. The `CutToClipboardCommand`, for instance, decorates a `RemoveCommand`. The `RemoveCommand` deletes a given set of objects from the model and defines those as its result; the decorator sets them as the current content of EMF's clipboard. Second, the method `getAffectedObjects()` is meant to identify objects that should be highlighted in the view, for instance by selecting them in a JFace viewer displaying the model. Both methods represent special scenarios that arise in EMF's application domain of building structured models for editors.

↰2.4.2

↰9.3.1

org.eclipse.emf.common.command.Command

public interface Command {
    ...
    Collection<?> getResult();
    Collection<?> getAffectedObjects();
}

Possibly external operations require further measures.

Eclipse's resources framework defines the structure of the overall workspace, with projects, folders, and files. The framework also includes `IUndoable`

↰7.10.2

Operations that represent changes to the workspace and that allow users to revert actions on those external entities.

These undoable operations by their nature act on an external model, which explains two deviations in the execute() method: First, a progress monitor parameter anticipates a possibly long runtime; second, the presence of an IStatus return value and a declared exception indicates that these commands can actually fail, perhaps due to external circumstances such as missing files. Of course, the concrete implementations should still ensure

↰1.5.6
↰6.3

that the model they work with is not corrupted—that they are exception-safe and preserve at least the model's invariants. Because the external state may have changed after the last undo(), commands are also given the chance to check that state in canRedo() before redo() gets called.

```
org.eclipse.core.commands.operations.IUndoableOperation

public interface IUndoableOperation {
    IStatus execute(IProgressMonitor monitor, IAdaptable info)
            throws ExecutionException;
        ...
    boolean canRedo();
        ...
}
```

Eclipse anticipates cross-model changes and a global history.

Many operations in Eclipse, such as refactorings on Java sources, in principle affect many files. Eclipse therefore tags each command which a *context* to which it applies. The context is then used to filter the available history.

```
org.eclipse.core.commands.operations.IUndoableOperation

boolean hasContext(IUndoContext context);
IUndoContext[] getContexts();
void addContext(IUndoContext context);
void removeContext(IUndoContext context);
```

For instance, suppose we create three classes A, B, and C, where B calls a method f() from A, but C does not. Then we use *Refactor/Rename* to rename the method f() to a method g(). Then the *Edit* menu for editors of A and B will show the entry "Undo rename method," while C shows the previous local modification to the source code there—the context of the renaming command includes the source files of A and B, but not of C.

9.6   Wrapping Up

This chapter touches on the core of professional software engineering. Any gifted layman can use the WindowBuilder to create a nice small application for a specific purpose, but it takes much more foresight to create a software product that can grow and change with the demands of its users, that can be maintained for years and decades, and that delivers its functionality reliably throughout.

Nevertheless, the chapter may appear surprisingly long when we reduce its content to the two fundamental concepts: Model-view separation enables testing to make the functionality reliable, and it liberates that functionality from concerns about the ever-changing user interface. Undoable operations are simply encapsulated as command objects, which are managed by a command processor.

↩9.1 ↩9.2.2

↩9.5

The challenge in this chapter is not the concepts, but their faithful rendering in concrete software: It is just too simple to destroy the principles and all their benefits by seemingly minor glitches in the implementation. After all, cannot a single reference to a view be tolerated in the model if it saves days of coding? Does it really matter if an observer interface is tailored to the user interface that we have to deliver in three days' time? Cannot repainting of changed data be much more efficient if the view remembers the changed data elements?

↩9.2.3

↩9.4.3

Professional developers know two things that will prevent them from falling into such traps. First, the extra effort of introducing model-view separation is rather extensive, but it is also predictable. Going through a series of well-known and well-rehearsed steps is psychologically less taxing than grappling with an endless list of poorly understood details. Second, they know the motivation behind all of those steps and see the necessity and implications of each. As a result, they perceive a proper overall structure as a necessary investment in achieving their future goals more easily. Both points together—the following of known steps and the understanding of implications—also enable professionals to be sure of their details, such as when recreating the previous and subsequent states in a command's `undo()` and `redo()` methods very precisely, if necessary by reasoning in detail about the contracts of invoked model operations. This chapter has introduced the landmarks for proceeding with forethought in this way.

↩9.4 ↩9.5.3

↩9.5.1

↩4.1 ↩4.2.2

Chapter 10

State Machines

Professional developers strive to create software that is correct. It is not too hard for even the ambitious amateur to achieve satisfactory responses for the most common use cases of a system, but it takes a professional to arrive at software that behaves as expected in all possible circumstances. Design-by-contract provides a solid reasoning framework for achieving this goal. Its cornerstone is the precise specification of single method calls, as shown in Fig. 10.1(a). In this model, some client accesses a service provider object. It passes arguments, obeying the method's pre-condition. The service provider must then deliver the promised result, as specified in the method's post-condition. Pre- and post-condition also capture the state of the service provider before and after the call, respectively: Many operations are not invoked for their return value, but for their effect on the target object.

↰4

↰4.1

(a) Contracts   (b) Events

Figure 10.1 Correctness and Events

Events and inversion of control challenge the fundamental assumptions of this approach, as illustrated in Fig. 10.1(b). In this scenario, a method call is no longer a service request, and there is not even a client expecting a specific answer. Instead, a method call is a notification that a certain event has taken place and the event-listener object must react appropriately, without being guided by the caller's expectations.

If contracts fail to capture the "appropriate reaction," a new framework for reasoning about correctness has to be found. This chapter presents a common and well-studied approach: *state machines*. State machines perceive an object as being in one of a number of abstract states. Each incoming event can send the object to a different state and trigger the execution of some action. The overall state machine then expresses the desired behavior, by capturing the details of these individual reactions to single events. This seemingly simple approach underlies the immmensely successful field of model checking, without which many of today's safety-critical software systems could not have been built.

⊞64,165,120,219

This chapter introduces the terminology and concepts of state machines as the core of the approach (Section 10.1), using the definitions of UML.

⊞47

It then traces these concepts to examples from the Eclipse platform and introduces additional details (Section 10.2). Finally, it discusses three approaches to implementing state machines faithfully (Section 10.3). In this last step, it turns out that contracts remain indispensable for precise reasoning, even if they fail to capture the relationship between event-source and event-listener in Fig. 10.1(b).

📖47,95

Throughout the chapter, we will use state machines to describe individual objects, in keeping with the subject of this book. In reality, they serve as a powerful tool at many levels of software design: They can capture the behavior of small embedded controllers and that of entire systems alike, and they cover implementation concerns and model-driven development as well as requirements analysis. We hope that the subsequent detailed treatment of their structure and meaning will give you the joy of discovering state machines hidden within many of your daily development tasks.

10.1   The Core: An Object's State and Reactions

↰1.1

Each object has a state, which (briefly put) is the sum of its fields' current contents. The challenge addressed by finite state machines is that very often the reaction of an object to an event will depend on its state.

To illustrate, let us consider a button in a toolbar, called a *tool item* in SWT. The tool item's reactions to mouse events are shown in Fig. 10.2. Since SWT treats widgets as black boxes and does not define the intermediate states, we borrow the terminology from Swing (see class ButtonModel): (a) The tool item starts in an *idle* state, where it paints itself as a flat area. (b) When the mouse moves in, the tool item acknowledges this by showing a pressable surface in state *rollover*. (c) When the user presses the left mouse button, the tool item gets *armed*, which means that releasing the

↰7.1

button now will fire the *clicked* (in SWT, *selected*) notification. (d) When the mouse moves out while the mouse button remains down, the tool item becomes *pressed*. In this state, releasing the mouse button will *not* fire the *clicked* notification. (e) State *pressed* differs from being *idle* in that simply reentering makes the tool item *armed* again, without repressing the mouse button.

(a) Idle   (b) Rollover   (c) Armed   (d) Pressed   (e) Rearmed

Figure 10.2 A Tool Item's Behavior

Events are significant external occurrences that trigger reactions.

The central element of the current chapter is the passive nature of objects, as indicated in Fig. 10.1(b). An event is "something that happens" and about which an object will be notified because it is relevant to the object. In the case of the tool item, the relevant occurrences, or *events*, are the mouse moves and clicks produced by the user.

📖47

Events are not always external occurrences. First, *time events* are generated just by elapsing of time, usually relative to entering the current state. Furthermore, the UML recognizes *signals* sent asynchronously by one object and received by another object, *messages* sent to an object to invoke a specific operation, and *changes* in state that cause a condition (i.e., a Boolean-valued expression) to become true. The cases of signals and messages are especially interesting, because they enable links between the state machines of different objects: When receiving an event, an object can decide to send a signal or message to another object, thus stimulating that object's state machine.

📖47 📖198(§13.3.27)
📖198(§13.2)

↰1.4.1

Finite state machines capture state-dependent behavior precisely.

Suppose you want to specify the tool item's behavior precisely—for instance, to describe a programming job to a different team. The screenshots and a textual description may be sufficient to get the idea across, but they are hardly a sound basis for actual work.

Fig. 10.3 shows a finite state machine for the tool item, using the UML notation. The rounded rectangles are the *abstract states*, or simply *states*, which represent the conceptual states from the above description. The interesting part is the object's behavior, which is captured by the *transitions* between those states, depicted as arrows. Each such transition is labeled with an event as its *trigger*: When the object is in the *source state* and the event occurs, then the transition is taken and the object ends up in the *target state*. One also says that the transition *fires*.

📖47

📖198(§15.3.14)

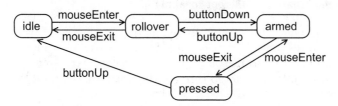

Figure 10.3 First Attempt at State Machine for a Tool Item

Let us align the drawing in Fig. 10.3 with the reactions from Fig. 10.2. Part (a) in Fig. 10.2 shows the *idle* state. After the mouse *enters* the button area, we reach state *rollover* in (b). When the left button is pressed *down*, the button is *armed* in (c). Moving the mouse in and out of the tool item switches between states *armed* and *pressed* in (d) and (e).

However, the state machine tells a more complete story, since the screenshots cannot show the internal state. For instance, what happens if a tool item is *pressed* and then the button is released—that is, if the event *button up* occurs? The screenshot does not change, but internally the tool item goes to state *idle*, as shown in Fig. 10.3. The state machine also clarifies that the only difference between states *armed* and *idle* consists of whether the mouse pointer is inside the tool item.

The machine's states abstract over an object's concrete field content.

The states in Fig. 10.3 derive from a previous textual description of a behavior. When read as specifications of a concrete object, their role is to arrive at a holistic understanding by suppressing the technical details of the object's concrete fields.

📖47 📖198(§15.3.11)

Toward that end, the UML understands a state as a point in time when an object waits for an event, when it performs an activity, or in general where some condition holds. The first point is the most prominent in the preceding example, as in many others: As long as no events arrive, the object just sits idle. Also, the "or" must be read inclusively: Frequently, an object performing an activity waits for an event that aborts the activity, and a specific assertion about the fields can be given that holds while the object is waiting for an event.

»10.2.2
↰4.1

📖47

💡 Another way of looking at states is to say that they encode the past history of received events: Each event can potentially change the state, so that the event gets recorded in the new state. This view is helpful because very often some expected reaction depends on a sequence of events—for instance, if the user has to press a button, then select an item from a list, and finally confirm the selection by pressing another button. Each state then represents an intermediate step in such a sequence.

A state must have an inherent meaning.

One crucial point is that states are not simply summaries of technical field contents. States must have meanings in themselves to achieve the overall goal: to allow us to reason about the behavior expressed by the state machine without having to go through the dreary details of a possible implementation.

»10.3

Let us look again at the example in Fig. 10.3. The crucial insight of the state machine is that "pressing a button" is not quite as simple as that after all: Users should be given the chance to cancel the process after they see from the visual feedback that they are about to trigger the button's action. The inherent meaning of the four states is clear: *Idle* means that nothing has happened and *armed* means that the button is ready to trigger its action. The other two states increase usability: *Rollover* indicates that the mouse cursor is inside the button area, which usually leads to some visual feedback. *Pressed* is an extra state that enables users to reconsider their intentions—the button will not trigger an action, but the user also has the choice of going back to *armed* by moving the mouse cursor back inside.

Effects at transitions capture the object's reactions.

So far, the example object's description in Fig. 10.3 is rather uninteresting: The internal state of the tool item changes, but the item does not show any outward reaction. Of course, it may choose to paint itself differently on the screen, but the main reason for using tool items in the first place is not expressed: The item should notify listeners when the user clicks with the mouse.

This omission can be remedied easily, as illustrated in Fig. 10.4. As shown in the figure, the transition from *armed* to *rollover* on the mouse event *button up* not only changes the state, but also has the *effect* named *fire*, separated from the trigger by a slash. For now, we read `fire` as a call to the standard notification method from the OBSERVER pattern.   ↩2.1

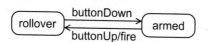

Figure 10.4 The Tool Item's Observable Reaction

Effects always run to completion.

Events relevant to an object can conceptually occur at any time, or even all the time: While the user moves the mouse, a new event signals the new mouse position every few milliseconds. In physical reality, a new event may thus easily overlap with the processing of the previous one. As a result, a naive reading of state machines could lead to the same event handler code being executed concurrently for different events.   ↩8

To obtain a simple explanation of a state machine's behavior, the complexities of concurrency must be avoided. The UML therefore specifies that   ↩8.2
effects always *run to completion*: Once an object has received an event, it performs the necessary processing, including any effects. The next event can be delivered to the object only after the previous one has been processed completely.

🔋 Run-to-completion is also the deeper reason behind SWT's event queue and event   ↩7.10.1
dispatch thread: Because the window system may detect events at any time, according to the user's input, these events get queued before being delivered one-by-one to the application's registered listeners.

»10.3

Align the implementation with the state machine.

State machines are popular as tools for expressing specifications because they can be aligned very closely with the implementation: Once the state machine is complete, it is a routine task to map it into concrete code implementing that specification. If the machine is sufficiently detailed, the code can even be generated automatically. Otherwise, one can think of encoding »10.3 states explicitly, either as `enums` or as objects in the STATE pattern. »10.3.2 In the following, we will apply the most common approach. In this strategy, the abstract states remain implicit in the code, as they merely provide a particularly intuitive way of explaining the object's concrete fields and their manipulation. We demonstrate the point and the close link between machine and code using a reimplementation of the tool item's behavior in a `CustomButton`.

States map to configurations of the object's fields.

We start by defining the object's state. Any definition of an object's fields must seek to simplify the internal algorithms. Fig. 10.3 provides a good hint: The arrows between the states nearly always come in symmetrical pairs. The reactions to the events therefore become simpler if each just has to toggle a switch: Is the mouse button currently down? Is the pointer inside the button? It also seems natural that being *armed* is special, because this state determines whether we fire an event to the listeners. We therefore introduce three corresponding fields:

---
custombutton.CustomButton

```java
private boolean mouseDown;
private boolean mouseInside;
private boolean armed;
```

The connection between the abstract and the concrete states can then be charted (Fig. 10.5). Specifically, the object is *idle* if all flags are `false`; it is *pressed* if the mouse is down but the pointer has run outside; and so on.

State	mouseDown	mouseInside	armed
idle	false	false	false
rollover	false	true	false
armed	true	true	true
pressed	true	false	false

Figure 10.5 Mapping Abstract States to Concrete States for the `CustomButton`

🔎 You will note immediately that the flag `armed` is really redundant: It is `true` exactly if `mouseDown` and `mouseInside` are both true. This could be expressed in a `private` method isArmed(). It is, of course, a matter of taste, but we feel that the methods' code becomes more readable when the special case is made explicit. In general, introducing redundant fields should be avoided, because every developer working on the class must be aware of the redundancy and the class invariants relating the fields.

↰4.1

The mapping from Fig. 10.5 can be traced to the code. The painting method must necessarily interpret the concrete state as an abstract state—for instance, to choose the correct background color. As shown in the following code, we first use red for the special state *armed*, and then differentiate between *rollover* (yellow) and *idle* (green).

```
custombutton.CustomButton.paintControl
if (armed)
    g.setBackground(getDisplay().getSystemColor(SWT.COLOR_RED));
else if (mouseInside)
    g.setBackground(display.getSystemColor(SWT.COLOR_YELLOW));
else
    g.setBackground(display.getSystemColor(SWT.COLOR_GREEN));
```

Events map to methods.

If the mouse events in Fig. 10.3 are relevant to the CustomButton, then the button must receive them. The standard way to achieve this is to have one method for each type of event and one method call for each event. The method is then responsible for implementing the appropriate reaction. As usual, we register a nested private listener for the raw SWT events and delegate the calls to corresponding handle methods in the outer class.

↰2.1.3

```
custombutton.CustomButton
public class CustomButton extends Canvas {
    ...
    protected void handleMouseDown() {
        ...
    }
    protected void handleMouseUp() {
        ...
    }
    protected void handleMouseEnter() {
        ...
    }
    protected void handleMouseExit() {
        ...
    }
}
```

Let us look at a few of these methods. The central one is certainly handleMouseup(), because it includes the only externally visible reaction in the special state *armed*: When the event occurs in that state, the fire() method is invoked (lines 2–3). Otherwise, only the flags are updated to reflect the new information about the mouse (lines 4–5). Note that this update is independent of the current state because of the clever choice of fields. That is, regardless of whether the object is in state *rollover* or *pressed*, it will end up in state *idle* (according to the mapping from Fig. 10.5).

custombutton.CustomButton

```
1 protected void handleMouseUp() {
2     if (armed)
3         fire();
4     setMouseDown(false);
5     setArmed(false);
6     redraw();
7 }
```

Another crucial point is the notification that the mouse enters. That event must be reacted to in two states (Fig. 10.3): In state *pressed*, the mouse is known to be down, and so the button becomes *armed* (lines 2–3). In any case, we note that the mouse pointer is now inside (line 5). Note also how the code makes sense without knowing the state machine: We could read lines 2–3 as "If the mouse button is already pressed, then the CustomButton becomes *armed* immediately."

custombutton.CustomButton

```
1 protected void handleMouseEnter() {
2     if (mouseDown) {
3         setArmed(true);
4     }
5     setMouseInside(true);
6     redraw();
7 }
```

These methods show that the implementation turns the intuitive reading of a state machine "inside-out": The diagram is read and understood starting with the states, then going on to the transitions emerging from these states when triggered by certain events. The implementation, in contrast, starts from the incoming events, in the form of method calls, and then goes on to differentiate between states within these methods. The STATE pattern remedies this mismatch, but at the cost of requiring some infrastructure.

» 10.3.4

State machines make the correctness of the code obvious.

The preceding code clearly reflects the state machine, and since the machine captures the button's expected behavior, the code is correct. As a conceptual tool, the state machine structures the code with the goal of making its correctness obvious.

» 10.2

In the inverse direction, it is often useful to explain the workings of existing code by overlaying it with a state machine. If one succeeds in constructing a machine that is implemented by the code, then one has gained a structure that explains the overall behavior at a glance.

State machines keep up a clean structure despite technical necessities.

Clearly, not all code can always be nice. Every framework and library that we use to get things done comes with its own technical details, obscurities, and idiosyncrasies. For instance, SWT has a slightly odd view on the `mouseEnter` and `mouseExit` events: When the user keeps a mouse button down while moving the pointer into and out of a widget, then the widget does *not* receive the events. The reason is that SWT stipulates that the widget will be tracking the mouse anyway during such drag gestures. This differs, for instance, from Swing's view, where enter and exit do have the expected purely geometrical meaning even if a mouse button is being held down.

   With state machines, the code can be kept in shape. The `handle` methods given earlier actually react to the *conceptual* events, as given in Fig. 10.3. In particular, enter/exit are read geometrically—even if we have not spelled this out, it follows from the discussion of Fig. 10.2. So far, it has been a coincidence that the conceptual events correspond one-to-one to SWT's concrete events. The odd behavior about enter/exit now breaks the rule, but all we have to do is find SWT events that we can *interpret* as the corresponding conceptual events. The following method does just that: It tracks the mouse motion and computes explicitly whether the new position is inside the widget.

```
                    custombutton.CustomButton.mouseMove
public void mouseMove(MouseEvent e) {
    boolean newInside = getClientArea().contains(e.x, e.y);
    if (mouseInside != newInside) {
        if (newInside)
            handleMouseEnter();
        else
            handleMouseExit();
    }
}
```

As a result, the technical obscurity is confined to this single method, while the state machine enforces a clear structure on the greater part of the class's code. What is more, that code is still seen to be correct by its close correspondence with the state machine.

Guards capture side-conditions on reactions.

Suppose that the `CustomButton` is frequently used to initiate dangerous tasks, so that under some circumstances, it must be "secured." A secured button must be sure never to notify its listeners and should not go to state *armed*.

   Guards are Boolean conditions that enable or prevent a transition from   47
being taken. They are noted in square brackets after the trigger of the

transition. Fig. 10.6 gives the current example: The crucial transitions between *rollover* and *armed* are now guarded by a flag `secured`. Guards are
evaluated whenever the trigger of the transition occurs. If they yield `true`
at this point, then the transition fires.

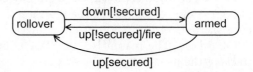

Figure 10.6 Securing the Custom Button with Guards

Guards can also be used to select one of several transitions triggered
by the same event. As long as the guards are mututally exclusive (i.e., at
most one can ever return `true` in any possible state of the object), the
state machine still has a well-defined, deterministic meaning. In Fig. 10.6,
the transition from *armed* to *rollover* must, of course, be made even if the
button is secured; however, it must not notify the listeners. The transition
from *rollover* to *armed*, in contrast, does not have to occur at all if the
button is secured—the event is just ignored.

⇄? Instead of modeling "being secured" as a side-condition to reactions, one might introduce it as a separate state *secured*. The other state, *ready*, contains the machine

≫10.2.3 from Fig. 10.3 as a nested state machine. New events *secure* and *unsecure* trigger the
transitions between these states.

The implementation of guards is straightforward: After it has been determined which transition is about to fire, one checks the guard. For instance, here is the handling of the `mouseUp` event in state *armed*; the fall-
through branch switches to state *rollover*, as before.

```
                    custombutton.CustomButton
protected void handleMouseUp() {
    if (armed)
        if (!secured)
            fire();
    setMouseDown(false);
    setArmed(false);
    redraw();
}
```

State machines are precise, but real applications require more elements.

This section has undertaken a brief survey of the central elements of state
machines and their meaning: Abstract states characterize points in an
object's lifetime, events are occurrences that objects must react to passively, and transitions describe these reactions through effects, possibly

using guards to constrain the behavior. Throughout, we have emphasized the connection of state machines and concrete code, which enables state machines to serve as detailed specifications of the expected behavior.

While these elements are useful and expressive, real-world situations require more detail. Notably, objects may perform ongoing activities while they are in a given state, or the behavior in that state may be specified further by nested state machines; it is also useful to execute effects whenever a state is entered or left. These elements can be understood as extensions of the basic model given here, and we introduce them in the next section.

10.2   State Machines in Real-World Scenarios

The key idea underlying state machines is rather straightforward and we have been able to apply it to the example of a button widget directly. Almost any practical example will, however, require more detailed specifications of the expected behavior. A major strength of UML is that it is a language made by practitioners for practioners. In turn, understanding its more advanced elements also means understanding how to cover more advanced examples. This section traces more elements through concrete examples from the Eclipse platform.

10.2.1   Additional Fundamental Elements

State machines are so successful as tools because most objects have state and many objects exihibit different reactions based on that state. Here is a simple example, the `ContentProposalAdapter` from the JFace framework. Fig. 10.7 shows a typical interaction sequence.

↰9.3

(a) We are about to enter "United States" as a country name.

(b) After pressing the pop-up trigger `Ctrl-Space`, we can select from a given list.

(c) Once the pop-up is shown, we can navigate within the list using the cursor up/down keys. Note that the keyboard focus remains within the text field, so the navigation is a feature of the `ContentProposal Adapter` and not built into the list. As we go on editing the text, the completion proposals are updated. However, when we press `Esc`, the pop-up is closed.

(d) Alternatively, we can press "tab" to switch the keyboard focus to the list (but we cannot return by a second "tab").

(e) Finally, whenever we choose a proposal, it replaces the current text. This result is, in fact, independent of whether we have pressed `Enter` in the text field (c) or in the list (d).

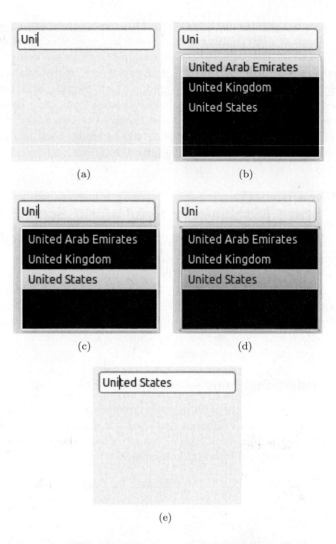

Figure 10.7 Auto-completion in JFace

State machines help in understanding existing code.

The class `ContentProposalAdapter` implements this behavior in about 2200 lines of code, with different listeners attached to different widgets. To get an overview, we summarize the specification in a state machine (Fig. 10.8). The machine distinguishes the different states of the pop-up window and a state where the target text field has been disposed. The transitions express the processing of user input: Pressing "enter" while the pop-up is open means accepting the proposal, pressing "tab" focuses the pop-up, and so on. The remaining new elements of the diagram will be discussed subsequently.

🔍 For the sake of simplicity, we have left out several details. For instance, the pop-up can be activated automatically when specific characters occur in the input. The important point is that the given machine captures the overall code structure and that the remaining details can be filled in appropriately.

Internal transitions trigger effects without leaving the current state.

The first extension to the notation is straightforward and already covers most of Fig. 10.8. *Internal transitions* take place within a state—that is, without leaving the state. They are written down within the state. In the example, state *pop-up open* handles key strokes in this way: While the pop-up remains open, the user can select a proposal; when the text to be completed changes, the proposals are updated. Internal transitions are full transitions in that they can also have guards, and different transitions triggered by the same event can be distinguished by mutually exclusive guards.

Enter and exit effects capture consistent actions conveniently.

The next new elements are *enter* and *exit effects*. Very often, some effect has to be executed whenever a state is entered or left. To avoid explicitly recording these effects at all incoming and outgoing transitions, they can be specified once in the state itself. For instance, when entering *pop-up closed*, the object will close the pop-up window if necessary. Likewise, when entering *pop-up open*, the pop-up window is created if necessary. The example does not contain exit effects; they are written analogously.

🔍 Enter and exit effects are written the same way as internal transitions are, such that `enter` and `exit` appear as special types of events. Their meanings are, however, quite different, and the UML distinguishes between an *internal activities compartment* for *entry*, *exit*, and *do* activities, and an *internal transition compartment* containing the transitions.

📖198

» 10.2.2

Well-written code naturally resembles a mapping of a state machine.

To show how the state machine structures the code, let us first consider the question of how the `ContentProposalAdapter` can receive the necessary events. Clearly, it must attach a listener to the target text field somewhere. Indeed, we find the following code, which covers most events in Fig. 10.8 through a listener for keystrokes and text changes. The omitted part is rather lengthy, consisting of approximately 100 lines. The state machine helps us in understanding the overall code because we know that these

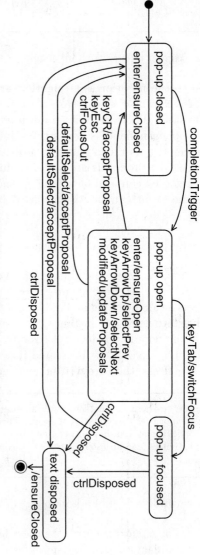

Figure 10.8 State Machine for JFace Auto-completion

100 lines will contain the details of the transitions, and we can skip them for now.

```
                 org.eclipse.jface.fieldassist.ContentProposalAdapter
private void addControlListener(Control control) {
    controlListener = new Listener() {
        ...
    };
    control.addListener(SWT.KeyDown, controlListener);
    control.addListener(SWT.Modify, controlListener);
}
```

The remaining events concern default selection events (i.e., the double-clicks) on the list of propsals. These are not delivered to the listener given in the preceding snippet, so we search on through the code. Sure enough, we find the corresponding listener, complete with the expected event handler, in the code creating the pop-up:

```
                 org.eclipse.jface.fieldassist.ContentProposalAdapter
proposalTable = new Table(parent, SWT.H_SCROLL | SWT.V_SCROLL);
setProposals(filterProposals(proposals, filterText));
proposalTable.setHeaderVisible(false);
proposalTable.addSelectionListener(new SelectionListener() {
    ...
    public void widgetDefaultSelected(SelectionEvent e) {
        acceptCurrentProposal();
    }
});
```

Let us now trace a few of the transitions. Most are associated with keystrokes, so their code will be found in the `handleEvent` method of the `controlListener` introduced earlier. The next code snippet, as usual, turns the state machine "inside-out," so the case distinction is first on the event, then on the state. We see that the state *pop-up open* is associated with the condition `popup!=null` (lines 4–7; no key events will be delivered if the state is actually *pop-up focused*, because then the keyboard focus is on the proposal table). State *pop-up closed* has only one outgoing transition (lines 8–16), so the code checks whether the event *completionTrigger* has occurred. More concretely, this means that the key combination `Ctrl-Space` for opening the pop-up has been pressed. If so, method `openProposal Popup()` creates the pop-up and finishes processing. (Setting field `doit` to `false` indicates that the event has been accepted.)

↰10.1
↠10.3.2

```
                 org.eclipse.jface.fieldassist.ContentProposalAdapter
1 public void handleEvent(Event e) {
2     switch (e.type) {
3     case SWT.KeyDown:
4         if (popup != null) {
5             ...  state 'pop-up open'
6             return;
7         }
```

```
8        if (triggerKeyStroke != null) {
9            if (
10               ...  keystroke is completion trigger
11           ) {
12               e.doit = false;
13               openProposalPopup(false);
14               return;
15           }
16       }
17       break;
18       ...
19   }
20 }
```

The openProposalPopup() method corresponds to the ensurePopup Open entry effect of state *pop-up opened* in Fig. 10.8: It does nothing if the pop-up already exists. Lines 7–12 show an interesting detail: To ensure that popup!=null is exactly the case if the pop-up exists, the code observes the closing of the pop-up shell and sets popup=null in this event.

org.eclipse.jface.fieldassist.ContentProposalAdapter

```
1 private void openProposalPopup(boolean autoActivated) {
2     if (popup == null) {
3         IContentProposal[] proposals = getProposals();
4         if (proposals.length > 0) {
5             popup = new ContentProposalPopup(null, proposals);
6             popup.open();
7             popup.getShell().addDisposeListener(
8                 new DisposeListener() {
9                     public void widgetDisposed(DisposeEvent event) {
10                        popup = null;
11                    }
12                });
13            ...
14        }
15    }
16 }
```

⌕4.1

Looking back on the previous two snippets, the condition on popup being null or not null clearly links to whether the pop-up is currently showing on the screen. Such a link is a typical class invariant:

(popup==null ∧ no pop-up showing) ∨ (popup!=null ∧ pop-up is showing)

≫10.3.2

We will come back to this insight later on.

State machines offer structure for the bumpy parts of the code.

It would seem at first that the controlListener described earlier is responsible for handling all events occurring on the text field. However, this is not the case. On closer inspection of the handleEvent() method, incoming events in state *pop-up open* are delegated to a TargetControlListener.

The method `getTargetControlListener()` creates an instance on the fly if necessary.

---
org.eclipse.jface.fieldassist.ContentProposalAdapter

```
if (popup != null) {
    popup.getTargetControlListener().handleEvent(e);
    return;
}
```

This delegation may be slightly unexpected from the point of view of event handling, but it is a standard coding idiom to encapsulate more complex algorithms into separate objects. The state machine from Fig. 10.8 ensures that we do not miss the bigger picture: The cases shown in the next code snippet correspond directly to transitions, both normal and internal from Fig. 10.8: `keyUp` moves the selection in the table, `keyCR` accepts the current proposal (if valid), and `keyTab` switches the focus to the completion list.

↰1.8.6

---
org.eclipse.jface.fieldassist.ContentProposalAdapter

```
private final class TargetControlListener implements Listener {
    public void handleEvent(Event e) {
        char key = e.character;
        ...
        if (key == 0) {
            int newSelection = proposalTable.getSelectionIndex();
            switch (e.keyCode) {
            case SWT.ARROW_UP:
                newSelection -= 1;
                if (newSelection < 0) {
                    newSelection = proposalTable.getItemCount() - 1;
                }
                break;
            ...
            }
            if (newSelection >= 0) {
                selectProposal(newSelection);
            }
            return;
        }
        switch (key) {
        case SWT.CR:
            e.doit = false;
            Object p = getSelectedProposal();
            if (p != null) {
                acceptCurrentProposal();
            } else {
                close();
            }
            break;
        case SWT.TAB:
            e.doit = false;
            getShell().setFocus();
```

```
              return;
        ...
    }
}
```

Self-transitions briefly leave and reenter the current state.

Internal transitions, as discussed earlier, execute some effect without changing the current state. In particular, they do not execute the enter and exit
effects. *Self-transitions*, in contrast, do leave the state briefly and the corresponding effects do occur. In Fig. 10.9, when the object receives event e,
effects a, b, and c are executed, in that order.

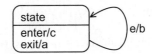

Figure 10.9 Self-Transition in a State Machine

Initial and final states delineate the state machine's processing.

This point explains the processing of events in Fig. 10.8 and links it to the
actual code. The overall machine has two more new elements, an *initial
state* and a *final state*. The initial state, depicted as a filled black circle,
designates the starting point of processing. The object starts its lifetime in
the initial state. The final state, depicted as a circle with an inner filled
circle, designates the end of the object's life cycle. The object cannot leave
the final state.

198(§15.3.8)   The initial state is only a *pseudostate*, because the object cannot remain in that state, but must go to some normal state immediately, without
waiting for an event. In the example, this transition goes to *pop-up closed*,
because initially there will be no pop-up.

🔎 An initial state can be left by several alternative transitions as long as their guards
are mutually exclusive, i.e. as long as the state machine remains deterministic.

Completion transitions fire when the state finishes its processing.

Transitions without events can occur at points other than the initial state.
Such transitions are called *completion transitions*, because they fire as soon
as their source state finishes processing and is therefore "ready to be left."
The processing can consist of some ongoing activity, or can be specified
➤ 10.2.2   more precisely by a nested state machine. The UML fits completion tran-
➤ 10.2.3 📖 198   sitions uniformly into the framework by introducing an implicit *completion
event*, which occurs whenever the processing in a state finishes. Completion
transitions are then just normal transitions triggered by a special event.

As a special case, if a state does not do internal processing, the completion event occurs as soon as the state has been entered—the object just passes through the state. Since completion transitions can have guards and effects, this construction can be useful for expressing sequential case distinctions with corresponding actions. In the example of Fig. 10.8, whenever the text field is disposed (event *ctrlDisposed*), the `ContentProposalAdapter` ends its life cycle. It briefly enters state *text disposed*, only to leave it immediately to dispose of any open dialog. The corresponding code was shown earlier in the method `openProposalPopup()`.

10.2.2   Ongoing Activities

Sometimes, jobs just take longer: because they involve complex algorithms, because they sift through a lot of data, or because they require access to slow media, such as the Internet. In the context of user interfaces, these jobs have to run in the background—that is, outside the user interface's ↰7.10 normal event dispatch thread. This is not all, however: The user interface code must also manage them. State machines can help here, by introducing special states where jobs get executed; they explain what will happen after a job finishes and in which cases it will be aborted.

For a real-world example, let us analyze the class `FilteredItems SelectionDialog` from the Eclipse platform. This class forms the reusable basis for various standard dialogs such as *Open Type* and *Open Resource*. The key challenge with these dialogs is that they have to filter a rather extensive set of possible items according to the user's current search expression. Since the search involves wildcards, prefixes, CamelCase support, and other possibilities, one cannot build a special index that filters items quickly enough to do everything in the event dispatch thread. The simple solution of installing a suitable `ViewerFilter` into a `TableViewer` does ↰9.3.1 not work out.

Instead, `FilteredItemsSelectionDialog` filters the items in the background and places them into a special `ContentProvider`. The actual filtering is, of course, specific to the type of objects being handled, such as Java types or Eclipse resources. It is therefore delegated to a subclass, in the manner of TEMPLATE METHOD (the `AbstractContentProvider` ex- ↰1.4.9 poses a single method `add()` for reporting a found element; it is therefore a client-specific interface). ↰3.2.2

---

org.eclipse.ui.dialogs.FilteredItemsSelectionDialog

```
protected abstract void fillContentProvider(
          AbstractContentProvider contentProvider,
          ItemsFilter itemsFilter,
          IProgressMonitor progressMonitor) throws CoreException;
```

🔎 Even without the timing issues, filtering and sorting would have to be handled by the dialog. As a further precaution to avoid swamping the event thread, the table viewer is created with flag SWT.VIRTUAL, so that only those items actually displayed on the screen get filled with text and icons. For obvious reasons, JFace viewers do not support filtering and sorting in conjunction with SWT.VIRTUAL.

The handling of the filtering and sorting is somewhat complex, because it has to cover various application scenarios encountered in the subclasses. Fig. 10.10 gives an overview. Whenever the search pattern is modified, the display is updated in four stages; the first three fill the content provider, while the last one *refreshing UI* displays the collected items. That last step is also the simplest: The state machine is drawn from the perspective of the user interface, assuming execution in the event dispatch thread. Refreshing the UI therefore blocks the processing, so that we can use a simple enter effect to execute the desired update. The details can be found in the nested class RefreshJob.

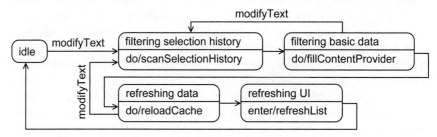

Figure 10.10 Example of Do Activities

Do activities are long-running, interruptable operations.

The first three states contain the new point of the current section: Their purpose is to execute a *do activity*, shown in the internal activities compartment of the state after reserved name do. A do activity is a long-running operation that can be interrupted by incoming events. It is long-running in the sense that unlike effects, it does not have to run to completion before the machine can go on processing events—that is, it does not have run-to-completion semantics.

In the example, each state is characterized by the condition that the filterHistoryJob, filterJob, or refreshCacheJob, respectively, is scheduled or running. All of these activities are implemented in nested classes derived from Job.

But let us trace the progress through the state machine step by step to understand how do activities and event processing interact. Initially, a change of the search pattern triggers the whole process. The event handler method delegates immediately to applyFiler().

↰10.2.1
▢47,198

↰7.10.2

org.eclipse.ui.dialogs.FilteredItemsSelectionDialog

```
pattern.addModifyListener(new ModifyListener() {
    public void modifyText(ModifyEvent e) {
```

```
        applyFilter();
    }
});
```

> ⌕ The method `applyFilter()` is also invoked at other points, such as when the dialog
> is restored with the previously used pattern. This behavior could have been captured
> using an initial state and a state *initializing dialog*.

Applying a filter then starts up the state machine. It is the central
event-processing method. In Fig. 10.10 the current state is left whenever
the user modifies the search pattern. In the code, the intermediate jobs are
canceled (lines 3–4). This cancellation accomplishes two things at once: It
interrupts any ongoing do activities according to the UML semantics and
switches the state. Then, to enter state *filtering selection history* and start
its do activity, the corresponding job is started (line 7).

```
                  org.eclipse.ui.dialogs.FilteredItemsSelectionDialog
1 protected void applyFilter() {
2     ItemsFilter newFilter = createFilter();
3     filterHistoryJob.cancel();
4     filterJob.cancel();
5     this.filter = newFilter;
6     if (this.filter != null) {
7         filterHistoryJob.schedule();
8     }
9 }
```

> ⌕ This implementation deviates slightly from the pure UML semantics. Specifically, a
> call to `Job.cancel()` does not stop the job immediately. Instead, it sends a signal to   ↰8.3
> the job, as a polite request to stop executing whenever convenient. A precise rendering
> would therefore have to wait for the job to actually finish before going on, using an
> `IJobChangeListener`. For the purpose of the dialog, it is sufficient that the next job is
> not started.

The remaining states are then arranged in a pipeline, linked by completion transitions. According to the meaning of completion transitions, the
current state is left as soon as its processing has finished. For instance,
the `FilterHistoryJob` effects the state change by scheduling the next job.
The remaining steps are very similar and we do not show them here.

```
            org.eclipse.ui.dialogs.FilteredItemsSelectionDialog.FilterHistoryJob
    private class FilterHistoryJob extends Job {
        private ItemsFilter itemsFilter;
            ...
        protected IStatus run(IProgressMonitor monitor) {
            ... perform the actual filtering
            filterJob.schedule();
```

```
              return Status.OK_STATUS;
          }
      }
```

In summary, do activities embed long-running operations into the context of state machines. Conversely, state machines provide a conceptual framework for understanding and managing long-running operations.

10.2.3   Nested State Machines

A natural description of an object's behavior often requires phrases involving "while." Here are some examples: "While the ATM holds onto the credit card, it accepts requests from the customer." Or: "While the browser is downloading a file, it repeatly stores the received data to disk." Some of such scenarios can be captured as do activities, but very often, this is too imprecise: Do activities are essentially opaque, black-box building blocks without inner structure. In other words, the framework of state machines cannot be used to specify them. In the two examples cited here, the handling of customer requests certainly involves several steps of selection, data entry, server communication, and so on. And even downloading a file can be split further into reading and interpreting the headers and perhaps opening a dialog box to ask for a file name. All of those can be explained as intermediate states.

↰10.2.2

Substates capture the behavior within a given state.

The UML introduces the concept of *substates* for expressing such behaviors. Each state can have nested substates, and these substates can be connected by transitions as usual. In effect, one can nest entire state machines within each state. A state that has substates is a *composite state*.

📖47

Let us introduce the concepts using the standard example of the ATM (Fig. 10.11). The ATM has two overall states, *idle* and *active*. It switches to *active* once a card is inserted and back to *idle* whenever the user presses the *abort* button, the entered card is found to be invalid, or processing finishes normally. State *active* has several substates, which capture the user interaction with the ATM. On entry, the card data is read. The nested state machine first validates the card data, then offers a menu, requests additional data for the chosen option, and finally processes the completed request. In the end, it asks whether the user wishes to continue.

While the meaning of the nested machine itself is straightforward, we have to take a closer look at the link between the substates and their surrounding states. First, and most obviously, entering the surrounding state through the transition on *cardInserted* starts the nested machine in its initial state. Conversely, the nested machine reaching its final state raises the completion event for the outer state. Next, when the outer state is left using a usual transition, such as on event *abort* in the example, then the current substate is left as well. Finally, when a transition from a substate leaves

↰10.2.1

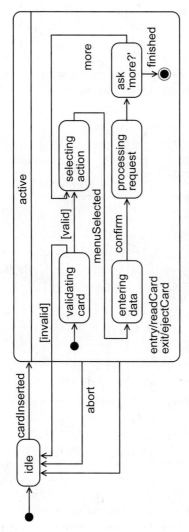

Figure 10.11 Example of Substates: ATM

the outer state, then the outer state is left as well. The example contains such a transition in the handling of invalid cards.

□198(§15.3.11)

As a result, transitions involving substates can always enter or leave several nested states at once. For each state entered or left, the corresponding entry or exit effect is executed. Fig. 10.12(a) illustrates this by an example. When the transition from *M* to *N* is taken, then the effects are executed in the order *exitM*, *exitA*, *enterB*, and *enterN*. It is also useful to visualize the hierarchical structure of states and substates as a tree [Fig. 10.12(b)]. Making a transition between two states or substates involves going upward through the levels toward a common ancestor state and then descending toward the target. Going upward through a state executes its exit effect; going downward executes the entry effects.

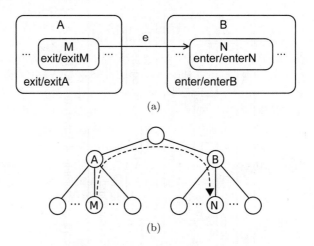

(a)

(b)

Figure 10.12 Entering and Exiting Substates

Orthogonal regions capture parallel and independent behavior.

Sometimes, an object must tackle several tasks at once, must keep track of the progress of independent processes, or simply comprises several independent aspects. The UML introduces *orthogonal substates* for such situations.

□47

We will outline this concept only very briefly and encourage you to read up on the details and extensions if you need to apply it. Fig. 10.13 illustrates the idea. Within state *A*, the machine has to accomplish two things *U* and *V*, each of which is described by its own state machine. The machines are contained within two *orthogonal regions*, separated by a dashed line. The meaning is clear: The transitions in one machine do not influence those in the other machine; rather, each machine holds its own independent state.

Orthogonal substates make state machines much more expressive. Previously, a machine was always in a single state, possibly nested inside some containing states. Those states always formed a linear path in the tree

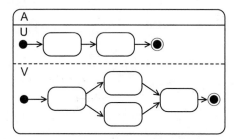

Figure 10.13 Orthogonal Substates

shown in Fig. 10.12(b). The UML calls them *active states*. With orthogonal   198(§15.3.11)
regions, several substates within a state can be active at the same time.
As a result, the overall set of active states will itself form a tree, the *state
configuration*. In this way, the states of the various aspects of an object can
be described in very great detail.

Note, however, that orthogonal substates do *not* introduce concurrency.   ↰8.1
Incoming events are still processed one-by-one, using run-to-completion semantics for effects.

10.3 Implementing Finite State Machines

We have introduced finite state machines as a framework for specifying the
behavior of objects. The implementation of these objects was, however, independent of the state machines: It could have been written, or indeed had
been written, without knowledge of the state machine, simply by following good coding practice. Now we will consider the case where the state
machine specifying the desired behavior is given and the object has to be
constructed. We start by examining a bit closer the approach followed so
far: States remain implicit and are identified by conditions on the object's
natural fields. Then, we give two canonical renderings, one using enums for
states and one using the STATE pattern. For simplicity, we will not deal
with nested state machines.   ↰10.2.3

10.3.1 Running Example: Line Editor

To enable a close comparison of the different techniques, we employ a small
running example [Fig. 10.14(a)], where the user can edit a line by dragging
its endpoints. The state machine is, of course, minimal [Fig. 10.14(b)]: The
LineEditor object has to remember only whether the user is currently
dragging a point. The transitions fire when the user presses or releases the
first mouse button, dragging an endpoint only if the cursor was above it.
The entry and exit effects on *dragging* concern the visual highlighting of
the endpoint.

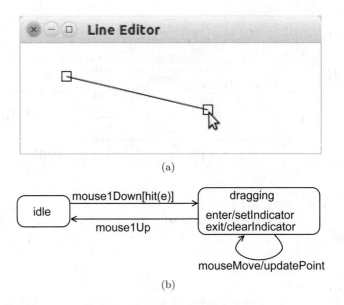

(a)

(b)

Figure 10.14 The Line Editor Example

↰3.1.4
↰7.8
The three implementations are based on a superclass `LineEditorBase`. It is a custom widget and provides a field `line` holding a `Line` object. The `Line` has two `Point` fields `p1` and `p2`. The base class handles the complete rendering. It requires the subclass to communicate the currently dragged point through the method `setDragIndicator()`.

linedit.base.LineEditorBase

```
protected void setDragIndicator(Point p) {
    this.dragIndicator = p;
}
```

Subclasses can also use the method `hit()` to test whether a mouse event took place near a given endpoint, and the method `clipLine()` to ensure that the line remains within the widget's screen area.

linedit.base.LineEditorBase

```
protected void clipLine()
protected boolean hit(MouseEvent e, Point p)
```

The overall shell in Fig. 10.14(a) then simply contains a `LineEditor` widget filling the entire client area.

10.3.2   States-as-Assertions

↰10.1 ↰10.2
In previous examples, we have linked the abstract states to the object's concrete fields through "conditions" that the fields fulfill. For instance, the

`ContentProposalAdapter` identified its states by checking the condition `popup==null`. We will now examine this approach further and give it a solid foundation by applying the established principles of design-by-contract. ↰4.1

Let us start with a natural implementation of a `LineEditor`. The central question is this: What does the object have to know to implement the behavior from Fig. 10.14(b)? Clearly, it must store the point being dragged, because otherwise it will not be able to modify it. In the state *normal*, this dragged point is, of course, invalid, so we set it to `null`. As a minor ↰1.8.9 consideration, we must keep the offset from the mouse pointer to the original position of the endpoint for correct positioning of that endpoint.

---
linedit.inv.LineEditor

```
private Point draggedPoint;
private int dX, dY;
```

This detail is best explained by the code accessing the fields `dX` and `dY`. Whenever the mouse moves, the currently dragged point must move along. Moving the center of the `draggedPoint` to the exact mouse position is not sufficient: If the user clicks some distance away from the center of the handle, the next mouse motion would move the handle abruptly by that distance. The offset resolves this problem: The mouse cursor always keeps its original distance from the center of the handle.

---
linedit.inv.LineEditor.mouseMove

```
public void mouseMove(MouseEvent e) {
    if (draggedPoint != null) {
        draggedPoint.x = e.x + dX;
        draggedPoint.y = e.y + dY;
        clipLine();
        redraw();
    }
}
```

We will now implement the various features of the state machine. For each step, we will follow a developer's intuition first. We will then continue to strengthen his foundation by relating it back to the conceptual framework of contracts. ↰4.1

Each abstract state is defined by an assertion about the object's fields.

To argue that the implementation is correct, we have to relate it back to the state machine. As a first step, we have to identify the abstract state that the object is in. Fortunately, this can be done by checking rather simple conditions:

$$normal \;\widehat{=}\; \texttt{draggedPoint==null}$$
$$dragging \;\widehat{=}\; \texttt{draggedPoint!=null}$$

But now let us be more precise. A "condition on an object's state"
is, of course, simply an assertion: It is a Boolean expression that can be
tested for truth at specific points in time. It is easy to rephrase the loose
correspondence given previously by defining assertions:

$$P_{\text{normal}} = \texttt{this}.\texttt{draggedPoint==null}$$
$$P_{\text{dragging}} = \texttt{this}.\texttt{draggedPoint!=null}$$

We will summarize this approach by the term *states-as-assertions*: Each
state is associated with a unique assertion.

The state assertions must be mutually exclusive.

Let us follow the thought of states-as-assertions one step further. One attraction of state machines is that the abstract states are disjoint; that is,
the object is always in a single, well-defined abstract state. For this to be
true, the assertions defining the abstract states must logically exclude one
another, meaning no two of them must ever be true at the same time. In
the current example, it is clear that

$$\neg(P_{\text{normal}} \wedge P_{\text{dragging}}) \tag{*}$$

The proof is simply that one just expands the definitions here. Other cases,
with more fields, may require a bit more thought. Also, with more than two
states, we must check each pair of them separately.

For practioners, this requirement touches the core of understanding their objects:
Objects very often take actions and decisions based on their fields' state. If we do
not have a clear grasp of the possible configurations, we will never be able to arrive at
consistent and complete case distinctions. Perlis has put this very succinctly: "Programmers are not to be measured by their ingenuity and their logic but by the completeness
of their case analysis."

It is a class invariant that one of the state assertions holds.

One point of state machines, then, is that the object is in at most one state
at a time. A second, complementary requirement is that the object always
is in one of the abstract states. In the current example, we must have that

$$P_{\text{normal}} \vee P_{\text{dragging}} \tag{**}$$

However, unlike the statement (*) given earlier, this one will usually not
be provable in itself. The current example is too simplistic to demonstrate
this—the single field is either `null` or it is not. But it is sufficient to have
two fields. For instance, the CCombo implementation considered previously
holds both a pop-up shell and a list contained in that shell. The widget has
two states: In state *open*, both fields are not `null`; in state *closed*, both are
`null`.

---
org.eclipse.swt.custom.CCombo

```
List list;
Shell popup;
```

However, there will always be brief periods of time when the one is `null` and the other is not, and during these intervals the object is not in a well-defined abstract state. For instance, when creating the pop-up window, the shell is necessarily created before the contained list widget:

---
org.eclipse.swt.custom.CCombo

```
void createPopup(String[] items, int selectionIndex) {
    popup = new Shell (getShell (), SWT.NO_TRIM | SWT.ON_TOP);
    ...
    list = new List (popup, listStyle);
    ...
}
```

The requirement that the object is always in one of the abstract states is therefore a statement about the object's consistency when the object is not currently working—it is a class invariant.   ↰4.1

💡 The run-to-completion semantics of event processing at this point ties in with the proof obligations for class invariants. The event is delivered to the object via a `public` method. Any `public` method can assume that the invariant holds initially and it must   ↰4.1 guarantee that the invariant holds at the end, when control returns to the caller. Since each event is processed to completion, the particular invariant given in (**) ensures that the object will again be in one of the abstract states afterward.

Temporary fields are linked to state assertions.

When using state machines to describe an object's abstract behavior, it is typical that the abstraction does not cover all fields. In the example, the fields `dX` and `dY` contain additional data tied to the *dragging* state. In fact, they are temporary and their content is undefined or invalid in state *normal*.

💡 State machines provide a good handle on temporary fields. Such fields should, of course, be avoided in general. However, they do occur rather frequently in objects that essentially implement state machines. It is a good practice to reset temporary fields to special values when they become invalid when leaving a state. Object references, especially, should be set to `null`, because this enables the garbage collector to clean up the referenced object if it is not used elsewhere.

Event handlers change the state implicitly.

Once we have mapped states to assertions, we can map transitions to concrete code. The transition from *normal* to *dragging* is straightforward: The

↰10.1

event becomes an event handler method, which starts out by determining the current state (line 2). The coding is, again, "inside-out": Reading the state machine goes from states to transitions and events; the code starts from the events and then distinguishes the states. Line 3 further checks that the left button is pressed, and lines 4 and 6 check the transition's guard.

---
linedit.inv.LineEditor.mouseDown

```
1 public void mouseDown(MouseEvent e) {
2     if (draggedPoint == null) {
3         if (e.button == 1) {
4             if (hit(e, l.getP1()))
5                 startDrag(l.getP1(), e);
6             else if (hit(e, l.getP2()))
7                 startDrag(l.getP2(), e);
8         }
9     }
10 }
```

The actual state change of the transition is then accomplished implicitly: Because the object's fields are modified, a different state assertion becomes true. The code exploits the symmetry between dragging the endpoints and calls a helper method `startDrag()`. That method switches the state (line 2) and executes the new state's enter effect (line 3). Finally, it handles the detail of keeping the mouse pointer offset.

---
linedit.inv.LineEditor

```
1 private void startDrag(Point p, MouseEvent e) {
2     draggedPoint = p;
3     setDragIndicator(p);
4     dX = p.x - e.x;
5     dY = p.y - e.y;
6 }
```

Guards become `if` tests.

↰10.1

The meaning of guards is linked to the occurrence of events: Whenever an event may trigger a transition, that transition's guard is reevaluated. The code in the snippet implements this approach directly in the `hit()` test in lines 4 and 6, exploiting the symmetry between dragging either of the points.

Enter and exit effects are inlined.

Another detail of this code is worth noting: A state's enter and exit effects ensure consistent behavior of the state machine. In other words, they are guaranteed to be executed regardless of how the state is entered or left. The code does not give the corresponding guarantees, so one has to be careful to inject the effects wherever the abstract state changes implicitly.

Factor changes of the abstract state into separate methods.

The `startDrag()` method has two merits beyond factoring out common code. First, the enter effect is sure to be executed in any case. Second, and more importantly, the method's name indicates the change of abstract state, which otherwise is only implicit. A team member looking through the code can understand lines 5 and 7 of method `mouseDown()` immediately, without going through the definitions of the state assertions.

With these points in mind, we introduce a corresponding method for going back to the *normal* state—that is, for leaving the special *dragging* state. Again, the exit effect is included:

---
linedit.inv.LineEditor

```java
protected void stopDrag() {
    setDragIndicator(null);
    dX = dY = -1;
    draggedPoint = null;
}
```

In general, it may be important to execute the exit effect before changing the state, because the effect might rely on the temporary fields valid in the state. This is the conceptual reason why we have chosen to invoke the effect first in this method, even if the implementation of `setDragIndicator()` happens not to access `dX` and `dY`. We also set these fields to `-1` to indicate that they are not valid.

With more than two states, a strict adherence to the proposed convention would require one enter method and one exit method per state. A transition then first leaves the source state and enters the target state. However, this coding idiom can easily clutter the code—and the goal of states-as-assertions, after all, is to let the state machine explain and structure the code while keeping it natural and readable at the same time. In most cases, longish methods with complex effects should be introduced, while simple state switches by setting single fields can be inlined.

Think about introducing methods for state assertions.

The assertions characterizing states remain implicit: One has to know them while writing and reading the code, but they do not occur in the code itself. There is, however, the chance that the code will become more readable if the states are made into concrete code elements as well—just introduce methods to execute the states' assertions. In the examples, this leads to the following code:

---
linedit.inv.LineEditor.inNormal

```java
private boolean inNormal() {
    return draggedPoint == null;
```

```
}
private boolean inDragging() {
    return draggedPoint != null;
}
```

The event handlers now reflect the state machine even more immediately. For instance, the code shown next can be read line-by-line to yield exactly the meaning of the transition from *normal* to *dragging*: "If we are in state *normal* and the first button is pressed, check whether an endpoint is hit. If so, change to state *dragging*."

↰10.1

linedit.inv.LineEditor

```
public void mouseDown(MouseEvent e) {
    if (inNormal()) {
        if (e.button == 1) {
            if (hit(e, l.getP1()))
                startDrag(l.getP1(), e);
            else if (hit(e, l.getP2()))
                startDrag(l.getP2(), e);
        }
    }
}
```

Again, these testing methods can have a downside. They may make the code more readable when looking at the state machine, but they may be artificial and meaningless for the developer who is not aware of the state machine. At the same time, the methods suggest to the informed reader that the code *should* be understood as an implementation of a state machine, so the educated maintenance programmer might start reconstructing the state machine on a whiteboard.

Implicit states enable you to take shortcuts.

Although usually the state machine will provide a consistent overview of a class, it can sometimes get in the way of obtaining clear and concise code. For instance, let us forget the state machine of `LineEditor` for a moment. We have introduced the field `draggedPoint` with the intention of having a handle on the point to be modified. With this understanding alone, the following code for event `mouseUp()` would be most readable, because it expresses a simple intuition: "Whenever the first button is released, stop dragging the point along." To understand this code, there is no need to know about the state machine. Also, the intuition does not mention any state at all: Releasing the mouse button stops the dragging process, whether such a process is currently going on or not.

linedit.inv.LineEditor

```
public void mouseUp(MouseEvent e) {
    if (e.button == 1) {
        setDragIndicator(null);
        draggedPoint = null;
```

```
        redraw();
    }
}
```

A similar case has been seen in the example `CustomButton`, where the event handlers did not switch between states of the conceptual machine, but merely recorded the current state of the mouse button and whether the widget is *armed*. ↰10.1

custombutton.CustomButton

```
protected void handleMouseDown() {
    setMouseDown(true);
    setArmed(true);
    redraw();
}
```

Both examples can be so concise because they exploit knowledge that is present at the implementation level but not in the abstract state machine. The `mouseUp()` method knew that there are only two states, and that it would not matter if field `draggedPoint` is set to `null` even if it was `null` before. The `handleMouseDown()` method exploits the symmetry in the transitions of the state machine.

States-as-assertions keep the code stand-alone.

As an overall summary, the main attraction of the states-as-assertions approach is that the state machine can serve to structure and to explain the code, but that it does not constrain the implementation: Special knowledge available at the implementation level can still be exploited and serves to keep the code natural, readable, and succinct.

As a further result, the code can still be understood without looking at the state machine. In practical development, this is often critical: The state machine might once have existed as a quick sketch on some long-erased white-board created during some long-forgotten team meeting. The code, however, lives on and needs to be maintained for years.

10.3.3 Explicit States

As a state machine gets complex, it becomes more and more important to match the code with the abstract view as closely as possible. Looking at some detail of the machine, the maintenance programmer will have to find the corresponding piece of code immediately and reliably. Toward that end, it can be useful to make the abstract state an explicit concrete field in the object.

For instance, the Graphical Editing Framework handles all user input through *tools*, such as selection of drawing elements, creation of specific elements, and so on. The treatment of mouse and keyboard events here is often very intricate. In fact, many tools will define multistep interactions, such as ▱214 when creating a new connection from some source to some target element in the drawing. The class `AbstractTool` therefore introduces an explicit field `state`, whose possible values are given by `final static` constants.

Making the state explicit places it at the center of reasoning.

In the example `LineEditor`, there are only two states. We encode them as `enum`s to allow for `switch` statements while keeping the code type-safe. Besides this abstract state, the object also has to keep the `draggedPoint` and offset (`dX`, `dY`) for the actual manipulation. The meaning of these fields is the same as before.

↰10.3.2

---
linedit.ids.LineEditor

```
private enum State { NORMAL, DRAGGING };
private State state;
private Point draggedPoint;
private int dX, dY;
```

The overall structure of the class is, of course, similar to the previous implementation: The object receives events, then makes a case distinction based on the state, and finally changes the state. The new point is the explicit `switch` statement on the current state.

---
linedit.ids.LineEditor.mouseDown

```
public void mouseDown(org.eclipse.swt.events.MouseEvent e) {
    switch (getState()) {
    case NORMAL:
        if (e.button == 1) {
            if (hit(e, l.getP1())) {
                setState(State.DRAGGING);
                initDraggedPoint(l.getP1(), e);
            } else
                ...   as before
        }
        break;
    case DRAGGING:
        break;
    default:
        throw new IllegalArgumentException();
    }
}
```

↰1.5.4

The `default` clause is, of course, not strictly necessary, because we know that only the two values of type `State` can ever occur. However, later extensions of the state space are simplified if new states without a corresponding handler are signaled immediately.

When ignoring the event in many states, use the fall-through semantics of the `switch` statement and place several `case`s directly behind each other, followed by a single `break`.

It is not always necessary to use a `switch` statement. GEF's tools, for instance, employ a method `isInState()` with usual `if` statements for testing the state. Following is the example of the event handler for mouse moves from the default `SelectionTool`. The code then becomes similar to that found in the previous section with explicit state-checking methods.

org.eclipse.gef.tools.SelectionTool

```
protected boolean handleMove() {
    ...
    if (isInState(STATE_INITIAL)) {
        ...
    } else if (isInState(STATE_TRAVERSE_HANDLE)) {
        ...
    }
    ...
}
```

Explicit states make the class structure more uniform.

The `switch` statement used in the example serves two purposes: It performs the case distinction step and at the same time ensures that the event is either handled or ignored in all possible states. This approach makes the format of the event-handling methods very uniform and predictable and helps the maintenance programmer in locating specific pieces of code.

Conversely, switches that ignore most of the states make the code almost unreadable, because they drown the really relevant bits in formal clutter. It is always possible to relegate these cases to the `default` clause, but this loses the automatic check for completeness.   ◀1.5.4

Explicit states require more class invariants.

One drawback of explicit states is that the object's remaining fields must always be interpreted with respect to the abstract state. In the example, the field `draggedPoint` must be read only in state `DRAGGING`, because it is invalid otherwise. In the previous implementation, this connection was immediate without further reasoning, because the content of `draggedPoint` determined the abstract state.

Technically, the connection must be captured as a class invariant: "If   ◀4.1
`state==State.DRAGGING`, then `draggedPoint` contains the target of the movement and `dX` and `dY` contain the offset." This means, however, that both the original developer and the maintenance programmer must be aware of this invariant, so it must be documented somewhere.

The looser connection between explicit state and the object's data can also be seen the following detail of the example code: Switching a state involves setting the state field and initializing the remaining fields. While it would be possible to extract these lines into a separate method, as is done for states-as-assertions, this would break the new focus on states and is usually avoided, for instance in GEF code.

linedit.ids.LineEditor.mouseDown

```
setState(State.DRAGGING);
initDraggedPoint(l.getP1(), e);
```

10.3.4 State Pattern

Both previous approaches to implementing state machines suffer from several drawbacks:

- Fields may be valid only temporarily, while the object is in specific states.

↰10.1

- Compared with the state machine, the code is structured inside-out; that is, the outer structure consists of event handler methods, which internally switch on the current abstract state.

- As a result, the behavior belonging to a state is scattered throughout the class.

- Furthermore, the necessary switch and if statements can quickly become hard to read.

- Extending the set of abstract states is very difficult, because one has to go through the entire class to adapt all case distinctions. Also, one must change the class invariant, which is always problematic.

📖100

These challenges are addressed by the STATE pattern. Its main idea is illustrated in Fig. 10.15: An object *context* implements a state machine, but the resulting code suffers from one or more of the just-identified problems. It therefore creates internal *concrete state* objects, one for each abstract state, and keeps a reference to the current state object. Each state object includes all the relevant information: Its fields hold the temporary values and its event handler methods implement the transitions from that state. The outer context object delegates all received events to the current state object.

PATTERN: STATE

To implement an object with complex state-dependent behavior, factor out the logic for each state into a separate *concrete state* object and let the main object delegate event handling to the current state object.

1. Define an abstract base class State that has one handler method for each expected event, as well as methods enter() and exit().

2. Give the context object a field `curState`.

3. Implement a state-switching method to set `state`.

4. Forward all incoming events to object `state`.

5. Implement the single states as subclasses of `State`.

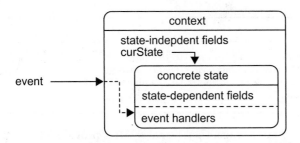

Figure 10.15 Idea Underlying the State Pattern

STATE introduces an event-handling infrastructure.

The main point of the pattern is that the implementation of the concrete   📖100
event-handling code can rely on a solid infrastructure for event handling in
general. Let us look at the steps one-by-one.

First, we introduce a base class of all possible states. States must be
able to handle all incoming events. Also, states will be notified when they
are entered and left.

---
linedit.state.LineEditor

```java
private abstract class State {
    public void enter() {}
    public void exit() {}
    public void mouseDown(MouseEvent e) {}
    public void mouseUp(MouseEvent e) {}
    public void mouseMove(MouseEvent e) {}
}
```

🔍 We use empty bodies rather than abstract methods because we expect many events
to be simply ignored in many states.

Next, we keep the current state in a field:

---
linedit.state.LineEditor

```java
private State state;
```

We finish the infrastructure with a method for switching the state. That
method also notifies the old and new states that they have been left and

entered, respectively. Note that this ensures that the enter and exit effects, coded in these methods, will be executed.

linedit.state.LineEditor

```
private void setState(State state) {
    this.state.exit();
    this.state = state;
    this.state.enter();
}
```

↰10.2.3

💡 Nested state machines complicate the proper handling of exit and enter actions further (Fig. 10.12 on page 546). The infrastructure of the STATE pattern can easily cope with that complexity if the tree of possible states [Fig. 10.12(b)] is reified into an object structure.

The context object can then lie back: After providing the infrastructure, it merely forwards all incoming events to the current state. Here are two examples:

linedit.state.LineEditor

```
public void mouseDown(MouseEvent e) {
    state.mouseDown(e);
}
public void mouseUp(MouseEvent e) {
    state.mouseUp(e);
}
```

↰4.1
↰4.2.4

💡 Both setState() and the event handlers rely on the class invariant that state is never null. This invariant is established in the constructor, as expected in design-by-contract:

linedit.state.LineEditor.LineEditor

```
state = new Initial();
state.enter();
```

Concrete state objects comprise all the logic for reacting in a given state.

State objects can now be self-contained definitions of the object's behavior in a given state. First, they can contain any necessary temporary fields:

linedit.state.LineEditor

```
private class Dragging extends State {
    private final int dX, dY;
    private final Point p;
    public Dragging(Point p, MouseEvent e) {
        this.p = p;
```

```
      dX = p.x - e.x;
      dY = p.y - e.y;
   }
   ...
}
```

🔍 We create a new instance for each state entered at runtime, in keeping with the
   fundamental assumption that objects are small and inexpensive entities. Alternatives ↩1.1
are discussed later.

Furthermore, the enter and exit effects from the state machine can now
be rendered directly as methods:

linedit.state.LineEditor.Dragging

```
public void enter() {
    setDragIndicator(p);
}
public void exit() {
    setDragIndicator(null);
}
```

Finally, and most importantly, the state itself handles outgoing transitions. Note that the implementation is no longer "inside-out": The logic for ↩10.1
identifying and firing transitions can start from the current state.

linedit.state.LineEditor.Dragging

```
public void mouseMove(MouseEvent e) {
    p.x = e.x + dX;
    p.y = e.y + dY;
    clipLine();
    redraw();
}
public void mouseUp(MouseEvent e) {
    setState(new Initial());
    redraw();
}
```

The other state Initial is much simpler: It waits for the user to press
the mouse button near an endpoint of the line and then switches to state
Dragging.

linedit.state.LineEditor

```
private class Initial extends State {
    public void mouseDown(MouseEvent e) {
        if (e.button == SWT.BUTTON1) {
            if (hit(e, l.getP1()))
                setState(new Dragging(l.getP1(), e));
            else if (hit(e, l.getP2()))
                setState(new Dragging(l.getP2(), e));
```

```
                                }
                            }
                        }
```

Keep preconstructed states for rapid switching.

📖100

↰1.6.2

For the small example with infrequent state changes, it was possible to create a new object for the target state in every transition. If transitions are very frequent, the overhead of creating and garbage collecting the state objects can become an issue. In this case, one can spend a bit more memory and preconstruct one object for each state in a `private` field. The initializations previously done in constructors then happen in life-cyle methods `init()`.

Use static state objects if they do not have temporary fields.

📖100

📖100

One optimization step further, if states do not have local, temporary data, they can be stored in `static` fields and shared by all instances of the context class. In this case, the context object has to be passed to every event handler method to enable the method to access the object's data and switch to different states. The result is similar to the FLYWEIGHT pattern, where shared objects are passed *extrinsic state* to each method invocation.

Think carefully before using the STATE pattern.

At first glance, the STATE pattern is the ideal solution to implementing state machines: The resulting object reflects the diagram directly, the logic does not have to be coded inside-out, the logic for each state is kept together in a single small class, and large and unreadable case distinctions are avoided. The set of states can even be extended later on, simply by adding new subclasses of `State`. This is particularly desirable if the requirements for the software are expected to change in the future.

However, the pattern also has a few drawbacks.

- It requires creating some infrastructure before starting on the first state. For small machines, this infrastructure dominates the actual logic.

- In many cases it is actually desirable to group the code by handled event, rather than by state; usual event-handling methods answer concisely the question "What happens if ... ?"

- The structure of the class is far removed from a natural, naive implementation, so that understanding it will require reconstructing the state machine.

- Because event-handling logic is strictly distributed between the different states, it is not possible to exploit symmetries and commonalities directly. As a result, the code is likely to become more redundant.

In the end, as usual in software engineering, you will have to weigh the benefits against the liabilities for the concrete implementation task at hand.

Part IV

Responsibility-Driven Design

Chapter 11

Responsibility-Driven Design

Design can be a rather elusive subject. Very often, one meets people who claim that some design is "elegant" or "crap," as the case may be, and who seek to substantiate that claim with rather abstract concepts such as "loose coupling" or the need for "shotgun surgery," respectively. It is not uncommon to have heated debates about, and almost religious beliefs in, certain design approaches.

From a more practical, down-to-earth point of view, design can be understood just as structuring the solution to a problem. From this perspective, we all design every day because we simply cannot avoid it. Before we start typing out any code, we make a plan, however briefly, about what we are going to type. For common problems, we reexecute time-proven plans from our existing repertoire. For larger problems that we have not solved previously, we may stand back and discuss alternative strategies, either by ourselves or within our team. For really long-term goals, we may take the time to explore existing systems and solutions.

Design is necessary because the solution to any practical problem is usually so complex that we, as human beings, cannot cope with all of its details at once. We have to summarize and abstract over some aspects to focus on and think clearly about others. The design helps us to place the current aspect into the larger picture. It keeps the overall software in shape while we work on a specific class, method, or internal data structure.

But design does not stop at creating just any solution. Usually, we look for a solution that is particularly "good" in some sense. It should be as simple as possible to reduce the implementation effort. At the same time, it may need to allow for easy extensions by new functionality or it may have to be reusable in several products. Necessarily, such extra demands also cost extra implementation effort, and this is where the disputes begin: Which design will offer the best cost/benefit ratio? Which one will be advantageous in the long run? Since such questions can be answered only with hindsight, we often have to rely on experience. Unfortunately, humans tend to prefer their own experience to that of others—quite often, squabbles about design are just another case of the not-invented-here syndrome.

To create and discuss designs, we have to create a suitable language for the task. Saying that objects contain data and the associated operations is certainly correct, but it remains close to the implementation. As a result, it becomes very hard to forget one object's details to focus on another object. There are many approaches to object-oriented design and they all come with their own terminology—the language that we choose tends to shape the way we think about a given problem.

32,264,55,263,262

For this book, we have chosen *responsibility-driven design*, because it has been very influential to the point where its terminology is now found throughout the literature on software engineering. The presentation is split into two chapters. This chapter gives an overview of designing with responsibilities. After introducing the core concepts in Section 11.1, we look more closely at the central strategy of assigning one main responsibility to each object in Section 11.2. To get more details, we then create a self-contained example application, a plotter for function graphs, in Section 11.3. Having mastered the technicalities, we finish by looking at a few indispensable strategies that help to find "good" designs in Section 11.5. While this chapter keeps at the level of individual objects and small groups of objects, the next chapter will look at building blocks at the architectural level and at more abstract design strategies.

11.1   The Core: Networks of Collaborating Objects

↰1.1

We started our investigation of object-oriented software development with the central assumption that objects are small and cheap entities, so that we can have as many as we like to solve a given problem. Having explored and mastered the technical details of the language, design-by-contract, and event-driven software, we are now in the position to ask: Which objects do I create to solve a given task? Which methods do they have?

Of course, it is very hard to come up with general recipes: Software development is and probably will always be a creative activity that involves experience, decisions, and sometimes even taste (although the last facet is grossly overrated—often it is merely a way of referring to one's accumulated experience without being able to pinpoint specific incidents or examples).

263,261

The literature gives many good guidelines on finding objects. They are most helpful when one already has some previous design experience. To gain this experience quickly, we will look at the design of Eclipse's *New Class* wizard: To become a good designer, there is nothing like imitating experienced professionals.

100

The presentation in this section proceeds in three steps. First, we look at the objects and their behavior in a concrete usage scenario to understand the overall approach. Second, we analyze the principles underlying the design. Finally, we examine a few general guidelines about the design process itself.

Software is a network of collaborating objects.

Let us plunge into the topic of design with an everyday example. Eclipse's *New Wizard* in Fig. 11.1(a) is reachable through the *New/Other . . .* entries of the *Package Explorer*'s context menu. (It is shown with indications of the internal structure for later reference.) The user can create virtually any kind of relevant file, complete with a sensible initial content. We will consider the example of creating a new Java class. When we select the *Class* entry in Fig. 11.1(a), the content of the dialog changes to the well-known class creation wizard in Fig. 11.1(b). The use case is simple enough, but how does the *New Wizard* accomplish the task?

When we look at class NewWizard, we find that it has something like 170 lines of code, including whitespace and comments. So all the complex functionality must reside somewhere else, and the NewWizard is only one piece in a larger design that provides the required functionality.

Digging through the different classes and objects involved reveals the structure shown in Fig. 11.2. Admittedly, it seems a bit complex, but the nine objects between them must accomplish the overall task of creating a new Java class through the dialog in Fig. 11.1. We will say that the objects *collaborate* toward that common goal. Collaboration usually consists   📖264,32,109
of simple method calls. To enable these calls, each object holds references to relevant other objects, so that the objects form the *network* (or graph structure) shown in Fig. 11.2. The idea of a network here also encompasses temporary references passed as parameters or stored in local variables.

We will now explain Fig. 11.2 briefly and will also link the explanation to the sources. The subsequent analysis of the underlying principles will justify the perceived complexity. We encourage you to refer back to Fig. 11.2 throughout the explanation, to validate the connections in detail.

The design must be traceable to the implementation.

It is a general principle that a good design is truly valuable only if it is   »11.5.4
also reflected in the code. After all, if the design does not explain how the code works, why bother with design in the first place? The term *traceability*   📖7,24
covers such relationships between different artifacts in software engineering processes.

Design creates mechanisms in which each object has its place.

To explain the overall network, it is best to follow the steps of the *New Wizard* chronologically, along the user experience. At the top of Fig. 11.2, the   ↰9.3.4
NewWizardAction can be placed in the menu or the toolbar. When clicked, it creates a generic WizardDialog, which is built to contain any kind of

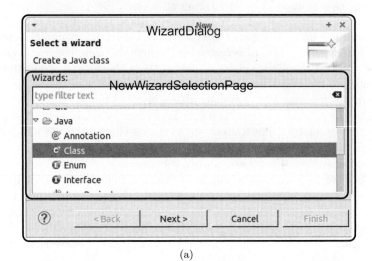

(a)

(b)

Figure 11.1 The New Wizard

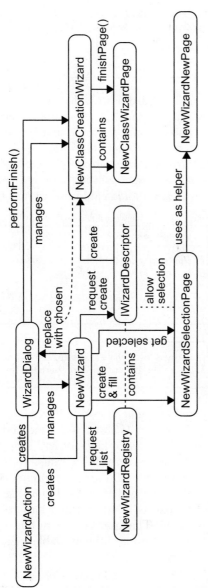

Figure 11.2 Structure of the New Wizard

IWizard. Leaving out the irrelevant code, the action's `run()` method is this:

---
org.eclipse.ui.actions.NewWizardAction

```java
public void run() {
    NewWizard wizard = new NewWizard();
    Shell parent = workbenchWindow.getShell();
    WizardDialog dialog = new WizardDialog(parent, wizard);
    dialog.open();
}
```

↰9.3

The framework of generic wizards is provided in the JFace layer. A JFace `Wizard` object is basically a container for *pages* and manages the switching between these pages. It also contains the code that gets executed once the user clicks the *Finish* button, in a method `performFinish()`. Each page can check whether the current entries are admissible and complete; also, each page is contained in one wizard, and it can dynamically compute the next page. The interface `IWizardPage` captures just this design:

---
org.eclipse.jface.wizard.IWizardPage

```java
public interface IWizardPage extends IDialogPage {
    public boolean canFlipToNextPage();
    public boolean isPageComplete();
    public IWizard getWizard();
    public IWizardPage getNextPage();
    ...   simple properties for name and previous page
}
```

↰3.2.7

⌕ The interface `IWizard` abstracts over the `Wizard` class to to decouple subsystems. Almost all concrete wizards in the Eclipse platform derive from `Wizard`.

The `NewWizard` is one particular wizard and extends `Wizard`. It organizes the overall process, as seen in its `addPages()` method in the next code snippet. First, it requests all available kinds of new files. Internally, these are termed—unfortunately—"new wizards," because technically they are, again, wizards. In the current context, they are represented by objects implementing `IWizardDescriptor`, which are held in a singleton `NewWizardRegistry` (which in turn collects them as extensions to a special extension point in the Eclipse IDE). The `NewWizard` contains a single page `NewWizardSelectionPage`, which displays the available wizard types, as seen in Fig. 11.1.

↰1.3.8
↠12.3.3.2

---
org.eclipse.ui.internal.dialogs.NewWizard

```java
public void addPages() {
    IWizardRegistry registry =
        WorkbenchPlugin.getDefault().getNewWizardRegistry();
    IWizardCategory root = registry.getRootCategory();
```

```
    IWizardDescriptor[] primary = registry.getPrimaryWizards();
    ...
    mainPage = new NewWizardSelectionPage(workbench,
                                selection, root,
                                primary, projectsOnly);
    addPage(mainPage);
}
```

The `NewWizardSelectionPage` delegates the actual display to a helper
class `NewWizardNewPage`. It creates that helper when it sets up its display   ↰7.1
in the `createControl()` method:

org.eclipse.ui.internal.dialogs.NewWizardSelectionPage

```
public void createControl(Composite parent) {
    newResourcePage = new NewWizardNewPage(this, wizardCategories,
                            primaryWizards, projectsOnly);
    Control control = newResourcePage.createControl(parent);
    ...
}
```

The crucial interaction occurs when the user selects a particular wizard from the list and clicks the *Next* button. At this point, the `NewWizard`
asks the `IWizardDescriptor` to create a wizard—in the current scenario
a `NewClassCreationWizard`, which has a single `NewClassWizardPage`
(see Fig. 11.2). All of this happens behind the scenes of the `NewWizard`
`Registry`. Since that class is all about the larger goal of extensibility, we
postpone its treatment and get on with the work: All that matters now is   ↠12.3.3.3
that we have a `NewClassCreationWizard`.

The link between the `NewWizardSelectionPage` and the selected follow-
up wizard happens through the mechanisms inside `WizardDialog`. As seen
in the interface `IWizardPage`, the dialog will ask each page whether it is
OK to switch to the next page and what that page will actually be. The
wizard selection page employs this mechanism to compute the desired page
dynamically, from the selected follow-up wizard.

org.eclipse.jface.wizard.WizardSelectionPage

```
public boolean canFlipToNextPage() {
    return selectedNode != null;
}
```

org.eclipse.jface.wizard.WizardSelectionPage

```
public IWizardPage getNextPage() {
    IWizard wizard = selectedNode.getWizard();
    if (!isCreated) {
        // Allow the wizard to create its pages
    }
    return wizard.getStartingPage();
}
```

↰1.4.1

🔍 Both of these methods are inherited from a generic `WizardSelectionPage`, but this is irrelevant at this point.

We now quickly summarize what happens when the user clicks the *Finish* button, leaving out the code for brevity. First, the wizard dialog invokes `performFinish()` on its current wizard. That wizard may be either a `New Wizard` or a `NewClassCreationWizard`, depending on whether the user has already clicked *Next*. The first case merely delegates to the second, so the call ends up with the `NewClassCreationWizard`, which through several indirections invokes the following method. There, finally, `fPage` is a `New ClassWizardPage` (see Fig. 11.2), which performs the actual creation of the source file.

```
org.eclipse.jdt.internal.ui.wizards.NewClassCreationWizard
```
```
protected void finishPage(IProgressMonitor monitor)
                throws InterruptedException, CoreException {
    fPage.createType(monitor);
}
```

↰9.1

»12.1

💡 The alert and suspicious reader will note that overall setup for creating a class source file actually breaks model-view separation: The code for creating the Java class is contained in the user interface plugin `org.eclipse.jdt.ui`. Since the class creation code is tightly linked to the options available on the wizard page, it would seem sensible to keep both together: If the options change, the code can easily change as well. The situation would be different if the Eclipse JDT included a full-fledged code generation component. That component would certainly have to be model-level, and then class creation would merely pick the right tools from the general functionality.

We have reached the end of this first part, in which we followed the workings of the class creation wizard once through the user experience. It has certainly proved to be a rather complex mechanism. Subsequently, we will see why the complexity is necessary and which general principles explain the chosen design.

Each object is a busy and efficient clerk in a larger machinery.

Even though the objects in Fig. 11.2 together accomplish the larger task of creating a new source class, the individual objects are not aware of this fact and do not have to be aware of it: Each one simply does its own job.

📖264,32

It is like a clerk who has a certain set of *responsibilities*. The overall "administration" is set up such that the machinery runs smoothly and all daily tasks are accomplished as long as each clerk fulfills its own responsibilities, or performs its own duties efficiently.

For instance, the `NewClassWizardPage` is responsible for creating a new source class, by first querying the user for the required parameters and

then creating the source file. It does not have to be aware of the context of
bringing up the pop-up dialog, selecting a file type, and so on. Indeed, it is
this focus on its own responsibilities that allows the class to be reused as   **»**12.4
part of several other wizards. Likewise, the `WizardDialog` is responsible for
managing pages and enabling the user to switch between them. It does not
care about the content of the pages, nor is it concerned with validating the
data the user enters: Those aspects are the responsibility of single pages.

The idea of "clerks" and "responsibilities" may at first sound a bit too abstract
to be helpful. But it is really just a metaphor: By saying that "an object is like
a busy and efficient person," we can transfer our understanding of busy and efficient
persons to the behavior of objects. If we can imagine how a person would handle a task,
we can better imagine how an intangible object would approach it. Metaphors are, in
fact, very common in software engineering. For example, design-by-contract transfers   **↰**4.1
our understanding of legal contracts to method calls. A level further down, we perceive
method calls and code execution as a "behavior" triggered by "messages" to an object. In   **↰**1.4.1
the area of network programming, a "socket" is a point for attaching network connections.
The term "connection," in turn, visualizes the perceived result of sending and receiving
sequences of data packets using the TCP protocol. In short, we use metaphors to link
the unknown, invisible software world to our everyday experience, thereby transferring
our understanding of one to the other.

Some objects perform managerial duties.

We have used the term "clerk" to invoke the image of a diligent, efficient
worker that goes about its daily tasks in a predictable manner. However,
the tasks themselves need not always be humble or basically stupid. In fact,
many objects display a great deal of "intelligence" in their implemented
logic. Also, many objects are more like managers, although their behavior
is still determined by strict rules. For instance, the `NewWizard` arranges for
things to happen, but it does not do any of these things itself. Such objects
will usually make decisions on behalf of and about other objects.   **↰**1.8.1

Roles are sets of responsibilities taken on by different objects.

Once we start thinking in terms of responsibilities, we quickly find that
different objects can take on the same set of responsibilities in different
situations. In the example, the `WizardDialog` can contain many kinds of
wizards, but all of those wizards must fulfill the responsibilities defined
by the interfaces `IWizard` and `IWizardPage`: The wizard must create and
manage a set of pages; each page must perform validation and must compute
the next page, and so on.

A *role* is a set of related responsibilities that can be fulfilled by different   📖263,211
objects. At the code level, roles usually map to interfaces or abstract base   **↰**3.2.10
classes, where the abstract methods capture the expected behavior of the
objects, to be filled in later by the concrete classes. For the purposes of

design, it is, however, better to postpone the definition of the interface and to focus on the conceptual responsibilities instead. That is, before deciding *how* a given service will be accessed, one has be very clear about *what* the service should actually be. Introducing too many implementation details too early tends to lead to premature restrictions of the design.

A role can serve as an abstraction over a number of special cases, such as for the wizards described earlier. The intuition is shown in Fig. 11.3(a), where the concrete collaborator of an object can be exchanged without the object noticing. Roles then lead to extensibility, because new objects fitting the role can be introduced at any time. They can also lead to reusability, because an object accessing a collaborator defined by a role can work with different collaborators in different scenarios.

»12.3
»12.4

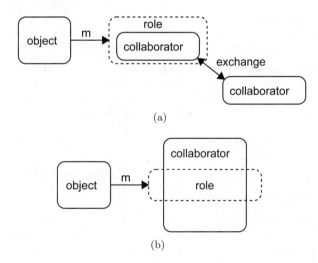

(a)

(b)

Figure 11.3 Illustration of Roles

📖211

A second intuition of roles is that they create slices of an object's behavior, as shown in Fig. 11.3(b). Usually a role does not prescribe the entire behavior of an object, but rather captures some aspect that is relevant in the current context. For instance, the `NewClassWizardPage` of the example contains all the logic for creating a new source file, yet the `WizardDialog` will be interested only in its ability as an `IWizardPage`: When the user clicks the *Next* button, the dialog requests the next page. This view on roles links back to the idea of client-specific interfaces, which carve out a particular aspect of an object's behavior for special usage scenarios.

↰3.2.2

---
org.eclipse.jface.wizard.WizardDialog

```
protected void nextPressed() {
    IWizardPage page = currentPage.getNextPage();
    if (page == null) { return; }
```

```
    showPage(page);
}
```

Fig. 11.3 might remind you of the illustration of the ADAPTER pattern in Fig. 2.10. In both cases, an object accesses a collaborator through a predefined interface. However, in the case of roles it is usually the object itself, rather than some artificial adapter, that provides the required methods. Also, the definition of the role usually predates that of the object. The link between the two situations is this: An adapter becomes necessary if an object fits the conceptual description of a role's responsibilities, but not its technical realization as an interface definition.

Design decisions must be based on concrete goals.

Before we examine the process of designing, let us reevaluate the setup in Fig. 11.2. When we started, it certainly seemed unnecessarily complex: Why not create a `NewClassCreationDialog`, in a single class, and be done with it? We could even use the WindowBuilder to assemble this dialog in a few minutes! Why bother to invent so many objects and so many intermediate steps that it becomes hard to see how the overall task is accomplished?   ↰7.2

The reason is very simple: The particular chosen distribution of responsibilities between objects attains several goals, which together make the Eclipse code base as a whole less complex, more maintainable, and more extensible.

- As a pervasive goal, the individual classes remain small because each object deals with only one main task. As a result, the maintenance developer has to understand less code when trying to debug or modify some functionality.   »11.2

- At the same time, the objects have disjoint responsibilities, so that the maintenance team knows where to look if some aspect of the behavior needs fixing.   »11.5.2

- The `WizardDialog` is a generic piece of infrastructure, which can be reused in many places. A special-purpose dialog assembled with the WindowBuilder could be used only once.   »12.4.2

- The `NewWizardRegistry` takes care of gathering contributed wizards for quite diverse file formats and other artifacts, such as example projects, from throughout the Eclipse platform. New plugins can offer new types of files by simply implementing the interface `INewWizard` and registering the implementation with extension point `org.eclipse.ui.newWizards`.   »12.3.3.3
»12.3.3

Properties such as extensibility and reusability characterize aspects of a software's internal quality that are quite independent of the quality perceived by the users. *Nonfunctional properties* (or *nonfunctional requirements*) capture precisely those aspects   ▢24

↰5.4.6

⌑24,59,218

of a system that are not covered by the use cases, which describe the system's reactions to external stimuli. Other nonfunctional properties include the perceived speed of the answers or the stability of the system. Many of these properties cannot be addressed by software design alone, but fall into the realm of software architecture.

Design must always be driven by such concrete demands; it is never an aim in itself. If someone tells you that his or her approach is simply "more elegant" or "cuter," be deeply suspicious: Chances are that the person is trying to sell you an overly complex solution that does not yield benefits in return for the greater implementation effort. Another trap is to make objects "reusable" by introducing "general" mechanisms right from the start, even if no reuse is planned for the foreseeable future and no one knows as yet the details of a possible reuse scenario. In all such situations, simply insist on evaluating the concrete mid-term savings of the approach. A good guideline is the "rule of three": You should have three concrete applications before setting out to define an abstraction. If the answer to these questions is insufficient, placate the team by pointing out that refactoring can always be done later to implement their ideas. Avoid speculative generality to stay productive.

»12.4

↰1.2.2
⌑92

⚠ Unfortunately, the human mind—and in particular the developer's mind—likes complex and creative solutions: When confronted with a simple everyday problem that looks rather dull, why not spice it up with a bit of intricate design? Try to avoid this temptation as far as humanly possible.

Objects know information, perform tasks, and make decisions.

We have introduced the approach of responsibility-driven design and have explored the need for explicit designs that also anticipate later reuse and changes. How, then, does one create such designs?

We have already examined the basic contributions of objects to a system briefly from a technical perspective. Let us now review them in the light of responsibilities. In general, the responsibilities of an object can be split into three categories:

↰1.8.1

⌑263

- An object may have to know information.

- It may have to perform tasks, mostly for others.

- It may have to make decisions affecting other objects.

Many objects have responsibilities from all three categories, although the last one is perhaps less frequent: Usually an object's decisions concern its own duties and its own internals. At the other end, objects that only hold information are very rare and should be avoided, since operations on the information are more challenging to code and cannot be encapsulated.

⌑92
↰1.1 ↰4.1

In the example, the `NewWizardRegistry` holds information about available file types, but it also gathers information from the various extensions

and wraps it into convenient `IWizardDescriptors`. The `NewClassWizard`   ↰2.4
`Page` holds the information about the new class's characteristics, allows the
user to edit that information, and creates the source file. The `Wizard` dialog
holds no "information" relevant to the user, but it decides when data must
be validated and when pages are flipped. It does so on behalf of the contained wizard and its pages, which are relieved from making these decisions
and can concentrate on their own contributions.

Having such categories helps in describing objects. For each object, ask
yourself what it has to know, what it contributes to the system's functionality, and in which way it is a manager making decisions of more strategic
importance.

Going one step further, objects often have mostly responsibilities from   📖261
only one category, which leads to the concept of *role stereotypes*: information holders, service providers, controllers, structurers, interfacers, and
coordinators. Their descriptions have been given earlier.   ↰1.8.1

Identify responsibilities and assign them to individual objects.

Responsibility-driven design then works from the tasks to be solved. In
the end, the application has to implement some desired functionality. That
functionality is often given by use cases, which describe possible interactions   📖147,47
of the users with the system: The users stimulate the system by their input
and expect some observable behavior in return. As a result, the software   ↰7.1 ↰10.1
becomes event-driven, which ties in with the view of objects responding to   ↰1.4.1
messages.

Designing then means breaking the functionality down into responsibilities—first into broad, comprehensive responsibilities that we assign to the
system's modules, and then into small-grained ones describing individual
steps or aspects of the overall solution. Those responsibilities get assigned
to individual objects.

Invent objects to take on responsibilities where necessary.

In the beginning, there are, of course, no objects that could take on the
responsibilities. During the design process, newly discovered responsibilities
may not fit in with any existing object. Inventing objects is therefore a
central activity in design. The basic idea is this:

If something needs doing, somebody has to do it.

Compare this to the real world: If the kitchenette in the office needs regular
cleaning, then someone must be responsible for it. There must be a well-
established mechanism that triggers the cleaning, because otherwise the
room quickly starts looking quite messy.

Let us try our hand at the example, by designing a *File Creation Wizard* from scratch. This wizard must show a list of file types, as well as *Next*

and *Previous* buttons, and must gather the correct extra information required for a specific file type. Fig. 11.4 shows a first attempt. The `File CreationWizard` manages the overall process. It uses a helper `FileType List` for the first step, because that is a self-contained task. Since the entry of the extra information depends on the file type, we create a role `Extra InformationPage` (the italics in the figure indicate that it is a role). Finally, knowing the benefits of model-view separation, we invent a role `Initial ContentCreator`, again with one kind of creator for each file type. The `FileCreationWizard` is responsible for transferring the entered extra information from the view-level `ExtraInformationPage` to the model-level `InitialContentCreator`.

Figure 11.4 First Attempt at a `FileCreationWizard`

Of course, this design is less elaborate than Fig. 11.2, but then we did not aim for reuse of the wizard dialog. Even so, we managed to observe model-view separation, so that the content creator can be tested on its own, without clicking through the wizard.

To sharpen the perception of what is specifically "object-oriented," let us stand back for a minute. All programming paradigms, such as object-oriented, procedural, or purely functional approaches, provide some way of subdividing the implementation of functionality. The crucial difference between the paradigms arises from the shape of subtasks that single implementation units can take on. In procedural programming, subtasks are algorithmic steps toward a solution. In purely functional programming, they are transformations of (mostly tree-shaped) values. In object-oriented programming, they are reactive entities that communicate via messages. To fully exploit objects, it is therefore best to postpone concerns about algorithmics and data structures during design: While it is necessary that the design *can* be implemented, and efficiently too, the focus must be on a sensible task assignment that can be understood on its own, without looking at any code.

> Do not assign the same responsibility to different objects.

The metaphor of "responsibilities" has a second important aspect: If a person is responsible for a given task, then the individual fulfills that task completely and reliably, and does not share that task with other people. Likewise, an object should be made the sole authority for its responsibilities. The obvious reason for this goal is that you will not have to write code twice or garble your design by copy-and-paste programming. One level

↰9.1

↰9.2.2

↰1.8.4

deeper, the exact details of responsibilities are likely to change. Confining
the changes to a single place keeps the software maintainable. As we will
see, however, this simple goal involves some rather subtle implications and
challenges.

»11.2.3
»11.5.5

Plan for collaboration to keep the responsibilities small.

Throughout the design, components and objects will rely on collaboration
to fulfill their responsibilities: An object never does things that another
object can already do. While identifying individual responsibilities, we will
therefore also plan for the necessary collaborations: If an object requires
help in its tasks, it must have a reference to the object that can provide
the help. The overall goal is to keep objects so small that their behavior
can be subsumed under a single, well-defined responsibility.

»11.2

In the running example from Fig. 11.2, the NewWizard relies on the
NewWizardRegistry to interact with the Eclipse extensions mechanism.
It delegates the task of displaying all found file types to the NewWizard
SelectionPage.

»12.3.3

At this point, it is important to recall the object-oriented view on methods. A method
call is not merely a technical invocation of a subroutine implementing a specific algorithm. It should instead be read as a message to which the receiver reacts appropriately,
at its own discretion. Since the ultimate responsibility for the reaction lies with the
receiver, it is also the receiver that decides which reaction will best suit the request.

◄1.4.1

Mechanisms structure sequences of individual collaborations.

Just as each object has few and small responsibilities, each individual collaboration between objects usually concerns a tiny aspect of the overall
application's functionality. It often takes the accumulated effect of many
collaborations between several objects to exhibit some desirable, externally
visible behavior.

»11.2

We will use the term *mechanism* for a sequence of logically connected
collaboration steps that together achieve a common goal. Mechanisms induce a switch of perspective: Rather than asking what a particular object
does and how it reacts, we ask how a particular overall reaction is achieved
through collaborations among possibly several objects. In UML, mechanisms are rendered as sequence diagrams. The comprehensive treatment
there underlines the importance of the concept.

☐47

In the example, one may rightly ask: How does a wizard-like dialog
ensure that the *Next* button is enabled only if the current page is filled
in with complete and valid data? The solution is that the current page
observes its input fields and invokes updateButtons() on its wizard container, which in turn calls the page method canFlipToNextPage(). But
this is not yet the whole story. Many concrete pages derive from Wizard

↰3.1.4

Page, and that base class provides some infrastructure. For instance, a flag isPageComplete captures the current status and updating the flag links in with the raw mechanism:

org.eclipse.jface.wizard.WizardPage

```
public void setPageComplete(boolean complete) {
    isPageComplete = complete;
    if (isCurrentPage()) {
        getContainer().updateButtons();
    }
}
```

↰2.1.4

⇄? Since the chosen mechanisms determine to a large degree the complexity of the implementation, it is important to consider alternatives. In the example, one could require the pages to act as Java beans and to inform PropertyChangeListeners about data modifications. The wizard container would then simply listen to the changes. However, there would always be only a single observer, and the page would have to translate SWT events to PropertyChangeEvents. The special-purpose communication through update Buttons() certainly reduces the overall implementation effort.

↰9.4.3

↰7.8

Another example of a typical mechanism is seen in the task of updating the screen after a change in the model. Fig. 9.14 (on page 500) explains how the discovery of a data modification after several intermediate steps leads to a callback to paintControl(). The mechanism is designed in this complex fashion to keep it general and to enable the window system to optimize the painted region in between.

Responsibilities and collaborations must make sense locally.

Mechanisms are necessary to structure and explain sequences of collaborations. However, they incur the danger that individual collaborations cannot be understood at all without also considering the larger picture. As a result, maintenance can easily become a nightmare: Having no time to read through the design documents or having mislaid these documents a long time ago, the maintenance developer must trace through the collaborations using a debugger to reconstruct the intentions of individual method calls.

↠11.2.1

The only way to avoid this problem is to constantly switch between the global perspective of mechanisms and the local perspective of responsibilities and collaborations of individual objects. It is a good exercise to "write" a mental documentation for individual objects from time to time: Can you still say in one or two sentences what the object or a particular method does *without* referring to the subsequent reactions of its collaborators? Only such localized descriptions ensure that the individual classes of the system can still be understood by the maintenance developer.

In the example, the mechanism for revalidating the data and enabling or disabling the wizard buttons can be documented locally. In the description of IWizardPage, and the base class WizardPage, one would have to (1) say that method canFlipToNextPage() must validate the data and (2) leave a remark that the object must invoke updateButtons() whenever the data has changed.

In the Graphical Editing Framework, one can still describe an individual "edit part" (i.e., the unit of composition of drawings) without understanding entire sequences of collaborations. It is necessary to understand only the edit part's expected reactions to specific stimuli, mostly sent as *Request* objects.

📖214

Disciples of other paradigms often bash object-oriented programming because of the necessity of combining several collaborations to achieve some overall effect. They complain that one never sees where anything particular gets done because so many objects are involved and each contributes so little. This perception has two possible sources. First, the particular design might be so bad that it is indeed impossible to understand the individual objects separately. Second, the developer in question might not be prepared to take the leap to the object-oriented way of thinking, where one focuses on individual objects and trusts subsequent collaborations to occur as would be expected. A similar case occurs for novices in functional programming, where many tasks are approached by (structural) recursion. A fundamental insight on recursion is this: Never think about a recursive function recursively. One does not understand a recursion by unfolding the calls a few levels deep. One has to focus on the contribution of the individual step, trusting the recursive calls to deliver the expected results reliably. Similarly, one understands a loop not by unrolling a few iterations, but rather by seeing the overall picture, as expressed in the loop invariant. In all three cases, the particular way of "seeing the point" in a solution requires some practice and experience with the particular units used for subdividing tasks.

↰4.7.2 📖144

CRC cards help to start designing.

Let us now turn to the design process itself. Design in many places is a creative, formally largely unconstrained activity. To introduce some structure, you can use *CRC cards*. The abbreviation stands for "class, responsibilities, and collaborators."

📖32

≫11.3.2

Here is how to start with CRC cards: You buy a few hundred medium-sized index cards and use one for each object or role that you identify. Each card gets subdivided as shown in Fig. 11.5. At the top of the card, you write the class name. A small right margin holds the collaborators, just to capture the overall graph structure from Fig. 11.2. The remaining area holds the responsibilities.

The cards in Fig. 11.5 capture the essence of the design: WizardDialog collaborates with the contained wizard and its pages, as well as with the outer Shell. It has to provide the outer frame for the actual wizard, and it initiates and decides about the flipping between pages. Also, it triggers data validation, by calling canFlipToNextPage() and isComplete() on pages. Each IWizardPage then has to create SWT widgets for data entry and must validate the data. It must dynamically provide the next and previous

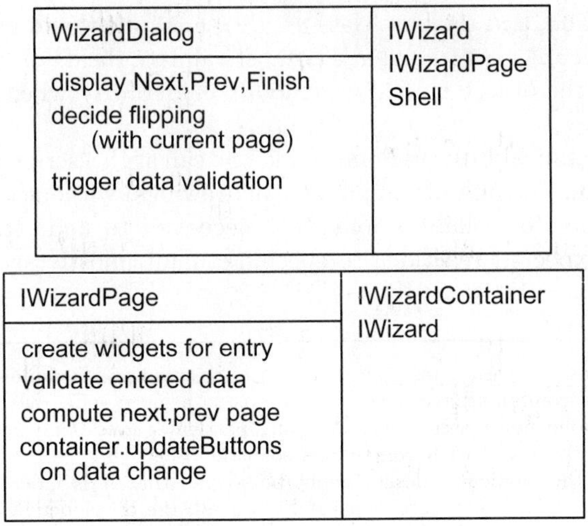

WizardDialog	IWizard
display Next,Prev,Finish decide flipping (with current page) trigger data validation	IWizardPage Shell

IWizardPage	IWizardContainer
create widgets for entry validate entered data compute next,prev page container.updateButtons on data change	IWizard

Figure 11.5 Example CRC Cards

pages in the sequence. Finally, it has to react to changes in the entered data by asking the container for revalidation.

Since CRC cards are cheap, lightweight, and easy to manipulate, they invite you to sketch designs quickly, and to throw away superseded versions of objects without regrets. Also, the limited area on the index cards forces you to split large classes—there is simply not enough space to describe too many or too complex responsibilities.

CRC cards establish a useful shape for thinking about design. Experienced designers and developers will often find that CRC cards assemble themselves in their heads and that they can type out the classes, or at least their `public` methods, immediately. CRC cards are an effective way of learning object-oriented design, but you must not feel constrained by the format for all times and in all situations.

📖 32

Start from your idea of a solution.

» 11.5.2

One important aspect of design is that it always captures one way of thinking about the given problem and one approach to solving it. Different people will understand a challenge differently, and they will arrive at different designs. One key contribution of a good design is that it captures the team's common understanding of the intended solution.

Before embarking on a design, you must have at least a general understanding of the overall solution strategy. Likewise, figuring out the details of the design is a good time for elaborating one's idea of the solution.

Design, evaluate, improve.

Design is always an iterative process. There is rarely one optimal solution, and in any case, one tends to forget important details when first designing networks of objects. As a result, one has to sketch out a few possibilities before deciding on their relative merits. CRC cards are just the tool for this kind of lightweight iteration.

Here are some evaluation criteria. Most fundamentally, one has to establish that the design solves the given problem: Will all the use cases be covered by the envisaged collaborations and mechanisms? Do all objects have access to the required collaborators? Beyond that, one can evaluate the match with object-oriented principles: Are the individual objects small and self-contained? Are they really reactive entities or are some objects merely storing information that other objects work on? Finally, there are possible strategic goals: Can the crucial components be rigorously unit-tested, by placing them in a test fixture? Does the design respect model-view separation? Can the implementation be extended to cover modified or additional use cases? Can parts of the implementation be reused in different contexts?

»11.2
▢92
↰5.1
↰9.1
»12.3
»12.4

Having the design available in some external form, such as CRC cards, enables us to point to special aspects and match them against our idea of desirable designs as well as against the given problem. Also, any implicit assumptions not yet worked out properly will be uncovered immediately.

The goal of these evaluations is to expose possible flaws early on, while changes are still quick and cheap. If we find that a missed use case does not fit the existing design only after completing substantial parts of the implementation, the effort to integrate it by changing the code structure will be much higher. Take the opportunity to seriously challenge your own designs through CRC cards.

Become aware of the decisions you make.

Designing always involves making decisions: Which object is responsible for which aspect of some reaction? Is a responsibility small enough to be carried by a single object or should it be split and distributed among collaborators? Do we need to generalize a solution to enable reuse later on while incurring some implementation overhead now?

To become good designers, we have to become aware of which decisions we make for which reasons. If we fail to see the necessity of a decision, we are likely to blunder on in one direction without even being aware of possibly smoother and shorter paths. If, in contrast, we have a bunch of alternatives right at our fingertips, we are more likely to come up with a useful design. We also gain the consolation that if we have taken the wrong turn at some point, we are not stuck but still have a number of alternative and promising paths left to explore.

»11.5

11.2   The Single Responsibility Principle

□170,172

If you are looking for a single guideline that will make a design come out "truly object-oriented," it is certainly the *Single Responsibility Principle*, abbreviated as SRP. Its diligent application will lead to small classes that collaborate in well-defined ways, and to software that is easy to change and to maintain.

↰1.1

11.2.1   The Idea

The Single Responsibility Principle states that each class should have only one responsibility and should delegate any tasks not related to that responsibility to its collaborators. For an illustration, let us go back to the wizard creating new files in Eclipse. With little time and little experience, we might just start on the user interface with the WindowBuilder and add the functionality to the event handlers as we go along. We will probably end up with the design in Fig. 11.6. The `FileCreationWizard` object displays a window with buttons for navigation; it looks through the registered file types; it allows the user to select a type; and finally it creates a wizard page to gather the information specific to the file type. Only that last task is delegated, and only by necessity: Because the information is different, we need different screens to collect it. Basically, this is an instance of the STRATEGY pattern.

↰11.1

↰7.1

↠12.3.3

↰1.3.4

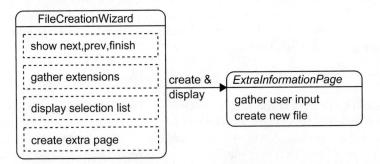

Figure 11.6 A `FileCreationWizard` with Too Many Responsibilities

Make each object responsible for one thing.

Obviously, the `FileCreationWizard` in Fig. 11.6 will be a huge class. We have surrounded its responsibilities with dotted lines to indicate that each will require several fields and methods in the implementation.

Suppose now that we "explode" this huge class into separate classes, one for each responsibility. We arrive at the design in Fig. 11.7. Basically, we have moved each thing that needs doing to a separate object that actually

↰11.1

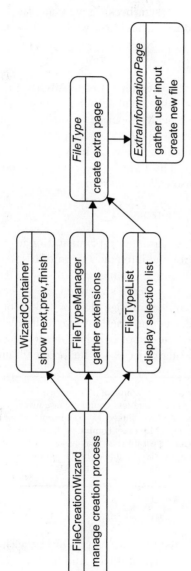

Figure 11.7 Refactored `FileCreationWizard`

does it. Only the `ExtraInformationPage` retains two responsibilities, because in this way it can apply the entered information directly during file creation. The similarity to Eclipse's own design in Fig. 11.2 (on page 571) is really quite remarkable: Although one could argue that we were bound to come up with the same design because we knew the original, the tasks in Fig. 11.6 really needed doing, and now we have done them.

The SRP keeps objects small and understandable.

A major benefit of applying the Single Responsibility Principle is that the code base of an object remains small: If independent tasks are distributed over several objects, then each of them has a simpler implementation. The code also becomes easier to understand, because the reader knows that any particular snippet must somehow fit in with the goal of fulfilling the object's one responsibility. This tight logical connection between an object's
»12.1.3 different code pieces is also called *cohesion*.

The SRP keeps objects maintainable.

The new design also clarifies the later implementation in two respects. First, it is clear where to look for the implementation of a specific piece of functionality that may need fixing or changing. This helps greatly in maintenance work. Second, the dependencies between the different tasks become clearer: Within the huge object in Fig. 11.6, any piece of code may access and manipulate any field, and any method may call any other method. In contrast, in the "exploded" design of Fig. 11.7, each object can access only
↰1.1 the `public` methods of other objects; the fields remain encapsulated.

↰4.1
↰4.1
A deeper reason that makes the "exploded" design desirable is that the clarification of dependencies leads to smaller and less complex class invariants. The fields needed for each responsibility in Fig. 11.6 are linked by consistency constraints (i.e., by class invariants). The invariant of the entire class combines these into a huge assertion. Each `public` method must prove that it establishes that assertion in the end. The developer must therefore understand the invariant completely to exclude any possible interactions, even if a `public` method touches only a very few fields.

Give each object a coherent overall purpose.

One question arises immediately: How can an object with only one responsibility ever get anything significant done? And how can a system consisting of only such minuscule objects ever fulfill its users' demands?

The answer is that the actual power associated with a responsibility depends largely on the granularity and abstraction level chosen for expressing the responsibility. The unit "responsibility" is a conceptual measure, not a technical one. For instance, the responsibility to gather existing extensions

in the designs of Fig. 11.7 and Fig. 11.2 involves a fair bit of data structures and boilerplate code, as well as some nontrivial knowledge about the
Eclipse API for accessing extensions. Still, it is one self-contained responsibility that the object `NewWizardRegistry` fulfills.

The Single Responsibility Principle is about logical cohesion: All tasks » 12.1.3 📖236
that an object undertakes must be subsumed under its responsibility, but
this does not mean that there is only a single task from a technical perspective. It might be better to say that an object has a single purpose,
which also captures a specific reason why the object must be present in the 📖92("Lazy Class")
system.

Learn to tell the stories of your objects.

Another helpful intuition is that of telling "stories." When we ask, "What's
the story behind this?" we actually mean this: What is a convincing explanation? Why should I believe the author? Why should I "buy" the argument?
A story is often related to a message: When a blog entry, for instance,
tells a good story, we mean that it has a point and states it clearly and
convincingly.

Telling "the story" of an object well means explaining what it does, why
it is a useful member of the community, why the implementation effort
is justified, and why its public API is exactly right. Imagine you have to
sell your objects to your teammates and you have only a few minutes to
convince them you did a great job. Which aspects would you emphasize?

The purpose of this exercise is to form a clear idea of each object's goals,
as well as of its limitations and the tasks it delegates to its collaborators:
Someone who knows his or her own expertise is better in focusing on this
area. It may take some time to find "the story" of your object, but it is 📖28
always worthwhile, since it helps you to focus, to find the "simplest implementation," and to communicate the results within the team.

Describe an object's purpose in a single sentence.

To check whether you have succeeded in assigning a single responsibility
to an object, try to summarize its purpose in one sentence. Here are some
examples from the original new wizard (Fig. 11.2):

- The `NewWizardRegistry` collects the declared extensions into a conveniently accessible data structure.

- The `NewClassWizardPage` enables the user to enter the parameters
  necessary for creating a new source file and then creates the file.

- An `IWizardDescriptor` encapsulates a declared file type to simplify
  setting up a wizard to handle the file type.

- A `WizardDialog` acts as a container for a concrete wizard with several
  pages.

An important point is that the one sentence must be a plain, short specimen. Once you start stringing together subclauses joined by "and," "if," and "but," you defeat the purpose of the exercise. Finding a sentence meeting this criterion is actually quite a challenge. The author admits freely that he had to fiddle with the formulation of the given examples to get there.

↰11.1

If you cannot come up with a short sentence that captures the object's purpose, the design may be flawed. A case in point is the `NewClassWizard` `Page`: Its description does contain an "and"—and we have already found that it violates model-view separation.

> Condense an object's single responsibility into the class name.

↰1.2.3

A single-sentence purpose is nice, but it is better still to condense the purpose even more by expressing it in the class name. For example, a `Wizard` `Dialog` is a dialog containing a wizard; a `NewClassCreationWizard` is a wizard responsible for creating a new source file with a Java class. Similarly, knowing that a "registry" in Eclipse parlance is something that manages specific objects, we see that the `NewWizardRegistry` manages extensions offering "new wizards." Renaming `NewWizardNewPage` to `NewWizard`

↰7.5

`SelectionPanel` would clarify that it is a composite widget offering several "new wizards" for selection.

11.2.2 The SRP and Abstraction

The Single Responsibility Principle has more benefits than just keeping the code base of individual classes small and coherent. An important aspect is that it guides developers toward creating useful abstractions.

> Assigning single responsibilities means understanding the solution.

↰11.2.1

You will quickly note that it is actually very hard to come up with a single sentence that describes an object well and comprehensively. The reason is simple: You have to identify the object's really important aspect from which all other aspects follow logically. In other words, you have to arrange your possibly many ideas about what the object does into an overall structure.

Once you succeed, however, you gain a better understanding of your object. The object is no longer a flat collection of tasks; instead, these tasks are interrelated. You know which ones are important and which ones are mere technical details; which ones are crucial and which ones are incidental; and which ones characterize your object and which ones it may share with other objects.

> The SRP helps to abstract over the technical details.

↰11.1

The Single Responsibility Principle also makes it simpler to understand the application's overall network of objects. Because you can summarize each object in one sentence, you can skip quickly from one object to the next without cluttering your mind with the technical details of each. Once your mind is freed from these details, it can hold more of the actual design.

The SRP helps in taking strategic design decisions.

Strategic insights and decisions are possible only at the level of abstraction created by brief summaries of objects. To make decisions, you have to juggle in your mind the design as it is, and most minds are not capable of holding too many details at a time. Brief summaries, in turn, are possible only if each object takes on only a small task, a single responsibility.

The SRP is indispensable in communicating the design.

There is nothing more boring and ineffective than listening to teammates expounding on the internals of their classes at the slightest provocation. Many developers fall for the temptation of boasting about their technical exploits.

The Single Responsibility Principle enables a team to communicate effectively: Because each team member prepares a one-sentence summary of his or her objects in advance, answers become shorter. Because the answers link directly to the overall system purpose, other team members can pick them up and store them away quite easily. In the end, the whole team gets   📖28 a pretty good overview of the system, without having to understand the technical details of every class.

The SRP also applies to class hierarchies.

The first association that springs to mind in connection with abstraction is inheritance. Since responsibility-driven design focuses on objects, rather than classes, we will look only at the basics. The Single Responsibility Principle applies to arranging code into classes, so it applies to hierarchies as well. From this point of view, each subclassing step and each level within   »11.4 the hierarchy has its own purpose and its own responsibilities. For an extended example, you can look at the hierarchy of editors in Eclipse and   »12.2.1.2 in particular the chain `EditorPart`, `AbstractTextEditor`, `StatusText Editor`, and `AbstractDecoratedTextEditor`.

11.2.3 The SRP and Changeability

It has been noted from the infancy of computer science that modularization is necessary because software probably needs to be modified during its lifetime. In his seminal paper, Parnas postulates: "The essence of in-   📖205 »11.5.1 formation hiding is to hide design decisions that are likely to change, and to make modules communicate through interfaces." It must be said that—

given Parnas's words were written in 1972—"design" means mostly design of data structures and algorithms. Still, the point is there: We make decisions now that we are pretty sure we will have to revise later on. How can we do this without breaking our product?

The SRP helps in restricting the impact of necessary changes.

172,170

In his presentation of the Single Responsibility Principle, Martin defines the term *responsibility* itself as "one reason to change." If each object has a single responsibility, then there is one kind of change that the object will absorb, one kind of change from which it insulates the rest of the system. The unit of task assignment coincides with the unit of changeability.

205

It is interesting to note that Parnas, in 1972, also made this connection: "In this context 'module' is considered to be a responsibility assignment rather than a subprogram." It seems that the metaphor of "responsibilities" is, indeed, very appropriate for reasoning about good software organization.

The Single Responsibility Principle does not immediately guarantee that changes will not ripple through the system. This outcome can be achieved only by striving for information hiding and designing for flexibility through-

11.5.1 12.2

out. However, the Single Responsibility Principle lays the foundation: When an object acquires a responsibility, it can and should become zealous about it and should not allow other objects to meddle with its own implementation decisions. Guarding these decisions as a private secret is the right step to take.

The SRP helps to locate the point of change.

11.2.1

At the same time, the Single Responsibility Principle helps one find the place that needs changing. Assigning a responsibility to an object also means that no other object will take on the same responsibility. If some behavior needs changing, we can quickly find the class that contains the code, through its one-sentence summary of its purpose.

Once we start looking into a class, we are sure that all the code we see is potentially affected by the change, simply because the class takes on only a single, coherent responsibility.

The challenge in design is to anticipate the probable changes.

How then, do we assign responsibilities? So far, we have proceeded largely by intuition. Now, we get a new criterion: Each responsibility should enclose one area where the software is likely to change. Anticipating such changes is far from simple. While we strive to find a solution for a given set of requirements, we have to think at the same time about similar solutions for similar requirements. A few heuristics will help to identify the critical points in the design.

- Experience in building a number of similar systems gives us a pretty good idea of the variability between different instances.

  □□70

- The insecurity we might feel in formulating and solving a specific problem can be a hint that we might have to revisit the code later on.

- If we have made a deliberate and well-informed decision between several alternatives, as professionals, we must be well aware that the others may come in handy later on.

- We are bringing in a library with which we have little prior experience. To make it simple to switch to a competitor, we hide all accesses in objects.

- Sometimes we deliberately build a suboptimal solution, perhaps even a mock object as a temporary stand-in for the the real and complex implementation.

  ↰5.3.2.1

From a language perspective, these guidelines are all about encapsulation of private elements behind the public facade of an object. Specifically, the remainder of the system can keep on using the same external interface as long as the internal implementation fulfills the established contracts.

↰1.1 ↠11.5.1

↰4.1

> The two notions of responsibility coincide naturally.

Fortunately, there is also a direct link between the intuitive approach of chopping up given requirements into individual responsibilities and the search for responsibilities as spots of likely change: Changes to a software are usually triggered by changes in the requirements. If these requirements vary only slightly, then chances are that they will fall under the same one-sentence summary of the object currently handling the requirement. The change then concerns only the internals of that object, and these internals are encapsulated within the object through its public interface. As a result, the remainder of the system is not affected, and the impact of the changing requirements is absorbed gracefully by the existing software structure.

11.3   Exploring Objects and Responsibilities

Having mastered the concepts and basics of responsibility-driven design as well as the all-important Single Responsibility Principle, we will now try out this approach on a self-contained project: a simple function plotter.

11.3.1   Example: A Function Plotter

Fig. 11.8 shows the overall application we will implement. In the lower-left corner, the user enters a formula, which then gets plotted in the main area above. In the lower-right part, the user selects the region of coordinates and the type of axis (simple or grid).

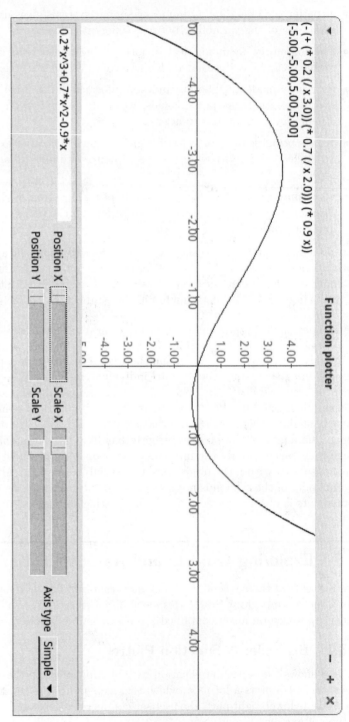

Figure 11.8 The Function Plotter Example

The whole thing seems simple enough, and you have probably implemented something like it just for fun in an hour or so. The challenge and goal here is not so much the functionality, but the design: How can we reuse the shift-reduce parser from the INTERPRETER pattern and the MiniXcel application? How can we keep individual aspects such as the certainly suboptimal choice of the plot region changeable? How can we build the application from small individual objects that collaborate only in well-defined ways? How do we shape those collaborations so that the objects remain as independent from one another as possible?

↰2.3.3 ↱9.4

↱12.1

We will see that to answer these questions satisfactorily, we have to tie together many individual design principles, design patterns, and elements of language usage that we have so far treated separately. Seeing them connected in a comprehensive example gives us the opportunity to explore their interconnections and synergies. At the same time, we will introduce more details about the known concepts.

The subsequent presentation focuses on the concrete code of the function plotter and justifies the design decisions from the resulting code structure. Afterward, we will give a brief summary of the development. To keep the wider view, you may wish to peek ahead at Fig. 11.11 on page 617, which depicts the main objects introduced and highlights their principal relationships.

↱11.3.4

11.3.2 CRC Cards

Before we can start, we need a better handle on design. The box-and-line drawings used in the presentation so far are all very well, but they hardly constitute a clean format for larger designs. At the other end of the spectrum, a semi-formal language like UML can easily stifle our insights and creative impulses.

📖47,198

Class, responsibilities, collaborators—CRC.

The insight that objects are characterized by their responsibilities and their collaborations has led to the proposal of writing down the *class*, the *responsibilities*, and the *collaborations* onto small colorful index cards—in short, *CRC* cards. We have seen the key idea of CRC cards already. In particular, Fig. 11.5 (on page 584) gives two simple examples. Now, we will add a few remarks on how to use them.

📖32

↰11.1

Use CRC cards to lay out candidate designs quickly.

Writing class names and responsibilities onto index cards may not seem such a great breakthrough at first. However, it turns out that the medium of CRC cards helps to push the design process in the right direction.

- Since CRC cards are small, there is no space to write up many or complex responsibilities. The medium enforces a sensible subdivision and drives us toward the Single Responsibility Principle.

↰11.2

- CRC cards are cheap and easy to manipulate. This encourages you to write up and explore alternative designs, and to discard those that prove wrong on closer inspection.

- CRC cards appeal to our visual and tactile understanding of situations. You can arrange tightly linked objects near each other, and stack a class and its helpers, or a role and its concrete realizations. You might also want to choose different colors for roles and concrete objects, for different types of objects such as boundary objects, or for the model-level and view-level objects.

↰11.1
↰1.8.7
↰9.1

- CRC cards can be moved around freely. This enables you to explore collaborations—for instance, by picking up one object and moving it temporarily near to its collaborator while describing a message, and then back to its original place in the design. You can also explore various configurations and layouts of the cards on a table and see which ones best reflect your intuition about the relationships between the objects.

- CRC cards are fun and lightweight. If design is a creative process, then its impetus must not be smothered under heavyweight design tools with strict usage guidelines and thick manuals. With CRC cards, you can just start designing the minute you have an idea or a problem.

↰11.1

In some sense, CRC cards play a role similar to that of metaphors in software engineering: Because software objects are invisible, intangible, and therefore largely abstract entities, it is good to link them to the concrete reality, with which most of us have extensive experience.

11.3.3   Identifying Objects and Their Responsibilities

Finding objects is not a simple task in general. It is not sufficient to look at the user interface or to model mere data structures from the application domain. We have to come up with a whole collection of objects that together set up a software machinery to fulfill the users' expectations. This also means that the ultimate source of all responsibilities of the system's objects is the set of use cases and the specified reactions: If something needs doing, somebody must do it. But the reverse is also true: If somebody does something, then the effort should better be justified by some concrete reaction that the system must implement.

↰11.1
▭263

↰11.1

Experienced designers carry with them a comprehensive catalog of their previous designs and model their new objects based on successful precursors. They know which kinds of tasks objects are likely to perform well and which objects are likely to be useful.

We will therefore provide some common justifications for why particular objects are present in a system and which kinds of purpose they fulfill. Part I has given a similar overview from a technical perspective, and it may be

↰1.8

useful to revisit it briefly. Now, we will reexamine the question from the
perspective of responsibilities, rather than class structure.

The presentation here proceeds from conceptual simplicity to conceptual abstraction—from the objects that are obviously necessary and easy
to recognize to the objects that emerge from some previous analysis. We
deliberately refrain from giving an overall picture up front, as we did for   ↰11.1
the introductory example. Instead, we follow the reasoning steps as they
could take place in the design process. In many steps, we make explicit the
connections to the general structuring principles introduced earlier on. We
hope that this arrangement will help you to apply similar reasoning within
your own projects. A summary of the development is given in Section 11.3.4.

11.3.3.1   Modeling the Application Domain

Any successful design will finally lead to software that fulfills all given requirements. For instance, one can start with use cases to trace the system's   ↰11.1 ↰11.3.2
reaction through the object collaborations. Alternatively, one may start
from the central business logic and the core algorithmic challenges. In any
case, the first objects that spring to mind emerge from the analysis of the
application domain—they are *domain objects*.

Represent concepts from the application domain as objects.

In the example, when we think about "plotting a function graph" as shown
in Fig. 11.8, we will at some point talk about a "plot region" as the ranges
in the x- and y-coordinates that are displayed on the screen. Translating
this concept into an object yields a simple bean that keeps the minimal and   ↰1.3.3
maximal coordinates:

```
                              fungraph.PlotRegion
public class PlotRegion {
    private double x0;
    private double x1;
    private double y0;
    private double y1;
    ...   constructor, getters, and setters
}
```

Another example is the function that gets plotted. Ideally, we would like
to plot functions $f\colon \mathbb{R} \to \mathbb{R} \cup \{\perp\}$, functions from the reals to the reals where
some values are undefined (value $\perp$). Of course, we use `double` to represent
$\mathbb{R}$. But beyond that, what is "the best" representation for the function
itself? A syntax tree? Some kind of stack machine code? Furthermore, do   ↰2.3.4
we have to implement the formula representation ourselves or will we find
a full-grown, reusable library? To defer such decisions, we introduce a role
Plottable Function: We simply specify how the function will behave without
deciding right now on its concrete class. The method `funValue()` in the
following interface captures the function f, with an exception signaling $\perp$.

Adding a self-description method is always useful for displaying information to the user.

computation.PlottableFunction

```
public interface PlottableFunction {
    String getDescription();
    double funValue(double x) throws Undefined;
}
```

One question is whether an explicit getDescription() method is useful, given that every object in Java has a toString() method that can be overridden. According to its API specification, that method is supposed to return a "a concise but informative representation that is easy for a person to read." Certainly, that statement is rather vague and open to interpretation. The general advice is to include all information useful for the human reader, if this is possible without returning unduly long strings. Then the object can be printed using System.out.println(), String.format(), and so on, and it will also display nicely in debuggers. For simple value objects, such as numbers, it may even be possible to provide a parsing function to recreate an equivalent object from the string representation. We would argue that toString() should be geared toward tracing and debugging scenarios: The end user is not concerned with objects, so a "representation of an object" is not useful in this situation. Instead, user interfaces require specialized external representations, so it is better to keep the two forms of "readable representation" separate in the code.

Starting with the application domain often means starting with the model.

In the context of model-view separation, we have advocated starting the application development with the functional core—that is, with its model. By focusing on the application domain, you will likely start with the business logic and therefore the model.

The application domain is a dangerous source of inspiration.

The PlotRegion object defined earlier is "lazy": It does not do anything, but merely holds some data. Such objects often result from a superficial analysis of the application domain, where we tend to describe things and concepts statically, by capturing their relevant attributes. Many things we find in the real world are not active themselves, but are manipulated by others. Think of bank accounts in a finance application, of hotel rooms in a booking system, or of messages in an email client. They all have perfectly clear relevance for the application, yet they are passive. As a result, they do not fit in with the view of objects as small and active entities.

Think about the software mechanisms throughout.

However, we can redeem the use of domain objects by simply asking: If the objects do exist in the system, which part can they play in the mechanisms of the software machinery?

In the case of the `PlotRegion`, a simple responsibility would be to keep interested objects informed about changes. In Fig. 11.8, both the central function graph and the plot region selector at the bottom must synchronize on the current plot region. Model-view separation, or more specifically the MVC pattern, tells us that in such cases it is best not to assume one flow of information, but rather to use a general OBSERVER pattern. For now, the user can only select the region in the special widget, but perhaps a later extension will allow the user to zoom in and out of the function graph by mouse gestures on the main display. The implementation is, of course, straightforward:

↰9.2.1
↰9.2
↰2.1

```
                        fungraph.PlotRegion
public class PlotRegion {
    ...
    private ListenerList listeners = new ListenerList();
    ...
    public void setX0(double x0) {
        this.x0 = x0;
        fireChange();
    }
    ...   fire, addListener, removeListener according to pattern
}
```

As a detail, we decide to use the simpler *pull* variant of the pattern, because a change in the region will require a full repaint of the function graph anyway, since incremental updates would be too complex.

↰2.1.3
↰9.4.3

```
                     fungraph.PlotRegionListener
public interface PlotRegionListener extends EventListener {
    void plotRegionChanged(PlotRegion r);
}
```

Software is rarely ever a model of reality.

The example shows clearly that the software machinery is quite distinct from any mechanisms found in the real world. Indeed, the reasons for introducing OBSERVER are strictly intrinsic to the software world and derive from the established structuring principles of that world. It would therefore be naive to expect that a close enough inspection of the application domain would yield a useful software structure.

⊞263

The only exceptions to the rule are simulations: If the application-domain objects do have a behavior that needs to be recreated faithfully in software, chances are that one can obtain a one-to-one match.

Application objects are good choices for linking to use cases.

Even if pure application objects are rare, they do have their merits when they fit naturally into the software machinery. For one thing, they enhance

□□24
the traceability of the use cases and requirements to the actual software. Once one has understood the use cases, one can also understand the software. If customers are technically minded, for instance in subcontracting parts of larger systems, they might care to look at the code themselves.

↰11.2.3
Furthermore, application objects may accommodate changes gracefully. If an application object reflects and encapsulates responsibilities derived from the application domain, then minor changes in the requirements are likely to be confined to the application object.

11.3.3.2 Boundary Objects

↰1.8.7
↰1.8.1
Another easily recognized source of objects is the system's boundary, which contains objects that are interfacers in the terminology of role stereotypes. Boundary objects hold a number of attractions:

- They often link to concrete external entities such as the application's file format, some XML transfer data, and so on. These entities may be available for inspection beforehand, so they can guide us in designing the software to process them.

- They are motivating because their reaction is visible externally and we may even demonstrate them to future users.

↰11.1
- The design process can start from the use cases. Since we encounter the boundary objects first, we have a clear picture of their reactions.

↰4.6
↰1.5.2
- They come with several predefined responsibilities. For instance, when they accept data from the user or other systems, they have to shield the system from possible failures, inconsistencies, and attacks.

- Their interface is often determined by libraries and frameworks. For instance, when using a SAX parser for XML files, we have to provide a `ContentHandler` to process the result. When writing a graphical user interface, we use SWT's widgets. When writing a web application, we
□□201
may use the servlet API.

Once the boundary objects are identified, we can start assigning responsibilities to them.

> Apply model-view separation to boundary objects.

↰9.2.2
□□201
An essential guideline for designing boundary objects is to use model-view separation, even if the boundary is not a graphical user interface. In particular, the boundary objects should be as small as possible. They should not contain any business logic, but only invoke the business logic implemented in a model subsystem. The benefits of model-view separation then carry over to different kinds of interfaces. Think of web services. Over time, many concrete protocols have evolved. If you keep the business logic self-contained, it becomes simpler to create yet another access path through a different protocol.

Make compound widgets take on self-contained responsibilities.

In the present example, the only boundary is the user interface. Since this is a common case, we explore it a bit further. As a first point, it is useful to create compound widgets that take on self-contained responsibilities. In the example, the user has to enter the function to be plotted in the lower-left region of the screen (Fig. 11.8). We invent an object `Formula Field` for the purpose.

↜7.5

---
dataentry.FormulaField

```
public class FormulaField extends Composite {
    private Text entry;
       ...
}
```

Once that object is in place, it can take care of more responsibilities. The formula string entered by the user needs to be parsed before the application can do anything useful with it. And if something needs doing, somebody has to do it—so why not the `FormulaField`? This choice is, in fact, supported by a second argument. Parsing includes validation, since a formula with a syntax error cannot be handled by the plotter at all. The general principle is that such validations take place in the system boundary. By having the `FormulaField` parse immediately and report any errors back to the user, the remainder of the system is shielded from invalid inputs altogether and can deal with clean abstract syntax trees.

⊞2 ↜2.3.3
↜11.1

↜1.8.7 ↜1.5.2

↜2.3.3

The `FormulaField` therefore includes a widget for error reporting and a field for the parsed result. (We will examine the aspect of reusing the previous parser implementation later on.) Whenever the user presses "enter" in the text field, the attached listener calls the method `reparseFormula()`. If there is no parse error, the new formula is stored and reported to any interested listeners (lines 10–12). Otherwise, the error message is displayed and a `null` object indicating an invalid formula is reported (lines 14–16). For model-view separation, note how the widget's listener orchestrates the application of the relatively complex, model-level parser.

》12.4.3
↜7.1

↜1.8.9

---
dataentry.FormulaField

```
1 private Label error;
2 private Expr formula;
3 ...
4 public Expr getFormula() {
5     return formula;
6 }
7 private void reparseFormula() {
8     Parser<Expr> p = new Parser<Expr>(new SimpleNodeFactory());
9     try {
10         formula = p.parse(entry.getText());
11         error.setText("");
12         fireChange(formula);
13     } catch (ParseError exc) {
```

```
14          error.setText(exc.getMessage());
15          formula = null;
16          fireChange(null);
17      }
18 }
```

↰2.1.4

⇄? You may rightly ask whether it is really sensible to implement OBSERVER here. In the actual application, there is only a single listener, and that object could have been made a direct collaborator of the FormulaField. We have used the more general structure for three reasons. First, it enables us to explain the FormulaField in a self-contained fashion, without forward references. This simple story in itself is an indication that our object has a clear purpose. Second, the FormulaField yields an example of the rather elusive concepts of loose coupling and reusability. Third, during the actual development of the example code, we wished to finish the "obvious" part beforehand, so that we actually did not know the later collaborator. Using OBSERVER was one way of postponing this decision.

↰11.2.1

↠12.1 ↠12.4

↠12.2

Introduce compound widgets for elements that are likely to change.

Another example of an obvious compound widget is the task of selecting the plot region: It has to be done somewhere, but there is as yet no object to do it. The naive solution is to just place a few sliders into the main window, according to the screenshot in Fig. 11.8, and somehow wire them up with the plot region.

The designed solution is to make a new object responsible for enabling the user to manipulate the plot region. The RegionSelector offers four sliders, two for the position of the graph and two for the scaling. The region is then updated whenever the sliders change. The nice thing is that now all the code concerned with the current region is confined in a single object, rather than being spread throughout the main window.

```
                    dataentry.RegionSelector
public class RegionSelector extends Composite {
    private Scale xPos, yPos, xScale, yScale;
    private PlotRegion region;
    ...
}
```

A second argument for introducing the extra object is that the selection mechanism is likely to change, because the current one has admittedly a rather poor usability. By making one object, and only one object, responsible for the user interface of the selection, we can substitute the interface once we get a better idea of what users really like to see here.

↰11.2.3

Merely pushing the four sliders into a surrounding widget is insufficient, however. The crucial point that insulates the remainder of the system from possible changes here is the lean and clear API that does not depend on the widget's internal details: The PlotRegion object was introduced and

↰11.3.3.1

defined long before we even thought about the necessity of manipulating the region!

💡 The idea of simply setting the `PlotRegion` to communicate the changes made by the user is a typical instance of a mechanism built into the software machinery. The overall goal is, of course, that the graph is repainted if the user changes the region. This is accomplished indirectly by making the `FunGraph` widget, to be described later, observe the `PlotRegion` object. The mechanism is, in fact, not very innovative, but is modeled after that of the MODEL-VIEW-CONTROLLER pattern.

↰11.1

↠11.3.3.3

↰9.2.1

11.3.3.3 Objects by Technical Necessity

Another set of objects that enter the design immediately are thrust upon you by the technical API of the frameworks and libraries that you are using. For instance, all elements of the user interface must be widgets, derived from the base class specified by the framework; when working with threads, you have to provide a `Runnable` that gets executed concurrently. In all such cases, the object must exist for technical reasons, but design is still necessary to decide which responsibilities the object will take on beyond the minimal API specified by the framework.

↰8

In the running example, the plotter must use custom painting to actually display the graph of the function. It registers a `PaintListener` on itself, which calls `paintComponent()`.

↰7.8

↰2.1.3

```
                          fungraph.FunGraph
public class FunGraph extends Canvas {
    ...
    protected void paintComponent(PaintEvent e) {
        ...
    }
    ...
}
```

When frameworks enforce specific objects, think about suitable responsibilities.

However, the implementation of `paintComponent()` depends on design decisions: Does the `FunGraph` itself draw the axis? Does it encapsulate the potential complexity of tracing out the graph in a separate object? The answers are seen in the code: The painting of the axis is delegated, but the actual graph is drawn directly.

↠11.3.3.7 ↰1.8.6

↠11.3.3.7

```
                          fungraph.FunGraph
protected void paintComponent(PaintEvent e) {
    ...
    if (axisPainter != null)
        axisPainter.paintAxis(this, g, r, region);
    ...
```

```
        paintFunction(g, r);
        ...
}
```

←11.3.3.1

»11.3.3.4

Painting the graph then involves tracing out functions $\mathbb{R} \to \mathbb{R} \cup \{\bot\}$, given by the interface `PlottableFunction` introduced earlier. We use a naive approach of walking from pixel to pixel on the x-axis, evaluating the function at each point, and connecting the points we find by (vertical) lines. The object `Scaler`, to be discussed in a minute, is a helper to convert between screen coordinates and real coordinates.

fungraph.FunGraph

```
private PlottableFunction fun;
    ...
private void paintFunction(GC g, Rectangle r) {
    Scaler scaler = new Scaler(region, r);
    int prevY;
        ...
    for (int x = r.x; x != r.x + r.width; x++) {
            ...
        double xp = scaler.toPlotX(x);
        double yp = fun.funValue(xp);
        int y = scaler.toScreenY(yp);
            ...
        g.drawLine(x - 1, prevY, x, y);
        prevY = y;
            ...
    }
}
```

←3.2.2

In this context, `PlottableFunction` is a client-specific interface. Anything that can evaluate and describe itself can be plotted by `FunGraph`.

11.3.3.4   Delegating Subtasks

So far, we have dealt with objects that were indicated by external circumstances: concepts from the application domain, parts of the user interface, and the API of employed frameworks. Now, we turn to the first objects that emerge from an analysis of the concrete problem at hand: helpers. Such objects are usually service providers; in the best case they are reusable.

←1.8.2 ←1.8.5

If some task admits a self-contained description, introduce an object.

Here, we see a prototypical application of the general principle: If something needs doing, somebody has to do it. Moreover, if you are able to describe a task in a single sentence, then this is a strong indication that a separate object, with a single responsibility, should take on the task.

←11.2.1

In the running example, we have to convert between pixel-based coordinates on the screen and `double` coordinates for evaluating the given function. Of course, the `FunGraph` could do this itself. But then, the task is a snug little piece of functionality that might as well be given to a separate object. Here is our code (leaving out the analogous case for the y-coordinates):

---

funcgraph.Scaler

```
class Scaler {
    private PlotRegion plot;
    private Rectangle screen;
    public Scaler(PlotRegion plot, Rectangle screen) {
        this.plot = plot;
        this.screen = screen;
    }
    public double toPlotX(int x) {
        return (double) (x - screen.x) / screen.width *
            plot.getXRegion() + plot.getX0();
    }
        ...
    public int toScreenX(double x) {
        return (int) ((x - plot.getX0()) / plot.getXRegion() *
                    screen.width + screen.x);
    }
        ...
}
```

Service providers are often passive.

The `Scaler` uses a `PlotRegion` object that is to be mapped to a rectangular screen area. Since a `PlotRegion` may change, the question is whether the `Scaler` should observe the changes. If this were so, then the `Scaler` itself would have to become observable to send messages when the result of scaling has changed. This would, in fact, make the `Scaler` an active, and therefore "better," object.

Although this idea is viable, it does not fit the `Scaler`'s purpose: The `Scaler` performs a computation, and that computation is stateless. The OBSERVER pattern, in contrast, is all about notifying interested objects about state changes.

Service providers, which act on behalf of a caller, are often passive. The collaboration can then be defined very precisely based on classical contracts. If the service providers do contain state (apart from caches, which are an internal technical detail not visible to clients), they would offer the OBSERVER pattern, which still keeps them independent of any concrete collaborators.

Passive service providers are found in great numbers in the Java library. `InputStreamReaders`, `Connections` to relational databases, `SimpleDate Formats`, a `Pattern` representing a regular expression—they all wait for their callers to ask them to perform their tasks.

↰11.3.3.1

↰2.1

↰4.1 ↰1.3.6

↠12.1

Active collaborators fit well with responsibility-driven design.

»11.3.3.6
↰11.3.3.2

It would be we wrong, however, to assume that most objects taking on
a well-defined subtask are passive. For instance, the `ApplicationWindow`
tying together the overall interface from Fig. 11.8 delegates the entry of
the formula to a `FormulaField` and the plot region to a `RegionSelector`,
as we have seen. These objects are very much active, as they react to user
↰1.8.7
input and pass on any information received in this way, after validating and
preprocessing it to fit the application's internal requirements.

Factoring out tasks opens the potential for reuse.

»12.4

In all cases, the fact that a task is taken on by a self-contained object opens
up the potential for reusing the implemented solution to the task. Had
we integrated the `FormulaField` and `PlotRegion` into the `Application`
`Window` and `FunGraph` objects, respectively, they could not have been ex-
↰1.8.5
»12.4.1 »12.4.3
tracted. From a technical perspective, having a functionality available in a
self-contained object is a prerequisite for reusing it. However, this alone is
insufficient—objects are usually not reusable per se.

Factoring out tasks provides for potential changeability.

↰11.2.3

Another benefit from moving subtasks into separate objects is that the current implementation can potentially be changed. First, if the new collabo-
↰1.1 »11.5.1
rators take encapsulation seriously, then their internals can be exchanged
at any time. For instance, the usability of the `RegionSelector` can be enhanced in any desirable way as long as the outcome of the selection is stored
in the target `PlotRegion`.

One step beyond, if it turns out that entirely different implementations
should coexist simultaneously so that the user can choose among them at
»11.3.3.7 ↰1.3.4 ↰3.2.1
runtime, one can introduce a new interface and let different objects implement that interface. As with potential reuse, the existence of the helper
»12.3
object is insufficient: Other objects must be able to reimplement the interface in a sensible manner, and the interface must be designed to be
reimplemented.

11.3.3.5   Linking to Libraries

A lot of things that need doing in the software world will actually have
been done already: by a teammate, by a different team in your company, by
some contributor from the open-source community, or by a special-purpose
company selling special-purpose components. Such ready-made solutions
are then offered as libraries or frameworks. In the following presentation, we
↰7.3.2
will talk about libraries, but note that the arguments apply to frameworks
as well.

Use libraries to boost your progress.

Responsibility-driven design is based on the principle that anything that needs doing must be done by some object. But this does not necessarily mean that one has to write the object from scratch. In many cases, it is better to look for a library containing a suitable object: You get the functionality almost for free. All you have to do is read a bit of documentation, look at a few tutorials, and there you are. Furthermore, a widely used library is also well tested. Any implementation you come up with will usually be more buggy in the beginning. And finally, the design of the library itself captures knowledge about its application domain. If it is a successful library, then its developer will have put a lot of thought into a suitable and effective API, efficient data structures, problematic corner cases, and so on. Before you could develop anything approaching its utility, you would have to learn as much about the application domain. We hope that these arguments will help you overcome the not-invented-here syndrome.

Place the library objects into your design explicitly.

But how does using a library relate to design? The library is, after all, finished. However, using a library should be an explicit decision of the development team. The team recognizes that a library offers an object that does something obviously useful. They would then write a CRC card for a library object and place it in into their current design. This step fixes one place in the design, and the remainder of the objects must be grouped ⬑11.3.3.3 around this fixed point. In fact, since applications usually use several different libraries, the situation can become more as illustrated in Fig. 11.9: The library objects are beacons that are linked by application objects to create a new overall functionality.

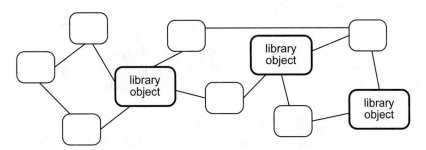

Figure 11.9 Library Objects in the Design

In the example, we recognize that we need to parse the formula that the user has entered. This responsibility was given to `FormulaField` widget ⬑11.3.3.2 earlier on. However, this does not mean that the developer of the widget

↰2.3.3
has to write a parser. In fact, we already have a suitable parser from earlier examples. The parser also comes with syntax trees `Expr` for simple arithmetic expressions, so that the `FormulaField` can deliver `Expr` objects.

↰11.3.3.3 ↰11.3.3.1
↰2.4.1
Now, we come to the point of linking the library into the existing design. Our `FunGraph` takes `PlottableFunctions` as input, so we will have to create an ADAPTER to make the objects collaborate. It takes an `Expr` and implements the interface's `funValue()` method by evaluating the expression.

```
                    computation.ExprAdapter
public class ExprAdapter implements PlottableFunction {
    private final Expr exp;
    public ExprAdapter(Expr exp) {
        this.exp = exp;
    }
    public double funValue(double x) throws Undefined {
        Valuation v = new Valuation();
        v.set(new VarName("x"), x);
        try {
            double res = exp.eval(v);
            if (Double.isInfinite(res) || Double.isNaN(res))
                throw new Undefined("not a number");
            return res;
        } catch (EvalError exc) {
            throw new Undefined(exc.getMessage());
        }
    }
    ...
}
```

Avoid letting the library dominate your design.

▭172(Ch.8)

▭215

When using a library, there is always the danger that the fixed objects it introduces into the design will dominate the subsequent design decisions. For instance, suppose you write an editor for manipulating XML documents graphically. You use a particular DOM implementation for I/O. If you are not very careful, you will end up with a design in which many application objects access the raw DOM objects representing the single XML nodes, simply because they are there and come in handy. This has several disadvantages:

- You cannot replace the library if it turns out to be buggy, misses important features, or is simply discontinued.

- The DOM objects cannot take on new responsibilities from your application, so that they cannot actively contribute to solving use cases. This restricts your opportunities of useful design.

▭92("Bad Smells")

- Beyond that, your own objects can also become ill designed. They work on someone else's data in a procedural fashion because they cannot delegate the processing to the library objects.

In the example, we have done the right thing, but for quite a different reason: We have introduced a `PlottableFunction` because we were not sure what a suitable implementation would be. Now it turns out that this extra work pays off: If we find a better parser or library of arithmetic expressions, we simply have to adapt the `FormulaField` as the producer, the `Expr Adapter` as the consumer, and the code that hands the `Expr` objects between them. But the central and most complex object, `FunGraph`, remains untouched.

↰11.3.3.1

↠11.3.3.6

⇄? The question arises of whether the `FormulaField` should provide `PlottableFunctions` directly, by wrapping them into `ExprAdapters` immediately after parsing. Then all changes would be confined to `FormulaField` and its helper `ExprAdapter`. Doing so would, however, tie the `FormulaField` to the context of plotting functions. It would not be usable if we wished to display, for instance, a tree view of the formula structure. In the end, there is a decision to be made; the important point is to recognize the decision and make it consciously.

↰11.1

The problematic dependency on libraries illustrated here will later lead to the more general Dependency Inversion Principle (DIP).

↠11.5.6 ▢170

Avoid cluttering your design with adapters.

Of course, there is a downside to the strategy of keeping your software independent from specific libraries: The ADAPTERs you introduce can easily clutter your design. You should always be aware that adapters do not contribute any functionality of their own, but merely stitch together different parts of the software. Just as any class must justify its existence by some concrete contribution, so must adapters.

↰2.4.1

In many cases, the library you choose will be essentially the only one or the best one for a given application domain. It is then not justified to introduce the extra complexity of adapters—you will not switch the library anyway. Just having an adapter because it leads to "decoupling" is usually a bad idea; it is just another example of "speculative generality."

↠12.2 ▢92

If you are using the best or the standard library, the opposite strategy will be more useful: Since the library's objects reflect a thorough design of its application domain, they can act as guides or anchors in your own design. By placing them into the network of objects early on (Fig. 11.9 on page 607), you are likely to fix important decisions in the right way.

Avoid dragging unnecessarily many libraries into a project.

A second snag in using libraries occurs in larger projects. Developers usually have their favorite libraries for particular application areas. For processing XML, for instance, there are many good libraries available. Also, there are always "cute" solutions to common problems that someone or other has used before. For example, there are compile-time Java extensions for generating getters and setters automatically for fields with special annotations.

With the number of available libraries constantly growing, there is the danger of stalling progress by relying on too many libraries. In such a case, all developers on the team will have to learn all APIs. You will have to keep track of more dependencies and check out updates. And if the developer who introduced his or her pet library into the project leaves, serious trouble can arise.

It is better to aim for consistency and minimality: Using the same solution for the same problem throughout a project's code base is always a good idea. Apply this principle to libraries as well. Also, for the sake of smoothing the learning curve, it may be better to spell out simple things like generating getters and setters instead of using yet another tool. If another library or tool seems necessary, be conservative, prefer standard solutions to "super-cool" ones, and find a consensus within the team.

11.3.3.6 Tying Things Up

So far, we have introduced objects that distribute among them the work arising in the given use cases. Once the distribution is complete, it is usually necessary to tie together the different parts into a complete whole. Such objects often fall under the role stereotype of structurers.

↰1.8.1

Create objects that are responsible only for organizing the work of others.

↰9.2.1

In the example, the `ApplicationWindow` creates the overall appearance of Fig. 11.8 by creating and linking the introduced compound widgets. Note how the `RegionSelector` and `FunGraph` share the `PlotRegion` to propagate the user's selection, following the MODEL-VIEW-CONTROLLER pattern.

```
                    main.ApplicationWindow
public class ApplicationWindow {
    ...
    protected void createContents() {
        shell = new Shell();
        ...
        PlotRegion r = new PlotRegion(-10, 10, -10, 10);
        ...
        FunGraph funGraph = new FunGraph(shell);
        funGraph.setPlotRegion(r);
        ...
        RegionSelector sel = new RegionSelector(entry);
        sel.setPlotRegion(r);
        ...
    }
}
```

↰2.2.1

The object `ApplicationWindow` is the owner of the different parts and links them as it sees fit. Quite a different kind of "tying together" of parts is seen when an object sits in the middle of several objects and links them

by actively forwarding messages or triggering behavior as a reaction to
messages received. Such an object is a MEDIATOR: It encapsulates the logic
for connecting other objects.

↰7.7

In the example, we introduce a `Mediator` object for demonstration purposes. It receives notifications when a new expression has been entered
and when a new type of axis has been chosen, in the lower-right corner of
Fig. 11.8. (We treat the handling of different axis types later in this section.) In both cases, the mediator passes the new choices to the `FunGraph`,
which will update the display.

≫11.3.3.7

```
main.ApplicationWindow.createContents
Mediator mediator = new Mediator();
...
mediator.setFunGraph(funGraph);
...
form.addExprListener(mediator);
...
ComboViewer chooseAxis = new ComboViewer(entry);
...
chooseAxis.addSelectionChangedListener(mediator);
...
```

The mediator is not typical, in that its reactions are somewhat simplistic and information flows in only one direction, toward the `FunGraph`.
Nevertheless, someone needs to organize this flow, so we have introduced
the new `Mediator` object. Also, the forwarding is not completely trivial,
but requires some adaptations: A newly selected axis must be extracted
from the selection event, and the raw `Expr` parsed by the `FormulaField`
must be wrapped to obtain a `PlottableFunction`.

📖100

≫11.3.3.7

↰2.4

```
main.Mediator
public class Mediator implements ExprListener,
                        ISelectionChangedListener {
    private FunGraph funGraph;
    public void setFunGraph(FunGraph funGraph) {
        this.funGraph = funGraph;
    }
    public void selectionChanged(SelectionChangedEvent e) {
        AxisPainter c = (AxisPainter)
            ((IStructuredSelection) e.getSelection())
                .getFirstElement();
        funGraph.setAxisPainter(c);
    }
    public void exprChanged(final ExprEvent e) {
        final Expr exp = e.getExpr();
        if (exp != null)
            funGraph.setFunction(new ExprAdapter(exp));
        else
            funGraph.setFunction(null);
    }
}
```

»12.1

↰1.3.4

↰1.8.4
↰11.3.3.1

⇄? You will have noticed a slight asymmetry in the design: The FunGraph observes the PlotRegion directly, but depends on the Mediator to supply the function and type of axis. Why does it not observe the FormulaField and the ComboViewer? Or conversely, why does the Mediator not also forward the PlotRegion to the FunGraph? The argument against the first modification is that the FunGraph becomes more closely coupled to its environment and is less reusable: While it does need a PlottableFunction and an AxisPainter, it does not care where they come from. It accepts them passively, as parameters to its behavior. The second modification, in contrast, is viable. It would treat the PlotRegion as yet another parameter to the FunGraph. However, there is a different mismatch: The function and the axis are designed as immutable value objects, while the PlotRegion is an active information holder. Passing the region around as a mere value then introduces an inconsistency there.

11.3.3.7   Roles and Changeability

↰3.2.1

↰11.1 ▭▭211

The objects treated previously have had concrete tasks that they fulfilled themselves or delegated to others. We will now venture a bit further afield and try our hand at (behavioral) abstraction: What if suddenly not one, but several possible objects can fill a place in the overall network and take on the associated responsibilities? In other words, what if we start designing roles, rather than single objects (see Fig. 11.3 on page 576)? Then we start collecting sets of related responsibilities without deciding immediately which object can fulfill them.

> Use roles to keep the concrete implementation of a task exchangeable.

↰7.8

»12.3.2

The function plotter contains an instance of such a challenge. The user can switch between different kinds of axes at runtime (see the lower-right corner of Fig. 11.8). Each axis looks slightly different on the screen, but the essential responsibility is clear: to overlay the display area with a coordinate system. Also, we make an axis responsible for describing itself. At the language level, we render a role as an interface, shown in the next code snippet. The getDescription() method is clear, but what are suitable parameters to paintAxis()? For technical reasons, we need the graphics context GC, and we also pass the screen area and the plot region, because the axis painter will need them for scaling its drawings. The first parameter fun Graph is introduced because in callbacks it is usually sensible to pass the context in which they take place.

```
fungraph.AxisPainter

public interface AxisPainter {
    String getDescription();
    void paintAxis(FunGraph funGraph, GC g, Rectangle screenRect,
                   PlotRegion region);
}
```

We render roles as interfaces because then an object implementing the interface
implicitly declares that it will fulfill the associated responsibilities faithfully. The very
same promise is expressed by the Liskov Substitution Principle as well as by contract
inheritance: When an object overrides a method, it must honor the contract associated
with that method; that is, it inherits the contract with the method.

↰3.1.1 ↰6.4

The STRATEGY pattern anticipates the design-level concept of roles at the language
level: Because the system contains alternative implementations of some task, we
abstract the commonality into a common superclass. In designing roles, we start from
the top and first ask what needs doing, before we start wondering who will eventually
do it.

↰1.3.4

Use roles to defer decisions about the concrete implementation.

Roles enable concrete objects to be exchanged later on. This is useful not
only if there are different implementations, but also if the only implementation should be exchanged later on. In the example, we were unsure how best
to represent a formula. We therefore introduced an interface that captures
just the responsibility that the object can somehow evaluate itself.

↰11.3.3.3

```
                    computation.PlottableFunction
public interface PlottableFunction {
    String getDescription();
    double funValue(double x) throws Undefined;
}
```

Roles very often specify only aspects of the object's overall behavior.

In both cases shown previously, the concrete implementation objects have
the only purpose of fulfilling the responsibilities associated with a role. In
the majority of cases, however, the concrete object has far more comprehensive responsibilities—those from the role capture only one aspect of the
overall behavior. An observer, for instance, is capable of receiving state
change notifications, but that is not its purpose; in fact, it needs the notifications only as auxiliary information precisely for fulfilling a different
purpose.

↰2.1

In fact, it can be useful to start designing roles and then to create objects
filling these roles with concrete behavior in a second step. This approach
will yield fewer dependencies between the objects so that the overall design
remains more flexible and will accommodate changes more easily. We have
seen this idea already in the context of client-specific interfaces. A different
perspective is offered by the Dependency Inversion Principle (DIP).

▯▯211

↰3.2.2
↠11.5.6

11.3.3.8   Neighborhoods: Subnetworks of Objects

📖263

One further element of responsibility-driven design remains to be discussed: *neighborhoods*. Very often, single objects are too small as units of design, because many objects have to collaborate to achieve a task of any size. When trying to flesh these objects out from the start, we can easily lose track of the application's overall structure.

Neighborhoods are groups of objects working on a common task.

Neighborhoods are groups of objects that collaborate closely to achieve a common overall goal. Fig. 11.10 gives the underlying structure. In the central, dashed area, a close-knit network of objects works on a task, while the outer objects consume their service through relatively few well-defined channels.

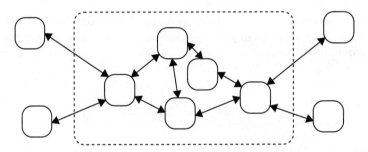

Figure 11.10 Neighborhoods

Objects collaborate more closely within a neighborhood.

The function plotter example is almost too small to demonstrate neighborhoods properly. However, the group of objects implementing the central plot area in Fig. 11.8 (on page 594) are certainly connected more closely among themselves than with the rest of the system: The FunGraph uses different AxisPainters for overlaying a grid, a Scaler for mapping coordinates from the screen, and a PlotRegion to maintain the coordinates to be displayed.

↰11.3.3.3
↰11.3.3.7

The outside world has to know next to nothing about these internal collaborations. The Scaler is package-visible and hidden altogether; the Plot Region and the AxisPainter are merely plugged into the FunGraph object. Furthermore, we can hide the exact nature of AxisPainters by making their concrete classes package-visible and exposing just the interface. Then, the FunGraph can be asked to provide all possible choices, so that the main ApplicationWindow merely has to plug them into the ComboBox Viewer shown in Fig. 11.8.

```
main.ApplicationWindow.createContents
```
```
ComboViewer chooseAxis = new ComboViewer(entry);
AxisPainter[] axisPainters = funGraph.getAvailableAxisPainters();
chooseAxis.setInput(axisPainters);
```

Neighborhoods have a common overall purpose.

Neighborhoods lift the idea of responsibilities to groups of objects. Just as
the Single Responsibility Principle demands that each individual object has   ↰11.2
a clearly defined purpose, so the objects in a neighborhood taken together
have a common, more comprehensive responsibility. In the end, the idea of
what a "single" responsibility really is depends on the degree of abstraction   ↰11.2.2
chosen in expressing the responsibility.

Neighborhoods may simplify outside access through designated objects.

Neighborhoods also shield the outside world from the internal complexities
of the contained subnetwork of objects. If the objects have few collaborations with the outside world, then the outside world has to understand only
these few collaborations and can leave the remaining ones alone.

   One step further, a neighborhood may choose to designate special objects through which all communication with the outside world is channeled.
The FACADE pattern expresses just this idea: to shield clients of a subsys-   ↰1.7.2
tem from its internal complexities.

Use modularization to enforce boundaries of neighborhoods.

Encapsulation at the level of objects means hiding the object's internal
data structures. Encapsulation at the level of neighborhoods means hiding
the internal object structure. The benefits of encapsulation then transfer to
the larger units of design: You can change the internals if you see fit, and
it becomes simpler to understand and maintain the overall system.

   Encapsulation for object structures is available at many levels. Nested   ↰1.8.8
classes are usually `private` anyway, and package-visible (default-visible)   ↰1.7
classes and methods can be accessed only from within the same package.
OSGi bundles in Eclipse help you further by exposing packages to other   ↠A.1
bundles selectively. Also, you may consider publishing only interfaces in   ↰3.2.7
these packages and keeping the implementation hidden away in `internal`
packages. The Eclipse platform uses this device throughout to keep the code
base maintainable.

11.3.4   Summing Up

The presentation of the function plotter's design has focused on the resulting code, because it is this code that needs to be developed and eventually

maintained. Now it is time to look back and to evaluate our design: Does it lead to an overall sensible structure?

Fig. 11.11 shows the principal objects in the design. The dashed objects are roles. The arrows with filled heads indicate access or usage. The arrows with open heads, as usual, denote subtyping. The dashed arrows mean that an access takes place, but only through an OBSERVER relationship or event notifications. Both dashed objects and dashed arrows therefore indicate a looser kind of relationship that does not entail an immediate dependency.

»12.1

Let us then check our design. The `FunGraph` implements the main functionality. It relies on several direct helpers: A `PlottableFunction` to obtain the values to be drawn and an `AxisPainter` to draw the co-ordinate grid according to the user's choice. Both are roles—that is, inter-faces at the code level—to keep the core functionality flexible. The `Plot Region`, in contrast, is an integral asset for drawing functions, so it is a con-crete class. However, the actual drawing is insulated from the challenges of coordinate transformations by accessing the `PlotRegion` through a `Scaler`. There are two choices of coordinate grids, both of which also access the `Plot Region` through a `Scaler`.

The remainder of the user interface components are grouped around the `FunGraph`. A `RegionSelector` contains the widgets to manipulate a `Plot Region`. Any changes are sent directly to `FunGraph` as notifications. This arrangement follows model-view separation, with the `PlotRegion` as the model. However, the `RegionSelector` is not a full view, because it does not listen to changes of the `PlotRegion`. This could, however, be accomplished easily if necessary.

The `ComboBox` for choosing the coordinate grid and the `FormulaField` are handled differently. Both report their values to a `Mediator`, which de-

◄1.3.4

cides what to do with them. In this case, it parameterizes the `FunGraph`.

The parsing of formulas, because of its complexity and a preexisting library, is isolated in one "corner" of the design: Only the `FormulaField` knows about parsing, and only the `Mediator` knows that behind a `PlottableFunction`, there is actually just a simple `Expr` object.

This summary is actually more than a convenience for the reader: When-ever you finish a design, it is useful to try to tell the overall story, to check whether the reasoning makes sense when told in a few words. If you are able to accomplish this, then the design is simple enough and understandable enough to be actually implemented.

11.4　Responsibilities and Hierarchy

Hierarchy and abstraction are at the heart of object-oriented programming. We have already examined at the language level the fundamental princi-ples governing the use of inheritance and interfaces. The Liskov Substitution Principle requires that an object of a subtype—a derived class or a class

◄3.1.1

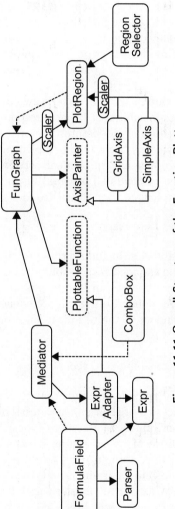

Figure 11.11 Overall Structure of the Function Plotter

↰3.2.1

implementing a given interface—can be used in all places where the super-type is expected. Behavioral abstraction complements this with the idea that superclasses and interfaces usually specify general reactions whose de-

↰6.4

tails can be implemented in different ways. Finally, the idea of contract inheritance makes these concepts precise by relating them to the pre- and post-conditions of individual methods.

It now remains to ask how hierarchy relates to responsibilities. The connection, of course, rests on the fact that responsibilities always specify aspects of an object's behavior and that hierarchy is one way of structuring this behavior. In expressing the earlier principles in terms of responsibilities, we will find that the new terminology also offers a new perspective on the previous ideas.

Before we start, we emphasize that inheritance and subtyping are not central to the idea of responsibilities. In fact, responsibility-driven design asks only what objects do and deliberately ignores how they have been

↰1.4.1

created: It is irrelevant whether a method's implementation is inherited or whether we need to introduce and implement certain interfaces to satisfy the compiler that a given method call is legal. Responsibilities help us free our minds from these implementation details to focus on the design itself.

All classes and interfaces have responsibilities.

All classes have responsibilities, including those used as base classes. Like-wise, all interfaces can be assigned responsibilities, because in the end they must be implemented by objects—an interface is merely a restricted way of accessing an object. As pointed out earlier, responsibilities relate to the concrete objects, independent of the technical questions of inheritance and subtyping.

Classes take on the responsibilities of their super-types.

The Liskov Substitution Principle demands that clients can work with sub-classes where they expect one of their super-types. This means that a class must take on all responsibilities of its super-types: When a client looks through the responsibilities of a super-type, it expects that the concrete

↰6.4

object will fulfill them. This is analogous to contract inheritance, so that we could say that responsibilities are inherited, too.

For instance, every SWT `Control` must notify interested listeners about

↰7.8

mouse movements, so a `Canvas`, which is used for custom widgets, must report mouse movements as well.

Roles capture behavioral abstraction.

↰11.1

We said earlier that roles are usually rendered as interfaces at the im-plementation level. Interfaces serve many different purposes, among them

↰3.2.1 ↰1.4.1

behavioral abstraction: The precise reaction of an object to an incoming message is left unspecified, so that each concrete class is free to react suitably.

Roles, as collections of responsibilities, can also exhibit this kind of abstraction. All that is necessary is to phrase the responsibilities in general, abstract terms. For instance, an `AxisPainter` in the function plotter example is responsible for painting a grid over the function graph, but that job description is so abstract that it allows for different concrete interpretations.

↰11.3.3.7

Even without deliberate generalization in the phrasing of responsibilities, roles should always be understood as behavioral abstraction. The intention of roles is that many different objects will fill them, so that it is usually not safe to presume any concrete reaction.

↰11.1

Inheritance allows for partially implemented responsibilities.

We saw in Part I that it is quite common for a class to leave some of its methods unimplemented. A class might leave the definition to the subclasses altogether, or it might leave out specific steps in a mechanism through TEMPLATE METHOD. In both cases, the superclass fixes responsibilities, but delegates their concrete implementation to the subclass.

↰1.4.10

↰1.4.9

Inheritance can structure responsibilities.

Of course, a subclass can also take on new responsibilities quite apart from those of its superclass: An SWT `Text` input field enables the user to enter text; a `Button` presents a clickable surface. Both show suitable indications of mouse movements and keyboard focus. None of this, however, belongs to the responsibilities of their common superclass `Control`.

With each level of the inheritance hierarchy, new responsibilities can be stacked upon the old ones from the superclass. Inheritance therefore helps to structure a class's responsibilities further, with the intention of sharing the responsibilities that are introduced higher up among many different classes.

Protected methods introduce hidden responsibilities.

Protected methods enable a special form of collaboration between a subclass and its superclass. On the one hand, the superclass can offer services that only its subclasses can use. On the other hand, through method overriding and abstract methods, the superclass can request services from its subclasses. Taken together, these mechanisms enable classes along the inheritance chain to have "private" responsibilities that are not visible to other objects.

↰3.1.2

↰1.4.8.2

↰1.4.11

↰1.4.9

Inheritance can be used for splitting responsibilities.

Taken together, the three previous points show the power of inheritance: It enables us to split the implementation of responsibilities of a single object

↰11.2

into separate pieces of source code. At each step, the responsibilities are self-contained and, ideally, small. As a result, the overall code base becomes more understandable, maintainable, and possibly reusable.

↰11.1

A larger example can be seen in the context of the class `NewWizard`. It uses a `NewWizardRegistry` to gather supported file types from the different plugins. That class is built in two inheritance steps, because different kinds of wizards are registered within the system. The `AbstractWizard Registry` simply keeps registered wizards in a list. Its subclass `Abstract ExtensionWizardRegistry` adds the responsibility of gathering these, but

»12.3.3

delegates the choice of the the type of wizard and their source extension point to its subclasses. The `NewWizardRegistry` then takes on this remaining responsibility.

> Be precise despite the abstraction.

Inheritance and hierarchy usually involve abstraction: The super-types specify responsibilities that comprise more cases, because they are implemented differently in the different subtypes. It is important not to confuse "abstract" with "vague" or "imprecise": If an abstract responsibility is imprecise, then it is unclear whether a subtype validates the Liskov Substitution Principle

↰6.4

and whether clients can rely on its behavior. The formulation of a responsibility must always be precise enough to allow precise reasoning about whether a subtype fulfills it properly.

11.5 Fundamental Goals and Strategies

It is really hard to say what makes a good designer and good designs. Of course, designs should be simple and easy to implement; they should follow established conventions and patterns; they should accommodate changes in requirements gracefully, simplify ports to different platforms, and so on. At a personal level, the designers should be able to communicate with different stakeholders; they should have a clear grasp of the strategic goals and overall architecture to make informed decisions; and so on. But these criteria are all rather abstract, and their application may depend in many cases on personal preferences and biases, as well as on one's own previous design experience.

▥92("Bad Smells")

Conversely, it is quite straightforward to say what makes a bad designer. Bad designers ignore the fundamental rules of their trade: They let objects access each other's data structures; they have no clear idea of what each object is supposed to do; their methods can be understood only by reading through the code; and they commit a multitude of other sins. In short, they create designs that result in completely unreadable, throwaway implementations.

This section gathers several fundamental requirements related to design. They have appeared as specific aspects and arguments in previous discussions, but now we switch perspective and put them at center stage. We also add more conceptual background, which would have been misplaced in the concrete previous settings.

11.5.1 Information Hiding and Encapsulation

The most fundamental principle of any software design—not just object-oriented design—is certainly information hiding. The size and complexity of modern software simply demands that we split up the implementation into chunks, or *modules*, which can be worked on independently by different team members or different teams. This is possible only if each team can focus on its own contribution and does not have to know the technical details of the other teams' modules. The information about what goes on in each module is hidden from the world at large. ▢▢205

> Information hiding goes beyond encapsulation.

Information hiding is not simply another name for encapsulation. Encapsulation is a language-level feature that controls access to part of a module's definition. For instance, the Java compiler will throw an error when you try to access an object's `private` fields from outside its own class. That is certainly very useful, in particular if some other team includes a tech guru who likes to tinker with other people's data structures. ▢▢216(§7.4,§7.6) ↰1.1

Information hiding means much more than just making an object's internals inaccessible. It means restricting the knowledge that other teams may have—or need to have—*about* your objects. So the information hidden is not the object's data, but your own team's information about why and how the object works.

🔎 Few software engineers, and indeed only a small part of the literature, will be so severe with their distinction between information hiding and encapsulation. Often the terms are used interchangeably, or encapsulation is used to encompass information hiding, because encapsulation, as we will see, is not useful on its own. So when someone says to you, "I have encapsulated this data structure," that statement usually implies "You're not supposed to know I used it at all" and "You can't hold me responsible if I trash the code tomorrow and do something entirely different." We make the distinction here mostly to highlight the extra effort a professional developer has to spend beyond making fields `private`. We will use "information hiding" when discussing design questions and "encapsulation" when discussing the implementation's object structures.

Suppose, for instance, that your team is responsible for your software's `AuthenticationService`, as shown next. The method `authenticate()` enables clients to check whether the given user can log on with the given password. Sometimes, other modules may need a complete list of users—for

instance, to display them to administrators. It is OK to have a method get
AllUsers() for this purpose:

```java
public class AuthenticationService {
    private List<User> users = new ArrayList();
    public boolean authenticate(String user, String password) {
        ...
    }
    public User[] getAllUsers() {
        return users.toArray(new User[users.size()]);
    }
    ...
}
```

↰1.3.3

↰1.7.1

Encapsulation is about technical security: The method getAllUsers()
copies the internal list to prevent other modules from smuggling in new
users. We can also make the setters in class User package-visible to prevent
other modules from changing user names and passwords.

Information hiding does more. It asks: What can the other modules learn
about the AuthenticationService? The method getAllUsers() tells
them that there is a global list of system users. Well, that was rather obvious
anyway. Or was it? As soon as you start linking to different LDAP or
ActiveDirectory servers, rather than finding users only in a local database,
you will not be able to assemble that list efficiently, so perhaps you have
already told too much, because you have barred yourself from one future
extension to the system.

Information hiding is also about the things you do not tell your colleagues. Suppose that for efficient lookup, you decide to keep the internal
list users sorted by the user names. Within your class, you can use binary search to find a user. Great. But it would really be unwise to meet
an other team over coffee and spill the beans: The next thing you know,
a different team might start using binary search on the result of getAll
Users()! Once again you have lost the chance of ever changing the "internal" order of users, because the information about this order is no longer
internal—it is no longer hidden information.

↰4.1

↰4.1

↰4.7
↰4.1

Information hiding also sheds new light on contracts and their usefulness in system
design. The assertions you state in pre- and post-conditions are all that other modules
will ever learn about your module's behavior. (Recall that the class invariant is a private
matter and is not disclosed.) If the post-condition of getAllUsers() in the example states
that the result is sorted by the user names, then this knowledge can be used by callers
for their reasoning. If it says nothing about the sortedness, the caller must not make any
assumptions in this direction (and your method does not have to prove sortedness).

Use encapsulation to express information hiding.

So information hiding is more than encapsulation, but the two are definitely related: Both are about keeping parts of your own implementation hidden, only at different levels of reasoning.

However, information hiding always comes first: You start by deciding what others may know about your implementation. This means that you have to formulate an information policy regarding your design and implementation decisions. Once you have established this policy, you must figure out how you can enforce it at a technical level through access restrictions. Not every detail can be enforced, such as the knowledge about the sortedness in the preceding example. However, modern programming languages are built with decades of experience in information hiding, so they offer pretty expressive mechanisms. It is worthwhile studying them in some detail. Here are some Java examples beyond the obvious `private` fields and methods: Package visibility keeps information between a set of related classes, `protected` keeps functionality confined to a class hierarchy, and interfaces can be used to hide away concrete classes and class hierarchies.

↰1.7.1
↰1.4.8.2
↰3.2.7 »12.2.1

Information hiding keeps the implementation changeable.

You recognize good information hiding in an object or a subsystem if you could change the implementation overnight without telling anyone and the system would continue to work as if nothing had happened.

↰11.3.3.8

The ability to throw away and recreate the implementation is essential to productivity, because it enables you to use the simplest thing that could possibly work until you find that it is not good enough after all. Without information hiding, you would have to think about and work hard on an optimal solution for every single object and every single task, because you would never be able to amend your choice later on.

📖28

In fact, this changeability is the main argument in Parnas's seminal paper on modules and information hiding. The information that must really be hidden is the design and implementation decisions that you make, because then you can revise these decisions later on, during software maintenance, without breaking the system.

📖205
»11.2.3 »12.1.1 »12.2

Assign responsibilities to match the goal of encapsulation.

The question is, of course, If encapsulation is about the implementation, why is it discussed so late in the book, rather than in Part I? The answer is simple: You have to prepare encapsulation by making a suitable assignment of responsibilities. If one object holds the data that another object works on, then there is little chance of encapsulating the choice of the data structure. If a class has so many responsibilities that it becomes large, then encapsulation is not useful, since it applies only between classes. These things are also known as "bad smells."

📖92

↰11.2

The Single Responsibility Principle counteracts many of these dangers. It ensures that classes remain small and have a well-defined purpose that can be expressed in one or two sentences. You can also easily recognize if two objects perform tasks that are too closely related or even duplicates.

↰1.8.1

If the Single Responsibility Principle guides you toward building small objects, then the next design question arises immediately: How can you come up with efficient collaboration steps that still keep internal objects really private? Perhaps you may even have to introduce a special information holder object that acts as a black box to the outside world.

Choose neutral data structures for argument and return types.

One step further, you may be in danger of leaking information about the internal data structures even if you are not leaking the data structures themselves. If your internal field holds an `ArrayList`, for instance, that fact should not show up in method signatures. Better to use a generic `List`, which also gives you the ability to wrap your internal list by `Collections.unmodifiableList()`. Or you might go for a copied array, created by `toArray()`, in the getter.

»12.2.1.1
📖172,44

Of course, the preference for neutral data types is not to say that you pass around only values of primitive types. That would be disastrous: It becomes hard to understand the contracts; the names of types cannot convey meaning; the compiler cannot check whether the right kind of data is passed; the data cannot take on responsibilities. Just don't choose overly concrete types that give away your implementation, that's all.

Make methods reflect conceptual operations.

Saying that you should not reveal the object's internals through its method signatures is a negative guideline. Here is a positive, and more constructive, one: If you are able to express an object's purpose concisely, then chances are you have taken the mental leap toward suppressing any details of possible implementations. Choosing the method signatures to hide these details then comes naturally: The methods are merely the technical way to gain access to an object's services.

↰11.2.2

We saw the same requirement earlier, in the approach of design-by-contract. There, we demanded that contracts be understandable from the object's specification, without considering its implementation. This was captured in the Precondition Availability Principle.

↰4.1

↰4.2.2

Take efficiency as a secondary aim.

The goals of information hiding and encapsulation often conflict with the goal of efficiency. Handing out references to the internal data structures is, of course, the access path that makes for the lowest runtime. When

thinking about encapsulation, we should therefore always be aware that ◀1.1
nowadays the most costly resource is development time, not execution time.
Furthermore, the really critical paths in terms of efficiency will show up only
under load, where they can be analyzed using a profiler. And even if you
do then find that an object with perfect encapsulation is on such a critical
path, you can often improve its performance by indexing and caching—   ◀1.3.6
that is, precisely those internal changes enabled by proper encapsulation.

> Encapsulation is the indispensable first step toward changeability.

The changes enabled by encapsulation are entirely local. In essence, you can
revise your decisions about how a single object will dispatch its responsibilities. Many more considerations, also about inter-object structures, apply   ▶12.1 ▶12.2
when you wish to keep the software flexible at a larger scale. Yet without achieving encapsulation properly first, these further measures cannot
be approached at all: In any case, there will be some object or interface
behind which the changeable part of the system remains hidden from the
clients. Gaining experience with achieving proper encapsulation in concrete
situations is a prerequisite for successful design in the large.

11.5.2   Separation of Concerns

The main point of design is to lend structure to the implementation. Without design, the implementation will look like one huge desert of code, where
interfaces between objects are defined sloppily and each line potentially interacts with every other line. *Separation of Concerns* is the principle that   📖78(Ch.27)
counteracts such disastrous outcomes. The goal is to break down the overall
problem into various aspects to keep the solution intellectually manageable.
Dijkstra, who first introduced the concept, has put this eloquently: 📖78(p.211)

> To my taste the main characteristic of intelligent thinking is
> that one is willing and able to study in depth an aspect of one's
> subject matter in isolation, for the sake of its own consistency,
> all the time knowing that one is occupying oneself with only
> one of the aspects. The other aspects have to wait their turn,
> because our heads are so small that we cannot deal with them
> simultaneously without getting confused. [...] I usually refer
> to [this] as "a separation of concerns" [...].

In our experience, unfortunately, many programmers have trained themselves to be able to keep a huge amount of detail in their heads at the same
time, and they pride themselves in being able to do so. Overcoming this
love for detail and retraining oneself to practice Separation of Concerns can
be challenging, but it is necessary to handle large and complex systems.

Implement distinct concerns in distinct parts of the software.

Any sizable piece of a software project will involve many different aspects. For instance, it will read and write data, perform computations on the data, access the network, and interact with the user. In many cases, it is useful to design the software such that each aspect, or concern, is handled by an entirely different subsystem.

↰9.1

One instance has been seen in model-view separation: The business logic and the user interface have so vastly different characteristics that it is best to keep them separate (see Fig. 9.1 on page 445). Likewise, it is useful to designate a "boundary" area where the software does all of its I/O and scrupulously checks all interactions with the outside world. Conceptually, this will keep the remainder free from checking the validity of data, so that the business logic can be implemented without distractions.

↰11.3.3.2 ↰1.8.7 ↰1.5.2

↰4.6

Separation of Concerns can suggest new subsystems.

Separation of Concerns acts as a repelling force between pieces of code. When you are implementing, or designing, one module with a clear purpose, and you find suddenly that you are thinking about an aspect that does not fit the purpose, it is time to push that aspect out into a separate module.

For instance, when your business logic needs to do logging for documenting its safety-critical decisions, you may find logging code splattered all over the nice, clean business logic code. It is much better to introduce a logging module that offers just the interface that the business logic needs to create the required documentation entries.

📖201

Another example may be access restrictions—for instance, in web applications. Security is so important that one cannot force authors of single pages to hand-code the security checks. It is better to implement a generic protection mechanism, possibly with declarative syntax for writing up constraints.

Separation of Concerns encourages the Single Responsibility Principle.

Separation of Concerns also works in the small, at the level of individual objects. Here, it complements the Single Responsibility Principle. Suppose an object is responsible for downloading a file from the web. Then it should probably not also be responsible for determining a viewer to display the file to the user. In this way, you will arrive at objects with a clear-cut purpose, just as recommended by the Single Responsibility Principle.

↰11.2

From a more general perspective, Separation of Concerns suggests to push apart those elements of functionality that are only vaguely connected. This step leaves together those elements that have a strong logical relationship. Separation of Concerns therefore leads to a higher cohesion of objects, modules, and subsystems.

↠12.1.3

Splitting concerns creates a need for communication.

Separation of Concerns is a useful and central principle, but it also comes with a few downsides. The first one is rather obvious: Because the different aspects of an overall goal are distributed between modules, these modules will have to communicate to achieve that goal.

If the necessary communication is complex, then nothing is gained. For example, the MODEL-VIEW-CONTROLLER pattern is often implemented in the DOCUMENT-VIEW variant, because the *View* and *Controller* share so   ◀9.2.8 many assumptions about the concrete screen display that it is often more sensible to merge them into a single object, leading to the DOCUMENT-VIEW variant.

Alternatively, the communication can happen through well-defined interfaces, which helps with encapsulating the details of the subsystems, so   ◀11.5.1 ◀11.2.3 that maintenance is simplified. The extra effort involved in enforcing Separation of Concerns may pay off later on.

Sometimes, the necessity of communication can lead to new and useful concepts. In compiler construction, for instance, one separates the concerns of parsing and   📖2 semantic analysis, such as type checking, in the front-end from the concern of code generation in the back-end. To do this, one has to introduce *intermediate languages* to pass information between the different phases. To make the compiler reusable, there is often one intermediate language that abstracts over the physical details of a specific CPU type, such as by assuming an unlimited number of registers. Optimizations are much easier in this intermediate language than they would be in the final machine code.

Watch out for duplicated or complicated functionality.

Another undesirable result of splitting a piece of larger functionality into separate concerns is that some functionality may have to be duplicated or newly introduced. This often happens because slightly different algorithms are required for similar data stored in different modules.

In the context of the MODEL-VIEW-CONTROLLER pattern, for example, large documents can be handled efficiently only by incremental screen   ◀9.4.3 updates. This means that the concern of "determining the changed model parts" has to be implemented twice: once at the level of the model itself and once to find the corresponding screen representation. For the second task, it might be necessary to keep a structure analogous to that of the model. An example can be found in the tree-structured edit parts of Eclipse's Graphical Editing Framework.   📖214

Watch out for cross-cutting concerns.

Some concerns do not lend themselves to being pushed out into a separate module. While these concerns do occur in many different places in the application, they are tied in with the local context so much that extracting them feels like doing violence to the code.

For instance, if an application accesses a relational database, it will have to create SQL statements in many places. The concern of "querying the database" is a cross-cutting issue. The obvious choice is to introduce a separate module that contains a method for each occurring SQL statement. However, this disrupts the original source code and does not help at all: A maintenance programmer can understand the code only by jumping to the new module.

> Be aware that concerns are a matter of perception.

📖267

Looking a bit more closely reveals the concern of producing *syntactically valid* SQL code for a specific query: Introducing a module that takes care of syntactic issues will simplify the remainder of the application. We might even rethink the entire idea of "accessing the database" by employing an

📖129 ↰5.4.9

object-relational mapping: The mapping layer can encapsulate the concern of database accesses altogether, while the application deals with only data access objects provided by the mapping layer.

In the end, the question of what a "concern" really is does not have an absolute answer. Designing also means identifying and phrasing subproblems, and identifying concerns to be treated separately is no different. Just as in the case of the Single Responsibility Principle, it is a good idea to

↰11.2.1

try to tell a self-contained story about a candidate concern. If you succeed, chances are you will also find a self-contained implementation in a separate module.

11.5.3   Compositionality

When developing object-oriented software, we frequently find that we are applying a principle from the area of mathematical proof: *compositionality*.

📖189

Compositionality in that context denotes the ability to finish subproofs about parts of a composite entity and then to derive in a single step, without the need for further insights, that a statement about the entity itself holds. The subproofs can simply be composed.

You are wondering what this might have to do with programming? Here is a first example: Java's type system. Type systems are defined such that

📖209

one can derive the type of an expression from the types of its subexpressions, without reexamining the subexpressions. For instance, knowing that hexRep is a method that takes a `long` and returns its hexadecimal representation as a `String` and that a+b yields a `long` value, we deduce that hexRep (a+b) must be a `String`.

We will now explore how the idea of compositionality links to object-oriented design in that it integrates previous strategies and goals into a common perspective.

Compositionality lets systems be created from atomic pieces.

Compositional reasoning always involves finding simple rules for combining partial results in a well-defined manner. Just think of the power of objects that can be combined so easily to achieve larger functionality! To create new software, you would simply take a few objects with clearly delineated behavior and "click them together" to achieve your goals. We will call objects that support such constructions *compositional*.

As a simple example, Java's I/O library features different `InputStreams` that can be combined to decode special file formats, including encrypted and compressed streams. Likewise, SWT user interfaces are created by combining atomic and compound widgets, and placing them on the screen using layout managers. These examples basically use object composition to achieve the purpose.

Here is a more advanced example. In the context of graphical editors, one can often modify short texts by *direct editing*: One clicks on a text, a small pop-up appears on top, and one types the new text. Eclipse's Graphical Editing Framework provides a class `DirectEditManager` for implementing this behavior. The class links to its context by three points: A `Graphical EditPart` is an element in the drawing representing a specific model element; a `CellEditorLocator` places the pop-up, usually relative to the edit part; and a `CellEditor`, such as `TextCellEditor` from the JFace framework, is used as the actual pop-up. The edit part, the cell editor, and perhaps also a generic cell locator can be reused. The `DirectEdit Manager` ties them together into a small network of objects that creates the overall user experience.

↰2.4.2
↰7.1
↰2.2
📖214

Compositionality requires the Single Responsibility Principle.

One aspect of compositional objects is that tasks are distributed among several objects, each of which makes a well-defined and small contribution. This goal is shared with the Single Responsibility Principle.

However, compositionality is more. It focuses on the single objects and seeks to find responsibilities that are meaningful in themselves, independent of the particular network in which the object is conceived.

↰11.2

Compositionality entails information hiding.

The attraction of compositional proofs is that subproofs remain valid independent of their context, and they never need to be reinspected when combining them into a larger proof. Objects can be compositional only if they can be understood without looking at their internals, which is precisely what information hiding is about.

↰11.5.1

Compositionality requires clear and general contracts.

The idea of "clicking together" objects works as intended only if the objects' interfaces are defined precisely, using contracts. Without clear contracts, objects cannot be combined without reconsidering their internal behavior, which is precisely what compositionality discourages.

Compositionality goes beyond contracts in that it demands general interfaces that are useful in many different situations. The JFace `TextCell Editor` in the direct editing example was never meant to be used in the context of graphical editors, but because its interface does not make specific assumptions about its underlying widget, it works for the GEF as well. The classical PIPES-AND-FILTERS pattern is so powerful because the filters, as the units of data processing, share a common data transfer format, so that they can be combined freely.

> Compositionality fosters reuse.

If objects "click together" well in one context, each implements an atomic contribution, and their interfaces are general enough, then it becomes more likely that individual objects become reusable.

However, compositionality does not require aiming at reuse. Even if objects fit well only within a single context, one still gains the other benefits described earlier.

11.5.4   Design-Code Traceability

In traditional software processes, design and implementation have been seen as consecutive steps: Once the design is complete, it remains only to implement it faithfully. Later on, the agile movement realized that the invariable problem of discovering design flaws too late is responsible for many failed software projects and broke up the strict sequence in favor of truly iterative development.

> The design must be reflected in the concrete code.

The goal is to create code that matches the design. We design to create an overall structure; to plan the implementation; to distribute work among teams; to communicate about our strategy; to maintain an overview of the code despite its technical complexity; to come back to the code during maintenance. All of this works best if we can point to some place in the design and find its concrete rendering in the code immediately. Maintaining mappings between different artifacts within the software development process is commonly called *traceability*.

> Anticipate the implementation while designing.

One of greatest dangers when first designing larger applications is that the design itself looks useful and sensible, but then its implementation turns out to be tricky or cumbersome. As the saying goes, "The proof of the pudding is in the eating."

The only realistic countermeasure is to think about the implementation in quite some detail while designing. During this process, one constantly switches between high-level planning and low-level implementation, until one is satisfied that everything will be all right.

☐☐263

Coplien has introduced the useful concept of *multiparadigm design*. He complements the standard approach of analyzing the application domain with the proposal of analyzing the *solution domain* with the same rigor. The solution domain comprises the language features available for the implementation. The goal is to find the most natural way of mapping the structure of the application domain to the available constructs of the solution domain.

☐☐71

Prefer short-term plans and validate them immediately.

Design-code traceability requires a lot of implementation experience to get it right the first time: One has to express the right structures in the code so that all technical details will fit in. Whenever you feel that the design of some subsystem or neighborhood is fixed, you might want to start implementing the design immediately, or at least write down the public API so that the network of objects compiles. Test-first comes in handy, because you not only see the static structure, but also can check out whether the design covers all functionality by suitable mechanisms.

↰5.2

↰11.1

Evaluate design decisions based on the resulting code.

In fact, the respective merits of alternative designs very often show up only in the implementation—for instance, in the amount of overhead required to achieve some desired generalization. When faced with a complex problem in an area where you have little implementation experience, it might be useful to write down some code for several alternatives to get a feeling for their feasibility.

11.5.5 DRY

Implementing the same functionality in different places is usually a bad idea: Development takes longer and if you find bugs or otherwise have to alter the functionality, you have to track down all the relevant places. Doing this is called "shotgun surgery" and it indicates that your design is not yet optimal. The positive formulation is simply this: "Don't repeat yourself" (DRY). Another one is "once and only once." So far, so obvious.

☐☐92

☐☐172

DRY is more complicated than it seems: It requires structure.

Copy-and-paste programming is an incredibly popular method of development. Indeed, many pieces of functionality are so complex that we are

happy and maybe lucky to get them right in one place. If we need the same
or similar functionality somewhere else, we just copy the code and adapt it
to the new context.

The reason for this deplorable state is that it takes thought and diligence
to come up with an object that is truly responsible for a task and solves it
once and for all. You have to define the task precisely, create an API, and
make the object accessible wherever its functionality is required. If you are
not sure of the task in the first place or, in the more likely case, do not
have the time to work it out in detail, DRY is incredibly hard to achieve.

↰11.1

Know the techniques for factoring out functionality by heart.

▱71

The first step toward achieving DRY is to know as many technical tricks
of achieving it as possible: Once you know the solution space to a design
problem, the design problem becomes much more tractable. For DRY, you
should be familiar with object-oriented techniques that help in factoring out
functionality: Simple methods or objects can capture algorithms, or maybe
the functionality can be seen as a stand-alone service; through inheritance,
a class can provide common behavior to clients, `protected` helper methods
to its subclasses, or larger mechanisms through the TEMPLATE METHOD
pattern. The more you become aware of these structures and the more you
practice them, the easier it becomes to avoid code repetition. Copy-and-
adapt is an effort, too, and if you can think of an alternative quickly, you
will use it.

↰1.4.8 ↰1.8.6 ↰1.8.2
↰1.8.5

↰3.1.3 ↰3.1.4
↰1.4.9

Design well-known parts carefully in a bottom-up approach.

When focusing on technical solutions only, you are likely to end up with
code that is not understandable. The goal is not to write nifty object-
oriented code, but rather to find an assignment of responsibilities so that
each class has a clear purpose.

↰11.2.1 ↠12.1.3

The best bet for achieving DRY is careful design. If during design with
CRC cards you find you have objects that are somehow similar, you can
probe their similarity and express it as a separate object without much
effort. If you do not succeed during design, you will never succeed during
coding, where you have to pay attention to all sorts of technical constraints
to avoid breaking the software. Work out the similarities you recognize at
once.

↰11.1 ↰11.3.2

Expressing similarities in objects is often a bottom-up activity. Design
usually starts from the use cases to make sure all requirements are covered. When expressing similarity, in contrast, you go away from concrete
goals and ask yourself which stand-alone piece of functionality would help
to achieve these goals later on. Very often, this involves looking out for
functionality you have already implemented somewhere else and know to
be useful.

For instance, many dialogs in Eclipse are of the filter-and-select variety: The user types some name, and the system provides a list of choices quickly. Since the designers recognized this similarity, they have provided a `FilteredItemsSelectionDialog` that you can adapt to your needs by subclassing. It uses TEMPLATE METHODS to provide a powerful infrastructure that supports your own implementations.

↰1.4.9

Refactor for the first (or second) copy.

In practice, the need for copy-and-paste often arises from new requirements that are introduced after the software is deployed. In such a situation, you may wish to quickly cover a new use case by adapting the solution to a similar one you already have.

At this point, you should sit back: Is it better to copy or to refactor? Copying is quick now, but you might pay a heavy price for it during maintenance. Refactoring requires more effort now, but you may create structure and stand-alone functionality that will come in handy later on. The problem with the decision is the "maybe" part of this process: It takes some experience to foresee the future development.

Many authors propose the heuristic that it is OK to have two copies of some functionality, because maintaining two copies is likely to be more effective than doing the refactoring. However, as soon as you create a third copy, you should refactor the code and replace all three copies with references to the common implementation.

Our personal experience is that it is useful to think about a refactoring even for the first copy. Usually, the need for copying shows that your design is incomplete, because you missed an opportunity to introduce an object or method with a single responsibility. Introducing a stand-alone object clarifies the design, if nothing more. In particular, you can choose an expressive name that helps maintenance developers to understand the software.

↰11.2.1

The choice between the two strategies depends on many factors, such as the size of the required refactoring, your familiarity with object-oriented techniques, and your prowess with the Eclipse refactoring tools. By learning and practicing refactoring often, you will make the balance shift toward refactoring, which improves both your development discipline and the code you produce. DRY is really a long-term goal.

DRY touches on reusability.

One key point is that DRY is really reuse in the small. You recognize a similarity and code the solution up so that it can be used in different places. As a result, the challenges of refactoring can also arise when applying DRY. For instance, we have used parsers for arithmetic expressions in several places throughout the book. Parsing is a simple enough and well-understood task, so one should think we have achieved DRY on our first try. For historical

↠12.4

↰2.3.3 ↰9.4.2 ↰11.3.3.1
📖2

reasons, which are so frequent in practice, this is not the case, and extensive refactoring and redesign were necessary to achieve DRY. Since it is somewhat intricate, the story will be told later on.

»12.4.3

11.5.6   The SOLID Principles

□170,169

We finish this overview with a collection of desirable design goals and principles for classes due to Martin. Their initials form the fitting acronym SOLID:

↰11.2
↰11.2.3

SRP   The *Single Responsibility Principle* is here expressed as "There should never be more than one reason for a class to change."

OCP   The *Open/Closed Principle* states that "A module should be open for extension but closed for modification."

↰3.1.1

LSP   The *Liskov Substitution Principle* states that "Subclasses should be substitutable for their base classes."

↰3.2.2

ISP   The *Interface Segregation Principle* states that "Many client-specific interfaces are better than one general-purpose interface."

DIP   The *Dependency Inversion Principle* demands, "Depend upon abstractions. Do not depend upon concretions."

We will not go into the implications of SRP, LSP, and ISP here because they have been treated already in detail. The remaining two principles, OCP and DIP, concern the higher-level structures created in the design process.

↰11.5.1

The OCP recognizes that the behavior of objects usually needs to be changed at some point. Because their internals may be complex, however, these changes should be effected without modifying the actual source code. In essence, the existing behavior can be extended to cover new aspects at specific points. The technical basis is polymorphism, which might also be exploited through a TEMPLATE METHOD or STRATEGY. In any case, we introduce general mechanisms so that objects can be adapted by adding facets of behavior without touching their original sources.

↰1.4.11
↰1.4.9 ↰1.3.4

↰11.2.3

Of course, the OCP involves a rather substantial design challenge: The possible points of change have to be anticipated in the original design. This means that the designer has to be aware of possible variants of the functionality currently being implemented and has to create a technical interface that fits all possible uses.

»12.1
↰4.1

The other new principle, DIP, highlights an important consequence of dependencies: When an object A depends on another object B, then A is likely to need changes if B changes. In a classical contract-based relationship between two objects, it is the caller that depends on the callee [Fig. 11.12(a)]: If the callee is forced to change its contract to accommodate new requirements, then the callee must be adapted as well.

However, when considering the overall architecture of an application, this is often unacceptable. Here, the caller implements some application-specific, high-level functionality based on some detailed service of the callee. It is then the high-level functionality that should determine the need for change, not the low-level details whose modifications might be somewhat arbitrary—for instance, if they reflect the underlying hardware or third-party code beyond our control.

The solution proposed by DIP is to introduce an interface and to let the high-level module define that interface [Fig. 11.12(b)]. When the low-level details change, we may have to introduce an adapter or develop some glue-code, but the overall application will remain intact. The dependency is effectively inverted, because now the lower-level functionality must follow the higher-level functionality.

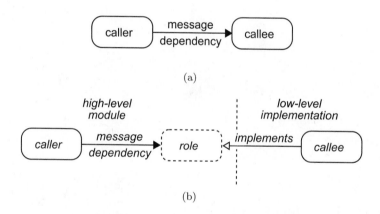

(a)

(b)

Figure 11.12 The Dependency Inversion Principle

We have already seen several applications of DIP. Most prominently, the OBSERVER pattern enables application objects to specify their mode of collaboration with dependent objects: They send out notifications about state changes without making assumptions about how these notifications will be used. In a specific instance, the model in the MODEL-VIEW-CONTROLLER pattern contains the business logic of an application, its most valuable part. That model remains insulated from changes in the rather volatile user interface.

↰2.1.2

↰9.2.1

↰9.2.2

The motivation for and assumption of DIP is that abstractions will be more stable than concrete implementations. Abstractions often capture time-proven concepts that have been applied successfully in different contexts, while the concrete implementations found by different development teams usually differ. By fixing the API of the concept in an interface and working only with APIs, one can make the overall application more stable.

Of course, DIP then incurs the rather challenging design problem of finding both the abstraction and its interface. Finding the abstraction requires a lot of literacy in computer science; defining the interface calls for a lot of experience with different implementation strategies.

Chapter 12

Design Strategies

Design is a challenging activity: We invent objects, distribute responsibilities, and define collaborations to solve a given real-world problem in software. In the process, we must make a vast number of decisions, each of which influences the outcome of the project: how well we fulfill the users' expectations; how quickly we can deliver the software; how much effort we have to spend; how easily the software can be adapted to new requirements; how long the software will remain usable; and maybe even whether the project is a success or a failure.

In the end, there is almost never a single best answer to the design questions that arise in this process. We have to make do with heuristics and often have to be content with steering in the right direction. We are always striving for the "best" design, but at the same time for the "simplest thing that could possibly work." We need to get the software finished quickly now, but we must also think ahead about later modifications. We might even be building only the first product from a larger product family.

To meet these challenges, we need a language for talking about designs as well as criteria for judging them to be "good" or "bad." And we need strategies that suggest routes that are likely to lead to good designs.

All of these strategies and judgements ultimately have to be measured against the resulting code: It is the code that must be developed, modified, maintained, and reused. It is the coding that consumes a project's resources and makes the software affordable or expensive, which makes it a throwaway bulk of nonsense or a neat, well-structured, maintainable piece of work. One important difference between expert designers and novice designers is that the experts have seen and solved so many problems in concrete code that they can predict the outcomes of their design decisions with some accuracy.

This chapter approaches the question of design strategies by focusing on the goals to be met: How can we achieve flexible solutions that allow modifications throughout the software's lifetime? How can we ensure that new functionality can be integrated with as little effort as possible? How can we build reusable components to reduce the overall cost of software development within our team or company? Each of these areas will be treated from the conceptual structure to the resulting code, using examples from the Eclipse platform. Indeed, analyzing and imitating the work of expert designers is the best way to become an expert oneself.

As we progress through the material, you will notice that we have actually discussed many of the conceptual considerations before. They have served to explain and to justify the language usage in Part I, they have guided the quest for precise contracts in Part II, and they have formed the basis of event-driven programming and model-view separation in Part III. Now, we set these individual points within the larger context of design.

12.1   Coupling and Cohesion

How do we recognize "good" design and why is a certain design "good" or "bad" in the first place? In the end, good design leads to code with desirable properties—code that is, for instance, changeable, maintainable, understandable, portable, reusable, and testable. But this is not very helpful: Once the implementation is ready, there is no use in talking about the design—if the design was "good," we are done; if it was "bad," there is nothing we can do about it. We need criteria for evaluating the design beforehand so that we can predict the properties of the resulting code.

Perhaps the most influential criteria for evaluating designs are *coupling* and *cohesion*. They were introduced early on in the study of "good" software structures and have proved helpful ever since. Briefly speaking, they address the central aspect of how "connected" different pieces code in a system are, where "connected" means that the pieces must be understood and maintained together. Coupling then captures the connectedness between modules, while cohesion captures connectedness within a module.

While this may sound rather straightforward, it turns out to be a challenge to define coupling and cohesion precisely and to apply them to concrete designs. Especially for coupling, the experts of the field will come up with so many facets that it seems implausible that one could ever find a one-sentence summary. We will first examine the agreed characterization of coupling as a factor that limits changeability: Software that is not changeable cannot be maintained, ported, and reused. Next, we take a conceptual step beyond and ask what brings about the coupling, besides the obvious technical dependencies. Then, we turn to the question of cohesion, before discussing the Law of Demeter, a helpful heuristic that limits coupling.

12.1.1   Coupling and Change

Changeability is a central property of software: We may get the requirements wrong, the requirements may change, or the context in which the software runs may change. In any case, our users expect us to come up with a cost-effective modification to our software so that it fits the new expectations.

Coupling describes the necessity of induced changes.

Coupling can be defined most easily by the necessity of propagating changes [Fig. 12.1(a)]: Component A depends on B—for instance, because A calls one of B's methods. It is also coupled to B if a change in B requires us to change A as well, as indicated by the shaded areas.

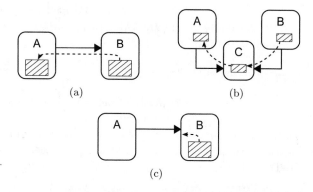

Figure 12.1 Coupling as Propagated Change

Coupling is problematic precisely because we will always make changes to our software. During development, we might remedy problems with earlier design or implementation decisions. After deployment, we must integrate new functionality or adapt existing points. Coupling then leads to an increase in both work and development costs.

The most basic form of coupling is easily recognized at the technical level. For instance, A is coupled to B in the following situations:

- A references a type name defined in B.
- A calls a method defined in B.
- A accesses a field or data structure from B.
- A instantiates a class defined in B.
- A extends a class or implements an interface from B.
- A overrides a method introduced in B.   ≫12.2.1.2

Whenever B changes the aspect that A references, then A has to change as well. For example, if a type name changes, all references must change; if a method gets a different name or different parameters, all calls must be adapted; and so on.

Coupling can occur through a shared third.

Coupling can also occur without a direct dependency between the modules in question. In Fig. 12.1(b), both A and B use a module C—for instance, as a service provider. Now some change in B might result in C being no longer good enough, so that it must be changed. In turn, this change may ripple through to A.

227

A special form of indirect coupling is *stamp coupling*. Here, both A and B use a common data structure C for communication. However, the data structure is not made for the purpose, as would be usual in passing parameters to methods. The data structure instead contains a number of aspects that are irrelevant to A and B. As a result, both modules become coupled to this fixed entity, and as a result to each other.

Dependencies do not always lead to strong coupling.

11.5.1

Of course, dependencies do not always lead to undesirable coupling [Fig. 12.1(c)]. If information hiding is taken seriously in the design of B, then some changes can be made to B without touching A. For instance, B's internal data structures, held in its fields and never exposed through public (or protected) methods, can usually be exchanged without A noticing.

Loose coupling means insulation from change.

In principle, then, any dependency might induce coupling, but some dependencies are more acceptable than others. The term *loose coupling* is used to describe situations such as in Fig. 12.1(c), where the dependency is designed such that we can get away with many changes to B without changing the remainder of the system. *Decoupling* then means breaking an existing coupling or preventing it from occurring.

11.5.1

However, loose coupling is not the same as information hiding, which also aims at enabling change. Information hiding describes the bare necessity of hiding internals, usually at the level of individual objects. Loose coupling concerns the design of the interface of objects and subsystems so that as many changes as possible can be made without changing the interface, and without adapting the specified method contracts. To be effective, loose coupling must usually be considered at the architectural level, when planning the overall system and its components.

4.1

12.2.1.4 11.5.6

One strategy for achieving loose coupling has been seen in the Dependency Inversion Principle (see Fig. 11.12 on page 635). Rather than making one subsystem A depend on the concrete implementation classes of another subsystem B, we introduce an interface between them that captures the expectations of A. As a result, B is free to change as much as possible; all that is required is that it still fulfills A's expectations.

3.2.7

Observer relationships are a standard means of decoupling.

12.2.1.8
2.1
2.1.2

One special case of achieving loose coupling is to channel collaboration through the OBSERVER pattern. The subject remains entirely independent of its observers, as long as the observer interface is, indeed, defined from the possible state changes to the subject.

12.2.1.9 93

A slightly more general view is to let an object define events that it passes to any interested parties. It does not care about these other objects at all; it merely tells them about important occurrences within its own life cycle.

Many architectural patterns are geared toward achieving loose coupling.

Since loose coupling is such an important goal in system design, it is hardly surprising that many architectural patterns achieve it in particular collaborations.

 59,101

For instance, the MODEL-VIEW-CONTROLLER pattern insulates the model from changes in the view. But the pattern does more: It also decouples the different views from each other, because each one queries, observes, and modifies the model independently. As a result, any individual view, as well as the overall application window, can change without breaking existing views. Note also that the essential decoupling step rests on the observer relation between the model and the view, as suggested earlier.

↰9.1

↰9.2.3

The PRESENTATION-ABSTRACTION-CONTROL (PAC) pattern decouples different elements of the user interface further by making them communicate through messages. In the LAYERS pattern, each layer insulates the higher ones from any changes in the lower ones; at the same time, each layer remains independent of its higher layers. The PIPES-AND-FILTERS pattern keeps individual data processing steps independent of both the other processing steps and the overall system structure.

▱59

»12.2.2

»12.3.4

Decoupling involves an effort.

Fig. 12.1(c) on page 639 is usually a too naive view: It assumes that B is already defined such that A remains loosely coupled. Very often, this is not the case. Decoupling must be achieved explicitly—for instance, through FACADE objects or through ADAPTERs that translate requests. In this context, a *mapper* is an adapter that translates requests in both directions. In general, such constructs are instances of *shields*; in other words, they are software artifacts that are introduced with the sole purpose of decoupling different objects or subsystems.

»12.2.1.6 ↰1.7.2 ↰2.4.1

▱93

▱225

In reality, decoupling by shields requires some infrastructure (Fig. 12.2). For A to access B in a loosely coupled manner, we have to define an interface I behind which we hide the possible changes. Then, we introduce an adapter (or mapper) C to actually implement the interface based on an existing B. The adapter also acts as the hinge that keeps A and B connected despite possible changes to B; these lead to changes in C, and only in C.

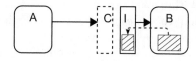

Figure 12.2 Shields for Decoupling

↰9.4.3

Beyond this, the subsystems A and B themselves will probably have to be more general, and therefore more complex, to communicate effectively through the interface I. As an example, decoupling the model from the view in the MODEL-VIEW-CONTROLLER pattern can involve substantial work to make repainting efficient. The work results from the necessity to translate model changes to screen changes, and vice versa, which could have been omitted if the model itself could contain the screen area associated with each model element.

Use decoupling to keep subsystems stand-alone.

↰11.3.3.5

You may ask, of course: If we know that B in Fig. 12.2 will have to implement I, why does it not do so directly? For one thing, it might be the case that B was created long before A and its special requirements were simply unknown at that time. For instance, B might be a library or subsystem taken over from a different project.

↰11.2
↰11.5.2

But even if B and A are designed at the same time, it is often sensible to keep B independent of A, because it enables B to remain self-contained and stand-alone. One good reason is that the team working on B remains free to choose the most sensible API from B's point of view. B can have a well-defined purpose and can be implemented and tested effectively. The underlying strategy here is simply Separation of Concerns. Or perhaps the interface I is not stable, because the demands of A are not known in all details. Getting B right and tested will then at least provide a reliable collaborator as early as possible.

»12.2.1.5 ↰3.2.7

Of course, you may also be planning to reuse B in a different project later on. In such cases, it is often useful to decouple subsystems A and B to keep them independent and stand-alone. The additional effort involved in creating the structure will pay off with the first restructuring of the system that becomes necessary.

Decoupling can be dangerous.

»12.3 »12.4
☐92

Loose coupling, like extensibility and reusability, often serves as an excuse for speculative generality. For example, creating the situation in Fig. 12.2 involves defining a nice, minimal interface I as well as the natural API for B, both of which can be intellectually rewarding challenges. The temptation of decoupling components for no other reason than decoupling them can be great at times. However, if no changes are likely to occur, then the effort of decoupling is spent in vain.

Beyond that, decoupling involves the danger of getting the interface I in Fig. 12.2 wrong. Within a system, you might simply forget to pass some parameter to a method; that is easily changed by Eclipse's refactoring tool *Change Method Signature*. Between systems, I would be a protocol, and changing it would require modifying the communication components on both ends. In any case, I must fulfill three roles at once: It must capture A's requirements; it must be implementable by B; and it must anticipate the likely changes to B from which A is supposed to be insulated. If you get the interface I wrong, the effort devoted to decoupling is lost. Also, changing I and C probably involves more effort than changing A would have required in a straightforward, strongly coupled connection from A to B.

12.1.2 Coupling and Shared Assumptions

The accepted characterization of coupling through changes from the previous section leads to a practical problem: How do you judge which changes are likely to occur, and how do you evaluate whether the changes will ripple through the system or will be "stopped" by some suitably defined API between modules? It takes a lot of experience to get anywhere near the right answers to those questions.

↰12.1.1

We have found in teaching that a different characterization can be helpful to grasp the overall concept of coupling. As we shall see, it links back to the original notion in the end.

Coupling arises from shared assumptions.

To illustrate, let us look at a typical example. The Java Model of the Eclipse Java tooling maintains a tree structure of the sources and binary libraries that the user is currently working with. The Java Model provides the data behind the *Package Explorer, Outline*, and *Navigator* views and it is used for many source manipulations. The implementation hierarchy below Java Element contains all sorts of details about caching and lazy analysis of sources and libraries. In an application of the BRIDGE pattern, a corresponding interface hierarchy below IJavaElement shields other modules from these details and exposes only those aspects that derive directly from the Java language, such as packages, compilation units, fields, and methods. Certainly, this is a prototypical example of decoupling.

↰9.1

↰3.1.5

⇥12.2.1.5
↰3.2.3

Now let us look a bit closer. For instance, an IMethod represents some method found in the sources and libraries. It has the obvious properties: a name, some parameters, and a return type. It also links back to the containing type declaration (i.e., the parent node in the tree), as is common with compound objects. But then there is one oddity: The return type is a String. What is that supposed to mean? Why don't we get the type's tree structure?

↰2.2

📖209,2

```
                    org.eclipse.jdt.core.IMethod
public interface IMethod extends IMember, IAnnotatable {
    IType getDeclaringType();
    String getElementName();
    ILocalVariable[] getParameters() throws JavaModelException;
    String getReturnType() throws JavaModelException;
    ...
}
```

Let us check whether the API is at least consistent. Sure enough, the ILocal Variables of the parameters also return their types as Strings!

---
org.eclipse.jdt.core.ILocalVariable

```
public interface ILocalVariable
    extends IJavaElement, ISourceReference, IAnnotatable {
    String getElementName();
    String getTypeSignature();
    ...

}
```

When we look at calls to these odd methods, we see that clients usually analyze the results immediately using some helper class, usually Signature or BinaryTypeConverter.

The explanation is simple: The Java Language Specification defines a neat, compact format for encoding Java types as strings. This format is also used in class files so it is easily extracted from the probably large libraries maintained in the Java Model. Because the Java Model must represent so many types, Amdahl's law suggests optimizing the storage requirements.

But let us see what effect this decision has on the classes involved (Fig. 12.3): All of them work on the common assumption that types are represented as binary signatures. The assumption ties them together.

🔍 We might think about replacing the word "assumption" with "knowledge." This strengthens the intuition that modules are coupled if their developers have to share some piece of knowledge or information for everything to work out. We have decided on "assumption" because "knowledge" implies some certainty, while "assumption" conveys the idea that software is very much a fluid construct, in which we make a decision today only to find we have to revise it tomorrow.

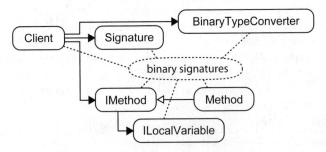

Figure 12.3 Coupling as Shared Assumptions

Shared assumptions imply coupling-as-changes.

Coupling-as-assumptions really means taking a step back from coupling-as-changes: If any of the classes in Fig. 12.3 were to deviate from the common

📖111

↰1.1

📖28

assumption that types are handled as in binary signatures, the other modules would have to follow suit to keep the API consistent.

Watch out for any assumptions shared between modules.

The benefit of focusing on shared assumptions is that developers are very familiar with assumptions about their software. They talk about the representation of data passed between modules, stored in files, and sent over the network. They think about invariants within objects, across shared objects, and within the inheritance hierarchy. They think about their objects' states, and about the allowed sequences of method calls. All of these details can lead to rippling changes, as you will have experienced in many painful debugging sessions.

↰4.1 ↰6.2.3
↰6.4.2 ↰10.1

In the end, coupling can be recognized, and possibly also tamed, even by modestly experienced developers. All that is required is that the developers become aware of their own assumptions. This does take a lot of discipline, but much less experience than anticipating the necessity and likelihood of changes. It is similar to learning contracts, which involves describing the program state at specific points in detail, rather than executing code mentally.

↰11.1

↰4.1

Shared assumptions shape the contracts between modules.

Another nice result of tracking assumptions is that the assumptions usually translate to code artifacts sooner or later. That is what traceability is all about: You express in code the decisions you make during the design phase. In particular, explicit assumptions help you define APIs that the client modules can understand and employ easily. If the assumptions are reasonable and you do not blunder in expressing them in concrete method headers, the method headers will be reasonable as well.

↰11.5.4

Shared assumptions help to distinguish between good and bad coupling.

Coupling is often seen as a measure of how "bad" a design is. Yet coupling is also necessary: Without it, there can be no collaboration. But why are some forms of coupling "tight" and therefore bad, whereas others are "loose" or "normal" and therefore acceptable?

📖223

Looking at the nature of shared assumptions can help to make that distinction. If the assumptions shared between two modules are obvious and unavoidable to reach the goal of collaborating, the resulting coupling is acceptable. If they are obscure and motivated by technical detail, the coupling should be avoided.

📖236(p.119)

This approach also links back to the Precondition Availability Principle from design-by-contract: The contract must always be specified in terms that the clients can understand. It is precisely the assumptions shared

↰4.2.2

by client and service provider that enable the client to make sense of the contract.

Decoupling means hiding assumptions.

Finally, thinking and talking about assumptions explicitly will also help to understand decoupling. Once you recognize an assumption that couples modules, you can start thinking about an API that is independent of that assumption and that would remain stable if you were to break the assumption in the future.

In the previous example of the Java Model API (Fig. 12.3 on page 644), the assumption was that types are represented and passed around as primitive `Strings`. We could apply a standard technique and wrap that data in objects of a new class `JavaType`. The API would become cleaner, as would the clients: `JavaType` could offer methods for analyzing and manipulating types, delegating the actual work to the existing helpers like `Signature`.

Coupling-as-assumptions can be traced through the literature.

Once you start to pay attention, you will find the idea of assumptions mentioned in connection with coupling in many places in the literature. However, this mostly happens by way of asides and informal introduction.

📖236(p.119)   Here are a few examples. In their seminal work, Stevens et al. see a large amount of shared information as a threat to good interface design: "The complexity of an interface is a matter of how much information is needed to state or to understand the connection. Thus, obvious relationships result in lower coupling than obscure or inferred ones." Assumptions that lead to

📖223   coupling can also be made about the software's application context: "For example, a medical application may be coupled to the assumption that a typical human has two arms because it asks the doc[tor] to inspect both arms

📖54,68,51   of [a] patient." A related classical insight, known as Conway's law, states that organizations tend to structure their software along their own structures: Departments and teams specializing in particular fields are assigned the modules matching their expertise. Decoupling happens by minimizing

📖26   the need for information interchange between teams. A recent proposal to quantify coupling measures "semantic similarity" through terminology contained in source names. It interprets this as an indication of how much domain knowledge is shared between different modules.

In short, the experts in the field are well aware of the roles that shared, and often implicit, assumptions play in the creation of coupling between modules. To become an expert, start paying attention to your own assumptions.

12.1.3 Cohesion

Good modularization is characterized on the one hand by loose coupling and on the other hand by high cohesion. While coupling describes relationships between modules, cohesion is a property of the individual modules.

☐☐236

Cohesion expresses that a module's aspects are logically connected.

When trying to understand or maintain a module from any sizable piece of software, we usually ask first: What does the module contribute? What are its responsibilities? The Single Responsibility Principle states that the design is good if there is a short answer.

↰11.1
↰11.2

The idea of cohesion takes the idea from classes to modules, which do not usually have a single responsibility, but a number of related ones. Cohesion then states that the different responsibilities are closely related to one another. In the end, one might even be able to come up with a more abstract description of the module that describes a "single" task. However, the abstraction level would be too high to be useful, so it is better to keep several smaller, highly cohesive responsibilities.

For instance, Eclipse's Java Model maintains the structure of the sources and libraries visible in the current workspace. Its responsibilities include representing the structure, parsing sources down to method declarations, indexing and searching for elements, tracking dependencies, generating code and modifying sources, reacting to changes in files and in-memory working copies, and several more. All of these are closely related, so it is sensible to implement them in one module.

There are other perceptions of high cohesion within a module. The module is stand-alone and self-contained. It is meaningful in itself. It captures a well-defined concept. These intuitions can help you recognize cohesion, or to diagnose problems in modules that lack cohesion.

Cohesion causes correlated changes.

We have characterized coupling by the effects of changes on other modules. Cohesion is often similar: Since the different responsibilities of a module are strongly related to each other, it is likely that changes in one place of the implementation will require other places to be touched as well. Although this sounds rather undesirable, the problem is outweighed by the possibility of sharing the implementation of the different aspects—for instance, through accessing common data structures and helper methods.

In fact, one viable heuristic for modularization is to place things that are likely to change together in a single module. For instance, a device driver module contains all the code that is likely to change when the hardware is switched. In contrast, any higher-level functionality that builds on the primitive data obtained through the device driver is better handled somewhere else, because then it can remain untouched even if new hardware is used.

Cohesion is not related inversely to coupling.

Even though coupling and cohesion are usually mentioned together as principles for modularization, and both can be connected to the necessity of changes to the software, they are complementary and orthogonal rather than linked. Low coupling does not make for high cohesion, and vice versa: It is obviously easy to scatter logically related functionality throughout the system and tie it together through loosely coupled collaboration. In the other direction, having a module with high cohesion does not say anything about its integration into the system. In the end, both properties must be achieved independently.

See cohesion and Separation of Concerns as opposite forces.

Even if loose coupling is not the inverse of high cohesion, it is useful to look further in this direction. Very often in design, we have to decide whether two pieces of functionality should reside in the same module (or class, component, subsystem, ...), or whether they are better split across different modules.

↶11.5.2
Cohesion can be seen as a force drawing the pieces of functionality closer together, into one module, if they are closely related [Fig. 12.4(a)]. In contrast, Separation of Concerns suggests that two distinct features, even if they are related and their implementations must collaborate, are better placed in distinct modules [Fig. 12.4(b)]. The opposite force to high cohesion then is not loose coupling, but Separation of Concerns. If we have decided on a split, loose coupling tells us how the modules should interact to keep them changeable.

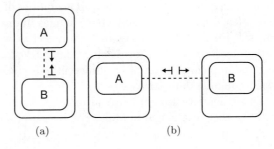

(a)   (b)

Figure 12.4 Cohesion and Separation of Concerns as Forces

An example is found in the MODEL-VIEW-CONTROLLER pattern. The
View and the *Controller* have quite distinct responsibilities: One renders
data on the screen, and the other decides about the appropriate reaction
to user input. Separation of Concerns suggests making them into separate
classes, as done in the classical pattern. At the same time, both are linked
tightly to the concrete display, because the *Controller* must usually interpret mouse gestures relative to the display and must often trigger feedback.
This cohesion of being logically concerned with the same display suggests
placing them in a single class—an arrangement that is found frequently,
namely in the form of the DOCUMENT-VIEW pattern.

↰9.2.1

↰9.2.8

> Tight coupling may indicate the potential for high cohesion.

We can gain a second perspective on the question of splitting tasks between
separate modules by considering the resulting coupling. If distributing tasks
would result in tight coupling, then it might be better to place the tasks
into the same module. It is then just possible that the tasks have so much
in common that they exhibit some cohesion as well.

For instance, the `NewClassWizardPage` from the introductory example
in Chapter 11 provides a form to let the user enter the parameters of a new
class to be created. It also creates the source of the new class. If we decide
to split these tasks, as suggested by model-view separation, then the two
are tightly coupled: Any change in the available options would require a
change to the code generator, and in many cases vice versa. It is better to
say that their common logical core, which lets the user create a new class,
leads to sufficiently high cohesion to implement both tasks in a single class.

↰11.1

12.1.4   The Law of Demeter

Pinning down the notion of "tight coupling" precisely can be rather challenging. Since designers may have different ideas about expected changes,
they may arrive at different evaluations of whether some link between objects is too "tight." An influential heuristic is the *Law of Demeter*, named
after the Demeter development environment in which it was first introduced
and supported. Its motivation is depicted in Fig. 12.5(a). Suppose object A
needs some functionality available in object D. It invokes getters to follow
the dashed path through the application's object structure and then uses
D's methods. The problem is that now A depends on the overall network
and the structure of all traversed objects, so that these structures cannot be
changed without breaking A. Such accessor sequences are also called "train
wrecks," because in the code they resemble long strings of carriages. More
strictly speaking, the law also excludes passing on references to internal
parts [Fig. 12.5(b); repeated here from Fig. 1.1]. It then does nothing else
but reinforce the idea of encapsulation in compound objects.

⊞158,172

↰1.3.3

⊞172

↰1.1

↰2.2.3

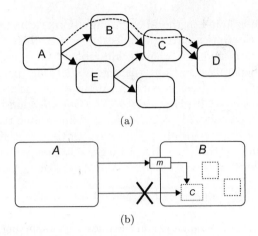

(a)

(b)

Figure 12.5 Motivation for the Law of Demeter

> Objects may work only with collaborators that have been made available to them explicitly.

The Law of Demeter is formulated to rule out such undesirable code, by defining a restricted set of objects with methods that a given method may safely invoke. The original presentation calls these "preferred suppliers" (i.e., service providers). More precisely, the Law of Demeter states that a method may access only the following objects:

1. `this`

2. The objects stored in fields of `this` (i.e., its immediate collaborators and parts)

3. The arguments passed to the method

4. The objects created in the method

5. Objects available globally—for example, as SINGLETONS

The overall intention is that an object may work with those collaborators that have explicitly been made available to it.

Note that objects returned from invoked methods are *not* included in the list of preferred suppliers. These objects are "fetched by force," not made available. As a result, the problematic getter sequences are ruled out.

> The Law of Demeter leads to encapsulation of object structures.

One way of looking at the Law of Demeter is to say that it provides an extended form of encapsulation. In Fig. 12.5(a), we wish to hide the existence of C from A. We hide information with the result that we can later change the object structure.

📖158

↰2.2

↰1.3.8

↰2.2.3

↰11.5.1

Information hiding within the individual objects is, of course, an orthogonal issue. In principle, compound objects encapsulate their internal helpers. The Law of Demeter goes beyond this in also applying to shared objects, such C in Fig. 12.5(a), which is shared between B and E.

↰2.2.3

The Law of Demeter encourages use of proper objects, rather than data structures.

The Law of Demeter forces developers to think of objects as service providers, rather than mere data structures that keep references to others. In Fig. 12.5(a), developers must design B in such a way that it is a useful collaborator to A, without exposing its own collaborators. B will therefore have clearly outlined responsibilities, ideally fulfilling the Single Responsibility Principle. It will most probably also be active and will aggregate services from its collaborators, rather than just delegating individual method calls.

↰1.8.2
↰1.8.3

↰1.1
↰11.2

Read the Law of Demeter as a guideline, not as a strict law.

The Law of Demeter is actually quite controversial, even if it is often cited. Already the original authors have recognized that following the law strictly has several undesirable consequences. Most important, since A is not allowed to reach beyond B in Fig. 12.5(a), B must provide all the functionality that A requires from C and D. Likewise, C must provide the functionality that B requires from D. In consequence, B and C have much larger interfaces than would be expected from their own purposes, and the objects no longer focus on their own tasks.

📖224
📖158

↰11.2 ↰1.1

The purpose of B might also be the selection of a suitable collaborator for A. In terms of role stereotypes, it might be a controller or a structurer. It might also be a factory for objects that hides the creation itself, but does not make any decisions. In all such cases it is, of course, mandatory to break the Law of Demeter.

↰1.8.1
↰1.4.12

To make this point clearer, let us look at an example where breaking the law actually achieves loose coupling. Eclipse contains many different kinds of editors, many of which share common abstract behavior: They expose some form of selection, provide an outline of their own content, deal with error markers, and so on. Since not all editors provide all aspects and their implementations will differ, Eclipse uses the EXTENSION OBJECTS pattern: Interested objects access an aspect of behavior through a generic `getAdapter()` method, specifying an interface for the kind of object requested. This induces loose coupling, because each client gets exactly the minimal interface that it requires. Sometimes the returned objects will already be part of the editor's infrastructure, and sometimes they are small adapters for accessing the editor's internal structures (see Fig. 12.2 on page 641).

↠12.2.1.9

↰3.2.2

↰12.1.1

12.2   Designing for Flexibility

The first goal of any software design must be to get the system to work,
spending as little effort on the implementation as possible. Next in line, the
second goal must be to keep the implementation changeable and flexible.
During development, it is common to find that the design or implementation is not working out exactly as planned or that requirements were
misunderstood in the first place. After deployment, new requirements also
keep arising all the time, and bugs and misunderstandings must be fixed
by adapting the implementation. The overall cost of a system is, in fact,
usually dominated by this kind of maintenance work. By keeping an eye
on flexibility from the beginning, we can significantly reduce these future
costs.

↰12.1

↰11.5.1

↰11.5.2 ↰11.2.3

Coupling and cohesion give us a good handle on the design decisions
to be made. Below these rather strategic—and perhaps a little abstract—
concepts, tactical considerations about proper information hiding, separation of concerns, and the Single Responsibility Principle go a long way in
achieving the goal. That is, if we get the individual objects "right," the
chances that the overall system remains flexible increase dramatically. This
section is about the strategic considerations that go beyond the tactical
ones.

> The overall goal for flexibility: localize decisions.

Information hiding is a very strict goal: An object must not reveal its internal implementation, not even accidentally such as through the return types
of getters. However, an object's public interface always reveals the object's
purpose: Which services will the object provide? Is it "intelligent," containing subtle or powerful algorithms, or is it rather "dumb," mainly keeping
data with a few operations to match?

When designing for flexibility, we cannot hide away all our decisions,
because some go into the interfaces of objects. Also, we must treat the
published interfaces as something fixed, something that we cannot change in
a hurry, because other objects rely on them. But we can aim at minimizing
the influence that changes in our decisions will have on these interfaces.
Likewise, we can confine or localize our decisions in larger software units,
such as by hiding objects behind interface definitions or publishing only
facade objects.

12.2.1   Techniques for Decoupling

🕮71

Professional design always involves the solution space: We have to be aware
of the technical tools that enable us to express our design in concrete code.
We therefore start out by gleaning a few tricks from the Eclipse platform.
Many of the points overlap with the usage of the relevant constructs from

Part I, but now we ask the reverse question: The focus is not on the possible applications of a construct, but rather on the constructs that fit a specific application—namely, that of achieving decoupling.

12.2.1.1 Using Objects Instead of Primitives

The most basic technique for keeping the implementation flexible is to avoid exposing primitive data types such as `int` or `String` and to define application-specific objects instead. This tactic is hardly worth mentioning, except that one is often faced with an awkward choice: to pass the primitive data along now and immediately, or to stop coding and start thinking about the meaning of the data and about an appropriate design for an object encapsulating the data. By placing data inside objects you can localize the decision about its representation, possible indexes and caches, and other facets, but it does take some time. Besides the encapsulation, you also gain the invaluable chance to express the data's purpose in the class name.   ↰11.2.1

12.2.1.2 Factoring Out Decisions: Composition and Inheritance

The guideline in regard to flexibility is to localize decisions. To design such that decisions can be revised means to find interfaces behind which the decisions can be hidden. With that approach, even if the decisions change, the interfaces can stay in place. At this point we need to talk about classes, even if otherwise we focus on objects: Classes are the units of code that may depend on the decisions.

> Factor out decisions into separate classes.

Suppose you are about to make a decision that you know may change in the future. In recognition of this fact, you create a separate class to which any code that depends on the decision will be confined. The class is a rigid container for the fluid consequences of the decision. Usually the new class must communicate with its surroundings. Now there are two ways to achieve this: composition and inheritance.

It is common consensus that inheritance introduces a strong coupling between the base class and its derived classes. We have discussed at several points that inheritance is, indeed, a powerful construct that needs some taming to be useful. The Fragile Base Class Problem highlights most clearly the idea of coupling as the inability to change the base class without breaking the derived classes. We have also seen that for this reason deep inheritance hierarchies are rather rare and should be avoided. But when exactly should we use composition, and when should we use inheritance?   📖44(Item 16) 📖232 ↰1.4.8.3 ↰3.1.2 ↰3.1.11 ↰12.1.1 ↰3.1.5

> Prefer composition for largely independent functionality.

Let us look at the example of source code editors in Eclipse. The base class `AbstractDecoratedTextEditor` introduces many elements that you will be familiar with from your daily work in Eclipse: the main source editing widget, the area for line numbers, and that for errors, warnings, tasks, and other elements on the right-hand side. The latter two areas are linked only very loosely to the editing functionality. In fact, they mainly have to scale their displays to match the size of the overall source code and the position of the editor's vertical scrollbar. It is therefore sensible to move them into separate custom widgets that can hide away decisions about the presentation of line numbers, errors, and so on.

↩7.8

---

org.eclipse.ui.texteditor.AbstractDecoratedTextEditor

```
public abstract class AbstractDecoratedTextEditor
                          extends StatusTextEditor {
    private LineNumberColumn fLineColumn;
    protected OverviewRuler fOverviewRuler;
    ...
}
```

🔍 The actual declared type of fOverviewRuler is IOverviewRuler, but that interface has only a single implementing class.

Prefer inheritance to assemble fragments that are linked tightly anyway.

The source code editors of Eclipse also show how inheritance can be used to localize decisions about different aspects of an object. For instance, the standard JavaEditor is assembled through several inheritance steps:

WorkbenchPart Provides the basic assets of windows in Eclipse, such as the title, tooltip, icon, and *site* for the integration with the context.

EditorPart Adds the element of an *editor input* of type IEditorInput. Editor inputs abstract over the concrete location of the file being edited. They can be saved and restored to maintain the workbench state across sessions.

AbstractTextEditor Assembles the main ingredients for source code editing, such as an ISourceViewer, font resources, and an IDocument Provider for accessing the document on the external storage.

↩9.3.1

StatusTextEditor Can replace the text editing widget with a page for showing error messages, such as the file being missing or exceptions being thrown during initialization.

AbstractDecoratedTextEditor Adds the right-hand-side overview rulers, line numbers, and support for displaying *annotations* such as errors, tasks, and changes on the edited source code.

JavaEditor Adds all the Java-specific elements, such as the outline page and a matcher for parentheses according to the Java syntax.

When going through these contributions, you will notice that the elements introduced in each step are tightly linked to those of the preceding steps. For instance, anything below the `AbstractTextEditor` will at some point or other access the `ISourceViewer` and the `IDocumentProvider`.

Also, it is quite common to create many cross-references between the different aspects. A prototypical case is seen in the `JavaEditor`. To maximize its support for the Java language, the editor requires a special source viewer. To introduce it, it overrides the factory method `createSourceViewer()`   ↰1.4.12 of `AbstractTextViewer`, as seen in the following code. Look closely at the required arguments to see how many of the elements introduced in the hierarchy are tied together to achieve the desired functionality. (The method `createJavaSourceViewer()` merely creates a `JavaSourceViewer`.)

org.eclipse.jdt.internal.ui.javaeditor.JavaEditor

```
protected final ISourceViewer createSourceViewer(
                Composite parent, IVerticalRuler verticalRuler,
                int styles) {
    ...
    ISourceViewer sourceViewer = createJavaSourceViewer(
        editorComposite, verticalRuler,
        getOverviewRuler(),
        isOverviewRulerVisible(),
        styles, store);
    ...
    return sourceViewer;
}
```

Use inheritance to optimize the public interface of objects.

The relationship between a base class and its derived classes includes a   ↰3.1.2 special, semi-private interface. It is given by `protected` services offered to   ↰1.4.8.2 the derived classes and hooks, mostly for TEMPLATE METHODS, that must   ↰1.4.9 be provided by the derived classes. In Part I, we emphasized the dangers of this special interface, because it offers privileged access to a class's internals, which can quickly destroy the class invariants.   ↰6.4.2

The perspective of localizing decisions now enables us to see the opportunity created by this intimacy: A class can make some aspects available to a few selected "friends" while keeping them hidden from the world at large. As a result, the public API can remain lean and focused (Fig. 12.6):   ↰11.2.1 It accepts only a few service calls that fit directly with the object's purpose,   ↰2.1 ↠12.2.1.8 and the callbacks are mostly notifications using the OBSERVER pattern. In contrast, the interface between base class and derived classes includes all kinds of links between the object's aspects, as we saw earlier. It also comprises many small-scale downward hooks and callbacks. Perhaps methods are even overridden on an ad-hoc basis to enforce a specific behavior. Without the special interface, all of this would have to be public and could not remain localized.

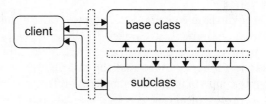

Figure 12.6 Optimizing the Public Interface

📖239

🌍 C++ `friend`s declarations serve the same purpose of keeping the general API lean but providing a selected few more rights. Something similar can, of course, be accomplished in Java with package visibility, albeit at a much coarser granularity.

12.2.1.3   Roles: Grouping Objects by Behavior

↰11.1

Roles in responsibility-driven design are sets of related responsibilities. They serve to characterize objects independent of their implementation class. At the language level, they map to Java interfaces. Roles usually abstract away many details of the object's behavior. Often, they describe behavior ↰11.3.3.7 that can be implemented in many different ways in different contexts. We have already seen that roles can keep objects exchangeable. In the current context, they can help to localize decisions behind a common abstraction that will be appropriate even if we have to reconsider a decision.

> Capture the minimal expected behavior in an interface.

You have to make a decision if you are faced with several alternative designs or implementations. By putting a role in front of the alternative you choose, you can keep the remainder of the system independent of your choice (Fig. 12.7).

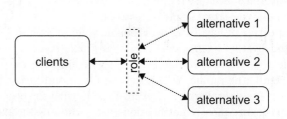

Figure 12.7 Hiding Alternatives Behind Roles

The challenge is, of course, to design the role. There are several approaches. Starting from the alternatives, you can think about their common📖70alities—the assumptions that will hold true regardless of the decision. On the one hand, this approach is quite straightforward and leads to powerful and extensive roles. On the other hand, there is the danger that tomorrow you might encounter yet another alternative that does not fit the bill.

In the other direction, you can ask what you actually wish to achieve with your design. What is the (main) purpose of the object or subsystem you are creating? What are the demands that the remainder of the system will have? This approach leads to roles that contain the minimal necessary responsibilities. It has the advantage that newly arising alternatives still match the demands, because they do fulfill the same overall purpose—otherwise, they would not be alternatives at all.

↰11.2.1

For an example, let us turn to Eclipse's *workspace*, which comprises all the resources such as projects, folders, and files accessible in the IDE. Internally, the workspace implementation is very complex, since it must keep track of resource modifications, symbolic links, locking, and many more details. To keep the exact implementation changeable, the designers have introduced an interface IWorkspace, which provides an abstract view on the available operations. It is minimal in the sense that all methods can be explained by the abstraction of a "workspace." Anything that is not in the abstraction is not in the interface.

We can only give the general flavor of the workspace abstraction here, using typical methods from the IWorkspace interface shown in the next code snippet. First, all resources are contained in a tree structure accessible below the workspace root. One can also observe resource changes, such as to keep user interface elements up-to-date. The workspace is responsible for running builders; usually this happens automatically, but builds can also be triggered. Any workspace modification should be wrapped in a IWorkspaceRunnable and should be specified further by the resources that it modifies (called the *scheduling rules*). The workspace will make sure that operations do not interfere with each other, so that the scheduling rules act as soft locks. The workspace can also check pre-conditions of intended operations—for instance, to validate a desired project location. Dialogs can use these methods to be robust and to ensure that subsequent operations will succeed.

↰2.3.1
↰9.1
↰8.1
↰4.1
↰4.6

```
                    org.eclipse.core.resources.IWorkspace

public interface IWorkspace extends IAdaptable {
    public IWorkspaceRoot getRoot();
    public void addResourceChangeListener(
        IResourceChangeListener listener);
    public void build(int kind, IProgressMonitor monitor)
        throws CoreException;
    public void run(IWorkspaceRunnable action, ISchedulingRule rule,
                    int flags, IProgressMonitor monitor)
            throws CoreException;
    public IStatus validateProjectLocation(IProject project,
                                           IPath location);
    ...
}
```

↰1.3.8

↰1.4.12

The question is, of course, how we will ever obtain an object filling the abstract role in Fig. 12.7. In the case of the resource plugin, a SINGLETON is justified because each Eclipse instance works on a single workspace (as in the following code). An alternative is to provide factory methods or abstract factories.

org.eclipse.core.resources.ResourcesPlugin

```
public static IWorkspace getWorkspace()
```

Enabling several or many alternatives leads to extensibility.

↰11.1

There are also many examples where all conceivable alternatives are actually valid. For instance, we started our exploration of responsibility-driven design with the question of how the dialog available through the *New/Other* context menu was ever to encompass all types of files available in Eclipse. The answer is that it doesn't. It merely defines a role "new wizard," with interface INewWizard, whose behavior is to ask the user for the file-specific information and then to create the file. Such situations, where different useful alternatives for a role can be implemented side-by-side, lead to extensibility of the system.

↠12.3

Provide a general default implementation of the interface.

↰3.1.4

In such cases, other team members or even your customers will supply the implementation or implementations of the role. You can make their task considerably easier if you provide a general default implementation as a base class. Its mechanisms can already work toward the common purpose of all alternatives you can think of.

12.2.1.4   Dependency Inversion

↰11.5.6

↰12.2.1.3

The Dependency Inversion Principle proposes to make central parts of an application depend on abstractions, rather than concrete implementations. Technically, this means introducing roles to capture the expected behavior of other subsystems. From an architectural perspective, it requires that you identify the possible variations in this behavior.

Dependency inversion is also a powerful technique for decoupling and for achieving flexibility. After identifying the parts where the implementation has to remain flexible, the remainder of the application must depend on these parts only through abstractions. An essential point is that applying the principle does not miraculously make "everything flexible." It is your own responsibility to choose carefully where the extra indirection through interfaces actually brings new benefits and where it simply obscures the sources.

Since the source code for this approach will look essentially the same as in previous sections, we will not provide an example here. Instead, we encourage you to go back to the snippets from the Eclipse platform and to view them as instances of dependency inversion—the change of perception is really quite startling and helpful.

12.2.1.5 The Bridge Pattern

On the one hand, inheritance induces strong coupling and comes with all the associated problems for changeability. On the other hand, it is a very neat and powerful implementation mechanism. The BRIDGE pattern aims at keeping the strong coupling hidden at least from the clients by introducing a self-contained abstraction. At the same time, it enables clients to use inheritance themselves.

↰12.2.1.2

▭100

PATTERN: BRIDGE

To keep the implementation of abstractions hidden from clients and to enable clients to add new subclasses themselves, introduce parallel class hierarchies for the abstraction and its implementation.

1. Define the abstraction hierarchy that clients will use.

2. Implement the abstraction in a separate hierarchy.

3. Provide factories that allow clients to obtain concrete implementations.

BRIDGE shields the clients behind a fixed abstraction.

A typical application of the pattern is seen in the design of the Abstract Window Toolkit (AWT), which was Java's first user interface framework and remains the technical basis of Swing. The overall goal is to enable AWT to choose a platform-specific implementation for each widget at runtime. These implementations are called *peers*, because they accompany the widgets created by the clients.

Let us trace the pattern's approach with the example of a `TextField`. AWT first creates an abstraction hierarchy for the clients, where `TextField` inherits from `TextComponent`, and `TextComponent` in turn inherits from `Component`, the base of all widgets in AWT. The actual handling of text takes place in the `TextComponent`. Note how the widget accesses its peer for the real operation: The widget, as perceived by the client, is only a handle on the real implementation.

↰3.2.3

```
                        java.awt.TextComponent
public class TextComponent extends Component implements Accessible {
    public synchronized String getText() {
        TextComponentPeer peer = (TextComponentPeer) this.peer;
        text = peer.getText();
        return text;
    }
}
```

```
    public synchronized void setText(String t) {
        ...
    }
    ...
}
```

The abstraction hierarchy is mirrored on the peers. `TextFieldPeer` derives from `TextComponentPeer`, which derives from `ComponentPeer`.

---
java.awt.peer.TextComponentPeer

```
public interface TextComponentPeer extends ComponentPeer {
    String getText();
    void setText(String l);
    ...
}
```

The implementation hierarchy remains hidden and changeable.

The real implementation of the AWT widgets is hidden in the bowels of the JRE library. Probably the methods of these objects are `native` anyway. For instance, the peer for a text field on Linux is called `XTextFieldPeer`. The clients are not concerned with that hierarchy at all, so it can be modified as necessary.

Link abstraction and implementation by a factory.

↰1.4.12
Since clients cannot create objects for the offered abstraction directly, the framework has to define an ABSTRACT FACTORY. In AWT, the factory is called `Toolkit`. Here is the case for the text field:

---
java.awt.Toolkit

```
public abstract class Toolkit {
    protected abstract TextFieldPeer createTextField(
                    TextField target) throws HeadlessException;
    ...
}
```

To simplify the API for clients, it is useful to hide the creation of implementation objects altogether. Here is the case of AWT: Whenever a widget is added to the widget tree and must be displayed, it constructs its peer on the fly.

---
java.awt.TextField

```
public void addNotify() {
    synchronized (getTreeLock()) {
        if (peer == null)
            peer = getToolkit().createTextField(this);
        super.addNotify();
```

```
        }
}
```

Clients can extend the abstraction hierarchy.

A central attraction of BRIDGE is that clients can introduce new cases into the abstraction hierarchy. In the case of AWT, they can implement their own types of widgets. In fact, the entire Swing framework relies on this ability: Its root `JComponent` derives from AWT's `Container`. As a result, Swing can, among other things, rely on AWT's low-level resource handling and painting facilities so that the native code written for the different window systems is reused.

↰7.5 ↰7.8

BRIDGE is usually a strategic decision.

The preceding code demonstrates a slight liability of BRIDGE: It tends to require a lot of extra infrastructure and many class and interface definitions. You should therefore not introduce BRIDGE lightly, but only if you see the concrete possibility that the implementation hierarchy will have to change at some point.

AWT is a case in point. Another example can be seen in the Eclipse Modeling Framework (EMF), which generates concrete classes from abstract UML-like models. In this process, it introduces a lot of boilerplate code and internal helper objects. All of those are not for consumption by the clients, but are necessary for setting up the complex and powerful runtime infrastructure that the EMF promises. Accordingly, the EMF generates a hierarchy of interfaces that reflects directly the properties, relationships, and subtyping given in the model. Clients access only these interfaces and will never depend on the intricate implementation details at all.

📖235

12.2.1.6   Boundary Objects and Facades

Objects are meant to form groups, or neighborhoods, of collaborators that work toward a common goal. Unfortunately, objects in such groups also have a natural tendency to cling together, and to glue surrounding objects to the group. To collaborate, objects need references, so that class names of collaborators are hard-wired into the objects. In the end, one tends to end up with an unmanageable lump of objects for an application.

↰1.1 ↰11.3.3.8

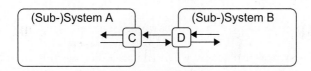

Figure 12.8 Boundary Objects Between Subsystems

📖24

»12.4

↰1.8.1

To avoid this, software of any size at all must be broken up into largely independent subsystems. Development can then be organized around this structure, and the design and implementation can proceed at least partly in parallel; in the best case, one may even reuse some subsystems between products. Ideally, collaboration between subsystems is then channeled through a few well-chosen and well-defined *boundary objects* (Fig. 12.8). Their role is that of interfacers that enable communication, but they also serve to protect and encapsulate the subsystem from the outside world, and shield it from changes elsewhere.

↰1.7.2
↰2.4.3
↰2.4.1

We have already seen several instances of boundary objects. For example, facades facilitate communication from clients to service providers inside a different subsystem. Remote proxies channel method invocations through byte streams. Adapters can bridge semantic gaps between object interfaces of different subsystems. All of these are, however, not very strict and rather incidental: They mainly perform those translations that are inevitable.

Boundary objects can define the clients' expectations.

One very good reason for introducing boundary objects is that the remainder of the subsystem may not yet exist. Suppose, for instance, that in Fig. 12.8 subsystem A is under development and relies on B. Unfortunately, B has been subcontracted to a different company and will not be available for a few months. In the current context, all decisions regarding B will be made elsewhere and must be localized in B.

↰5.3.2.1

It is then useful to design boundary objects D through which all calls to B will be channeled. Be very careful and diligent about their API, but only mock up their behavior for the time being. The unique chance here is that you can define the objects D according to your own expectations, creating a "wish list" for the later functionality. You can even hand the classes to the other company and ask for a proper implementation.

Boundary objects can insulate subsystems from changes elsewhere.

Very often, one of the subsystems in Fig. 12.8 is somewhat volatile. It may be a third-party library under active development, a prototype that will eventually evolve into a real implementation, or even a mock-up that so far answers only a few well-defined requests. For instance, if B is volatile but keeps the behavior of boundary object D consistent throughout the changes, then A can remain stable.

Boundary objects can confine unknown or complex APIs.

One particular instance occurs when you are quite unsure about some API you have to use. You know that you can accomplish some task, but you do not yet know the best, the most idiomatic, the most well-established way of doing it. In terms of the overall guideline of localization, you cannot decide what the best implementation really is. Just working on this basis means spreading your shallow knowledge throughout your production code: After you have learned more about the API, you will have to go back and perform massive shotgun surgery.

📖92

Suppose, for instance, that we want to write an editor for an XML document containing the description of vector graphics, similar to SVG. Model-view separation demands that the user interface observes the XML document. But then neither the standard `Document` nor `Element` provides methods for adding and removing listeners! After some web searching, we find that `EventTarget` is the thing we need. But then the event model of the W3C DOM specification does look somewhat complex and also a bit intimidating.

↰9.1

So we start thinking about a subsystem "picture DOM" that encapsulates the handling of standard DOM objects as representations of pictures. One particular boundary object will hide the complexity of the native event model. What we really want is to be notified about the "obvious" tree manipulations through a standard OBSERVER pattern. So we start by defining the listener interface, which also belongs to the boundary of the "picture DOM."

↰2.1
↰2.1.2

```
pictures.picturedom.DOMModificationListener
```
```
public interface DOMModificationListener {
    void nodeInserted(Element elem, Element parent);
    void nodeRemoved(Element elem, Element parent);
    void attributeModified(Element elem, Attr attr);
}
```

Then we create the facade object itself according to our expectations.

```
pictures.picturedom.PictureDOMFacade
```
```
public class PictureDOMFacade implements EventListener {
    ...
    private ListenerList listeners = new ListenerList();
    private Document doc;
    ...
    public void addDOMModificationListener(
        DOMModificationListener l) {
        ...
    }
    public void removeDOMModificationListener(
        DOMModificationListener l) {
        ...
    }
    ...
}
```

It is only when implementing the facade that we have to understand the DOM event model. In fact, it is sufficient to understand it partially: If later on we learn more, we will then be in a position to adapt the implementation without touching the remaining system. Upon searching for references to the EventTarget interface in the Eclipse platform code, we find that we will have to register for all relevant events separately. The events are named and it seems that no constants are available. This does look messy! Fortunately, we are sure we can change the code if we happen to learn we overlooked something.

---
pictures.picturedom.PictureDOMFacade

```java
public static final String DOM_NODE_INSERTED = "DOMNodeInserted";
public static final String DOM_NODE_REMOVED = "DOMNodeRemoved";
    ...
public static final String[] EVENTS = { DOM_NODE_INSERTED,
        DOM_NODE_REMOVED, DOM_ATTR_MODIFIED };
private void hookDocument() {
    if (doc == null || listeners.isEmpty())
        return;
    EventTarget target = (EventTarget) doc;
    for (String evt : EVENTS)
        target.addEventListener(evt, this, false);
}
```

The final step is to translate the native notifications into the desired ones. Here we go—once again the code is open for future improvements.

---
pictures.picturedom.PictureDOMFacade.handleEvent

```java
public final void handleEvent(Event evt) {
    if (evt instanceof MutationEvent) {
        MutationEvent mut = (MutationEvent) evt;
        if (DOM_ATTR_MODIFIED.equals(mut.getType())) {
            fireAttributeModified((Element) mut.getTarget(),
                    (Attr) mut.getRelatedNode());
        } else
            ...
    }
}
```

Combine boundary objects with roles for further abstraction.

📖172(Ch.8)
↩12.2.1.3

It is often useful to combine the technique of boundary objects with the definition of roles for their minimal expected behavior. The Eclipse platform uses this throughout. For instance, JavaCore creates Java model elements that are specified through interfaces. Similarly, the ResourcesPlugin doles out handles to concrete resources, but the static types are always interfaces.

Boundary objects can isolate subsystems from failures elsewhere.

↩4.5

Quite apart from the structural benefits of explicit boundary objects, they also have advantages at runtime. As we have seen, effective development and efficient execution always require a good deal of trust: The non-redundancy principle demands that methods never check their pre-conditions, and every caller relies on invoked methods to actually establish the post-conditions they promise. In cross-module calls, this may not always be justified; perhaps the "other" developers do not share our understanding about the contracts.

↰4.1

For instance, the `NotificationManager` sits on the boundary of the Eclipse resource management. Objects from all over the application register to receive change events, and the manager sends these out in due turn. This sending step is a bit dangerous: If any of the listeners throws an exception, it might upset the consistency of the resource data structures. At this crucial point, the notification manager prevents this dangerous outcome from happening by wrapping the notification through `SafeRunner`.

```
                    org.eclipse.core.internal.events.NotificationManager

private void notify(
      ResourceChangeListenerList.ListenerEntry[] resourceListeners,
      final IResourceChangeEvent event, final boolean lockTree) {
   for (int i = 0; i < resourceListeners.length; i++) {
      SafeRunner.run(new ISafeRunnable() {
         public void run() throws Exception {
            listener.resourceChanged(event);
         }
      });
   }
}
```

12.2.1.7 Factories

A particularly strong form of coupling arises from the creation of objects: Java gives us only one chance of setting an object's type and general behavior—namely, by choosing its class at creation time. Enabling flexibility here means introducing factory methods or abstract factories. The term "virtual constructor" for a factory method summarizes the benefit very clearly: We are suddenly able to override the creation step itself. Since we have already seen many examples, both in the small and in the large, we merely point out the power of the technique here.

↰1.4.12

↰1.4.12

Another connection is worth mentioning: Factories work best when combined with roles. The return type of a creation method must be general enough to enable different implementations. Specifying an abstract base class rather than an interface constrains the choice of implementations. Even so, it keeps the overall structure less abstract and more tangible and might improve understandability.

↰12.2.1.3

↰3.2.10

12.2.1.8 Observers

Most collaborations have very concrete participants: One object requires a service of a second object or notifies that object about some event. Both objects are designed at the same time and in lockstep to ensure the collaboration is smooth and effective. While elaborating the different use cases

↰11.1

↰11.3.2
↰4.1 ↰6.1.2 ↰6.1

with CRC cards, we trace through these concrete collaborations. One step further toward the implementation, we design the contracts of the method calls to achieve a sensible distribution of work between the caller and the callee.

Observers enable flexible collaborations and flexible behavior.

↰2.1
↰2.1.2

The OBSERVER pattern offers the chance of more flexible collaboration schemes. At its core, the subject specifies the observer interface by considering only its own possible modifications, but never the concrete expected observers. As a result, the subject knows next to nothing about its observers. In turn, new observers can be added in a very flexible manner and existing observers can be changed without breaking the subject.

↰2.1.3

At the same time, the commonly used push variant of the pattern provides the observers with so much detailed information that they are really well informed about the subject. It is almost as if the subject is constantly collaborating with its observers, since the most significant occurrences in an object's life are usually connected to its state.

An observer can then implement quite complex functionality based on the information it receives. For instance, by observing Eclipse's resources, one can update the user interface or compute and track meta-information about files. Just look through the callers of addResourceChange Listener() in IWorkspace to get an impression of the breadth of the possible applications.

12.2.1.9　Inversion of Control

The OBSERVER pattern introduces callbacks. As we saw in the previous section, these can be helpful for achieving flexibility. However, the callbacks are restricted to changes in an object's technical state. One step beyond, one can ask which events within an object's life cycle may be relevant to others, even if the object's state does not change. A flexible system then emerges, because the events are detected and distributed regardless of their receivers.

An event-driven style keeps objects loosely coupled.

↰12.1

Suppose we apply this idea to the "big players" in a network (Fig. 12.9). These objects may use local helpers, indicated with thin dashed lines. But it is the big players that tie together the overall system, by communicating among themselves. Now, rather than sending messages tailored to the receivers, they send out events about themselves without caring about the receivers. The receivers react to the events and broadcast new events about themselves. As the thick dashed lines indicate, the "big" objects remain largely independent and are coupled very loosely, because none of them makes too many assumptions about the event receivers.

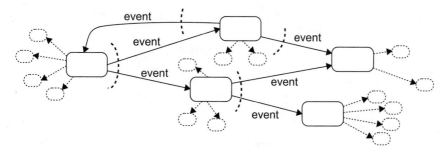

Figure 12.9 Flexibility Through Inversion of Control

We may ask, for instance, why SWT is such a flexible and versatile ↰7.1
widget toolkit. It is certainly not its artistic quality and beauty—SWT
does nothing about that anyway. SWT's widgets are flexible because they
offer so many different events capturing possible user interactions. As a
result, almost any application functionality can be built on top of SWT,
because that functionality can be triggered at the right moments.

The object-oriented perspective on method calls is message passing. We do not think ↰1.4.1 ▯109
about technical aspects such as call stacks, dynamic dispatch, and parameter passing,
nor do we expect a particular piece of code to be executed for a method call. Instead,
an object sends out a message and trusts the receiver to take the appropriate action.
The attraction of this fundamental notion becomes even clearer in the light of event-
based communication. Messages can then be understood as "I think something like this
should happen," rather than "Please do this for me." With this looser interpretation,
the receiver is more flexible in its reactions. If applied throughout the design, the looser
interpretation leads to more flexible systems.

Inversion of control keeps the system flexible.

Events also come with inversion of control: It is the sender of the event, not ↰7.3.2
its receiver, that determines when a reaction or functionality is required. In
Fig. 12.9, the receivers are content knowing that an event has occurred, but
they do not inquire about the exact internal circumstances in which this
has happened. In the end, inversion of control, rather than the events themselves, makes for the increased flexibility, because many different behaviors
can be attached to an event source. ↠12.3.2

Let us look at a concrete example, the *Outline View* of Eclipse. That
view somehow manages to show the structure of any type of file, whether it
contains Java sources, XML data, or a bundle manifest. How does this work?
The construction assembles the view by inheritance. The class `Content` ↰12.2.1.2
`Outline` derives from `PageBookView`. That class tracks the currently active
editor and caches a *page* for each of the views and editors. All pages are
contained in a *page book* and the currently required one is brought on top.

↰7.1

To keep informed about the active editor, the `PageBookView` registers a listener when it shows itself on the screen:

org.eclipse.ui.part.PageBookView

```
public void createPartControl(Composite parent) {
    book = new PageBook(parent, SWT.NONE);
    ...
    getSite().getPage().addPartListener(partListener);
    ...
}
```

»12.3.3.4

⌕ The *site* of a view is the context in which it is shown and gives the view access to its surroundings. The *page* of a workbench window contains all views and editors.

Here is the first case of flexibility brought about by inversion of control: The overall workbench window does not care about exactly which views are shown. The notifications about the active view or editor work equally well for all of them.

↰2.1.3

The events about part changes arrive, through a private anonymous class, at the method `partActivated()` in `PageBookView`. At this point, the `PageBookView` decides that a new page must be created if it does not exist.

org.eclipse.ui.part.PageBookView

```
public void partActivated(IWorkbenchPart part) {
    ...
    PageRec rec = getPageRec(part);
    if (rec == null) {
        rec = createPage(part);
    }
    ...
}
```

Here, the second instance of inversion of control occurs: The `PageBookView` decides that a page must be created and its `createPage()` method calls the following `doCreatePage()`. In other words, the class asks its concrete subclass to actually provide the page:

org.eclipse.ui.part.PageBookView

```
protected abstract PageRec doCreatePage(IWorkbenchPart part);
```

At this point, we find inversion of control a third time: The `Content Outline` view asks the currently active editor for an `IContentOutline Page` (lines 2–3); then it asks the retrieved page to render itself within the page book (line 7)—the fourth specimen of inversion of control.

org.eclipse.ui.views.contentoutline.ContentOutline

```
1 protected PageRec doCreatePage(IWorkbenchPart part) {
2     Object obj = ViewsPlugin.getAdapter(part,
```

```
3                             IContentOutlinePage.class, false);
4       if (obj instanceof IContentOutlinePage) {
5           IContentOutlinePage page = (IContentOutlinePage) obj;
6           ...
7           page.createControl(getPageBook());
8           return new PageRec(part, page);
9       }
10      return null;
11  }
```

Inversion of control localizes decisions.

But let us go back to the overall guideline: To keep a system flexible, try to localize decisions. The example of the outline view shows clearly how inversion of control achieves this. Each step makes one decision, but delegates others to the respective callee. The workbench window's page delegates reactions to the user's switching of the active editor; the PageBook View delegates the creation of a particular page; the ContentOutline asks the current editor to provide the actual page. The decision of what to do in each step rests with the object taking the step and does not depend on the other objects involved.

From a different point of view, the scenario and the techniques can be seen as a case of extensibility: The PageBook caters to many types of pages; the ContentOutline works with different kinds of editors. Then, the overall strategy is covered by the INTERCEPTOR pattern. You may want to peek ahead now or to come back later to explore this link in more detail.

» 12.3
» 12.3.2

12.2.2 The Layers Pattern

Developers like to think in terms of high-level and low-level aspects of their software. For example, the business logic is high-level, the necessary networking is low-level. JFace is more high-level than SWT, because we connect widgets directly to the application's data structures instead of placing strings and images into the widgets. In addition, the user interface focuses on a pleasant user experience and delegates the details of processing to the model.

↤9.3

↤9.1

It is often useful to apply Separation of Concerns along these lines—that is, to treat high-level aspects in one module and low-level aspects in another. As the previously mentioned examples show, the perspective determines precisely what is high-level and what is low-level. The perspective is based on an implicit measure of "abstraction" (Fig. 12.10):

↤11.5.2

📖59

(a) The business logic assumes that it can send data over the network, but it is not concerned with the wires that transport the data.

(b) An application may be using a library of standard graph algorithms, which in turn relies on the basic data structures from the JDK.

(c) JFace provides mechanisms for mapping data to SWT widgets and spares the application the direct setting of strings and images; the SWT layer in turn spares JFace the details of the native window system and makes it platform-independent.

(d) The user interface orchestrates only the processing steps available in the model.

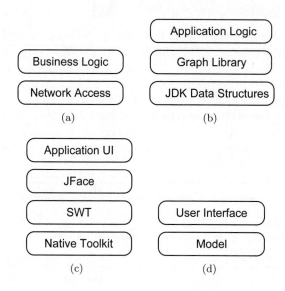

Figure 12.10 The Layers Pattern

📖101,59

The LAYERS pattern captures this idea. The notion of "layers" is, indeed, folklore in development practice. The pattern adds several details that the naive view neglects. These details are, however, crucial to gain the full benefits of a layered design.

PATTERN: LAYERS

Structure a system by splitting its functionality into a stack of layers according to a chosen abstraction criterion.

1. Choose and fix a suitable abstraction criterion.

2. Align the functionality along the scale of abstraction.

3. Split the functionality into layers, focusing on cohesion.

4. Define the interfaces between adjacent layers.

The presentation in [59] proposes nine steps in the implementation. We have sum-marized them here to give a better idea of the overall intention. We will later fill in the details.

Fig. 12.11(a) gives the overall idea of the pattern. We arrange the re-sponsibilities we find into modules along an increasing level of abstraction. The lowest module is layer 1. Each layer communicates only with its ad-jacent neighbors. In particular, a layer never reaches more than one layer away. Fig. 12.11(b) adds further details about that communication. Very often, the downward calls constitute service requests: to send data over the network, to display specific data on the screen, or to perform a particular computation on the application data. Upward calls, in contrast, are very often notifications, such as about the availability of network data, about clicks in the user interface, or changes to the data stored in the model.

The attentive reader will note immediately that the JFace/SWT example violates   ↰9.3.1
the principle of never "going around" layers from Fig. 12.11(a), since the application will, indeed, access SWT widgets directly. We will come back to this point later.

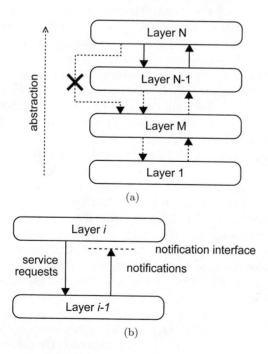

Figure 12.11 The Layers Pattern

↰12.1

We will now examine these aspects in greater detail and analyze their impact on the success of applying the LAYERS pattern. Decoupling is a cross-cutting concern: The particular structure from Fig. 12.11(a) enables higher-level and lower-level parts of the system to vary independently.

Formulate the abstraction criterion carefully.

The central choice in implementing the pattern is the abstraction criterion: It determines the order of the layers and the distribution of responsibilities between them. The criterion very often is just the amount of technical detail to be considered, such as when placing network functionality in a layer below the application's business logic. But it may actually require some thinking to come up with a coherent solution.

To see the impact of the chosen abstraction criterion, let us reexamine a well-known and seemingly obvious example: the user interface stack of native toolkit, SWT, JFace, and application UI depicted in Fig. 12.10(c). The underlying abstraction criterion is the "amount of technical detail."

↰9.1

A completely different sequence of layers results from starting with the principle of model-view separation. That principle suggests that the foundation is the application's business logic, so let us change the abstraction criterion to "distance from the business logic."

Fig. 12.12(a) shows the result. The actual SWT interface is as far removed from the application model as possible and the intermediate layers connect the two endpoints. With a bit of imagination, even the communication between the layers can be interpreted as service requests and notifications: When the user clicks a button, this is a service request that gets translated through the layers to an eventual change of the application

↰9.2.1

model. In the reverse direction, the MODEL-VIEW-CONTROLLER pattern suggests that change notifications travel upward until eventually they reach the SWT widgets. All in all, the layering resulting from the new abstraction criterion expresses much better the ideas and design choices of model-view separation.

Even so, this interpretation of services and notifications is a little forced. At the technical level, as shown in Fig. 12.12(b), the "notifications" from the application's special UI objects to the JFace viewers and from there to the SWT widgets are actually simple method calls and therefore service requests. In the other direction, the "service requests" from SWT and JFace to the application layer are actually transported through OBSERVERS—that is, they are notifications. Even if the new criterion explains the software structure well, we will not be able to claim the benefits of LAYERS, such as the exchangeability of the lower layers.

This example shows that the abstraction criterion is not arbitrary, but rather must be formulated explicitly and with care. On the one hand, seemingly obvious criteria may have alternatives. On the other hand, not all criteria lead to a proper implementation at the technical level.

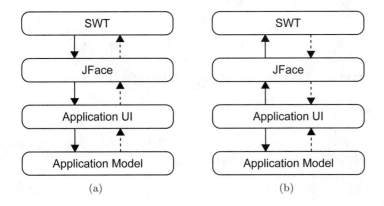

Figure 12.12 Alternative View on Layers Involving JFace

Split the functionality into layers.

After defining an abstraction criterion, we start with responsibility-driven   ↰11.1
design, using the layers as units instead of objects. However, we get some
more help than from CRC cards alone: Whenever we find a new responsibility, we can place it by the linear measure of the abstraction criterion.
We are not designing a full network of objects, but a linear stack with very
restricted interactions. Very often, responsibilities will "fall" close to each
other in this placement. In the example of network access, establishing a
connection is naturally close to sending data over the connection. The layers
then arise from clusters of responsibilities.

Maximize the cohesion of each layer.

In general, the number and the exact boundaries of the layers require some
thought. It might even take some adjustments to the formulation of the
criterion to reach a convincing structure.

Take the example of wizards in user interfaces. Should they be placed
in the JFace or the SWT layer in Fig. 12.10(c)? In principle, a wizard is
just a special compound widget that contains a series of pages to be displayed; it has nothing to do with mapping the application data. Wizards
should therefore be in the SWT layer. However, we want the SWT layer to
be minimal, because it must be cloned for different window systems. The   ↰7.4
somewhat generic criterion "technical detail" used earlier should be made
more precise as "distance to the native widget toolkit": Mapping data is
still a step above accessing the native widgets, but wizards are not actually
offered as native widgets, so they are just one notch further up the abstraction scale and can be moved to the JFace layer, where they are shared
between platforms.

The general goal is, of course, not some conceptually "pleasing" assignment of responsibilities to layers. Instead, the goal is to maximize the cohesion within layers. Each layer then establishes one self-contained, meaningful abstraction step along the scale of the criterion, and it contains all the necessary software machinery to take this step effectively.

↩12.1.3

Design the intralayer structure carefully.

We have often seen beginners present a thoroughly designed layers concept for an application as a preparation for a lab exercise, only to end up with the most disastrous code base in the final submission. The reason is that they stopped thinking after having "fulfilled" the exercise's goal of a layered design.

↩11.1

The layers are just the first step. They set the general scene, but you still have to fill in the objects and collaborations within the layers to make the software work smoothly. Think of all the details of JFace's rendering of wizards: the concrete dialogs, the interfaces of single pages and wizards, and the abstract base classes for implementing the interfaces easily. Without this careful work, introducing a JFace layer does not help at all.

Design the layer interfaces carefully.

The specific form of interaction between adjacent layers, which is shown in Fig. 12.11(b) on page 671, is responsible for many of the benefits of the LAYERS pattern. Here is the first point:

A layer is not aware of the identity of the next higher layer.

Fig. 12.11(b) demands that a layer communicate with its upper neighbor only through an interface specifically designed for the purpose. A layer is not aware of the exact identity of the next layer up, because that identity is hidden behind the interface. Think of a networking layer. It serves all kinds of applications as diverse as web browsers, telephone conference software, and remote sensing technology.

↩12.2.1
↩2.1.2

💡 We have seen the power of special-purpose interfaces several times in the techniques for decoupling. In particular, the OBSERVER pattern designs the observer interface from the perspective of the subject alone, without making assumptions about possible observers. This coincides with the idea of notifications for LAYERS. Similarly, the

↩11.5.6

Dependency Inversion Principle focuses the design on some important functionality and specifies its requirements on its collaborators.

Lower layers are insulated from higher-level changes.

The definition of a special notification interface for upward calls shown in Fig. 12.11(b) creates the immediate benefit of making lower layers independent of higher layers. As a result, the lower layers can be developed and tested independently. The technical, basic, detailed functionality is then stable and available early on in the project.

Higher layers can be insulated from lower-level changes.

In the other direction, higher layers are insulated from changes in the lower layers. With respect to the general guideline of localizing decisions, it is precisely the less abstract, the more intricate, and the potentially more obscure functionality that remains changeable. This is certainly a very desirable outcome for any design. But let us look at the details of why this really works out—it is easy to get them wrong in the implementation.

The fundamental approach is that each layer communicates only with its direct neighbors, so that changes further down in the stack will not affect its functionality. The most famous example is, of course, the Internet Protocol stack [Fig. 12.13(a)]. The success of the Internet depends crucially on the fact that the lowest *link* layer, which deals with the physical networks to which a host is attached, can be exchanged: It must only relay packages, but the *IP* layer, which handles the global routing of packages, does not care whether a LAN, WLAN, or VPN is used for this purpose.

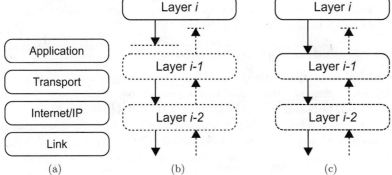

Figure 12.13 Exchangeability of Lower Layers

Of course, the exchangeability of lower layers does not come for free. One has to fix an interface on which the higher layer can rely [Fig. 12.13(b); dashed layers are exchangeable]. In effect, the interface defines a standard that any implementors of the layer have to obey. Defining the interface can be quite a challenge—the definition of the Internet Protocol as we know it took more than two decades, from the first research to the robust protocols.

Locally, one can resort to taking an existing layer with its working upward interface, and replace only its implementation [Fig.12.13(c)]. This idea
is seen in the design of the SWT layer: The classes' public interfaces are the
same on each window system, but their implementation must be developed
nearly from scratch for each one.

↰7.4

Do not bypass layers.

We emphasize that all of the previously mentioned benefits result from
the fact that layers communicate only with their immediate neighbors and
therefore form a linear stack. Accessing lower layers directly destroys the
benefits [see also Fig. 12.11(a)].

Layers can enable reuse of lower-level modules.

A further huge benefit gained by layers is the potential for reuse. Because a
layer is not aware of the identity of its higher neighbor, chances are that it is
reusable in a different context. Examples have been seen in Fig. 12.10(a)–(c)
on page 670, where the lower layers contain reusable functionality.

It is again important to choose the right abstraction criterion. Rather
than considering technical detail, distance to the user interface, or something similar, one must use the generality of the provided functionality.
Also, one has to choose the specific layer interfaces to match this generality. For instance, the SWT widget set is reusable only because it is designed
carefully to capture the requirements of standard desktop applications. The
layer of network sockets is so successful because its generic byte streams enable applications to encode their data as they see fit.

📖237

Translate errors to match the abstraction level.

One detail of a layer's interface that often gives away the novice is error
handling. In general, errors must match the purpose of the component that
raises them. Otherwise, the clients cannot interpret them properly. In the
case of layers, errors must therefore match a layer's abstraction level. Errors
received from lower-level layers must usually be translated.

↰1.5.1

Handle errors in the lowest possible layer.

Layers offer a unique chance of shielding an application from low-level errors
altogether. For instance, the IP layer of the Internet stack [Fig. 12.13(a)]
does not guarantee delivery. The TCP protocol on the next higher *transport*
layer makes up for this shortcoming by arranging redelivery of unacknowl-
edged packets. If some layer is therefore able to recover from the errors
received from a lower level, it should do so.

📖237

Relaxed layers can mitigate some problems with strict layers.

Adhering to the communication discipline between layers strictly can lead to several problems. Very often, lower layers define extensive interfaces that enable their clients to take advantage of all technical details they have to offer. Higher-level layers then abstract over these details and the extra functionality is lost. For instance, the native widgets encapsulated by SWT offer all platform-specific features. However, SWT carefully exposes only those features that can be used reliably across platforms.

In general, all the functionality required by higher layers must be passed on throughout the stack. Sometimes, this is undesirable because it pollutes the higher-level interfaces with low-level detail, even if only some clients require them. The RELAXED LAYERS pattern acknowledges this by allowing direct accesses around layers [contrary to Fig. 12.11(a)]. 59

The JFace layer is a good example (Fig. 12.14). It relies on SWT for ↰9.3 the actual display of data, but does not hide that layer completely. The application still specifies layouts and visual attributes on the basic SWT ↰7.1 widgets, and it is always aware of the SWT-level widget tree. As a result, JFace can focus completely on adding higher-level services, which minimizes the implementation effort.

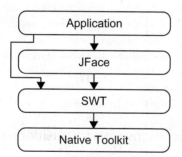

Figure 12.14 Relaxed Layers in SWT/JFace

Beware of rippling changes.

Layers are a folklore concept, and any team facing the design of a larger system will probably first think about chopping the task up into layers, if for no other reason than to separate the high-level (interesting) tasks from the low-level (tedious) tasks. It is very important not get carried away by enthusiasm at this point: All the benefits of the pattern rely on the stability of the layers' interfaces. Once some interface of a low layer changes, chances are that the higher-level layers need to change as well. In fact, the pattern increases coupling rather than decreasing it. It is therefore very important ↰12.1.1 to plan the layers conscientiously from the start, rather than to start coding with a vague intuitive understanding.

> In agile development, create LAYERS in vertical slices.

In many other places, we have pointed out the benefits of agile development and in particular of the approach of building "the simplest thing that could possibly work." The LAYERS pattern introduces a possible snag here: The design guidelines imply that we find a perfect and fixed set of layers and their interfaces before we implement the internals. This goes against the grain of agile development.

↰5.4.5

The solution is to apply another principle, that of delivering a useful increment of functionality in each iteration. Rather than designing the layers completely, we again let concrete use cases and test cases drive the design. In this way, we create a small part of each layer's interfaces and implementation in each iteration. Effectively, we develop the stack of layers in small, vertical slices.

12.3 Extensibility

↰12.2

Changeability is a crucial nonfunctional property for any professional software. One particularly important kind of changeability is extensibility. New use cases and new requirements keep arising all the time once a system is deployed. Very often, it is only at this point that users begin to realize what *could* be done in software—and then they continue asking for new features all the time. This section examines architectural approaches to extensibility, after providing an introduction to its technical aspects.

12.3.1 Basic Techniques and Considerations

One of the great attractions of object-oriented software development is that objects offer strong support for extensibility. At the most basic level, instantiating objects clones their functionality; extensibility here means doing the same thing as often as the users wish for. The technical basis for supporting entirely new use cases of a system is polymorphism: Similar kinds of objects can be created by overriding particular methods to inject new behavior.

↰1.4.1

↰3.1.11 ↰3.1.4 ↰3.1.6

Because undisciplined coding quickly leads to problems, we have already examined many guidelines and techniques that tame polymorphism:

↰3.1.1 ↰6.4

- The Liskov Substitution Principle dictates that new objects must obey the general behavior expected from their super-types. The interaction between subclass and superclass should be defined explicitly through protected methods.

↰3.1.2

↰1.4.9

- The TEMPLATE METHOD pattern designates specific hook methods where subclasses can place new functionality without breaking the superclass mechanisms.

- The EXTENSION OBJECTS pattern enables an object to expose new functionality without having to extend its interface.   ↰3.2.2 ↰3.2.5

- The COMPOSITE pattern supports new kinds of nodes in tree-structured data such that recursive operations work smoothly for the new cases.   ↰2.3.1

- The VISITOR pattern simplifies the introduction of new operations on fixed object structures.   ↰2.3.2

- The OBSERVER pattern transmits messages to any new kind of interested object. New behavior can then be attached in an event-driven way.   ↰2.1 ↰12.2.1.8 ↰7.1

- The STATE pattern covers extensions of behaviors of individual objects that are essentially state-dependent.   ↰10.3.4

Extensibility: to be able to do similar things again with little additional work.

The techniques listed previously may seem rather comprehensive and their scope may seem promising. Perhaps it is, after all, very simple to build extensible systems, if we just combine the right techniques?

Unfortunately, this is not the case. The overall goal of extensibility is much broader than just making the implementation "flexible" at sufficiently many points or providing enough "hooks" where new code can be injected into the existing mechanisms.

Extensibility must aim at making extensions simple, while not overly complicating the design and implementation of the basic application. This means that the appropriate techniques must be applied at well-chosen spots; applying them throughout clutters the sources and makes it almost impossible to find the right spot to hook up a desired extension. Furthermore, the precise API of callbacks must be thought through in detail—extensions must be provided with enough information to go ahead with their tasks, yet they must not be overwhelmed. In the end, extensibility is attractive only if extensions are simple and follow well-defined patterns.

Extensibility requires keeping the application's code base stable.

One of the crucial challenges of extensibility is to keep the overall application stable. Almost any software is "extensible" in the sense that it can be restructured and rewritten to accommodate new functionality. True extensibility means that no extra work on the existing code base is required to incorporate such additions. If this cannot be achieved, nothing is won and much is lost by trying for "extensibility": The overhead for extensible mechanisms must be invested, but it never pays off, because each addition requires still more work on the base application. In other words, designing for extensibility involves a high potential for "speculative generality."   📖92

⬑7.3.2

»12.3.3.5

Extensions are best integrated by inversion of control.

Extensions are kept simple if they perform just a small and well-defined task at specific, well-defined points. Inversion of control is a prime approach to achieving this goal: The application takes care of running the software, and the extension can hang back until it is called.

To illustrate the previous two points, here is a prototypical example of a well-designed API for extensions. Eclipse's Java editor includes a most powerful completion pop-up. As we saw in Part I, the "completions" can be rather complex code patterns. To keep the main Java plugin small, the pop-up offers an extension point to which other plugins can contribute. The API is straightforward and minimal: Whenever the pop-up opens, the extension will be asked to supply proposals as self-contained objects. The given `context` contains the document and the current cursor position, so that the provider can pick up any textual context it requires.

```
org.eclipse.jdt.ui.text.java.IJavaCompletionProposalComputer
```
```
public interface IJavaCompletionProposalComputer {
    List<ICompletionProposal> computeCompletionProposals(
                            ContentAssistInvocationContext context,
                            IProgressMonitor monitor);

    ...

}
```

Anticipate the kinds and forms of additional behaviors.

One fundamental prerequisite for creating an extensible application is knowing which types or forms of extensions will likely be useful. If the scope is too broad, the individual extension becomes too complex. If it is too small, desirable extensions may not be possible. You can make accurate predictions only if you have worked on a variety of applications in the same area and know the variations in features that are likely to be required.

Solve two or three scenarios by hand before implementing extensibility.

Abstraction is always a challenging task to complete, and the abstraction over the desirable extensions is no exception. The "rule of three" applies, as usual: It is a good idea to build two or three instances manually, perhaps even choosing between them with crude `if-then-else` constructs. This implementation gives you two crucial insights. First, you know that the extensibility will really be necessary, because you know five to ten similar pieces of functionality that would be useful. Second, you get a good feeling for the technical requirements of all this functionality. Your chances of getting the extension interface right increase dramatically with this approach.

12.3.2   The Interceptor Pattern

There are many forms and variants of mechanisms that make a software extensible, but they all share a few common central characteristics. Knowing these characteristics will help you understand the concrete extensibility mechanisms—the individual API elements and code snippets will fall into place almost at once. The INTERCEPTOR pattern gives the overall picture.   📖218

PATTERN: INTERCEPTOR

Allow new *services* to be added to a *framework* such that the *framework* remains unchanged and the *services* are called back when specific events occur.

🔍 The term "framework" is typically used in the sense of a semi-complete application   ↰7.3
that captures the mechanisms common to a family of applications in a reusable form.
Here, the term focuses on the aspect of inversion of control: The framework defines the   ↰7.3.2
overall computation and calls back to the new services at its own discretion. The pattern
also applies to ordinary software that is to be extensible at certain points.

The central elements of the pattern, which are also the recurring elements of extensible software, are gathered in Fig. 12.15(a). We will now describe them one-by-one, going left-to-right, top-to-bottom. As a running example, we will again use the Java auto-completion mechanism. Since our   ↠12.3.3.5
aim is to obtain a common blueprint for the later studies, we will not go
into the details of implementing the INTERCEPTOR pattern.   📖218

Interception points designate useful hooks for adding new services.

The pattern's first insight on extensibility is that one has to provide specific, well-defined points within the software that will receive the extensions. If we just provide arbitrary hooks in arbitrary places, the software becomes unmaintainable, because the services know too much about its existing internal structure. The pattern calls these points of extensibility *interception*   ↰12.1.2
points because the services intercept the normal processing: They receive the control flow and perform their computation before the software resumes its operation. Fig. 12.15(a) indicates the control flow as a dashed, curved path.

In the running example, the interceptor must implement the interface `IJavaCompletionProposalComputer`. The service produces a list of proposals for the pop-up dialog.

```
           org.eclipse.jdt.ui.text.java.IJavaCompletionProposalComputer

public interface IJavaCompletionProposalComputer {
    List<ICompletionProposal> computeCompletionProposals(
                        ContentAssistInvocationContext context,
```

```
                     IProgressMonitor monitor);
        ...
}
```

In practice, each interception point will offer several logically related callbacks, which are rendered as methods in a common interface that the service has to implement. The pattern calls these sets of callbacks *interception groups*. We have omitted the other methods in the interface in the preceding code snippet for brevity, but they are there.

»12.3.3.5

Context objects enable interceptors to query and influence the framework.

A new service must usually interact with the framework to request data or to influence the future processing. Toward that end, the framework passes a *context object*, which offers a selection of access paths to the framework's internals without revealing them. The context object can be seen as a FACADE; its API is usually specified through an interface to decouple the interceptors from the framework's implementation.

↰1.7.2 ↰3.2.7 ↰12.2.1.3

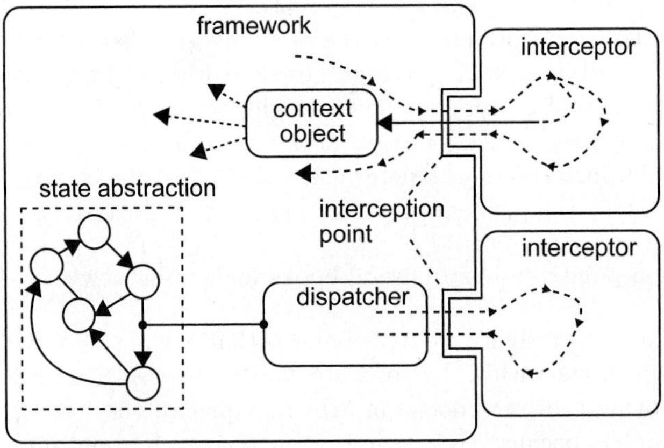

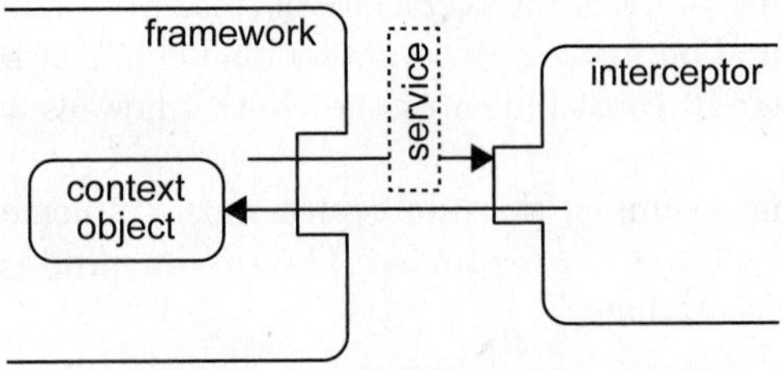

Figure 12.15 Overview of the Interceptor Pattern

In the example, the `ContentAssistInvocationContext` passed to the method `computeCompletionProposals()` gives access to the textual context where the completion was requested.

Extensibility works best with lean interfaces for interaction.

Fig. 12.15(b) summarizes the interaction between framework and interceptors. The framework invokes callbacks on the interceptors through a designated service interface; the interceptors in turn can access selected functionality from the framework through the context object. The point of the illustration, and indeed of the pattern, is that the interaction remains lean and focused, since all possible calls are specified by only two interfaces. In the example, knowing `IJavaCompletionProposalComputer` and `Content AssistInvocationContext` is sufficient to understand the interception point.

🔎 In fact, both the context object and the service interface in the example of Java completions are subclassed, so that more specific services are accessible on both sides. This is an instance of the EXTENSION INTERFACE pattern.

»12.3.3.5

↰3.2.5

💡 The INTERCEPTOR pattern focuses on black-box frameworks. The lean API makes for easy extensibility.

↰7.3.3

Callbacks to services occur for specific transitions in the framework state.

One crucial question with any arrangement for callbacks is when the callbacks will actually take place: the implementors of the interceptors can provide their services reliably only if they can be sure that callbacks will occur as expected.

The pattern proposes to create an abstraction on the framework's internal state in the form of a state machine [Fig. 12.15(a), lower half]. Since it is only an abstraction, it can be published to implementors of interceptors without revealing the framework's internals. The state machine can, in fact, be read as a specification of the framework's behavior, which will be useful in any case.

↰10.1

The link between the framework state and the interception points is established by the transitions of the state machine. Special transitions that are potentially relevant to new services are reported as events and lead to callbacks.

We examined the state machine for completion pop-ups in Fig. 10.8 on page 536. When the transition from a closed to an open pop-up window is made, the framework will request the completion proposals. While

the pop-up remains open, the internal transition on text modifications will
again request the updated completions.

🔍 The state machine abstracts over such details as delays, timeouts, and progress
monitors. It highlights the points where the callbacks will occur.

Dispatchers manage interceptors and relay events.

Finally, there is a lot of boilerplate code involved in managing the interceptors attached to each interception point. The pattern proposes to see this
management as a self-contained responsibility and to assign it to special
dispatcher objects. The dispatchers also have methods that relay an event
to all registered interceptors, by invoking the respective callback methods.

» 12.3.3.2
In the example, a (singleton) object `CompletionProposalComputer`
`Registry` gathers and maintains the service providers implemented by different plugins. The completion pop-up can access them depending on the
document partition (e.g., source code, JavaDoc).

org.eclipse.jdt.internal.ui.text.java.CompletionProposalComputerRegistry

```
public final class CompletionProposalComputerRegistry {
    private final List<CompletionProposalComputerDescriptor>
                    fDescriptors;
    List<CompletionProposalComputerDescriptor>
        getProposalComputerDescriptors(String partition)
    ...

}
```

The dispatch of the callbacks is implemented for each computer separately, by `CompletionProposalComputerDescriptor`. The two classes
together therefore form a typical dispatcher mechanism.

org.eclipse.jdt.internal.ui.text.java.CompletionProposalComputerDescriptor

```
final class CompletionProposalComputerDescriptor {
    private IJavaCompletionProposalComputer fComputer;
    public List<ICompletionProposal> computeCompletionProposals(
            ContentAssistInvocationContext context,
            IProgressMonitor monitor)
    ...

}
```

Interceptors usually have an explicit life cycle.

Interception points usually specify further callbacks that are independent of
the framework's state transitions but concern the interceptors themselves.
The interceptors are notified when they are hooked to and unhooked from
the framework, or when they are no longer required. The context object
may also be passed to an initialization step.

In the example, the proposal computers are notified about the start and end of completion sessions. This enables the computers, for instance, to prepare for quick proposal retrieval by indexing and to discard any created indexes later on.

```
org.eclipse.jdt.ui.text.java.IJavaCompletionProposalComputer
```
```java
void sessionStarted();
void sessionEnded();
```

12.3.3   The Eclipse Extension Mechanism

The success of the Eclipse IDE is largely founded on its general mechanism of extension points: Any plugin in the platform can allow other plugins to contribute functionality at specific points. Examples are the items for menus and context menus, proposals for the Java editor's completion pop-up, available database types in the *Data Source Explorer*, and many more. The mechanism is often said to be complex and cumbersome, but usually by people who insist on editing the `plugin.xml` files by hand, rather than through the provided editors. The conceptual basis and the practical use of the mechanism are really rather straightforward and neat.

The first goal of this section is to demonstrate the simplicity of the mechanism itself, by first introducing its concepts and then giving a minimal example. Having cleared away the technical issues, we can concentrate on the real challenge of building extensible systems: One has to find an API for extensions that is general enough to cover all expected applications, but specific enough to keep the individual extensions small and straightforward. We will examine some existing extension points from the Eclipse IDE to approach this rather advanced topic on solid ground.

↰12.3.1

12.3.3.1   Overview

If extension points allow plugins to contribute new functionality at specific points, the key question is this: What does a typical piece of "contributed functionality" look like? At its heart, it usually consists of some callback that implements the new functionality. Many extensions can also be specified partly by data, which is often simpler than having an object return the data. For instance, a menu item is described by a string and an icon, beside an action object that implements the expected reaction.

↰9.3.4

  ⌕ Eclipse introduces yet another form of declarative indirection through *commands*.   ▥174
    The concrete code is contained in *handlers* for commands. This indirection helps in declarative bindings—for instance, from keystrokes to commands.

Extension points accept combinations of data and classes.

Fig. 12.16 illustrates the idea of passing data and code in the larger context of the overall mechanism. Some plugin A decides that it can accept contributions at some extension point E. Think of the Java completion pop-up that shows arbitrary lists of completion items. The plugin specifies a data format F and an interface I that all contributions must match. A plugin B that declares an extension must provide concrete data D and a class C implementing the interface I.

📖174
»12.3.3.2

The Eclipse platform then does the main part of the job: It links all extensions belonging to an extension point across all installed plugins. It even keeps track of changing sets of extensions when plugins are dynamically added, removed, and updated. As we shall see later, the infrastructure that Eclipse provides makes it very simple for plugin A to retrieve all extensions to access their contributions.

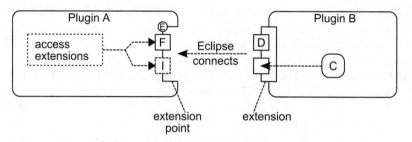

Figure 12.16 Extension Points in Eclipse

🔎 Just in case you are wondering: Of course, extensions can also accept several pieces of data and several classes at once. Each plugin can also have several extension points and several extensions. Finally, it is common for a plugin to extend its own extension points, usually to establish some basic functionality.

Extension points use data attributes to enable lazy loading.

↰1.1

Even if we do not usually talk about efficiency, we have to do so now to help you write professional extensions: The distinction between data and objects as attributes of extensions is key for the efficiency of the extension mechanism.

Think of a menu item sitting deep inside the menu hierarchy. It may never be invoked at all, or it may be invoked only in very special situations. To display the item, it is sufficient to know its icon and text. The actual action implementing the functionality is not required until the user happens to click on the menu item. The class mentioned in the extension needs to be loaded into memory before that.

This issue does not matter so much for single classes, but a large system will contain many thousands of such event handlers that should remain inactive until they are needed. And the OSGi framework used for managing

»A.1

Eclipse's plugins can do even more: A plugin from which no class has ever been instantiated does not have to be loaded at all. Since loading a plugin involves much analysis of its structure, this is a huge benefit. It is only this setup that allows you to have hundreds of plugins installed without paying with an enormous cost at startup time: The PHP plugin will be loaded only when you open the first PHP source file; the WindowBuilder is read in only when you try to edit a user interface widget graphically.

↰7.2

Learn to use the Eclipse tool support.

When developing Eclipse plugins with extensions, the same kind of editing steps recur very often. We will show the basic usage of the *Plugin Manifest Editor* later with a concrete example. You should also investigate the *Plugins* view, from which you can easily access the core information about existing plugins. In many situations, you can take a shortcut to the information you are looking for by using the two tools described next.

»12.3.3.2

TOOL: Search for Plugin Artifacts

The *Search/Plug-in* menu opens a search dialog that can be used to find plugins, extension points, and extensions by identifiers and parts of identifiers.

TOOL: Open Plugin Artifact

To jump quickly to a plugin, extension, or extension point, use *Navigate/Open Plugin Artifact* (Ctrl-Shift-A). The selection dialog performs quick filtering over the declarations in the workspace.

12.3.3.2 A Minimal Example

The Eclipse extension point mechanism is made to support big applications. Big mechanisms are best explained by tracing their workings through a minimal, but typical example. We will use a demo "service" provider that computes some result. See Section A.1.2 for working with plugin projects in general.

Capture the behavior of extensions with an interface or abstract base class.

The interface that follows captures the expectation for the provided "service." It plays the role of *I* in Fig. 12.16. We will later add a description of the service as a string to illustrate the use of data slot *F* in Fig. 12.16.

```
extpoint.IDemoHook
public interface IDemoHook {
    String computeResult();
}
```

↰3.2.10

In principle, the behavior of extensions can also be described by abstract base classes. Using interfaces has, however, the advantage of decoupling plugins. The implementation of the interfaces can still be simplified by

↰3.1.4

providing a basic infrastructure in base classes.

> 🔎 Specifications of extension points can give both an interface and a base class for just this scenario. When you let the plugin manifest editor create the class for you, as shown later, you get a class extended to the base class and implementing the interface.

Keep declared extensions in a data structure.

Before we approach the actual connection at the center of Fig. 12.16, it is useful to look at the remainder of the implementation within the plugins A and B to get a firm grip on those details.

When retrieving the contributions, plugin A will keep them in a local data structure. In the example, it is a list of simple Contribution objects.

```
                          extpoint.DemoApp
private class Contribution {
    String description;
    IDemoHook hook;
    ...
}
private List<Contribution> contributions =
                new ArrayList<Contribution>();
```

In the end, the contributions will be invoked whenever their functionality is required. Usually, this happens by a simple iteration, as seen in the next code snippet for the example.

```
                          extpoint.DemoApp
private void invokeContributions() {
    for (Contribution c : contributions) {
        String descr = c.getDescription();
        String result = c.getHook().computeResult();
        ...  Use description and result
    }
}
```

Extensions provide contributions by implementing the given interface.

The plugin offering a contribution implements the interface, as seen next. The description string will be added in a minute.

```
                          extprovider.DemoExtension1
public class DemoExtension1 implements IDemoHook {
    public String computeResult() {
        return "Demo extension 1";
```

```
    }
}
```

These steps have established the main points of the connection we are interested in: the implementation of new functionality, its description in a generic interface, and its use by invoking a callback method.

Use the plugin manifest editor to define extension points.

It remains to inject a concrete `DemoExtension1` object into the list `contributions` introduced earlier. This step is the responsibility of the Eclipse mechanism (see Fig. 12.16). In Eclipse, each plugin can contain a file `plugin.xml`, which declares both the extension points and the extensions that the plugin offers. The structure of the `plugin.xml` file is rather too detailed for editing by hand, so Eclipse provides extensive support for its modification. The *Plugin Manifest Editor* keeps track of the structure ≫A.1.2 and understands the definitions of extension points needed to provide specialized editing support. Just click on the `plugin.xml` or the `MANIFEST.MF` of a plugin to bring up the editor. We will show only screenshots of this editor for the examples to encourage you to forget about the XML files immediately. The screenshots are also cropped slightly to save space and to focus on the essentials.

In the example, we first define the extension point E in Fig. 12.16. The definition consists of an entry in the `plugin.xml` [Fig. 12.17(a)], which references an *extension point schema* in a separate XML file [Fig. 12.17(b)]. The editing is largely done through context menus: To create a new extension point or extension, use the context menu on the list; to specify an extension further, select the extension and use its context menu.

Extension point schemas capture your structural assumptions about extensions. They work analogously to XML schemas or DTDs; that is, they specify the allowed structure of the extensions' declarations. For the minimal example, we specify that the extension consists of a sequence of one or more `hookProvider` elements. Each such element has attributes `description` and `class`, which have types *string* and *java*, respectively. The type assignment is not shown, because it is straightforward: Just select the attributes of `hookProvider` in Fig. 12.17(b) and fill in the details that the editor shows. The `class` attribute is described further by the expected interface `IDemoHook` that extensions must implement.

🔎 The attribute name `class` for designating executable code is customary, but not mandatory. Any attribute can be assigned type *java*.

🔎 Extension points are declared with local IDs such as `demoExtensionPoint`. References in extensions are always global, prefixing the local ID with the plugin name (see Fig. 12.18 for the example).

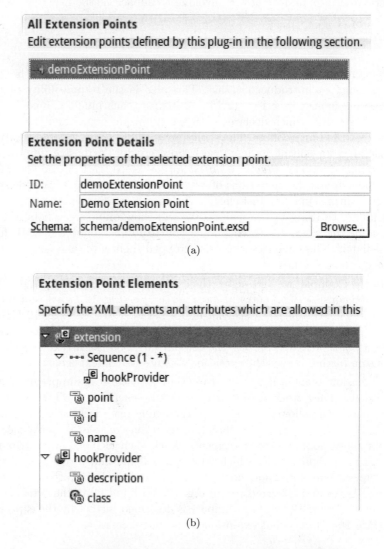

All Extension Points

Edit extension points defined by this plug-in in the following section.

◂ demoExtensionPoint

Extension Point Details

Set the properties of the selected extension point.

ID:	demoExtensionPoint
Name:	Demo Extension Point
Schema:	schema/demoExtensionPoint.exsd	Browse...

(a)

Extension Point Elements

Specify the XML elements and attributes which are allowed in this

▽ 🔲e extension
　▽ •••• Sequence (1 - *)
　　　🔲e hookProvider
　　🔳 point
　　🔳 id
　　🔳 name
▽ 🔲e hookProvider
　　🔳 description
　　🔳 class

(b)

Figure 12.17 Working with Extension Points in Eclipse

Use the plugin manifest editor to link extensions to extension points.

At the other end of the example, we wish to declare extensions that contribute new functionality (see plugin B in Fig. 12.16). Again, the editor in Fig. 12.18(a) provides thorough support. It interprets the schema from Fig. 12.17(b) to display fields *description* and *class* in Fig. 12.18(b). The *Browse* button is preconfigured to accept only classes implementing `IDemo Hook`. When creating a new extension [through the context menu of the extension point in Fig. 12.18(a)], the *class* link in the details even pops up a preconfigured *New Class* wizard.

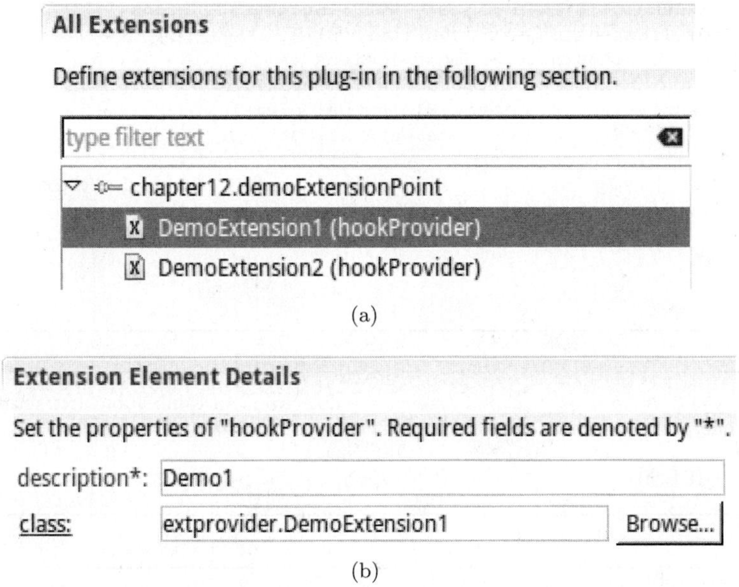

All Extensions

Define extensions for this plug-in in the following section.

| type filter text   ⊗ |

▽ ◇= chapter12.demoExtensionPoint
    ⊠ DemoExtension1 (hookProvider)
    ⊠ DemoExtension2 (hookProvider)

(a)

Extension Element Details

Set the properties of "hookProvider". Required fields are denoted by "*".

description*: Demo1

class: extprovider.DemoExtension1   Browse...

(b)

Figure 12.18 Working with Extensions in Eclipse

The tool support in Eclipse makes extensions a lightweight mechanism.

These few steps finish the connection between the plugins. Using Eclipse's tooling, they take no more than a few minutes once the interfaces and classes on both sides have been created—just don't try to edit the `plugin.xml` files by hand.

Gathering all extensions for an extension point is straightforward.

From the setup in Fig. 12.16, it remains only to actually retrieve the contributions for the extension point. The required logic largely consists of boilerplate code. In the end, line 13 in the following code dumps each contribution separately into the list `contributions` introduced earlier. Before that, the code in lines 3–9 asks the platform for all extensions and traverses them. As can be gathered from Fig. 12.18(a), each extension has several elements, represented as `IConfigurationElements`. Each such element gives us access to the attributes and also helps us to interpret them: We get the description as a `String` in Line 10 and an instance of the `class` given in Fig. 12.18(b) in line 12.

extpoint.DemoApp

```
1  protected void queryExtensions() throws CoreException {
2      IExtensionRegistry registry = Platform.getExtensionRegistry();
3      IExtensionPoint extPoint = registry
4          .getExtensionPoint("chapter12.demoExtensionPoint");
5      IExtension[] extensions = extPoint.getExtensions();
6      for (IExtension ext : extensions) {
7          IConfigurationElement[] elems =
8              ext.getConfigurationElements();
9          for (IConfigurationElement e: elems) {
10             String descr = e.getAttribute("description");
11             IDemoHook obj =
12                 (IDemoHook) e.createExecutableExtension("class");
13             contributions.add(new Contribution(descr, obj));
14         }
15     }
16 }
17
```

»12.3.3.3 If you develop several related extension points, you can think about extracting the boilerplate code into reusable helper classes. For instance, the platform uses the (internal) `AbstractWizardRegistry` for different kinds of wizards that can be hooked into the IDE. Its `addExtension()` method performs the traversal for all cases.

»A.1.1 The method `createExecutableExtension()` is more than a convenience: You cannot simply get the class name as a `String` and then use `Class.forName()` to load and later instantiate the class. The reason is that OSGi associates a special class loader with each plugin. It enforces the access restrictions given in the plugin's `MANIFEST.MF` file; only packages exported explicitly can be accessed from the outside. The method `createExecutableExtension()` therefore runs with the class loader of the plugin declaring the extension to have access to all of its defined classes. Furthermore, the OSGi class-loader allows only acyclic dependencies between plugins, as defined in the `MANIFEST.MF`. The plugin declaring the extension must, however, usually depend on the plugin declaring the extension point; its classes must implement the interfaces given in the extension point schema. The method `createExecutableExtension()` therefore accesses the class against the direction of the plugin dependencies.

📖81 Traversing the registered extensions involves a performance bottleneck. Since the number and sizes of plugin manifests `plugin.xml` in the system have become rather huge, the platform's extension registry keeps them in memory only briefly. If the registry is required afterward, all manifests must be reloaded completely. The iteration given earlier must therefore not be run frequently. A common technique is to initialize the ↰1.6.1 `contributions` lazily when they are first requested. An alternative would be to run the loop when the plugin gets initialized, but this has the drawback of making startup slower.

12.3.3.3 The Case of New Wizards

After seeing the extension mechanism at work, let us turn to the conceptual challenges of extensibility. We started our investigation of object-oriented design with the example of the *New Wizards* in Eclipse. The overall mechanism for creating new file types was rather elaborate, as shown in Fig. 11.2 on page 571. Nevertheless, it had the advantage of being extensible: If some part of the IDE introduces a new type of file, it can also introduce a corresponding *New Wizard* to help the user create and initialize such a file. We will now examine how this goal of extensibility ties in with the Eclipse mechanisms.

↰11.1

Enable extensions by decoupling parts of mechanisms through interfaces.

As a first step, we split the network of objects shown in Fig. 11.2 along the involved plugins (Fig. 12.19). The generic mechanisms for having all kinds of *New Wizards* in the IDE is implemented in `org.eclipse.ui`. Here, we find the action to trigger the dialog and the management of the extensions. The `WizardDialog` itself is reused from the JFace layer. On the other side of Fig. 12.19, the Java tooling in `org.eclipse.jdt.ui` supplies the specifics of creating a new source file with a class definition.

↰9.3

Between the two plugins, the interfaces `IWizard` and `INewWizard` (which is actually a tagging interface extending `IWizard`) hide the concrete implementation classes and decouple the `org.eclipse.ui` plugin from the provider `org.eclipse.jdt.ui`. It is this decoupling that enables arbitrary other plugins to create their own wizards and to integrate them with the existing infrastructure.

↰3.2.8

Real-world extension points are no more complex than the minimal one.

To understand the interaction between the plugins in more detail, let us look at the definition of the extension point `org.eclipse.ui.newWizards`. The main points of its schema are shown in Fig. 12.20(a): The `class` must implement `INewWizard` [Fig. 12.20(b)]. The attributes `name`, `icon`, and `category` are data elements that describe the wizard for the user's benefit.

Manage extensions in separate objects and base classes.

As a final level of detail, we will dig down into the code that actually creates the connection between the two plugins in Fig. 12.19. We saw earlier that the plugin declaring the extension point must actively look for all extensions (Fig. 12.16 on page 686). The implementation in Eclipse takes into account that much code in a naive implementation is actually boilerplate and factors this code out into reusable helper objects and reusable base classes. It is worth studying this infrastructure: It helps when one is implementing new extensions, and more importantly it demonstrates how professionals capture common logic and keep variabilities apart.

↰12.3.3.1

↰12.3.3.2

↰1.8.5 ↰3.1.4

↰12.2.1.2 📖70

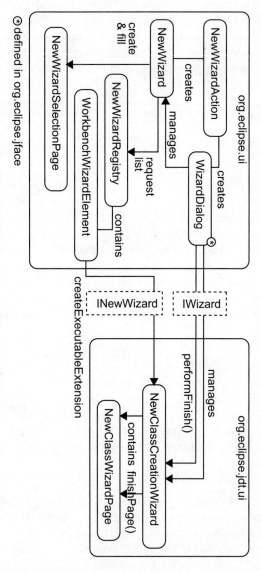

Figure 12.19 The New Class Wizard as an Extension

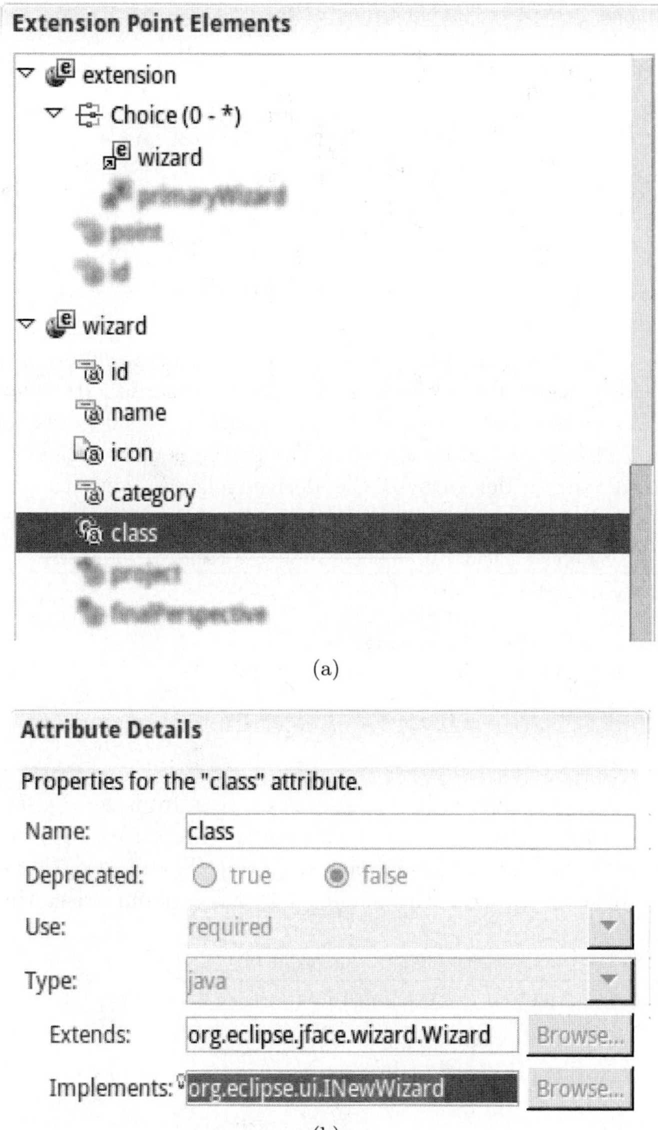

Extension Point Elements

▽ ⓔ extension
　　▽ 🔀 Choice (0 - *)
　　　　🔲ⓔ wizard
　　　　　 primaryWizard
　　　　　 point
　　　　　 id
▽ ⓔ wizard
　　　 @ id
　　　 @ name
　　　 @ icon
　　　 @ category
　　　 @ class
　　　 project
　　　 finalPerspective

(a)

Attribute Details

Properties for the "class" attribute.

Name:	class
Deprecated:	○ true ◉ false
Use:	required ▼
Type:	java ▼
Extends:	org.eclipse.jface.wizard.Wizard Browse...
Implements:	org.eclipse.ui.INewWizard Browse...

(b)

Figure 12.20 Definition of the New Wizard Extension Point (Abbreviated)

For the *New Wizards*, the class `NewWizard` initiates this processing of extensions when the wizard dialog is opened.

```
                    org.eclipse.ui.internal.dialogs.NewWizard
public class NewWizard extends Wizard {
    ...
    public void addPages() {
        IWizardRegistry registry =
            WorkbenchPlugin.getDefault().getNewWizardRegistry();
        IWizardCategory root = registry.getRootCategory();
        IWizardDescriptor[] primary = registry.getPrimaryWizards();
        ...
    }
    ...
}
```

In fact, the `IWizardRegistry` here is implemented by `NewWizard Registry`, which derives from `AbstractExtensionWizardRegistry`. That class is also used for import and export wizards. Its method `do Initialize()` is called during lazy initialization. It delegates the actual work to a `WizardsRegistryReader`. (The methods `getPlugin()` and `get ExtensionPoint()` delegate to the derived classes, here to `newWizard Registry`.)

↶1.6.1

```
              org.eclipse.ui.internal.wizards.AbstractExtensionWizardRegistry
protected void doInitialize() {
    ...
    WizardsRegistryReader reader =
        new WizardsRegistryReader(getPlugin(),
                                  getExtensionPoint());
    ...
}
```

The class `WizardsRegistryReader` derives from `RegistryReader`, which is a helper that basically encapsulates the processing loop for extensions shown in the minimal example. Using TEMPLATE METHOD, the specific subclasses process the single elements—in our case, the wizard contributions.

↶12.3.3.2 ↶1.4.9

```
                   org.eclipse.ui.internal.registry.RegistryReader
public void readRegistry(IExtensionRegistry registry,
                         String pluginId,
                         String extensionPoint) {
    IExtensionPoint point = registry.getExtensionPoint(
                                  pluginId, extensionPoint);
    IExtension[] extensions = point.getExtensions();
    extensions = orderExtensions(extensions);
    for (int i = 0; i < extensions.length; i++) {
        readExtension(extensions[i]);
    }
}
```

We stop at this point, because the remainder is clear: Through a number of indirections introduced by TEMPLATE METHOD, the wizard extensions arrive back in `WizardRegistryReader`, which creates `WorkbenchWizard Elements`. If you are interested, use the tools *Open Declaration* and *Open Implementation* to trace the calls through the sources.

This setup might seem unduly cumbersome: Why should a sane designer dispatch a simple iteration through the extensions up and down through an inheritance hierarchy rather than implementing a quick-and-dirty solution? More critical team members might even ask who will ever understand this mess. The answer is that object-oriented systems are not understood by tracing method calls at all. Instead, they are understood by looking at the responsibilities of the different objects and their distribution across an inheritance hierarchy. In the end, the goal is to enact the Single Responsibility Principle: Each class in the hierarchy addresses a single task, which maximizes the cohesion within the classes of the system. Try to check this out in the example; you will find that the design obeys the single-sentence rule for describing an object's purpose.

↰11.1
↰11.4
↰11.2
↰12.1.3

↰11.2.1

12.3.3.4 The Case of Views in Eclipse

Designing useful extension points hinges on finding a clean abstraction that covers the intentions of many possible extensions. The challenge is to find that abstraction, to formulate it succinctly, and to express the behavior in an interface. Aiming for the Single Responsibility Principle helps a lot. Here is a concrete example.

↰11.2.2

> Views are just windows that appear in the Eclipse IDE.

You are familiar with *views* from your everyday work in Eclipse. The *Package Explorer*, the *Console*, the *Variables*, and many more—they all provide extra information that is useful while editing or debugging sources. Views are, of course, not the only kind of windows in Eclipse. For instance, the actual sources are accessed in *editors*, which appear in the central *editor area*. We focus on views here because they are a little simpler and still exhibit the essential aspects.

Let us examine the software infrastructure that makes it simple to add a new view. Fig. 12.21(a) shows the extension point `org.eclipse.ui.views`. The central attribute is a `class` deriving from `ViewPart` [Fig. 12.21(b)] or implementing `IViewPart`, as explained in the documentation of the extension point. We will look at their methods in a minute. The remaining attributes of the extension point describe the view using simple data such as a name, an icon, and a category to be used in menus and the *Show View* dialog. The `class` will not be loaded until the view is shown.

↰12.3.3.1

`ViewParts` can be edited with the WindowBuilder. The tool then fills in the creation of the SWT widget tree but leaves you free to implement the other methods as necessary.

↰7.2

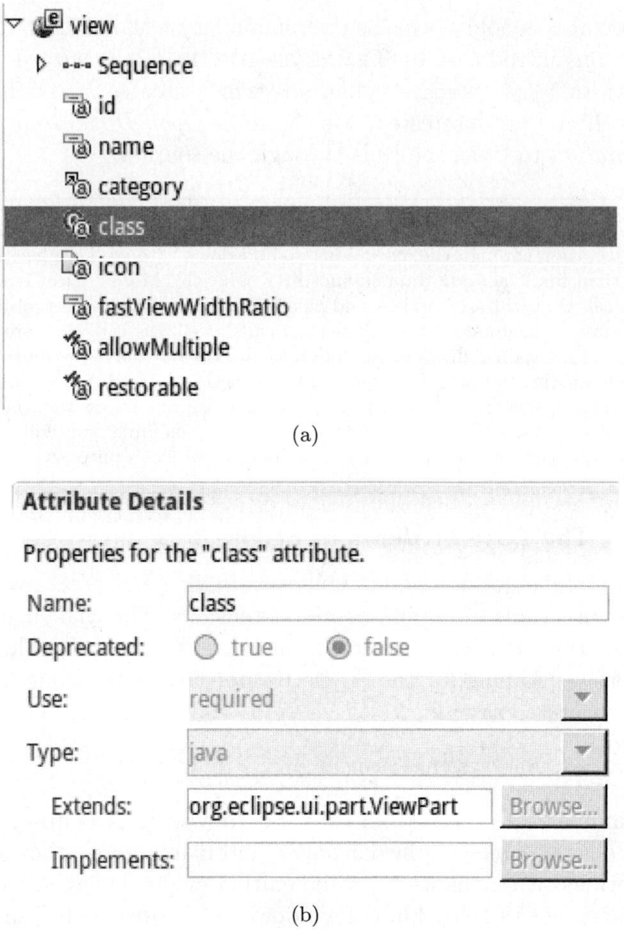
view
Sequence
id
name
category
class
icon
fastViewWidthRatio
allowMultiple
restorable
(a)
Attribute Details
Properties for the "class" attribute.
Name:
class
Deprecated:
true
false
Use:
required
Type:
java
Extends:
org.eclipse.ui.part.ViewPart
Browse...
Implements:
Browse...
(b)

Figure 12.21 **The Extension Point `org.eclipse.ui.views`**

»A.1.2 The extension point and some infrastructure are defined in the plugin `org.eclipse.ui`. If you wish to build a new view, be sure to include that plugin in your dependencies. The online supplement contains a minimal example `MiniView` with which you can start playing around.

Ask yourself about the minimal requirements on extensions.

Let us now look at the structure of a view in more detail. Most facets result from the fact that Eclipse shows views in tab folders and decorates them with a title, an icon, and a tooltip. The interface `IWorkbenchPart`, from which `IViewPart` derives, deals with these general aspects. The view ↰7.1 also has to create its SWT widget tree. The method `dispose()` is a life-cycle callback enabling the view to clean up—for instance, by de-registering listeners or freeing resources. Method `setFocus()` allows the view to move the keyboard focus to some default widget when the user clicks on the view title. The view must notify Eclipse about its properties. Views have only a title; editors additionally can be dirty or change the edited resources, as seen in their interface `IEditorPart`. The super-interface `IAdaptable` has already been discussed.

↰1.1
↰7.4.1

↰2.1

↰3.2.2

---
org.eclipse.ui.IWorkbenchPart

```
interface IWorkbenchPart extends IAdaptable {
    public String getTitle();
    public Image getTitleImage();
    public String getTitleToolTip();
    public void createPartControl(Composite parent);
    public void dispose();
    public void setFocus();
    public static final int PROP_TITLE =
        IWorkbenchPartConstants.PROP_TITLE;
    public void addPropertyListener(IPropertyListener listener);
    public void removePropertyListener(IPropertyListener listener);
    public IWorkbenchPartSite getSite();
}
```

The last method `getSite()` in this code needs some more background. Each view and each editor in Eclipse is anchored to the *site* at which it currently appears. The site enables each window to access its own context on the screen. For instance, the *page* contains all views and editors and manages their layout; the *workbench window* holds the top-level shell with menu, toolbar, and status bar.

▭174
↰7.1

The site is passed to the view during initialization. Since its type differs between editors and views, the corresponding life-cycle method `init()` is declared in the `IViewPart` interface shown next. The methods dealing with `IMemento`, as well as the interface `IPersistable`, enable a view to save and restore its own state between IDE sessions. Eclipse manages the mementos for all views, which again simplifies the creation of new views.

↰1.6.2

↰9.5.1

---
org.eclipse.ui.IViewPart

```
public interface IViewPart extends IWorkbenchPart, IPersistable {
    public void init(IViewSite site) throws PartInitException;
    public void init(IViewSite site, IMemento memento)
                                throws PartInitException;
    public void saveState(IMemento memento);
    public IViewSite getViewSite();
}
```

⊕ The VIEW HANDLER pattern provides an abstract analysis of applications managing internal windows. It explains the general form of protocols that negotiate the life cycle and manipulation of these windows.

▭59

↰12.3.1

↰3.1.4

↰1.8.6

↰12.3.2

Aim at making extensions simple.

So why does this setup simplify the creation of new views? The answer is clear: Eclipse provides a substantial amount of machinery for showing and managing individual views; it even takes care of any internal state that the view might wish to preserve between sessions. All that Eclipse asks for in return is a little collaboration at those points that are really special for each view: the title, the SWT widget tree, the handling of their state, and so on. But Eclipse does even more. The `ViewPart` base class provides the infrastructure for the menial tasks such as managing the property listeners. In the end, developers of views can really concentrate on their own tasks and can trust Eclipse to integrate their views into the overall IDE.

12.3.3.5   Completion Proposals

One of the most versatile features of Eclipse's Java editor is its completion pop-up. It does more than simply list the names of types, methods, and fields: It also includes common code patterns such as a `main()` method, `System.out.println()`, or `Runnables`, and goes on to code recommenders supplying example snippets for API usage. This large variety of functionality could never be maintained effectively in a monolithic implementation, because the Java editor component would become huge. Instead, the editor provides a common abstract structure of proposals that subsumes all individual entries.

The example is particularly interesting in the current context, because it demonstrates the step away from the concrete functionality to the abstract structure of expected functionality. It also shows how additional infrastructure classes can bridge the contrasting goals of an abstract, general API and the simplicity of extensions. Compared with the earlier analysis of the same example, we therefore switch our perspective and focus on the abstraction, rather than on the mechanics.

Proposals are provided dynamically, depending on the pop-up's context.

Let us start from the goal: We want to show the pop-up window that you are familiar with. Many of the proposals will be generated dynamically, such as by looking up field and method names in the Eclipse Java Model. The extension point `org.eclipse.jdt.ui.javaCompletionProposalComputer` [Fig. 12.22(a)] therefore accepts sequences of objects implementing the interface `IJavaCompletionProposalComputer` [Fig. 12.22(b)].

That interface is simple enough: Each completion proposal computer at the core provides a list of `ICompletionProposals`, given a context in which the completion takes place. The context includes, among other things, the text document and completion position, so that the textual context can be accessed directly. The `sessionStarted()` and `session Ended()` callbacks are life-cycle methods that notify the computer when a

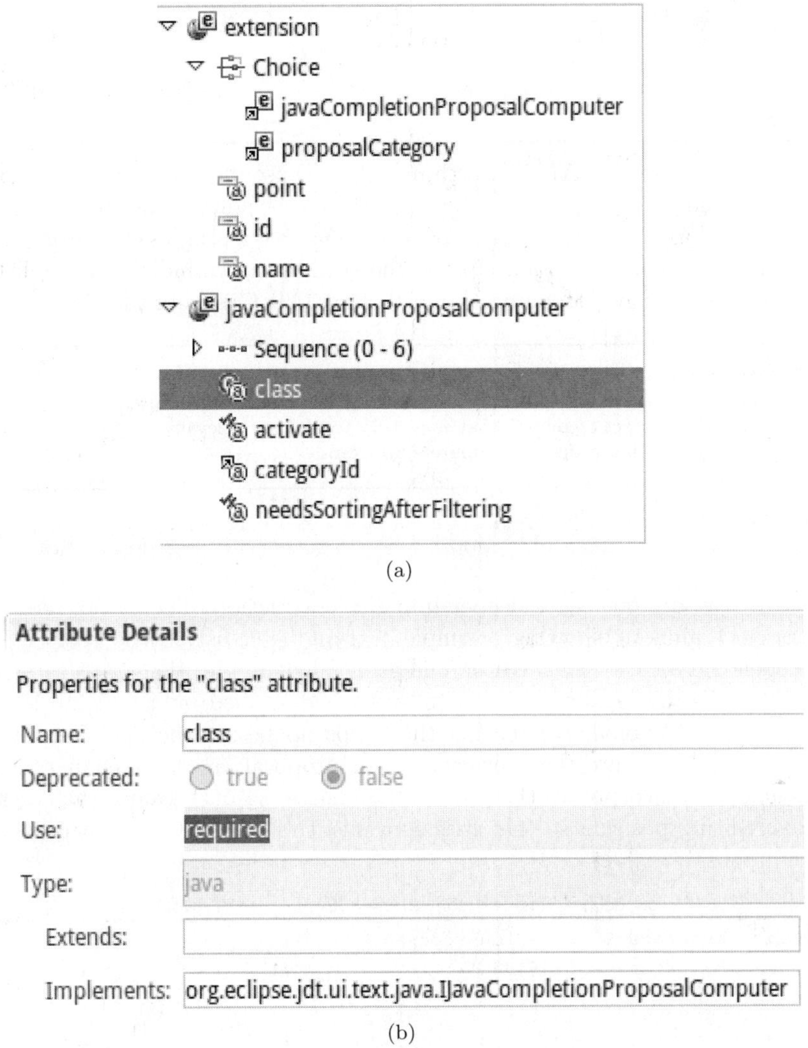

(a)

Attribute Details

Properties for the "class" attribute.

Name: class

Deprecated: ○ true ● false

Use: required

Type: java

Extends:

Implements: org.eclipse.jdt.ui.text.java.IJavaCompletionProposalComputer

(b)

Figure 12.22 Extension Point for Java Completions

pop-up is shown and is removed, respectively. This enables the computer to allocate resources or caches temporarily and free them once no completion operation is immediately pending. The computer can provide an error message explaining why it has not been able to find any proposals.

```
org.eclipse.jdt.ui.text.java.IJavaCompletionProposalComputer
public interface IJavaCompletionProposalComputer {
    List<ICompletionProposal> computeCompletionProposals(
                        ContentAssistInvocationContext context,
                        IProgressMonitor monitor);
```

```
    void sessionStarted();
    void sessionEnded();
    String getErrorMessage();
      ...
}
```

↰7.10.2

One detail of this API is worth noting, because it demonstrates the experience that is required for designing extensible systems: The core method `completeCompletionProposals()` is also handed a progress monitor. The designers have obviously anticipated the need to search indices or raw lists of items, maybe even opening and analyzing JAR files from the class path.

> ℗ If you wish to implement new proposals, note that the `context` passed to the callback is actually a `JavaContentAssistInvocationContext`. That object already holds some analysis of the syntactic context that may help to identify relevant proposals quickly. Please look at existing proposal computers for example usages.

A proposal is an executable modification together with its description.

↰9.3

Let us now dig one layer deeper into the abstraction. The `ICompletion Proposal` aims at showing a simple text-and-icon list to the user. It is independent of the Java editor and is defined in the JFace abstraction over SWT's raw text widgets. A proposal is described by a text, an icon, and some additional information that pops up beside the list. The final two methods capture the execution of the proposal: `apply()` changes the document to incorporate the proposal; `getSelection()` guides the editor to an editing position so that it is convenient for the user after accepting the proposal.

```
          org.eclipse.jface.text.contentassist.ICompletionProposal

public interface ICompletionProposal {
    String getDisplayString();
    Image getImage();
    String getAdditionalProposalInfo();
    void apply(IDocument document);
    Point getSelection(IDocument document);
      ...
}
```

↰1.8.6

The first interesting point in this API is the generality of the `apply()` method. Many proposals are about completing some method or type name. Focusing on those would lead to a method `getCompletionString (prefix)`, which would be simple to implement, because it does not involve any logic about the context. However, that design would not cover the more advanced cases such as wrapping code in `Runnables`. By comparison, the general version can be hard to implement if each type of completion proposal would actually have to manipulate documents. The solution is to

provide base classes with infrastructure that keeps the API general but ↰3.1.4
simplifies the common case. Here is the `apply()` method in `Completion`
`Proposal` that keeps simple proposals purely data-driven; one simply has
to store the textual replacement in fields.

---
org.eclipse.jface.text.contentassist.CompletionProposal

```
public void apply(IDocument document) {
    try {
        document.replace(fReplacementOffset, fReplacementLength,
                         fReplacementString);
    } catch (BadLocationException x) {
        // ignore
    }
}
```

The new cursor position is set to the end of the proposal, so that the user
can continue typing immediately.

---
org.eclipse.jface.text.contentassist.CompletionProposal

```
public Point getSelection(IDocument document) {
    return new Point(fReplacementOffset + fCursorPosition, 0);
}
```

Use extension interfaces for backward compatibility.

Another interesting point of the completion API is that it has already been
updated seven times to provide more advanced feedback for the user and
more detailed control over the application of proposals. This goes to show
that even experts are not omniscient and cannot anticipate all desirable
application scenarios of an API. The EXTENSION INTERFACE pattern can ↰3.2.5
be used to keep existing proposals working while new proposals can take
advantage of the new facilities. Look through the interfaces `ICompletion`
`ProposalExtension`, `ICompletionProposalExtension2`, and so on for
the details: There are special provisions for an on-the-fly validation, selection by trigger characters, disabling auto-application, styled strings rather
than plain text for displays, and more.

Extension interfaces complicate the reusable mechanisms.

EXTENSION INTERFACE ensures backward compatibility, but it comes with
a price: The code invoking the new functionality must use case distinctions
and downcasts. As a result, it quickly becomes very complex. In the exam- ↰3.1.9
ple, extension 6 introduces styled strings—for instance, to highlight parts
of a proposal in boldface font. The code that displays a proposal must take
this new capability into account whenever it looks for the display string.
Lines 5–9 in the following code perform the check and downcast; the meanings of the variables in lines 3–4 depends on the case distinction.

org.eclipse.jface.text.contentassist.CompletionProposalPopup

```
 1  private void handleSetData(Event event) {
 2      ...
 3      String displayString;
 4      StyleRange[] styleRanges = null;
 5      if (fIsColoredLabelsSupportEnabled
 6              && current instanceof ICompletionProposalExtension6) {
 7          StyledString styledString =
 8              ((ICompletionProposalExtension6) current)
 9                  .getStyledDisplayString();
10          displayString = styledString.getString();
11          styleRanges = styledString.getStyleRanges();
12      } else
13          displayString = current.getDisplayString();
14      ...
15  }
```

Strike a balance between simplicity now and later.

The discussion so far highlights a central dilemma when designing the API of extensions: You can start out with the cost of a simple, straightforward definition that works for all cases currently on the radar, or you can invest more time to build for more sophisticated applications that might arise in the future. The second choice clearly comes with the cost of a higher implementation complexity, while the first choice involves the danger of deferring that complexity to the future, where the amount of work and the ugliness of the code will be very much increased.

28   In the end, there is no general guideline. The idea of building the simplest thing that could work may help a bit: "Work" can be read to mean "cover all desirable extensions," an understanding that asks you to look conscientiously for applications that you do know about. "Simplest" then means to ask which collaborations are really indispensable for these applications. Styled strings are a case in point: Eclipse's auto-completion capability would still be immensely useful, even if slightly less beautiful, without them. Since they involve advanced uses of the SWT `Table` widget, it is a good idea to defer their addition until some users actually ask for them.

12.3.3.6 Extension Points and Extensibility

The Eclipse mechanism for extensions is great as a mechanism: It is conceptually clean, poses few restrictions on the format of extensions, and comes with a lot of supporting infrastructure and IDE support. It is certainly worth studying by itself, as an example of craftsmanship in software design. We learn even more, however, by taking a step back and asking how it contributes to the overall goals of extensibility and, one level beyond, to decoupling in general.

Extension points keep extensions small and simple.

One of the main requirements for extensibility is that one can add new func- ↰12.3.1
tionality in a simple and well-defined way. If you look back at the examples ↰12.3.3.2 ↰12.3.3.3
so far, especially to Fig. 12.19 on page 694, you will notice that almost the
entire overhead for making things extensible lies with the provider of the
extension point. The individual extensions consist of objects implementing
usually small interfaces. Registering these objects with the mechanism is
done through a few mouse clicks using Eclipse's editors.

Extension points help to keep the extensible plugin stable.

Extensibility requires that the application's code base remain stable despite ↰12.3.1
the added functionality. The Eclipse mechanism encourages the necessary
decoupling in that it forces the plugin offering the extension point to define
an interface or abstract base class that captures all of its expectations (see
Fig. 12.16 on page 686). Defining this abstraction can be hard, but at least
it is approached early on, before many extensions exist that must possibly
be rewritten. The design of this interface is best achieved by asking about
the future behavior that extensions are expected to exhibit. ↰3.2.1

From one perspective, extensibility therefore leads to an instance of the
Dependency Inversion Principle. In this case, the main application is the ↰11.5.6
stable, crucial, valuable part of the software. The extensions are incidental
details whose implementation must not influence or constrain the design of
the main application.

Extension points encourage decoupling through interfaces.

The necessity of specifying an interface or abstract base class as the single
link between the plugins participating in an extension implicitly introduces
decoupling between the modules. On the one hand, changes are likely to re- ↰3.2.7 ↰12.1.1
main confined in the individual extensions. On the other hand, the interface
makes explicit the assumptions that the participating plugins share. ↰12.1.2

12.3.4 Pipes and Filters

Many applications today feature graphical user interfaces and are largely
event-driven. Nevertheless, the good old input–process–output model still ↰7.1
holds its own at the heart of many computations. Indeed, the advent of
affordable multicore and multiprocessor hardware has made the model ever ⊞57,207,8
more important: Throughput in bulk processing of data is best obtained by
organizing the processing steps in producer–consumer chains in which data ↰7.10.1
is copied along. In this way, each processor can run at full speed, without
being hampered by waiting for locks on shared data structures. The PIPES- ↰8.1
AND-FILTERS pattern captures the essence of such data processing systems. ⊞101,59

Networks of filters and pipes make for extensible systems.

Fig. 12.23 illustrates the idea of the pattern. Data flows into the system, often at several points (A and B). Then it is split and recombined through several processing steps (C, D, E) and finally the results leave the system, perhaps again at several points (F, G).

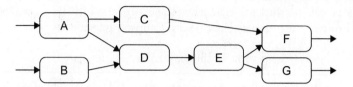

Figure 12.23 A Network of Filters for Data Processing

The nodes A–G are called *filters*. Filters receive data, process it, and hand the resulting data on. Filters at which the data enters the system are called *sources*; those where the data leaves the system are called *sinks*. The connections between the filters are called *pipes*. Briefly put, they are responsible for transporting the data between the processing steps. If the network is simply a linear sequence of filters, one speaks of a *pipeline*.

The most famous examples of pipelines are perhaps the versatile UNIX text processing tools. Suppose you have received the year's banking transactions as a CSV file, with one transaction per line. Now you wish to know which people you have sent money to most often. Here is the trick: Fetch the data from disk (`cat`), splice out the relevant columns (`cut`), and select only those with a negative flow (`grep`). Finally, you splice out only the names (`cut`) and count the number of occurrences. This works most simply by sorting (`sort`) and counting the number of consecutive lines with the same content (`uniq -c`). As a final touch, you sort numerically by the number of transactions, in descending order (`sort -nr`).

```
cat transactions.csv|cut -f6,8,9|grep -e '-[0-9.]*$'\
   |cut -f1|sort|uniq -c|sort -nr
```

PATTERN: PIPES-AND-FILTERS

The PIPES-AND-FILTERS approach provides a structure for systems that process streams of data. The *filters* process the data; the *pipes* connect the filters and transport the data from one filter to the next. Filters form a directed acyclic network, where *sources* receive data from the outside and *sinks* pass the result on to other systems.

59

The pattern provides extensibility in two directions. First, one can introduce new kinds of processing steps by implementing new types of filters and inserting them into the network. Second, one can recombine existing filters to add new processing steps to existing data flows. As a further benefit, the pattern enables the rapid construction of new applications from a toolbox of existing filter types.

To reach these goals, three technical constraints have to be observed: a common data format, the nature of data as streams, and the resulting need for incremental processing. We will introduce these requirements now, before proceeding to a more detailed analysis of the pattern itself.

All filters share a common data format for input and output.

The pattern's first and main constraint concerns the format of the data. To enable the free combination of existing filters and the easy integration of new filters, they have to agree on a common data format: The output of any filter must be a suitable input to the next.

In many applications, the data is just a sequence of bytes—that is, one filter produces bytes to be consumed by the next one. However, the bytes usually have further structure. For instance, when processing audio data, the bytes encode samples, but they must be grouped according to the number of bits per sample and maybe further into blocks with checksums to enable error correction. UNIX text processing tools read text files and produce text files, but they usually work on lines terminated by a linefeed (LF) character. Database systems, in contrast, work in terms of pages or individual records of fixed formats.

Assume that the data arrives in the form of a potentially infinite stream.

A further central point of the pattern shapes the later implementation decisions to a large degree: One assumes that the data is large or even unbounded. A *stream* is such a potentially infinite sequence of data items. For instance, when building the audio processing software for a conference system, you can never be sure whether the current speaker will ever stop. And even if the data is known to end at some point, it may be infeasible to store a modified copy at each filter.

Filters aim at incremental processing for low latency.

The way to cope with large or unbounded data is to process it *incrementally* (Fig. 12.24): Each filter reads just enough data to be able to perform its computation, does all the processing, and passes the result on to the next filter as soon as it is done.

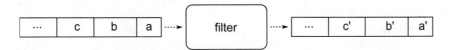

Figure 12.24 Incremental Processing of Data Streams

In effect, the first pieces of the result stream appear at the sinks of the overall filter network at the first possible moment. The time taken for a piece of data to travel through the network is called the network's *latency*. In many applications, such as real-time signal processing, a low latency is crucial to achieve a satisfactory user experience. But even in data processing systems and application servers, it is a good idea to start sending data over the network as soon as possible: Transmitting the computed data will take some time, and during that time the next batches of data can be processed. As a result, the overall time that elapses before the user sees the complete web page is minimized.

Pipes synchronize processing between filters.

Having set the goals, we can now come back to the elements of the pattern. First for the more obscure ones: If all the processing is done by the filters, what is the purpose of the pipes? What do they contribute?

Pipes are responsible for transporting the data between filters. This also means making sure that no data gets lost, even in unfavorable circumstances where the producer is much quicker than the next consumer in the network. Simply dropping data is usually not an option. Instead, the pipes have to synchronize the processing between filters so that fast producers get slowed down a bit and quick consumers get to wait until new data is available.

The simplest form of pipes occurs with *passive filters*. Here, the transport of data happens by method calls. Either the consumer asks the producer for new data or the producer delivers new data to the consumer. In any case, the method call will not return until the operation is complete. This type of filter can be studied by examining the readers and writers of Java's I/O library. For instance, it is instructive to study how the GZIP OutputStream and GZIPInputStream achieve an on-the-fly compression and decompression of byte data.

↞8.1
With *active filters*, in contrast, each filter runs in a separate thread. It usually has a main loop that repeatedly reads data from its input, processes it, and writes it to the output. Active filters support parallel and distributed processing. To synchronize active filters, the pipes must buffer incoming data. They keep the consumer waiting if no data is available and stop the producer when the buffers are full. We have already studied the standard

↞8.3
BlockingQueue implementations that fulfill this purpose.

Pipes can also include buffering to improve the *throughput* of the overall network. The throughput is the amount of data processed in a given time. This amount is maximized if all filters run in parallel and at top speed. To do so, they must have sufficient input data and must hand on their data without delay. Such a scheme will work as intended only if the pipes buffer data to level out temporary discrepancies in processing speed.

↞11.5.2
In summary, pipes are not merely auxiliary connectors. They form the backbone of the overall application. They also establish a separation of

concerns: The filters can assume that their input data is available and will be transported reliably, so that they can focus on the actual processing of the data.

Filters implement elementary processing steps.

When designing with the Pipes-and-Filters pattern, it is important to get the granularity of the filters, and therefore that of the individual processing steps, right. If you have just a few large-scale blocks, the pattern structures your application, but you do not gain the ability to recombine filters into new applications quickly. If you have a huge number of tiny microprocessing steps, the time spent in transporting the data dominates the overall runtime.

A good guideline is to look at the application domain. Which kinds of "operations" on data are discussed there? Which elementary steps are mentioned in the descriptions of overall systems? Making the meaning of operations—rather than the size of their implementations—the unit of filters helps to strike a balance between the extremes. At the same time, it ensures that the structure of the network resembles the description of the desired application.

Filters are reusable between applications.

We have placed Pipes-and-Filters into the context of extensibility, because its central feature of a common data format shared between filters makes it simple to extend the toolkit of filters. However, there is a second major gain: Once the filters have been developed, they can be reused in new applications.

»12.4

Pipes-and-Filters enables rapid prototyping and product lines.

Furthermore, the overall structure and the strong basis established by the pipes makes it simple to assemble applications quickly, either for rapid prototyping or in the sense of product lines, where a number of very similar software products must be maintained side-by-side.

Pipes-and-Filters focuses on stateless computing.

Objects are usually stateful, which enables them to be self-contained and active entities. It must be said, however, that purely functional, immutable objects do have some advantages when it comes to debugging complex computation processes.

↰1.1
↰1.8.4

The main point of the Pipes-and-Filters pattern is the transformation of data, and that data is stateless: You can inspect the input and output data of filters and be sure that the same stream of input data will lead to the same stream of output data. Filters are essentially functions from their inputs to their outputs. For the implementation, this means that even if you do pass objects along the pipes, you must not modify them as long as any other filter might have access to them.

However, the filters themselves can and very often will, in fact, be stateful. As a result, even if the same group of bytes repeats at different positions within the overall stream, different output may result. For instance, compression algorithms usually optimize their dictionaries dynamically. Encryption algorithms even take great care to avoid repeating the same output for the same input in different positions.

PIPES-AND-FILTERS defines specific responsibilities and collaborations.

At first glance, PIPES-AND-FILTERS is not particularly object-oriented: After all, object design is first of all about behavior and not about data. However, the pattern can also be understood as a particular style of assigning responsibilities and defining collaborations. The responsibility of each filter is a particular data transformation. All collaborations rely on handing on data for further processing.

📖92

Of course, a central objection remains: Published data structures are usually considered a "bad smell" in a design. However, we must make a fine distinction. The published part of the data is what the system is all about: An audio system processes audio data, a database management system processes tuples, and so on. The internal state and data of the individual filters, in contrast, is still private. This distinction aims at the question of

↰11.5.1 ↰12.1.1

which aspects are likely to change. We practice information hiding because we wish to change an object's implementation if necessary while the remainder of the system remains untouched. But we will never try to turn an audio system into a database management system, so it does not really matter if their central data structures are published and therefore fixed.

12.4   Reusability

Reusability is all about solving a problem once and for all. Indeed, computer science itself would be nothing without software reuse. In the beginning, when we punched our source code into cards, reuse happened through "libraries," where one could literally borrow a batch of cards and pack it with one's own computation jobs. Since then, we have come a long way: Libraries are just JAR files that we download from the web, possibly even using an

📖173

automatic build system such as Maven. Nevertheless, creating reusable software and reusing software created by others is still a tough job. Even if the technical challenges are largely solved, the conceptual ones have increased with the growing size and complexity of the systems we build.

12.4.1 The Challenge of Reusability

Let us start from a simple definition: Reusable software solves a particular problem and works in many contexts. You can just use the off-the-shelf software in your own applications. Unfortunately, this characterization assumes that the software already exists. To get a grasp on the process of creating reusable software, it is better to start from one application. Assume for a moment that you are thinking about a task for an object and you suddenly realize that this task will reoccur in many places. How do you transform that insight into reusable software?

Reuse means extracting a component and embedding it into a new context.

Fig. 12.25 illustrates the core of the reuse challenge. We have written a component R for one system, but we think it is reusable somewhere else. In a truly object-oriented design, R is embedded in a network of objects: A accesses R as a service provider, indicated by the direction of the arrow. B additionally expects some callbacks, such as notifications about state changes. On the right-hand side of Fig. 12.25, R itself uses collaborators to fulfill its responsibilities. It calls on C for some aspects and collaborates with D more closely, including some callbacks.

↰11.1

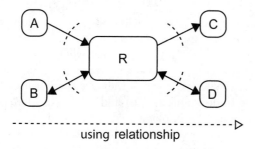

using relationship

Figure 12.25 The Challenge of Reuse

The challenge of reusing R in a different context then is that we have to cut these connections as sketched by the dashed lines and reestablish them in the new context, with different objects. This perspective of extracting R from its original context is useful even if you have not yet implemented R: You will find R first useful at one place of a design, and only then will you start thinking about making it reusable in other places.

Single objects are usually not a suitable unit of reuse.

Before we proceed, it must be clear that the component R in Fig. 12.25 is usually not a single object but really a group of objects that together accomplish a purpose that is worthwhile reusing—the Single Responsibility Principle would not allow for anything else, because it keeps objects small

↰11.2

↰1.7.2

and focused. In particular, R will have internal collaborations. C and D stand for the external ones that vary between contexts. However, it might be a good idea to make the functionality of R accessible through a FACADE object to keep the API simple for the users A and B.

Enable reuse by designing general and conceptually clean APIs.

Replacing object A in Fig. 12.25 means designing the API of R such that it is generally useful. A prime example is the operating system API for accessing data in the form of byte streams. It has survived since the 1960s and even transfers to TCP network connections, because it is lean, clean, and general: Making the byte the smallest unit of information enables any application A to encode and decode its own data structures by marshaling them into some convenient format, while the operating system R serves all applications the same way.

Reusability often induces inversion of control.

↰7.3.2

Inversion of control is a characteristic of frameworks that distinguishes them from libraries: Frameworks implement generic mechanisms that work on their own. The application's own logic is called back only at specific and well-defined points.

Fig. 12.25 shows that this principle evolves naturally when designing reusable objects. In the figure, collaborators C and D must be plugged into R in each new context. They get called back whenever R judges this to be useful. Only reusable components R that rely entirely on their own objects for help do not have such callbacks—they are the libraries.

↰12.1.1

The challenge in designing R is to find interfaces for C and D such that these collaborators can be implemented easily by different users of R. One particular aspect, which will arise in many later examples, is the question of which information R must pass to C and D. If R makes available too much or reveals its own details, it cannot change. If it offers too little information, C and D cannot implement any useful functionality and R is not reusable.

The remainder of this section explores examples of reusable components to make more concrete these challenges and their solutions.

12.4.2   The Case of the Wizard Dialogs in JFace

↰9.3
↰11.1

To start with reuse, let us look at an example of a successful, polished component: the `WizardDialog` object provided in the JFace layer. We have already seen it at work in the `NewWizard` mechanism of Eclipse, which enables users to create arbitrary files with dialogs specific to the type of file. The overall network of objects is rather complex, because it obeys the Single Responsibility Principle and aims at several higher-level goals (Fig. 11.2 on page 571). One of these goals is the reusability of the wizard infrastructure.

↰11.2

Let us now examine the relationships of the `WizardDialog` to the other classes of the overall structure. Fig. 12.26 casts the first dialog page for selecting the type of file [Fig. 11.1(a) on page 570] into the general structure of the reuse scenario from Fig. 12.25.

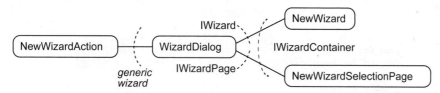

Figure 12.26 Reusing the `WizardDialog` for New Wizards

Provide a simple service API for accessing reusable components.

On the left-hand side of Fig. 12.26, the `WizardDialog` offers a general and straightforward service API for showing wizards. In this API, one creates the dialog, passes an `IWizard`, and opens the dialog. The specific wizard becomes part of the dialog and the dialog starts managing the wizard.   ↰2.2.1

```
                    org.eclipse.ui.actions.NewWizardAction
NewWizard wizard = new NewWizard();
 ...   initialize the NewWizard
WizardDialog dialog = new WizardDialog(parent, wizard);
dialog.create();
 ...
dialog.open();
```

This is simple enough. The crucial design decisions take place on the right-hand side of Fig. 12.26: How will the generic `WizardDialog` and the specific contained wizard object collaborate to provide the overall user experience?

Keep the interfaces for callbacks conceptually clean.

In the direction from the `WizardDialog`, the interfaces `IWizard` and `IWizardPage` capture the expectations of the dialog toward the specific wizard provided by the concrete application. First, there are some lifecycle methods that connect the wizard to its container and set up and tear down the wizard (lines 2–5). We will discuss the interface `IWizardContainer` further later in this section. Next up, the dialog enables navigation through the pages by its *Next* and *Previous* buttons; it calls back on the wizard to decide on the actual page selected (lines 6–9). Finally, the dialog has buttons *Finish* and *Cancel*. It lets the wizard decide whether the *Finish* button should be active, based on whether sufficient information is available to finish immediately (line 10). Finally, it notifies the wizard when one of the buttons is actually clicked.

```
                   org.eclipse.jface.wizard.IWizard
1 public interface IWizard {
2      public void setContainer(IWizardContainer wizardContainer);
3      public IWizardContainer getContainer();
4      public void createPageControls(Composite pageContainer);
5      public void dispose();
6      public IWizardPage[] getPages();
7      public IWizardPage getStartingPage();
8      public IWizardPage getNextPage(IWizardPage page);
9      public IWizardPage getPreviousPage(IWizardPage page);
10     public boolean canFinish();
11     public boolean performCancel();
12     public boolean performFinish();
13         ...
14 }
```

🔍 The alert reader will notice some apparent redundancy between the method get
   Pages() and the subsequent ones. The difference is in their semantics. The method
getPages() returns the pages in the physical order of their creation, while getStarting
Page(), getNextPage(), and getPreviousPage() represent the logical order in which the
pages appear in the wizard. For instance, some steps may be optional depending on
previous user input. It is instructive to look through different implementations within
the Eclipse platform. (Use the tool *Open Implementation* from page 180.)

↰12.4.1   This interface underlines the earlier statement that reusable object-
oriented components usually introduce some level of inversion of control. It
is the wizard that decides when pages flip, what the next page will be, and
when the overall operation should be triggered. The application—that is,
the software reusing the dialog—has to wait until it is called back.

Aim at covering all application scenarios.

The methods omitted in the presentation of IWizard so far deal with seemingly minor issues of the graphical presentation. However, they demonstrate
a further challenge in creating truly reusable components: It is not sufficient
to target 90% of the possible applications; one must reach 100% to avoid
forcing clients to adopt copy-and-paste programming in more subtle cases.
      In the case of wizards, it is useful to specify the window title and the
color of the upper part of the dialog. Also, the appearance of the help,
next, and previous buttons might not be sensible for all wizards. Finally, if
wizards perform long-running jobs, the user will appreciate the display of
a progress bar.

```
                   org.eclipse.jface.wizard.IWizard
public String getWindowTitle();
public RGB getTitleBarColor();
public boolean isHelpAvailable();
```

```
public boolean needsPreviousAndNextButtons();
public boolean needsProgressMonitor();
```

The other interface `IWizardPage` was discussed earlier (see page 572). ↰11.1
It is worth reexamining its methods from the perspective of reusability:
What does the `WizardDialog` expect of the single pages of a contained
wizard?

Strike a balance between completeness and effort.

The general aim is to cover 100% of the later applications. But hold on for
a minute—this is quite some deviation from the earlier principles. What
about "build the simplest thing that could work" and "you ain't gonna need
it (YAGNI)"? There are really three answers.

The first answer is: Very often, covering 95% of the applications is good
enough, because these are all the scenarios you are ever going to need in your
software. And creating a component that covers 95% is often substantially
simpler than building one to cover 99% or 100%. So you should still be
building the simplest possible thing.

The second answer is that building frameworks and reusable software
shifts the priorities slightly: If you decide to build a reusable component,
then do it once and be done with it. Reusability introduces an extra effort
and you should make sure that the effort is spent well.

The third answer is: If you find it hard to create a reusable component that covers even 95% of the applications, then you probably should
not try to create it right now. Perhaps it is better to follow the "rule of
three": Build three concrete applications by hand before attempting the
abstraction.

Think carefully about the information and services offered to callbacks.

But the right-hand side of Fig. 12.26 holds yet another challenge: Not only
does the `WizardDialog` call back on the wizard and its pages for specific
events, but it also offers services to the wizard. These services are given
by an interface `IWizardContainer`, so that wizards can also be shown in
other contexts. Through the interface, the wizard can access the shell—for
instance, to show pop-up dialogs. It can also directly influence the page ↰7.6
shown by the wizard, in case the concrete data entered by the user or any
errors require a deviation from the standard, linear page sequence. The final
`update ...` methods are really notifications sent to the dialog: Whenever a
page detects that the data has changed in a significant way, it must notify
the dialog that the display must be updated.

---
org.eclipse.jface.wizard.IWizardContainer

```
public interface IWizardContainer extends IRunnableContext {
    public Shell getShell();
    public IWizardPage getCurrentPage();
```

```
    public void showPage(IWizardPage page);
    public void updateButtons();
    public void updateMessage();
    public void updateTitleBar();
    public void updateWindowTitle();
}
```

The challenge of reusability is perhaps most prominent in these service interfaces for collaborators. Let us go back to the general situation in Fig. 12.25 on page 711, which is also reflected in Fig. 12.26.

The services for A and B on the left-hand side are really clear-cut, because they derive from the purpose of the reusable component R itself. The interfaces from the component R to its collaborators C and D on the right-hand side of Fig. 12.26 are also rather straightforward, because they can be defined along the minimal requirements of the component. But the final interfaces, from collaborators C and D to the reusable R are really hard: There are no general guidelines that would enable us to gauge the expectations and requirements of these collaborators. Only experience and analysis of concrete usage scenarios will tell. In fact, even in the case of the Wizard Dialog, it was only later on that the designers recognized that wizards might wish to adapt the dialog size to cater to pages of varying sizes. They captured this new service in the extension interface IWizardContainer2:

»12.4.4

↰3.2.5

---

org.eclipse.jface.wizard.IWizardContainer2

```
public interface IWizardContainer2 extends IWizardContainer {
    public void updateSize();
}
```

↰11.1

⇄? We have already discussed (page 582) that the update ... methods in IWizard Container could be replaced by making the dialog a generic observer. We have dismissed this approach because it would complicate matters and there would always be only one observer, contrary to the intentions of the OBSERVER pattern.

↰2.1.4

The current question of reusability offers yet another perspective if we ask a new question: Which object should determine the callback interface? The OBSERVER pattern insists that the subject, in this case the contained wizard, define the callbacks according to its possible state changes. However, we are building a generic WizardDialog that must be reusable in different scenarios (Fig. 12.25). Since that object is in the focus of the design, the Dependency Inversion Principle suggests that the WizardDialog should also define the notification methods.

↰2.1.2

↰11.5.6

↰12.3.2 ↰7.3.2

💡 A further view of the IWizardContainer derives from the fact that the wizard uses it to access its context, in this case the WizardDialog in which it happens to be displayed. In the INTERCEPTOR pattern, the WizardDialog plays the role of a framework linking to some application-specific functionality by inversion of control. In such situations, callbacks usually receive a *context object*, which enables them to query the framework's status and to influence the framework's behavior.

12.4.3   Building a Reusable Parser

To appreciate the challenge of reuse fully, one cannot simply look at polished examples of reusable components. One has to struggle through the process of creating such components, even if it means grappling with the details of API design and performing many tedious refactorings.

↰12.4.1

Let us therefore go back once more to the example of the function plotter, through which we explored the challenges of responsibility-driven design itself. There, we reused the `Parser` from the section on tree structures and the MiniXcel application. The process of creating this parser is instructive. On the one hand, the example is small enough to get through by tactical considerations, taking one step after the other. On the other hand, it does include some of the real-world obstacles to reuse. We also use the example to formulate and explore a few fundamental guidelines for reusability.

↰11.3

↰11.3.3.1 ↰2.3.3
↰9.4

> Design the services of reusable components along established concepts.

So, let us picture `Parser` as the component R in Fig. 12.25. We start designing on the left-hand side of the figure. To arrive at a general service API for the parser, we ask: What does a parser really do for its clients? Well, it transforms a string conforming to some formal grammar into an abstract syntax tree (AST). Since we are mainly aiming at arithmetic expressions, this would suggest roughly the following interface:

📖2

```
public class Parser {
    ArithmeticExpression parse(String expr)
    ...
}
```

It is usually a good idea to start designing reusable components from generally known concepts, such as "parsing." Other developers will easily understand the purpose and usage of the component. Also, well-known concepts are well known precisely because they tend to pop up in many different contexts. The potential for reuse is then particularly high.

> Mold the concept into an API carefully.

The API presented earlier involves a rather subtle problem: We cannot simply fix the type of the syntax tree, because MiniXcel and the function plotter differ in the detail of cell references and variables. Some tools, such as ANTLR, circumvent such questions by using generic structures of nested linked lists. But this approach prevents the use of the COMPOSITE pattern, which neatly embeds recursive operations into the recursive object structure.

📖206
↰2.3.1

The only solution to defining the AST properly is to let the client do it: Only the client knows the best structure for the syntax trees for the language it is parsing. We render this idea in the API by parameterizing the `Parser` by the type `T` of these trees. The parser will then juggle around AST nodes without inspecting them. If you are wondering how the parser will ever create objects of type `T`—we will come to that in a minute. For now, recognize that the `Parser` has become an object encapsulating a (semi-) complex algorithm in a simple method `parse()`:

↰1.8.6

parser.Parser

```
public class Parser<T> {
    ...
    public T parse(String expr) throws ParseError {
        ...
    }
    ...
}
```

Design collaborators as roles, starting from general concepts.

Let us now turn to the collaborators `C` and `D` in Fig. 12.25—that is, to those objects whose services the reusable component `R` itself requires from the context for proper operation. Since they vary between contexts, technically `R` has to access them through interfaces. The interfaces capture the expected behavior without constraining the implementation.

↰3.2.1

It is important to realize that, again, these interfaces must derive from a conceptual understanding of roles: Concrete objects `C` and `D` will fulfill the requirements not by coincidence, but only if the roles' responsibilities can be implemented in different but meaningful ways.

↰11.3.3.7

The reusable `Parser` must somehow construct the syntax tree. However, it cannot do so itself because the tree's type `T` is left open. For this scheme to work, the parser needs a collaborator to undertake the construction—an ABSTRACT FACTORY. The collaborator is passed to the parser's constructor to create the object structure sketched in Fig. 12.25.

↰1.4.12

parser.Parser

```
private NodeFactory<T> factory;
public Parser(NodeFactory<T> factory) {
    this.factory = factory;
}
```

What, then, is a suitable set of methods for the `NodeFactory`? Conceptually, the parser recognizes constructions in arithmetic expressions, each of which ends up as a node in the AST. It is therefore sensible to introduce one method for each type of syntax construct recognized. The parameters contain a description of the construct. The last method creating "references" involves a deliberate generalization, which is often necessary for successful reuse in different contexts. We discuss the details next.

---
parser.NodeFactory

```
public interface NodeFactory<T> {
    T createNumber(double num) throws ParseError;
    T createBinaryOperator(String op, T left, T right)
        throws ParseError;
    T createFunctionApplication(String fun, List<T> args)
        throws ParseError;
    T createReference(String token) throws ParseError;
}
```

⇄? One point worth discussing is the type of `op` in method `createBinaryOperator()`.
Technically, a shift-reduce parser will recognize only a fixed set of operators, because
it needs to assign a precedence to each of them. An `enum` type would therefore probably   📖2
be more suitable. We have left our first version of the API here to raise precisely this
discussion about a necessary decision, rather than presenting a polished version that
glosses over it. Also, you may want to try your hand at a further generalization: Why
not parameterize the parser from the online supplement by using an `OperatorTable` that
maps operator symbols to precedences? The parser can then classify any consecutive
sequence of punctuation characters as an operator.

The implementation of reusable components should reflect the used
concepts.

The construction and handling of AST nodes in the `Parser` is a good
example of a collaboration between a generic, reusable component R and
its application-specific helpers C and D in Fig. 12.25.

In principle, a shift-reduce parser reads through the input string from   📖2
left to right. It groups the characters into *tokens* such as numbers and
operators. When it finds a leaf node, such as a variable or a number, it
pushes the node on a stack, because it cannot know whether the node is
the right operand of the previous operator or the left operand of the next.
For instance, in `a+b+c`, `b` belongs to the left operator to yield the result
`(a+b)+c`. In contrast, in `a+b*c`, `b` must be kept until `c` has been seen to yield
`a+(b*c)`. Keeping a node for later reference is called a *shift* step. Creating
a new node from an operator and its operands is called a *reduce* step.

Our `Parser` keeps the currently recognized subexpressions on an *operand
stack* and the currently open binary operators on an *operator stack*.

---
parser.Parser

```
private Stack<Op> operatorStack = new Stack<Op>();
private Stack<T> operandStack = new Stack<T>();
```

When it encounters a number, it pushes a node on the operand stack:

---
parser.Parser.endToken

```
if (NUM_PATTERN.matcher(tokStr).matches()) {
    operandStack.push(factory.createNumber(Double.parseDouble(
                                            tokStr)));
}
```

Reducing means finishing a subexpression by creating a new node for the syntax tree. The parser pops an operator and its two operands. It calls on the factory to create the node for the syntax tree. That node becomes a newly found operand to surrounding operators.

parser.Parser.reduceUpTo

```
T r = operandStack.pop();
T l = operandStack.pop();
String op = ((BinOp) operatorStack.pop()).op;
operandStack.push(factory.createBinaryOperator(op, l, r));
```

The interesting point about this implementation is that it works entirely at the level of shift-reduce parsing, without any thoughts about the applications of function plotting or spreadsheets. In our experience, one indication that you got your abstraction right is that your code reflects your understanding of the concepts you have chosen as the basis of your reusable component.

↰11.2

In fact, this focus on the abstract concepts is a prime example of the Single Responsibility Principle. Previously, we have applied the principle to split separate tasks into separate objects or classes. Now we see that it also serves to separate the abstract mechanisms from the concrete applications. While previously the split was vertical, putting one task beside the other, the new split is horizontal, in the sense of the LAYERS pattern: It puts the high-level mechanisms above the low-level details and the common aspects above the variations between the applications.

↰12.2.2
▢70,71

Creating a reusable API requires experience and deliberate generalization.

Reusability to novices often seems to be the ultimate goal in software design: What can be more elegant than a general solution that you build once and never have to touch again? Besides, the personal prestige to be gained from finding such "ultimate" solutions is extremely attractive.

To counteract such misconceptions, we reveal that the solution presented here is the *third* attempt at building a shift-reduce parser. We have never said to ourselves, "Hey, parsing is cool and we have some experience, so let's build a reusable parser so we never have to do it again." In fact, our previous experience with parsing told us precisely that such a component could *not* be built easily. Here is the story of how we arrived at the Parser class through repeated refactoring and generalization.

↰9.4

The first parser version dates back to a lecture from 2006. It had a hard-coded syntax tree for the MiniXcel application, which the students were to use in a project. In a later lecture in 2008, we asked the students to come up with the syntax tree for simple arithmetic expressions and introduced the type parameterization and the node factory. In essence, this carved out the reusable concept of shift-reducing parsing from the tangle of interacting objects within MiniXcel. Only after this step did the scenario resemble Fig. 12.25, with the Parser class in the position R.

Nevertheless, there remained one reference to the original MiniXcel context: For lack of time, the second version still accepted cell references like A3 or B$2. The NodeFactory had the two creation operations shown in the following code snippet, and we simply asked the students to ignore the one for CellRefs in the exercise. While this version was reusable enough for the purpose, we would certainly not commit it to paper.

```
T createVariable(String name) throws ParseError;
T createReference(CellRef r) throws ParseError;
```

The third version prepared for this book required a major refactoring to get rid of the dependency on CellRefs scattered through the implementation and to come up with the general creation for "references," whether they are variables or cell references. The reusable parser's collaborator Node Factory, indicated as role C in Fig. 12.25, now creates the appropriate node, or throws a parse error if the format is unexpected. For convenience, here is the generalized method from the NodeFactory once more:

parser.NodeFactory

```
T createReference(String token) throws ParseError;
```

In many situations, you will find that generalizing the API of a reusable component also requires generalizing its internal mechanisms, because the existing ones take shortcuts only valid in the special case treated so far— after all, the guideline is to build the simplest thing that could possibly work.

For instance, the old parser distinguished variables and cell references first lexically, by whether they were uppercase or lowercase. In a second step, variables before an opening parenthesis were taken to be function names. Since this distinction between uppercase and lowercase characters is invalid for general "references," the new parser stores any characters that are neither whitespace nor reserved characters in a string buffer token. When it hits an opening parenthesis afterward, it checks whether the token is a valid function name. For any other special character or whitespace, it delegates the recognition of the token to the NodeFactory's create Reference() method.

parser.Parser.endToken

```
if (inFunPos) {
    if ((m = FUN_PATTERN.matcher(tokStr)).matches()) {
        operatorStack.push(new Fun(m.group(), operandStack.size()));
    } else {
        error(pos - token.length(), pos, "illegal function name");
    }
} else {
    operandStack.push(factory.createReference(tokStr));
}
```

> Generalize such that the previous applications remain covered.

The purpose of the whole generalization effort is, of course, to use the same code for different applications. In this book, we would like to use the `Parser` for the trees in Chapter 2, for MiniXcel in Chapter 9, and for the example of the function plotter in Section 11.3. The fundamental principle is always "don't repeat yourself" (DRY): Once you start on copy-and-paste programming, you have to keep changes and bug fixes coordinated. The effort of generalizing at the first instance of reuse may be well spent, because you save on maintenance, and may even find further places in the system where the reused component can be deployed.

↰11.5.5

The challenge was, of course, to keep the original MiniXcel application working while refactoring for the new uses. To avoid losing time in debugging the online supplement for Chapter 9, we started by extending the existing test suite for the parser before attempting any changes. Generalizing is a large effort itself. You should not increase it by breaking the product at the same time.

↰5.4.8

12.4.4 Strategies for Reuse

As the examples in the previous subsections have shown, reusability is a complex and challenging goal. At the same time, it often requires large investments in a general software infrastructure that complicates the code base. Worse still, the investments may never pay off because the "reusable" components turn out not to cover all expected applications. Because every component is essentially special, it is very hard to come up with general guidelines on how to proceed toward successful reuse. This section gives a few general hints.

> Reusability is not an aim in itself.

☐258

The first pitfall to be avoided is apparently a human weakness: Developers love to come up with "elegant" solutions, in particular if they can define "elegance" according to their own personal taste. Reusability always has a strong attraction here: You can do a thing once and never have to bother with it again. However, reusability invariably takes development time away from the concrete application functionality, because it requires generalization and abstraction. It simply does not do to waste development time on "reusable" components if these are never reused. The danger of running into "you ain't gonna need it" (YAGNI) is very high.

↰12.4.3
☐228

> Make reusable design pay early.

The first guideline is therefore to evaluate the potential of a reusable component early on, before you start to design or to implement. Try to be completely fair: Count the possible scenarios where the component applies. Estimate the ease of use and the savings in development time in each scenario.

Gauge the simplicity of reusing compared to hand-coding the functionality:
If the configuration of the reusable component is very complex, this indicates that the variability between the uses exceeds their commonality and   □□70
the basis for reusability is rather weak. In many cases, you will find but a
few application spots, so you must aim at making the generalization pay
early on.

　　To avoid personal biases, you should also discuss the proposed component with your teammates. If they find applications or expect them to arise
from their experience, the probability that your component will actually be
useful increases dramatically.

Do the simplest thing that could possibly work.

One particular temptation in designing for reusability is to get carried away
with abstraction. While you are implementing a reusable component, you
will come across many hooks that might be useful in some future application. However, you should focus on the usage scenarios you have identified
and leave other generalizations until later. A good constraining idea is to
start testing your component immediately: If you have to write a test for   ↰5.2
each adaptation point, you will think twice about whether you really need
the generality.

Aim for cohesion and conceptual clarity.

The other point that helps to focus the design is cohesion. Do not try to   ↰12.1.3
build the ultimate solution that anticipates every possible detail of every
possible application scenario. Instead, define the purpose of your component
clearly and then build only those features that are covered by the purpose.
This guideline is useful in object-oriented design in general, but it is even   ↰11.2
more important when designing for reusability: Because you are dealing
with more abstract mechanisms, it is harder to judge whether a particular
piece of functionality is really required.

Keep reusable components decoupled from their context.

The initial intuition in Fig. 12.25 hints at the need to decouple a reusable   ↰12.1
component from its context, because the component will have to work in
many different scenarios. It is useful to keep this caveat in mind when
creating CRC cards for the component: Think about the minimal assump-   ↰12.1.2
tions that enable your component to work. Once you have written code, it
becomes much harder to reduce these assumptions.

Design reusable components along established concepts.

A good guideline for finding parts of the implementation that make reuse
worthwhile is to look at general concepts, both from the application domain
and from computer science. A parser for arithmetic expressions might come   ↰12.4.3

in handy, as could a framework for rendering charts from raw data. Eclipse is all about editing code, so a custom-tailored, powerful `SourceViewer` will be required. Proven concepts such as graphical editing might also warrant a general implementation.

Once you have found the central concept of the reusable component, you should also get a precise idea of where the reusable functionality ends: Which services does the component comprise? Which parts of the behavior will differ between the uses and should better be implemented elsewhere? Which aspects have a default implementation that can be overridden?

Look for available reusable components first.

Once you have formulated the concept you want to capture, you should sit back and browse for available libraries and frameworks that already cover that concept. If you do find a solution, you do not save just the implementation effort; you also save the effort that is required for first understanding the problem at the necessary level of abstraction. Do not insist on making all the initial blunders yourself, and do not fall for the not-invented-here syndrome. Of course, the available components might not have exactly the API that you would have built, but that can often be solved by creating a few ADAPTERS.

Reusability is not a technical issue.

Many novices like reuse because it gives them license to try their hand at all kinds of nifty indirections and patterns that object-oriented programming has to offer. They often start by generalizing the implementation without having a clear understanding of the abstraction they are aiming at.

Professionals start from the conceptual questions, which give them a clear picture of the commonalities between the different uses of a component. Only then do they start to think about how the differences, or variabilities, between these uses can be captured technically: Should they use TEMPLATE METHOD, STRATEGY, OBSERVER, plain collaboration through interfaces, or abstract base classes? The trick is to start from the client's perspective: Which API will be easiest and best for your teammates when they start using your component?

Build a toolbox that helps to build your applications.

One effective way of recognizing candidates for reusable components is to be perceptive in your daily work. If you find that you have implemented variations of some piece of functionality several times, chances are that you will encounter it some more later on. You can then start to think about the concepts that are common to all occurrences and to turn them into reusable components.

214

↰7.3

↰11.3.3.5

↰12.2.1.6 ↰2.4.1

71,70
↰1.4.8 ↰1.8.5 ↰3.1.4
↰1.1

The general idea is that you are building a toolbox that helps you build your applications. Fill the toolbox while you go on with your daily work. This will also help you to focus on the essentials and to avoid over-designing. It will encourage you to forge only tools that you can use immediately.

Start from working code and concrete mechanisms.

Another approach is to let reusable functionality find you, rather than actively searching for it. While aiming for DRY, you can try to generalize existing objects so that they cover more and more situations. The `Parser` example shows that this can be done gradually, incorporating one new application after the other. If you keep testing diligently, you will start saving implementation effort almost immediately, because you avoid the bugs introduced by copy-and-paste programming. And the more you master the Eclipse refactoring tools, the more progress you make. Throughout the process, be sure to identify concepts in your implementation; then you can refactor to exhibit those concepts more clearly.

↰11.5.5
↰12.4.3

Practice reuse in the small.

Software engineering, like any craft, is often a matter of practice and experience. Designing reusable components is particularly tricky, so you should give yourself the time to learn. Design individual objects, then compound objects, then small neighborhoods. Afterward, you can go on to components.

Part V

Appendix

Appendix A

Working with Eclipse Plugins

Eclipse is not just a great IDE. It does more than simply support many languages and tools. It is also extensible by nifty add-ons created for special purposes. Beyond all of this, it is also a strong basis for building stand-alone applications for end-users. It offers a vibrant community and a rich ecosystem of reusable off-the-shelf components, both open source and commercial. The technical basis for all of this is Eclipse's powerful plugin mechanism. It enables the assembly of largely independent components into consistent overall applications.

This appendix introduces the mechanism and the tools of the plugin development environment (PDE). The goal is to enable you to work with the book's sample code and to start creating your own plugins. At the same time, we want to contradict the myth that plugins are complex and unwieldy beasts that suck up valuable development time. In many cases, it is the incomplete tutorials on the web, which fail to mention the possible technical stumbling blocks or leave out crucial insights, that are responsible for these losses.

The Eclipse plugin mechanism consists of two layers (Fig. A.1): At the bottom, the OSGi layer offers the typical features of a module system such as dependencies, versioning, and explicit exports. It also takes care of class loading and access to resources such as images. All of this is described in the META-INF/MANIFEST.MF file of each plugin. The OSGi implementation Equinox is part of the normal Eclipse platform. On top of this, Eclipse adds its own specific extension point/extension mechanism. The declarations are given in a file plugin.xml in each plugin using extensions. Because OSGi has laid a very solid foundation, this second layer is actually very thin.

📖203

📖175,65

↰12.3.3

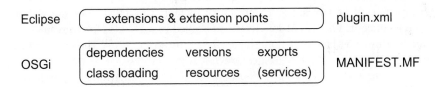

Figure A.1 The Levels of OSGi and Eclipse

This appendix focuses on the OSGi layer, because the editing of the file plugin.xml has already been covered in some detail.

↰12.3.3

🔎 OSGi includes support for *services* (Fig. A.1), which are defined by Java interfaces and can then be implemented by any bundle that is loaded into the OSGi runtime. This introduces dependency inversion: Code consuming the service is no longer tied to a specific implementation and therefore remains more flexible. Because Eclipse itself does not use services extensively, we will not cover them here.

↰11.5.6
↰12.2.1.4

Bundles and plugins are technically the same thing.

For historical reasons, the Eclipse and OSGi layers use different terminology: Where Eclipse talks of "plugins," OSGi talks of "bundles." Within the Eclipse context, they are technically the same thing. If you like, you can say that an Eclipse plugin at the higher level is technically represented as an OSGi bundle at the lower level, with an additional optional `plugin .xml` file. The distinction appears both in the documentation and in the sources, because the Equinox API refers to "bundles," while class names from the Eclipse IDE often include the term "plugin."

Throughout the appendix, we will also introduce the relevant Eclipse tools as we go along. The central entry point is the plugin manifest editor.

TOOL: Plugin Manifest Editor

An Eclipse plugin is described mainly through the files `META-INF/ MANIFEST.MF` and `plugin.xml`. Clicking on either of these opens the *plugin manifest editor*, which provides access to all relevant aspects of a plugin.

A.1   OSGi: A Module System for Java

The plain JVM comes with a sophisticated idea: The classes of a running application are fetched on demand by dedicated *class loader* objects. Basically each class is tagged at runtime with its own class loader, and when a class references another class, it asks its own class loader to provide it. Unfortunately, that's it. There are no further features that enable encapsulation at the level of "modules"; in fact, the JVM does not define such a concept. Classes usually come packaged in JAR files for convenience, but at runtime they share one huge, flat namespace. Only the established naming conventions for packages prevent frequent clashes.

↰11.5.1

Of course, this is quite unacceptable for larger applications, in particular if they are assembled from independently developed plugins. For instance, the naming conventions for packages do not help if two plugins happen to require different versions of the same library. Also, conventions are guidelines but they can be circumvented: You can access a package-visible class or method contained in any library simply by placing your own class in a package with the same name—even if you use a different JAR file.

OSGi provides a proper module system for Java.

The OSGi layer of Eclipse provides all of these missing features.

A.1.1   The Structure of OSGi Bundles

OSGi calls a module a *bundle* (Fig. A.2). Each bundle contains a tree of packages and subpackages with classes, as usual. It can also contain libraries in the form of JAR files. These libraries are hidden from other bundles, so that different bundles can use different versions of the same library. A bundle makes explicit which packages it wishes to *export*; the others remain hidden, as indicated by dashed lines in Fig. A.2. A bundle can declare *dependencies* on other bundles. It can then access the exported packages of those bundles.

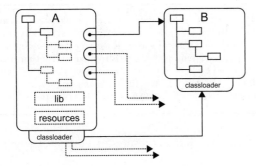

Figure A.2 A Bundle in OSGi

𝒫 OSGi is very powerful and flexible and the preceding description glosses over many of its capabilities. For instance, a running application *can* contain different versions of the same plugin, but it usually doesn't. One *can* export the packages contained in a bundle's libraries, but one usually doesn't. One *can* import named packages, rather than depending on bundles, but one usually doesn't. The purpose of this section is to give a thorough overview of OSGi, but without wading through all the details.

⚠ Here is the first stumbling block: If a bundle has unsatisfied dependencies at runtime, Equinox will not load it. Any dependent bundles will also be skipped. However, the startup process of the application will still continue. When you get `ClassNotFound` `Exceptions`, you should check the startup log messages—perhaps the relevant bundle has not been loaded at all.

A bundle's manifest contains a self-description.

Each OSGi bundle describes itself through a file `META-INF/MANIFEST.MF`. That file gives the bundle's name, identifier, version, dependencies, and exports, among other things. We will explicitly not show these files to discourage you from working with the raw text. Use the plugin manifest editor instead.

The OSGi class loaders enforce the module system's access restrictions.

If OSGi offers theses expressive extra features, one might expect that it requires complex modifications to the JVM. However, this is not the case at all. The Equinox implementation just uses a single crucial observation: Because all class loading happens through class loaders, it is sufficient to make these class loaders enforce the access restrictions. At runtime, the Equinox implementation creates a dedicated, special-purpose class loader for each bundle (Fig. A.2). It is wired up with the class loaders of required bundles to propagate requests.

⚠ The class loading process is often perceived as problematic, because even compiling code can fail with an obscure `ClassNotFoundException` at runtime. First, it is important to think about the general setup: Have you got the dependencies and their versions right? Is a required bundle perhaps dropped at runtime because of missing dependencies, as explained earlier? Are the libraries included in the build, as will be explained later? If all else fails, you can use the class `org.eclipse.osgi.framework.debug` `.Debug` and set its static field `DEBUG_LOADER` to `true` to trace the search for classes.

OSGi provides a runtime infrastructure for bundles.

OSGi can be understood as a runtime infrastructure that manages the loaded bundles. It represents bundles as `Bundle` objects, and you can access these bundles by calling `Platform.getBundle()` with a bundle's name. In addition to other things, the bundles then give access to their contents: One can load (exported) classes and query the resources along the usual path, through the bundle's class loader. Alternatively, one can search the bundle's entries directly.

---

org.osgi.framework.Bundle

```
public interface Bundle extends Comparable<Bundle> {
    Class<?> loadClass(String name) throws ClassNotFoundException;
    URL getResource(String name);
    Enumeration<URL> getResources(String name) throws IOException;
    URL getEntry(String path);
    Enumeration<URL> findEntries(String path, String filePattern,
                                 boolean recurse);
    ...
}
```

🔎 The URLs returned from these methods are usually internal. To get the content of a retrieved resource, use the URL's `openStream()` method. If you must have the actual disk location, you can use the `FileLocator` class from the `org.eclipse.core.runtime` plugin. It translates URLs to an external format if possible. There is a serious catch, however: When launching an application or a JUnit test from within Eclipse, the bundles are loaded from the development workspace directly, so the resources are actually files. When packaging bundles in JARs and installing them, however, the URL translation suddenly fails because the resources are located within JARs. Consequently, using File Locator is rather problematic. If you still insist that you must have the files, you can export a plugin through a *feature* and select the option "Unpack the plug-in archive after installation" in the feature definition file.

»A.2.1 »A.2.2

174 »A.3

OSGi also defines an explicit life cycle for bundles and allows bundles to be loaded and unloaded dynamically. The bundles themselves are notified if they declare an *activator* class. The activator must implement the following simple interface:

| org.osgi.framework.BundleActivator |

```
public interface BundleActivator {
    public void start(BundleContext context) throws Exception;
    public void stop(BundleContext context) throws Exception;
}
```

Eclipse provides an implementation Plugin, which keeps a reference to the bundle upon startup. It is then not necessary to go through the Platform to find the bundle.

| org.eclipse.core.runtime.Plugin |

```
public abstract class Plugin implements BundleActivator {
    public void start(BundleContext context) throws Exception {
        bundle = context.getBundle();
        ...
    }
    public final Bundle getBundle() {
        if (bundle != null)
            return bundle;
        ...
        return null;
    }
    ...
}
```

It is a common practice for a plugin's activator to provide a static reference to the bundle object and to expose the bundle symbolic name as a constant. Here is the example of the JavaCore plugin:

| org.eclipse.jdt.core.JavaCore |

```
public final class JavaCore extends Plugin {
    public static final String PLUGIN_ID = "org.eclipse.jdt.core" ;
    public static JavaCore getJavaCore() {
        return (JavaCore) getPlugin();
    }
    ...
}
```

Fragments are merged into their host bundles at runtime.

Sometimes it is useful to split the implementation of one logical bundle over several physical bundles. For instance, a bundle might have to be complemented by translated language files. Or, like the SWT bundle, it might contain platform-specific code that must be loaded according to the current operating system and hardware.

Fragments address these scenarios. They are packaged into independent JAR files, so that they can be distributed and deployed on their own. At runtime, their content its merged virtually into a designated *host* plugin: The classes share a common class loader and namespace. When requested, they are loaded from the host or the fragment, as the case might be.

A.1.2   Working with Bundles in Eclipse

When you think of the powerful plugins available for the Eclipse IDE, you may be left with the impression that plugins themselves are heavyweight and complex. This is not the case.

Plugin projects are small and lightweight.

A project in Eclipse consists of a top-level folder and a tiny XML file named `.project`. A Java project adds an XML file `.classpath` for internal purposes and an `src` folder. A plugin project requires only one additional file, the `META-INF/MANIFEST.MF` with the bundle's self-description. If you add extensions or extension points, a top-level `plugin.xml` will be created automatically. That's it. Setting up this structure is really simple.

↩12.3.3

TOOL: Creating an OSGi Bundle

Use the *New Project* dialog (*File/New/Project*) or in the package explorer use *Context Menu/New/Project* and choose *Plug-in Project*.

TOOL: Converting a Java Project to a Bundle

Select the project in the package explorer and choose *Configure/Convert to Plug-in Projects* from its context menu.

Some people might suggest that the manifests of Eclipse plugins are very complex and cumbersome to work with. When you hear such a remark, just ask these people how they edit the `MANIFEST.MF` and `plugin.xml` files. Very often you will find that they use a text editor. Don't do that.

The Eclipse tooling makes a bundle's structure easily accessible.

The plugin manifest editor in Eclipse gives easy access to all the relevant information. Let us look through the manifest of the Java IDE's central ingredient, the `org.eclipse.jdt.core` plugin. The *Overview* page contains the plugin's ID, name, version, and activator [Fig. A.3(a)]. The

Dependencies contain the IDs of the required bundles [Fig. A.3(b)]. Working with these entries is obvious from the user interface. Of course, the *Add* button for dependencies pops up a filtering selection dialog, so that typos are excluded.

General Information
This section describes general information about this plug-in.

ID:	org.eclipse.jdt.core
Version:	3.9.2.v20140114-1555
Name:	%pluginName
Vendor:	%providerName
Platform Filter:	
Activator:	org.eclipse.jdt.core.JavaCore Browse...

☑ Activate this plug-in when one of its classes is loaded

☑ This plug-in is a singleton

| Overview | Dependencies | Runtime | Extensions | Extension Points | MANIFEST |

(a)

Required Plug-ins

Specify the list of plug-ins required for the operation of this plug-in.

⬚ org.eclipse.core.resources [3.3.0,4.0.0)	Add...
⬚ org.eclipse.core.runtime [3.3.0,4.0.0)	Remove
⬚ org.eclipse.core.filesystem [1.0.0,2.0.0)	
⬚ org.eclipse.text [3.1.0,4.0.0)	Up
⬚ org.eclipse.team.core [3.1.0,4.0.0)	Down
	Properties...

| Overview | Dependencies | Runtime | Extensions | Extension Points | MAI |

(b)

Figure A.3 Basic Properties of Bundles

🔍 The Eclipse support also covers refactoring. When you rename a bundle in the workspace, the manifests of all dependent bundles are updated automatically. The same holds for exported packages, to be discussed next.

Exported packages are given on the *Runtime* page.

A slight confusion may arise from the placement of a bundle's exported packages. These are accessible through the *Runtime* tab, which may sound somewhat too "dynamic" for an essentially static visibility restriction—but there it is. The user interface is otherwise straightforward (Fig. A.4). The *Add* button shows a selection dialog, as would be expected.

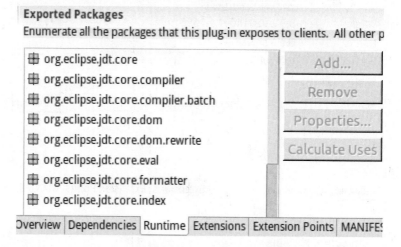

Figure A.4 Exports of a Bundle

Enclosed libraries are entered in the *Runtime* and *Build* pages.

Bundles can contain and enclose libraries (Fig. A.2). By convention, they are packaged in a top-level folder `lib`. This point requires a bit of caution when working with bundles, because entries in three different places have to agree for everything to work out correctly. The plugin development tools do a great job most of the time, but one has to be aware of the background connections, especially when changing the libraries. The three places in question are as follows:

Manifest Class Path The bundle's `MANIFEST.MF` file lists the library JARs in the *Classpath* section of the *Runtime* tab. Fig. A.5(a) shows the Hibernate example from Chapter 5. These entries are evaluated by the OSGi runtime environment when it constructs the bundle's class loader.

Build Specification The bundle's `build.properties` file, accessible through the *Build* page [Fig. A.5(b)], must list the JARs for inclusion in the packaged bundle. These entries are used during packaging. When they are missing, the bundle does not physically contain the libraries referenced in the manifest, so they will not be found after all.

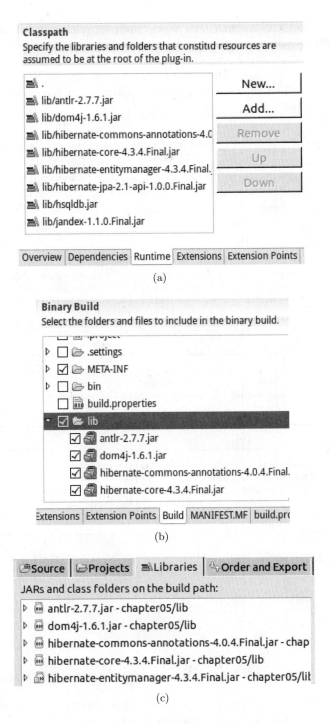

Figure A.5 Enclosing Libraries in Bundles

Compilation Class Path The Java compiler's class path, accessible through the usual *Project Properties* dialog or the *Configure Build Path* entry in the project's context menu [Fig. A.5(c)], must list the same JARs again. The IDE's compiler treats plugin projects as Java projects and does not look into the special bundle manifests.

The *Runtime* page of the manifest editor is the primary source.

The plugin development tooling regards the *Runtime* page of the manifest file as the primary source. When a JAR file is added there, it automatically gets added in the other two places as well. However, when removing or exchanging library files, one sometimes has to work by hand. Because failures are rather annoying and have subtle explanations, we list the most common stumbling blocks.

⚠ It is not sufficient to use *Add to build path* from the context menu of the project. Although the code will compile, it will not run as a proper plugin. Unfortunately, it *will* run if you start a normal Java main class from the plugin, because the Java launch configuration takes the compilation class path into account. This can be quite confusing in the beginning.

» A.2.5

⚠ When the entry on the *Build* page is missing, the plugin will work when launched from within Eclipse, but not when packaged and deployed in a stand-alone Eclipse instance. The reason is that the special launching class loaders look into the plugin projects directly without considering the `build.properties` file.

» A.2

⚠ You must include the entry "." in the bundle class path, unless the bundle class path is completely empty. If you have library entries but not the root ".", the bundle's own classes will not be loaded. Unfortunately, the plugin development environment often removes this entry accidentally when manipulating the list of libraries. Look in the `MANIFEST.MF` text file to make sure the entry is present and to correct any problems.

When something compiles but does not run, you can try the following tool, which will remove any unwarranted entries from the build path.

TOOL: Update Class Path from Plugin Manifest

To synchronize the Java class path with the plugin manifest, choose *Plugin Tools/Update Classpath* from the plugin project's context menu.

The *Extensions* and *Extension Points* are declared in the `plugin.xml`

↰12.3.3

The manifest editor also provides the pages *Extensions* and *Extension Points*. These have already been covered in the treatment of the Eclipse extension mechanism.

There are, however, two technical points worth noting. First, the `plugin` `.xml` file is created only when the first extension or extension point is declared. The second point is really a stumbling block.

⚠ Make Eclipse plugins *singleton* bundles. While the lower-level OSGi runtime does allow different versions of the same bundle to be loaded simultaneously, this is not possible with the Eclipse extension mechanism. Be sure to tick the check box *This plug-in is a singleton* in the manifest editor's *Overview* page.

A.1.3   OSGi as an Application Platform

OSGi also provides a new entry point for applications, as a replacement for the plain Java `main()` method. Just implement `IApplication` and start computing. The following code may look small in size, but Eclipse itself starts up from `IDEApplication`, which also implements the interface. When implementing stand-alone applications based on the Eclipse Rich Client Platform, this is your starting point.

📖174

```
                            osgi.HelloWorld
public class HelloWorld implements IApplication {
    public Object start(IApplicationContext context)
        throws Exception {
        System.out.println("Hello, world!");
        return null;
    }
    public void stop() {}
}
```

🔍 The interface `IApplication` is defined in bundle `org.eclipse.equinox.app`, but most of the time classes from `org.eclipse.core.runtime` are required anyway, so it is a safe bet to list that bundle in the dependencies. It also includes the OSGi basics.

To be able to launch the application, you have to do one more thing: You have to create a simple extension in the plugin manifest editor (Fig. A.6).

↰12.3.3.1

⚠ Be sure to give the extension point `org.eclipse.core.runtime.applications` itself a readable ID attribute. That attribute will be used for selecting the application during launch.

»A.2.3

A.1.4   Defining Target Platforms

In the real world, versioning is of supreme importance. When you write plugins and ship them to users, you can never be sure which exact configuration their IDEs really have. At the very least, you should think carefully about your plugins' minimal requirements. Do you develop for, say, the

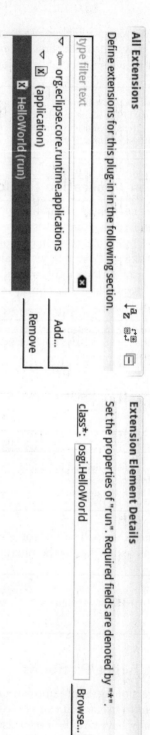

Figure A.6 Declaring an OSGi Application to Eclipse

Eclipse Kepler or Juno releases and thereby exclude users still working with the Indigo release? Professionals are usually not following the latest development snapshots, because they cannot afford to lose valuable time on the latest bugs in their tools. To maintain consistency within a team, larger organizations may be rather conservative about migrating even to the next stable Eclipse release.

Do not work against your development installation.

When you do nothing about versions, you do the worst thing possible: Your plugins are compiled and deployed against the collection of plugins within your running Eclipse instance. If you happen to follow the latest patches for some tools, your code will be compiled against those. Also, any plugin dependency you enter in the manifest editor will automatically be tagged with the version from the snapshot plugin. As a result, the plugins will not work correctly in your users' IDEs. This is a road to disaster for your project.

↰A.1.2

Establish a stable baseline by using target platforms.

Fortunately, the Eclipse plugin tooling recognizes the importance of proper version management. It enables you to define a *target platform* consisting of a selection of plugins against which your plugins will be compiled and which will also be used for launching and building. You can even define several target platforms and switch between them—plugins are always identified by their symbolic name and their expected versions.

To define a target platform, create an empty general project to contain the definition file. Although you can place the file anywhere, it keeps things nice and clean if you use a separate project. Then use *New/Other/Plug-in Development/Target Definition* to create the actual definition file and edit its contents.

The simplest way to create a stable baseline for your development is to list a stable release as the source of the target platform. Fig. A.7 shows the definition for the example code accompanying the book. We deliberately use the rather old Indigo release here to follow up the point made in the introduction to this subsection: Very often, you cannot expect your customers to use the newest tools. When you click the *Add* button and enter an update site, you can choose the required plugins just as in the software installation wizard.

Creating a target definition can take quite some time, because the selected plugins will be downloaded from the Internet. It is, however, time well spent: Without an explicit target, you simply cannot do any professional software development.

The current target platform is a global choice.

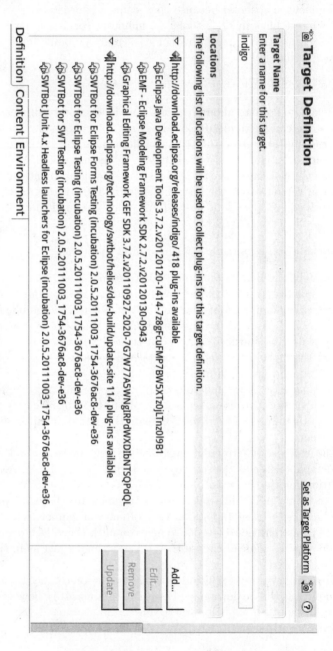

Figure A.7 Defining a Target Platform

Mostly a software project will have a single target platform and will be managed in a dedicated Eclipse workspace anyway. Eclipse therefore has only a single global setting for the target platform. It is accessible through the general workbench *Preferences* dialog (Fig. A.8). The *Running Platform* is not usually a good choice, so you quickly *Add* the newly created one and set it as the default.

Eclipse will recompile all plugins in the workspace against the new target. It will also launch your application against this target. As a result, you can be sure that your customers, who are still stuck with the Indigo release, will see exactly the same behavior as you see during testing and debugging.

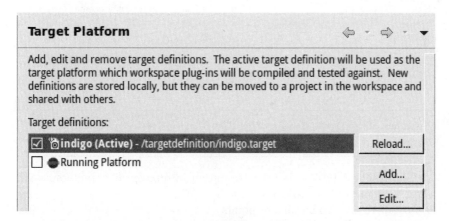

Figure A.8 The Target Platform in the Preferences

Establish a target platform before starting on your plugins.

The target platform is used in many places throughout the plugin development tooling. One particular point is that the manifest editor will, by default, set the required version of a newly created dependency to the version found in the target platform. It is really annoying if you find you have to downgrade all versions by hand after you choose a new target.

Reload the target platform after changing it.

If you edit a target definition after first creating it, the plugin tooling sometimes does not pick up the new content in all places. In particular, plugins that are obviously present sometimes fail to show up in the manifest editor's *Add Dependency* dialog. Simply clicking the *Reload* button in the selection page (Fig. A.8) fixes such issues. As a shortcut, you can click the *Set as target platform* link at the top of the target platform editor.

A.2   Launching Plugins

Having created a few plugins, you will want to see them run. Here are a few steps matching common scenarios. The first and smallest set of steps, for JUnit plugin tests, also discusses the selection of plugins for launch configurations in general.

A.2.1   JUnit Plugin Tests

Running a JUnit plugin test is simple enough:

> **TOOL: Starting Unit Tests for Plugins**
>
> Select *Run As ... /JUnit Test Case* from the test class's context menu, either in the package explorer or in the editor. You can also press Alt-Shift-X T to launch the test, which is particularly convenient during editing of tests. When applying these steps to packages or projects, Eclipse will execute all contained test classes.

⚠ Be sure not to choose *Run As/JUnit Test*. That mode does not set up the plugin's expected working environment such as an Eclipse workspace.

Beyond these basics, JUnit tests must run quickly. If it takes ages for a test to come up, you will not run the test frequently and it is not very useful. There are two important points to be observed in regard to ensuring a quick startup time. First, make sure that the run configuration's *Main* tab selects a headless execution—that is, that an execution that does not start up a user interface before running the tests (Fig. A.9). Of course, this approach works only if your test does not rely on the workbench window.

Figure A.9 Launching Headless JUnit Tests

Second, minimize the number of plugins that must be loaded and initialized. On the *Plugins* page of the launch configuration, go through these steps (or create the launch configuration from scratch): Select *Deselect all*, then select the plugin under test, and finally select *Add Required Plug-ins*.

⚠ Be sure to uncheck the point *Add new workspace plug-ins to this launch configuration automatically* on the *Plug-ins* page. Otherwise, your startup times will deteriorate whenever you create new plugins. Also, the new plugins may rely on dependencies that have not yet been established, which may break the launch configuration.

⚠ When you change any of the dependencies of your application's bundles, the launch configuration *does not change accordingly*. The result is that some bundles are silently not loaded because their dependencies are not satisfied. (There are log messages to this effect on the console, though, when you look closely.) This results in odd behavior and missing functionality. For instance, your new editor for some file type may suddenly be no longer available. Just open the launch configuration and click *Add Required Plug-ins*.

A.2.2 Contributions to the Eclipse IDE

Many plugins are actually contributions to the Eclipse IDE, so you have to test them within that context. The plugin tooling makes it simple to start up a separate IDE, complete with workspace, Java Development Tools, and so on. Just create a new launch configuration of type *Eclipse Application* and choose `org.eclipse.ui.ide.workbench` as the OSGi application to be started on the *Main* page (Fig. A.10). Alternatively, you can run the product `org.eclipse.platform.ide` by choosing it in the *Product* selection box (grayed out in Fig. A.10).

Figure A.10 Launching an IDE with Your Plugins

Of course, starting the workbench takes as much time as your normal Eclipse startup. This may be too long for brief debugging cycles. If you want to minimize the number of plugins on the *Plugins* page for a quicker startup, be sure to include the `org.eclipse.ui.ide.application` and its dependencies. Unfortunately, you will also have to add the basics, such as the plugin for the *Project Explorer* (`org.eclipse.ui.navigator` and dependencies) and the Java Development tools (`org.eclipse.jdt.ui` and dependencies) by hand. ↰A.2.1

It may be better to switch over to selecting entire *features* in the *Plugins* page. Features group plugins according to an end user's perspective. For instance, a normal working environment can be constructed from the features `org.eclipse.jdt` for the Java Tooling and `org.eclipse.platform` for the overall IDE. Adding the required features gives a complete launch configuration, as shown in Fig. A.11. Recall from Section A.1.4 that we ↠A.3

deliberately chose the outdated Indigo platform because some of our customers are still stuck with that release.

↰A.1.4

💡 Another, very viable method is to minimize the target platform itself to contain the minimal working environment that you expect your users to have. Then you can simply launch with all present plugins; you do not have to go through further minimization steps.

A.2.3   Eclipse Applications

📖174

↰A.1.3

The Eclipse platform enables you to write entire applications from scratch. While they can make use of the rich selection of available plugins, they do not have to look like an IDE at all. In fact, a minimal application is nothing more than a main class implementing `IApplication`.

You can start such applications through the launch configuration type *Eclipse Application*. The selection of plugins is the same as in the previous sections. The only difference is that you choose your own application, as declared in the extension point `org.eclipse.core.runtime.applications`, on the *Main* page (Fig. A.12).

A.2.4   Installing Plugins in the Workspace

One attractive feature of the plugin development environment is that you can very quickly write your own development tools. For instance, the code snippets in this book were retrieved from the example sources and formatted into the book's LaTeX directory by a special-purpose builder. In another project, we wrote a small translator that turns HTML templates into Java classes while creating the DOM trees. The resulting Java classes are then compiled by Eclipse's own Java builder. Just think of all the new opportunities to speed up your work!

> **TOOL: Install Plugins in the Running Workbench**
>
> From a plugin project's context menu, choose *Export/Plug-in Development/Deployable plug-ins and fragments*. The wizard will build the plug-ins and place them into the current workspace so that they become available after you restart the IDE.

»A.3

⚠ This approach is actually a massive shortcut, which circumvents the usual packaging of plugins into features and features into update sites, which is followed by installing the content of the resulting update site into the IDE properly. When starting out on a real-world project that you will ship to others, be sure to go all the way early on.

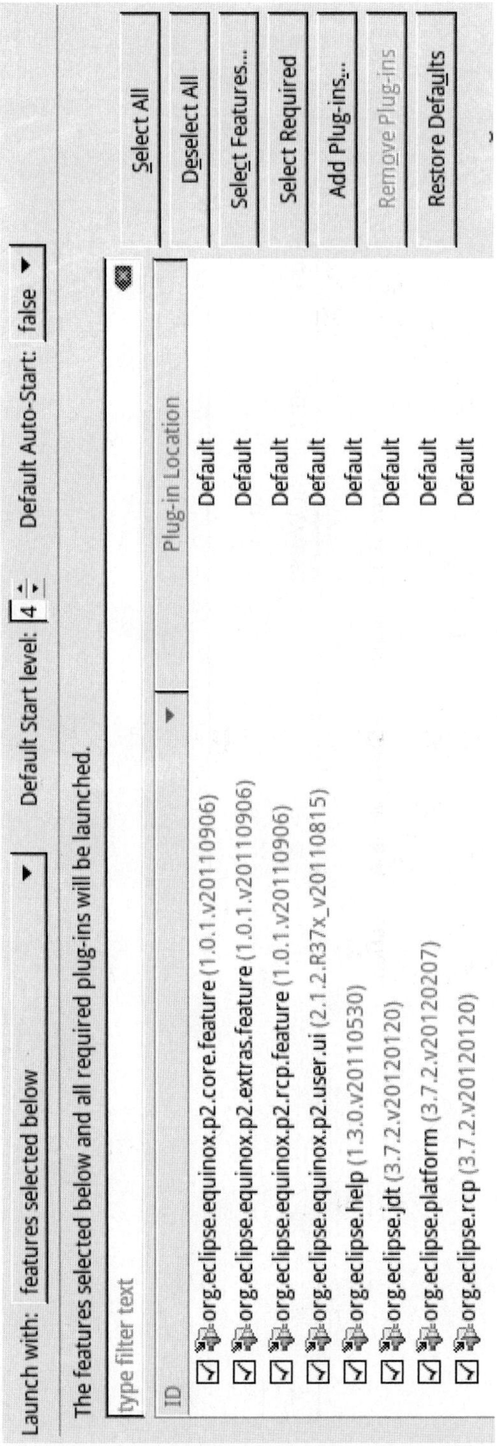

Figure A.11 Launching an IDE with a Set of Features from the Target Platform

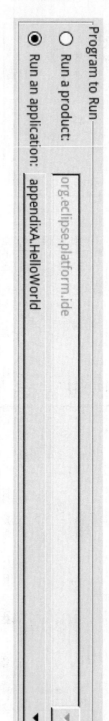

Figure A.12 Launching a Stand-alone Application

A.2.5 Java Programs

When your application does not use the Eclipse runtime infrastructure at all, the plugin development tools also allow you to start a class with a normal `main()` method. The tooling will analyze the dependencies and will add the JAR files containing required plugins to the normal Java class path. In this manner, you can, for instance, start an SWT/JFace application as if SWT and JFace were part of the normal Java library. The advantage of this approach is that startup is incredibly fast and lightweight.

↰7.1 ↰9.3

⚠ This shortcut is useful mainly for experiments and demos. We mention it here to give you a quick access path to the user interface examples in the book. Whenever you want to hand your application to users, you will have to gather all the required JAR files yourself and create a launching script to feed them into the JVM. You will also have to take care of picking the platform-specific fragments—for instance, for the SWT native widgets. In such cases, it is much better to spend the little extra learning effort and use the OSGi infrastructure properly.

↰7.4

💡 If you like the speed of pure Java applications but want to retain the full plugin infrastructure for your application, just work hard on minimizing the required plugins. Starting up a pure OSGi application, without a full Eclipse workspace and resource management, does not take significantly longer than starting with a raw Java main class.

A.3 Where to Go from Here

As a professional plugin developer, you cannot get around the challenges of the last mile: How will your plugins be shipped to their users? How will you provide timely updates with bug fixes? How can you make sure that your own stand-alone OSGi applications will run on different platforms, even if they do contain platform-specific bundles such as SWT?

We will not cover these topics here, because this is a book on object-oriented development and its concepts, not about the details of the Eclipse platform itself. To give you a head start, let us briefly look at the main ingredients of a solution:

📖174

Features Plugins and bundles are useful as technical packaging mechanisms, because they support modular programming, information hiding, and separation of concerns. They are, however, too fine-grained for consumption by the end user. For instance, an end user will want to add "the Java Tools" to the Eclipse IDE, without asking whether they are split across plugins according to model-view separation. *Features* are sets of plugins that are installed together. Features can have dependencies on other features, so that Eclipse installs these automatically as well.

↰11.5.1
↰11.5.2

↰9.1

Update Sites Eclipse defines a standard format for websites offering plugins and features for download. Within Eclipse, you can describe such *update sites* through *update site projects*, which reference plugins and features from your workspace. An export wizard then takes care of assembling all the necessary artifacts into an overall ZIP file, which you can unpack on a web server.

Products The Eclipse Rich Client Platform is made for building standalone applications that do not even have to look like an IDE anymore and do not have to rely on a workspace. You can bring up any user interface you like and just pull in those aspects that you require. A *product* is a selection of plugins or features. Eclipse can automatically create a native launcher, complete with icons and other branding that you specify, and will include the correct native plugin fragments for different platforms from its *delta pack*.

Headless Builds Once you start on serious projects, it becomes cumbersome to click through the export wizards to create update sites. The professional way is to set up a build server that pulls in the sources from a version control system, compiles all plugin projects, and packages everything up neatly into an update site. Perhaps you will even publish the nightly build automatically to your project website. For a solid solution, look at Tycho, which integrates the special requirements of building and deploying Eclipse plugins into the generic build process of the Maven build tool.

📖248

📖173

Bibliography

[1] Martin Abadi and Luca Cardelli. *A Theory of Objects*. Monographs in Computer Science. Springer, 1996.

[2] Alfred V. Aho, Monica S. Lam, Ravi Sethi, and Jeffrey Ullman. *Compilers: Principles, Techniques and Tools*. Addison-Wesley, 2007.

[3] Bowen Alpern, Anthony Cocchi, Stephen Fink, and David Grove. Efficient implementation of Java interfaces: Invokeinterface considered harmless. In *Proceedings of the 16th ACM SIGPLAN Conference on Object-Oriented Programming, Systems, Languages, and Applications*, OOPSLA '01, pages 108–124, New York, NY, 2001. ACM.

[4] Bowen Alpern, Anthony Cocchi, David Grove, and Derek Lieber. Efficient dispatch of Java interface methods. In *Proceedings of the 9th International Conference on High-Performance Computing and Networking*, HPCN Europe 2001, pages 621–628, London, UK, 2001. Springer.

[5] Pierre America. Designing an object-oriented programming language with behavioural subtyping. In J. W. de Bakker, Willem P. de Roever, and Grzegorz Rozenberg, editors, *REX Workshop*, volume 489 of *Lecture Notes in Computer Science*, pages 60–90. Springer, 1990.

[6] Gregory R. Andrews. *Concurrent Programming: Principles and Practice*. Addison-Wesley, 1991.

[7] Giulio Antoniol, Bruno Caprile, Alessandra Potrich, and Paolo Tonella. Design-code traceability for object-oriented systems. *Annals of Software Engineering*, 9(1-4):35–58, 2000.

[8] Apache. The Apache Hadoop library. http://hadoop.apache.org.

[9] Apache Struts. http://struts.apache.org/.

[10] Apache. Apache POI: The Java API for Microsoft documents. http://poi.apache.org, 2014.

[11] Apache. Apache Tomcat. http://tomcat.apache.org, 2015.

[12] Andrew W. Appel and Sandrine Blazy. Separation logic for small-step C minor. In Klaus Schneider and Jens Brandt, editors, *Theorem Proving in Higher Order Logics, 20th International Conference*, volume 4732 of *Lecture Notes in Computer Science*. Springer, 2007.

[13] Apple.   OS X frameworks.   `https://developer.apple.com/library/mac/documentation/MacOSX/Conceptual/OSX_Technology_Overview/SystemFrameworks/SystemFrameworks.html`, 2015.

[14] Apple.   What are frameworks?   `https://developer.apple.com/library/mac/documentation/MacOSX/Conceptual/BPFrameworks/Concepts/WhatAreFrameworks.html`, 2015.

[15] Krysztof R. Apt and Ernst-Rüdiger Olderog. *Verification of Sequential and Concurrent Programs.* Springer, 2nd edition, 1997.

[16] Joe Armstrong, Robert Virding, Claes Wikstrom, and Mike Williams. *Concurrent Programming in Erlang.* Prentice Hall, 2nd edition, 1996.

[17] Franz Baader and Tobias Nipkow. *Term Rewriting and All That.* Cambridge University Press, Cambridge, 1998.

[18] Ralph-Johan J. Back, Abo Akademi, and J. Von Wright. *Refinement Calculus: A Systematic Introduction.* Springer, Secaucus, NJ, 1998.

[19] David F. Bacon, Stephen J. Fink, and David Grove. Space- and time-efficient implementation of the Java object model. In *Proceedings of the 16th European Conference on Object-Oriented Programming*, ECOOP '02, pages 111–132, London, UK, 2002. Springer.

[20] Anindya Banerjee, David Naumann, and Stan Rosenberg. Regional logic for local reasoning about global invariants. In Jan Vitek, editor, *ECOOP 2008—Object-Oriented Programming*, volume 5142 of *Lecture Notes in Computer Science*, pages 387–411. Springer, 2008.

[21] Michael Barnett, Robert DeLine, Manuel Fähndrich, K. Rustan M. Leino, and Wolfram Schulte. Verification of object-oriented programs with invariants. *Journal of Object Technology*, 3(6):27–56, 2004.

[22] Mike Barnett, Bor-Yuh Evan Chang, Robert DeLine, Bart Jacobs, and K. Rustan M. Leino. Boogie: A modular reusable verifier for object-oriented programs. In *4th International Symposium on Formal Methods for Components and Objects*, volume 4111 of *Lecture Notes in Computer Science*. Springer, 2006.

[23] Mike Barnett, K. Rustan M. Leino, and Wolfram Schulte. The Spec# programming system: An overview. In Gilles Barthe, Lilian Burdy, Marieke Huisman, Jean-Louis Lanet, and Traian Muntean, editors, *CASSIS 2004, Construction and Analysis of Safe, Secure and Interoperable Smart Devices*, volume 3362 of *Lecture Notes in Computer Science*, pages 49–69. Springer, 2005.

[24] Len Bass, Paul Clements, and Rick Kazman. *Software Architecture in Practice.* Addison-Wesley, 2nd edition, 2003.

[25] Florian Battke, Stephan Symons, and Kay Nieselt. Mayday: Integrative analytics for expression data. *BMC Bioinformatics*, 11(1), 2010.

[26] Fabian Beck and Stephan Diehl. On the congruence of modularity and code coupling. In *Proceedings of the 19th ACM SIGSOFT Symposium and the 13th European Conference on Foundations of Software Engineering*, ESEC/FSE '11, pages 354–364, New York, NY, 2011. ACM.

[27] Kent Beck. *SmallTalk Best Practice Patterns*. Prentice Hall, 1997.

[28] Kent Beck. *Extreme Programming Explained: Embrace Change*. Addison-Wesley, 1999.

[29] Kent Beck. *Test Driven Development: By Example*. Addison-Wesley, 2002.

[30] Kent Beck. *JUnit Pocket Guide*. O'Reilly, 2004.

[31] Kent Beck. *Implementation Patterns*. Addison-Wesley, 2007.

[32] Kent Beck and Ward Cunningham. A laboratory for teaching object-oriented thinking. *SIGPLAN Notices*, 24(10), October 1989.

[33] Kent Beck and Martin Fowler. *Planning Extreme Programming*. Addison-Wesley, 2001.

[34] Kent Beck and Erich Gamma. JUnit cookbook. `http://junit.org`, 2014.

[35] Jon Bentley. Programming pearls: Little languages. *Communications of the ACM*, 29(8):711–721, August 1986.

[36] Josh Berdine, Cristiano Calcagno, Byron Cook, Dino Distefano, Peter W. O'Hearn, Thomas Wies, and Hongseok Yang. Shape analysis for composite data structures. In *CAV 2007*, volume 4590 of *Lecture Notes in Computer Science*. Springer, 2007.

[37] Josh Berdine, Cristiano Calcagno, and Peter W. O'Hearn. Smallfoot: Modular automatic assertion checking with separation logic. In Frank S. de Boer, Marcello M. Bonsangue, Susanne Graf, and Willem P. de Roever, editors, *Formal Methods for Components and Objects, 4th International Symposium (FMCO)*, volume 4111 of *Lecture Notes in Computer Science*. Springer, 2005.

[38] Josh Berdine, Cristiano Calcagno, and Peter W. O'Hearn. Symbolic execution with separation logic. In Kwangkeun Yi, editor, *Programming Languages and Systems, Third Asian Symposium (APLAS)*, volume 3780 of *Lecture Notes in Computer Science*. Springer, 2005.

[39] James M. Bieman and Josephien Xia Zhao. Reuse through inheritance: A quantitative study of C++ software. In M. H. Samadzadeh and Mansour K. Zand, editors, *Proceedings of the ACM SIGSOFT Symposium on Software Reusability (SSR'95), Seattle, WA, ACM SIGSOFT Software Engineering Notes*, pages 47–52, August 1995.

[40] The BioJava project. `http://www.biojava.org`, 2014.

[41] bioKepler: A comprehensive bioinformatics scientific workflow module. `http://www.biokepler.org`, 2014.

[42] Richard Bird. *Introduction to Functional Programming Using Haskell.* Prentice Hall, 2nd edition, 1998.

[43] Dines Bjørner. TRain: The railway domain: A "grand challenge" for computing science and transportation engineering. In René Jacquart, editor, *IFIP Congress Topical Sessions*, pages 607–612. Kluwer, 2004.

[44] Joshua Bloch. *Effective Java.* Addison-Wesley, 2nd edition, 2006.

[45] Daniel G. Bobrow, Linda G. DeMichiel, Richard P. Gabriel, Sonya E. Keene, Gregor Kiczales, and David A. Moon. Common Lisp object system specification. *SIGPLAN Notices*, 23(SI):1–142, September 1988.

[46] Sascha Böhme and Michał Moskal. Heaps and data structures: A challenge for automated provers. In Nikolaj Bjørner and Viorica Sofronie-Stokkermans, editors, *23nd International Conference on Automated Deduction (CADE 23)*, volume 6803 of *Lecture Notes in Computer Science*, pages 177–191. Springer, 2011.

[47] Grady Booch, Ivar Jacobson, and James Rumbaugh. *The Unified Modeling Language User Guide.* Addison-Wesley, 2nd edition, 2005.

[48] Grady Booch, Robert A. Maksimchuk, Michael W. Engle, Bobbi J. Young, Jim Conallen, and Kelli A. Houston. *Object Oriented Design with Applications.* Addison-Wesley, 3rd edition, 2007.

[49] Richard Bornat. Proving pointer programs in Hoare logic. In *Mathematics of Program Construction*, 2000.

[50] Tim Boudreau, Jaroslav Tulach, and Geertjan Wielenga. *Rich Client Programming: Plugging into the Netbeans Platform.* Prentice Hall, 2007.

[51] Ivan T. Bowman and Richard C. Holt. Software architecture recovery using Conway's law. In *Proceedings of the 1998 Conference of the Centre for Advanced Studies on Collaborative Research.* IBM Press, 1998.

[52] Gilad Bracha. Generics in the Java programming language. Tutorial, http://www.oracle.com/technetwork/java/index.html, March 2004.

[53] Gilad Bracha, Martin Odersky, David Stoutamire, and Philip Wadler. Making the future safe for the past: Adding genericity to the Java programming language. In Craig Chambers, editor, *ACM Symposium on Object Oriented Programming: Systems, Languages, and Applications (OOPSLA)*, pages 183–200, Vancouver, BC, 1998.

[54] Frederick P. Brooks. *The Mythical Man-Month: Essays on Software Engineering, Anniversary Edition.* Addison-Wesley, 2001.

[55] Timothy A. Budd. *Object-Oriented Programming.* Addison-Wesley, 1991.

[56] Lilian Burdy, Yoonsik Cheon, David Cok, Michael D. Ernst, Joe Kiniry, Gary T. Leavens, K. Rustan M. Leino, and Erik Poll. An overview of JML tools and applications. *Software Tools for Technology Transfer*, 7(3):212–232, June 2005.

[57] Michael G. Burke, Kathleen Knobe, Ryan Newton, and Vivek Sarkar. *The Concurrent Collections Programming Model.* Technical Report TR 10–12, Department of Computer Science, Rice University, Houston, TX, December 2010.

[58] R. M. Burstall. Some techniques for proving correctness of programs which alter data stuctures. In B. Meltzer and D. Michie, editors, *Machine Intelligence 7.* Edinburgh University Press, 1972.

[59] Frank Buschmann, Regine Meunier, Hans Rohnert, Peter Sommerlad, and Michael Stal. *Pattern-Oriented Software Architecture: A System of Patterns*, volume 1. Wiley & Sons, 1996.

[60] Giuseppe Castagna. Covariance and contravariance: Conflict without a cause. *ACM Transactions on Programming Languages and Systems*, 17(3):431–447, May 1995.

[61] Raymond Chen. Why is the function SHStripMneumonic misspelled? `http://blogs.msdn.com/b/oldnewthing/archive/2008/05/19/8518565.aspx`, 2008.

[62] Yoonsik Cheon, Gary Leavens, Murali Sitaraman, and Stephen Edwards. Model variables: Cleanly supporting abstraction in design by contract: Research articles. *Software: Practice and Experience*, 35(6):583–599, May 2005.

[63] Keith L. Clark and Sten-Ake Tärnlund, editors. *Logic Programming.* Academic Press, London, UK, 1982.

[64] E. M. Clarke, E. A. Emerson, and A. P. Sistla. Automatic verification of finite-state concurrent systems using temporal logic specifications. *ACM Transactions on Programming Languages and Systems*, 8(2):244–263, April 1986.

[65] Eric Clayberg and Dan Rubel. *Eclipse Plug-ins.* Addison-Wesley, 3rd edition, 2009.

[66] Ernie Cohen, Markus Dahlweid, Mark Hillebrand, Dirk Leinenbach, Michał Moskal, Thomas Santen, Wolfram Schulte, and Stephan Tobies. VCC: A practical system for verifying concurrent C. In *Theorem Proving in Higher Order Logics, 22nd International Conference (TPHOLs)*, volume 5674 of *Lecture Notes in Computer Science.* Springer, 2009.

[67] Ernie Cohen, Michał Moskal, Wolfram Schulte, and Stephan Tobies. A precise yet efficient memory model for C. In *4th International Workshop on Systems Software Verification (SSV 2009)*, ENTCS. Elsevier Science B.V., 2009.

[68] Melvin Conway. How do committees invent? *Datamation*, 14:28–31, 1968.

[69] William R. Cook, Walter L. Hill, and Peter S. Canning. Inheritance is not subtyping. In *Proceedings of the 17th ACM SIGPLAN-SIGACT Symposium on Principles of Programming Languages*, pages 125–135, San Francisco, CA, 1989. ACM.

[70] James Coplien, Daniel Hoffman, and David Weiss. Commonality and variability in software engineering. *IEEE Software*, pages 37–45, November 1998.

[71] James O. Coplien. *Multi-Paradigm Design for C++*. Addison-Wesley, 1998.

[72] Thomas H. Cormen, Charles E. Leiserson, and Ronald L. Rivest. *Introduction to Algorithms*. MIT Press, Cambridge, MA, 1990.

[73] Ádám Darvas and K. Rustan M. Leino. Practical reasoning about invocations and implementations of pure methods. In Matthew B. Dwyer and Antónia Lopes, editors, *FASE*, volume 4422 of *Lecture Notes in Computer Science*, pages 336–351. Springer, 2007.

[74] Ádám Darvas and Peter Müller. Reasoning about method calls in interface specifications. *Journal of Object Technology*, 5(5):59–85, June 2006.

[75] Leonardo de Moura and Nikolaj Bjørner. Z3: An efficient SMT solver. In C. R. Ramakrishnan and Jakob Rehof, editors, *Tools and Algorithms for the Construction and Analysis of Systems (TACAS)*, volume 4963 of *Lecture Notes in Computer Science*, pages 337–340. Springer, 2008.

[76] David Detlefs, Greg Nelson, and James B. Saxe. Simplify: A theorem prover for program checking. *Journal of the ACM*, 52:365–473, May 2005.

[77] Edsger W. Dijkstra. Guarded commands, nondeterminacy and formal derivation of programs. *Communications of the ACM*, 18:453–457, August 1975.

[78] Edsger W. Dijkstra. *A Discipline of Programming*. Prentice Hall, 1976.

[79] Dino Distefano, Peter W. O'Hearn, and Hongseok Yang. A local shape analysis based on separation logic. In Holger Hermanns and Jens Palsberg, editors, *Tools and Algorithms for the Construction and Analysis of Systems (TACAS)*, volume 3920 of *Lecture Notes in Computer Science*, pages 287–302. Springer, 2006.

[80] Robert Eckstein, Marc Loy, and Dave Wood. *Swing*. O'Reilly, Sebostopol, CA, 2nd edition, 2002.

[81] Performance bloopers. http://wiki.eclipse.org/Performance_Bloopers, 2009.

[82] Eclipse. The EclipseLink project. http://www.eclipse.org/eclipselink/, 2013.

[83] Eclipse SWTBot. http://eclipse.org/swtbot/, 2014.

[84] Eclipse. SWT snippets. http://www.eclipse.org/swt/snippets, 2015.

[85] ECMA. ECMAScript language specification: Edition 5.1, 2011. http://www.ecma-international.org/publications/standards/Ecma-262.htm.

[86] Ramez Elmasri and Shamkant B. Navathe. *Fundamentals of Database Systems*. Benjamin/Cummings, 2000.

[87] ESA. Ariane 5: Flight 501 failure. http://esamultimedia.esa.int/docs/esa-x-1819eng.pdf, July 1996.

[88] J.-C. Filliâtre. *WHY: A Multi-language Multi-prover Verification Tool.* Research Report 1366, LRI, Université Paris Sud, March 2003.

[89] Cormac Flanagan, K. Rustan M. Leino, Mark Lillibridge, Greg Nelson, James B. Saxe, and Raymie Stata. Extended static checking for Java. In *Programming Language Design and Implementation*, PLDI 2002, 2002.

[90] Robert W. Floyd. Assigning meanings to programs. In J. T. Schwartz, editor, *Mathematical Aspects of Computer Science*, volume 19 of *Proceedings of Symposia in Applied Mathematics*, pages 19–32, Providence, RI, 1967. American Mathematical Society.

[91] Internet Engineering Task Force. Rfc 1122: Requirements for Internet hosts—communication layers. `http://tools.ietf.org/html/rfc1122`, October 1989.

[92] Martin Fowler. *Refactoring: Improving the Design of Existing Code.* Addison-Wesley, 2000.

[93] Martin Fowler. Reducing coupling. *IEEE Software*, 18(4):102–104, July 2001.

[94] Martin Fowler. *Patterns of Enterprise Application Architecture.* Addison-Wesley, 2002.

[95] Martin Fowler. *UML Distilled: Applying the Standard Object Modeling Language.* Addison-Wesley, 3rd edition, 2004.

[96] Gottlob Frege. *Begriffsschrift, eine der arithmetischen nachgebildete Formelsprache des reinen Denkens.* Verlag von Louis Nebert, Halle, 1879.

[97] Garry Froehlich, H. James Hoover, Ling Liu, and Paul Sorenson. Designing object-oriented frameworks. In Saba Zamir, editor, *Handbook of Object Technology*, pages 491–501. CRC Press, 1998.

[98] Eric Gamma. The Extension Objects pattern. In Robert C. Martin, Dirk Riehle, and Frank Buschmann, editors, *Pattern Languages of Program Design 3*. Addison-Wesley, MA, 1997.

[99] Erich Gamma and Kent Beck. *Contributing to Eclipse: Principles, Patterns, and Plugins.* Addison-Wesley, 2004.

[100] Erich Gamma, Richard Helm, Ralph Johnson, and John Vlissides. *Design Patterns: Elements of Reusable Object-Oriented Software.* Addison-Wesley, 1995.

[101] David Garlan and Mary Shaw. *An Introduction to Software Architecture.* Technical Report CMU-CS-94-166, School of Computer Science, Carnegie Mellon University, Pittsburgh, PA, 1994.

[102] Holger Gast. Lightweight separation. In O. Ait Mohamed, C. Muñoz, and S. Tahar, editors, *Theorem Proving in Higher Order Logics 21st International Conference (TPHOLs 2008)*, volume 5170 of *Lecture Notes in Computer Science*. Springer, 2008.

[103] Holger Gast. Reasoning about memory layouts. *Formal Methods in System Design*, 37(2-3):141–170, 2010.

[104] Holger Gast. Developer-oriented correctness proofs: A case study of Cheney's algorithm. In Shengchao Qin and Zongyan Qiu, editors, *Proceedings of 13th International Conference on Formal Engineering Methods (ICFEM 2011)*, volume 6991 of *Lecture Notes in Computer Science*. Springer, 2011.

[105] Holger Gast. Structuring interactive correctness proofs by formalizing coding idioms. In Jörg Brauer, Marco Roveri, and Hendrik Tews, editors, *6th International Workshop on Systems Software Verification, (SSV 2011)*, volume 24 of *OpenAccess Series in Informatics*. Schloss Dagstuhl: Leibniz-Zentrum für Informatik, 2011.

[106] Holger Gast. *Functional Software Verification by Symbolic Execution in Classical Logic*. Habilitationsschrift. Mathematisch-Naturwissenschaftliche Fakultät, Universität Tübingen, Tübingen, Germany, 2012.

[107] Holger Gast. Semi-automatic proofs about object graphs in separation logic. In Stephan Merz and Gerald Lüttgen, editors, *Automated Verification of Critical Systems*, AVoCS '12, 2012.

[108] Carlo Ghezzi and Dino Mandrioli. Incremental parsing. *ACM Transactions in Programming Languages and Systems*, 1(1):58–70, 1979.

[109] Adele Goldberg and David Robson. *Smalltalk-80: The Language and Its Implementation*. Addison-Wesley, 1983.

[110] Michael J.C. Gordon. Mechanizing programming logics in higher order logic. In *Current Trends in Hardware Verification and Automated Theorem Proving*, pages 387–439. Springer, 1989.

[111] James Gosling, Bill Joy, Guy Steele, Gilad Bracha, and Alex Buckley. *The Java Language Specification: Java SE 7 Edition*. Addison-Wesley, 2013. http://docs.oracle.com/javase/specs/.

[112] Mark Grechanik, Collin McMillan, Luca DeFerrari, Marco Comi, Stefano Crespi, Denys Poshyvanyk, Chen Fu, Qing Xie, and Carlo Ghezzi. An empirical investigation into a large-scale Java open source code repository. In *Proceedings of the 2010 ACM-IEEE International Symposium on Empirical Software Engineering and Measurement*, ESEM '10, pages 11:1–11:10, New York, NY, 2010. ACM.

[113] Philipp Haller and Martin Odersky. Event-based programming without inversion of control. In *Proceedings of the 7th Joint Conference on Modular Programming Languages*, JMLC'06, pages 4–22, Heidelberg, Germany, 2006. Springer.

[114] Morten Borup Harning. An approach to structured display design: Coping with conceptual complexity. In Jean Vanderdonckt, editor, *CADUI*, pages 121–140. Presses Universitaires de Namur, 1996.

[115] John L. Hennessey and David A. Patterson. *Computer Architecture: A Quantitative Approach*. Morgan Kaufmann, San Francisco, CA, 2nd edition, 1996.

[116] Joel Henry and Donald Gotterbarn. Coupling and cohesion in object-oriented design and coding. In *Proceedings of the 1996 ACM 24th Annual Conference on Computer Science*, CSC '96, page 149, New York, NY, 1996. ACM.

[117] James Henstridge. GIMP Python documentation. http://www.gimp.org/docs/python, September 2014.

[118] Frederick Herzberg, Bernard Mausner, and Barbara B. Snyderman. *The Motivation to Work*. Wiley, New York, NY, 2nd edition, 1959.

[119] C. A. R. Hoare. An axiomatic basis for computer programming. *Communications of the ACM*, 12(10):576–580,583, October 1969.

[120] Gerard J. Holzmann. The model checker SPIN. *IEEE Transactions in Software Engineering*, 23(5):279–295, May 1997.

[121] Peter V. Homeier and David F. Martin. Mechanical verification of mutually recursive procedures. In *Proceedings of the 13th International Conference on Automated Deduction*, CADE-13, pages 201–215, London, UK, 1996. Springer.

[122] John E. Hopcroft, Rajeev Motwani, and Jeffrey D. Ullman. *Introduction to Automata Theory, Languages, and Computation*. Addison-Wesley, 2nd edition, 2003.

[123] Daniel H. H. Ingalls. Design principles behind Smalltalk. *BYTE Magazine*, 6(8), August 1981.

[124] Bart Jacobs and Frank Piessens. Verification of programs using inspector methods. In E. Zucca and D. Ancona, editors, *Proceedings of the Eighth Workshop on Formal Techniques for Java-like Programs*, pages 1–22, 2006.

[125] Bart Jacobs, Jan Smans, and Frank Piessens. A quick tour of the VeriFast program verifier. In *Proceedings of the Eighth ASIAN Symposium on Programming Languages and Systems*, APLAS 2010, 2010.

[126] Bart Jacobs, Jan Smans, and Frank Piessens. VeriFast: Imperative programs as proofs. In *VS-Tools Workshop at VSTTE 2010*. (No formal proceedings), 2010.

[127] java.net. Project JAXB. https://jaxb.java.net, 2013.

[128] JBoss. Hibernate: Getting started guide (version 4.3). http://docs.jboss.org/hibernate/core/4.3/quickstart/en-US/html/, 2014.

[129] JBoss. Hibernate: Relational persistence for idiomatic Java. http://www.hibernate.org/orm/documentation/5.0/, 2013.

[130] Ralph E. Johnson. How to design frameworks. *Tutorial Notes OOPSLA*, 1993.

[131] Ralph E. Johnson. Components, frameworks, patterns (extended abstract). In *Proceedings of the 1997 Symposium on Software Reusability*, pages 10–17, Boston, MA, 1997. ACM.

[132] Ralph E. Johnson and Brian Foote. Designing reusable classes. *Journal of Object-Oriented Programming*, 1(2):22–35, 1988.

[133] Richard Jones and Rafael Lins. *Garbage Collection: Algorithms for Automatic Dynamic Memory Management*. Wiley & Sons, 1996.

[134] Ioannis T. Kassios. Dynamic frames: Support for framing, dependencies and sharing without restrictions. In Jayadev Misra, Tobias Nipkow, and Emil Sekerinski, editors, *FM 2006: Formal Methods*, volume 4085 of *Lecture Notes in Computer Science*, pages 268–283. Springer, 2006.

[135] Richard Kelsey and Jonathan Rees. A tractable scheme implementation. *Lisp and Symbolic Computation*, 7(1):315–335, 1994.

[136] Gregor Kiczales and John Lamping. Issues in the design and specification of class libraries. In *Conference Proceedings on Object-Oriented Programming Systems, Languages, and Applications*, OOPSLA '92, pages 435–451, New York, NY, 1992. ACM.

[137] Gavin King, Pete Muir, Jozef Hartinger, Dan Allen, David Allen, Nicola Benaglia, Gladys Guerrero, Eun-Ju Ki, Terry Chuang, Francesco Milesi, and Sean Wu. CDI: Contexts and dependency injection for the Java EE platform. `http://docs.jboss.org/weld/reference/latest/en-US/html/`, April 2014.

[138] Gerwin Klein, June Andronick, Kevin Elphinstone, Gernot Heiser, David Cock, Philip Derrin, Dhammika Elkaduwe, Kai Engelhardt, Rafal Kolanski, Michael Norrish, Thomas Sewell, Harvey Tuch, and Simon Winwood. seL4: Formal verification of an OS kernel. *Communications of the ACM (CACM)*, 53(6):107–115, June 2010.

[139] Donald E. Knuth. Notes on the van Emde Boas construction of priority deques: an instructive use of recursion, March 1977. Classroom notes, Stanford University, Stanford, CA; see `http://www-cs-faculty.stanford.edu/~uno/faq.html`.

[140] Donald E. Knuth. Structured programming with go to statements. In Edward Nash Yourdon, editor, *Classics in Software Engineering*, pages 257–321. Yourdon Press, Upper Saddle River, NJ, 1979.

[141] Donald E. Knuth. Literate programming. *Computer Journal*, 27(2):97–111, May 1984.

[142] Donald E. Knuth. *The TEXbook*. Addison-Wesley, 1986.

[143] Donald E. Knuth. *The Art of Computer Programming, Volume 2: Seminumerical Algorithms*. Addison-Wesley, 3rd edition, 1997.

[144] Andrew Koenig and Barbara E. Moo. *Accelerated C++: Practical Programming by Example*. Addison-Wesley, 2000.

[145] Keith Kowalczykowski, Kian Win Ong, Kevin Keliang Zhao, Alin Deutsch, Yannis Papakonstantinou, and Michalis Petropoulos. Do-it-yourself data driven web applications. In *Fourth Biennial Conference on Innovative Data Systems Research*, CIDR 2009. `http://www.cidrdb.org/`, 2009.

[146] Glenn E. Krasner and Stephen T. Pope. A cookbook for using the model-view controller user interface paradigm in Smalltalk-80. *Journal of Object Oriented Programming*, 1(3):26–49, August 1988.

[147] Philippe Kruchten. *The Rational Unified Process: An Introduction*. Addison-Wesley, 3rd edition, 2003.

[148] Doug Lea. *Concurrent Programming in Java: Design Principles and Patterns*. Addison-Wesley, 2nd edition, 1999.

[149] Gary T. Leavens, Albert L. Baker, and Clyde Ruby. JML: A notation for detailed design. In Haim Kilov, Bernhard Rumpe, and William Harvey, editors, *Behavioural Specifications for Business and Systems*. Kluwer, 1999.

[150] Gary T. Leavens, Albert L. Baker, and Clyde Ruby. Preliminary design of JML: A behavioral interface specification language for Java. *SIGSOFT Software Engineering Notes*, 31(3):1–38, 2006.

[151] Gary T. Leavens and Yoonsik Cheon. Design by contract with JML. http://www.jmlspecs.org/jmldbc.pdf, January 2006.

[152] Gary T. Leavens, K. Rustan M. Leino, and Peter Müller. Specification and verification challenges for sequential object-oriented programs. *Formal Aspects of Computing*, 19(2):159–189, 2007.

[153] Dirk Leinenbach and Thomas Santen. Verifying the Microsoft Hyper-V hypervisor with VCC. In Ana Cavalcanti and Dennis Dams, editors, *FM 2009: Formal Methods*, volume 5850 of *Lecture Notes in Computer Science*, pages 806–809. Springer, 2009.

[154] K. Rustan M. Leino and Peter Müller. A verification methodology for model fields. In Peter Sestoft, editor, *European Symposium on Programming*, volume 3924 of *Lecture Notes in Computer Science*, pages 115–130. Springer, 2006.

[155] K. Rustan M. Leino and G. Nelson. Data abstraction and information hiding. *ACM Transactions on Programming Languages and Systems*, 24(5), 2002.

[156] T. C. Lethbridge, J. Singer, and A. Forward. How software engineers use documentation: The state of the practice. *Software, IEEE*, 20(6):35–39, 2003.

[157] Nancy G. Leveson and Clark S. Tyler. An investigation of the Therac-25 accidents. *IEEE Computer*, 26(7):18–41, 1993.

[158] Karl J. Lieberherr and I. Holland. Assuring good style for object-oriented programs. *IEEE Software*, pages 38–48, September 1989.

[159] Tim Lindholm, Frank Yellin, Gilad Bracha, and Alex Buckley. *The Java Virtual Machine Specification, Java SE 7 Edition*. Addison-Wesley, 2013.

[160] Barabara Liskov. Data abstraction and hierarchy. *ACM SIGPLAN Notices*, 23(5):17–34, 1988.

[161] Barbara H. Liskov. *CLU Reference Manual*. Number 114 in *Lecture Notes in Computer Science*. Springer, 1981.

[162] Barbara H. Liskov and Jeannette M. Wing. A behavioral notion of subtyping. *ACM Transactions on Programming Languages and Systems (TOPLAS)*, 16(6):1811–1841, November 1994.

[163] Tim Mackinnon, Steve Freeman, and Philip Craig. Endo-testing: Unit testing with mock objects. In Giancarlo Succi and Michele Marchesi, editors, *Extreme Programming Examined*, pages 287–301. Addison-Wesley, 2001.

[164] David Maier and David S. Warren. *Computing with Logic: Logic Programming with Prolog*. Benjamin/Cummings, Menlo Park, CA, 1988.

[165] Zohar Manna and Amir Pnueli. *The Temporal Logic of Reactive and Concurrent Systems*. Springer, New York, NY, 1992.

[166] Jeremy Manson, William Pugh, and Sarita V. Adve. The Java memory model. In *Proceedings of the 32nd ACM SIGPLAN-SIGACT Symposium on Principles of Programming Languages*, POPL '05, pages 378–391, New York, NY, 2005. ACM.

[167] Claude Marché and Christine Paulin-Mohring. Reasoning about Java programs with aliasing and frame conditions. In Joe Hurd and Thomas F. Melham, editors, *Theorem Proving in Higher Order Logics*, volume 3603 of *Lecture Notes in Computer Science*, pages 179–194. Springer, 2005.

[168] Nicolas Marti, Reynald Affeldt, and Akinori Yonezawa. Formal verification of the heap manager of an operating system using separation logic. In Zhiming Liu and Jifeng He, editors, *8th International Conference on Formal Engineering Methods (ICFEM)*, volume 4260 of *Lecture Notes in Computer Science*. Springer, 2006.

[169] Robert C. Martin. Design principles and patterns. `http://www.objectmentor.com/resources/articles/Principles_and_Patterns.pdf`, 2000.

[170] Robert C. Martin. *Agile Software Development: Principles, Patterns, and Practices*. Prenctice Hall, 2002.

[171] Robert C. Martin. Professionalism and test-driven development. *IEEE Software*, 24(3):32–36, May 2007.

[172] Robert C. Martin. *Clean Code*. Prentice Hall, 2009.

[173] Apache Maven project. `http://maven.apache.org/`, 2014.

[174] Jeff McAffer, Jean-Michel Lemieux, and Chris Aniszcyk. *Eclipse Rich Client Platform*. Addison-Wesley, 2010.

[175] Jeff McAffer, Paul VanderLei, and Simon Archer. *Equinox and OSGi: The Power Behind Eclipse*. Addison-Wesley, 2009.

[176] Farhad Mehta and Tobias Nipkow. Proving pointer programs in higher-order logic. In F. Baader, editor, *Automated Deduction: CADE-19, 19th International Conference on Automated Deduction*, volume 2741 of *Lecture Notes in Computer Science*, pages 121–135. Springer, 2003.

[177] Farhad Mehta and Tobias Nipkow. Proving pointer programs in higher-order logic. *Information and Computing*, 199(1–2):200–227, 2005.

[178] Erik Meijer, Maarten Fokkinga, and Ross Paterson. Functional programming with bananas, lenses, envelopes and barbed wire. In *Proceedings of the 5th ACM Conference on Functional Programming Languages and Computer Architecture*, pages 124–144, New York, NY, 1991. Springer.

[179] Marjan Mernik, Jan Heering, and Anthony M. Sloane. When and how to develop domain-specific languages. *ACM Computing Surveys*, 37(4):316–344, December 2005.

[180] Bertrand Meyer. *Eiffel: The Language.* Prentice Hall, 1992.

[181] Bertrand Meyer. *Object-Oriented Software Construction.* Prentice Hall, 1997.

[182] Betrand Meyer. Applying "design by contract". *IEEE Computer*, 25(10):40–51, October 1992.

[183] Scott Meyers. *Effective C++: 55 Specific Ways to Improve Your Programs and Designs.* Addison-Wesley, 3rd edition, 2005.

[184] Microsoft. .NET compiler platform ("Roslyn"). `https://github.com/dotnet/roslyn`, 2015.

[185] Leonid Mikhajlov and Emil Sekerinski. A study of the fragile base class problem. In Eric Jul, editor, *ECOOP'98—Object-Oriented Programming, 12th European Conference*, volume 1445 of *Lecture Notes in Computer Science*, pages 355–382. Springer, 1998.

[186] Robin Milner. A theory of type polymorphism in programming. *Journal of Computer and System Sciences*, 17:348–375, 1978.

[187] P. Müller. *Modular Specification and Verification of Object-Oriented Programs*, volume 2262 of *Lecture Notes in Computer Science*. Springer, 2002.

[188] Peter Müller, Arnd Poetzsch-Heffter, and Gary T. Leavens. Modular specification of frame properties in JML. *Concurrency and Computation: Practice and Experience*, 15(2):117–154, 2003.

[189] Sara Negri and Jan von Plato. *Structural Proof Theory.* Cambridge University Press, 2001.

[190] Java Source Net. Open source parser generators in Java. `http://java-source.net/open-source/parser-generators`, 2013.

[191] Tobias Nipkow. Winskel is (almost) right: Towards a mechanized semantics textbook. *Formal Aspects of Computing*, 10:171–186, 1998.

[192] Tobias Nipkow and Gerwin Klein. *Concrete Semantics: A Proof Assistant Approach*. Springer, 2014.

[193] James Noble, Jan Vitek, and John Potter. Flexible alias protection. In Eric Jul, editor, *ECOOP'98–Object-Oriented Programming, 12th European Conference*, volume 1445 of *Lecture Notes in Computer Science*, pages 158–185. Springer, 1998.

[194] Martin Odersky, Lex Spoon, and Bill Venners. *Programming in Scala*. Artima, Walnut Creek, CA, 2nd edition, 2010.

[195] Peter W. O'Hearn, John C. Reynolds, and Hongseok Yang. Local reasoning about programs that alter data structures. In *Proceedings of the 15th International Workshop on Computer Science Logic*, number 2142 in *Lecture Notes in Computer Science*, pages 1–19. Springer, 2001.

[196] Chris Okasaki. *Purely Functional Data Structures*. Cambridge University Press, 1999.

[197] Kenneth Ölwing. How to correctly and uniformly use progress monitors. `https://www.eclipse.org/articles/Article-Progress-Monitors/article.html`, January 2006.

[198] OMG. OMG unified modeling language, superstructure: Version 2.4.1. Technical report, Object Management Group (OMG), August 2011. `http://www.omg.org/spec/UML/2.4.1/Superstructure/PDF`.

[199] Oracle. Java SE 6 hotspot virtual machine garbage collection tuning. `http://www.oracle.com/technetwork/java/javase/gc-tuning-6-140523.html`, 2006.

[200] Oracle. Expression Language specification, version 3.0. `http://java.net/projects/el-spec/`, 2013.

[201] Oracle. *The Java EE 7 Tutorial*, September 2013. `http://docs.oracle.com/javaee/7/tutorial/`.

[202] Oracle. JavaBeans spec. `http://www.oracle.com/technetwork/java/javase/documentation/spec-136004.html`, October 30, 2013.

[203] OSGi website. `http://www.osgi.org`, 2014.

[204] Susan Owicki and David Gries. An axiomatic proof technique for parallel programs. *Acta Informatica*, 6:319–340, 1976.

[205] D. L. Parnas. On the criteria to be used in decomposing systems into modules. *Communications of the ACM*, 15(12):1053–1059, December 1972.

[206] Terence Parr. *The Definitive ANTLR Reference: Building Domain-Specific Languages*. Pragmatic Bookshelf, 2007.

[207] Frank Penczek, Wei Cheng, Clemens Grelck, Raimund Kirner, Bernd Scheuermann, and Alex Shafarenko. A data-flow based coordination approach to concurrent software engineering. In *Data-Flow Execution Models for Extreme Scale Computing*, DFM 2012, pages 36–43, September 2012.

[208] Alan J. Perlis. Epigrams on programming. *ACM SIGPLAN Notices*, 12:7–13, September 1982.

[209] Benjamin C. Pierce. *Types and Programming Languages*. MIT Press, Cambridge, MA, 2002.

[210] Ed Post. Real programmers don't use Pascal. *Datamation*, 29(7), 1983.

[211] Trygve Reenskaug, Per Wold, and Odd Arild Lehne. *Working with Objects: the OORAM Software Engineering Method*. Manning Publications, 1995.

[212] John H. Reppy. *Concurrent Programming in ML*. Cambridge University Press, 1999.

[213] John C. Reynolds. Separation logic: A logic for shared mutable data structures. In *Proceedings of the 17th Annual IEEE Symposium on Logic in Computer Science*, LICS 02, 2002.

[214] Dan Rubel, Jaime Wren, and Eric Clayberg. *The Eclipse Graphical Editing Framework (GEF)*. Addison-Wesley, 2012.

[215] S3C. Document object model. http://www.w3.org/DOM/, 2009.

[216] Stephen R. Schach. *Object-Oriented and Classical Software Engineering*. McGrawHill, 8th edition, 2010.

[217] Norbert Schirmer. *Verification of Sequential Imperative Programs in Isabelle/HOL*. PhD thesis, Technische Universität München, Munich, Germany, 2005.

[218] Douglas Schmidt, Michael Stal, Hans Rohnert, and Frank Buschmann. *Pattern-Oriented Software Architecture: Patterns for Concurrent and Networked Objects*. Wiley & Sons, 2000.

[219] Klaus Schneider. *Verification of Reactive Systems: Formal Methods and Algorithms*. Springer, 2004.

[220] Arne Schramm, André Preußner, Matthias Heinrich, and Lars Vogel. Rapid UI development for enterprise applications: Combining manual and model-driven techniques. In *Proceedings of the 13th International Conference on Model Driven Engineering Languages and Systems (MODELS '10)*. Springer, 2010.

[221] Ken Schwaber and Jeff Sutherland. The Scrum guide: The definitive guide to Scrum: The rules of the game. http://www.scrumguides.org/, July 2013.

[222] Chris Sells and Ian Griffiths. *Programming WPF*. O'Reilly, 2007.

[223] Coupling and cohesion. http://c2.com/cgi/wiki?CouplingAndCohesion, 2014.

[224] Law of Demeter revisited. http://c2.com/cgi/wiki?LawOfDemeterRevisited, 2014.

[225] Shield pattern. http://c2.com/cgi/wiki?ShieldPattern, 2014.

[226] Singletons are evil. http://c2.com/cgi/wiki?SingletonsAreEvil, 2014.

[227] Stamp coupling. http://c2.com/cgi/wiki?StampCoupling, 2014.

[228] You aren't gonna need it. http://c2.com/cgi/wiki?YouArentGonnaNeedIt, 2014.

[229] Ben Shneiderman and Catherine Plaisant. *Designing the User Interface: Strategies for Effective Human–Computer Interaction.* Addison-Wesley, 2009.

[230] Jan Smans, Bart Jacobs, and Frank Piessens. Implicit dynamic frames: Combining dynamic frames and separation logic. In *Proceedings of the 23rd European Conference on ECOOP 2009: Object-Oriented Programming*, Genoa, pages 148–172. Springer, 2009.

[231] Jim Smith and Ravi Nair. *Virtual Machines: Versatile Platforms for Systems and Processes.* Morgan Kaufmann, San Francisco, CA, 2005.

[232] Alan Snyder. Encapsulation and inheritance in object-oriented programming languages. In *OOPLSA '86 Conference Proceedings on Object-Oriented Programming Systems, Languages and Applications*, pages 38–45, New York, NY, 1986. ACM.

[233] Ian Sommerville. *Software Engineering.* Addison-Wesley, 2010.

[234] Simon St. Laurent, Edd Dumbill, and Eric J Gruber. *Learning Rails 3.* O'Reilly, 2012.

[235] Dave Steinberg. *EMF: Eclipse Modeling Framework.* Addison-Wesley, 2nd edition, 2008.

[236] W. P. Stevens, G. J. Myers, and L. L. Constantine. Structured design. *IBM Systems Journal*, 13(2), 1974.

[237] W. Richard Stevens. *UNIX Network Programming.* Prentice Hall, 1990.

[238] W. Richard Stevens. *Advanced Programming in the UNIX Environment.* Addison-Wesley, 1992.

[239] Bjarne Stroustrup. *The C++ Programming Language.* Addison-Wesley, 3rd edition, 1997.

[240] Bjarne Stroustrup. Exception safety: Concepts and techniques. In Alexander B. Romanovsky, Christophe Dony, Jørgen Lindskov Knudsen, and Anand Tripathi, editors, *Advances in Exception Handling Techniques*, volume 2022 of *Lecture Notes in Computer Science*, pages 60–76. Springer, 2000.

[241] Sun. Java code conventions. http://www.oracle.com/technetwork/java/codeconventions-150003.pdf, April 1999.

[242] Richard E. Sweet. The Mesa programming environment. In *Proceedings of the ACM SIGPLAN 85 Symposium on Language Issues in Programming Environments*, SLIPE '85, pages 216–229, New York, NY, 1985. ACM.

[243] Clemens Szypersky, Dominik Gruntz, and Stephan Murer. *Component Software.* Addison-Wesley/ACM Press, 2nd edition, 2002.

[244] Taligent. Building object-oriented frameworks. `http://lhcb-comp.web.cern.ch/lhcb-comp/Components/postscript/buildingoo.pdf`, 1997.

[245] Simon Thompson. *Haskell: The Craft of Functional Programming.* Addison-Wesley, 2nd edition, 1999.

[246] Harvey Tuch, Gerwin Klein, and Michael Norrish. Types, bytes, and separation logic. In Martin Hofmann and Matthias Felleisen, editors, *Proceedings of the 34th ACM SIGPLAN-SIGACT Symposium on Principles of Programming Languages,* POPL '07, 2007.

[247] Thomas Tuerk. A formalisation of Smallfoot in HOL. In S. Berghofer, T. Nipkow, C. Urban, and M. Wenzel, editors, *Theorem Proving in Higher Order Logics, 22nd International Conference (TPHOLs),* volume 5674 of *Lecture Notes in Computer Science.* Springer, 2009.

[248] Tycho: Building Eclipse plug-ins with Maven. `http://www.eclipse.org/tycho/`, 2014.

[249] Arie van Deursen, Paul Klint, and Joost Visser. Domain-specific languages: An annotated bibliography. *SIGPLAN Notices,* 35(6):26–36, June 2000.

[250] Hibernate ORM. `http://hibernate.org/`.

[251] Jsr-000299 web beans. `https://jcp.org/aboutJava/communityprocess/final/jsr299/index.html`, December 2009.

[252] The spring framework. `http://spring.io/`, 2014.

[253] David von Oheimb. Hoare logic for mutual recursion and local variables. In C. Pandu Rangan, V. Raman, and R. Ramanujam, editors, *Foundations of Software Technology and Theoretical Computer Science,* volume 1738 of *Lecture Notes in Computer Science,* pages 168–180. Springer, 1999.

[254] David von Oheimb. Hoare logic for Java in Isabelle/HOL. *Concurrency and Computation: Practice and Experience,* 13(13):1173–1214, 2001.

[255] W3C. XSL Transformations (XSLT) version 2.0. `http://www.w3.org/TR/xslt20/`.

[256] W3C. Document object model events. `http://www.w3.org/TR/DOM-Level-2-Events/events.html`, 2000.

[257] Tim A. Wagner and Susan L. Graham. Incremental analysis of real programming languages. In *Proceedings of the ACM SIGPLAN 1997 Conference on Programming Language Design and Implementation,* PLDI '97, pages 31–43, New York, NY, 1997. ACM.

[258] Gerald M. Weinberg. *The Psychology of Computer Programming.* Van Nostrand Reinhold Company, New York, NY, 1971.

[259] Frank White. *The Overview Effect: Space Exploration and Human Evolution.* American Institute of Aeronautics and Astronautics, Reston, VA, 2nd edition, 1998.

[260] Mats Wirén. Interactive incremental chart parsing. In *Proceedings of the Fourth Conference on European Chapter of the Association for Computational Linguistics*, pages 241–248, Manchester, UK, 1989.

[261] Rebecca Wirfs-Brock. Characterizing classes. *IEEE Software*, 23(2):9–11, 2006.

[262] Rebecca Wirfs-Brock. A tour of responsibility-driven design. Tutorial at International Conference on Object-Oriented Programming, Systems, Languages, and Applications, OOPSLA 2006, Portland, OR, 2006.

[263] Rebecca Wirfs-Brock and Alan McKean. *Object Design: Roles, Responsibilities, Collaborations.* Addison-Wesley, 2003.

[264] Rebecca Wirfs-Brock and Brian Wilkerson. Object-oriented design: A responsibility-driven approach. In *OOPSLA '89 Conference Proceedings*, pages 71–75, 1989.

[265] Xerox. AspectJ: Crosscutting objects for better modularity. `http://www.eclipse.org/aspectj`, 2013.

[266] Fan Yang, Nitin Gupta, Chavdar Botev, Elizabeth F. Churchill, George Levchenko, and Jayavel Shanmugasundaram. WYSIWYG development of data driven web applications. *Proceedings of the 34th International Conference on Very Large Data Bases (VLDB)*, 1(1), 2008.

[267] `Zend_Db_Select` from the Zend framework. `http://framework.zend.com/manual/1.12/en/zend.db.select.html`, 2014.

[268] The Zend framwork. `http://framework.zend.com/`, 2014.

[269] ZEST. Zest: The Eclipse visualization toolkit. `http://www.eclipse.org/gef/zest/`, 2013.

Index

REGISTER YOUR PRODUCT at informit.com/register

Access Additional Benefits and SAVE 35% on Your Next Purchase

- Download available product updates.

- Access bonus material when applicable.

- Receive exclusive offers on new editions and related products.
  (Just check the box to hear from us when setting up your account.)

- Get a coupon for 35% for your next purchase, valid for 30 days. Your code will
  be available in your InformIT cart. (You will also find it in the Manage Codes
  section of your account page.)

Registration benefits vary by product. Benefits will be listed on your account page
under Registered Products.

InformIT.com–The Trusted Technology Learning Source

InformIT is the online home of information technology brands at Pearson, the world's foremost
education company. At InformIT.com you can

- Shop our books, eBooks, software, and video training.
- Take advantage of our special offers and promotions (informit.com/promotions).
- Sign up for special offers and content newsletters (informit.com/newsletters).
- Read free articles and blogs by information technology experts.
- Access thousands of free chapters and video lessons.

Connect with InformIT–Visit informit.com/community

Learn about InformIT community events and programs.

informIT.com
the trusted technology learning source

Addison-Wesley · Cisco Press · IBM Press · Microsoft Press · Pearson IT Certification · Prentice Hall · Que · Sams · VMware Press